D1552077

A HISTORY OF THE UNITED STATES AIR FORCE

1907—1957

By

ALFRED GOLDBERG

Editor

WILHELMINE BURCH	GEORGE F. LEMMER
R. FRANK FUTRELL	ARTHUR K. MARMOR
CLEMENT L. GRANT	WAYNE E. SCRIVENER
HAROLD LARSON	JOHN C. WARREN

D. VAN NOSTRAND COMPANY, INC.

PRINCETON, NEW JERSEY

TORONTO   LONDON

NEW YORK

D. VAN NOSTRAND COMPANY, INC.
120 Alexander St., Princeton, New Jersey (*Principal office*)
257 Fourth Avenue, New York 10, New York

D. Van Nostrand Company, Ltd.
358, Kensington High Street, London, W.14, England

D. Van Nostrand Company (Canada), Ltd.
25 Hollinger Road, Toronto 16, Canada

———

———

Published simultaneously in Canada by
D. Van Nostrand Company (Canada), Ltd.

———

Library of Congress Catalog Card No. 57-14552

———

PRINTED IN THE UNITED STATES OF AMERICA

Foreword

In this Golden Anniversary year of the United States Air Force, it is most fitting that an account of the achievements of this first half-century be made a matter of permanent record. The Air Force bears a heavy responsibility in the defense of the Free World in an era when a technological revolution in the art of war is coupled with increasing international tension. The future of our service, and of those institutions with whose defense it is charged, depends to a high degree on the wisdom and imagination with which we face unprecedented challenges. For a solid basis of experience it is well to look to the lessons of history. Hence I commend this volume to all who have a deep and abiding interest in American airpower — to those of us who wear the Air Force uniform, to our brothers-in-arms of the reserve components, to those who support Air Force activities in other capacities. It is a proud chronicle of the past and a valuable tool for the future.

THOMAS D. WHITE
Chief of Staff
United States Air Force

September 6, 1957

Preface

The year 1957 marks the fiftieth anniversary of military aviation in the United States. It also marks the tenth anniversary of the establishment of the Department of the Air Force and the United States Air Force. These events were the inspiration for the preparation of this history of the US Air Force and its antecedent organizations.

For a long time there had existed a need for a general history of the Air Force and its predecessors. The best work to date, the multivolume *Army Air Forces in World War II,* covers only a brief part of the fifty-year history of the Air Force. From both within the Air Force and without, there had been frequent requests for a one-volume history. These requests, together with the need for an authentic and comprehensive history to honor the anniversary dates in 1957, led to the decision in 1956 to have the USAF Historical Division prepare such a history for the Office of Information Services, Office, Secretary of the Air Force.

The authors were chosen from among the historians in both the Washington and Air University offices of the USAF Historical Division. In most cases, their chapters represent the fruits of a minimum of five years of research and writing in their particular specialties. The chapters on the decade 1947-57, although more detailed than the earlier ones, cannot be considered other than a preliminary history of the period. Written mainly from unclassified sources, they provide an introduction to the subject that should prove helpful to both the public and future scholars. Aside from time and space, the chief limitation has been security, which regretfully but necessarily required the omission of much important information and analysis. At some future date, when security restrictions no longer apply to the documents of this period, it will be possible to prepare a more definitive history of the US Air Force. Meanwhile, the present history can serve the useful purpose of bringing to the people of the United States as much of the story as can be told now.

Because of time and space limitations, certain arbitrary decisions about the scope of the volume had to be made at the beginning. It was decided to place the emphasis on the decade after the establishment of the US Air Force in 1947. The *Army Air Forces in World War II* had already told the definitive story of the years 1939-45. The USAF Historical Division had in preparation a history of the Army air arm for the period 1861-1939 which will eventually appear in one or two volumes. On the other hand, there existed no general history of the period after World War II, and it was here that the need for informing the public seemed the greatest. But the US Air Force of 1947-57 could be best understood in the light of its previous history and tradition, and for this reason it was thought desirable to include an account of its forty-year heritage.

Many people contributed to the inception of this history. Maj. Gen. Jacob E. Smart, Assistant Vice Chief of Staff, Col. Lawrence F. Loesch, then Secretary of the Air Staff, and the Office of Information Services endorsed the project, and Gen. Thomas D. White, then Vice Chief of Staff, directed that it be undertaken. At the Air University, Col. Curtis D. Sluman, Director of the Research Studies Institute, and Dr. Albert F. Simpson, Chief of the USAF Historical Division, assigned historians to the project and gave them generous support. Maj. Wayne E. Scrivener, Chief of the Air University Historical Liaison Office, wrote the chapter on leaders and was enthusiastic and unflagging in his devotion to the project.

Individual acknowledgment is due many members of the staff of the USAF Historical Division. The most important contribution of all was made by Mrs. Wilhelmine Burch, who did a prodigious and masterful job in collaborating on almost every phase of the editorial task. Besides the authors, valuable assistance was provided by Maj. George P. Lescanec, Miss Marguerite Kennedy, and especially Miss Adele Abramson and Mr. David Schoem. Mr. Schoem gathered statistical information and much of the organizational data for the book. Miss Abramson supervised the typing, proofreading, and checking of the many drafts of the manuscript and carried much of the burden of preparing the index. Dr. Henry L. Bowen, Dr. Robert D. Little, Mr. Max Rosenberg, Dr. Ralph D. Bald, and Mrs. Juliette Hennessy read portions of the manuscript and made constructive criticisms that helped improve the final product. The expert typing of the various drafts of the chapters was handled by Miss Norma Martin, Mrs. Edna M. Barnette, Miss Sara Venable, Mrs. Margie McCardel, Mrs. Dorothy Turner, Mrs. Kathleen Chandler, and Mrs. Lois Lynn.

Others who read and criticized individual chapters were Col. John C. Pitchford, Lt. Col. Gore Roberts, Mr. Murray Green, and Capt. James F. Sunderman, all of Headquarters USAF. A special word of acknowledgment is due Captain Sunderman of the USAF Office of Information Services, who guided the project through a myriad of administrative details with great tact and assurance. Mr. John J. McLaughlin, Administrative Assistant to the Secretary of the Air Force, helped greatly by giving freely from his storehouse of knowledge about the work of the Office of the Secretary during its first decade. Mr. William Weitzen, Deputy Assistant Secretary of the Air Force for Research and Development, answered numerous questions about his specialty quickly and accurately and with the utmost courtesy.

Because there are so many of them, it is impossible to acknowledge individually the staff and command historians—at Headquarters USAF and throughout the Air Force—who prepared the histories on which much of this book is based. Their continuing efforts are the best assurance that the Air Force will be able to present to the American people comprehensive and accurate histories in the future as in the past.

ALFRED GOLDBERG
Editor

August 10, 1957

The manuscript prepared by the USAF Historical Division for the USAF Office of Information Services forms the basis for this history in its final form.

The editors of AIR FORCE *Magazine*, in whose pages this history originally appeared, wish to take this opportunity to commend the Historical Division for achieving so monumental a task in such a comparatively short space of time. It was our responsibility to perform the final editing, select the illustrations, write the captions, and shepherd the material through final design and layout. In this task we were greatly aided by the devoted efforts of our editorial assistants: Mrs. Nellie M. Law, Mrs. Peggy M. Crowl, and Mrs. Michael Burdett Miller. Design and layout were the work of MacLeod, Sanders, Noe, and Kirwan, Inc., Washington, D. C. We are also indebted to the following for supplying the photographs that appear in this history:

Pictorial Records Branch, Photographic Records and Services Division, US Air Force

Photographic Branch, Editorial and Publication Division, Office of the Chief of Military History, US Army

The Bettmann Archive, New York, N. Y.

The Library of Congress, Washington, D. C.

The National Advisory Committee for Aeronautics, Washington, D. C.

The National Archives, Washington, D. C.

The Smithsonian Institution, Washington, D. C.

JAMES H. STRAUBEL
Editor, AIR FORCE *Magazine*

JOHN F. LOOSBROCK
Managing Editor

RICHARD M. SKINNER
Assistant Managing Editor

Contents

Orville and Wilbur Wright make man's first powered flight at Kitty Hawk, N. C., December 17, 1903. Orville took the controls on the first flight. The machine stayed aloft for twelve seconds and traveled a distance of 120 feet.

The Early Days

THE EPIC flight of Wilbur and Orville Wright at Kitty Hawk, N. C., on December 17, 1903, climaxed centuries of effort by man to conquer the air. To the future it bequeathed the new weapon of airpower that was destined to revolutionize warfare within the brief span of half a century.

From Versailles to Kitty Hawk

The ancestors of the airplane were the balloon and the glider. The balloon came first, in 1783. On September 19, at Versailles, France, the Montgolfier brothers' balloon soared aloft, carrying a sheep, a rooster, and a duck as passengers. Once more at Versailles, on October 15, Jean François Pilâtre de Rozier became the first human being to ascend into the atmosphere. These flights dispelled the popular fear that life could not exist in the atmosphere above the earth's surface and fired the imaginations of other Frenchmen. Within fifteen months, in January 1785, Jean-Pierre Blanchard made the first balloon crossing of the Channel from England to France. The military possibilities of the new device were not lost on such astute scientific observers as Benjamin Franklin and Louis-Bernard Guyton de Morveau, the eminent French chemist.

It was fitting that the first military use of the balloon should have occurred during the era of the French Revolution. In 1794 the French organized what may be considered the world's first air force—the Aerostatic Corps—and for several years it served with distinction in the field against the Austrians. But after Napoleon came to power in 1798, he abandoned the balloon, and the corps played no part in his remaining campaigns. Napoleon's neglect of balloons is ironic, for the outcome of the Battle of Waterloo in 1815 might have been different if Napoleon had used balloons to observe the terrain and enemy movements.

Blanchard, of English Channel fame, made the first successful balloon flight in the United States—from Philadelphia into New Jersey—in 1793, with George Washington and other dignitaries in attendance. Ballooning in the United States made progress during the first half of the nineteenth century, but proposals to use balloons against the Seminole Indians in 1840 and the Mexicans at Vera Cruz in 1846 were not accepted by the Army. It was not until the Civil War that the eager balloonists received their chance.

The North used balloons almost from the beginning of the war. The most successful civilian balloonists with the Union Army were John La Mountain and Thaddeus S. C. Lowe. In September 1861, Lowe became head of the Army's first air arm—the Balloon Corps of the Army of the Potomac. During the Richmond campaign of 1862 the corps operated frequently over the lines, and its observations were of value to Union commanders. Some of Lowe's balloons were used in the West as well. The Confederacy used a few balloons, but there is little mention of them after May 1862. Changes in Union Army commands in 1863 brought in generals who were not interested in the balloon, and Lowe's corps was disbanded in June 1863. Wartime experience demonstrated the value of the balloon for making aerial observations, reporting observations to the ground by telegraph, and directing gunfire successfully.

In the years between the Civil War and the Spanish-American War in 1898, the tiny US Army served essentially as a frontier police force. The Indian campaigns were wars of movement, and there appeared to be little that the balloon could do under such conditions. But there were still Army officers who remembered balloons from the Civil War and were impressed by the fact that many European armies had balloon corps. One of these officers—Brig. Gen. Adolphus W. Greely, Chief Signal Officer from 1887 to 1906—established a balloon section in the Signal Corps in 1892. After the outbreak of the Spanish-American War the Signal Corps shipped its one balloon to Cuba, where it operated in the Santiago area, observing the Spanish forces and directing artillery fire in the Battle of San Juan Hill. Spanish fire riddled the balloon when it was moved too close to enemy lines, and it was withdrawn, thereby ending the aerial phase of the war.

One more significant aeronautical development occurred before the advent of the airplane. This was the steerable airship or dirigible—a rigid or nonrigid balloon, eventually of cylindrical shape—driven by propellers attached to cabins beneath the bag and powered by gasoline engines. The successful pioneers of this lighter-than-air ship at the turn of the twentieth century were the German Count Ferdinand von Zeppelin and the Brazilian Alberto Santos-Dumont. Zeppelin's great airships were to bomb London and Paris during World War I—the beginning of strategic air bombardment. Although dirigibles were flown in exhibitions in the United States shortly after 1900, it was not until 1908 that the Signal Corps secured the money to buy Army

1

In 1783, near Paris, an intrepid Frenchman named de Rozier made history by ascending eighty-four feet in this balloon.

France's use of balloons to observe Austrian lines in Battle of Fleurus in 1794 helped French win the battle.

George Washington was on hand when Jean-Pierre Blanchard, who'd already flown the English Channel, made first balloon flight in US, from Philadelphia to New Jersey, 1793.

Dirigible No. 1. But the airship was soon destined to be overshadowed by the airplane, and the Army bought no more dirigibles until World War I.

Efforts to build a successful flying machine had been going on during much of the nineteenth century. Early experimenters like Otto Lilienthal of Germany, Percy S. Pilcher of Great Britain, and Octave Chanute and John Montgomery of the United States built and flew gliders as the first step toward a powered flying machine. Others—Sir Hiram Maxim of Great Britain, Clement Ader of France, and Samuel P. Langley—attempted at the start to equip a plane with an engine.

Langley, a bona fide scientist and Secretary of the Smithsonian Institution from 1887 to 1906, began his experiments in aerodynamics in 1885. In 1896 one of his steam-driven model airplanes flew three-quarters of a mile along the Potomac River. At the instigation of General Greely and other officers, the Army gave Langley $50,000 in 1898 to investigate and build a full-size test machine. Two trial flights of Langley's airplane—the Aerodrome A—in 1903 failed because the launching apparatus did not work. Congressmen and the public criticized the Army for having squandered money on such an impossible invention, and the embarrassed War Department refused Langley any further support. Eleven years later, in 1914, Glenn Curtiss successfully flew the Langley plane after a number of structural changes had been made in it.

And so to Wilbur and Orville Wright fell the glory of making the first successful airplane flight—at Kitty Hawk, N. C., on December 17, 1903. The first flight over the sand dunes by Orville lasted twelve seconds and covered a distance of 120 feet. In the fourth and last flight of the day, in raw and windy weather, Wilbur flew 852 feet in fifty-nine seconds. The Wrights had spent four years of patient study, investigation, and experimentation with gliders at Kitty Hawk and at their home town of Dayton, Ohio. They had even built their own twelve-hp. engine. Theirs was a remarkable scientific achievement and undoubtedly the last of such magnitude to come from what amounted to a home workshop.

Birth of the Army Air Arm

Few recognized the revolutionary implications of the beginning of powered flight by a heavier-than-air flying machine. The news of this and subsequent flights, as the Wright brothers made their machine into a practical airplane, met with disbelief, skepticism, and disinterest. A half

The Smithsonian Institution

Professor Thaddeus Lowe, who later headed Army's first air arm, readies his balloon *The Great Western* for an ascent at Philadelphia in the period just before Civil War.

century later, such an epochal feat would have occasioned a tidal wave of publicity, but the fact is that few people knew about it even after several years had passed. The future commander of the Army Air Forces, Henry H. Arnold, at the time of his graduation from West Point in 1907, did not know what the Wrights had done at Kitty Hawk during his plebe year. As one acute observer put it, the "birth of aviation was forced on an unbelieving world."

Among the believers in the new invention was the government of Great Britain, which late in 1904 sent a representative to inquire about purchase of the plane. Preferring that their own country have first use of their invention, during 1905 the Wrights twice offered it to the US Army. But the agency charged with investigating new military devices, the Board of Ordnance and Fortification, was still smarting from the Langley incident. Skeptical that the airplane even existed, the board would not state the performance requirements for a flying machine when the Wrights asked them to do so in October 1905. By this time the French as well as the British were negotiating with the Wrights.

President Theodore Roosevelt had to intervene to bring the War Department and the Wrights together. Prominent members of the Aero Club of America told Roosevelt about the invention in the spring of 1907, and he directed the Secretary of War, William H. Taft, to investigate the possibilities. After correspondence and conferences with Wilbur Wright, the War Department in late December 1907 called for bids on an aircraft that could carry two persons at a speed of at least forty miles an hour for 125 miles. Three bids, including that of the Wrights for $25,000, were accepted in February 1908. Only the Wright plane was ever delivered and accepted.

The US Army had not kept up with the greatly accelerated aeronautical activity in Europe after 1900. The balloon detachment of the Signal Corps was virtually nonexistent after 1898. Not until 1907 was the Army sufficiently impressed by the great new aeronautical developments to take the first step toward building an air arm. On August 1, 1907, the Signal Corps established an Aeronautical Division to take "charge of all matters pertaining to military ballooning, air machines, and all kindred subjects." Capt. Charles de F. Chandler was detailed in charge and Cpl. Edward Ward and First-Class Private Joseph E. Barrett were assigned to the division. When the first-class private "went over the hill" shortly afterward, the Army's air arm lost half of its enlisted strength.

Pending receipt of a flying machine, the Signal Corps expanded its balloon activities and experimented with bal-

This US Army Signal Corps airship causes a flurry of interest among the citizens of Des Moines, Iowa, in 1909.

One of the forerunners of the Wright brothers, Britain's Percy Pilcher, poses with his glider and a helper, 1896.

Among the early experimenters was Octave Chanute, a close friend of the Wright brothers, here making a glider test.

loon photography and radio reception. The dirigible accepted in 1908 was used for instruction and exhibition, and a number of officers later qualified as airship pilots.

In August 1908 the Wrights brought their plane to Fort Myer, Va., just across the Potomac from Washington, for pre-test flights. They had modified their 1905 model to carry two people, installed a thirty-hp. engine, and made other changes. The plane was a pusher type, with the engine and propeller placed behind the pilot and his passenger. Like its Wright predecessors, this plane was mounted on skids and launched from a monorail starting track.

The series of flights, beginning September 3, thrilled the thousands of spectators who thronged to Fort Myer and

In the Civil War, the North used balloons more extensively than the South. Above, during the battle of Fair Oaks, members of the Union's Balloon Corps inflate the *Intrepid*.

effectively dispelled the skepticism and disbelief about the very existence of the flying machine that had persisted even until then. The flights came to a tragic end on September 17 when the plane crashed, severely injuring Orville Wright and fatally injuring his passenger, Lt. Thomas E. Selfridge. Selfridge, an aviation enthusiast, had been associated with Alexander Graham Bell in aeronautical experiments. Only a few months before, in May 1908, he had become the first US Army officer to make a solo flight in a powered flying machine—the *White Wing*—developed by Bell and his associates.

In June 1909 the Wrights came back to Fort Myer with an improved version of their 1908 plane for official War Department tests before acceptance. After a full month of practice hops, Orville Wright, with Lt. Frank P. Lahm as a passenger, made the first official test flight on July 27— establishing a world's record of one hour, twelve minutes, and forty seconds for a two-man flight. On July 30, an excited crowd of 7,000 watched the final test—a cross-country speed flight from Fort Myer to Alexandria, Va., five miles away. Accompanied by Lt. Benjamin D. Foulois, Orville Wright averaged 42.5 mph on the flight, enough to win a bonus of $5,000 above the contract price of $25,000. The next day the Washington *Evening Star* announced that the "Wright machine is now 'Aeroplane No. 1, Heavier-than-air Division, United States aerial fleet.'" The Army accepted the Wright plane on August 2.

A Few Men and a Few Planes

Now that it had an "aerial fleet," the Army needed pilots. As part of the original contract the Wrights had agreed to teach two officers to operate the machine. In October 1909, Wilbur Wright trained Lieutenants Lahm and Frederic E. Humphreys at a field at College Park, Md., near the present site of the University of Maryland. Both officers soloed and were pronounced pilots on October 26, after a little more than three hours apiece of actual flying time. Lieutenant Foulois returned from France in time to be trained by Wright and Humphreys but did not solo.

The Army lost its total air strength temporarily after Lahm and Humphreys crashed in the plane on November 5. Neither was hurt, but the Signal Corps lost them both shortly afterward when they returned to their regular assignments. Lahm went back to the Cavalry in compliance with the "Manchu Law," the popular name for an Army regulation which limited a line officer to four consecutive years of detached duty. At the time Army gossip had it that he was relieved from flying duty because he had taken a woman up in the plane. Humphreys rejoined the Engineers. Thus the Army was left with neither a usable plane nor a fully qualified pilot.

While the plane was being repaired the Army decided to move flying operations to Fort Sam Houston, Tex., for the winter. The planes of the day—made of wood and cloth and held together by wire—were too frail to be flown without great hazard in the wintry winds of the Washington area. Furthermore, since the pilots had no appropriate winter clothing, it would have been most uncomfortable to fly in the damp cold at College Park. Even during the good weather of the summer and early fall the pilots had been careful to restrict their flying to early morning and late afternoon, when the air was more likely to be calm. As the only Army officer on flying duty, Foulois, assisted by a party of enlisted men, packed up the plane and took it to Texas, arriving there in February 1910.

Foulois resumed flying on March 2. Since he had no instructor, all of his flights were, perforce, solos. He got his instruction from the Wrights by mail, becoming the first correspondence-school pilot in history. But the Wrights also sent an instructor who helped Foulois master the dif-

In the years of study and experimentation before their first successful powered flight, the Wrights used gliders to test their theories. Here's Wilbur in the 1902 glider.

The Wright brothers picked the sandy wastes of Kitty Hawk, N. C., for their camp because of the favorable winds. The tests led, in December 1903, to man's first powered flight.

H. H. Arnold, the future commander of the AAF, sits at the controls of a a Wright Type B airplane at the Wright Flying School, Dayton, where he learned to fly in 1911.

The Smithsonian Institution

President Theodore Roosevelt took an early interest in
military flying, backed the purchase of the first Army
plane. Above, in the Wright airplane, St. Louis, 1910.

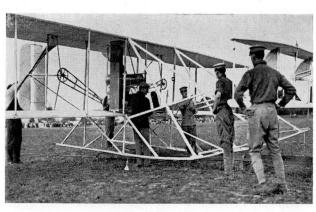

The Wright plane, later accepted by the Army, is readied
for a cross-country test flight on July 30, 1909, from
Fort Myer to Alexandria, Va., a distance of five miles.

In a crash on September 17, 1908, at Fort Myer, Va.,
Orville Wright barely escaped with his life, while his
passenger, Lt. Thomas E. Selfridge, was fatally injured.

At the flying field at College Park, Md., Wilbur Wright
taught Lahm and Humphreys to fly in 1909. Above, in 1911,
Lt. Henry H. Arnold poses in the Wright Type B airplane.

Orville Wright at the controls of the Wright brothers'
plane over the gate to Fort Myer, Va., in August 1908.
The Army accepted its first flying machine a year later.

First man to head the Aeronautical Division of the Signal Corps, Capt. Charles de F. Chandler (fifth from left),
later commandant of College Park, Md., flying school,
poses with (from left) Lt. Frank Lahm, Navy Lt. G. C. Sweet,
Maj. C. McK. Saltzman, Maj. George O. Squier, Lt. Benjamin D. Foulois, and 2d Lt. Frederic E. Humphreys.

ficult art of landing. This probably prolonged the lives of
both Foulois and the plane. The fast-aging plane had been
damaged and repaired or rebuilt several times because of
landing accidents. Between March and September, Foulois
made sixty-one flights. Until 1911 the Army had only the
one pilot and the one plane.

While waiting for the War Department to buy some
more planes, the Signal Corps had use of another machine
through the generosity of Robert F. Collier, the publisher.
Collier bought a Wright Type B airplane early in 1911 and
lent it to the Signal Corps for use at Fort Sam Houston.
It was none too soon, for "Aeroplane No. 1" was so far gone
that even the Wrights recommended against rebuilding it.
On May 4, 1911, the War Department approved restora-

With his original ground crew, Lt. Benjamin D. Foulois (second from right) stands in front of the Wright Type B airplane, stationed at Fort Sam Houston, Tex., 1910.

tion of the plane to its original condition and transfer to the Smithsonian Institution for permanent exhibition. And so, in October 1911, after two years of service, the Army's first airplane became a museum piece.

At the beginning of 1911, the US Congress had not yet appropriated a single dollar specifically for aeronautics. Even the money to purchase the Wright plane had come mostly from an experimental fund. The Signal Corps got maintenance money for flying out of a general fund intended for maintenance of military telephone and telegraph installations. At Fort Sam Houston, during 1910, only $150 was available for aviation gasoline and repairs. In order to keep flying, Foulois had to pay some expenses out of his own pocket. Despite a marked lack of enthusiasm for aeronautics among many of the Army's line officers, the Signal Corps had tried hard to get funds to expand its aviation activities, requesting $200,000 in each fiscal year beginning in 1908. The typical congressional reaction to these requests was probably expressed by the member who reportedly asked, "Why all this fuss about airplanes for the Army? I thought we already had one."

In March 1911, Congress finally appropriated $125,000 for Army aeronautics, with $25,000 to be made available immediately. Chief Signal Officer James Allen quickly ordered five new planes at a cost of about $5,000 each. A Wright Type B and a Curtiss airplane were delivered at Fort Sam Houston in April. The Curtiss plane, also a pusher, was the Army's second airplane.

Glenn Curtiss, pioneer flyer and manufacturer, moved his flying activities to California for the winter of 1910-11 because of the favorable flying conditions there. He established a flying school camp on North Island in San Diego Bay, about a mile from the city of San Diego, and invited the Army and Navy to send officers for free instruction as airplane pilots. Three Army officers stationed in California —Lts. Paul W. Beck, G. E. M. Kelly, and John C. Walker, Jr.—were chosen from some thirty who applied. They were ordered to San Diego in January 1911.

Since the Curtiss plane was only a one-seater, the student had to learn to handle it himself, using the "grass-cutting" or "short-hop" method. First he learned to handle the controls. Then with the foot throttle tied back to limit ground speed to fifteen miles per hour, the student began by taxiing up and down the field in as straight a line as possible. When he reached the end of the field, he got out of the plane, picked up the front end, swung it around in the opposite direction, and taxied down to the other end. His first flight at ten feet off the ground had to be a solo.

In April 1911, Beck, Kelly, and Walker joined Foulois at Fort Sam Houston, where they found on hand the Wright Type B and the Curtiss. The first fatality in flying training occurred on May 10 when Lieutenant Kelly crashed. The commanding general at Fort Sam Houston then prohibited further flying from his drill ground, which was being used as the flying field. Fortunately, the Signal Corps now had

funds for aeronautics, and it had already begun to build a flying school back at College Park, near Washington, D. C. The men and planes moved to College Park from Texas in June and July, and flying training was resumed as soon as the first plane arrived and was assembled. Foulois was ordered to duty with the Militia Bureau in Washington in July and did not return to aviation duty until December 1913.

The Flying Schools

Captain Chandler, who resumed his position as chief of the Aeronautical Division in June 1911, also served as commandant of the flying school at College Park. In addition to Beck, now a captain, there were also Lts. Henry H.

Lts. Henry H. Arnold and Thomas DeW. Milling, who had both learned to fly at the Wright School in Dayton, qualified as military pilots at College Park, Md., in 1911.

A number of aviation careers began at the school at Augusta, Ga., though unseasonably bad weather there during the winter of 1912 hampered operations. Above, in 1915.

Arnold and Thomas DeWitt Milling, both of whom had been trained to fly at the Wright School at Dayton in May, and Lt. Roy C. Kirtland. Since the Army had no prescribed test for qualification as an airplane pilot, it adopted the regulation of the Fédération Aeronautique Internationale as administered by the Aero Club of America. Arnold and Milling passed the tests in July and the others qualified during August and September.

Among the achievements of the flyers at College Park during 1911 were a "long," forty-two-mile cross-country flight to Frederick, Md., record-breaking altitude flights to 3,260 and 4,167 feet by Arnold, aerial photography experiments, and testing of a bombsight invented by Riley E. Scott, a former Army officer. The sight showed considerable promise, but the War Department refused to purchase it. Scott had to discontinue his experiments in order to enter a competition in Europe, where he won a $5,000 prize with his invention.

San Diego, Calif., became the site of the Army's first permanent aviation school. This is what the hangar line looked like in 1914, as war was breaking out in Europe.

Frank Lahm, with one Wright Type B airplane, opened a flying school in the Philippines, near Manila, in 1912.

Once again the men and planes moved south as winter came on—this time to Augusta, Ga. Flying activities were severely restricted from January to March 1912 by heavy snows, rains, and floods. Some of the pilots, trained on one type of plane, learned to fly the other, and some new student officers began their aviation careers at Augusta. In April 1912 the school moved back to College Park.

The availability of funds had a benign influence on Army aviation activities during 1912. At least a dozen more lieutenants were ordered to aviation duty and sent to airplane manufacturing plants for shop and flying courses—a newly inaugurated policy. At College Park the Army pilots pioneered in night flying and experimented in firing a machine gun from a plane. On June 2, Captain Chandler fired the Lewis gun, a low-recoil machine gun invented by Col. Isaac N. Lewis, from a plane piloted by Lieutenant Milling. The results were so good that the aviators requested ten more guns for further experiments, but the Ordnance Department could not supply them because the Lewis gun had not been adopted for Army use. The Lewis gun eventually became standard armament on Allied planes during World War I.

A detachment of several pilots, including Foulois who had been ordered to flying duty for the occasion, took two planes to Connecticut for maneuvers with ground troops in August 1912. Their reconnaissance flights were generally successful when the weather was good, but in bad weather they could not see anything from the prescribed minimum 2,000-foot altitude. The highlight for the flyers occurred when advancing Red forces captured Foulois and his plane after he landed to send a telegram to the Blues, informing them that their flanks were in danger.

By November 1912 the College Park school had grown to fourteen flying officers, thirty-nine enlisted men, and nine airplanes, including hydroplanes. One of the hydroplanes, built by the Burgess Company, was the Army's first

tractor plane, so-called because the propeller was mounted in front of the plane and pulled it through the air instead of pushing from the rear.

As winter came on, the Wright planes and the pilots went back to Augusta, while the Curtiss planes and pilots went west to San Diego at the invitation of Glenn Curtiss. From this small beginning, San Diego eventually grew into the Army's first permanent aviation school.

Flying activities at Augusta were hampered by weather and mechanical trouble, but the five flyers on hand gained experience. At the end of February 1913 their stay was suddenly cut short by orders to report to the 2d Division at Texas City, Tex. Relations with Mexico had become strained when the United States refused to recognize the revolutionary regime of Gen. Victoriano Huerta, who had seized power on February 22.

Chandler and his men assembled at Texas City early in March and organized as a provisional unit—the 1st Aero Squadron—in order to operate more effectively with the 2d Division. The Signal Corps felt, too, that the time was ripe to establish an air organization capable of military operations in the field. It could not expect much from the tiny handful of men and planes at Texas City, but from the standpoint of making a beginning toward organizational and operational development the Signal Corps was probably right. Luckily, the 1st Aero Squadron was not put to the test of combat operations since hostilities with Mexico did not occur, but the pilots were able to spend a good deal of time in the air, especially on cross-country flights.

For still another reason it was fortunate that the 1st Aero Squadron was not put to the test of battle. The unit's morale was low because of accidents and dissatisfaction with aviation leadership all the way up to the top in Washington. The pilots on the border sent the Chief Signal Officer, Brig. Gen. George P. Scriven, a round-robin letter. According to Arnold, then on duty in Washington, the letter demanded changes in "top aviation personnel in Washington, changes at Texas City, changes at the school at San Diego, and even stated who was to be put where!" Most of the demands were granted.

This was the first of a series of incidents that were to earn for the Army's flyers a reputation as prima donnas among the general staff. The exasperated Chief Signal Officer later described the flyers as being "deficient in discipline and the proper knowledge of the customs of the service and the duties of an officer." It was inevitable that Army aviators should want flyers to command them. This feeling grew stronger as time passed, and eventually it became a major factor in the gradual attainment of autonomy by the air arm.

The crisis with Mexico spent itself during the spring of 1913. On June 15 most of the men and planes of the squadron moved on to the aviation school at San Diego, leaving behind a small detachment of three pilots, twenty-six enlisted men, and two planes. At San Diego, they joined forces with the rest of the Army's air strength, which had been gathering at North Island since December 1912.

Actually, the San Diego school did not represent the Army's total aviation strength in 1913. In addition to the small detachment left behind at Texas City, two overseas training schools had been established—one in the Philippines and one in Hawaii. Lahm, who had been transferred to the Philippines at the end of 1911, opened a flying school at Fort William McKinley near Manila in March 1912 at the request of the Signal Corps. Using one Wright Type B plane, during the next two years Lahm trained several pilots, including Lt. Herbert A. Dargue, who was destined to become an outstanding leader of the Air Corps. The school at Fort Kamehameha, in Hawaii, established in the summer of 1913 under Lt. Harold Geiger, was less successful because of troubles with the seaplanes used for training, lack of facilities, and the treacherous winds in the area. The Kamehameha school lasted for little more than a year.

The Signal Corps decided to concentrate aviation training at San Diego and to abandon the field at College Park, where so much of early aviation history had been made. In December 1913 the Signal Corps designated North Island as the Signal Corps Aviation School. At the time, there were twenty officers on aviation duty there. In addition to flying training, the school began to emphasize ground training, in classes under such distinguished scientists as Albert F. Zahm of the Smithsonian, William F. Durand of Stanford University, and William J. Humphreys of the US Weather Bureau.

Special activities included minefield detection flights for the Navy, further experiments with the Riley Scott bombsight and parachutes, and new Army altitude and cross-country record flights. Once in a while, cross-country flyers from San Diego would have to land in plowed fields from which they could not take off. Their planes would have to be disassembled and shipped by rail to San Diego, where they could be put together again. Those were the days before instrument panels, and the flyer had to carry his own watch, compass, and aneroid barometer.

The Congressional Charter

By 1914 certain distinct trends had emerged from the confusion and uncertainty of the early beginnings of Army aviation. These pointed to a future of enormous promise. The state of the art had advanced rapidly, and unorthodox and freakish designs were giving way to machines based on sounder aerodynamic principles that would eventually lend themselves to standardization. Although the commercial value of the airplane had not yet been demonstrated, the military importance was beginning to be more fully appreciated, and governments were spending increasing amounts on aviation.

Other countries made far greater progress than did the United States. As early as 1911, five countries had more certified pilots, France's 353 contrasting with twenty-six in the United States, of whom only eight were military. It is estimated that between 1908 and 1913, Germany spent $22 million on military and naval aviation; France, $22 million; Russia, $12 million; and even little Belgium, $2 million. During the same period the United States spent $430,000.

By 1914 the United States had lost the leadership in aeronautics with which the Wrights had endowed it—and especially did it fall behind in military aviation. In 1914 the US Army never had more than twenty serviceable airplanes, as compared with about 100 serviceable machines in the British Royal Flying Corps and still larger numbers in the French and German armies. Safe from attack behind its ocean barriers, the United States lacked the intense spirit of international competition that pervaded the military establishments of the European powers in the years before the Great War. The American tradition of preparing for war only after it had begun would endure for yet another war.

In addition to money and planes there was the problem of getting and keeping pilots. Much of the difficulty arose from the dangers of flying, to which the high fatality rate—twelve killed out of the first forty-eight officers detailed to flying duty—was an eloquent witness. The tragic deaths in these early years were probably unavoidable because of the experimental nature of the flying machines. Information about flying could come only from actual experience, and the early pilots were truly pioneers—if not guinea pigs—in accumulating the data that permitted safer and more effective flying in the future. But with each fatality the War

First professional recognition for pilots came in 1912, when the rating of Military Aviator was established and qualified flyers were authorized to wear these badges.

Department became more reluctant to detail officers from other arms and services to flying duty. Furthermore, few volunteered because, as Capt. William Mitchell said, "They do not see any future in it."

In 1912, qualified pilots were awarded badges as Military Aviators and recognized professionally. A year later, Congress authorized thirty-five percent extra pay for a maximum of thirty officers regularly assigned to flying duty, and the Chief Signal Officer called attention to this new incentive in his efforts to attract volunteers.

But underlying most of the difficulties encountered by Army aviation was the lack of a clearly defined status and function within the service. Aeronautics was clearly a costly business, in terms of manpower, materiel, and facilities, and the Signal Corps found it increasingly difficult, in the face of congressional and public indifference, to support its fledgling air arm. Many flyers felt that Army aviation would never make satisfactory progress until it was given specific statutory recognition, with specified duties and strength. A bill introduced into the House of Representatives in 1913 called for removing aviation from the Signal Corps and establishing it as a separate arm of the Army. The War Department opposed the bill, and among the opponents were Foulois and Mitchell. Only one pilot—Beck—favored separation from the Signal Corps. The others felt that aviation had not yet developed to the point of becoming a separate arm or service of the Army.

Legislation finally enacted on July 18, 1914, gave statutory recognition to Army aviation, putting it on a firm and permanent basis. The act created the Aviation Section of the Signal Corps with an authorized strength of sixty officers and 260 enlisted men. It was "charged with the duty of operating or supervising the operation of all military aircraft, including balloons and aeroplanes, all appliances pertaining to said craft, and signaling apparatus of any kind when installed on said craft; also with the duty of training officers and enlisted men in matters pertaining to military aviation." The act limited officers to unmarried lieutenants of the line, provided for flying pay, and established the aeronautical ratings of Junior Military Aviator and Military Aviator.

Technical and Tactical Advances

In spite of a lack of funds and genuine support, in spite of inferior equipment and difficult manpower problems, Army aviation had made some progress by 1914. The primitive machines of 1911-12 were giving way to faster and safer aircraft. In 1914 the Signal Corps condemned the pusher-type plane that had accounted for most of the fatalities. The pusher had an unfortunate habit of diving and

Curtiss biplane in flight. Pusher-types, with engine behind pilot, proved dangerous, fell out of favor in 1914.

Curtiss tractor plane, purchased by the Army in 1914, was among first of its kind to be ordered by the government.

Here's the famous Curtiss JN-4A, "Jenny," one of the series of trainers used to turn out pilots in World War I.

crashing, probably because of an inherent weakness in the elevators. On such occasions, the engine would usually tear loose from the rear of the plane and ram into the pilot and passenger.

Condemnation of the pusher-type planes in 1914 left the Army with only five training planes at San Diego, and even these had to be reconditioned if they were to be of any use. The training program kept going with the help of a sport plane purchased from Glenn L. Martin at Los Angeles and converted into a satisfactory dual-control trainer. In 1914 the Army also ordered from Curtiss the JN-1, first of a series of trainer planes that were to become affectionately known to a whole generation of student pilots as the "Jenny."

The Army's difficulties with its assortment of early aircraft made a convincing case for settling on a standard airplane that would meet the tests of safety and performance. A competition among aircraft manufacturers in October 1914 produced only one plane—the Curtiss—that met specifications of four hours of nonstop flight and a 4,000-foot climb in ten minutes while fully loaded. But airframe and engine development moved too fast to permit standardization, and the individual manufacturers were too small to build planes in quantity.

Although its problems and its lack of funds persisted, the Aviation Section expanded its organization and its field activities. In December 1914, General Scriven stated that for an adequate air force the Army needed four squadrons of eight planes each with approximately fifty percent re-

serve planes—or a grand total of fifty airplanes—and twenty officers and ninety enlisted men per squadron. By September 1915, Scriven had raised his sights to eighteen squadrons of twelve planes each. Although information from Europe about the technical aspects of the air war was hopelessly inadequate, the Army had acquired some idea of the vast growth in the size of the forces involved, and Scriven's recommendations reflected this knowledge. But it required America's entrance into the war to bring about an expansion of Army aviation on such a scale.

The 1st Aero Squadron, which had existed off and on in some form since early 1913, reorganized at San Diego in September 1914 on a more official basis in accordance with a War Department order. It had sixteen officers, seventy-seven enlisted men, and eight airplanes. Under Captain Foulois, the squadron engaged in training and testing activities during 1914-15. In the years immediately preceding the entrance of the US into the war in Europe, this squadron represented the tactical air strength of the Army.

Meanwhile, relations with Mexico had once more reached a critical stage following the Tampico incident in April 1914. The 1st Aero Squadron immediately sent a detachment of five officers and three planes to Galveston, Tex., to join the US expedition against Vera Cruz, but it arrived too late to catch the transport and the planes were never unpacked. The detachment returned to San Diego in July. With the emergence of Pancho Villa as a revolutionary leader in Mexico, the Texas border once more became an area of tension and potential conflict.

Still another detachment from the 1st Aero Squadron—this time two officers and a single plane—went to Texas in April 1915. Operating from Brownsville, Lieutenants Milling and Byron Q. Jones reconnoitered the border area and were fired on by Villa's men.

In July the whole squadron moved from San Diego to Fort Sill, Okla., to take part in fire-control operations with the field artillery. The experience of Milling and Jones at Brownsville had shown that the airplane and field artillery did not work together effectively. Part of the squadron was dispatched to Brownsville once again in August. This, together with mechanical troubles, prevented any real progress at Fort Sill. In November, with winter coming on, the squadron made its first mass cross-country flight—439 miles, but not nonstop, to Fort Sam Houston at San Antonio. Meanwhile, the detachment at Brownsville flew a number of reconnaissance missions, but trouble with the planes once more limited their effectiveness, and they rejoined the squadron at San Antonio before the end of 1915.

On the Mexican Border

Within a few months of its arrival at Fort Sam Houston, the 1st Aero Squadron became the first and the only American tactical air unit prior to World War I to be tested under full field conditions. On March 9, 1916, Pancho Villa, the most notorious of the freebooting revolutionary leaders opposing the Carranza regime in northern Mexico, raided Columbus, N. M., and killed seventeen Americans. Provoked to retaliatory action, the United States government ordered Brig. Gen. John J. Pershing to organize a force of 15,000 troops to pursue Villa into Mexico and take him dead or alive. Ordered almost immediately to Columbus, the 1st Aero Squadron arrived there on March 15. Foulois had ten pilots, eighty-four enlisted men, and eight planes. Eventually, in May, the unit reached a strength of sixteen officers and 122 men.

Operating in the high winds of the mountains of northern Mexico, the squadron's handful of battered airplanes never had a real chance. On the very first squadron flight on March 19, from Columbus to the advanced base at Casas Grandes, Mexico, one plane had to turn back, one cracked up in a forced night landing, and the other six were forced down by darkness, four of them managing to stay together. This experience established the pattern of future operations. The planes could not get across the 10,000- to 12,000-foot mountains of the area on reconnaissance flights; they could not battle the terrific air currents and whirlwinds; and they could not fly in the high winds, dust storms, and snow storms. Short flights in good weather, with mail and dispatches, appeared to be about as much as could be expected.

Some of the flyers had experiences that bordered on comic opera. Two planes landed at Chihuahua City in Mexico to deliver duplicate dispatches to the American consul there. One was fired on by mounted *rurales*, and Foulois was arrested and jailed. Eventually, he was released by the local Mexican commander. Meanwhile, a crowd surrounded the machines, burned holes in the wings with cigarettes, slashed the fabric with knives, and removed nuts and bolts. Both planes took off, but one was forced down almost immediately when the top section of the fuselage blew off, damaging the stabilizer. The pilot, Lieutenant Dargue, had to stand off the threatening crowd until Mexican soldiers arrived to guard the plane. The plane was repaired, and Dargue took off at 5:30 the next morning to avoid the mob.

By April 20, only two planes were still operational, and these were taken to Columbus where they were condemned and destroyed. The replacement planes proved no more adaptable to field service in Mexico than had their predecessors. Although the squadron continued to be based at Columbus until early 1917, its operations over Mexico diminished after the summer of 1916. But many new planes did arrive, and the squadron used these in experimental and testing activities.

The Eve of War

The near-fiasco of the 1st Aero Squadron's operations in Mexico, at a time when aviation in Europe was daily demonstrating its great combat potential, served to dramatize the appalling shortcomings of Army aviation. The degree to which American airplanes had fallen behind European planes in performance was brought home to Congress and the public in a way that the warnings of the Chief Signal Officer and other Army officials had never been able to do. Word about the unhappy lot of the flyers in Mexico got back to Washington, and in August 1916, Congress provided what was then a huge sum— $13,281,666—for military aeronautics.

The Army desperately needed the money to train more flyers and buy better planes. Unfortunately, the better planes were not available because the American aircraft industry had fallen far behind in its development and production of airplane engines, the key to improved performance. The best engines had come from Europe even

Lt. Herbert Dargue, standing by his damaged plane during 1916 punitive expedition into Mexico, was threatened by mob at Chihuahua City. Mexican soldiers arrived to guard the plane, which was repaired and flown safely out next day.

Purchase of Martin T. T. with Curtiss OX-2 engine marked first time one company supplied the airframe, another the engine.

before 1914, but by 1916 the belligerent countries needed more engines than they themselves could produce. Such planes as American manufacturers built for the Allies usually had European engines installed in them after their arrival abroad.

Technical assistance of the highest order was on the way for American aeronautics, but it came too late for World War I. In March 1915, Congress created the National Advisory Committee for Aeronautics (NACA) "for the supervision and direction of scientific study of the problems of flight, with a view to their practical solution" and to "direct and conduct research and experiment in aeronautics." Unfortunately, NACA did not get its great Langley Memorial Aeronautical Laboratory at Langley Field, Va., into use until after World War I ended, but from then on it was the country's greatest force for aeronautical research and development.

The National Defense Act of 1916 increased the strength of the Aviation Section and established a reserve corps of officers and enlisted men. In a number of states, air units had been organized by flying enthusiasts, assisted by the Aero Club of America, a great force for aeronautical progress in the United States during these years. These units provided their own planes, often at their own expense. The only one ever officially recognized by the War Department as a National Guard unit was mustered into federal service in 1916 for a period of several months. In 1917 these air units and the reserve corps were an important source of manpower for the Aviation Section.

The expansion of Army aviation planned in 1916 was eventually overtaken by the events of 1917, but the Signal Corps made definite progress in adding training facilities and forming new aero squadrons by April 6, 1917. The school at San Diego had forty-five officers in training in October 1916, and a new school was established at Mineola, N. Y., to train candidates for the reserve corps and the National Guard. A new flying school was opened at Essington, Pa. In addition, civilian flying schools began training reservists for the Aviation Section late in 1916. Some Army officers learned to fly at their own expense. Among them was Maj. William Mitchell, assistant chief of the Aviation Section, who, in the fall of 1916, commuted on weekends from Washington to the Curtiss school at Newport News, Va.

In 1916 the War Department authorized the organization of seven aero squadrons of twelve planes each—four in the United States and three in the overseas departments. In addition to the 1st Aero Squadron, the 3d, 4th, and 5th would be stationed in the United States. The 2d Aero Squadron, which already had a company on hand, would be brought up to strength in the Philippines, the 6th Squadron would be stationed in Hawaii, and the 7th in Panama. All of the squadrons were in existence early in 1917, but only the 1st was fully organized and equipped, and even its equipment left much to be desired. Plans for further expansion of the Air Service to twenty squadrons were still in the paper stage at the outbreak of World War I.

American aircraft manufacturing on the eve of World War I was limited, at best. Here's a view of the Wright plant.

It was inevitable that aircraft, originally thought of as observation craft, should be used for bombing. This is a scene at an American bombing school in World War I.

Chapter 2

The Air Service in the Great War

THE achievement of Army aviation and the American aircraft industry in World War I was never as great as the promise. The task that the Army air arm set itself, at the insistent urging of the Allies, proved to be beyond the capabilities of the country because it was not possible to overcome in a brief nineteen months the effects of almost a decade of neglect and unpreparedness. Not until 1917 did America fully realize the extent to which it had fallen behind Europe in aeronautics. The resources on hand were not a broad enough base on which to build the enormous structure projected.

The resources in April 1917 were indeed meager. The Aviation Section had 131 officers, practically all pilots and student pilots, and 1,087 enlisted men. It had fewer than 250 planes, none of which could be classified higher than trainer by European standards. Its balloon strength totaled five. It had no bombers, fighters, or any of the other combat types that had been fighting the air war in Europe. It had only one fully organized and equipped combat squadron. The American aircraft industry had delivered to the Army in 1916 only sixty-four planes out of 366 ordered—and this represented the output of nine different factories. Furthermore, the performance of these planes, especially the engines, could not be compared with that of their European counterparts.

Clouds of Planes

Even more embarrassing than the almost complete absence of any tangible air strength, which, after all, could be blamed on the repeated failures of Congress to appropriate money for Army aeronautics, was the absence of plans and programs for building an air force that could fight in Europe. And perhaps most embarrassing of all was the lack of knowledge on which to base the program. According to one Army flyer, "Not a single air officer in Washington had even seen a fighting plane." The Army had failed to send trained observers abroad to gather even the limited information that could be gotten about technical and operational aspects of the war in Europe. Much

By the time of the Meuse-Argonne offensive, above, formations of hundreds of planes were fighting the air war.

of the fault here lay with the Allies, who exercised strict censorship of aviation information and refused to permit American air observers to visit the front. The British did not repeat this mistake in World War II, and the exchange of technical information between the United States and Great Britain was of great mutual benefit in 1940-41.

The idea of planning for a war before it began was still new to the Army and alien and repugnant to much of the public. There is a story that when newspapers published accounts of war planning by the War Department in 1916, President Wilson himself was indignant and outraged. The Chief of Staff and the Secretary of War had to explain to him that such planning was necessary and proper. At this time, "The War Department was concerned only with the mobilization of manpower."

The effort to provide a General Staff that would pull together the uncoordinated and often conflicting agencies of the War Department had been none too successful in the thirteen years since this change had been made. Congress was suspicious of this "foreign innovation" and limited the number of General Staff officers stationed in Washington. In 1917 the number was twenty. It was little wonder that there was a lack of coordinated planning and that it took the War Department the better part of a year to put its house in order. If the Aviation Section did not know what it needed to fight the war, neither did the

Army or Navy—nor the country as a whole—have any notion of what was required.

The original Army mobilization plan, which concerned itself only with manpower, contemplated an Army of 1,000,000, of which aviation would be "a relatively insignificant part." And the initial appropriations for aviation after our entrance into the war—$10.8 million in May and $43.4 million in June—appeared to confirm the minor role planned for aviation by the General Staff. On May 1 the Chief Signal Officer proposed to add six aero squadrons and two balloon squadrons to the seven aero squadrons already formed, but even this modest increase would have to await legislation. Fortunately, there were already forces at work that would lift Army aviation out of its obscurity and raise it to the highest priority among American war programs.

American artillery roars into action on the Meuse, 1918. Meanwhile, airpower was keeping the enemy off balance.

Although the press and the public were enthusiastic about expanding the air arm, it was the insistent urgings of the French and British that tipped the scales on the side of aviation. The Allies rejoiced when the United States entered the war on April 6 and hastened to place their technical knowledge at our disposal. Within three weeks, large and well staffed missions from both France and Great Britain had arrived in Washington to appeal for full American participation in the fighting in Europe. They felt that the United States could help most effectively by sending a powerful air force to help the hard pressed Allies on the Western Front in 1918. In a cable to President Wilson, received on May 26, 1917, Premier Alexandre Ribot of France proposed a program that became the initial basis for the expansion of Army aviation. Ribot asked that an American "flying corps" of 4,500 planes, 5,000 pilots, and 50,000 mechanics be placed in France during 1918 in order to "enable the Allies to win the supremacy of the air."

This proposal called for producing 16,500 planes during the first six months of 1918, far more than anyone had previously considered. The National Advisory Committee for Aeronautics had taken the lead in coordinating plans for aircraft production, and on April 12, 1917, it had recommended a program for producing 3,700 planes in

1918, 6,000 in 1919, and 10,000 in 1920. But the War Department disregarded this plan in preparing early in June a detailed program for Army aviation based on the French recommendation. A group of officers headed by Foulois drafted the program in a few days in an atmosphere of great pressure in which the "one thought was the supreme opportunity and the supreme need for haste." The program provided for 22,625 airplanes and almost 44,000 engines, plus eighty percent spare parts, which equaled another 17,600 airplanes. Although 12,000 were to be for use in France, the exact types were not yet known.

The magnitude of the program was enough to give pause to all but the most optimistic aviation enthusiasts. From the first Wright plane in 1903 through 1916 the American aircraft industry had produced fewer than 1,000 military and civilian planes; now it was being asked to produce 22,000 military planes in one year. France itself, in three years of war, had not produced as many planes as it was asking the United States to produce in one. The French had 1,700 airplanes at the front and 3,000 training planes behind the lines.

But Secretary of War Newton D. Baker approved the program before formal action by the General Staff and submitted legislation to Congress. It was greeted enthusiastically by the press and the public. The thought of great fleets of American planes turning the tide of battle in Europe fascinated almost everyone for a while. The Chief Signal Officer, Brig. Gen. George O. Squier, was so carried away by the dazzling vision that he appealed to the country to "put the Yankee punch into the war by building an army in the air, regiments and brigades of winged cavalry on gas-driven flying horses."

Secretary Baker announced on June 18: "The War Department is behind the aircraft plans with every ounce of energy and enthusiasm at its command. The aircraft program seems by all means the most effective way in which to exert America's force at once in telling fashion." Caught up in the atmosphere of fervor and buoyant hope, Congress rushed through an appropriation of $640 million for aeronautics in fifteen days, and President Wilson signed the act on July 24. It was the largest sum for a single purpose ever appropriated by Congress up to that time. It provided the foundation for the aircraft program, but it came a full 3½ months after the declaration of war.

With ample money, and hope for the future, the Aviation Section secured approval in August of a program for raising 345 combat squadrons, forty-five construction companies, eighty-one supply squadrons, eleven repair squadrons, and twenty-six balloon companies. Of these, 263 combat squadrons were intended for use in Europe by June 30, 1918, and the remainder in the United States, Panama, and the Pacific. But the high hopes of the summer faded rapidly as all production programs fell far behind.

Aircraft production lagged badly, and by December 1917 both civilian and military officials realized that we owed it to our Allies as well as to ourselves to lower the goals to more realistic levels. After consulting with General Pershing's headquarters in France early in 1918, the War Department approved a new program of 120 combat squadrons to be at the front in Europe by January 1, 1919. In August 1918, Pershing and the War Department agreed on a final program calling for 202 squadrons to be at the front by July 1, 1919. There would be sixty pursuit, forty-nine corps observation, fifty-two Army observation, fourteen day bombing, and twenty-seven night bombing squadrons, plus 133 balloon companies. Although only forty-five combat squadrons got to the front by November 11, 1918, the final program of 202 might have been met by July 1, 1919, if the war had lasted.

Emergence of the Air Service

US Army aviation never fulfilled the promises made on its behalf by civilian and military leaders alike in 1917—whether it was producing planes, raising squadrons, or "crushing the Teutons." But it underwent profound changes during the war that decidedly improved its position and pointed the way to future greatness. From the standpoint of the future, one of the most important changes occurred in the organizational structure.

The existing aeronautical organization at the beginning of the war was completely inadequate to meet the demands made upon it. The War Department had neither the knowledge nor the experience to direct the huge air program, and lacking precedent to serve as a guide, defense officials tended to think of the air setup as semidetached from the rest of the war effort.

The key problem from the beginning was production. To help the Army and Navy in this field, the Council of National Defense established the Aircraft Production Board in May 1917. Congress gave this agency legal status as the Aircraft Board on October 1. Under the chairmanship of a leading industrialist, Howard E. Coffin, the board advised the military services on quantity production and all related materiel problems. After October, when it came under the Secretaries of War and Navy, it tended to advise rather than "supervise and direct" as the law provided. Nevertheless, the Aircraft Board and its growing staff did the basic planning of the aircraft production effort and saw it through the first year of the war.

Within the War Department the General Staff had no real experience in air matters and was busy with other more familiar problems. The Signal Corps, under pressure to produce results, expanded the Aviation Section quickly and reorganized it into a number of divisions, all of which were individually responsible to the Chief Signal Officer himself, General Squier. This officer found himself in the unenviable position of personally supervising two major programs, of which the air was by far the larger. As Arnold later recalled, "The situation . . . was more a state of affairs than a chain of events."

By the spring of 1918 the aviation program was in great trouble. Production had not begun to approach the widely heralded goals, and the public optimism of the preceding year quickly gave way to painful disillusion. With this hard swing of the pendulum came investigations and charges that the agencies handling the program were inefficiently organized and administered. The outcome was a sweeping reorganization of the whole aeronautical structure of the War Department.

After preliminary steps, on May 21, 1918, President Wilson transferred aviation from the Signal Corps to two agencies under the Secretary of War: the Bureau of Aircraft Production and the Division of Military Aeronautics. The latter, under Maj. Gen. William L. Kenly, just returned from France, was responsible for training and operations. The new Bureau of Aircraft Production, formed from the old Equipment Division of the Signal Corps, was assigned "full and exclusive jurisdiction and control over production of aeroplanes, engines, and aircraft equipment" for the Army. Since its head, John D. Ryan, former president of the Anaconda Copper Co., was also chairman of the civilian Aircraft Board, a close and helpful connection existed between the two agencies. On May 24, the War Department officially recognized the Division of Military Aeronautics and the Bureau of Aircraft Production as constituting the Air Service, but it did not choose to appoint a chief of the Air Service to coordinate their activities.

The absurdity of not providing for close coordination

Bettmann Archive

Despite ambitious goals, American aircraft production was beset by problems. Above, aircraft parts are assembled.

of two such interdependent agencies soon became too obvious to be tolerated. On August 27 the President appointed Ryan as Director of Air Service and Second Assistant Secretary of War, the latter position assuring him enough prestige to make his weight felt. While the appointment was a step toward representation of aeronautics at a higher level, it may also have been designed to forestall creation of a separate department of aeronautics, for which there was a good deal of sentiment in Congress.

The new organization emerged late in the war, when many of the worst difficulties had already been, or were about to be, overcome. The end of the war prevented the Air Service from making a record in 1919 that would have at least partially vindicated the original claims on behalf of aviation.

The Planes

American airplane production during the war was a failure when judged by original goals and promises. But it was a substantial achievement when compared with the records of the other warring countries. During its nineteen months in the war, the United States produced fifty percent more planes than did Great Britain during its first thirty-one months of war—and Great Britain was the largest Allied producer.

The large appropriations for aircraft and the extravagant production programs of 1917 created rose-colored clouds which temporarily obscured the fact that the American aircraft industry could not produce 22,000 planes in the first year of war. In March 1917 there were only twelve companies capable of producing planes for the government, and their total production during 1916 had been less than 400 planes of all kinds.

Other factors were scarcely less important in their effect on production. Raw materials were often inadequate to meet the enormously increased demand. Drastic action had to be taken to ensure an adequate supply of spruce—the tough, resilient wood that was superior to all others for the construction of airplanes. The government, in effect, took over and operated the spruce industry in Oregon and Washington. The Air Service assigned more than 27,000 officers and enlisted men to the Spruce Division of the Aircraft Board. Working in the forests, mills, and railroads, they helped the industry increase production by 2,500 percent.

Civilians and military alike recognized from the beginning that the greatest problem would be production of combat planes fit for use in Europe. None had ever been produced in this country, and no one had the technical knowledge to do it quickly. There were not even any designs for such planes. The greatest deficiency was in engines. In 1917 the United States produced no engines that combined the light weight and high horsepower needed for use in combat planes.

The United States had to turn to its Allies for planes to equip its units on the front and for the technical knowledge that would enable it to produce combat planes for itself. The advice and guidance was sometimes more than a little tinged with self-interest and often showed a lack of real knowledge of the situation in America. But without the assistance of the Allies, the Air Service could not have made the gallant, albeit brief, combat record that it did.

COST OF REPRESENTATIVE AIRCRAFT, 1918

PLANE	COST	
Curtiss JN-4A	$ 5,550.00	
Curtiss JN-4H	8,042.61	
Thomas-Morse S-4B	7,750.00	
Dayton-Wright DH-4	5,750.00	Plus cost of one Liberty engine ($4,600 to $5,300)
Curtiss SE-5	7,442.61	
Handley-Page	48,000.00	Plus cost of two Liberty engines
Martin Bomber	40,000.00	Plus cost of two Liberty engines
Standard E-1 (M-Defense)	6,975.00	With Le Rhone 110 engine
Caproni	15,000.00	Plus cost of three Liberty engines
Curtiss R-4	19,148.62	
Spad	10,242.61	

The National Archives

Many of the US combat planes had to come from the Allies. From the British the US purchased 143 Sopwith F-1 Camels.

To gather vital technical information, the Army sent a large mission to Europe in June 1917, headed by Maj. Raynal C. Bolling, a newly commissioned but long-time civilian leader in aeronautics. As a result of the mission's findings, the aircraft production authorities decided to build training planes initially and to buy pursuit planes chiefly from the French. Pursuit designs changed so rapidly that it was considered impracticable to manufacture them so far from the fighting front. The French agreed in August to produce for the United States almost 6,000 planes—chiefly Spads, Nieuports, and Bréguets—plus some 8,500 engines, to be delivered by July 1, 1918. The United States would supply the raw materials.

Deciding the kinds of combat planes the United States should produce was a difficult problem. Efforts to standardize fighting planes during the war were unsuccessful because of rapid technical changes. During this relatively early stage of aeronautical development—1914-18—the British and French each developed more than fifty different types of fighting planes, the Italians more than thirty, and the Germans more than twenty-five. The United States used nine types of combat planes purchased from the Allies.

After much discussion and controversy, the Americans settled on the de Havilland 4 (DH-4), a two-place reconnaissance bomber of English design, for production in the United States. Eventually, American companies also placed the British Handley-Page bomber and the Italian Caproni bomber in production, but only the DH-4 was produced in quantity. The other programs were overtaken by the Armistice before any real progress was made. Production of other European models—including the Spad, Bristol, and Lepere—was considered or even undertaken in American factories, but none ever reached the production stage, usually because of technical problems. The only American-designed combat plane developed during the war was the two-engine Martin bomber, built around the American Liberty engine. This plane did not get beyond the development stage before the end of the war, but it became the standard bomber of the Air Service in the early 1920s.

Certainly the outstanding contribution of the United States to aeronautical development during the war was the Liberty engine. Designed and produced in America, it was good enough to be sought after by the Allied countries. There is a story that two engineers designed the Liberty engine in two days at the end of May 1917 in a suite at the Willard Hotel in Washington. This is only partly true because engineers from a number of companies and from the US Bureau of Standards also did a great deal of work on the engine. Produced in two versions—eight-cylinder and twelve-cylinder—the Liberty was destined to be the standby of the Air Service for more than a decade. In addition to the Liberty, American engine manufacturers during the war also produced

The National Archives

One of the popular pursuit types bought from the French was the Nieuport 28, shown here. The US purchased 297.

The National Archives

Between September 1917 and the Armistice, the Air Service received 4,881 French-built aircraft. Some were Spad 16s.

The only American-designed combat plane developed during the war, the two-engine Martin bomber, came into use in the early 1920s. Above from left, with the MB-1 in 1918, Lawrence Bell, Eric Springer, Glenn Martin, Donald Douglas.

in quantity two other domestic engines, the Curtiss and the Hall-Scott, and a number of foreign types, including the Hispano-Suiza, Gnome, and Le Rhone.

Beginning in the spring of 1917 the aircraft industry expanded feverishly, and sometimes haphazardly, in an effort to do its enormous job. Existing companies increased their capacities many times over, and a host of new companies came into the industry. But the narrow base of this expansion and the intricacies of the technical problems involved in putting new and foreign airplane and engine designs into production defeated the wholehearted efforts that most companies made to reach their goals.

In January 1918, production in the United States was at a monthly rate of only 700 engines and 800 planes, of which some 700 were primary trainers. Not one combat plane had been completed, and not one plane had been shipped to France. The country was aware in a vague way that the aircraft program was behind schedule, but even congressmen of the "watchdog" type were not especially disturbed. Ironically, the War Department itself touched off the uproar over aircraft production. It announced on February 21 that the first American-built planes were "en route to the front in France," implying carelessly that this was five months ahead of schedule. Actually, only one DH-4 had been shipped from Dayton. It did not leave Hoboken, N. J., until March 15, and the ship that carried it was torpedoed off the Azores. The first American DH-4 did not fly in France until May 17.

The revelation that the program was actually failing, instead of marching ahead as the War Department had implied, led to rumors that were followed by congressional and presidential investigations. Charges of graft and sabotage proved to be utterly false, but the presidential investigating committee, headed by Charles Evans Hughes, eventually strongly criticized the indecision, delay, defective organization, lack of knowledge and experience, and conflict of judgment that characterized the program.

During the war, the US produced a total of more than 3,000 British-designed DH-4s, two-place reconnaissance bombers.

Many pilots called the Bristol two-place biplane the best all-round fighter-reconnaissance plane of the war.

Reorganization of the aircraft production machinery in the spring of 1918 brought renewed, if more sober, confidence in the ability of the aircraft industry to make a real contribution to the war effort. The basic problem was to shift quickly from production of trainers, of which there were plenty, to production of combat planes, especially the DH-4, which was adapted to the Liberty engine. The success of the shift is shown by the increase in DH-4 production from fifteen in April 1918 to 1,097 in October. In all, the United States produced well over 3,000 DH-4s before the Armistice on November 11. To these may be added about 7,800 primary and advanced training planes, most of them the famous JNs or Jennies, plus a few hundred combat-type planes other than the DH-4, almost all of them experimental or test planes. The best estimates of production put the over-all total for the war period at more than 11,000 planes, as against 27,000 originally ordered.

Engine production from July 1917 through November 29, 1918, totaled approximately 32,000, of which almost half were Liberty engines and a quarter OX-5s, a Curtiss-produced engine used in trainers. The remaining 8,000 engines were foreign types, principally Hispano-Suizas and Le Rhones. One other type of aircraft—the balloon—played a prominent role in the air war in Europe and was produced in quantity. The country turned out more than a thousand balloons, including some 650 of the observation type.

Although training planes were indispensable to the building of an air force, the real measure of aircraft production had to be in terms of the number of planes it could put into the fighting in France. It was here that the greatest failure occurred. Of the almost 6,300 planes delivered to the American Expeditionary Forces (AEF) in France, only some 1,200 (all but three of them DH-4s) came from the United States. Almost 4,800 came from the French, but most of these were training planes. Perhaps a truer index of the American contribution is the actual aircraft strength in US units in the Zone of Advance on November 11, 1918. Of 1,005 planes, 325 were American-built DH-4s, and all the rest were foreign-built planes, chiefly Spads and Salmsons; of 740 planes actually in squadrons at the front, only 196 were DH-4s. During their seven months of combat action in France, American pilots flew foreign planes most of the time. And since the French and British naturally kept their best planes for themselves, the Americans often found themselves flying outmoded types.

It is perhaps only fair to note that the tightness of shipping and the priority given shipment of ground forces in 1918 played a part in retarding the movement of American-built combat planes to France. The record would probably have been better had there been more shipping available when the planes began to roll off the lines.

And the United States was not alone in its failure to meet goals for aircraft production and expansion of air strength. In August 1917 the Bolling Mission had contracted for the French to deliver to the AEF in France 5,875 planes and 8,500 engines by July 1, 1918, but only one-quarter of the planes could be delivered in time and the United States canceled the contract before it expired. Nor did the French reach the combat strength they promised themselves. They never met their program of 4,022 planes at the front by April 1, 1918, for at the end of the war they had only 3,321 planes at the front.

Training

Fortunately, the human material from which to build an air force was not only available but willing. The air war in Europe had a strong romantic appeal for young men stirred by tales of the daring, individualistic feats of the great air aces—Georges Guynemer, René Fonck, and Charles Nungesser of France; Baron Manfred von Richthofen, Oswald Boelcke, and Max Immelmann of Germany; Albert Ball and Edward Mannock of Great Britain; and William A. Bishop of Canada. Between July 1917 and June 1918 more than 38,000 of the finest of America's youth volunteered for flying training in the Army. Transforming this raw manpower and many other thousands into trained flyers and ground crews was the most staggering task faced by the Air Service.

With its tiny handful of 1,200 officers and men and its three flying fields as a nucleus, the Army's air arm began in April 1917 an expansion requiring it to multiply itself

France's René Fonck

Canada's Billy Bishop

Germany's Max Immelmann

Germany's Von Richthofen

more than a hundred and fifty times over in little more than nineteen months. At the beginning there existed no real knowledge of what it would take to produce pilots who could fly in combat on the Western Front. No American military pilots had ever engaged in combat and few, if any, had even flown in a combat plane. In fact, the Army had not one worthy of the name. Only from the Allies could there come the information and assistance that the United States needed to establish an effective training program.

The Aviation Section made certain basic decisions early, even before the full scope of the expansion became known. Training would have to be standardized; the personalized methods of prewar years would not serve to train thousands of pilots quickly. There would be three phases of flying training—ground, primary, and advanced. Most advanced training would be done overseas—in Great Britain, France, and Italy—where the right types of planes and experienced instructors were available. Large numbers of officers would be commissioned direct from civilian life in order to provide the planning and ground staffs needed for the expansion of the new training program.

After Foulois and others inspected the Canadian flying training system in April 1917, the Aviation Section took steps to launch the various phases of the training program.

World War I training field. American pilots were trained both in the US and in Europe. Some 15,000 cadets entered primary, and more than 10,000 pilots were finally trained.

Hiram Bingham, a Yale professor commissioned in the Signal Corps, played a key role in the training program. Before the end of May, Bingham had started ground schools for cadets at six leading American universities— Massachusetts Institute of Technology, Cornell University, Ohio State University, and the Universities of Illinois, Texas, and California. Until the end of the program after the war, these six schools and two others—Princeton University and the Georgia School of Technology—received almost 23,000 cadets and graduated more than 17,500. The original eight-week curriculum was later increased to twelve and was of great value in giving the cadets a theoretical basis for flying training.

The expansion of primary flying training could not be done as quickly because most of the fields had to be built first. Meanwhile, the Canadians provided flying facilities in Canada during the summer months of 1917 in return for the use of American fields in the south during the winter. By the middle of December 1917, fifteen flying fields were in use, including some that were to become permanent landmarks of the air arm: Chanute, Selfridge, Kelly, and Scott. Wisely, the War Department built most of the fields in the southern states where flying conditions were good all year round. Ultimately, there were twenty-seven flying fields in the United States and another sixteen in Europe.

At the primary flying schools in the United States, cadets could earn their wings in six to eight weeks, after a total of forty to fifty hours of flying, usually in the JN-4. Rated as Reserve Military Aviators (RMA), they received twenty-five percent flying pay. In all, almost 15,000 cadets entered the primary flying schools in the United States, and 8,688 received the RMA rating. Others received their training at overseas schools, making a total of more than 10,000 pilots trained during the war.

Training of Americans in Europe was handicapped by lack of facilities, late arrival of cadets, and the more urgent needs of the Allied air services, which naturally had first claim on planes and flyers. But cadets arrived in France as early as August 1917, and eventually some 2,500 came from the United States or were recruited in France. Unfortunately, more than a thousand of these cadets who arrived during 1917 had to spend months waiting at Issoudun, Tours, and St. Maixent before they got a chance to begin training. Meanwhile, they were called on for construction work, cooking, guard duty, and any other jobs that needed to be done. Because they received the then handsome pay of $100 per month, they became known at Issoudun as the "Million Dollar Guard."

The Air Service, American Expeditionary Forces, began building its own schools in France in August 1917, since the French schools could not handle the expected arrivals. Eventually sixteen fields—of which Issoudun was the largest and best known—were used to train American flyers. By November 1918 the American schools could give about 2,000 pilots a month their final or "refresher" training. In all, more than 8,000 pilots and observers received some form of flying training in France, the Air Service schools accounting for almost 1,700 fully trained pilots and 850 observers. About 500 Americans received all or part of their flying training in Great Britain, and a few hundred more at two schools in Italy. The greatest

Brooks Field, Tex., one of the twenty-seven flying fields the US used for training pilots in World War I. The War Department built most fields in southern states, where flying conditions were generally good all year round.

Balloons played an important, if unspectacular, role in the war. Balloon training was completely separate from the rest of the Air Service training program. Above, training balloon observers over a suburb of London.

contribution of these foreign schools was to give American pilots the feel of the planes they would fly in combat—planes that were not available in the United States.

But the French and British did not have enough training schools to handle the Americans, and the training establishment in the United States had to take over the greater part of advanced pilot training. Specialized advanced schools were set up, beginning with the first observer school in September 1917. Aerial gunnery schools were also set up, and all flying personnel were supposed to have courses in gunnery, an absolute requirement for combat service.

Flyers alone did not make an air force. Engineers, supply and administrative officers, mechanics, and a host of other specialists and nonspecialists were needed on the ground if the air mission was to be fulfilled. The remarkable development of aerial photography and radio created a demand for large numbers of officers and enlisted men trained in these specialties. Schools for the various officer specialties were established at airfields or at educational institutions, and thousands completed the courses during 1917-18.

Any hope that enough mechanics could be obtained from civilian life was dispelled by the autumn of 1917. Schools

American aviators at French training school, Tours, in 1918. Here, they prepare to fly in a flimsy, French-built Morane *rouleur*. Training in the foreign schools gave the Americans the feel of the planes they would fly in combat.

had to be opened to train enlisted men in a wide variety of specialties, including airplane engines, armament, armor, propellers, machine guns, ignition, welding, instruments, sail-making, vulcanizing, and copper work. At first, men were trained at factories and at northern flying fields that had to be closed down for the winter. Beginning in December 1917, heavy reliance was placed on large technical institutions to operate schools for the Air Service. By May 1918 more than 10,000 men had been trained at these various schools, more than half of them at the technical institutions. This met the most immediate needs. In June the Air Service concentrated all training of mechanics at its two large schools at St. Paul, Minn., and Kelly Field, Tex., and closed the others down. More than 7,600 men had been graduated from the various courses at these two schools by the end of the war.

The British also helped train American mechanics and other ground personnel at fields and factories in Great Britain. This was of mutual benefit as it helped relieve the British labor shortages also. Large numbers of mechanics were also trained at French factories and at American schools in France. Whole squadrons were trained in this manner.

Balloons played an important, if unspectacular, role in the war, and there was a constantly growing need for them. Balloon training remained completely separate from the rest of the Air Service training program. Special balloon schools trained pilots and observers and offered technical courses to the enlisted men of the balloon companies. Some balloon observers received their training in France. Up to the Armistice, balloon schools in the United States turned out 751 trained officers. The Air Service formed eighty-nine balloon companies of which thirty-three went overseas. Two companies were formed in France. By the end of the war the balloon force had a strength of more than 17,000 officers and men in the US and abroad.

Air Service, AEF

On April 6, 1917, there were five US Army aviation officers in Europe. Three were attending French flying schools; one was an assistant military attaché in London; and the fifth was an air observer in Spain. But the observer in Spain was the energetic and aggressive Maj. William Mitchell, and he lost no time in getting permission to visit the front as an observer.

The National Archives
Though American planes in combat were only ten percent of Allied air strength, Air Service pilots fought well.

During the next few months Mitchell studied the air war intensively, visiting airfields, depots, and headquarters, spending ten days at the front and flying over the front lines. On his own initiative, and with French help, he drew up and sent to the War Department on April 20 a plan for the organization of an American air force in France. He followed this with a steady flow of reports on almost every aspect of the air war. It is likely that he had a hand in developing the aviation program for the United States laid down in the Ribot cable of May 26. By the

THE WESTERN FRONT IN WORLD WAR I

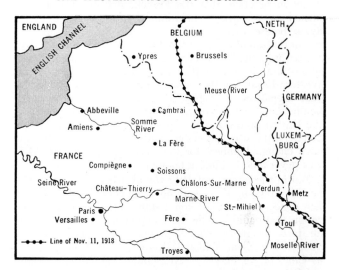

time Pershing arrived in France with the staff of the American Expeditionary Forces in June, Mitchell was not only the best-informed but probably the best-qualified man to serve as Aviation Officer, AEF.

Mitchell presented Pershing with a proposal for an Air Service composed of two distinct forces. One consisted of squadrons attached to the ground armies, corps, and divisions and under the control of ground commanders. The other force consisted of "large aeronautical groups for strategical operations against enemy aircraft and enemy materiel, at a distance from the actual line." The bombardment and pursuit formations making up this force "would have an independent mission . . . and would be used to carry the war well into the enemy's country."

Here was clearly foreshadowed the classic controversy over the proper role of airpower that was to agitate the American military establishment for so many years. The heart of the controversy was destined to be the concept of strategic bombardment. Mitchell's ideas reflected the powerful influence of the foremost prophet of airpower of his time, the advocate of strategic bombardment and unified air command—Maj. Gen. Hugh M. "Boom" Trenchard, commander of the British Royal Flying Corps.

Pershing appointed a board of officers, including Mitchell, to recommend the composition and organization of the Air Service, AEF. The board began with the assumption that "a decision in the air must be sought and obtained before a decision on the ground can be reached." Therefore, it recommended a strategic force of thirty bombardment groups and thirty fighter groups and a second force of a size based on the strength of the ground forces to which it would be attached. Pershing did not accept the board's recommendations. The first program for the Air Service which he did approve provided only for units of the second type. Although later programs included bombardment and pursuit squadrons, at no time was permission granted to establish an American strategic bombardment force.

Actually, the composition of the Air Service in France was probably determined more by the nature of the aircraft obtainable than by programs or tactical doctrine. The programs adopted by Pershing's staff had some influence on aircraft production in the United States in 1918, but the hard fact remained that most of the American squadrons flew foreign aircraft in combat. The Americans had to take what the Allies could spare them over and above their own sometimes-desperate needs.

The Bolling Mission, which provided most of the technical guidance for the American aircraft program in 1917, could not help but be impressed by the emphasis, in theory if not in practice, that the French, British, and Italians placed on strategic bombardment. But there had to be flyers before there could be an Air Service, and this meant that training planes would have to be given priority, at least initially. The American ground armies would need supporting air units if they were to do their part on the Western Front. For these reasons, the Bolling report to the War Department in July 1917 gave third priority to bombers and fighters for a strategic air force. By the time the United States was in a position to begin turning out bombers, the war had ended, and since the Allies did not have enough bombers for their own programs, the AEF was never able to build a bomber force of its own.

But in the summer of 1917 the aviation officers at AEF headquarters in Paris had no planes—only plans. Their first concern was to develop a staff and command organization that could handle the complex task of building an air force from scratch. On September 3, Pershing appointed Brig. Gen. William L. Kenly, a field artillery officer, as Chief of Air Service, AEF. Bolling served as assistant chief in charge of supply, while Mitchell became Air Commander, Zone of Advance. In November, Foulois, already a brigadier general, arrived in France with a ready-made headquarters staff of 112 officers and 300 enlisted men. After he thoroughly inspected aviation activities, Foulois succeeded Kenly as Chief of Air Service, AEF.

Building the Air Service in France proved to be a painful and halting process. Aside from the difficulties inherent in developing any military organization under the intense pressure of war, jealousy and friction within the Air Service further complicated matters. Air and ground officers were often at loggerheads. Earlier arrivals resented later ones (many of whom were newly commissioned civilians), and at the higher echelons such key officers as Bolling and Mitchell could not agree on their respective responsibilities.

By the spring of 1918 the lack of progress, aggravated to be sure by production failures at home and delays in French deliveries, could no longer be ignored. Pershing regarded the Air Service headquarters staff as a "lot of good men running around in circles." In May 1918, he brought in as Chief of Air Service a West Point classmate and senior Corps of Engineers officer, Brig. Gen. Mason M. Patrick. Pershing reasoned that Patrick would be able to stand above the strife of the ambitious young air officers, almost all of whom—including Mitchell and Foulois—were under forty.

Mitchell was subordinated to Foulois, who was placed in charge of aviation at the front in June with the title of Chief of Air Service, First Army, but it was difficult for the two to work together. The colorful, dashing Mitchell, determined to cut red tape and get things done no matter how, was bound to clash with the more studious and orthodox Foulois. Eventually, in an unusual act of self-denial, Foulois recommended that Mitchell be given the combat command and asked for himself the position of Assistant Chief of Air Service under Patrick. This change, in August, paved the way for Mitchell to become what he had wished to be all along—the outstanding American air combat commander of the war.

In May 1918, General Pershing brought in Brig. Gen. Mason M. Patrick to be Chief of Air Service, AEF.

When, in August 1918, Billy Mitchell became Chief of Air Service, First Army, his wish to be the outstanding American air combat commander was fulfilled.

The Smithsonian Institution

From this point on, the combat forces expanded rapidly, and new combat air commands were organized as new American armies came into the field. In October, Col. Frank P. Lahm became Chief of Air Service, Second Army; and Mitchell, newly promoted to brigadier general, rose to Chief of Air Service, Army Group, on October 14. Pershing had told Patrick that he wanted Mitchell to command the combat forces at the front. Another pioneer Army flyer, Col. Thomas DeWitt Milling, succeeded Mitchell at First Army. The establishment of Air Service, Third Army, just before the Armistice, completed the air organization at the front as of November 11, 1918.

The Armistice saw the Air Service beginning to fulfill the promise expected of it. There were 58,000 officers and men in the Air Service in France, about 20,000 in training in England, and a small number in Italy. For every plane at the front, the Air Service estimated it needed thirty-five to forty men.

Air War in France

The US Air Service made its combat record in World War I in a period of only seven months—from April to November 1918. It had required a full year for American aero squadrons to reach the point where they could support American ground forces at the front.

Aside from the logistical and training difficulties, there was a major difference of opinion between the AEF and the Allies, and this further delayed the appearance of American units. The French and British, already drained of their best men and hard pressed by the Germans, looked on the American forces, both ground and air, as providing a fresh and growing manpower pool from which to draw replacements for their tired and depleted units. They wished to attach American battalions to French and British divisions and individual American pilots and observers to British and French air squadrons.

Pershing resisted strongly, and his insistence on a separate American army responsible for a separate sector of the front ultimately gave the Americans an opportunity to prove that they could fight as an independent force. But, meanwhile, the desperate manpower needs of the French and British in the face of powerful German attacks could not be ignored. Beginning in the fall of 1917, US battalions and regiments served as parts of French and British divisions until they could be reunited into American divisions and eventually into the first US Army on August 10, 1918.

The experience of the Air Service followed the over-all pattern. Most of the American flyers and mechanics available for service at the front in late 1917 and early 1918 were trained in Europe. The Allies naturally wanted to use the young and fresh Americans to reinforce their own units, hoping to bolster Allied morale and discourage the Germans. Then, too, the Americans had as yet no combat planes of their own, and there was no other way in which they could get the combat experience they needed. The logic of this arrangement could not be disputed, and it was adopted as an interim measure, to be followed by the grouping of trained Americans into squadrons for use on French and British fronts. Later, when the American armies were formed, the American squadrons would be used with them.

There was little doubt that the Americans would fight well in the air. Since 1915, American volunteers had been flying with the French and British. Although the members of the Lafayette Escadrille were the most famous, many others had also won enviable reputations. After America entered the war, ninety-three trained pilots transferred to the Air Service and another twenty-six to the US Navy, while a number remained with the French. In February

American volunteers were in combat as early as 1915, many as members of the famed Lafayette Escadrille. Above, Raoul Lufbery sitting in the cockpit of his Nieuport, 1916.

1918 the flyers of the Lafayette Escadrille became the nucleus of the 103d Pursuit Squadron, the first American squadron to fly as a unit in action. The 103d continued to serve with the French, since no other American squadrons were yet ready for action. In order to take advantage of the experience of the transferred pilots, the Air Service eventually distributed most of them through new American units as squadron commanders and flight leaders.

The 1st Aero Squadron, of Mexican border memory, arrived in France under the command of Maj. Ralph Royce on September 3, 1917—the first American flying unit to reach Europe. After training at French schools, it received French planes and further training as an observation squadron. Additional American squadrons arriving in France during the fall and winter followed a similar pattern of training. In preparation for the eventual transfer of a sector of the front to the American ground and air units, the Allied High Command decided that American units should be gradually concentrated in the Toul area, toward the eastern end of the vast front stretching from the Channel coast to Switzerland. The front in eastern France, comparatively quiet since the first year of the war, appeared to be a good place for blooding the new American forces.

The American buildup in the Toul sector began in February 1918 with the arrival in the Zone of Advance of the 95th Pursuit Squadron. The 94th Pursuit Squadron joined it on March 5, but neither unit had machine guns for the Nieuport fighters they were flying. In spite of this deficiency, which could have meant the difference between life and death, they began flying pursuit patrols over the lines on March 15. When the machine guns finally arrived, the 95th found that it still could not start regular operations because most of its pilots had never received instruction in gunnery. They had to be sent back to a French aerial gunnery school, leaving to the 94th the honor of being the first American-trained pursuit squadron to fight at the front. This famous "Hat-in-the-Ring" squadron, later commanded by Capt. Edward V. Rickenbacker, began its operations on April 3. On April 14, Lts. Alan F. Winslow and Douglas Campbell shot down the squadron's first two German planes. The 95th returned to the front on April 25, and the two squadrons were subsequently formed into the 1st Pursuit Group. The tendency toward larger units was almost inevitable as the number of squadrons was increased; eventually, groups were organized into wings.

Meanwhile, the 1st Aero Squadron had arrived in the

Eddie Rickenbacker, center, and other pilots of the 94th Pursuit Squadron, first American-trained squadron to get into combat. Famous as "Hat-in-the-Ring" squadron, it was later commanded by Rickenbacker, top US World War I ace.

Members of the 11th Aero Squadron of the Air Service, which later was the 11th Bombardment Squadron, line up with their DH-4s at base in France, in 1918. The comic-strip character "Jiggs" was retained as the squadron insignia.

Toul sector on April 4, and on April 15 its pilots flew Spad two-seaters in the first reconnaissance missions over the lines. Two more squadrons arrived before the end of May, and the three were formed into the 1st Corps Observation Group, under French tactical control. Earlier, in March and April, balloon companies had begun operating with American divisions near Toul. The first day bombardment squadron to go into action was the 96th. Flying in French Bréguets, the 96th began its operations in the Toul sector by raiding the railroad yards at Dommary Baroncourt on June 12. By the middle of June, therefore, representative units of all four elements of the Air Service had gone into action around Toul.

In a desperate effort to smash the Allies before American resources could permanently tip the scales against them, the Germans launched a series of mighty offensives in March 1918 that reached a furious climax in the Marne-Champagne battle of July. At the beginning of the offensive, the Germans used massed airpower for the first time. Some 300 planes seized control of the air and attacked Allied troop movements. It required a still larger concentration of Allied planes to recapture control of the air. This lesson was taken to heart by all of the American air leaders.

At the end of June, American ground and air units moved to the vicinity of Château-Thierry, at the tip of the great salient the Germans had driven into the French lines. The American air units—1st Pursuit Group and 1st Corps Observation Group—together with some French units, were organized into the First Brigade under Mitchell and given responsibility for a portion of the battle area. Conditions were far different from those on the quiet Toul front. Great battles raged almost continually for weeks on end. The Germans had local superiority in the air because of greater numbers and the high quality of their *Jagdstaffeln* —pursuit squadrons. Outnumbered and facing superior planes—especially the latest version of the Fokker—the American pursuit pilots often found themselves outmatched. It was difficult to protect the observation planes in their missions behind the German lines, and formations of squadron size or larger became necessary.

The First Brigade found itself on the defensive throughout a five-week period during which the German attack was stopped and thrown back. The First carried out its primary mission of supplying information to the ground forces, but at a heavy cost in both observation and pursuit planes. In the most important offensive action of the air campaign, American pursuit planes joined British bombers and pursuits in attacking the large German supply base at Fère-en-Tardenois. Allied losses were heavy, but the attack forced the Germans to use fighters to protect their

One of the hottest American pilots was Frank Luke. He shot down two other German planes and two balloons the same day that he downed this German reconnaissance plane.

British BE-2C. Throughout much of the war German equipment, especially the Fokker planes, proved superior to the equipment used by the Americans and Allied pilots.

This is the Fokker D-VII biplane, which many called the best single-seater of the war. In one month in 1918, this German fighter brought down a total of 565 Allied planes.

supply bases, weakening their strength over the front. The experience at Château-Thierry was a hard one, but it prepared the American flyers for future campaigns as the Toul sector never could have done.

In August, Patrick placed all American air units along the French front under the Air Service, First Army, with Mitchell as commander. These units had increased steadily during July and August, and Mitchell organized them, along with a number of French groups, into three wings—pursuit, observation, and bombardment. Most of his bomber groups and some of his pursuit and observation groups were French. In all, the Air Service, First Army, had forty-nine squadrons, of which only about half were American. Mitchell also controlled a French aerial division with more than forty additional squadrons, and he had the cooperation, but not the use, of nine British bombardment squadrons from Trenchard's Independent Air Force recently organized for strategic bombardment of Germany. Mitchell massed most of this strength behind an eighty-mile front manned by the US First Army and a French army corps under Pershing.

The Allied forces prepared to wipe out the St.-Mihiel salient, which had been sticking into the French lines for four years. For several weeks before the attack began on September 12, the Air Service made ready for the assault. It succeeded in limiting enemy reconnaissance and collected the information needed by the ground commanders without arousing strong enemy suspicion of the American concentration. A significant measure of the degree of tactical surprise attained was the overwhelming superiority of the American and French forces at the beginning of the action—almost 1,500 planes against an estimated 295 German planes. For this campaign Mitchell had what was up to that time "the largest aggregation of air forces that had ever been engaged in one operation on the Western Front at any time during the entire progress of the war."

For the first time the Americans had numerical superiority in the air. Mitchell used it to capture and maintain the offensive in spite of increasing opposition, including some of the best German pursuit units from other parts of the front. During the first two days of the battle, bad weather kept most of the planes on the ground, but their many attempts to carry out missions showed that the American flyers had gained greater experience and confidence. With better weather on September 14 and 15, Mitchell could put his plans in motion.

About a third of his force—some 500 observation and pursuit planes—operated in support of the ground forces. The remainder struck behind the German lines, bombing communications and installations and strafing German columns. These attacks met strong German reaction in the air, and losses were heavy on both sides. The American day bombardment units met the strongest German opposition, and their losses were likewise heavy. But the over-all results were good, since the Germans had been kept on the defensive and most of the action had taken place well behind their lines.

In September the Allies were advancing almost everywhere along the line. The success at St.-Mihiel confirmed an earlier decision that the next American assault should be along the sector from the Meuse to the Argonne—in eastern France. After the Americans consolidated their lines on the St.-Mihiel front, the ground and air units disengaged themselves and moved into the Meuse-Argonne area. Once more, as at St.-Mihiel, the air units attempted to preserve secrecy. The Americans refrained from flying, other than as observers in French planes, until the attack was launched on September 26. They spent much of their time in training exercises with artillery and infantry units, a need revealed during the St.-Mihiel campaign.

For this final campaign, Mitchell had a smaller force than at St.-Mihiel, but it was augmented during October and November by new American units. His initial strength was more than 800 planes, of which almost 600 were American. Here again, Mitchell sought every opportunity to concentrate his forces for large blows at the enemy, instead of parceling them out among the divisions and corps, where coordination of their activities was always most difficult. By incessant assaults on the German rear, he planned to keep the enemy on the defensive and prevent an attack on the American lines.

From the beginning of the offensive on September 26, the bombers played a key part in establishing air superiority over the battle area. The biggest air battles were usually provoked by these bomber raids, for the Germans regarded them as a serious threat. The largest and perhaps most successful of the missions took place on October 9, when a force of 200 Allied bombers, accompanied by 100 pursuit planes and fifty three-place planes flying in two echelons, struck a concentration point where the enemy was forming for a counterattack. The bombers dropped more than thirty tons of bombs in the face of strong attacks by German fighters. Other "huge" formations of up to 190 planes hit sensitive targets behind the lines on October 30 and November 4. To cope with these assaults the Germans reinforced their fighter units, and the American day bombers suffered grievous losses on a number of their missions.

Pursuit planes escorted bombers and observation planes, and protected balloons. They also patrolled aggressively to force the Germans to fight. Some students of the air war believed that the low-flying patrols operating throughout the offensive in spite of bad weather proved "the outstanding success" of the campaign. From September 26 to October 1, American fighters claimed 100 hostile planes, and twenty-one balloons shot down. The 1st Pursuit Group, under Mitchell's control, operated over the battle lines against enemy planes and balloons, establishing a degree of air superiority that heartened the ground troops.

Capt. Eddie Rickenbacker was credited with shooting down twenty-six enemy planes, probably downed many others.

THE AIR SERVICE IN THE GREAT WAR   27

The observation squadrons were more successful in working with the infantry and artillery than they had been at St.-Mihiel. They defended themselves better and adopted aggressive tactics, attacking enemy machine-gun emplacements and strongpoints. Their greatest successes came in spotting enemy artillery and reporting visual reconnaissance. In this work, the balloon squadrons, of which there were twenty-three at the front by Armistice Day, also played an important part.

On November 11, 1918, Mitchell was Chief of Air Service, Army Group, directing the operations of the air services for the First and Second Armies and readying a third for action. He had forty-five combat squadrons at the front, with 767 pilots, 481 observers, and twenty-three aerial gunners. Two of these units—the British-trained 17th and 148th Pursuit Squadrons—had just rejoined the American forces after serving with the RAF on the British front since July 1918.

American officers continued to fly as individuals with Allied air forces even after American units appeared in strength at the front. In Italy, Capt. Fiorello H. La Guardia led a detachment of eighteen bomber pilots into action against the Austrians in June 1918. In all, more than sixty-five American pilots saw action on the Italian front, flying Caproni bombers.

The combat record in France was not statistically impressive. The 740 American planes in squadrons at the front on November 11, 1918, constituted a little more than ten percent of the total aircraft strength of the Allies. The Air Service carried out 150 separate bombing attacks during which it dropped about 138 tons of bombs and penetrated as far as 160 miles behind the German lines. American losses in combat were 289 planes and forty-eight balloons, including fifty-seven planes piloted by officers flying with the British, French, and Italians. A number of the 237 American officers and men killed in battle certainly

could have been saved if the Air Service had required the use of the parachute. Although the German flyers used parachutes in the closing stages of the war, the Allied air forces refused to adopt them. The aviators themselves stubbornly rejected them—partly because of skepticism and partly because of a "freakish pilot fetish that it was a sign of cowardice and lack of confidence in one's ability and equipment."

American pilots had confirmed claims of 781 enemy planes and seventy-three balloons shot down, but the true totals were less because of duplicate claims. The "Golden Age" of individual aerial combat, World War I saw the glorification of the fighter ace. Such American flying heroes as Capt. Eddie Rickenbacker, Maj. Raoul Lufbery, and Lt. Frank Luke became better known to the American public than all except a handful of American generals. No fewer than seventy-one Americans qualified as aces—each shooting down five or more enemy aircraft. Altogether, they shot down some 450 planes and fifty balloons.

Among the American aces of World War I were Capt. Elliott Springs (left) and Lt. George Vaughn. Each downed twelve German planes, and in addition Vaughn got one balloon.

The National Archives
Raoul Lufbery, taken the day before he died in combat, in May 1918. He coached Rickenbacker in air war techniques.

The National Archives
Carefree Frank Luke died fighting a one-man war. He downed four planes, fourteen balloons in seventeen days.

Between

World Wars

THE MORE thoughtful air leaders came out of the Great War with the profound conviction that airpower would be the dominant weapon of the future. Although the American experience in the war had been brief, it had been sufficient for them to glimpse the awesome potential of the air weapon. Men like Mitchell had the ideas, but they did not have the weapons to prove their theories. And they would have to wait two decades before aeronautical development could begin to catch up with their ideas. The years from 1919 to 1939 were hard for the young apostles of airpower, and they often despaired. But technology was on their side, and the time would come when the machines would bear out their words.

The Mitchell Era

With the end of the war, the Air Service had to face the sober realities of life in the peacetime US Army. The wartime machinery of expansion had to be thrown into reverse and the entire establishment reduced to what Congress considered a normal peacetime size.

Orders for 13,000 planes and 20,000 engines were canceled within a few days of the Armistice. Demobilization of most of the nearly 200,000 men in the Air Service also began immediately, and by June 30, 1920, there were fewer than 10,000 officers and men on hand. Ninety percent of the aircraft industry that had sprung into existence during the war was liquidated by 1920, and the remainder could expect little help from military orders. For more than a decade the Air Service would be using planes and engines left over from the war. Furthermore, the sale of large numbers of surplus military planes and equipment, a major job for the Air Service, met much of the civilian demand for planes, further reducing the market.

In January 1919 the Air Service and the General Staff made plans for a postwar aviation force of 24,000 officers and men. When Congress appropriated less than a third of

the money asked for the Air Service, this planned strength had to be cut in half in 1920. Furthermore, the Director of Air Service reported, "Not a dollar is available for the purchase of new aircraft."

The Fight for Airpower

Even before the war ended there was a great deal of discussion about the postwar organization of the air arm. Proposals for a separate Department of Aeronautics from congressmen and from a board appointed by Secretary of War Baker met resistance from the War Department, which insisted that the Air Service must remain a part of the Army. Baker himself opposed an "independent department of air." Yet he recognized that "the art [aviation] itself is so new and so fascinating, and the men in it have so taken on the character of supermen, that it is difficult to reason coldly, and perhaps dangerous to attempt any limitation upon the future based even upon the most favorable view of present attainment."

Congress agreed with Baker and with Pershing, who stated that "an air force acting independently can of its own account neither win a war at the present time nor, so far as we can tell, at any time in the future." The Army Reorganization Act of 1920 made the Air Service a combatant arm of the Army, with an authorized strength of 1,516 officers and 16,000 enlisted men, including a maximum of 2,500 cadets. This was out of 280,000 authorized for the whole Army.

Although regarded by many air officers—Foulois and Mitchell had been most outspoken—as a crushing defeat of their hopes for a separate air force, the new law did apply some lessons learned from the war. Indeed, the Air Service was unique among the combatant arms, for it was given control of research and development, procurement, and supply of aircraft and directly related equipment in addition to its personnel and training functions. The legislation did away with the dual organization developed in 1918 and ensured unified control of the most important aspects of the air mission. In addition, it met other complaints of the aviators by authorizing flight pay amounting to fifty percent of base pay and requiring the tactical units to be commanded by flyers. The Chief of the Air Service was given the rank of major general and the Assistant Chief that of brigadier general.

The blueprint of the tactical organization called for twenty-seven squadrons in seven groups under two wings. The fifteen observation and four surveillance squadrons emphasized the Army support role; four pursuit and four bombardment squadrons rounded out the force. One unit, equipped with Martin MB-2s, was labeled a heavy bombardment squadron and proudly pointed to as the first and only one in the Air Service. Balloons still had a place in the picture, and thirty-two companies were planned.

The General Staff insisted that the tactical squadrons operate under control of the ground commanders, as integral parts of divisions and corps. This dashed the hopes of air officers who believed that World War I experience, particularly at St.-Mihiel, had demonstrated the correctness of two basic principles as the best means of supporting the ground battle: concentration of forces under centralized control and priority of operations against the enemy air force. Tactical units in the United States were placed under the commanders of the nine Army corps areas that had been set up after the war. These commanders had air officers on their staffs as advisers. The Chief of the Air Service kept command of the training schools, depots, and other activities, which were exempted from corps area control.

Thus, Secretary Baker's young "supermen" of the Air Service lost out to the General Staff and its supporters on almost every major point at issue. Indeed, there was strong difference of opinion among the air officers themselves. Maj. Gen. Charles T. Menoher, Chief of the Air Service, opposed a separate air force in 1919-20, feeling that the air arm was not yet ready for that stature. And even the radicals—Mitchell, Foulois, Arnold, and others—were not always consistent or certain of what they wanted. But there emerged from the heat of the controversy that raged for a half-dozen years a number of ideas that eventually became basic doctrine for the air arm.

At the center of the struggle stood one of the most popular and colorful figures of the recent war—the "Fighting General"—Billy Mitchell. It was inevitable that a man of his audacious and outspoken temperament should become the leader of the fight for greater recognition of airpower. As Assistant Chief of Air Service from 1920 to 1925 he was the "gadfly of the General Staff and the hero of the Army's flyers." Convinced of the greatness of airpower's destiny and ambitious that the air arm be given a major role in national defense, Mitchell became a crusader and ended a martyr.

The heart of the problem was whether the air arm had an independent mission that would warrant its separation from the Army and Navy. Army generals and Navy admirals, with few exceptions, denied that either the experience of the past or the prospect of the future supported the idea of air operations independent of surface forces. It was true that American air experience in World War I had been confined almost entirely to use of observation and pursuit aviation over the ground battle area, and even many air officers felt that support of ground operations would continue to be the chief mission of the air arm. An independent mission, of course, meant bombardment of enemy cities and industries, and the Air Service had done hardly any of this during the war.

But other air forces had engaged in strategic bombardment during World War I, and their experience could be studied. The Germans had begun attacks on London as early as 1915, and the British had been driven by public demands for retaliation to organize the Independent Air Force under Trenchard in June 1918 to bomb the German

Convinced of the greatness of airpower's destiny and ambitious that the air arm be given a major role in national defense, Mitchell became a crusader, ended a martyr.

cities. Actually, the French as well as the British had considered bombing German industry in 1915-16, but they lacked the bombers, and the demands of the ground war always outweighed other requirements. Between June and November 1918, the British made a good beginning toward bombing industrial cities in western Germany, and at the time of the Armistice, Trenchard was all set to send his Handley-Page bombers on a spectacular mission against Berlin.

In October 1918 the Allied High Command established the Inter-Allied Independent Air Force, which might well have carried out a sustained bombing offensive against German industry but for the Armistice. Trenchard, its commander, conceived his mission to be "the breakdown of the German Army in Germany, its government, and the crippling of its sources of supply." In this effort, the US Air Service would have participated—production of Handley-Pages and Capronis permitting. Had the war lasted well into 1919, Mitchell might have had historical evidence to support his theories, and the subsequent history of military aviation in the United States would have been different.

Actually, the US Air Service in France had developed a doctrine of strategic bombardment before the end of 1917. In what has been called the "earliest, clearest, and least known statement of the American conception of airpower," Lt. Col. Edgar S. Gorrell, chief of the Strategical Aviation Branch of the Air Service in France, recommended in December 1917 the bombing of German commercial centers and communications in order to strangle the German army. The destruction of German industrial power was vital, Gorrell said, because the ground war was stalemated. Furthermore, the Germans might well attempt to destroy Allied industrial power. Unlike Trenchard, who proposed widespread, light attacks with civilian morale as the chief target, Gorrell recommended round-the-clock saturation attacks to overwhelm defenses and wreck production facilities. His plan included major groups of targets. The plan was never put into effect for reasons previously indicated.

In the 1920s, the climate of opinion in the United States was not favorable for military theories that smacked of the total-war concept. When Secretary of War Baker denounced the idea of attacking civilian populations, he undoubtedly reflected the opinion of most military and civilian leaders of the Western world. It was easier to "convince doubters of the technical potentialities of aircraft than it was to gain acceptance of strategic bombing as a decent means of fighting." Under the circumstances, it is hardly surprising that Mitchell's ideas of total war failed to win support and that civilian and military authority alike rejected strategic bombardment as an independent mission for an air force.

But Mitchell persisted. He was especially certain that the bomber spelled the end of seapower. His vision of airpower rather than naval power as the defender of the American coasts touched off a feud with the Navy that was all the more aggravated by his successful bombing tests against Navy ships. After a great deal of haggling between them, the Air Service and the Navy held a test off the mouth of the Chesapeake Bay in July 1921. Bombers from Langley Field, Va., sank three German vessels, including the powerful battleship *Ostfriesland*. In tests off Cape Hatteras in September 1923, Air Service bombers sank the obsolete US battleships *Virginia* and *New Jersey*.

It was true, of course, that the targets were sitting ducks—they were motionless, unarmed, and unmanned. But even while the Navy was discounting the ability of bombers to destroy surface vessels able to maneuver and defend themselves, it was busy taking the lesson to heart and laying the foundations of its own airpower. It required the devastating shock of Pearl Harbor to drive the lesson home beyond question, but from the 1920s the aircraft carrier was destined to be the prime weapon of seapower. Mitchell's hope that the Air Service would get the mission of coast

In bombing test against US warships, a Martin MB-2 bomber scores direct hit with phosphorus bomb on the USS *Alabama*.

defense was utterly frustrated by the Navy, and up to Pearl Harbor there still existed no clear-cut system of joint Army-Navy coastal defense.

The failure of his crusade fed Mitchell's impatience and led him into impetuous indiscretions that brought about his downfall. He wrote and spoke bitterly about the deficiencies of the Air Service and denounced the arch conservatives in the Army and Navy who stood in the way of reform and progress. In April 1925, at the expiration of his term as Assistant Chief of Air Service, he was sent to San Antonio, Tex., in his permanent grade of lieutenant colonel as air officer of the corps area. From here he continued to

The German battleship *Ostfriesland*, called "unsinkable," staggers under bomb impact from Mitchell's bombers, 1921.

Billy Mitchell, in uniform, and his supporters used his court-martial in 1925 as a public forum for their views.

loose blasts against Army and Navy authorities that could no longer be overlooked by his superiors.

After the loss of the Navy dirigible *Shenandoah* in a storm in September 1925, Mitchell issued a prepared press statement in which he spoke of the high command of the Army and Navy as being guilty of "incompetency, criminal negligence, and almost treasonable administration of the National Defense." The court-martial he had been inviting took place in Washington in November and December 1925 and served as a public forum for his ideas and those of his adherents in the Air Service—almost all of its officer corps. Since both President Coolidge and Secretary of War John W. Weeks had called for the court-martial, the conclusion was a foregone one. Found guilty and suspended from duty for five years, Mitchell resigned in 1926 to continue his fight on the outside. Within the Air Service the fever subsided, but only temporarily, for the germ was still there.

State of the Air Service

Many conditions in the Air Service that Mitchell criticized were beyond the power of the War Department to remedy. It was true that aviators had to fly old World War I crates because there was no money to buy new planes. But the whole Army suffered from severe cutbacks in funds after World War I, and the General Staff felt that the Air Service should take its share of the cut.

In 1921 the serviceable planes on hand and in storage consisted of some 1,500 Jennies for training, 1,100 DH-4Bs for observation, 179 SE-5 pursuit planes, and twelve Martin MB-2 bombers. Most of them were obsolescent and should have been replaced. There were no less than 330 crashes in these old planes between July 1, 1920, and June 30, 1921. Sixty-nine men were killed and twenty-seven severely injured—a large toll for a force that had fewer than 900 pilots and observers.

By July 1, 1924, the aircraft strength had fallen to 1,364 planes. Of these, only 754 were in commission, including 457 observation, fifty-nine bomber, seventy-eight pursuit, and eight attack planes. During most of the 1920s the total offensive strength of the Air Service in the United States consisted of one pursuit, one attack, and one bombardment group. There was also one pursuit squadron and one bombardment squadron in each of the three overseas depart-

ments. But most of the strength was in observation units.

By contrast with this composition, Maj. Gen. Mason M. Patrick, Chief of the Air Service from 1921 to 1927, kept recommending that in a "properly balanced Air Service twenty percent of the total strength should be made up of observation units and the remaining eighty percent devoted to 'Air Force' or combat aviation." In spite of general recognition that pursuit planes had emerged from the war as the dominant aircraft type, the lack of funds prevented securing new planes in quantity, and the existing imbalance could not be overcome for a long time.

With the bleak experience of the past in mind, General Patrick observed in 1925 that there was not enough money to "provide aircraft in numbers adequate to equip completely the present tactical units, much less to provide a war reserve." The only alternative, he reported, was to "continue experimentation and research until the best types of planes" had been developed and to be prepared to build them in quantity in the event of war.

On hand, in the years after World War I, were more than 1,100 DH-4Bs, which, though obsolescent, saw wide use.

For a few years after 1918 the momentum the war had given to research and development within the Air Service persisted, and the Engineering Division at McCook Field, Ohio, continued to report significant progress. Air Service engineers designed and actually built twenty-seven airplanes of all types at McCook Field between 1919 and 1922. After 1923, experimental activities declined for lack of money. Although the Air Service devoted almost twenty-five percent of its 1924 appropriation to research and development, the amount came to only $3 million. A small nucleus of officers and civilians carried on at McCook Field, working on such problems as bombsights, aircraft cannon, all-metal planes, and more powerful engines. Manufacturers took over most of the work of designing planes, guided by Air Service specifications.

In the decade after the war, development of aircraft, especially bombers, was disappointing to many air leaders. The experimental Barling bomber (XNBL-1) of 1923, a triplane weighing more than 42,000 pounds, could not get enough power out of its six Liberty 12A engines to fly even 100 miles an hour or to fly over the Appalachians on the 400-mile flight from Dayton to Washington. But it furnished the engineers lessons which were later of great value. The two-engine NBS-4 Condor, perhaps the best bomber of the 1920s, had a top speed of 100 miles per hour and a radius of action of less than 300 miles. This was hardly a weapon to meet Mitchell's prescription for airpower.

The principal pursuit model of the mid-1920s, the PW-8 Hawk, could get up to 178 miles per hour and 22,000-foot altitude, and it had a range of 335 miles. The difference in performance between the two types underlined the continuing superiority of pursuit over bomber and explains the emphasis on pursuit aviation during the 1920s. One other relatively new aircraft type emerged—the attack plane, designed for low-altitude attack in immediate support of ground troops. But the earliest, specially designed attack plane, the A-3 Falcon, did not appear in numbers until the late 1920s. It carried 600 pounds of bombs, had a range of 630 miles and a top speed of 140 miles per hour.

Nor was there ever enough money during these years to reach the strength authorized by Congress in 1920. A number of the flyers temporarily commissioned in 1917-18 had remained in active service for a time after the war, and some of these were commissioned in the Regular Army in

The years after World War I soon made the SE-5 obsolete.

The Martin MB-2 bomber came along too late for the war.

In the '20s came experimental all-metal planes like CO-1.

Barling bomber looked impressive but lacked performance.

The Curtiss A-3 Falcon was designed for low-level attack.

The Curtiss Condor ushered in the age of the big bomber.

Curtiss P-1 was a refinement of the PW-8 Hawk of the '20s.

Lt. John A. Macready (left) and Lt. Oakley G. Kelly, flying a fuel-laden Fokker T-2 transport, made the first nonstop flight from New York to California, in May 1923.

1920. Among them were some of the greatest of the future leaders of the Air Force: George C. Kenney, Ira C. Eaker, Muir S. Fairchild, Claire L. Chennault, Barney M. Giles, Ennis C. Whitehead, Kenneth B. Wolfe, and James H. Doolittle.

But the Air Service was dependent on a constant influx of young pilots because flyers were not considered fit for combat after the age of thirty-five. West Point could not meet the demand, so the Air Service continued, on a much reduced scale, the aviation cadet system developed during the war. Young men from civilian life were trained as pilots at Air Service schools and commissioned as reserve officers. Some of them were given a few years of active duty with the Air Service.

Although the Air Service was authorized up to 2,500 cadets, funds were never made available for this number. During the year ending June 30, 1921, graduates from cadet training numbered 190 airplane and fifteen airship pilots, and at no time up to 1939 were there more than 700 cadets enrolled in any one year. Nevertheless, the system provided a large reserve pool of trained pilots who would be available for immediate duty in time of war. In 1926 the Air Service had a reserve of almost 7,000 officers, many of whom were not pilots. The other source of reserve strength was the National Guard, whose air units were chiefly observation squadrons.

The training establishment took on a permanent form in 1922. Primary training was given at Brooks Field and advanced training at Kelly Field—both at San Antonio, Tex. Scott Field, Ill., offered balloon training, and Chanute Field, Ill., had technical schools for both officers and enlisted men. An engineering school was conducted at McCook Field, Ohio. The Air Service Tactical School at Langley Field, Va., trained officers as higher-unit commanders and taught the tactical employment of military aviation. The Tactical School moved to Maxwell Field in 1931. At this school originated most of the important studies and statements of air doctrine during the two decades between wars.

The Accomplishments

Although the accomplishments of the Air Service were sometimes obscured by the tempests that whirled about it during the Mitchell era, the small band of flyers and me-

chanics proved their wholehearted dedication to their profession over and over again. In spite of their worn-out planes and equipment, they made spectacular pioneering flights and continually pushed forward the frontiers of aeronautics.

The postwar "spectaculars" began with a 4,000-mile flight across the continent by four JN-4H airplanes seeking information for the establishment of air routes and landing fields, one of aviation's greatest needs. In the autumn of 1919, two flyers and two mechanics in a Martin bomber made a flight "round the rim" of the United States—9,823 miles. In a lighter vein was Maj. Henry H. Arnold's race against pigeons in 1921—from Portland, Ore., to San Francisco. Happily for the Air Service, he won the race.

The Air Service held its own in the making and breaking of world records for altitude, speed, and distance, although the intense competition among nations meant that records seldom remained in one place very long. Air Service racing pilots set new speed records in 1925, when Lts. Cy Bettis and Jimmy Doolittle won the Pulitzer and Schneider Cup races within two weeks.

But the major efforts went into long-distance and endurance flights. America's vast distances required long-range airplanes before aviation could truly come of age. And the ideas of Mitchell and his followers would have meaning only when planes could prove their ability to reach out to distant points beyond the continent. The first nonstop flight across the country—from New York to San Diego, Calif., in May 1923—pointed the way to the future. Lts. Oakley G. Kelly and John A. Macready made the 2,520-mile flight in twenty-six hours and fifty minutes in an Army T-2 transport. In June the Air Service made its first successful in-flight refueling test, and two months later, in August, Lts. Lowell H. Smith and John P. Richter set a new world's endurance record by staying aloft for thirty-seven hours and fifteen minutes in a DH-4 over San Diego with the help of refueling from another DH-4. This technique was to prove of immense importance in future military aviation —especially in the 1950s.

One of the most stirring feats of the period was the dawn-to-dusk flight by Lt. Russell L. Maughan from New York to San Francisco on June 23, 1924. In a Curtiss PW-8, he flew the 2,670 miles, with five stops, in twenty-one hours and forty-eight minutes. In the same year Air Service flyers made the first round-the-world flight—in 175 days. After careful and extensive planning and preparation, eight flyers took off on April 4 from Seattle, Wash., in four specially built Douglas World Cruiser planes. Two of the four planes made the entire journey—more than 26,000 miles— returning to Seattle on September 28. Less than thirty-three years later, in January 1957, three Air Force B-52s, with the help of aerial refueling, circled the globe in forty-five hours, flying 24,325 miles without landing.

There were other less remarkable activities that also contributed to the advancement of military aviation and, indeed, of all aeronautics in the 1920s. Air Service pilots and planes pioneered many of the airways across the United States, collecting valuable data and spotting airfield locations. Great strides were made in day and night aerial photography and in the use of radios in planes. Using bombers as well as transports, the Air Service moved men and supplies among its bases by air, foreshadowing the enormous air transport operations of the future. Along the still disturbed Mexican border, Mitchell started an aerial border patrol in 1919 to police the air from Brownsville, Tex., to San Diego, Calif. Flying twice daily from each direction, the patrols spotted illegal border crossings and discouraged marauding bands by a show of military force.

The Air Service also showed how the airplane could be used for social and economic purposes. In 1918, Army pilots and planes had inaugurated the airmail service,

Lts. Lowell Smith and John Richter set world's endurance record in their DH-4, in first use of aerial refueling.

The Smithsonian Institution

In 1924 Lt. Russell L. Maughan flew his PW-8 from coast to coast in less than twenty-two hours with five stops.

First round-the-world flight was made in 1924 by four Douglas World Cruisers, like this one, in total of 175 days.

turning it over to the Post Office Department after a few months. In 1919 the Air Service began flying aerial patrols over the forests of the Far West, detecting fires and directing fire fighters. The Forest Service eventually took over this work, but the Army flyers had saved thousands of acres of timber worth many millions of dollars. To help the Department of Agriculture in its battle against the boll weevil, Army planes sprayed cotton crops in Louisiana in 1924-25, laying the foundation for the large civilian dusting and spraying enterprises of later years.

Although the superiority of the airplane over lighter-than-air craft had been proved during World War I, the balloon and the dirigible still had their military uses. The Air Service had operated no dirigibles during the war, and afterward it agreed that the Navy should have exclusive responsibility for rigid airships. Work with semirigid and nonrigid airships brought no important results, and the crash of the Air Service's semirigid *Roma* in 1922 did not help the dirigible program. Only one other semirigid—the RS-1—was flown later, the Air Service placing emphasis on the balloon.

Peacetime flying activities, even including ballooning, drained the air arm of some of its best men. Unlike the other branches of the Army, the flying service was hazardous in peacetime as well as wartime, and there had to be a steady influx of officers and men to replace those killed in aircraft crashes.

The Army air arm lost some of its potentially great leaders in this manner during the 1920s and 1930s. Outstanding in this group were Lt. Col. Horace M. Hickam,

Pilots and mechanics of 1924 round-the-world flight pose with one of the World Cruisers after the 26,000-mile flight.

The Morrow Board, shown arriving in a Douglas transport for the International Races, at Mitchel Field, N. Y., in October 1925, rejected the idea of a separate air force but recommended that the name be changed to the Air Corps.

Capt. Ernest E. Harmon, Col. William C. McChord, Lt. Eugene H. Barksdale, Col. Leslie MacDill, and Maj. Harold Geiger.

A Decade of Patience and Progress, 1925-35

The agitation of the Mitchell era was not without its minor gains for the Air Service. The Lassiter Board, a group of General Staff officers, recommended to the Secretary of War in 1923 that a force of bombardment and pursuit units be created to carry out independent missions under the command of an Army general headquarters in time of war. The Lampert Committee of the House of Representatives went far beyond this modest proposal in its report to the House in December 1925. After eleven months of extensive hearings, the committee proposed a unified air force independent of the Army and Navy, plus a department of defense to coordinate the three armed forces.

But another board, headed by Dwight W. Morrow, had already reached an opposite conclusion—and in only 2½ months. Appointed in September 1925 by President Coolidge to study the "best means of developing and applying aircraft in national defense," the Morrow Board issued its report two weeks before the Lampert Committee's. It rejected the idea of a department of defense and a separate department of air, but recommended that the air arm be renamed the Air Corps in order to give it more prestige, that it be given special representation on the General Staff, and that an Assistant Secretary of War for air affairs be appointed.

Officially, the Air Service had been seeking a status somewhere between the two extremes of the Morrow and Lampert reports. Since 1924, General Patrick had been urging creation of an Air Corps directly responsible to the Secretary of War. He wanted a separate budget for aviation and a single air commander to control all air operations. In short, as he put it, he wanted a "status in the Army similar to that of the Marine Corps in the Navy Department." The Morrow Board report provided the War De-

partment with official support for its strong opposition to such proposals.

The Air Corps Establishment

Congress, too, accepted the Morrow Board ideas. The Air Corps Act of July 2, 1926, changed the name of the Air Service to the Air Corps, "thereby strengthening the conception of military aviation as an offensive, striking arm rather than an auxiliary service." The act created an additional Assistant Secretary of War to help foster military aeronautics, and it established an air section in each division of the General Staff for a three-year period. Other provisions required that all flying units be commanded by rated personnel and that flight pay be continued. There were to be two additional brigadier generals as assistant chiefs of the Air Corps. The position of the air arm within the War Department remained essentially the same as before, and once more the hopes of the air officers had to be deferred. Even the new position of Assistant Secretary of War for Air, held by F. Trubee Davison from 1926 to 1932, did not help very much.

Perhaps the most promising aspect of the act for the Air Corps was the authorization to carry out a five-year expansion program. Between 1920 and 1926, along with the rest of the Army, the Air Corps had suffered from a chronic lack of funds. Accordingly, it had never reached the strength authorized by the Army Reorganization Act of 1920, and in 1926 it had only 919 officers and 8,725 enlisted men, including 142 flying cadets, instead of the 1,516 officers and 16,000 enlisted men originally authorized. Its "modern aeronautical equipment" consisted of sixty pursuit planes and 169 observation planes, but "no bombardment or attack planes considered standard." Only 115 of the training planes could be called modern. Total aircraft strength was under 1,000. Clearly there was need for expansion and re-equipment if the nation was to have an effective air arm.

Lack of funds caused the beginning of the five-year expansion program to be delayed until July 1, 1927. The terminal date was accordingly set back to June 30, 1932. The goal eventually adopted was 1,800 serviceable airplanes with 1,650 officers and 15,000 enlisted men, to be reached in regular increments over the five-year period. But even this modest increase never came about as planned because adequate funds were never provided.

The Air Corps blamed the Office of the Secretary of War and the Bureau of the Budget for the cuts in its appropriation requests. The cuts by these two offices averaged almost forty percent over the five-year period. This unhappy situation reinforced the Air Corps' firm belief that it should have a separate budget. It should be noted, however, that the last two fiscal years of the program came after the onset of the depression, and funds for military expansion were not likely to be looked on with favor by either the administration or Congress. Most of the expansion in personnel actually took place during the first three years—1927 to 1930.

By June 30, 1932, the Air Corps had 1,305 officers and 13,400 enlisted men, including cadets. Planes on hand numbered 1,709. The forty-five airplane squadrons included four attack, twelve bombardment, sixteen pursuit, and thirteen observation. There were also two airship and two balloon squadrons. The gain over the 1927 strength of thirty-six airplane squadrons was chiefly in pursuit and bombardment units.

There were other gains of lasting importance, especially in training and logistics. In August 1926 the Air Corps Training Center was established at San Antonio. Under the command of Brig. Gen. Frank P. Lahm, it included the primary and advanced flying schools and the School of Aviation Medicine. This concentration under a single chief permitted closer coordination and control of training activities—to the advantage of the whole program. And within a few years, funds at last became available for the great flying center at San Antonio which had been proposed as far back as 1913. Randolph Field, the "West Point of the Air" of the 1930s, was dedicated on June 20, 1930, and became the headquarters of the Air Corps Training Center and the site of the primary flying school in 1931. The advanced training school was close by at Kelly Field.

But no sooner was the handsome new field ready for use than depression economies forced a reduction in the training program to graduate only 150 flying cadets per year. From the ranks of the cadets who passed through the Air Corps flying schools in the 1920s and 1930s came many of the future leaders of the Air Force: Curtis E. LeMay, Edwin W. Rawlings, Joseph H. Atkinson, Elwood R. Quesada, Thomas S. Power, and Donald L. Putt.

The Air Corps also put its logistical organization on a firmer footing with the establishment of the Materiel Division at Dayton, Ohio, on October 15, 1926, and with the appointment of Brig. Gen. William E. Gillmore as chief. A year later the division moved from McCook Field to a new and modern plant at Wright Field, which became thereafter the symbol of Air Corps logistics.

Out of Wright Field came the engineers and logistic experts who paved the way to future greatness for the air arm. These men rarely received the public acclaim accorded the more spectacular feats of the combat flyers and commanders. Leaders like Gillmore, Augustine W. Robins, Oliver P. Echols, William F. Volandt, Alfred J. Lyon, and Edward M. Powers made vital contributions to the logistical progress of the Air Corps in the 1920s and 1930s. And the engineers, both military and civilian, guided the technical development that provided the superior equipment which helped to win World War II. Outstanding among the engineering officers were Clinton W. Howard, Leslie MacDill, Franklin O. Carroll, Grandison Gardner, George W. Goddard, and Laurence C. Craigie; among the civilians were Albert W. Stevens, John B. Johnson, Ralph M. Ferguson, Adam Dickey, Opie Chenoweth, Clarence Clawson, Samuel Burka, and John Lamphier.

At Wright Field were the laboratories and testing facilities that contributed so much to the technical progress of the Air Corps. From Wright, the Materiel Division directed the work of procurement districts and the field depots, which provided supply and maintenance services to combat and training units in the United States. Civilians performed most of the work at the depots. Beginning in 1931 these depots—at Fairfield, Ohio; Middletown, Pa.; San Antonio, Tex.; and San Diego, Calif.—were linked together by an air transport supply service operating on a regular schedule. The Materiel Division had a degree of technical control over other depots in the overseas departments.

The dead hand of World War I equipment, especially engines, was not entirely lifted from the Air Corps until the 1930s, and until then it greatly affected the development and procurement of airplanes. Because the continued use of the World War I engines had hurt the US aircraft engine industry, Congress prohibited the production of new airplanes using Liberty engines. As late as 1930 the Air Corps still had more than $40 million worth of Liberty engines in stock, which it planned to use as spares.

Aeronautical Progress

The small band of Air Corps flyers continued to perform valuable peacetime services for the nation and to expand the limits of aeronautical knowledge. In 1927-28, as part of a continuing activity, the Air Corps photographed 35,-000 square miles in various parts of the United States for the War Department and other government agencies. For a period in 1929 the 3d Attack Group and the 12th Observation Squadron, operating from Fort Huachuca, Ariz., protected the border from air and ground raids by renegades from Mexico. In one of the most gratifying missions of the period, Air Corps bombers dropped food to Indian villages in Arizona, New Mexico, Colorado, and Utah, isolated by blizzards during the winter 1932-33.

There was notable progress in long-distance and endurance flying. On June 28, 1927, Lts. Lester J. Maitland and Albert F. Hegenberger flew a trimotor Fokker monoplane, the *Bird of Paradise*, 2,418 miles nonstop from Oakland, Calif., to Hawaii in twenty-five hours and fifty minutes. One and a half years later the Air Corps claimed a new world endurance flight record when the *Question Mark*, commanded by Maj. Carl Spaatz and including Capt. Ira C. Eaker and Lt. Elwood R. Quesada among its crew, stayed aloft for almost 151 hours between January 1 and 7, 1929, over Los Angeles, using the refueling technique developed in 1923. The flight of ten B-10 bombers to

A top aviation event of the '20s was Lindbergh's flight.

In 1929, the *Question Mark*, here refueling over San Diego, set new endurance record of almost 151 hours in the air.

From left, Capt. Ross Hoyt of refueling plane, Ira Eaker, General Fechet, Carl Spaatz, Elwood Quesada, M/Sgt. Hooe.

Alaska in 1934 tested the idea of reinforcing outlying possessions by air. Led by Lt. Col. Henry H. Arnold, the thirty officers and enlisted men made an 8,290-mile round trip in July and August, flying nonstop over water from Juneau, Alaska, to Seattle on the way back.

The B-10, an all-metal two-engine monoplane with a speed of more than 200 miles per hour and a ceiling of 28,000 feet, showed the heartening progress in aircraft development since the DH-4 and the Curtiss Condor bombers of the 1920s. All-metal construction, pioneered by Hugo Junkers in Germany, had come to be accepted by all of the leading air forces of the world. The steady increases

in horsepower per pound of engine weight were indispensable to the development of bigger, faster airplanes. Other significant developments included the controllable pitch propeller, retractable landing gear, improved bombsights, gun turrets, and electrically operated bomb racks.

The steady improvement in aircraft performance of the late 1920s and 1930s had a profound effect on the Air Corps. The believers in long-range bombardment—bomber commanders like Maj. Hugh J. Knerr and Lt. Col. Clarence C. Culver—had persisted in requests for planes designed solely for bombardment. Since most earlier bombers had been designed to be used for other purposes also, they could not be as effective as planes designed specially for bombing. The Boeing B-9 and the Martin B-10 of the early 1930s were important steps toward true bombardment aircraft, and they revived the hopes and aspirations of the men who believed in strategic bombardment.

Bomber development was so greatly accelerated that the new bombers were almost as fast as the best pursuits. Until this time, the pursuit plane had enjoyed a wide margin of superiority over the bomber, giving the opponents of strategic bombardment one of their most telling arguments. Now it appeared that the heavily armed bomber might be able to hold its own against the pursuit plane, and there were those who maintained that the days of pursuit aviation as the dominant factor in air warfare were drawing to an end.

The exuberant hopes raised by the B-9 and B-10 caused the Air Corps to press for the development of bigger and better bombers. Many of the leaders, including General Foulois—Chief of the Air Corps from 1931 to 1935—harbored a passionate determination to prove the validity of the airpower ideas so long derided by orthodox military men. They saw themselves on the verge of great aeronautical developments that could provide them with the planes they had lacked during the controversies of the 1920s. They did not have long to wait.

Other events after 1930 also helped to create a favorable climate for the acquisition of long-range bombers. An agreement in January 1931 between Gen. Douglas MacArthur, Chief of Staff of the US Army, and Adm. William V. Pratt, Chief of Naval Operations, gave the Army air arm responsibility for land-based air defense of the coasts of the United States and the overseas possessions. Two years later, in January 1933, the War Department officially stated that the role of Army aviation would include long-range reconnaissance and operations "to the limit of the radius of action of the airplanes."

In 1934, Lt. Col. Henry H. Arnold, top center, led flight of B-10s to Alaska and back in test of aerial resupply.

The "big-bomber" look was evolving in the 1930s, though in the Boeing B-9 the open cockpit was still fashionable.

Enclosed cockpits and retractable landing gear were features of Martin B-10.

General Foulois.

In maneuvers along the west coast in 1933, the Air Corps demonstrated that it could concentrate air units quickly for defense of the coasts. The maneuvers also showed the need for aircraft capable of long-range operations against enemy invasion fleets. They proved, to the satisfaction of the Air Corps, the desirability of forming a General Headquarters (GHQ) air force—a central striking force under the top command of the Army. Such a force would require long-range bombardment and observation aircraft to perform its mission of defending the United States and its possessions from seaborne attack. After these encouraging developments the Air Corps moved quickly to begin development of long-range bombers.

The GHQ Air Force

The emergence of the heavy bomber in 1935 coincided with the advent of the GHQ Air Force. The circumstances leading up to the two events were closely related and actually influenced each other. The idea of an "air force," separate from the support aviation assigned to Army units, had been urged on the War Department by Patrick and his successor, Maj. Gen. James E. Fechet, Chief of the Air Corps from 1927 to 1931. But the Army General Staff had not been able to see what mission the air arm could have apart from Army support. Nor did it agree that aviation should be concentrated under a single air command for use in the field. Now, the growing importance of coastal defense provided the Air Corps with a mission that could be carried out independently of the ground armies, thus helping pave the way for the GHQ Air Force.

By 1933 the Army was planning to reorganize its ground forces in the United States into an "integrated machine" of four field armies. In answer to a War Department query

as to how it might fit best into the new program, the Air Corps recommended a GHQ air force with bombardment, attack, and pursuit planes under its control for coastal defense.

A War Department board headed by the Deputy Chief of Staff, Maj. Gen. Hugh A. Drum, reviewed the Air Corps proposal in October and endorsed the idea of a GHQ air force, although it did not accept the emphasis placed on airpower by the Air Corps. Nevertheless, it recommended that the force be used for both tactical and strategic operations, including attacks on major installations in enemy territory. Although the Drum Board estimated that 2,320 planes would be required by the Air Corps, it recommended a strength of only 1,800 on the grounds that any additional planes, as well as additional manpower, would have to be at the expense of the rest of the Army.

While the War Department debated the proposed reorganization, the nation's attention was focused on the Air Corps by its unfortunate experience in carrying the mail during the winter and spring of 1934. In February 1934, Postmaster General James A. Farley canceled the government's airmail contracts with the commercial airlines because he was convinced that the contracts had been drawn up in violation of the law. To keep the service going, the Post Office asked the Air Corps to deliver the mail. What followed was the most ill-fated peacetime venture in the history of the Air Corps.

Without proper planes, equipment, ground organization, or experience in this kind of transport operations, the flyers attempted to carry on a service that the airlines had taken years to develop. On top of these troubles, the first flights on February 19 coincided with the beginning of a period of freezing blizzards, ice storms, squalls, and wind storms

General Fechet.

Loading the airmail in Denver. Bad weather and poor equipment combined to doom this venture.

from one end of the country to the other. The crashes began almost immediately, and within three weeks nine flyers had been killed flying mail. Public reaction, at first angry and annoyed, soon changed to concern about the adequacy of the training and equipment of the Air Corps. But for the tragic loss of life, the airmail episode might be considered a blessing in disguise for the Air Corps. It spurred the creation of two special investigating bodies that helped to focus attention on the inadequacies of American aviation and clinched the arguments for creation of a GHQ air force.

Almost a month before the Air Corps was mercifully relieved of the airmail job in May, a War Department board began to study the operations of the Air Corps and its proper relation to civil aviation. Headed by former Secretary of War Newton D. Baker, the board made its report in July. It rejected both a unified defense department and an independent air force. It denied most of the claims for airpower made by Air Corps officers and their adherents and clearly expressed its attitude: "Independent air missions have little effect upon the issue of battle and none upon the outcome of war." But the Baker Board did recommend creation of a GHQ air force made up of air combat units and capable of operating either independently or in cooperation with the ground forces.

It has been suggested that the Baker Board endorsed the GHQ air force idea in an effort to weaken the case for a separate air force and to head off a possible recommendation by still another board—the Federal Aviation Commission—for separation of the Air Corps from the Army. When this latter group—known as the Howell Commission after its chairman, Clark Howell—reported in January 1935, it refrained from comment because the Army had already ordered the creation of the GHQ Air Force, and the commission felt that the experiment should be given an adequate trial.

On the last day of 1934 the War Department ordered the creation of the GHQ Air Force as of March 1, 1935. The new command went to Brig. Gen. Frank M. Andrews, a member of the General Staff and one of the ablest officers in the Air Corps. From his headquarters at Langley Field, Va., Andrews concentrated the scattered tactical units under three wings, at Langley, Barksdale (La.), and March (Calif.) Fields.

Struggle for the Heavy Bomber, 1935-39

The history of the Army's air arm in the years immediately preceding World War II is, in essence, an account of the struggle to develop and use the long-range bomber. The great hopes for airpower, excited by the GHQ Air Force

and the B-17, were frustrated for most of this period. Only in 1939, when the European war was already looming on the horizon, did the natural and artificial obstacles to the growth of the Army air arm begin to disappear.

Air leaders had accepted the GHQ Air Force, but they were not enthusiastic about it as a solution to their problems. It was a compromise of what most of them really wanted, and it created new problems that seriously affected the organization and operation of both the GHQ Air Force and the Air Corps. At best, it was a step toward a more fundamental change, and General Andrews as well as the successive chiefs of the Air Corps—General Foulois, Maj. Gen. Oscar Westover (1935-38), and Maj. Gen. Henry H. Arnold—accepted it as such, sincerely.

Westover, a great stickler for observance of channels of military authority, normally tended to accept the *status quo* and strongly opposed ideas looking toward separation of the air arm from the Army. Andrews stood on the opposite side. While giving the new organization an honest and genuine trial, he became increasingly convinced of the need for greater autonomy. The strong differences between Westover and Andrews on this paramount issue inevitably sharpened some of the other issues that arose between their commands. Air officers tended to favor whichever camp they were assigned to, and the rivalry expressed itself in the efforts of each to absorb or control the other.

The difficulties of the GHQAF experiment stemmed largely from the divided authority to which it was responsible. For tactical training and employment it was under the control of the General Staff in peacetime and a theater commander in time of war. For administrative matters the tactical bases were responsible to the Army corps area commanders; and for supply and training the GHQ Air Force came under the control of the Chief of Air Corps. Here was plenty of room for discord, and the history of both

General Andrews.

General Westover.

the Air Corps and the GHQ Air Force can be told in terms of the attempts to reunify the air arm. Andrews repeatedly pointed out the absurdities resulting from this divided authority and urged corrective action. Some base commanders reported to four different superiors, the fourth being the chief of the Materiel Division of the Air Corps, who was responsible for maintenance.

Repeated recommendations from both Andrews and Westover failed to remedy the situation. The only improvement before 1939 was the exemption of GHQAF stations from corps area control except for court-martial jurisdiction. Finally, with the completion of Andrews' tour as commander on March 1, 1939, the GHQ Air Force was made responsible to the Chief of Air Corps, General Arnold, rather than the General Staff. The new arrangement permitted a closer coordination of personnel, training, and equipment functions at a crucial time—on the eve of an expansion that would continue until the powerful air weapon of World War II had been forged. The 1939 arrangement was not destined to last long, for the next three years saw the great changes in the structure of the War Department which finally brought forth the Army Air Forces—a step just short of an independent air arm.

The B-17

In the final analysis, the future of the air arm would be determined by the weapons that it could develop, acquire, and operate. And above all other weapons, the long-range heavy bomber could confirm the tenaciously held Air Corps belief in an offensive, independent role for airpower.

The more favorable attitude of the War Department in 1933 toward long-range planes made it possible for the Air Corps to press forward with the development of the plane that was to make history as the Flying Fortress. Taking advantage of a design competition that year for a multiengine bomber, the Air Corps encouraged Boeing, the only company to propose a design of more than two engines, to go ahead with a four-engine plane of advanced design. The prototype of this bomber—the Boeing 299—was based largely on a transport development by the company.

Designated the XB-17 by the Air Corps, the plane began its test flights in July 1935. In August it flew nonstop from

Bombers like the Keystone didn't meet needs of the 1930s.

Seattle to Dayton—2,100 miles at an average speed of 232 miles per hour. Although the original model crashed and burned at Wright Field on October 30, 1935, it had proved itself, and its purchase was assured. In the years that followed, the B-17 became a symbol of both vindication and promise to the air arm. It pointed the way clearly and directly toward an airpower mission independent of surface forces—either land or sea.

Actually, even before the B-17 appeared on the scene, the Air Corps had stated a requirement for a bomber far advanced beyond the Flying Fortress. Known as Project A, this plane was to have a maximum range of 5,000 miles and speed of 200 miles per hour, with a 2,000-pound bomb load. It was to have the ability "to reinforce Hawaii, Panama, and Alaska without the use of intermediate servicing facilities." In May 1934 the General Staff approved as its tactical mission "the destruction by bombs of distant land or naval targets." Boeing began development of the plane in June 1934, and the Air Corps contracted for one Project A plane, designated the XB-15, in June 1935. The plane flew for the first time in 1937, but it was too large for the power plants then available. The B-17 benefited from early work done on the XB-15, and the B-29 later was the offspring of Project A.

While the ambitious Project A was moving along, the War Department approved a contract in October 1935 with the Douglas Aircraft Company for the design of a still larger experimental bomber—the XB-19. One model eventually flew in 1941, but the 212-foot wingspan and

Boeing 299, introduced in 1933, was redesignated the XB-17 and began test flights in 1935. Its purchase gave new promise to the air arm.

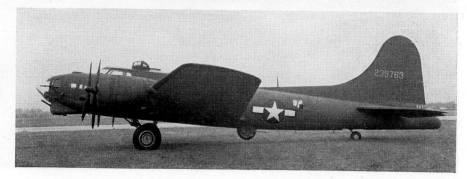

When war broke out, the B-17's silhouette had changed, but it was a new look that would be recognized the world over.

In 1937, the Air Corps was impressed by the giant Boeing XB-15, but it did not have the performance of the B-17.

160,000-pound maximum gross weight proved to be too much for the best engines then available. As with the XB-15, the engineering knowledge derived was invaluable in the development of the B-29 and the B-36.

Between 1935 and 1939 the B-17 was the air arm's chief hope for the immediate future. So encouraging had been the tests of the XB-17 in 1935 that the Air Corps recommended purchase of sixty-five B-17s in place of 185 other planes during fiscal year 1936. The War Department reduced the number to thirteen, even though an investigation showed that there had been no mechanical failure in the crash of the original model in October 1935. The contract signed in January 1936 resulted in the delivery of thirteen B-17s between January and August 1937.

To men like Arnold, to Andrews and his chief of staff, Col. Hugh J. Knerr, the B-17 was a vision of the promised land. In 1936 Andrews recommended formation of two B-17 groups—one for the east coast and one for the west. The Air Corps asked for fifty B-17s to be purchased in fiscal year 1938, but the General Staff preferred the two-engine B-18 as adequate for the Army's mission. Andrews

asked in 1937 that in the future his bombardment units be equipped only with four-engine bombers, but the total number on order in 1938 was only forty, and none of these was delivered until 1939.

Between 1933 and 1936 the General Staff had been comparatively generous in authorizing the series of bomber development projects. The Air Corps had been receiving the lion's share of the Army research and development budget all along, and the approval, for instance, of more than $600,000 for Project A had represented a good ten percent of the total Army development budget for a year. But a number of circumstances coming to a head between 1936 and 1938 combined to put a brake on the developmental work and to blight entirely the hope of equipping GHQAF bomber units with the B-17.

In the first place, the Army had been guided ever since 1919 by the national policy of arming for defense only. This was why the Air Corps invariably justified its requests for long-range bombers in terms of coastal defense and reinforcement of outlying possessions, rather than in terms of offensive action. This policy, carried to ridiculous extremes at times by both the government and the public, denied the Army, and especially the Air Corps, the weapons it needed even for adequate defense.

Second, the General Staff became concerned in 1936 about the equipment for the ground forces and determined to hold research and development to a minimum, devoting the maximum amount of money available to purchase of existing new types of equipment. For the Air Corps, this meant a scaling down of its development activities. From almost $6 million for the year July 1, 1935-June 30, 1936, its research and development appropriations declined to $3.5 million for the period July 1, 1938-June 30, 1939—the year of Munich and the rape of Czechoslovakia. E. I. du Pont de Nemours and Company spent twice as much for the same purpose during 1939. The General Staff refused to approve projects for developing heavy bombers beyond the XB-15 and XB-19 or for the purchase of additional improved B-15s. This was consistent with an Army view that the Air Corps had been "led astray by the allurement of a quest for the ultimate in aircraft performance at the expense of practical military need."

Third, the policy of getting the maximum amount of new weapons with the funds available also prevented the Air Corps from getting the B-17s it desperately wanted. The General Staff decreed that the Air Corps should buy

Engineering knowledge gained from the huge Douglas XB-19 proved valuable in the design of the later B-29 and B-36.

Air Corps said it needed fifty B-17s in 1938. Army General Staff said twin-engine Douglas B-18s (above) were adequate.

more small bombers, like the two-engine B-18, instead of the larger and more expensive B-17. This decision was no doubt influenced by the Army fear that overemphasis on heavy bombers would detract seriously from the ability of GHQ Air Force to carry out its prime mission of supporting the ground forces.

Finally, the major Army air mission of defending the coasts was undermined by a verbal agreement between the Chief of Staff and the Chief of Naval Operations in May 1938 that limited the Air Corps to operational flights of no more than 100 miles off shore. This action followed the successful "interceptions" by three GHQAF B-17s of the Italian liner *Rex* some 725 miles east of New York. Air Corps leaders believed that the Navy, alarmed by the implications of the flight, protested to the Army and that the 100-mile order followed. In its willingness to go along with the Navy's desire to have responsibility "for operations not only upon the ocean but in the air above the ocean," the General Staff may well have been influenced by the prevailing Army opposition to the long-range bomber. The agreement deprived the long-range bomber of one of its chief reasons for existence and threatened to cripple the GHQ Air Force.

Opposition to the long-range bomber reached its peak in the spring of 1938 when Secretary of War Harry H. Woodring directed the Air Corps to confine its bomber estimates for fiscal year 1940 to light, medium, and attack bombers. In a classic statement in May 1938, the Deputy Chief of Staff, Maj. Gen. Stanley D. Embick, summed up the position of the General Staff on heavy bombers as follows:

"(1) Our national policy contemplates preparation for defense, not aggression, (2) Defense of sea areas, other than within the coastal zone, is a function of the Navy, (3) The military superiority of . . . a B-17 over the two or three smaller planes that could be procured with the same funds remains to be established, in view of the vulnerability, air base limitation and complexity in operation of the former type. . . . If the equipment to be provided for the Air Corps be that best adapted to carry out the specific functions appropriately assigned it under Joint Action . . . there would appear to be no need for a plane larger than the B-17."

On the eve of Munich, the Air Corps was deprived of the mission for which it had ostensibly developed the B-17, and it was forbidden to purchase any B-17s beyond the forty already ordered. Not only did Andrews and Knerr fail to get their heavy bombers, but it appeared that they

had blighted their careers for good by their persistent opposition to official policy. At the end of his tour as commanding general of the GHQ Air Force on March 1, 1939, Andrews reverted to his permanent rank of colonel, and the Army assigned him to the same post to which Mitchell had been sent in 1925. Knerr was retired on grounds of ill health. Within a few years, both were to be fully vindicated and promoted to posts of high responsibility in the Army.

Beginning of Rearmament

During the crisis over Czechoslovakia in the summer and fall of 1938, Adolf Hitler and the Luftwaffe demonstrated that airpower had become a powerful factor in international relations—if only as an instrument of blackmail. Fortunately for the United States, President Roosevelt recognized the significance of the Luftwaffe's role. According to his confidant and adviser, Harry Hopkins, the President was "sure then that we were going to get into war and he believed that airpower would win it."

Roosevelt's first concern was to build up US aircraft production in order to help equip the French and British air forces as well as our own. Both France and Great Britain, alarmed by the strength of the Luftwaffe, had already turned to American manufacturers to help them make up their production deficits. But Roosevelt correctly perceived that only American air rearmament could provide an increase in aircraft production on the scale likely to be required in the future. The first step toward US air rearmament had already been taken with the passage of the Naval Expansion Act of May 1938. Recognizing the near-obsolescence of the whole naval air arm, the act included a maximum 3,000-plane program.

Virtually assured of a favorable reception by the White House, the Air Corps drafted plans during October 1938 for a force ranging up to 7,000 planes. At a conference with his military advisers, Roosevelt asked the War Department to prepare a program for an Air Corps of 10,000 planes, of which 3,750 would be combat planes. He emphasized strongly the need for greatly increased aircraft production. Among those present were Maj. Gen. George C. Marshall, the new Army Deputy Chief of Staff, and Maj. Gen. Henry H. Arnold, who had become Chief of the Air Corps after the tragic death of General Westover in an airplane crash on September 21, 1938. An air veteran who had somehow survived the hazards of flying in the early days, Arnold knew that airplanes alone did not make an air force. He impressed on the President at this time

When GHQ Air Force B-17s intercepted liner _Rex_ 725 miles east of New York, the long-range implications were obvious.

and later that a well-balanced air force required air bases and trained men also.

The need for similar increases in the ground forces compelled changes in the plans to use for the Air Corps alone the additional $500 million the President planned to ask from Congress. The President receded somewhat from his former position and agreed that only $300 million should be used for the Air Corps and that only $180 million of the amount should go for combat planes. The practical outcome, therefore, was to place a limit of 6,000 planes on the program which was to be presented to Congress.

In a special message to Congress on January 12, 1939, the President stated flatly that "our existing [air] forces are so utterly inadequate that they must be immediately strengthened." Congress responded quickly, passing the necessary legislation on April 3. It authorized $300 million for an Air Corps "not to exceed _six thousand_ serviceable airplanes." The program actually adopted by the Air Corps and War Department was for 5,500 airplanes, the most they could get with the money. This meant that the Air Corps would be able to buy 3,251 planes during the next two years, twice as many as it had on hand at the beginning of 1939. By June 30, 1941, the Air Corps hoped to have a balanced force of 5,500 planes with a strength of 48,000 officers and men, plus the necessary equipment to operate such a force.

In the face of such positive recognition of the potentialities of airpower, the Army was forced to reexamine the restrictions it had placed on its air arm. In March 1939 an Air Board began studying how to best use aircraft in hemisphere defense. On September 1, the first day of the war in Europe and his first day as Chief of Staff, Gen. George C. Marshall reviewed the board's report for the Secretary of War and concluded that it established "for the first time a specific mission for the Air Corps." The strategy of national defense was broadened to include the whole Western Hemisphere. For guarding the approaches to the United States from the Caribbean and Latin America, the board looked to the long-range airplane. Its flexibility of movement and its striking power pointed up the need for acquiring outlying bases to extend even farther its radius of action. The Air Corps now had a mission demanding the fullest development of the long-range

bomber, so recently rejected as an appropriate weapon for the US Army.

Air Corps emphasis on the long-range bomber, although justified by later events, adversely affected the development of fighter planes. While the B-17 was the outstanding bombardment plane in the world from the time of its emergence until the B-29 appeared, American fighters lagged behind those of the RAF and the Luftwaffe from 1935 until the P-47 and the P-51 entered battle in 1943. As the B-17 demonstrated its potential prowess in the late 1930s, Air Corps leaders came to assume "the ascendancy of bombardment over pursuit." There can be no doubt that this attitude hindered the development of fighter planes. This belief that big bombers could be made to go as fast as pursuits and could defend themselves against fighters contributed much to the failure to provide escort fighters for the heavy bombers in the early years of World War II—one of the biggest mistakes of the air war. The tendency to downgrade fighter aviation, opposed bitterly by the outstanding fighter specialist, Capt. Claire L. Chennault, extended also to interceptors, with the result that the Army Air Forces had no adequate night fighters in action until 1944.

The fighter planes that were to carry the burden during the first two years of the war—P-39, P-40, and P-38—were designed in 1936-37, but they were not ready when the war in Europe began. The P-38 did not get into action until late 1942. Unquestionably, the limited funds available for development and the use of a large portion of these funds for heavy bomber development, hindered the fighter program.

The attack bombers, which became the medium bombers of World War II, fared better than did the fighters between 1935 and 1939. The A-20 was originally designed by Douglas in 1937 for the French Air Force. The Air Corps bought the B-25 and the B-26 right off the manufacturers' drawing boards in 1938 and 1939. All three aircraft met most of the requirements for tactical bombers during World War II.

But all these planes belonged to the future. Of the types of planes on hand in the Air Corps on September 1, 1939, only one—the B-17—flew as a first-line plane after Pearl Harbor. And there were only twenty-three B-17s on hand in September 1939. The B-24, running mate of the B-17 during the war, was hardly off the drawing boards at the time. The standard bomber was the B-18, a two-engine plane greatly inferior to the B-17 in performance. The A-17 was the standard attack plane, and the P-36 the standard fighter. The three standard models comprised 700 of the 800 first-line combat aircraft of the Air Corps. By the time of Pearl Harbor they were all obsolete.

President Roosevelt had these planes in mind in January 1939 when he referred to the "antiquated weapons" of the Air Corps. So did General Andrews when he described the US Army air arm as a "fifth-rate air force." A comparison with the British and German air forces as of September 1939 reveals the extent to which American military aviation had lagged. The 26,000 officers, cadets, and enlisted men in the Air Corps included approximately 2,000 pilots and 2,600 aircraft mechanics. The Luftwaffe had a strength of more than 500,000, including 50,000 to 75,000 aircrewmen alone. The RAF had more than 100,000 officers and men.

The numerical inferiority of the Air Corps in first-line planes—800 as against 4,100 for the Germans and 1,900 for the British—was actually worse than it appears because the planes themselves were inferior. The Spitfire and the Hurricane of the RAF and the Messerschmitt-109 of the Luftwaffe could fly faster and higher than the latest model P-36 and carried more armament. The German attack bombers —the Junkers-87 Stuka and the Junkers-88—outclassed the A-17 in every respect. Only the B-17 was superior to the best British and German bombers of the time.

Fortunately for the Air Corps and the country, we did not have to fight in 1939, or the sad experience of 1917 might well have been repeated. More than two years would elapse before the Pearl Harbor catastrophe. In the interval, there would be time for rearmament and industrial mobilization. But in 1939 we still had only the plans and programs. The substance of airpower was yet to come.

Generals Arnold and Marshall began working together on Air Corps expansion plans at White House conference in 1938.

Curtiss P-36 was the standard first-line fighter aircraft in 1939. By Pearl Harbor time, it and its mates were obsolete.

Chapter 4

WORLD WAR II | 1939-45

Poland to Pearl Harbor

1939-41

THE United States was unprepared for war in 1939, but not for lack of warning. For eight years the comparatively stable and law-abiding world order of the 1920s had been under open attack by nations that regarded existing treaties simply as obstacles to the fulfillment of their ambitions. Beginning with the Japanese conquest of Manchuria in 1931, the pattern of aggression had unfolded steadily as the Italians and the Germans swallowed up their helpless victims.

A Distant Drum

Until September 1939 the American people, though frequently stirred to moral indignation, had felt little more concern over the expanding epidemic of aggression than if it had been on another planet. The nation was lulled by a deep-seated conviction that so long as the American and British fleets held the seas, the United States was invulnerable to attack.

The defense establishment reflected national policy. On the eve of the war, the US Navy was possibly the largest in the world. By contrast, the US Army was a little cadre of about 200,000 men, including the 26,000 who composed its air arm. Any talk of expansion still roused dark suspicions of militarism. When General Arnold went before Congress in the summer of 1939 to ask for more aircraft, the question was still: "I want to ask you—who [sic] are we going to fight?"

In Europe, Adolf Hitler had no doubts about whom he was going to fight. His tanks and planes crossed the Polish border on September 1. Two days later the British and French, who had promised to aid Poland if she were attacked, honored their pledge by declaring war on Germany. A second World War had begun. What followed was an exhibition of something new in warfare. The Luftwaffe destroyed the Polish Air Force of fewer than 500 antiquated planes at the outset; then it held the Polish armies paralyzed while fast-moving columns, spearheaded by pan-

zer divisions, swept around them and destroyed them piecemeal. In sixteen days, Poland was hopelessly defeated.

The fall of Poland shocked American complacency, and the President seized the opportunity to initiate changes in the iron restrictions of the neutrality laws. After fierce debate, Congress enacted a new "cash and carry" law in November, allowing belligerents to buy arms in the United States if they paid in cash and took the goods home in their own ships. Since German shipping had been swept from the seas, the beneficiaries of the new policy were England and France. Both nations desperately needed aircraft to catch up with the Luftwaffe, and the American aircraft industry appeared to be their best hope.

Although the British aircraft industry had expanded miraculously from 150 planes a month in 1938 to 700 a month at the outbreak of war, it could not catch up with the rapidly mounting needs of the Royal Air Force. French production remained pitifully small. By the close of 1939 the two Allies had ordered 2,500 aircraft in the United States; before the end of March 1940 they had arranged for the purchase of 8,200 combat planes of the latest types. Such orders, piled on top of the Air Corps twenty-four-group program adopted in the spring of 1939, gave a tremendous boost to the American aircraft industry. From a production rate of 100 military aircraft per month in 1938, the industry reached 402 in April 1940 and was tooling up to produce at double that rate. Tested in battle in Europe, future American planes would be well adapted to modern air combat.

But the French and British were already too late. In April 1940 the Germans seized Norway—a victory largely made possible by the Luftwaffe. In May they overwhelmed neutral Holland and Belgium, and in June they drove the British from the continent at Dunkirk and conquered France. In two months they had changed the course of history.

Rearmament Programs

Not since the Civil War had the American public suffered such a shock as when France fell. Almost overnight,

Debris at Wheeler Field, Oahu, T. H., is mute evidence of US unpreparedness and impotence on December 7, 1941.

The RAF's Spitfire was a fine interceptor but when war broke out in Europe in '39, British had only a handful.

In a weird kind of aerial shorthand, these contrails over London spelled out the desperateness of Battle of Britain.

national defense became a national concern. The Air Corps, so recently an ugly duckling, was transformed into a public favorite. With the scream of German dive bombers whining in their ears, congressmen clamored for the best air force money could buy. When General Arnold went before Congress in June he was told that any appropriation he needed would be forthcoming. "All you have to do is ask for it," said Senator Henry Cabot Lodge, Jr.

What was to be done with this blank check? On May 16, President Roosevelt had called for an air force of 50,000 Army and Navy planes supported by an annual production capacity of 50,000 military planes. The hard fact was that neither an air force nor an aircraft industry on that scale could be bought off the shelf for all the gold in Fort Knox. Under intense pressure to state specific requirements, the War Department asked for 18,000 planes by April 1, 1942, and a production capacity of 18,000 planes a year for Army use by the same date. The President approved the program on June 18. On June 26, General Marshall approved the First Aviation Objective, under which the Air Corps was to have 12,835 planes and fifty-four combat groups by April 1942. Almost 4,000 combat aircraft and 220,000 officers and men would be needed for this air force.

From June 1940 onward, appropriation was heaped upon appropriation and program upon program. The fifty-four-group program was hardly under way before Arnold's staff began planning a still larger force. The need for a larger force was demonstrated to the satisfaction of the War Department, which approved the Second Aviation Objective in March 1941. This program provided for eighty-four combat groups by June 30, 1942, to be equipped with 7,800 combat planes and manned by 400,000 officers and men. In July 1941, authorization for Army and Navy aircraft reached 50,000.

By this time, circumstances required a new statement of long-term US production objectives. The Lend-Lease Act of March 1941 and a greatly expanded heavy bomber program had led to greatly increased demands for munitions. Faced with these growing demands, President Roosevelt asked the Secretaries of War and Navy on July 9, 1941, to prepare an estimate of "over-all production requirements required to defeat our potential enemies." The report, presented to the President on September 11, included an AAF section prepared by the Air War Plans Division and known within the AAF as AWPD/1.

Drafted in a single week in August by a group of brilliant younger officers—Lt. Cols. Harold L. George and Kenneth N. Walker and Majs. Laurence S. Kuter and Hay-

When the scream of German dive bombers, like these JU-87Ds, fell on congressional ears, the pursestrings loosened, and appropriation followed appropriation.

"Rosie the Riveter" joined B-17 production lines as the American aviation industry moved to meet the demands of war.

wood S. Hansell, Jr.—AWPD/1 proved to be a remarkably accurate forecast of AAF strategy and requirements for a simultaneous war against Germany and Japan. The major contribution of the AAF would be a strategic bombing offensive. To carry out its missions, the AAF would need 239 combat groups and 108 separate squadrons, 63,467 planes of all types, and 2,164,916 men. If an all-out effort were started immediately, the planners predicted that the air offensive against Germany could reach full power in April 1944. This prediction, as well as the statement of total requirements, proved to be just about right. The AAF eventually had a peak strength of 2,400,000 men, 243 combat groups, and nearly 80,000 aircraft.

Growing Pains

Meanwhile, in the summer of 1940, the road to rearmament was beset with pitfalls and bottlenecks. To begin with, the aircraft manufacturers were reluctant to accept new contracts unless they could be assured of guarantees against the risks involved. Since there were laws that set limits on armament contracts, the manufacturers asked for relief on the grounds that they could not estimate costs accurately in a period of rising prices. Already operating at capacity because of the heavy British orders, they would have to build new factories and enlarge old ones to meet the new production goals. This the manufacturers feared to do, for they had seen much of the aircraft industry go bankrupt after World War I, and they had no desire to risk a similar fate. Meanwhile, with thousands of planes to be bought, it took seven weeks to let contracts

for thirty-three combat planes, and by August 20, contracts for only 343 had been placed in a period of 100 days.

Legislation permitted the cost of new plants to be amortized within five years, instead of the normal sixteen to twenty. Combined with other financial buffers and inducements this helped to dispel fears of overexpansion, but only after several months of delay. Even then, since few companies could provide the gigantic sums required, the government usually had to provide credit through the Reconstruction Finance Corporation or build facilities at its own cost and lease them to the producers.

When the contracts had been signed and financing arranged, the construction work could begin, a task full of technical problems and increasingly hampered by shortages of materials and skilled workmen. It took an average of twenty-three months for a new engine factory to get into full operation, thirty-one months for an assembly plant. Not one of the new plants authorized after June 1940 had produced a single combat plane when the Japanese struck at Pearl Harbor, but their production was to be the mainstay of the American offensives during the last two years of the war.

Because of earlier expansion and improvements in mass production techniques, the number of military aircraft produced in the United States rose from 402 in April 1940 to 2,464 in December 1941. But less than half of the new planes went to the Army air arm. It received 9,932 of the 22,077 military aircraft delivered between July 1940 and December 1941, while the British Empire obtained 6,756 and the US Navy got 4,034. Saving England from defeat was manifestly important, but the US contribution was at

Randolph Field, Tex., the "West Point of the Air" (seen over a trainer's wing), was nucleus of expanded pilot training.

a heavy cost to its own rearmament. At the time of Pearl Harbor the nation still did not have enough of the right kinds of aircraft to outfit fifty-four combat groups.

Less complex than the task of aircraft production, but in some ways fully as difficult, were the jobs of building bases and training flyers and technicians. In 1939 the continental United States had only seventeen Army air bases and four depots. The famous names and mellow brick façades of these installations could not conceal the fact that many of them had been unimproved and ill maintained for two decades. The Air Corps training program ranked second to none in quality, but it graduated fewer than 300 pilots a year. From this to the housing and training of eighty-four combat groups was a mammoth step. Nevertheless, by December 7, 1941, there were 114 major Army air installations within the continental United States, and legislation was well advanced to permit construction of fourteen new air bases and improvement of fourteen others to meet the eighty-four-group goal.

The growth of pilot training programs was fantastic. Pilot training objectives leaped from 300 a year to 1,200 a year before the end of 1939, to 7,000 a year in June 1940, to 12,000 a year under the First Aviation Objective in July 1940, and finally on February 14, 1941, to 30,000 pilots a year, or 100 times the original level. General Arnold had foreseen in 1938 the need for mass production of pilots and resolved to use civilian schools for primary flight training. He persuaded several to invest in the necessary facilities before any governmental action had been taken. As he later recalled, "I told them I didn't have any money but was sure I could get the support of Congress. . . ." They took his word, Congress approved, and nine schools went into operation under contract in the summer of 1939. By the time of Pearl Harbor, forty-one primary schools were in operation. Besides providing a ready-made instrument for quick expansion, the civilian contractors did their job well.

With civilian schools taking over primary training, the Air Corps could handle the essentially military programs of basic and advanced flying training in its existing schools at Randolph, Kelly, and Brooks Fields until the huge expansion in the summer of 1940. Then new training bases began to spring up like mushrooms, mostly in the South and Southwest where the climate permitted year-round flying. Eight were in operation under the fifty-four-group program, and twenty more—authorized under the eighty-four-group program—were completed or under construction by the end of 1941.

Training programs for other flying personnel—bombardiers and navigators—and for mechanics and technicians were also developed, although somewhat more slowly. Between 1939 and March 1941 the demand within the Air Corps for mechanics and technicians shot up from 1,500 to 110,000 a year.

To the multitudes of Americans who passed through them in the grim days after Pearl Harbor, the names of early training fields and schools like Luke, Mather, Keesler, Chanute, and Lowry conjure up a variety of memories. Some were dustbowls and some were swamps. Some men slept in ivy-covered brick barracks, others in tarpaper huts and winterized tents. Everywhere was breathless haste. As General Arnold reported, "It was not unusual to find a training field with dozens of planes flying above it, bulldozers on the ground finishing the earthwork, cement

New training bases turned out pilots by the thousands, stressed physical fitness as well as flying aptitude.

mixers turning out concrete for runways yet to be built, and men in the open still clearing the brush off what had been grazing land." One might add that in 1941 the training base that had "dozens of planes" was a fortunate one, indeed.

By December 1941, after two and one-half years of effort, the expansion of the Army air arm was beginning to shift out of low gear. The force already in being had grown to sixty-seven combat groups—eighteen deployed on overseas bases, 28½ in strategic reserve in the United States, and 20½ still in operational training. The number of officers and men had risen to 354,000. More than 9,000 pilots had received their wings, and some 59,000 mechanics and technicians had been graduated from training schools. The greatest shortage was in combat aircraft. Of 2,846 first-line combat planes on hand just before Pearl Harbor, only 1,157 were actually fit for battle against an enemy armed with modern weapons.

As the Army air arm expanded, its importance to national defense increased proportionately, and in November 1940, Arnold became Acting Deputy Chief of Staff for Air. His dual position as Marshall's deputy and as Chief of Air Corps, plus his cordial personal relationship with Marshall, permitted Arnold to give a measure of unity and direction to air policy. But delays and confusion multiplied as the ever increasing volume of Air Force business continued to pass through a maze of War Department channels. By the spring of 1941, Marshall had become convinced that he could get better results by giving more unity and authority to the air arm.

The appointment on April 10 of Robert A. Lovett to the long-vacant post of Assistant Secretary of War for Air was a major step. An efficient and tactful advocate of airpower, Lovett had been serving since December 1940 as Special Assistant to the Secretary of War to expedite air matters. At the same time, Marshall initiated a general reorganization and pushed it forcefully. Army Regulation 95-5, issued on June 20, 1941, created the Army Air Forces (AAF), headed by a Chief who was also the Deputy Chief of Staff for Air. As Chief, Arnold coordinated and directed both the Air Corps and the Air Force Combat Command (new name of the GHQ Air Force) and all other air elements. The AAF was also to have its own staff, but the regulations did not specify the relationship of this Air Staff to GHQ (the Army's top field command, established in 1940). This was an inevitable source of future friction.

By 1941, growth of the AAF had created serious organizational problems that required the establishment in March of four numbered air forces—the First and Third in the Northeast and Southeast, the Second and Fourth in the Northwest and Southwest. This change grew out of a concern over continental defense and a decision by Marshall on February 28 that air defense should be a responsibility of the Army air arm. On April 12 the War Department directed each numbered air force to organize a bomber command and an interceptor command to meet the need for "offensive and defensive task forces larger than single wings." Each of the bomber commands would serve as a support command to one of the four field armies responsible for ground defense. The interceptor commands had charge of air defense activities including aircraft warning and antiaircraft units. The question of command relationships between the field army and the numbered air force remained wide open, but the War Department obviously intended that they should work together closely.

Additional links in the chain of command also had to be added in the realm of noncombat activities under the Air Corps. On March 26, 1941, the Air Corps set up the Technical Training Command to direct the huge new programs for schooling ground crews and technicians. Although the flying training centers were kept under direct supervision

Robert A. Lovett became Assistant Secretary of War for Air in April 1941.

of the Chief of Air Corps for ten more months, their growth finally forced the establishment on January 23, 1942, of a Flying Training Command.

The old Materiel Division had to be split to handle the enormous volume of business coming its way. In March 1941 the Air Corps Maintenance Command was created to take over supply and maintenance, leaving the Materiel Division free to concentrate on procurement and research and development. The new organization, redesignated in October as the Air Service Command, had its headquarters at Wright Field, Ohio, next door to the Materiel Division. Another new agency, the Air Corps Ferrying Command, was established on May 29, 1941, to fly aircraft overseas for delivery to the British.

Hemisphere Defense

In the atmosphere of isolationism that prevailed until 1940, the United States had limited its overseas deployment to the Panama Canal and to the island fortress of Hawaii, sending only token forces to defend the Philippines. In July 1939, only 3,991 Army air personnel were overseas. Then, the German victories in Europe transformed hemisphere defense from a dead issue to a national watchword. The Nazi slogan, "Tomorrow the World," became credible enough to make the United States anxious to bolster its Atlantic defenses.

There were two possible routes for a German invasion of the Western Hemisphere. One was the island bridge formed by Iceland, Greenland, and Newfoundland across the North Atlantic. The second was from Africa to the corner of Brazil that jutted out into the Atlantic within 1,900 miles of the great base at Dakar in French West Africa. The Caribbean also required attention, not because of any real prospect of invasion, but because it could not be closed to German raiders until air and sea bases were built on the island chain that guarded the entrance to this vital area.

The United States took a tremendous step toward defense of both the North Atlantic and the Caribbean with the famous "destroyers for bases deal," announced by President Roosevelt on September 3, 1940. Under this agreement the British received fifty old destroyers, which they urgently needed, and, in return, gave to the United States ninety-nine-year leases on eight bases in British possessions of the Western Hemisphere. As a result, by the end of 1941 the AAF had squadrons or detachments on reconnaissance duty at Gander in Newfoundland and at four bases on British possessions in the Caribbean. A base in Dutch Guiana was also acquired and occupied by agreement with the Dutch government-in-exile.

Greenland lay outside the American sphere of defense

until March 1941 when Germany extended the combat zone to include both Iceland and Greenland. Then the United States extended its hemisphere defense area to include Greenland, and on April 9 the Danish minister in Washington signed an agreement giving the United States the right to build bases there. The Army Air Forces found promising sites for airfields at Narsarssuak on the southern tip of Greenland and at a point on the west coast just within the Arctic Circle.

The War Department gave this construction such high priority that in spite of great difficulties the field at Narsarssuak (later famous in the AAF by its code name of Bluie West 1) was well advanced by the end of the year. The base was also carefully stocked with supplies, an important consideration, for, as the commander wrote, "Nothing is available locally except drinking water and sand and rocks." As yet the air garrison consisted only of aviation engineers plus a few weather and communications men.

Iceland had been occupied by the British in May 1940, but as the war went on they grew increasingly anxious to withdraw their garrison for use elsewhere. Therefore, in July 1941, at the request of both England and the Icelandic government, which in May had declared its independence of German-occupied Denmark, the United States sent a brigade of Marines to Iceland to replace the British. On July 25 the air echelon of the AAF's 33d Pursuit Squadron, equipped with thirty P-40s, moved to the island by aircraft carrier. There it operated with RAF units under combat conditions.

In the Caribbean the greatest progress in air defense between 1939 and 1941 took place on the island of Puerto Rico. An emergency strip at Borinquen Field was transformed with haste and efficiency into a major air base, and another good airfield, Losey, was also completed before 1942. By the spring of 1941, air strength on the island had been built up to a composite wing. There were some 300 Army aircraft in the Caribbean area just before Pearl Harbor, but 183, including all the heavy bombers (eight B-17s) and most of the best fighters (P-40s), remained bunched around the Panama Canal at France,

Albrook, and Howard Fields. When the Caribbean Defense Command was set up in the spring of 1941, Maj. Gen. Frank M. Andrews became its commander. It was fitting that Andrews should be the first air officer to hold a theater command.

On November 1, 1940, air units in Hawaii were organized into the Hawaiian Air Force under the Hawaiian Department. At the end of the year the new air force had only 117 aircraft—none of recent vintage—but it grew rapidly thereafter. By December 6, 1941, the islands had the greatest air strength of any comparable area either in the United States or its overseas possessions—231 military planes of which about half were modern. Among them were twelve B-17Ds, which had been sent to Hawaii in the belief that their long range would make them particularly valuable in defense of the islands. The 19th Bombardment Group, under the command of Lt. Col. Eugene L. Eubank, had flown twenty-one of the big planes without accident from California to Oahu on May 13-14, setting a record for mass overwater flights.

On the eve of hostilities the Hawaiian Air Force, under Maj. Gen. Frederick L. Martin, included the 18th Bombardment Wing, at Hickam Field outside Honolulu, and the 14th Pursuit Wing, at Wheeler Field about fifteen miles from Hickam. One pursuit squadron was training at Haleiwa, a small outlying field.

Until the summer of 1941, American plans called for no more than a holding action in the Philippines. Up to November 1940 the air defense of the islands was in the hands of one squadron of aged bombers and twenty-eight obsolete P-26s. Some reinforcements did arrive during the next six months, and a Philippine Department Air Force was organized on May 6, 1941.

In a radical change of policy, the United States decided in June to garrison the Philippines strongly and to base a large number of heavy bombers there. On July 26, General Marshall ordered the mobilization of the Philippine army and the creation of a new command, the United States Army Forces in the Far East, to direct the forces of both the Philippine Commonwealth and the Philippine Department. Gen. Douglas MacArthur was recalled to active duty

Up to November 1940 our fighter strength in the Philippines consisted of twenty-eight obsolete Boeing P-26s.

to head the new command. On August 4 the Philippine Department Air Force became the Air Force, United States Army Forces in the Far East.

As the Japanese became increasingly aggressive in southeast Asia during the summer and fall of 1941, the AAF hurried substantial air reinforcements to MacArthur. Among them was the 14th Bombardment Squadron, commanded by Maj. Emmett O'Donnell, Jr., which set out on September 5 from Hickam Field to the Philippines via Midway, Wake, New Guinea, and Australia. A week later all nine of its B-17s landed safely at Clark Field, Manila, after one of the most remarkable flights of the prewar period. The 19th Bombardment Group took off from California in twenty-six B-17s on October 22, followed the route pioneered by O'Donnell's squadron, and arrived at Clark Field on November 6. By December the AAF had about 265 combat planes in the Philippines, but the only first-line aircraft were thirty-five B-17s and 107 P-40s. Of these, thirty-one P-40s were not yet in combat units.

Headquarters AAF decided to reorganize its forces in the Philippines in keeping with its projected strength and sent a senior officer, Maj. Gen. Lewis H. Brereton, to serve as MacArthur's air commander. Brereton assumed his new post on October 7, and on November 16 his command was reorganized and redesignated as the Far East Air Force.

Brereton inherited a multitude of problems and deficiencies. He had no money for building dispersal areas for the B-17s at Clark Field. Revetments had been authorized so late and were built so slowly that only two were ready by December. Uncamouflaged, the big planes could be seen from the air as far as twenty-five miles away. Brereton, concerned about their exposed position, sent sixteen of them south on December 5 to a sod field under development at Del Monte on the island of Mindanao. The air warning system was operating twenty-four hours a day in December, but its communications were both inefficient and unreliable. Also, not more than two radar warning sets were in operation, one at Iba, and one outside Manila. Pursuit pilots could not go much higher than 15,000 feet without oxygen, but only Nichols Field had even a small supply of it.

Marshaled in ominous readiness on Formosa, the Japanese had more than 150 short-range Army planes and 300 first-line naval aircraft, including 184 Zero fighters. Wonderfully maneuverable, these fast-climbing planes could reach a speed of 350 miles an hour and were heavily armed with two twenty-two-mm. cannon and a pair of machine guns. Veiled in more than oriental secrecy, the Zero was little known in the United States and was to be a most disagreeable surprise to American pilots.

The logical route for a Japanese invasion of the Western Hemisphere was via the Aleutians and through Alaska. Before air units could be deployed to Alaska, suitable airfields had to be built. The territory had none worthy of the name in 1939. Funds for a base near Anchorage, disapproved by the House appropriations committee in the spring of 1940, were hastily provided after the German blitz. Work then began almost immediately on what later became Elmendorf Field. In all of Alaska, at the beginning of the war, the AAF had only thirty-two aircraft—all out of date—in three squadrons commanded by the 28th Composite Group.

Overseas Air Routes

A rather special phase of prewar overseas operations was the ferrying of American-built planes to friendly nations, beginning in November 1940. Because the British found it hard to supply pilots, Arnold proposed that ferrying as far as overseas departure points be done by the Air Corps. His idea won approval, and, in June 1941, Col. Robert Olds took over the new Air Corps Ferrying Command. In its first six months of operations, the command delivered about 1,350 aircraft. Most of the pilots were on short tours of temporary duty from the Air Force Combat Command.

From its beginning the Ferrying Command had as its secondary mission the establishment of air transport service overseas. Before the year was out its transport work was approaching its ferrying activities in importance. The command began its overseas flights on July 1, 1941, when Lt. Col. Caleb V. Haynes took off from Bolling Field, Washington, D. C., bound for Scotland. The British dubbed the service the "Arnold Line." In 1941 this northern route ran from Bolling to Montreal to Gander Lake, Newfoundland, then to Prestwick Airport, at Ayr in Scotland. The bases in Greenland, which later served to break the long Atlantic hop, were not ready in 1941, and the airfields in Iceland could not handle big planes.

A second overseas route was developed to span the South Atlantic. Though much longer than the northern route, it was particularly useful for flights to Africa and the Middle East and also as a means of reaching England without risking the winter storms of the North Atlantic. Ferrying operations began in June 1941 when a subsidiary of Pan American Airways undertook to deliver twenty transport aircraft to the British in Africa. Civilian pilots flew all the planes to Africa over a route from Miami to Lagos, on the Nigerian coast, with stops at Trinidad, at Belem and Natal in Brazil, and Bathurst, Gambia. On June 26 the AAF made permanent arrangements for Pan American, again acting through subsidiaries under government contract, to set up regular ferry and air transport services to Africa and, in addition, to take over existing British ferrying and transport operations across central Africa to Egypt.

When the situation in the Middle East became critical in the fall of 1941, the United States became interested in developing a military air transport service to Cairo. To test the feasibility of such a service, Colonel Haynes, with Maj. Curtis E. LeMay as copilot, set out from Bolling on August 31 in a B-24 of the Ferrying Command. They flew the southern route from Florida to West Africa via Brazil and across Africa to Cairo, went on from Cairo to Basra on the Persian Gulf, and returned to the United States the same way to complete an unprecedented and thoroughly successful 26,000-mile trip.

In November the War Department decided to open a regular military service to Cairo. Beginning on November 20, the Ferrying Command flew a few Liberators to Cairo for use by the British in the Middle East. This was the first ferrying done by the AAF outside the Western Hemisphere and required presidential sanction. Although the actual volume of operations across the South Atlantic and through Africa in 1941 was small, the installations and organizations in being and the experience gained proved invaluable when the United States found itself at war.

After 1939 the Air Corps repeatedly requested acquisition of a chain of island air bases in the Pacific over which long-range bombers could fly to the Far East. Until the summer of 1941 the War Department turned down all requests, but once it was decided to make the Philippines a stronghold, development of a Pacific air route got top priority. The prime need was a fairly direct path from Hawaii to Australia that would avoid Japanese forces in the Caroline and Marshall Islands. The Chief of Staff approved AAF recommendations for such a route on October 3, 1941. Australia, New Zealand, and the Free French collaborated in a project to build by January 1942 at least one 5,000-foot runway each on Canton Island, Christmas Island, the Fiji Islands, New Caledonia, and at Townsville on the east coast of Australia.

Steps Toward Alliance

The fall of France forced the independent British and the isolationist Americans into increasingly close military cooperation for mutual protection. As a first step, three American military observers were sent to London on August 6, 1940. It was a sign of the times that the triumvirate included an air officer, Maj. Gen. Delos C. Emmons, then commander of the GHQ Air Force.

At the end of 1940 the British sent a staff delegation to Washington to discuss mutual problems, including the possibility that the United States might be drawn into the war. In a series of conversations, military representatives of the two countries laid down the blueprint of an Anglo-American alliance, carefully avoiding any political commitments. The reports of these discussions, issued on March 27 and 29, 1941, under the short titles ABC-1 and ABC-2, specified that in the event of war "the High Command of the United States and the United Kingdom will collaborate continuously in the formulation and execution of strategic policies and plans." Strategy was to start from the premise that "the Atlantic and European area is to be considered the decisive theater."

Initially, American ground forces would be employed defensively, but bombardment units were to operate offensively "in collaboration with the Royal Air Force against German military power at its source." On the question of command, a frequent source of friction between allies, the conferees agreed to divide the world into areas and to specify for each where primary responsibility would lie. Except in the Far East, the power designated as responsible for an area would have full strategic command over all allied forces in it, but would exercise authority over the forces of allies only through their commanders. The detailed planning that made up the bulk of the reports was soon outdated, but the fundamental assumptions governed the future conduct of the war. Such a working partnership naturally called for permanent and formal contact between the British and American military establishments. This began in May when the British Joint Staff Mission arrived in Washington and a group of American "Special Observers" went to London. The importance of American airpower to the ABC plans was indicated by the selection of an air officer, Maj. Gen. James E. Chaney, as Special Army Observer. A further indication was the presence of Arnold as the American air representative at the Atlantic Conference between Roosevelt and Churchill in August 1941. It established a precedent that carried over into the Joint and Combined Chiefs of Staff organizations set up early in 1942.

Relations with Russia were peculiarly difficult. The suspicious government of the Soviet Union asked much and offered nothing. Yet its hundreds of divisions and thousands of planes were needed to keep the Nazis from winning control of all Europe. Arrangements for British and American aid to Russia were embodied in the First Soviet Protocol, signed on October 1, 1941, unaccompanied by either military or political agreements. According to the protocol, the United States would furnish 1,800 planes within nine months.

Disaster at Pearl Harbor

In both the Atlantic and the Pacific during the fall of 1941 the United States edged closer to war. Tension mounted in the Atlantic as German U-boats attacked American naval vessels escorting convoys to the United Kingdom. In the Pacific, Japan's move into Indochina appeared to be merely the prelude to further aggression in southeast Asia, with the Netherlands Indies as the chief prize.

American action in July to halt the Japanese advance by imposing economic sanctions had merely convinced the Japanese extremists, headed by Gen. Hideki Tojo, that they would have to defeat the United States to gain their ends. In November, they decided that war with the United States was inevitable.

On November 3 the Imperial Navy approved a plan to begin war in the Pacific with a surprise attack on Pearl Harbor by a carrier task force. Two days later Adm. Isoroku Yamamoto notified the fleet: "War with Netherlands, America, England inevitable." When Japanese negotiators in Washington failed to get American agreement to Japanese terms for a *modus vivendi* in the Pacific, the Japanese government on November 30 officially decided on war. On December 1 the Japanese government sent the final radio order for the attack on Pearl Harbor to the special task force that had set sail for Hawaii on November 26.

At Honolulu, on the main island of Oahu, the American military chiefs had been notified by Washington on November 24 that the Japanese might make "a surprise aggressive movement in any direction." On November 27, Washington sent two stronger messages. One, specifically called a war warning, ordered an "adequate defensive deployment." Adm. Husband E. Kimmel, Commander in Chief of the Pacific Fleet, put the fleet on first-class alert. Lt. Gen. Walter C. Short, the Army commander, decided without consulting his air commander, General Martin, that an alert against sabotage would suffice.

Neither Kimmel nor Short, or their staffs, ever believed that the Japanese would strike at Hawaii. At the beginning

Every battleship in the Pacific Fleet was either sunk or damaged in the tragically successful Japanese sneak attack on Pearl Harbor. This view shows plume of smoke from the battleship *Arizona*, on fire and sinking with the bulk of its crew either dead or trapped inside the ship.

The AAF lost 152 out of 231 planes on December 7. These are B-17s going up in smoke after the attack on Hickam Field.

of December the war plans officer of the Pacific Fleet told Kimmel and Short that there would "never" be an attack on Pearl Harbor by air. Short testified later that when the attack took place he "could scarcely believe it."

In November 1941 the US government knew, thanks to its decoding of Japanese messages and other intelligence sources, that Japan was on the verge of military action. But apparently everyone expected a strike in the Far East, probably against Malaya and the Indies, possibly against the Philippines. Japanese deployments in the southwest Pacific were known to Washington. But the Japanese had been successful in concealing the existence of the Pearl Harbor task force. The attack on December 7 came as a complete surprise.

At 0653 on the morning of Sunday, December 7, a destroyer on patrol outside Pearl Harbor reported firing on a Japanese submarine. Ranking naval officers received the report with skepticism and awaited confirmation before taking any action. At 0702 a private, tinkering with a radar set at Kahuku Point after his duty had ended, spotted a big formation of aircraft approaching from the north about 130 miles away. Excitedly, he telephoned the Information Center. Unfortunately, the one officer there, an inexperienced lieutenant on hand for training, assumed that the blip was made by B-17s due from the mainland or by Navy planes, about which the Army seldom got any information. He did not report it.

At 0755, Japanese planes attacked Hickam Field. Other formations struck Wheeler Field and the naval air bases at Ford Island and Kaneohe and the ships in Pearl Harbor. These first attacks, which did most of the damage, were carried out by a force of 183 Japanese planes launched at 0600 from six well-escorted Japanese aircraft carriers some 200 miles north of Oahu. A second wave of 170 planes followed about an hour later.

The defending air units were taken completely by surprise. Of more than 100 combat-worthy Army pursuit planes on Oahu, only twenty-five got into the air, mainly against the second wave of attackers. The Navy and Marines fared worse. Not one of their planes in Hawaii was able to take to the air. The AAF's 47th Pursuit Squadron at the outlying field of Haleiwa, which the Japanese had neglected to attack, put up most of the air resistance. Lt. George S. Welch took to the air about 0815 and later claimed four Japanese planes shot down.

Much to their own amazement, pilots of twelve B-17s flying in from California found themselves in an air battle. Without ammunition, their guns in cosmolene, and their rear armor displaced to make way for extra fuel, they were in bad shape for a fight, but the Japanese, intent on their prescribed targets, paid little attention to them. Their biggest problem was to find a safe place to land. By good luck and good piloting only one incoming B-17 was destroyed and three badly damaged.

The last of the invading aircraft swung out to sea about 0945, its mission accomplished. Such was the confusion and the havoc the Japanese had wrought that not until 1100 did a bomber take off in pursuit. The search was in vain. The enemy fleet escaped unseen.

For this daring raid, the Japanese carrier force paid an insignificant price—twenty bombers, nine fighters, and fifty-five men. About twenty more planes cracked up in landing on their carriers. The task force had achieved results beyond its wildest dreams. Only seventy-nine of the 231 AAF aircraft that had been on hand at daybreak remained usable. Of 169 naval aircraft on Oahu, eighty-seven had been destroyed. As for the great Pacific Fleet, all its battleships had been sunk or crippled. For a long time to come the burden of naval defense in the central Pacific would rest on the three US aircraft carriers that had been at sea when the Japanese struck.

In a White House ceremony, May 1942, President Roosevelt congratulates Lt. George S. Welch for his four victories over Japanese planes during Pearl Harbor attack, as family and congressmen from Delaware, Welch's home, look on.

Symbolic of the air war above Europe are these B-17s of
the Eighth Air Force. Contrails curving upward were made
by escort fighters accompanying bombers in raid on Germany.

Chapter 5

WORLD WAR II | 1939·45

War in Europe

FOR MANY months after Pearl Harbor the misfortunes of their forces in the Pacific held the attention of the American people, and sheer necessity forced the government to divert large forces to the Far East. Nevertheless, because the defeat of Germany still held top priority, military leaders made plans to build up strength in the United Kingdom for a landing in France in the fall of 1942 or the spring of 1943. During this buildup, known as Bolero, no ground operations in Europe or Africa were to be undertaken by the United States except in emergency.

But in the summer of 1942, German forces were sweeping across the Ukraine, and the Russians demanded an immediate Anglo-American offensive to help divert enemy strength from Russia. The British wanted action to ease the pressure on their Eighth Army, which had been beaten in the Libyan desert by the German Afrika Korps and driven back to El Alamein, the last defensible position short of the Nile. Churchill proposed an invasion of French North Africa, an enterprise that he described as relatively easy and not likely to delay Bolero. His brilliant advocacy persuaded Roosevelt to the African venture before the end of July 1942.

The Eighth Air Force

Meanwhile, American forces were moving to England by sea and air under the Bolero program. Plans called for all air units to fly their planes to Britain over the North Atlantic ferry route, but in fact many went by sea. The only fighters to make the trip by air in 1942 were the two-engine P-38s. Before winter weather halted the flights in December, 882 AAF planes—chiefly B-17s and C-47s—had flown to England. The accident rate was five percent— only half of what had been predicted. American heavy bombers were concentrated north of London, in the area known as East Anglia.

In February 1942, Arnold had sent Brig. Gen. Ira C. Eaker to England to establish a bomber command headquarters and to prepare for the arrival of the combat units. In May, Eaker took command of the advance echelon of the

After the first all-American raid on *Festung Europa*, Brig. Gen. Ira Eaker (right) checks in with Maj. Gen. Carl A. "Tooey" Spaatz, then commander of the Eighth Air Force.

Eighth Air Force, which had been chosen to fight the air war from England. The Eighth's commander, Maj. Gen. Carl Spaatz, arrived in England in June and opened his headquarters on the eighteenth at Bushy Park, on the outskirts of London.

The honor of being the first AAF unit to fight in western Europe fell to the 15th Bombardment Squadron. After arriving in England in May it trained with the RAF, flying British Bostons (A-20s). On July 4, six crews of the 15th flew with the RAF in a low-altitude attack against airdromes in Holland. Unexpectedly intense flak brought down two American planes and spoiled the accuracy of the bombing. Nevertheless the mission was the forerunner of great things to come.

The AAF put its faith in daylight precision bombing. Spaatz and Eaker counted on the quality of their crews, the firepower of the B-17, and the accuracy of the Norden bombsight. The British had grave doubts, for they had found night bombing both safer and more economical. Supporting their case was the grim fact that missions deep into Germany would have to fly unescorted, for the Allies had no long-range fighter. But the Americans, hopeful that bombers could fight their way to the target without escorts, were determined to give daylight bombing a thorough trial. During August, the Eighth Air Force and the RAF worked out plans for a coordinated day-night bomber offensive in which each would use its own methods.

The 97th Bombardment Group, commanded by Col. Frank A. Armstrong, Jr., flew the first American heavy bomber mission from England on August 17, 1942. Twelve B-17s, with Eaker riding in the *Yankee Doodle*, lead plane of the second flight, attacked the marshalling yards at Rouen-Sotteville in France, while six others flew a diversionary sweep. Escorted by a strong RAF Spitfire formation, they bombed accurately against slight opposition and came back almost untouched. Within the next three weeks the Fortresses flew ten more small missions against objectives within easy fighter radius of England. Flying in summer weather, they were so accurate that Eaker estimated his men might be able to put forty percent of their bombs within a 500-yard radius of the aiming point. But when the mission on September 7 encountered bad weather, the bombing accuracy declined alarmingly. Only two B-17s had been lost in the eleven missions, but as yet the Germans were merely feeling out the characteristics of the plane.

The decision to mount an invasion of North Africa in

Big names and big news. Lt. Gen. H. H. "Hap" Arnold and Brig. Gen. Jimmy Doolittle, then commanding Twelfth AF.

the fall of 1942 meant that the Eighth Air Force would lose a large part of its strength to the new invasion air force —the Twelfth—commanded by Brig. Gen. James H. Doolittle. On September 8, Spaatz ordered that all air operations be subordinated to preparations for the invasion of North Africa. Because of this restriction and a spell of stormy weather, the Eighth completed only three more missions before the end of October. In the most important of these, an attack on Lille on October 9, it dispatched 108 heavy bombers. In fierce attacks, German fighters shot down four bombers and threw the rest into confusion. Only nine bombs hit within 500 yards of the aiming points, and the effect of the bombing on German war production was slight. Such results indicated that the great expectations roused by earlier missions might have to be revised. And the shift of emphasis from the United Kingdom to North Africa meant that the Eighth Air Force would have to play a secondary role in military operations until the summer of 1943.

Crisis in the Middle East

Even before the Eighth Air Force arrived in the British Isles, events in the Middle East had provided the prelude for the North African campaign. In June 1942, when Gen. Erwin Rommel's Afrika Korps drove across the Libyan desert to El Alamein, the only American air strength in the area was a detachment of B-24s at Khartoum, commanded by Col. Harry A. Halverson. At British urging, the B-24s remained in the Middle East instead of going on to China, as originally planned. On their first mission, flying from Egypt, twelve Liberators bombed the important oil refineries at Ploesti in Rumania on June 12, 1942, but did little damage. None of the planes was shot down, but one crash-landed and four were interned in Turkey.

A few days later an urgent appeal from Churchill for help in the Middle East won from the United States a promise of immediate air reinforcements from India and an agreement that nine AAF combat groups would be sent to Egypt as soon as possible. General Brereton flew to Egypt from India with every usable B-17 he had—nine war-weary Fortresses. When he arrived in Cairo on June 28, he ordered the activation of the US Army Middle East Air Force (USAMEAF). This became the Ninth Air Force in November.

By mid-August 1942 the 98th Bombardment Group (H), 12th Bombardment Group (M), and the 57th Fighter Group had arrived in the Middle East from the United States. The heavy bombers struck at ports and shipping along Rommel's long supply lines. The mediums and fighters went into action during September with the RAF's Desert Air Force in support of Lt. Gen. Bernard L. Montgomery's Eighth Army. In the great battle of El Alamein (October 24-November 5) the Ninth Air Force helped break the back of the Afrika Korps. After that victory they shared in the pursuit of Rommel's forces through Libya, to Tripoli, and beyond. Meanwhile, more combat groups had joined the Ninth and entered the battle. By February 1943, Rommel had retreated to Tunisia and was preparing to make a stand in the French fortifications called the Mareth Line. At that point the campaign merged with another, which had begun when the Allies invaded French North Africa.

North Africa

Operation Torch, the Allied invasion of North Africa on November 8, 1942, was the first major amphibious operation of World War II in the European theater. For so important a venture it was mounted in great haste. With the appointment of Lt. Gen. Dwight D. Eisenhower as commander on August 7, 1942, Allied Force Headquarters (AFHQ) promptly began preparations in London for landings in Algeria by forces from the United Kingdom. In September the Allies belatedly decided to land a task force from the United States near Casablanca, on the coast of French Morocco. Inevitably the creation and embarkation of that force were attended by great confusion. Plans were vague, for nobody could foresee whether the French would resist. Even more important, what would the Germans do— rush troops into Tunisia or launch a flank attack through Spanish Morocco?

The French did put up a fight, but it was brief and for the most part half-hearted. Algiers fell on D-day, Oran on November 10. On the next day, French forces in Morocco surrendered on orders from the commander of all French forces, Adm. Jean Darlan, who had been captured in Algiers. The only AAF combat unit to fly in support of the initial operations was the 31st Fighter Group. On November 8 it flew from Gibraltar to Tafaraoui near Oran, where it was engaged by French Dewoitine airplanes as it was

Castel Benito Airfield, Libya, once the pride of Mussolini's empire, was bombed out, rehabilitated, used against Axis.

landing. The next day it turned back a column of the Foreign Legion marching toward Oran.

In Tunisia, Admiral Darlan's orders to surrender were disregarded, because the Germans, beginning on November 9, had flown in enough troops to overawe the French authorities. The question was whether the Allies could take Tunisia before the Germans rushed in enough troops to hold it. Allied mobile units rushed eastward from Algiers, and paratroops dropped at Bône, Youks-les-Bains, and Souk-el-Arba to seize key points. On November 28, advance units pushed to within twenty miles of Tunis, and the British and Americans seemed to have victory in their grasp. But they did not have enough strength on the spot even to hold what they had gained. During the next two days the Germans drove the Allies back and inflicted heavy losses on British paratroopers dropped south of Tunis on the twenty-ninth.

The winter storms that set in a few days later bogged down Allied supplies and reinforcements and grounded Allied aircraft. Rainy weather speedily reduced their only two forward airfields, Souk-el-Arba and Youks, to the consistency of soup. The Germans, who held several hard-surfaced fields in Tunisia, were scarcely affected. American and British troops, plagued by German dive bombers, seldom saw a friendly plane and naturally felt that their air forces were neglecting them. But once a fighter plane got stuck in the Tunisian mud, not even direct orders from a corps commander could have boosted it into the air.

For various reasons some ground commanders at first exercised operational control of tactical aircraft, but they tended to dissipate the scanty aircraft strength against unsuitable objectives or on routine patrols. After General Spaatz arrived in Africa on December 3 to act as Eisenhower's deputy for air, this situation was gradually corrected. The doctrine eventually established gave the tactical air commander full control of all his units in close cooperation with the ground commander he was supporting.

In February 1943 the Anglo-American air commands in northwest Africa merged for operational purposes into a single organization, Northwest African Air Forces (NAAF), headed by General Spaatz. Most of its strength was divided

Bulldozers worked overtime filling bomb craters in hastily improvised, dirt-runway airfields to support African push.

between the Northwest African Strategic Air Force, under General Doolittle, and the Northwest African Tactical Air Force commanded by Air Vice Marshal Sir Arthur Coningham, who had led the RAF Desert Air Force across North Africa. NAAF, Ninth Air Force, and the RAF forces in the Middle East and on Malta were coordinated by a small supervisory headquarters, Mediterranean Air Command (MAC), under Air Chief Marshal Sir Arthur W. Tedder, one of the great military leaders of the war.

On February 14, after Rommel's forces had made contact with the Axis troops already in Tunisia, the enemy launched an offensive in a weakly defended area in central Tunisia, broke through Kasserine Pass, and almost took the important base at Youks before being stopped. Then the Allies, having built more than a dozen forward airfields and assembled powerful air and ground forces, took the initiative. During March they won air superiority over Tunisia in a determined counterair campaign. At the end of the month Montgomery's Eighth Army, with aircraft and artillery blasting a path ahead of it, broke through the Mareth Line from Libya. While the Eighth Army pressed north, Allied airmen proceeded to isolate the enemy bridgehead so that it could neither be maintained nor evacuated.

Because Tunis and Bizerte had already been well pounded, Spaatz directed air operations mainly against Sicilian ports and against sea and air traffic. In March, B-17s of the 301st Group destroyed some thirty acres of dock area at Palermo. In a particularly notable mission— the "Palm Sunday Massacre" of April 18—American fighters shot down more than fifty out of a hundred German JU-52 transports over the Mediterranean off Tunisia. After a new series of counterair missions, which forced the enemy to evacuate most of his planes to Sicily, the Allies began their final ground offensive on April 22. Supported by as many as 2,000 aircraft sorties a day, they gradually pried the Germans from their entrenchments in the hills and broke out onto the coastal plain early in May. Penned against the sea, 270,000 Axis troops were forced to surrender.

Sicily and Italy

In January 1943 at the Casablanca Conference, the British and American leaders had decided to follow Tunisia with the conquest of Sicily. This would not only be a blow to Italy but would relieve an acute shipping shortage by opening the Mediterranean narrows to Allied convoys. The

NORTH AFRICAN, MEDITERRANEAN, AND EUROPEAN THEATRES—WORLD WAR II

ner of Sicily, beyond the radius of fighter support from area eventually selected for assault was the southeast cor- Tunisian bases. Thus it was important to take the Italian fortress island of Pantelleria, midway between Africa and Sicily, not only to deny it to the enemy but to use it as a fighter base to supplement RAF fighters on Malta. NAAF planes hammered Pantelleria for a month, dropping 6,200 tons of bombs in over 5,000 sorties. Under this rain of explosives the garrison ran up the white flag on June 11, just as assault forces were approaching. Air action alone had conquered Pantelleria.

As a necessary preliminary to the invasion of Sicily, an Allied air campaign put out of operation all but a handful of the thirty-one airfields on the island, destroyed about 1,000 planes, and forced the enemy to evacuate most of his remaining aircraft. Thanks to this air superiority, only a dozen of the 3,000 ships that carried the American Seventh Army and the British Eighth Army to Sicily on July 10 were sunk by enemy air action, and those mainly at night. Although NAAF pilots did not have bases nearby, they flew 1,092 sorties on D-day to protect the convoys and beaches and more thousands of sorties during the next three days.

By July 14, daylight air opposition over Sicily had practically ceased. Thereafter, Allied aircraft ranged as far as France, attacking bases from which enemy air attacks on Sicily had been or might be made. For weeks at a time Allied ground troops never saw an enemy plane. This was NAAF's great contribution to the Sicilian campaign. Effective attacks on the railway system in Italy helped convince the Nazis that Sicily could not be adequately reinforced and so could not be defended.

The Allied airborne operations in the Sicily campaign were singularly unfortunate. An American paratroop regiment, dropped the night before D-day, was scattered far and wide because high winds had driven the troop carriers off course. And nearly half of a glider-borne British brigade came down at sea, because in the darkness the gliders had been released too far offshore. Later, two missions were fired upon and dispersed by Allied gunners who mistook the identity of the planes. Despite some valiant individual feats of arms, the operations were too costly to have been worthwhile.

Although a German counterattack on July 11-12 temporarily threatened the American beachhead, Allied victory in Sicily seemed assured when fighter planes landed at Pachino on the thirteenth. The Nazis fought to hold a defense line anchored on the crags of Mt. Etna while evacuating their forces across the Strait of Messina. The Allies cracked the German line after hard fighting in which NAAF contributed devastating strikes against such strongholds as Troina and Randazzo. They took all Sicily by August 18, but the Germans had extricated most of their troops, ferrying them to Italy at night under cover of an extraordinary concentration of flak. Allied aircraft sank at least twenty-three ships but could not stop the withdrawal.

The defeat in Sicily, coupled with air bombardment of the Italian peninsula, proved too much for the tottering government of Benito Mussolini. On July 25 he was forced to resign. His successors sued secretly for peace and on September 3 signed an armistice. Although the Germans took over the country, their hold appeared precarious.

To take advantage of this situation and to make the best use of the powerful forces assembled in the Mediterranean, the Allies invaded the Italian peninsula. On September 3, after strong air and artillery preparation, the British Eighth Army crossed the Strait of Messina. On September 9 the American Fifth Army landed at Salerno to take the great port of Naples and to cut off German forces engaging the British. The latter hope faded quickly because the few Germans in southern Italy had withdrawn hastily, blowing the bridges behind them.

Bombs away over Axis installations in Sicily. The campaign was short but fierce, and most of the Nazis got away.

Where do we go from here? Generals Eisenhower and Arnold, perhaps discussing the next move, at Castelvetrano, Sicily.

The Allies, who had hoped to achieve surprise at Salerno, found the beaches there well guarded. They gained a foothold but progress was slow. It was impeded not only by ground opposition but by air attacks on a scale of more than 100 sorties a day. Air defense of the Salerno beachhead posed a difficult problem. The Germans still had strong air forces in Italy, and the nearest Allied fighters, based 180 miles away in Sicily, were limited in what they could do. The US Navy provided four escort carriers and one big one as cover for the assault. Although NAAF and the Navy flew an average of about 800 sorties a day to protect the beachhead, they could not keep enough planes over it at any one time to prevent German hit-and-run raids, especially since the mountainous terrain made radar ineffective.

After receiving substantial reinforcements, the Germans launched a vigorous counterattack on September 12 and came close to breaking through to the sea the next day. To counter this threat a regiment of American paratroops was dropped very accurately behind the lines on the night of the thirteenth. By morning it had reinforced the weak sector of the front. The next night, another regiment successfully jumped in the same spot.

Throughout the fourteenth and fifteenth, NAAF made an all-out effort to aid the troops on the beachhead, flying over 3,400 sorties, most of them in direct support. Bomb concentrations averaging 760 tons to the square mile combined with naval and ground fire to stop the German offensive. On the sixteenth, Lt. Gen. Mark W. Clark's Fifth Army regained the initiative and made contact with the Eighth Army that had been working its way up the Italian boot. Spaatz's airmen then turned their attention to the remaining enemy airfields south of Rome. In two days of bombing and strafing they destroyed some 300 aircraft and gliders and reduced the number of sorties against the

Arched remnants of an ancient Roman aqueduct cast patterned shadows as Fifteenth Air Force B-17s roar overhead.

North American B-25s over fuming Mt. Vesuvius, on their way north to bomb German forces at Monte Cassino, Italy.

Allied armies to around thirty a day. Meanwhile, American fighters were flying in to operate from bases in the Salerno area. Thereafter, the Allies had and kept air superiority over Italy.

The Fifth Army took Naples on October 1, and the Eighth Army, driving up the east coast, took a valuable group of air bases around Foggia from which strategic bombers could pound central Europe. But before the Allied

armies got much farther they were stopped by the German fortifications known as the Gustav Line. The jagged Italian mountains and the exceptionally bad winter weather also came to the aid of the enemy.

At Cairo in December 1943 the Americans and British decided to curtail their efforts in Italy and begin shipping troops to the United Kingdom for a cross-channel invasion of the continent. Among the commanders moving to England were Generals Eisenhower, Spaatz, and Doolittle and Air Chief Marshal Tedder. Another outcome of the Cairo Conference was a merger of NAAF and MAC into Mediterranean Allied Air Forces (MAAF), a true Allied theater air headquarters with control of all Allied air forces everywhere in the Mediterranean.

General Eaker came from England in January 1944 to take charge of MAAF and of its American component, Army Air Forces/Mediterranean Theater of Operations (AAF/MTO). Under him, in command of Mediterranean Allied Tactical Air Force and of its American component, the Twelfth Air Force, was Maj. Gen. John K. Cannon. The XII Bomber Command had been transformed in November into the Fifteenth Air Force, a strategic bomber force like the Eighth. Maj. Gen. Nathan F. Twining, who had headed the Thirteenth Air Force in the Solomons, took command of the Fifteenth and of Mediterranean Allied Strategic Air Force.

Although the Mediterranean had become a subsidiary theater, the Allies still hoped to take all Italy and were determined to keep the German forces there under pressure. During the winter they made several unsuccessful efforts to pierce the Gustav Line. One such assault was coordinated with a landing on January 22, 1944, at Anzio behind the enemy lines. But the Fifth Army's frontal attack on the Gustav Line failed. Cooped up in a small beachhead that was raked from end to end by artillery, the troops at Anzio had no base from which supporting aviation could operate. To blast a way through the Gustav Line, MAAF bombers on March 15 thoroughly pulverized the key town of Cassino. This, too, failed to pierce the German lines because, among other reasons, the Allied followup infantry attack was both too late and too little.

On March 19, MAAF launched a different kind of operation, a coordinated air offensive, later called Strangle, against the railroads supplying the German forces and, secondarily, against roads and shipping. Italy, with its few north-south routes heavily interspersed by bridges and tunnels, was a promising setting for such an interdiction campaign. This had already been proved by the success of more limited operations against railroads in 1943. MAAF flew about 50,000 sorties in Strangle up to May 11, 1944. Most profitable of these were fighter-bomber attacks on bridges. These attacks badly crippled the Italian railway system within a few days, and by the end of the campaign, rail traffic in central Italy had practically ceased. By May, less than 4,000 tons of supplies a day were reaching the fourteen or fifteen German divisions at the front. Most of this was delivered by trucks moving at night.

Such a pittance could not maintain the Germans in battle. When the Allies launched a new drive on May 11, German resistance speedily crumbled. Anzio was relieved on the twenty-fifth, and Rome fell on June 4, two days before the Normandy invasion. Throughout June and July the Germans were kept on the run. MAAF's 280 combat squadrons flew 50,000 sorties in June alone, mainly in support of the advance. Direct support was lavish, well coordinated, and precisely directed by "Rover Joes," mobile, forward control parties in jeeps equipped with radios. Use of controllers to solve the problems of direct support had been one of the important developments of the Mediterranean war.

In harassing the retreating foe, pilots became fiendishly skilled at creating roadblocks and then working over the resultant traffic jams. They reported 5,000 enemy vehicles destroyed in the offensive's first six weeks. Farther ahead, Allied planes knocked out all but three of the bridges over the Po but could not halt a limited flow of supplies at night over ferries and pontoon bridges. Though the retreat cost them heavily, the Germans skillfully withdrew most of their forces to a new line in the high mountains south of the Po, between Pisa and Rimini. There they held firm, partly because nine Allied divisions and considerable air resources had been diverted from the Italian campaign for an invasion of southern France in August.

During the autumn and winter of 1944-45, MAAF operated almost unopposed over northern Italy, where the Germans clung desperately to their mountain line. The ground campaign was one of grim, drab attrition, but MAAF wrecked the enemy lines of communication from the front to the Alps and made it dangerous for even a single bicyclist or mule driver to travel by daylight in the Po Valley. When the Germans were finally driven from their mountain strongholds in April 1945, they collapsed utterly. They could not move enough materiel back across the Po to go on fighting.

Strategic Bombardment from Torch to Overlord

From the invasion of North Africa until the spring of 1943 the Eighth Air Force accomplished little. Diversion of heavy bombers to Torch and to other theaters kept its combat strength between two and six groups of bombers. Because of supply shortages and maintenance difficulties scarcely half its aircraft were operational. Only on rare

All that was left of Monte Cassino after it was bombed to rubble in attempt to dislodge German troops sheltered there.

occasions could it mount a hundred-plane mission. More-over, the winter weather over northwest Europe turned out to be even worse than expected. In some months fog and clouds grounded most of the Eighth's scheduled missions. Weather, combined with faulty equipment, spoiled many operations by making pilots turn back or lose their way.

To crown it all, two-thirds of the bomber effort was wasted on submarine bases and yards. These operations had been given top priority because the U-boats were sink-ing Allied shipping at a fearful rate, but the pens and yards were unsuitable targets. The sub pens, built of im-mensely thick reinforced concrete, proved almost invul-nerable. The U-boat construction yards were easy to dam-age but also easy to repair. Not until June 1943, when the submarine menace had been averted by other means, were the bombers relieved of this fruitless task.

Eaker, who had succeeded Spaatz as commander of the Eighth, restricted most missions to targets in France and the Low Countries. The Eighth did not make its first at-tack on Germany proper until January 27, 1943, when it hit the U-boat yards at Wilhelmshaven.

Long missions proved especially hazardous, for the bombers had no nose turrets to protect them from frontal attack. And the Eighth's fighters could escort them hardly 200 miles. Some protection was obtained by packing about eighteen bombers into a tight formation called a combat box and stacking two or three boxes vertically in what was known as a combat wing. Nevertheless, losses on operations beyond escort radius often ran above ten percent. In an otherwise successful mission against an aircraft factory in Bremen on April 17, sixteen of 106 bombers were lost. Anticipating a sustained bomber offensive, the Nazis had built up in the West a defensive fighter force of 500 (soon more than 700) planes that could be concentrated wherever

needed by means of an excellent warning and control sys-tem. Antiaircraft fire around the enemy's industrial centers was bound to be intense, but the great danger was the fighters.

As summer approached, the prospects for a decisive bomber campaign brightened. Doubled in strength by the addition of six heavy bomb groups, the Eighth looked for-ward to making the most of the long days ahead. In May the Combined Chiefs of Staff gave high priority to a Com-bined Bomber Offensive to be waged by the Eighth and the RAF Bomber Command against Germany. The chief objectives of the Eighth Air Force were to be the German aircraft, ball-bearing, and oil industries. Destruction of any one of these three target systems could win the war, but to destroy more than a few outlying plants would require ex-tremely long and dangerous missions deep into hostile territory.

The first stage of the Combined Bomber Offensive is well symbolized by its two most important and tragic opera-tions: the Ploesti mission of August 1, 1943, and the Regensburg-Schweinfurt mission of August 17. Both were fairly successful. Both were unbearably costly. Neither could be followed up as it should have been, primarily be-cause the AAF was not yet ready to try such difficult ven-tures on other than a one-shot basis.

Ploesti, in southeastern Rumania, was of prime impor-tance as the source of a third of Germany's oil. Too far away to be attacked from England, it could be reached from North Africa. The Ninth Air Force assembled two B-24 groups of its own and three on loan from the Eighth Air Force at bases near Bengasi in Libya. In an effort to achieve surprise, the bombers would cross Rumania at mini-mum altitude in complete radio silence, turn beyond the town of Floresti, and strike at their targets from the north-

Roosevelt and Churchill with Allied leaders at Casablanca Conference. From left, Lt. Gen. H. H. Arnold, Adm. Ernest J. King, Gen. George C. Marshall, Adm. Sir Dudley Pound, Gen. Sir Alan Brooke, and Air Chief Marshal Sir Charles Portal.

Consolidated-Vultee B-24s fly through heavy flak to drop their bombs on the oil refineries at Ploesti, Rumania.

west. Unfortunately, the lead groups made their turn too soon and, before they knew it, were on the outskirts of Bucharest, to the south of Ploesti. This alerted the whole defense system, and the attacks had to be made through a terrific concentration of flak. German fighters also appeared in strength and, though too late to have much effect on the bombing, took a heavy toll of the bombers. Of the 177 Liberators dispatched on the mission, no fewer than fifty-four were lost. About forty percent of the cracking and refining capacity of Ploesti had been destroyed, but the enemy, undisturbed by further attacks, succeeded within a few months in getting production back almost to its former level.

The Regensburg-Schweinfurt operation from England was a bold test of the effectiveness of the German fighter defense system. Plans called for the bombers to penetrate 200 miles into Germany to reach Schweinfurt and 100 miles farther to Regensburg. The Regensburg formations would avoid the hazards of a return trip across Germany by flying on southward to bases in Algeria. By flying immediately after the Regensburg force, the Schweinfurt contingent hoped for a comparatively clear path, since much of the German fighter effort would have been committed against the earlier mission. Messerschmitt works at Regensburg and Wiener Neustadt built nearly half of Germany's single-engine fighters. Schweinfurt produced half of her ball-bearing output. Allied experts believed that destruction of these factories would profoundly reduce the enemy's capacity to wage war.

On the morning of August 17 the Regensburg task force of 146 bombers took off from its bases in England. No sooner

had the escort turned back near the border between Belgium and Germany than enemy fighters attacked ferociously and continuously for an hour and a half. German controllers directed fighters to the scene from as far away as the Baltic and held them on station awaiting their turns. Spotters who flew along just out of range of the bombers told the waiting fighters when and where to strike. The Germans used all sorts of tactics, but as usual the exposed top and bottom squadrons of the combat wing were favorite targets. The high squadron was often hit in screaming dives, the low by assailants who approached head-on, then swept down and out. Twenty-four bombers were destroyed, most of them before reaching the target. Apparently not expecting such a deep penetration, the Nazis shot their bolt too soon, for as the bombers approached Regensburg the fighter attacks slackened, enabling the bombardiers to take good aim. Their accurate releases damaged every important building in the Messerschmitt plant at Regensburg. Then, while the fighter packs waited for them to run the gantlet back to England, the Americans soared over the Alps and proceeded unopposed to Africa. They landed with the incredulous relief of men "who had not expected to see another sunset."

Most unluckily the Schweinfurt mission was delayed 3½ hours by unfavorable weather, so by the time it reached Germany the enemy fighter force was rested, refueled, and ready to go again. Attacks began as soon as the bombers reached the Rhineland and continued with scant intermission until they were over the Channel on the way home. Of 230 bombers dispatched, thirty-six were lost and many more were crippled. Formations broke and crews became

Flaming Schweinfurt, one of the tough targets of the war.

exhausted. Nevertheless, eighty direct hits were made on the two principal ball-bearing plants.

These missions to Schweinfurt and Regensburg were Pyrrhic victories. One week of such operations would wipe out the Eighth Air Force. Nevertheless, hoping for better fortune, Eaker and his bomber commander, Brig. Gen. Frederick L. Anderson, risked more deep penetrations on October 9 to targets in Poland and East Prussia, on the tenth to Münster, and on the fourteenth to Schweinfurt again.

The second Schweinfurt mission furnished final and terrible evidence of the perils in unescorted daylight bombing attacks against German industry. The raid cost sixty of the 291 Fortresses employed. In return, about thirty-five German fighters were shot down—not a profitable exchange. Once more the fighters began their attacks near the German border and sustained them with only one significant break until the bombers met friendly fighters on their way back.

The enemy's tactics followed a new and deadly pattern. Alternate waves of single-engine fighters attacking from the front and twin-engine fighters lobbing rockets from the rear would concentrate on a single formation, usually the lowest. The rockets proved dangerously effective in loosening the tight American combat boxes. Once a formation broke, packs of fighters would set upon isolated stragglers like wolves on wounded deer. Probably because a sharp change of course near the target caught some German controller by surprise, fighter attacks slackened as the Fortresses approached Schweinfurt, enabling the bombers to make a well concentrated and destructive attack. The results of the mission frightened the Germans into undertaking an expensive program of dispersion, but purchases from Switzerland and Sweden enabled them to avoid any serious shortage of bearings.

For several months after the Schweinfurt operation the Eighth Air Force avoided unescorted missions deep into Germany. Bad weather also interfered with operations, but the Eighth continued the bomber offensive by using pathfinder tactics. Planes equipped with an airborne radar called H2X led formations to bomb through overcast skies on targets as far away as Münster. Being invisible from the ground, the bombers were safer on such missions, especially when jamming devices such as chaff (strips of aluminum foil that gave radar echoes) were used to baffle the enemy warning and gun-laying radar. However, since H2X was hard to master, radar bombing lacked precision. Less than half of the radar missions were successful, but that was vastly better than no missions at all.

Meanwhile, the Combined Bomber Offensive was reassessed in the closing months of 1943. The verdict was discouraging. German industrial capacity had merely been dented; German fighter production was about to be expanded; the German fighter force opposing the bombers was stronger than in June. This last was the most painful

discovery of all, for if AAF estimates of German losses had been even half correct, the Luftwaffe would long since have ceased to exist. The trouble was that every German fighter shot down by a bomber formation might be separately claimed by dozens of gunners and, after a long air battle, interrogators could not untangle the duplication. And finally, the daylight bomber offensive could not succeed without long-range escort fighters.

Related to these disappointments was a shake-up in command at the end of 1943. Eaker, who had headed the Eighth Air Force for more than a year, was sent to Italy. Doolittle took over the Eighth, and a new headquarters, United States Strategic Air Forces in Europe (USSTAF), under Spaatz, was set up in England to coordinate the operations of the Eighth and Fifteenth Air Forces. Arnold urged the new commanders to press their offensive and win air superiority so that the projected invasion of the continent could take place. He wrote on December 27, "This is a MUST. . . . *Destroy the enemy Air Force wherever you find them, in the air, on the ground and in the factories.*"

By this time the Eighth had at last obtained the long-range escort fighters it so desperately needed. The AAF had made a major blunder in not developing these planes earlier, but from June 1943 it worked feverishly to extend the range of the P-38, P-47, and P-51. The first P-51 Mustangs to arrive in England flew with the bombers to Kiel and back on December 13. The Mustang was to prove the answer to the long-range escort problem. "Little Friends" to the bombers, "Indianer" to the Nazis, the escorts soon taught the enemy to keep his distance. One of the oldest Mustang outfits, Col. Donald J. Blakeslee's 4th Fighter Group, claimed 156 kills in its first month of long-range escort operations.

When the opportunity to strike a massive blow at the German aircraft industry came in February 1944, the Eighth was prepared. It had been growing rapidly during the winter as new bomber and fighter groups arrived in a steady stream from the United States. On February 20, Spaatz's deputy for operations, Maj. Gen. Frederick L. Anderson, decided to take advantage of good weather and launch the first of a series of long-planned attacks which became known as the "Big Week." Doolittle sent out more than 1,000 bombers escorted by hundreds of fighters against the German aircraft factories. Between February 20 and 25 the Eighth Air Force flew 3,300 bomber sorties and the Fifteenth 500 against a dozen factories, while the RAF helped out with five massive night attacks. Fighters flew some 3,500 sorties in support of the Eighth and Fifteenth. The Big Week cost the Allies six percent of the bombers employed, but it set back enemy aircraft production by two months at a critical time.

Next, the Eighth went after "Big B"—Berlin itself. When Mustangs appeared over Berlin on March 4 the Germans knew that thereafter the Americans would be able to bomb targets anywhere in Germany. On March 6 and 8 more than 1,000 bombers struck at Berlin. In spite of heavy losses, Spaatz and Anderson resolutely continued their campaign, sending every flyable bomber against high-priority targets as often as they could.

The American fighters switched to the attack, flying ahead of the bombers to seek out the enemy fighters and destroy them. Attacks on such a scale ate up German fighter strength at a rate that the Luftwaffe could not endure. It lost about 800 day fighters in the West during February and March and began to run out of competent pilots. Thereafter the German Air Force declined rapidly in effectiveness. The Americans had won air superiority. This can hardly be overemphasized, for it was the foundation of practically all of the later Allied successes in both air and ground offensives.

Long-range escort fighters, like these North American P-51s, proved to be the answer to bomber losses over Germany.

Republic P-47, another workhorse of Western Europe.

Douglas A-20s of Ninth Air Force nick German defenses on northern French coast in pre-D-day softening-up mission.

The Invasion of Western Europe

While Spaatz's bombers and fighters were breaking the back of the Luftwaffe, the Allies moved ahead rapidly with their preparations for the liberation of western Europe. In anticipation of the mighty Overlord operation, the AAF had set up the Ninth Air Force in England in October 1943. The Ninth took its name, its commander —General Brereton—and some key personnel, including an outstanding fighter commander—Brig. Gen. Elwood R. Quesada—from its predecessor in the Mediterranean. Otherwise it was a new creation. Composed of medium bombers, fighter-bombers, and troop carriers, it eventually grew into the largest single tactical air force in the world.

The Supreme Allied Commander, General Eisenhower, set up his headquarters in England alongside Spaatz's USSTAF headquarters in January 1944. In addition to the Ninth and the British 2d Tactical Air Force, Eisenhower also had "direction" of the American and British strategic air forces after the middle of April. This permitted the maximum concentration of strength in support of Overlord.

Allied air preparations for Overlord had three primary objectives—isolation of the assault area from German ground reserves, isolation from enemy air reinforcements, and destruction of coastal defenses and radar that might endanger the success of the attack. In a tremendous campaign to paralyze the French railroads, Allied bombers dropped 76,000 tons of bombs. At first, rail centers were the principal targets, but attacks on bridges proved so profitable that mediums and fighter-bombers of the Ninth Air Force and the British 2d Tactical Air Force switched to bridge targets with spectacular results. By D-day— June 6—every bridge over the Seine below Paris had been destroyed. The whole railway system was in such a mess that most of the German reserves had to walk into Normandy after D-day.

To protect the invaders against the Luftwaffe, the American and British air forces pounded airfields within 130 miles of the proposed beachhead for three weeks immediately preceding the assault, dropping a total of 6,700 tons of bombs. This campaign made the forward German airfields untenable, so that the Luftwaffe was able to fly only a few sorties against the Allied invasion forces on D-day.

During the preinvasion period the Eighth Air Force continued its attacks on German industries in a successful attempt to keep the German fighters committed to the defense of their homeland and to continue the attrition that was wearing them down. It is significant that the Eighth's missions over Germany were often strongly opposed, while the heavy preinvasion operations over France seldom encountered an enemy plane.

Last and probably least helpful of the preinvasion operations were attacks on coastal defenses. There was a great deal of extra effort here because in order to conceal the location of the assault, the Allies flew two missions against defenses outside the landing area for every one within it. The bombers did particularly valuable work against radar warning stations, destroying about eighty percent of those between the Channel Islands and Ostend, Belgium. Combined with jamming and other precautions, this enabled the Allies to take the enemy by surprise.

Still another major bombing effort was made against the launching sites for the V-1, a small pilotless jet aircraft with a ton of explosives in its nose. In December 1943 the Allied air forces had started bombing these sites, but the V-1 remained so much of a menace that the sites received top priority in April. In the six months before D-day, Allied aircraft flew 25,000 sorties and dropped 36,000 tons of bombs on the sites. Though the sites were hard to see and hard to hurt, the bombings, coupled with damage done to the French railways, set back the missile program by at least three months. The first V-1 did not hit England until a week after D-day. This delay may have decided the fate of the invasion. Eisenhower declared later that if the Germans had been able to use the V-1 a few months sooner, Overlord would have been "exceedingly difficult, perhaps impossible."

On June 6, 1944, the Allies stormed the beaches of Normandy. Summer gales made the assaults difficult but threw the enemy off guard and kept his patrol boats and reconnaissance planes from venturing out. Planes of IX Troop Carrier Command and two RAF groups dropped paratroops of three airborne divisions between

An A-20 attack on Nazi supply lines in the Cherbourg peninsula. Ninth Air Force played big role in tactical support.

midnight and dawn. In the morning, after a heavy air and naval bombardment, five divisions landed on beaches between Caen and Montebourg. Although the paratroops were somewhat dispersed, they served as a valuable screen for Allied troops and helped them gain firm footholds near Caen and Carentan. Elsewhere the Germans very nearly repulsed an American assault on Omaha Beach. But under a tremendous umbrella of fighter cover furnished by 171 squadrons, the Allies made good all their landings. Only a handful of German planes ventured within reach of the patrols, and only one or two got through to attack the convoys. The Eighth and Ninth Air Forces each had more than 3,000 planes to throw into the battle immediately. Between them, they flew 8,722 combat sorties, and the RAF, during the day, flew 5,676.

In the weeks that followed, German attempts to fly fighter forces into Normandy failed miserably, and the Allies retained overwhelming air superiority. As a result they poured troops ashore as fast as their boats could shuttle. At the same time, the continuing interdiction campaign against all means of transportation into northwestern France slowed German deployment against the beachhead to a fatal degree. No trains moved across the Seine and few over the Loire. The Nazis had planned to mass twenty-five divisions by D-plus-ten for a counteroffensive, but only fourteen were on hand at that time, and they were battered, tired, and ill-supplied. The Allies,

V-1 "buzz bomb" plunges into Piccadilly area in London.

Normandy. Deliberately scuttled Liberty ships form a makeshift breakwater to ease task of unloading cargo craft.

Martin B-26, called "Flying Prostitute."

Douglas A-26 Invader, medium bomber.

Ninth AF Republic P-47 is outlined against the explosion of its own target —a German ammunition truck. Despite flaming debris, pilot got home safely.

Lockheed P-38 Lightnings form striking geometric pattern over France.

on the other hand, had sixteen divisions ashore as early as D-plus-five and by June 26 had put a million men into Normandy. They used their ground and air superiority to push westward according to plan and take the port of Cherbourg on June 27, but until late July the stubborn German defense kept them bottled up in Normandy.

As the invasion air force for the Americans, the Ninth went all out to move its combat units, especially the fighters, across the Channel to Normandy. Thanks to the extraordinary efforts of IX Engineer Command, an emergency strip was completed on D-day. The first squadrons started using landing strips in Normandy on June 13, and by July 31 all but one of the Ninth's eighteen fighter-bomber groups were in France. The medium bombers came later, but the fighter-bombers were on hand for the great sweep across France to the German border during August and September.

On July 25 a prodigious saturation bombing of five miles of the front near St.-Lô by some 1,500 Eighth Air Force heavy bombers and more than 900 mediums and fighters of the Ninth Air Force paved the way for an American breakout. Once the hole was made, tank columns of Lt. Gen. George S. Patton's Third Army raced south-

ward across Normandy and into Brittany. With each column went an air support party and a patrol of fighter-bombers, ready to reconnoiter or to blast enemy resistance at a word from the support party. Such scattering of fighter resources would have been wasteful, even dangerous, had the Luftwaffe still been a serious threat, but that threat had been broken.

On August 7 the enemy, under orders from Hitler himself, used all available armor and artillery in an effort to drive through Mortain to the sea at Avranches and cut off the American spearheads. A resolute ground defense, strongly supported by fighter-bombers, stopped the Nazis and threw them back. Meanwhile, the British from the north and the Americans from the south had begun a huge pincers movement which threatened to trap almost all of the Germans engaged in Normandy. The panzers, trying to squeeze their way out of the almost closed Falaise-Argentan pocket, made perfect targets for Allied planes, which bombed and strafed them into piles of junk. Eisenhower compared the scenes he saw along the roads to something out of Dante's Inferno. The German resistance was broken at Falaise. What was left of the German forces fled headlong across France and Belgium to the shelter of the Siegfried Line.

Famous names and famous faces gather for conference at an advanced headquarters somewhere in Europe. From left, Generals Carl Spaatz, George Patton, Jimmy Doolittle, Hoyt Vandenberg, and O. P. Weyland, all top US combat leaders.

During his lightning drive across France from Brittany to the Moselle, Patton had relied on the fighter-bombers of XIX Tactical Air Command to protect his exposed southern flank along the Loire River. XIX TAC took such a heavy toll of one of the largest German columns retreating from southern France toward Dijon that the German commander surrendered without any ground action. Appropriately, the commander of XIX TAC, Brig. Gen. Otto P. Weyland was invited to be present at the Beaugency bridge ceremonies when almost 20,000 Germans surrendered on September 16.

Immediately behind the racing Allied armies came the

tactical air forces, operating from hastily repaired or improvised fields as close to the forward columns as they could get. In a period of some seven weeks under a new commander, Maj. Gen. Hoyt S. Vandenberg, the Ninth Air Force moved its fighter-bombers from the beachhead across France and into eastern Belgium—400 to 500 miles —with as many as four or five stops in between. This remarkable feat of tactical mobility was made possible by the herculean efforts of the aviation engineers and the logistical units of the Ninth.

In an effort to knife into Germany quickly, the Allies on September 17 attempted an airborne operation to seize

Germans were first to put an operational jet fighter into the air, the twin-engine Messerschmitt-262 (above).

a sixty-mile salient, including a bridgehead over the Rhine at Arnhem, in Holland. The initial phase of the operation was brilliantly executed. But unexpectedly stiff resistance and the delay of airborne reinforcements because of clouds and fog prevented it from succeeding. The troops put down at Arnhem were thrown back across the Rhine with heavy losses, and the Nazis established themselves from the North Sea to Switzerland in defensive positions against which the Allied armies struggled with only limited results throughout the autumn.

Meanwhile, on August 15, American and French forces from the Mediterranean had landed on the French Riviera. The Fifteenth Air Force bombed southern France intensively before the landings, and the Twelfth Air Force was spectacularly effective in its support and interdiction missions. As part of the initial assault, American troop carriers dropped more than 5,000 paratroops. After taking Marseille, the invasion forces raced up the Rhone Valley and linked up with Eisenhower's forces by September 11. Spearheaded by XII Tactical Air Command, they had liberated more than half of France in less than a month. They had also opened an important new supply line for the Allied armies in eastern France.

During November and December 1944, Hitler scraped together his reserves for one last attempt to turn the tide of battle by an offensive through the Ardennes forest area of Belgium. He hoped to split the Allied armies by capturing the important communications center of Liége and the great port of Antwerp, the supply key to Eisenhower's armies. Striking through a thinly held sector of the Ardennes, powerful German armored forces took the Americans by surprise and advanced as much as fifty miles before being stopped. But they failed to take any major objectives during this advance, and when American paratroops of the 101st Airborne Division repulsed them at the key road junction of Bastogne, their fate was sealed.

In this famous Battle of the Bulge, the Nazis were at first protected from air attack by a week of cloudy weather, but on December 23, while they were still advancing toward the Meuse River, the skies cleared and remained clear for five days. During that time the Ninth Air Force flew an average of 1,000 fighter-bomber sorties and 400 medium bomber sorties a day against the Bulge. The B-26s and A-20s concentrated on interdiction of the railroads leading into the Ardennes, while the Eighth Air Force put 14,000 tons of bombs on rail centers and marshalling yards farther back. Fighters swarmed like mosquitoes over the enemy columns creeping along narrow roads in the Belgian hills. Cut off from fuel and even food, snarled in colossal traffic jams, and decimated by bombing and strafing, the twenty-five German divisions in the Bulge collapsed in the face of Allied counter-attacks.

The Luftwaffe was also beaten. Out in strength to support the Nazi offensive, it flew more than 600 sorties on December 17 and 800 on the twenty-third. Though it did considerable damage, it suffered heavy losses because of the inexperience of its pilots. On December 24, 1,400 of Doolittle's heavy bombers struck crippling blows at eleven airfields and cut in half German air operations over the Bulge. The enemy retaliated on January 1 with a strike by 700 planes against Allied airfields. The Nazis destroyed 156 aircraft, but they lost even more. It was the Luftwaffe's last major effort.

The enemy still had other trump cards, but he never got a chance to play them. Prewar research had given the Germans a long lead in the development of jet aircraft and guided missiles. But during the early years of the war Adolf Hitler, confident of blitzkrieg victories, had curtailed the development of new weapons, including missiles and jets. Later, after the value of the jets had been proved, he had wasted time trying to convert his best jet fighter, the ME-262, into a ground-support bomber. Thus a weapon that might have restored air superiority to the Reich was not put in quantity production until it was too late.

In 1945 the same shortages of fuel and pilots that grounded conventional aircraft in Germany also grounded the jets. A handful did operate and flew rings around everything they met, but they were too late to affect the course of the war. On occasions when it seemed that the jets might interfere with Allied operations, they were disposed of on the ground by massive attacks on their bases.

The V-1 attack on England between June and September 1944 did a great deal of damage, but not enough to interfere with the progress of the invasion. Early in September the Germans started firing their V-2 rockets against England. The V-2 had a range of some 200 miles, reached an altitude of fifty to fifty-six miles and a speed of 3,600 miles per hour. It carried almost a ton of explosives. But it, too, came too late to be decisive, even though it caused much damage in the London area and to Antwerp. The errors of the all-knowing dictator made Germany a few months too late with the weapons that might have altered the course of the war if they had been put into earlier use.

Parachutes fill the sky over the coast of southern France as C-47s drop men and supplies to join Normandy invaders.

Maj. Glenn Eagleston, Ninth AF ace, here with others from his squadron, describes a successful attack on Nazi communications and supply lines during Battle of the Bulge.

Strategic Bombardment, Overlord to V-E Day

Although the first duty of the heavy bombers throughout the summer of 1944 was to support the ground campaign, USSTAF and RAF Bomber Command continued to attack strategic targets in Germany. The Eighth Air Force had almost 2,000 four-engine bombers, Fifteenth Air Force almost 1,000, and RAF Bomber Command 1,100. The Eighth Air Force alone dropped 230,000 tons of bombs in the five months from May through September. Thanks to fair weather and lack of fighter opposition most of its planes reached their objectives and bombed with devastating results. The percentage of losses declined greatly, but flak barrages had grown heavier and made most of the strategic missions still dangerous. The worst month was July, when the Eighth lost 324 planes, the Fifteenth 318. For many weeks the Fifteenth was actually losing more men than were the two Allied armies fighting in Italy.

These losses were rewarded by a clear-cut strategic victory—the shattering of the German oil industry. The Eighth began the campaign against the synthetic oil industry in Germany with a smashing attack against plants at Merseburg-Leuna and other cities on May 12. Further attacks, coupled with the Fifteenth's great campaign against Ploesti, cut the enemy's oil output in half by June. From then on, oil got top-target priority, so that by September production had shrunk to a quarter of normal. Of twenty-four synthetic oil plants, the Eighth Air Force had put all but a few out of business, and the Fifteenth's sustained assaults had practically ended production at Ploesti

before Rumania surrendered late in August. German motor traffic ground to a halt. Gasoline had to be hoarded for weeks at the cost of all ordinary operations for any large movement. This was particularly true of the Ardennes offensive. Indeed, one purpose of the offensive was to fill

Heavy attacks on rail yards played jackstraws with engines.

Hit by flak over Italy, a B-24 catches fire and plunges to ground. Two men managed to bail out.

Almost perfect photographic timing caught these sticks falling from Flying Fortress bomb bays.

the Nazis' fuel needs through the capture of Allied stocks near Liége.

Lack of gasoline actually robbed the Germans of the fruits of a production victory. In spite of the fact that the Allies had bombed aircraft factories on a scale second only to the oil plants, Karl Saur, the director of German fighter production, had worked such miracles of concealment and dispersal that in September 1944 Germany produced 4,000 fighters. Yet this wealth of planes had to sit on the ground most of the time with empty tanks. Such efforts as that of November 2, when the Nazis put 400 planes in the air and shot down twenty-six bombers, had to be interspersed by periods of a fortnight or more in which Allied bomber missions seldom saw an enemy aircraft. Moreover, the Germans had to stint on pilot training to save fuel, with the result that the combat effectiveness of their fighters fell lower and lower.

During the winter, clouds forced the Americans to do eighty percent of their bombing by radar, and the Germans succeeded in boosting oil production slightly. But by April 1945 the continuing and overwhelming attacks had cut output to a mere five percent of normal. Coupled with greatly intensified bombing of the German railroad system and canals during the winter of 1944-45, this shortage of fuel strangled the German economy. Transportation in Hitler's Reich slowed almost literally to a walk, and without transportation Germany was ceasing to be an industrial nation. In the first strategic bombing campaign in history it was inevitable that some unprofitable objectives would be chosen. It was probably inevitable that political and military pressures would divert

the heavy bombers to some unsuitable tasks, such as close support or the bombing of the sub pens, but in the end they had found the enemy's vitals and struck home.

Victory in Europe

By the end of 1944, Germany was like a beaten boxer, unable to do more than cover up and hang on. In January and February 1945 the Allies pushed through the Rhineland. In March they made four separate crossings of the Rhine, all with astonishing ease. On April 1 they encircled the Ruhr, Germany's richest industrial area, and with it 400,000 of Hitler's best remaining troops. Above them, the Anglo-American air forces ruled the skies.

In April the last German defenses in the West crumbled, and American tank columns, covered by fighter-bombers and moving so fast they had to be supplied mainly by air, plunged across southern Germany into Austria and Czechoslovakia. Meanwhile a Russian offensive, begun on January 12, had rolled from Warsaw to the Oder River. Americans and Russians met at the Elbe on April 25, and on May 7 the Nazi government surrendered unconditionally.

Airpower was decisive in the conquest of Germany. Great credit must go to the Allied armies and navies, but they could hardly have set out from England had not Allied airpower first established superiority over the Luftwaffe. Airpower shielded them, guided them, and cleared a path for them. And it was airpower that ultimately broke Germany's capacity to resist by denying it fuel and transportation.

Large-scale air attacks on Wesel, paving the way for the Rhine jump-off, left the city bomb-pocked and pulverized.

Chapter 6

W O R L D   W A R   I I | 1 9 3 9 · 4 5

War in the Pacific

THE ATTACK on Pearl Harbor was but the first of a series of shocks that rocked the United States during the first six months of the war. One after another, American possessions in the Pacific fell before the rampaging Japanese forces. Only in the Philippines were the Americans and Filipinos able to put up a prolonged resistance.

Disaster in the Philippines

The Japanese were not able to attack the Philippines and Pearl Harbor simultaneously. Because of the time difference, it was still dark in Manila in the early morning of December 8, and effective air attack was not practicable. By about 0400, MacArthur and his air commander, Brereton, received word of the attack on Pearl Harbor. Unlike Kimmel and Short in Hawaii, the American commanders in the Far East had time to act. With their two squadrons of B-17s at Clark Field, north of Manila, and two more at Del Monte, far to the south on the island of Mindanao, they might have found out what the Japanese were up to or have struck the first blows against the enemy. They did neither. By the time they made up their minds later in the day to attack Formosa, it was too late.

As precautionary measures, two pursuit squadrons took off on patrol about 0800, and the two squadrons of B-17s at Clark Field were ordered into the air. By 0830 all were flying except two that were being camouflaged and one that was out of commission.

Highly mechanized warfare against a primitive backdrop. The marriage of the bulldozer and the airplane perhaps best symbolizes Pacific campaign, a war of jungles and islands.

In midmorning, MacArthur gave Brereton permission to use the Fortresses at Clark for a strike just before dark against known Japanese airfields on Formosa. All but two of the B-17s landed to prepare for their mission. It seemed safe to land at Clark because it was logical to suppose that if the Japanese had intended a major air attack that day they would have launched it early to give the defenders the least possible time for preparation. The Japanese had indeed planned to send off a mission at dawn but had been delayed until about 0915 by a heavy fog. By 1045, when the Fortresses finished landing at Clark, a force of 108 bombers and eighty-four Zero fighters was well on its way from Formosa.

The radar set at Iba Field, on the coast west of Clark, spotted the enemy a good way off and reported to air headquarters that at 1127 the approaching formations were seventy miles from Lingayen Gulf. The radar men faithfully tracked the Japanese until a bomb killed them at their post, but their efforts were in vain. Communications on Luzon, which had always been unsatisfactory, broke down almost completely after 1130, a circumstance later attributed to wire-cutting and radio-jamming by Japanese agents. During the next hour, confusion reigned at Clark Field.

At 1233 a formation of fifty-four Japanese bombers with an escort of fifty Zeros flew over the fighter field at Iba and dropped a row of bombs straight across the field from 28,000 feet, too high for interception by the American fighters. What the bombers left, the Zeros strafed. Iba was completely destroyed.

About 1235, men at Clark Field looked up from their tasks as the base alarm sounded to behold Japanese bombers high in the northwest. Four pilots of the 20th Squadron, which had just finished refueling after spending most of

THE PACIFIC AND CHINA-BURMA-INDIA THEATERS OF OPERATIONS—1941-45

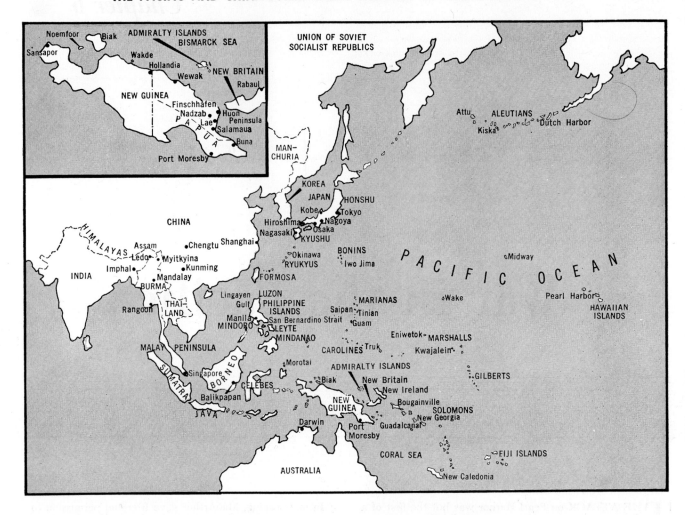

the morning on patrol, zoomed down the runway and into the air. The control tower gave one frantic call, "All pursuit to Clark." Next minute, bombs rained down on the field in a precise and accurate pattern. After the bombing, Zeros strafed back and forth for at least half an hour, concentrating on the B-17s. When they had finished, the field lay in ruins, its buildings gutted, not one plane flyable. A towering pillar of black smoke from Clark's burning fuel dump marked the grave of the American bombers. The four P-40s cleared the runway in time to make kills. Lt. Randall B. Keator scored the first kill, and Lt. Joseph H. Moore accounted for two more.

The smashing second blow expected next day did not come. Wind and rain grounded the Japanese bombers. During the afternoon and night of December 9, fourteen Fortresses flew up from Del Monte for a mission against Formosa. Instead, they went out next morning to hit large Japanese convoys heading for the northern coast of Luzon, but they had little success. Fighters did better. The only big kill was made at the cost of his own life by Lt. Samuel H. Marrett, commander of the 34th Pursuit Squadron, who took his plane in at masthead height to attack a 10,000-ton vessel and was caught in the blast when the ship exploded. After their attack against the convoys, the B-17s withdrew to Mindanao, a wise move in the light of subsequent events.

A dozen Zeros strafed the fighter base at Del Carmen, west of Clark Field, on the afternoon of December 10, destroying practically all the planes on the field. Less than half an hour later a force of about 100 Japanese bombers and 150 fighters attacked Nichols Field and the naval base at Cavite, badly damaging both. Although most of the bombers flew too high to be intercepted, the remaining

American fighters tangled with the Japanese escort in a wild melee. Three American pilots were killed, and at least eight more bailed out or crash-landed. The defenders destroyed more Japanese aircraft than they lost, but they could ill afford their own losses.

On the night of the tenth, Brereton had eighteen B-17s left, and only twelve were operational. Of the fighters, only twenty-two P-40s and eight P-35s remained. The pursuits were ordered to fly no more combat missions because they were too few to achieve significant results in combat operations and they were urgently needed for reconnaissance. Thereafter, with only minor exceptions, the Japanese had unchallenged control of the air over the Philippines.

From MacArthur down, the beleaguered garrison on Luzon dreamed of huge American convoys steaming into Manila Bay with reinforcements. But shipments to the Philippines were diverted elsewhere because of Japanese air and naval superiority, and only a trickle of supplies arrived by submarines and blockade runners. On December 24 the War Department notified MacArthur that it intended to concentrate its Far East airpower in Australia because it was impossible to stage fighter aircraft to Luzon.

After a series of landings, the most important in Lingayen Gulf, Japanese troops swept across Luzon so easily that MacArthur's chief ground commander, Maj. Gen. Jonathan M. Wainwright, became fully convinced of "the futility of trying to fight a war without an Air Force." Japanese occupation of bases on Luzon endangered Del Monte on Mindanao, so between December 16 and 18 the B-17s there were sent south to Australia.

The remaining American forces on Luzon withdrew on December 24 to the island fortress of Corregidor in Manila

Bay and to the rugged peninsula of Bataan on the northwest side of the bay. By holding out in these key points they denied Manila to Japanese shipping and pinned down large forces that the Japanese might have used for conquest elsewhere. Half-starved and wracked with malaria and dysentery, the defenders of the peninsula held out until April 9, the Corregidor garrison until May 6. Most of the Air Corps officers and men fought as infantry for lack of planes. The few planes still on hand continued to fly missions. Almost to the end, they managed to make some attacks from Corregidor despite fantastic difficulties.

For six months after Pearl Harbor the Japanese swept everything before them with astounding ease. The lightly garrisoned islands of Guam and Wake fell within a few days. Taking full advantage of their control of the air and sea, the Nipponese drove the Americans, British, Dutch, and Australians from one line of defense after another. Filtering through the jungles of Malaya, their troops captured the "impregnable" fortress of Singapore on February 15, 1942. Less than a month later, they completed the conquest of the Netherlands Indies. Small amphibious forces seized footholds on New Britain, on New Guinea, and in the Solomon Islands, bases from which the Japanese might attack Australia directly or isolate it by an advance into the Fiji Islands or New Caledonia. Marching westward from Thailand, Japanese armies took Rangoon on March 8, conquered practically all of Burma, and isolated China by cutting the Burma Road.

Japan had carved out a huge empire rich in the natural resources it had so long craved, but there was a flaw in the structure that would eventually be fatal. The long sea lanes were extremely vulnerable, and avenging American and Allied submarines and aircraft set out to destroy the precious shipping without which the empire could not endure.

Turn of the Tide

Although Japanese conquest was running at floodtide during the early months of the war, the Americans chose to launch their first counterstroke against Japan itself. On April 18, 1942, Lt. Col. James H. Doolittle led sixteen AAF B-25s from the US Navy aircraft carrier *Hornet* in a spectacular low-level attack against Tokyo and other targets in Japan. All sixteen planes were lost in bad weather over China, but most of the crews were saved. Although the attack did only minor damage, it profoundly affected Japanese strategy. It probably caused the Japanese to keep at home four Army fighter groups that were badly needed in the South Pacific during 1942-43. It also spurred on the Japanese to expand their perimeter still farther in order to

keep the Americans beyond reach of the home islands. The Tokyo raid was followed within a few weeks by the Japanese reverse at the Battle of the Coral Sea, off the southeast coast of New Guinea, on May 7-8. The two events were important factors in the Japanese decision to bring the American Pacific Fleet to battle by an attack on Midway Islands. If the American carriers could be destroyed, the Pacific would become a Japanese lake.

The Battle of Midway on June 3-4, 1942, was a great victory for American naval airpower. Three American carriers destroyed four Japanese carriers while losing one of their own. The powerful Japanese fleet, including six battleships, dared not face the two remaining American carriers and turned homeward in retreat. The day of the battleship was done, and airpower would rule the oceans of the world thereafter.

In conjunction with the attempt against Midway, a Japanese force attacked Dutch Harbor in the Aleutians and landed troops on Kiska and Attu islands. They remained on the islands, under frequent attack from the Eleventh Air Force, until 1943 when American forces recaptured Attu and forced them to withdraw from Kiska.

Meanwhile, Australia was being prepared as the major base for Allied resistance. American forces secured the islands along the vital routes to Australia, and reinforcements poured into the southwest Pacific. One-half of the troops and a third of the cargo sent overseas from the United States during the first three months of 1942 went to Australia. In addition to three American fighter groups, fifty heavy bombers and replacement fighter planes arrived to bolster the air defenses of the subcontinent. But once Australia's minimum requirements had been met, the policy of concentrating strength against Germany went into effect, and supplies and reinforcements for the southwest Pacific were small by comparison with Europe. It was the grievance and the glory of the commanders in the Pacific that they eventually fought great offensive campaigns with resources supposedly adequate only for defense initially and for limited offensives thereafter.

MacArthur arrived in Australia from the Philippines on March 17 and soon after became commander of the Southwest Pacific Area, with Australian as well as American troops under him. The Netherlands Indies had already been lost, and the Japanese were eying the approaches to Australia. For two months, operations north of Australia were insignificant as the Japanese gathered their strength for an assault on the key to northern Australia: Port Moresby, on the southeast coast of New Guinea. On May 7 and 8, in the Coral Sea southeast of New Guinea, an American naval task force turned back a powerful Japanese amphibious

After a raid, Consolidated B-24s of Eleventh Air Force return to their lonely airstrip in the desolate Aleutians.

Jimmy Doolittle's daring raid on Tokyo from the decks of the carrier *Hornet* in 1942 was a psychological success.

In the bitter battle for Guadalcanal, air operations from much-bombed Henderson Field were indispensable to victory.

Generals George C. Kenney (left) and Ennis Whitehead were the architects of the air victory in the Pacific theater.

force headed for Port Moresby. It was a strategic victory for the Allies, even though the US carriers did not win a clear-cut tactical victory over the enemy.

The Solomons and New Guinea

In the course of their headlong plunge into the South Pacific, the Japanese occupied Guadalcanal and other strategic islands in the Solomons, from where they could threaten the lifeline to Australia. Acting on strategic directions from the Joint Chiefs of Staff, Adm. Chester W. Nimitz, commander of the Pacific Ocean Areas, ordered the capture of Guadalcanal, to be followed by further operations through the Solomons and New Guinea to Rabaul on New Britain. Rabaul was the anchor of the Japanese position in the southwest Pacific.

The US Navy directed the campaign for the reconquest of the Solomons. After the First Marine Division landed on Guadalcanal on August 7, the Americans won the drawn-out race with the Japanese for reinforcement and supply. Henderson Field on Guadalcanal was indispensable to victory, for the island could not have been taken without the help of the Navy, Marine, and AAF flyers who won control of the air over the island. Victory was assured in November when American ships and planes destroyed all eleven transports in a Japanese fleet carrying 13,500 reinforcements to the island. But the Japanese did not give up Guadalcanal until February 1943, and they made strong air attacks on Henderson Field for some months after that.

From Guadalcanal the Marine and Army troops, under the over-all command of Adm. William F. Halsey, went on to capture remaining Japanese strongholds in the Solomons. The year-long campaign resulted in the capture of New Georgia Island and the Empress Augusta Bay region of Bougainville, which completed the sealing-off of the Japanese remaining on bypassed islands in the Solomons. The Thirteenth Air Force, under Maj. Gen. Nathan F. Twining, worked closely with Marine and Navy air units to provide the air support for this extended campaign. A handful of AAF bombers performed valuable service on long-range reconnaissance and bombardment missions.

Before the battle for Guadalcanal had even begun, the Japanese started their final bid for Port Moresby, this time by land. In July 1942, from the tiny settlement of Buna on the north side of New Guinea, they began a drive southward on a trail that led through the jungles and over the Owen Stanley mountains of Papua to Port Moresby. By September, they had crossed the mountains and were within thirty miles of their goal.

In this crisis, Maj. Gen. George C. Kenney, sent out as a trouble shooter, became commander of the Allied Air

Forces in the area. In September he organized the American units in Australia and New Guinea into the Fifth Air Force. Since his headquarters at Brisbane, in Australia, was far behind the battle zone, Kenney set up an advanced headquarters in New Guinea under Brig. Gen. Ennis C. Whitehead, who remained Kenney's No. 1 combat commander throughout the war. Kenney inspected the demoralized remnants of the 19th Bombardment Group, which at that time had only four of its thirty-two battered B-17s in flyable condition, watched P-39s at Port Moresby making futile attempts to intercept Japanese bombers flying far above P-39 ceiling, and decided, as he later wrote, "No matter what I accomplished, it would be an improvement."

Kenney's basic strategy was simple and orthodox: "To take out the Jap air strength until we owned the air over New Guinea." The Fifth Air Force concentrated on attacks against airfields at Buna and Lae to drive the enemy "off our front lawn." Runways were knocked out by B-17s and B-25s using conventional bombing techniques. To destroy aircraft on the ground Kenney introduced new tactics and new weapons. Beginning in September 1942, A-20 attack bombers made low-altitude strikes with fragmentation bombs attached to parachutes and armed with instantaneous fuzes. For this purpose the A-20s, which had origi-

A P-38, one wing torn by flak, limps home. Once the Lightnings entered the war, American air superiority widened.

nally carried only four thirty-caliber machine guns, had four additional fifty-caliber guns packed into their noses. The modification was invented and supervised by Maj. Paul (Pappy) Gunn, who had joined the AAF during the Philippine campaign and had since made a fabulous reputation as a flyer and mechanical wizard.

By mid-September the Fifth Air Force had won command of the air over New Guinea, partly, to be sure, because the Japanese had their hands full in the Solomons. The time was ripe for an Allied offensive. Kenney demonstrated the value of air transport by ferrying about 4,500 fresh troops from Australia to New Guinea to help push the Japanese back along the Buna trail. Then, while the ground forces plodded slowly forward, his troop carriers flew two regiments over the Owen Stanley mountains to jungle airstrips within a few miles of Buna. In a characteristic last-ditch defense the Japanese held out at Buna until January 2, 1943.

The most important contribution of the Fifth Air Force to this campaign was maintaining control of the air. Japanese attacks against the ground forces were few and ineffective. After the P-38 Lightnings went into action in December 1942 the American margin of air superiority over the Japanese widened steadily.

In the jungles and mountains of New Guinea, air supply proved second in importance only to control of the air. When Japanese air attacks upset plans to supply the troops in northern Papua by sea, air transport made up the deficit by flying in about 2,450 tons of supplies to airstrips on the north coast between November 13 and January 23.

After the loss of Buna the Japanese fell back on their main base at Lae. In February, intelligence reports based largely on air reconnaissance indicated that the enemy would make a major effort to reinforce Lae. Ready for the occasion was a new weapon that Kenney called his commerce destroyer. The ingenious "Pappy" Gunn had designed to Kenney's specifications a modified B-25 with eight machine guns packed into its nose where one had been before. Using the technique of low-altitude skip bombing, the Fifth Air Force bombers were ready to take a toll of Japanese convoys off New Guinea.

The Japanese attempted to reinforce Lae as predicted. On March 1, a B-24 spotted a convoy carrying a Japanese division in the Bismarck Sea north of Cape Gloucester, New Britain. For three days American and Australian planes attacked the sixteen ships in the convoy. The B-25s

In attack on Karas, Dutch New Guinea, a Douglas A-20 is caught by Japanese flak, plunges smoking into the sea.

Their shipping took such a beating in Battle of Bismarck Sea that Japanese ceased trying to run convoys to Lae.

A Fifth Air Force minimum-altitude attack on Japanese airstrip west of Wewak. B-25 (left) has just unloaded bombs.

B-25s wing toward Rabaul while, below, an American invasion convoy casts its wakes on way to strike Green Islands.

Iron-nerved P-38 pilot, Capt. Richard I. Bong, soon topped
Rickenbacker's World War I record of kills, went on to
shoot down forty planes to become America's all-time ace.

and A-20s did the most effective bombing, and P-38s provided cover for some of the attacks. Only four destroyers
escaped; the rest of the convoy was sunk. Known as the
Battle of the Bismarck Sea, even though the decisive action
took place after the convoy had passed into the Solomon
Sea, this victory ended Japanese attempts to run convoys
in to Lae. Thereafter they relied mainly on barges.

Plans made in the spring of 1943 provided that while
Admiral Halsey's Marine and Army troops advanced
through the Solomons, MacArthur's men would drive west
along the north coast of New Guinea. Their next objectives
were Salamaua and Lae, lying respectively 150 and 175
miles west of Buna. But first, Kenney wanted to neutralize
the strong Japanese air strength at Wewak, 300 miles west
of Lae. On August 17 and 18, Fifth Air Force bombers
swept "like a giant scythe" over airfields at Wewak, destroying 175 planes on the ground.

With the Japanese air threat sharply reduced, the Allies
moved against Lae by sea and air, temporarily bypassing
Salamaua where the Japanese had concentrated the bulk of
their troops against the Americans and Australians who
had been maintaining pressure on them. The American
503d Parachute Regiment and a battery of Australian artillery dropped at Nadzab, about nineteen miles northwest of
Lae, in one of the classic airborne operations of the war.
Lae fell on September 16. Resistance at Salamaua had been
broken two days earlier.

MacArthur hastened to exploit the weakening Japanese
position by further advances up the Markham Valley and
to Finschhafen, on the tip of the Huon Peninsula opposite
New Britain, by October 2. These new positions permitted
the Fifth Air Force to support advances northward into
New Britain or westward toward Wewak. In October 1943
the Fifth was called on to neutralize Japanese air and naval
strength at the key port of Rabaul in support of Halsey's
assault on Bougainville in the Solomons. Kenney began a
drive to win control of the air over all New Britain and
New Ireland and to put the two islands under air blockade.
The task was not easy, for Rabaul alone was protected by
367 antiaircraft guns and an estimated force of 124 bombers
and 145 fighters based at five neighboring fields.

In conjunction with Thirteenth Air Force and Navy

planes from the Solomons, the Fifth eventually destroyed
Japanese air strength on New Britain and ruined Rabaul.
By mid-December, Allied control of the air was strong
enough to permit an invasion of New Britain to secure
positions from which Allied shipping could be protected.

While Army and Marine troops took the Arawe Peninsula and Cape Gloucester during the winter of 1943-44,
the air forces from the Solomons were finishing off Rabaul.
A sustained offensive of almost 6,000 bomber and fighter
sorties in the first fifty days of 1944 shattered Japanese
resistance. Rabaul was left a battered ruin. There was no
need to capture it.

As 1944 began, the Japanese still held most of New
Guinea with about 70,000 troops and with considerable
air strength, concentrated mainly at Wewak and 250 miles
farther west at Hollandia. But the hardest going was over.
The enemy was weakening. He no longer had to be rooted
out of each position. American air and naval strength would
permit bypassing many Japanese strongpoints. Cut off from
their supplies, the Japanese would rot in the jungle. To
complete the isolation of the Japanese on New Britain and
in the Solomons and to cut the communications of all the
Japanese left in New Guinea, the Allied forces took the
Admiralty Islands, northwest of New Britain, by the end
of March 1944.

Bypassing Wewak and other intermediate positions, the
Allied forces aimed next at the Japanese stronghold of Hollandia. Because this was beyond the normal range of the
P-38, the Japanese had believed that the Americans could
not gain aerial superiority over Hollandia, without which
they could not risk a landing. But the Fifth had added new
wing tanks that extended the range of the P-38s to 650
miles. With the Lightnings escorting them all the way,
B-24s, B-25s, and A-20s destroyed Japanese air strength
on the ground at Hollandia in a three-day blitz through
April 1, 1944. Later, the Allies found 340 airplanes mol-
dering around Hollandia. Another fifty had been destroyed
in the air. The cost to the Fifth was two Lightnings. And
during this campaign an iron-nerved P-38 pilot, Capt.
Richard I. Bong, surpassed Eddie Rickenbacker's World
War I record by shooting down his twenty-seventh plane
on April 8.

After the occupation of Hollandia and its airfields in
April, the Allied forces took, in quick succession, a series
of islands off the northern coast of New Guinea—Wakde,
Biak, and Noemfoor. The islands were important chiefly
because they already had airstrips or could be developed
into air bases. The pattern of operations was the same for
each campaign. Fifth Air Force bombers would soften up
the defenses with heavy attacks, and Navy vessels would
bombard the islands just before the troops landed. In every
case the landings were virtually unopposed, although fierce
fighting usually developed inland. When the American 41st
Division went ashore on Biak without ground or air opposition on May 27, the division commander signaled, "My
hat is off to the Air Force."

The seizure of Noemfoor on July 2 climaxed a three-
month campaign during which MacArthur's forces had advanced more than 800 miles by adroitly using control of
the air to neutralize and then bypass enemy surface forces.
One more hop at the end of July gave them Sansapor on
the western tip of New Guinea with little more than a
skirmish. Behind them was half a Japanese army, and in
New Britain, New Ireland, and the Solomons some 80,000
Japanese troops still held out. Such powerful remnants had
to be watched and contained. But, isolated in the jungles
without planes and almost without heavy weapons, the
efforts of these Japanese forces were like the convulsive
struggles of a beheaded snake. The Allies had a firm grip
on all they needed of New Guinea. Ahead lay the Philippines.

With the end of the Solomons campaign, the Thirteenth Air Force came under Kenney, who organized the Far East Air Forces in June 1944 as an over-all headquarters to control the Fifth and the Thirteenth. The Thirteenth, commanded by Maj. Gen. St. Clair Streett, moved forward gradually to New Guinea and joined in the operations against the Japanese from its new location. Whitehead took over the Fifth from Kenney.

The Philippines and Okinawa

Once victory in New Guinea loomed ahead, the Joint Chiefs of Staff authorized MacArthur to retake the Philippines. MacArthur's forces first needed advanced bases, so in September they captured Morotai, southeast of Mindanao. The Fifth Air Force had been waging an air campaign against Japanese air strength on Mindanao since early August in preparation for an invasion.

The original plan called for a landing on Mindanao, but the spectacular success of US Navy carrier sweeps in the Philippines and an optimistic report that the key island of Leyte was virtually undefended led to a decision to bypass Mindanao and go after Leyte in October. Under the protection of a huge Navy task force, the US Sixth Army went ashore on Leyte on October 20, meeting heavy opposition shortly after from the 20,000 Japanese troops on the island.

While the battle raged on Leyte, most of the desperate Japanese fleet sallied forth to make an all-out attack on the task force. It was thoroughly beaten by Vice Adm. Thomas C. Kinkaid's Seventh Fleet and Admiral Halsey's powerful Third Fleet in the Battle of Leyte Gulf. But Halsey, with most of the fast carriers, permitted himself to be decoyed northward, leaving the beachhead without sufficient protection. When he steamed northward on October 24 to intercept the Japanese decoy force, he believed that the fleet he had repulsed earlier had turned back from its attempt to pass through San Bernardino Strait. But the Japanese admiral did not turn back and, but for the heroic resistance of a few escort carriers of the Seventh Fleet, he might have played havoc with the shipping off the beaches. A further crisis arose when most of the carriers had to be prematurely withdrawn for refueling. The engineers rushed through a single fighter strip at Tacloban, and Fifth Air Force P-38s flew in on October 27, barely in time to provide air defense for the beachhead.

For a week or two the air battle over Leyte was hotly contested, but once there were enough airfields for American fighters, the Japanese were again outclassed. Fifth Air Force pilots shot down 314 enemy aircraft over Leyte before the end of 1944 while losing only sixteen planes. They also began a devastating campaign against Japanese airfields in the islands.

From Leyte the next hop was to Mindoro, well suited as an advanced air base for a landing on Luzon. When Mindoro was invaded on December 15 the enemy still resisted vigorously in the air. Japanese suicide planes made severe attacks on Allied convoys heading for Lingayen Gulf to make the initial landings on Luzon. But after MacArthur's troops surged ashore at Lingayen on January 9, 1945, Japanese airpower was quickly shattered and the remaining enemy aircraft were evacuated. Air attacks had put some 1,500 planes out of action. The enemy had poured planes into the islands by the hundreds only to have them destroyed on the ground by FEAF and US Navy planes, often before they had made a single sortie.

Almost no air opposition was encountered during the Luzon campaign. The Fifth Air Force concentrated its efforts on ground support, which the Joint Chiefs of Staff later described as the most strikingly effective of the Pacific war. Among the most spectacular of the support operations was a successful paratroop drop on February 16 to take the little fortress island of Corregidor. By the beginning of March, the capture of Manila had been completed and the reconquest of the Philippines assured.

The Philippine campaign greatly weakened the Japanese in the western Pacific and speeded up the tempo of American operations. From the central Pacific, Admiral Nimitz mounted an invasion of Okinawa, main island of the Ryukyus, on April 1, 1945. In American hands, Okinawa, only 400 miles south of Japan, could become a main base for the invasion of Japan proper—the climactic action of the war. The Japanese garrison on Okinawa resisted the US Tenth Army with more than usual skill and tenacity.

Kamikazes inflicted the heaviest losses of the war on the American fleet. Japanese pilots deliberately crashed their explosive-laden planes into targets, especially ships. The Japanese had reached back into their medieval past for this suicide tactic because they were no longer able to meet the American flyers in the air. In all, the Japanese made about 1,900 such sorties during the Okinawa campaign. These attacks were especially serious because the ground troops on the island depended for air support on US Navy

Japanese cargo ship carrying reinforcements to Leyte is target for this B-25 attack at little more than mast-top height.

A lighter moment as Pacific air war leaders get together. From left, Maj. Gen. Willis H. Hale, Gen. George C. Kenney, Lt. Gen. Ennis C. Whitehead, Maj. Gen. Paul B. Wurtsmith, and Brig. Gen. Thomas D. White, now USAF Chief.

carriers during the early days of the campaign. On April 7 a tactical air force, composed of Seventh Air Force and Marine units, began arriving and thereafter gave sustained and effective support to the ground troops. The conquest of the island was not completed until June 21.

The Ryukyus quickly became a springboard for the invasion of Japan. Whitehead sent his Fifth Air Force units into the islands to join those of Brig. Gen. Thomas D. White's Seventh Air Force, which came under the command of FEAF in July. An enormous airfield building program—probably the largest aviation engineering project ever attempted in so short a time—was undertaken. The Fifth and Seventh Air Forces attacked Kyushu—the southernmost island of Japan—the China coast, and enemy shipping wherever it could be found. The buildup in Okinawa was proceeding at a tremendous rate when the Japanese surrendered in August. FEAF's advance guard would fly over Tokyo in transport planes instead of the bombers and fighters that had carried them so far from Australia and the Solomons.

China-Burma-India

By June 1942 the Japanese had conquered Burma and severed China's one remaining lifeline—the Burma Road. The advance of the Japanese to the frontiers of India had been halted more by the monsoon rains than by Allied resistance.

In addition to the Royal Air Force, air opposition to the Japanese in Burma had come from the American Volunteer Group (AVG), more familiarly known as the Flying Tigers. A retired Air Corps officer with long experience in China,

Claire L. Chennault, had organized the group on behalf of China to defend the Burma Road and provide the Chinese armies with air support. After fighting gallantly in defense of Burma, the Flying Tigers pulled back into China in April, and Chennault was recalled to active duty and promoted to brigadier general by the AAF. The AVG flyers were inducted into the AAF in July. At the time, Chennault had an effective strength of thirty P-40s and seven B-25s. The AAF sent additional combat groups, and early in 1943 the Fourteenth Air Force was established in China with Chennault as commander.

The desperate situation in Burma had forced the AAF to send Brereton and the remnants of his air units from the Netherlands Indies to India in March 1942. Brereton took command of the new Tenth Air Force at New Delhi on March 5, but he resumed his travels again in June when the AAF ordered him with all of his B-17s to the Middle East to shore up the defenses of Egypt. The Tenth was left without a single operating combat unit in India.

From the first, the air transport operations from India to China were as important as the AAF's combat mission in the theater. Without air transport, China could not stay in the war. The loss of Burma, and especially the key airfield at Myitkyina, forced the air transports to fly the "Hump" route to China, over an uncharted extension of the Himalayas with passes 14,000 feet high flanked by peaks towering to 16,500 feet. Crews forced by accident or enemy action to take to their parachutes might land on ice fields or in jungles inhabited by head-hunters. The monsoon season brought wild storms to the mountains, with heavy clouds and winds over 100 miles an hour. Under these circumstances, the C-47s had great difficulty in hauling any appreciable tonnage into China.

Under the control of the global AAF Air Transport Command (ATC) after December 1, 1942, the India-China Wing slowly increased its lift during 1943, reaching 2,800 tons in February, still below the minimum of 3,500 tons promised Chiang Kai-shek in 1942. For an effective effort, the wing needed better airfields in Assam, on the northeastern frontier of India, and larger planes—especially the four-engine C-54. With additional transports on hand, the lift over the Hump reached 7,000 tons in October 1943 and averaged more than 12,000 tons a month during the first six months of 1944. In July 1945 the transports carried the tremendous total of 71,000 tons across the Hump.

Until very late in the war, Allied operations in China, Burma, and India (CBI) were muddled and impeded as nowhere else by a tangled chain of command, conflicts of

Flying Tiger AVG pilots run for their Curtiss P-40s.

Transports supplied China across the Himalayan "Hump."

national policy, and personal feuds among the commanders. Maj. Gen. George E. Stratemeyer, who commanded the American air forces in the theater between 1943 and 1945, described the organization as a strange animal that was "all headquarters and no hindquarters." In addition, the theater had a very low priority. Both the Tenth Air Force in Burma and India and the Fourteenth Air Force in China were small even by Pacific standards and dwarfs compared to the forces fighting in Europe. The primary purpose of the Allied effort in CBI was not to win the war but to hold the enemy in check while victory was achieved elsewhere.

In China the Fourteenth Air Force showed great skill in holding its own against heavy odds. Chennault, a brilliant tactician and aggressive commander, carried the war to the enemy, strafing targets as far away as Shanghai and attacking Japanese shipping off the coast of China. Without the help of the Fourteenth, the Chinese armies would have had almost no air support against the Japanese.

In Burma, the Tenth Air Force and the RAF gradually won air superiority over the Japanese. Medium bombers and fighter-bombers carried on energetic campaigns against river traffic, bridges, and railroads. American and British transport planes saved a large British force in the Indian border area around Imphal by flying in whole divisions of reinforcements and more than 20,000 tons of supplies after it had been encircled by a Japanese offensive in March 1944. For weeks, the British army of 150,000 men was maintained solely from the air. Then, in May and June, the British Fourteenth Army broke the siege and drove the Japanese back. But for the complete Allied control of the air, the Japanese would have probably taken Imphal and won a major victory.

In March, Allied troop carrier units and a special American air commando group carried out a daring operation far behind the Japanese lines in central Burma. They landed in the jungles some 10,000 of British Maj. Gen. Orde C. Wingate's raiders, popularly known as Chindits. These long-range penetration groups, supplied entirely from the air, struck at vital Japanese supply lines, endangering the enemy's position in Burma.

In northern Burma an American-trained Chinese corps and an American regiment, "Merrill's Marauders," sustained mainly by airdrops, advanced through the jungles from Ledo and took the airfield at Myitkyina in May 1944. With the help of huge quantities of supplies airlanded at Myitkyina, the corps reopened the Burma Road to China in January 1945. However, the tonnage brought over the road from then to the end of the war did not equal that flown over the Hump in a single month.

The British Fourteenth Army, after long years on the defensive, took the offensive late in 1944 and drove the Japanese mercilessly before it. Preceded by bombers and fighters of the Tenth Air Force and the RAF, the British captured Mandalay in March 1945, Rangoon in May, and drove the remnants of the Japanese forces out of Burma. Liberators pounded Japanese depots and installations during the campaign. Japanese airpower was completely broken, and the enemy could muster barely fifty planes for the defense of Burma. The tactical air forces were deadly in close support, harrying the enemy and slaughtering thousands of Japanese soldiers. This campaign was remarkable because most of the supply of the Army was by air. In April 1945, the Anglo-American Combat Cargo Task Force supplied no fewer than 356,000 advancing troops by air.

In China, by contrast, the Japanese began a series of offensives in the spring of 1944 to secure north-south railroad communications and to drive the Fourteenth Air Force from its forward bases. Rolling over the weary and demoralized Chinese armies, these offensives were highly successful. By the end of the year they had forced Chennault's flyers deep into the interior of China. To retrieve the situation, ATC and troop carrier planes flew two of the American-trained Chinese divisions in Burma back to China in December 1944. Ably supported by the Fourteenth Air Force, these troops launched a counteroffensive in May 1945 and retained the initiative from then on. The Fourteenth Air Force and the transport pilots on the Hump route kept China in the war. A high-ranking Japanese officer stated after the war that had it not been for the Fourteenth Air Force "we could have gone anywhere we wished [in China]."

The Strategic Bombardment of Japan

From the very beginning of the B-29 in 1939-40, air leaders like Arnold and Spaatz had felt that one of its chief uses might well be the bombardment of Japan. When the four-engine Superfortress proved itself worthy of mass production in 1943, Arnold and his advisers were more convinced than ever. But although the B-29 was a great

East meets West on an Indian airstrip. Runways for modern aircraft were laboriously hacked out with primitive methods.

advance over the B-17 and the B-24, it still had an effective combat radius of only 1,600 miles, and in 1943 the United States held no bases that close to Japan. China was the only area from which attacks against the heart of Japan might be mounted, and the logistical problems of flying from there were immense.

There was still another route whereby the B-29s might attack Japan. This was from islands in the central Pacific, most notably the Marianas, some 1,500 miles southeast of the main Japanese island of Honshu. But in 1943 the Marianas were still in Japanese hands and so were the Gilberts and Marshalls to the east, both of which would have to be taken before the Marianas could be assaulted. Admiral Nimitz, commander of all American military forces in the area, had plans for moving through the central Pacific toward the China coast and Japan itself, but such a campaign would take time. And the AAF wanted to send the B-29s into battle early in 1944 with the hope of finishing off Japan by strategic bombardment.

In spite of the great difficulties of using the B-29s from India and China, the President approved an AAF project, called Matterhorn, for using B-29s to bomb Japanese steel plants. The bombers would be based in India and would be staged through Chengtu, in central China. Preparations for supporting the XX Bomber Command—the parent organization for the B-29s—began in late 1943, but the planes did not begin to arrive in India until April 1944. By then the AAF had come to realize more fully the immense problems involved in building huge air bases in India and China and in transporting the necessary supplies to China. As it turned out, the B-29s had to fly most of their own fuel and supplies to the advanced bases in China. They probably flew more transport than bomber missions. It was appropriate that during this period the command should be headed by Brig. Gen. Kenneth B. Wolfe, an outstanding logistical officer who had supervised the production of the B-29.

Although it appeared in the spring of 1944 that US forces would take the Marianas during the summer, the AAF determined to go ahead with B-29 operations from China. By this time, Arnold and his staff regarded Matterhorn as an interim phase in the use of the B-29, since they had already determined that the Marianas should be the chief base once they were taken. Accordingly, the Superfortress campaign from India and China did not last long enough to get the maximum benefits from the elaborate preparations made for XX Bomber Command. And it is doubtful that the effort could have been much greater without an inordinate increase in the logistical support of the big bombers.

During the course of its operations in the CBI—from the

An India-based B-29 of XX Bomber Command dumps its load on Rangoon, Burma. First B-29 operations of the war were in CBI, accumulating much valuable operational experience.

first attack, against Bangkok on May 27, 1944, to the last, against Singapore on March 30, 1945—XX Bomber Command averaged only two sorties per plane per month. The four groups in the command flew most of their missions against targets other than Japan and, indeed, dropped only 800 tons of bombs on Japan itself. The B-29s made their first attack against Japan on June 15, 1944, when they bombed the steel mills at Yawata. Under a series of commanders including Maj. Gen. Curtis E. LeMay, the command gained a great deal of experience and knowledge that it passed on to other B-29 units preparing for combat. From the CBI it would move to the Marianas in 1945 and participate in the final assault against Japan.

The invasion of the Marianas in June 1944 climaxed a campaign begun in November 1943, when the Army, Navy, and Marines had joined forces to take three of the Gilbert

In Marianas, Seventh AF mechanics watch P-47s return from a mission.

LeMay and Arnold inspect Guam base.

Night firebomb attacks on Japanese cities proved a potent weapon. This is Osaka, gutted after only four such missions.

Japanese landmark, Mt. Fujiyama, from nose of a B-29 on first raid over Japan since Doolittle's mission. Weather was bad, results poor.

Islands. By 1944 the US Navy had built up a force of more than fifty aircraft carriers while Japan had been building about half a dozen. The overwhelming power of the US Navy prevented the Japanese from counterattacking when Marine and Army troops seized strategic Kwajalein and Eniwetok in the Marshalls in February 1944. Navy carriers provided the air support for these operations. The Seventh Air Force, under Maj. Gen. Willis H. Hale, played a creditable part in softening up the islands for the invaders.

The invasion of the Marianas was a huge enterprise carried out by a task force bigger than the whole Japanese Navy. In preparation, heavy bombers of the Seventh and Thirteenth Air Forces flew great distances in a difficult and sustained bombing campaign to neutralize the great Japanese bastion of Truk in the Carolines. From Truk the Japanese could have menaced the flank of the invasion fleet. A few days after the landings began, the powerful force of American carrier planes annihilated the air strength of a Japanese fleet that attempted to attack the invasion fleet.

After several weeks of hard fighting, Saipan fell in July and Guam and Tinian in August. Navy, Marine, and Seventh Air Force planes provided the air support. The AAF greeted the victories enthusiastically, for the islands provided the springboard for the strategic bombardment of Japan.

But the B-29s still needed bases to fly from. The Twentieth Air Force, commanded by Arnold himself, had taken over control of all B-29s and operated as a global air force with the approval of the Joint Chiefs of Staff. XXI Bomber Command was to control three very heavy bomber wings in the Marianas, and Arnold wanted bases for these wings. Later, more bases were needed for additional wings. Construction lagged behind schedule and delayed the planned buildup of air units. Much of the credit for pushing the construction through must go to Lt. Gen. Millard F. Harmon, commanding general of the AAF in the Pacific Ocean Areas. Eventually there were five great airfields, each of them occupied by a whole B-29 wing: two on Guam, one on Saipan, and two on Tinian. At each field there would be as many as 180 B-29s and 12,000 men.

The B-29s started arriving on October 12, when the commander of XXI Bomber Command, Brig. Gen. Hay-

wood S. Hansell, Jr., brought *Joltin' Josie, The Pacific Pioneer*, into Saipan. On their first mission on October 28, the B-29s flew to Truk, but only fourteen of eighteen planes bombed the target, with indifferent success. After a series of training missions against Truk and other islands, the B-29s started the campaign against the Japanese homeland on November 24. Brig. Gen. Emmett O'Donnell, commander of the 73d Wing, led 111 B-29s against industrial targets in Tokyo, but only eighty-eight of the planes were able to bomb. Results were poor, partly because of bad weather to and over the target. This was the first attack on Tokyo since the Doolittle raid in April 1942.

For several months Hansell sent his bombers on daylight precision raids against industrial targets, chiefly aircraft factories, but the results did not meet expectations. The slow buildup of B-29 strength, lack of escort fighters, bad weather, "deplorable" bombing accuracy, a high abortive rate, and losses of planes at sea had all contributed to the poor showing. But Arnold was impatient for results, and in January 1945 he ordered LeMay from India to Guam to succeed Hansell as commander.

Many damaged Superforts were lost on the return flight from Japan because there was no place to land other than the ocean. The air-sea rescue service did an excellent job of rescuing the crews, but even so there were still substantial losses. The answer to the problem was to occupy Iwo Jima, a rocky volcanic island in the Bonins about midway between the B-29 bases and Japan. It was made to order as a base for escort fighters—another deficiency Hansell had faced—and as an intermediate waypoint for B-29s.

B-24s of the Seventh pounded the island continually for nineteen out of twenty days before the Marines landed on February 19, 1945. The bloody battle that followed lasted four weeks instead of the estimated three or four days. The engineers moved in quickly and developed landing strips for the B-29s. By the end of the war about 2,400 Superforts had made emergency landings on Iwo. Probably many of the 25,000 crewmen involved would have been lost but for Iwo Jima. The Chief of Naval Operations, Adm. Ernest J. King, estimated that the lives saved "exceeded the lives lost [4,900] in the capture of the island itself."

By 1945 the planners and analysts at Headquarters AAF had become interested in the possibilities of incendiary

A P-51 takes off from hard-won Iwo Jima. The dearly bought island base proved worth the battle, since from it escort fighters could operate over Japan and crippled bombers could find a refuge on the long flights back to base.

bombing attacks against the large Japanese cities. LeMay, an experimenter by nature, tried a few such missions in February 1945. In March, he made one of the most important decisions of the war—to use the B-29s in low-level night attacks with incendiaries against the terribly vulnerable Japanese cities. By coming in at low altitudes the planes could carry larger bomb loads. The first attack by 334 B-29s on March 9 burned out 15.8 square miles in the heart of Tokyo and took the lives of more than 80,000 people. It destroyed about one-fourth of all the buildings in Tokyo.

The remarkable success of the Tokyo mission established the pattern for the fire-bomb campaign against Japan's urban areas. Four more attacks followed in rapid succession, and by March 20 the Superforts had wiped out thirty-two square miles of buildings in the industrial areas of Tokyo, Nagoya, Osaka, and Kobe. Because the Japanese defenses against night attack were poor, the B-29s suffered

minor losses in these and subsequent attacks. So confident were the Americans that they stripped most of the B-29s of their guns and ammunition and filled them up with more bombs. The P-51 escort fighters were superfluous almost as soon as they began flying from Iwo Jima in the spring.

In the last few weeks of the war, the bombers even dropped leaflets naming Japanese cities to be attacked and warning the civilian population to flee. By the end of the war the Superforts had dropped 145,000 tons of bombs on Japan and had destroyed about 105 square miles in the center of Japan's six most important industrial cities. Dozens of smaller cities were also devastated, and in one of them, Toyama, 99.5 percent of the built-up area was laid waste.

In July, General Spaatz, fresh from victory in Europe, took over control of all B-29 operations in the Pacific. In addition to the Twentieth Air Force in the Marianas, he controlled the Eighth Air Force, which was to operate with B-29s against Japan from the Ryukyus. By June the four

In July 1945 General Spaatz arrived, fresh from victory in ETO, to take charge of B-29 operations. From left, Generals Nathan Twining, Curtis LeMay, Spaatz, Barney Giles.

It was all over but the shouting when General Douglas MacArthur (right) arrived at Atsugi Airdrome, Tokyo, on August 30, 1945, after the Japanese surrender. On hand to greet him were Spaatz (left) and General Kenney of FEAF.

End of World War II and dawn of the nuclear age, all wrapped up in Hiroshima's historic mushroom cloud.

groups from India had joined the Twentieth, and more units had come from the United States. Strength in the Marianas grew to almost a thousand bombers, and as many as 625 B-29s flew to the attack on a single day.

In addition to the assault against the Japanese cities, the Superforts also carried out other missions. Probably the most successful of these "diversions," as the AAF regarded them, was the aerial mining of the waters around Japan, especially the Shimonoseki Strait. The Twentieth Air Force flew 1,528 mining sorties in 1945 and planted more than 12,000 mines. Estimates credited the mines dropped by the B-29s with sinking about 800,000 tons of shipping, even more than the Navy's submarines sank during the 4½-month period. But the submarine had all along been the most potent weapon in destroying Japanese shipping, which had been reduced to 1,500,000 tons afloat in August 1945. The bombing and the blockade were bringing Japanese production to a standstill by August, with many war industries operating at less than twenty-five percent of capacity.

It was obvious to Japanese leaders that Japan could be destroyed by starvation and bombing even without an invasion. But influential groups of Japanese militarists, determined to fight to the bitter end, delayed surrender. The final blow that persuaded the nation to come to terms was the atomic bomb. On August 6, 1945, the B-29 Enola Gay, piloted by Col. Paul W. Tibbets, Jr., dropped the first atomic bomb—destroying 4.7 square miles of the city of Hiroshima and killing more than 70,000 people. A second atomic bomb, dropped on Nagasaki on August 9, convinced the Japanese leaders of the futility of further resistance. On the same day, the Soviet Union invaded Manchuria. The Japanese government decided on August 10 that it must surrender. The formal ceremony came in Tokyo Bay on September 2, when General MacArthur received the Japanese envoys for the surrender aboard the battleship Missouri.

Chapter 7

W O R L D   W A R   I I | 1 9 3 9 - 4 5

The War at Home

THE American people heard the tragic news from Pearl Harbor and the Philippines with shock but also with confidence that they would avenge their losses. Airpower had made the Japanese successes possible—and the United States took the lesson to heart. After blitzkrieg in Europe and catastrophe in the Pacific, the country knew that the airplane was the first line of national defense, whether it flew from an aircraft carrier or from a land base. Airpower's mobility would permit it to strike the first American blows against the German and Japanese homelands and to turn the tides of aggression in the Pacific, North Africa, and Europe.

Air Defense of the United States

But in December 1941 public morale was shaken by the Japanese successes, and many expected bombing attacks on the continental United States. Blackouts became familiar, and false alarms were not uncommon. The memorable "Battle of Los Angeles" on February 25, 1942, had all the sound and fury of a real raid, although no enemy planes appeared. Actually, except for German submarines shelling a few islands in the Caribbean, the eastern United States was not seriously threatened, but Japanese carriers could have launched a mission against the west coast without much risk until the Battle of Midway in June.

On December 7, 1941, the AAF had only forty-five modern fighters, ten heavy bombers, and seventy-five medium bombers defending the Pacific Coast. Effective use of these planes was greatly handicapped by the weak-

Training new pilots for the greatly expanding air arm became one of the most important jobs on the home front.

ness of the warning system, then in its infancy. There were only six radar stations on the west coast; the equipment was crude, the operators unskilled. And the planes themselves lacked equipment, bombs, and ammunition. On the Atlantic Coast, the situation was even worse, for the fighter planes on hand were too few for adequate defense and almost useless at night or in bad weather.

Soon after Pearl Harbor the War Department designated the Eastern and Western Defense Commands as theaters of operations. In the East, interceptors of the First Air Force provided protection from air attack; in the West, the Fourth Air Force patrolled the coastal areas. By 1943 the AAF had seventy-five radar stations in operation, while a million and a half civilian ground observers manned thousands of observation posts. American radar research caught up with the British, who had given valuable help in 1940 and 1941, and American factories were turning out radar equipment by the carload in 1943. And most important of all, the AAF was winning control of the skies over Europe and the Pacific to an extent that made any risk of bombing of the United States increasingly remote.

As a result of decisions by the Joint Chiefs of Staff, the AAF began dismantling its air defense system in September 1943 and substituting a standby system. The First and Fourth Air Forces, which had increasingly been used by the AAF for fighter training, returned to the AAF from their assignments to the defense commands. During the summer of 1944 the AAF inactivated most of the aircraft warning system, and by the end of the war not one radar station was in regular operation. By contrast, in May 1944, Germany had 2,100 antiaircraft batteries, 360 searchlight batteries, and more than 1,200 fighter planes arrayed in defense of the Reich. As General Arnold observed, the best defense in air warfare is a good offense.

THE NUMBERED AIR FORCES AROUND THE WORLD—1945

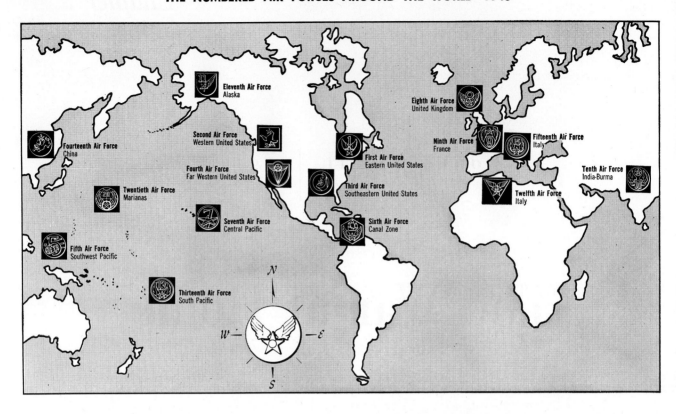

Eleventh Air Force
Alaska

Second Air Force
Western United States

Fourth Air Force
Far Western United States

Fourteenth Air Force
China

Twentieth Air Force
Marianas

Seventh Air Force
Central Pacific

Fifth Air Force
Southwest Pacific

Thirteenth Air Force
South Pacific

First Air Force
Eastern United States

Third Air Force
Southeastern United States

Sixth Air Force
Canal Zone

Eighth Air Force
United Kingdom

Ninth Air Force
France

Fifteenth Air Force
Italy

Twelfth Air Force
Italy

Tenth Air Force
India-Burma

After Midway, any effective air attack on this country was highly improbable. In a last fantastic effort to strike at the continental United States, the Japanese began in November 1944 to send bombs over the United States at high altitude in wind-borne paper balloons. Inherently inaccurate, these balloons did little damage, although the enemy dispatched 9,000 of them.

The AAF Against the U-Boats

The AAF shared in still another and unexpected defensive responsibility—the protection of shipping against German submarines in the Atlantic and Caribbean. The war against submarines was an important part of the war against Germany, for until mid-1943 the U-boats posed the greatest menace to the buildup of forces in the United Kingdom and the Mediterranean area. When war came, the Navy found its preparations to deal with U-boats quite inadequate. During the next five months, while American vessels were being sunk wholesale within sight of the coast, the Navy could not even escort coastal convoys.

Answering the Navy's appeal for help at the very beginning of the war, the AAF began sending planes on antisubmarine patrols off the east coast on December 8, 1941. By mid-January 1942 the I Bomber Command had nine B-17s and a hundred other aircraft engaged in this work. Planes of I Air Support Command and, later, some of the Civil Air Patrol also helped to cover waters near the coast. The Navy directed these operations on a rather indefinite basis until March, when the Eastern Sea Frontier, a Navy command, received full operational control of AAF units operating over the sea for protection of shipping. AAF task forces, at Navy request, also hunted subs in the Gulf of Mexico and the Caribbean, where they came under the control of the Navy's sea frontier commanders in those areas.

Recognizing its special function, the AAF redesignated I Bomber Command on October 15, 1942, as the AAF Antisubmarine Command (AAFAC). By that time the AAF and the Navy had driven the submarines from the Atlantic Coast. After January 1943 the U-boats did not sink a single merchant ship within 600 miles of a US aircraft base, whereas forty-six ships had been sunk in coastal waters in May 1942. From the coastal areas, the German U-boat wolfpacks shifted their operations to the convoy lanes between the United States and Europe, where they enjoyed great success against Allied shipping during the first half of 1943. To fight them, AAFAC increased its strength to twenty-five squadrons, fifteen equipped with B-24s.

Six of these B-24 squadrons, carrying special long-range search equipment, operated during 1943 from bases in Newfoundland, England, and North Africa. There were few places in the Atlantic where submarines could escape observation by the long-range Liberators. Together with the escort carrier and microwave radar, they made it possible to harry the submarines from the seas. When the Navy won permission to take over all antisubmarine B-24s,

The Air Force pioneered the use of the long-range bomber in antisub warfare. Here, an attack on a German U-boat.

AAFAC was relieved of its maritime responsibilities. On August 31, 1943, it rejoined the First Air Force as the I Bomber Command. The pioneer work of the AAF's Liberators bore good fruit, for the long-range bomber ultimately ranked second only to the carrier plane as a submarine killer. During the war, British and American shore-based aircraft sank more German submarines than did the surface vessels of both navies put together.

Production and Logistics

In terms of production, Pearl Harbor was a stimulant rather than a blow to the United States, for it jolted the Arsenal of Democracy into an all-out effort. President Roosevelt reorganized the machinery for industrial mobilization in January 1942 and gave the War Production Board real power to get the job done. The board acted quickly to convert civilian industries to munitions production. One of its first steps was to stop the output of automobiles, thus freeing the giant automotive industry for conversion. By June 1942 the industry was devoting all of its resources to the production of airplanes and other munitions.

The American Federation of Labor and the Congress of Industrial Organizations promised not to strike—and, according to the US Department of Labor, "during the entire war period few if any strikes were authorized by the na-

B-29s in Boeing plant, 1943. Aircraft plants went on a round-the-clock basis in 1942, in 1943 employed 2,100,000.

tional or international unions." Factories ran twenty-four hours a day six or seven days a week. Men spent as much as eighty hours a week on the job without complaint. Women joined the war effort by the millions. At one time they comprised nearly half the civilian employees of the Air Service Command. Meanwhile, the civilian share of the national output was being squeezed down from eighty-five to fifty percent to permit industry to meet the huge munitions programs.

While "decadent democracy," as the Nazis referred to the United States, was driving itself to such efforts, Germany was fighting a one-shift war in its factories, still relying on Hitler's intuitive genius to win the war. Not until 1943 did the Germans begin to make the effort the Americans had made in 1942, and by that time "Rosie the Riveter" and the pallid crews of the graveyard shift had given the United States a decisive lead.

The aircraft production program consistently received priorities at or near the top among American munitions programs, but never the "national first priority" asked by AAF planners immediately after Pearl Harbor. The only really serious shortage of materials was in aluminum,

which persisted until the summer of 1943. At the end of 1943, the labor force in the aircraft industry reached a peak of 2,100,000 men and women. This force was generally ample in numbers, but it consisted largely of recruits working on highly simplified tasks under the direction of the small cadres of experts on whom the aircraft industry had relied before the war. Fortunately, the development of mass production methods and a gradual rise in experience greatly increased the workers' efficiency.

By 1944, labor costs per pound of airframe had shrunk to one-third of what they had been in 1941. The number of man-hours needed to make a B-17 fell from 55,000 to 19,000. The Ford plant at Willow Run, Mich., showed what assembly-line methods could do. After many early difficulties, Ford turned out 5,476 B-24s in 1944-45. At its peak, Willow Run's monthly production of four-engine bombers was greater than the entire annual output of military planes by the prewar aircraft industry. Willow Run's production of 92,000,000 pounds of airframe weight in 1944 almost equaled that of the whole Japanese aircraft industry and was more than fifty percent of the 175,000,000 pounds produced by Germany in that year.

But the established manufacturers of the prewar industry carried the main burden of aircraft production. During the period July 1, 1940, to August 31, 1945, the eleven leading companies delivered 229,554 planes, as follows:

North American	41,188
Consolidated Vultee	30,903
Douglas	30,696
Curtiss	26,154
Lockheed	18,926
Boeing	18,381
Grumman	17,428
Republic	15,603
Bell	13,575
Martin	8,810
Chance Vought	7,890

Douglas, Consolidated, Boeing, and North American produced more than fifty percent of the total airframe weight during 1940-44, with North American ranking fourth, because most of its output was fighters and trainers.

The United States spent $45 billion for aircraft during the war, about a quarter of the cost of the whole munitions program. In return the nation got nearly 300,000 military aircraft for its Army, Navy, and Allies. Up to V-J Day the AAF accepted delivery of 158,880 planes, including 51,221 bombers and 47,050 fighters. Bomber production included 3,760 B-29s, 18,188 B-24s, and 12,677 B-17s. The fighters produced in largest quantities were the P-47 with 15,485, the P-51 with 14,501, and the P-40 with 13,700. Among the transports, the reliable C-47 ranked first with 10,245. Production rose from 2,464 planes in December 1941 to a peak of 9,113 planes in March 1944. During the same period airframe weight shot up from 6,121 tons to 44,454 tons. The much greater percentage increase in airframe weight clearly indicated that the larger planes—bombers and transports—were being produced in greater quantities. The annual rate of production in March 1944 was almost 110,000 planes. By that time the United States was producing a greater weight of airframe than all the rest of the world put together.

Mass production required standardization, and this prevented the constant modification necessary to maintain superiority. Throughout the war, combat aircraft were in a state of constant competitive evolution, for survival often depended on the quick addition of an extra gun or a new gadget. The AAF solved the problem by leaving the factories undisturbed and setting up its own modification centers. Although twenty-eight centers were established,

AAS FACTORY ACCEPTANCES OF AIRCRAFT BY TYPE: JANUARY 1940-AUGUST 1945

Includes Lend-Lease and experimental airplanes and US-financed Canadian production

Year	Very Heavy Bombers	Heavy Bombers	Medium Bombers	Light Bombers	Fighters	Reconnaissance	Transports	Trainers	Communications	Total
1940	—	60	62	891	1,422	65	233	2,320	1	5,054
1941	1	313	460	2,396	3,784	203	398	8,036	270	15,861
1942	3	2,576	3,271	4,055	9,102	223	1,738	16,978	3,146	41,092
1943	92	9,393	5,413	5,175	17,628	284	6,817	19,491	4,307	68,600
1944	1,161	14,887	5,228	3,861	24,174	95	9,276	7,578	3,696	69,956
1945 (Jan-Aug)	2,507	3,771	1,636	1,732	12,149	247	4,236	1,309	2,138	29,725
Total	3,764	31,000	16,070	18,110	68,259	1,117	22,698	55,712	13,558	230,288

AIRPLANES ON HAND IN THE AAF BY MAJOR TYPE: JULY 1939-AUGUST 1945

Year As of June 30	Very Heavy Bombers	Heavy Bombers	Medium Bombers	Light Bombers	Fighters	Reconnaissance	Transports	Trainers	Communications	Total
1940	—	54	478	166	477	414	127	1,243	7	2,966
1941	—	120	611	292	1,018	415	144	4,124	53	6,777
1942	—	846	1,047	696	2,950	468	824	12,610	1,732	21,173
1943	2	4,421	4,242	1,689	8,010	486	4,268	22,849	3,051	49,018
1944	445	11,720	5,427	2,914	15,644	1,056	9,433	27,907	4,211	78,757
1945 As of Aug. 31	2,865	11,065	5,384	3,079	16,799	1,971	9,561	9,558	3,433	63,715

COSTS OF REPRESENTATIVE AIRCRAFT, WORLD WAR II

Airplane	Cost	Airplane	Cost	Airplane	Cost
Very Heavy Bombers		**Fighters**		C-47	85,035
B-29	$509,465	P-38	$ 97,147	C-54	259,816
		P-39	50,666		
Heavy Bombers		P-40	44,892	**Trainers**	
B-17	187,742	P-47	83,001	PT-13, PT-17, PT-27	$ 9,896
B-24	215,516	P-51	50,985	PT-19, PT-23, PT-26	15,052
				BT-13, BT-15	23,068
Medium Bombers		**Reconnaissance**		AT-6	22,952
B-25	116,752	OA-10	207,541	AT-7, AT-11	68,441
B-26	192,427				
		Transports		**Communications**	
Light Bombers		C-43	27,332	L-4	2,701
A-20	100,800	C-45	48,830	L-5	8,323
A-26	175,892	C-46	221,550		

AAF depots, both within the United States and overseas, did much additional modification, especially on bombers.

Early in the war there was undoubtedly too much emphasis on production of complete aircraft, too little on procuring the spare parts and equipment needed to keep them flying. The resultant shortages led to widespread cannibalization—the destruction of some planes to provide parts for others. Occasionally, too, the "numbers racket"—the urge to meet numerical objectives—kept obsolescent planes in production when effort might better have been shifted to new projects. Generally, however, the AAF continued to produce some old models because commanders in the Pacific or North Africa felt that a P-39 or a P-40 in time would save nine future fighters. The astonishing thing is not that there were some failures and some misplaced emphasis but that so few "lemons" got into quantity production. Certainly few gambles have been better justified than the contracts for 1,644 B-29s entered into by the AAF before the first Superfortress was even flight-tested in September 1942.

Aircraft were used up fast. Until late in the war, the life expectancy of a heavy bomber in the Eighth Air Force was about forty-seven missions. The AAF lost 22,948 planes in combat operations, and thousands more in accidents. Planes grew "war weary" rapidly from combat damage and the wear and tear of combat operations. The AAF reached its peak inventory of almost 80,000 planes in July 1944. When the war ended, it had 33,235 first-line combat aircraft.

Any of the AAF's World War II aircraft would seem old-fashioned to a young jet pilot of the 1950s. All were propeller-driven and powered by gasoline-fueled reciprocating engines. Heavy bombers and some transports had four engines, the rest one or two. All the combat planes were covered with an aluminum skin. Fastest was the P-51, which could do almost 500 miles an hour in level flight. Some fighters could go above 40,000 feet, but only the B-29 bomber could stay that high for long, because it alone had a pressurized cabin.

Development of jet aircraft in the United States got under way in 1941, somewhat later than in Germany and England. With British assistance the AAF made such rapid progress that in October 1942 Col. Laurence C. Craigie successfully flew the first American jet—the Bell XP-59A. A prototype of the P-80 jet fighter, rushed to completion in 145 days by Lockheed, flew on January 8, 1944. But various "bugs," including an inordinate fuel consumption, kept the P-80 from being distributed to tactical units until December 1945. Some were tested overseas during the war, but none saw combat. Both the Germans and the British started flying jet aircraft in combat during 1944.

The problems of AAF supply were prodigious. The Air Service Command—"the stockroom and garage" of the AAF— had to stock some 500,000 different items and send them overseas. The changing character and tempo of the war frustrated attempts to plan the flow of goods on the basis of previous consumption. Stocks ample for a quiet winter could be used up in a week of all-out offensive. Changes in tactics, like General LeMay's shift to incendiary bombing of Japanese cities, resulted in sudden, huge demands for items little used before. The Air Transport Command flew more than 45,000 tons of AAF materiel overseas after January 1943 to meet emergency needs.

The Air Service Command gradually gave up logistical forecasting and based shipments of maintenance or technical supplies mainly on the requisitions of the overseas commands. It met requirements so effectively that lack of parts grounded less than one percent of the planes of the Eighth Air Force in England during the second half of 1944. Only 0.3 percent of the B-29s of XXI Bomber Command in the Marianas were grounded for lack of parts in June 1945.

The AAF laid heavy emphasis on proper aircraft maintenance, since it often meant the difference between life and death for an aircrew. Huge depots and mobile units in overseas theaters became highly efficient at keeping the planes flying. It took about five planes in the theater to keep three planes in combat. During the last year of the war, the AAF maintained about 24,000 planes overseas—almost twice the prescribed unit-equipment strength of the combat groups.

The Service Expands

Phenomenal as AAF growth had been before Pearl Harbor, the expansion afterward was far greater. Roughly speaking, the Army's air arm quadrupled during the next three years. On January 14, 1942, President Roosevelt approved schedules calling for production of 45,000 combat aircraft (including transports) in 1942 and 100,000 in 1943. Linked to this action was a new program to expand the AAF to 115 groups within the year.

In August and September 1942, at the President's request, the Air Staff calculated the number of planes that this country would have to produce in 1943 in order to gain "complete air supremacy over the enemy." It recommended that the United States produce 131,000 military aircraft in 1943 and that the AAF expand by the end of that year to 2,734,000 men and 281 tactical groups. But this estimate had to be scaled down to meet the needs of the ground forces and the Navy. On the advice of the War Production Board, the Joint Chiefs of Staff reduced objectives for 1943 to 107,000 military aircraft, of which 85,000 were actually produced. General Arnold accepted a goal of 273 AAF groups as "the saturation point for American airpower."

The AAF almost achieved this goal on paper, for at one time it did officially have 269¼ groups. But the maximum operational strength, attained in March 1945, was 243 tactical groups, of which 224 were then overseas. Of the groups overseas at that time, the European area had 149, the Pacific area fifty-two, the CBI twenty-one, and Alaska two. Group strength by types was as follows:

Very heavy bombardment 25
Heavy bombardment 72
Medium bombardment 20

First US-built jet, Bell's XP-59, powered by two GE J-31 engines. Never operational, it was a valuable guinea pig.

Cadets and instructors head for their training aircraft at Randolph Field, Tex., to log a chunk of flying time.

Light bombardment	8
Fighter	71
Reconnaissance	13
Troop carrier	29
Composite	5
TOTAL	243

In March 1944, at the climax of the training program, the AAF reached a personnel peak of 2,411,294–306,889 officers and 2,104,405 enlisted men—about thirty-one percent of the entire strength of the US Army. Of these, eighty-two percent of the officers and seventy-seven percent of the enlisted men belonged to the Air Corps. The rest were members of the Signal Corps, the Engineers, the Quartermaster Corps, and other arms and services with the AAF.

The rise of the engineers was particularly remarkable.

At the beginning of the war, there were few specialized aviation engineers. One regiment had been provided for such work in the spring of 1941. In 1944 the AAF had more than 100,000 engineers. Rarely needed in the days of peace, they had come into their own in the Pacific, in North Africa, and in western Europe, when victory often depended on how fast airfields could be built.

Air and Ground Training

Before Pearl Harbor, no aspiring youth could hope to become an aviation cadet until he was more than twenty years of age and had completed two years of college or had passed a special examination. Applicants who met these requirements had to be approved by cadet examining boards and by the Office of Chief of Air Corps. Quotas grew after 1939, but admissions were still limited. A few days after the nation entered the war the AAF wiped out all quotas, empowered the examination boards to give final approval to candidates, and substituted a qualification test for the college education previously required. Shortly thereafter the age limit was dropped from twenty to eighteen.

These measures gave the AAF all the cadets it could use. A flood of applications showed the impact of the air age on the imagination of the American people. Thousands of young men chose to "live in fame or go down in flame" as AAF pilots rather than accept deferment or take their chances in the draft. But since there was no assured reservoir to draw on, this flood could be followed by a drought. To stabilize the flow of applicants into training, the AAF created an Air Corps Enlisted Reserve on April 1, 1942. This was a pool of approved applicants whose cadet training was deferred. They received the option of continuing their studies, remaining in civilian employment, or enlisting for active duty, pending future admission to cadet training.

During 1942 the shortage of draftable manpower became so acute that in November the government lowered the draft age from twenty to eighteen and in December it terminated voluntary enlistment. Men enrolled for the draft could no longer enlist in the arm or service they preferred before being called up. These measures forced the AAF to get its flyers via the selective service system or by recruitment within the Army, instead of picking the cream of the crop before it could be drafted. While theoretically fair, this worked a hardship on the AAF, because its quotas did not contain enough first-rate men to meet the need for pilots.

By the spring of 1943 the supply of potential pilots in the Air Corps Enlisted Reserve was running out. Opening aviation cadet training to all draftees who wanted to fly and met the qualifications provided the eventual remedy. In October 1943, aviation cadet examining boards began giving both qualifying and physical examinations at the reception centers. From then on, there was no lack of prospective flyers. Indeed, in the later stages of the war the number of cadets once again had to be limited.

Before the war, the handful of bombardiers and navigators had been drawn mainly from cadets eliminated from pilot training. War and the advent of the heavy bomber created a great demand for bombardiers and navigators. The AAF met these requirements by giving newly appointed cadets a series of aptitude tests, the so-called "classification battery." Then, on the basis of service quotas, aptitudes, and, to some extent, individual preference, the men would be assigned to training as pilots, bombardiers, or navigators, or would be eliminated from the program.

The tempo of pilot training under the Flying Training

AAF trained 700,000 men in aircraft maintenance during the war. Motto above puts burden on these young mechanics.

Command accelerated under the pressures of war. Primary, basic, and advanced training, which together had formerly taken a year, were cut to nine weeks each, plus nine weeks added for preflight training. Even so, American pilots still got 360 hours in the air during training, three times as much as their German opponents. Between July 1939 and August 1945, 193,444 pilots were graduated from flying school, and 124,000 trainees washed out, mostly during primary training.

Washouts got a second chance, as bombardiers or, less often, as navigators, if their aptitude ratings showed sufficient promise. Training programs for bombardiers and navigators ran twenty-four weeks or less, and the washout rate generally ran around fifteen percent. In all, more than 45,000 bombardiers and 50,000 navigators were graduated during the war. Training programs were also provided for certain specialists like radar operators and the flight engineers of the B-29s, and flexible gunnery courses were given to the enlisted members of the bomber crews.

Proud young pilots who had won their wings still faced transition training in the planes they would use in combat. Finally, they had to learn to work together in organized units. New units were usually built around cadres drawn from parent groups, but when most experienced outfits were being rushed overseas, it was neither convenient nor safe to draw cadres from them. Accordingly, early in 1942 the AAF set up specialized parent groups called operational training units (OTUs) to provide cadres and supervise the training of newly created units. Later, when the AAF needed individual replacements rather than new organizations, it set up replacement training units (RTUs) from which individual pilots or crews could be drawn to fill the ranks of the fighting squadrons.

The First and Fourth Air Forces handled most of this operational training for fighters, the Second Air Force for bombers, and I Troop Carrier Command for transport crews, with special emphasis on preparation for airborne operations. Advanced training for the OTU cadres was given by the AAF School of Applied Tactics at Orlando, Fla.

The Technical Training Command schooled nonflying officers and enlisted men. Its huge task was more important than people generally realized, for the AAF needed seven "guys on the ground" for every man in the air, and four of them had to be specialists. Practically all enlisted men began their service careers with four weeks (later eight weeks) at a basic training center where they received physical conditioning and rudimentary military training. Then, those who already possessed usable skills and those classified as fit only for routine duties were assigned to operating units. The rest went to technical schools to become mechanics, radio operators, or any other of the multitude of specialists required by the AAF. By far the biggest of these programs was the 112-day basic mechanics course. No fewer than 700,000 men were graduated from courses in aircraft maintenance during the war.

Schools for ground officers, nonexistent in the prewar Air Corps, were established and expanded to provide men for new tasks and free flyers from extra responsibilities. Training of weather officers, begun in 1940, expanded enormously before the market for meteorologists became glutted in 1944. As planes grew increasingly complex and pilots and ground crews less experienced, pilots could no longer adequately supervise maintenance. To solve this problem, the AAF began to offer courses for aircraft engineering officers in 1941. The need for "chairborne" administrators prompted the creation of the Officer Candidate School at Miami Beach, Fla., in February 1942. An Officer Training School, also in Miami, provided a mild form of basic training for civilians who had been given direct commissions.

Organization

The status of the Army Air Forces for the remainder of the war was settled by the War Department reorganization of March 9, 1942. This thoroughgoing change created autonomous and coequal commands within the War Department: Army Air Forces, Army Ground Forces (AGF), and Services of Supply, redesignated Army Service Forces (ASF) in 1943. The Operations Division of the War Department General Staff became the command post for

General Arnold and Maj. Gen. Barton K. Yount (center), in command of the Flying Training Command, together with some training leaders at Columbus, Miss., in 1942. At left, Brig. Gen. Howard Davidson of Technical Training Command. Second from right, Brig. Gen. Thomas J. Hanley of Air Staff; right, Maj. Gen. Ralph Royce, of Maxwell Field.

General Marshall, planning the strategy and supervising its execution. The three major commands exercised responsibility for administration, supply, organization, and training within the United States.

The Army Air Forces of March 1942 was a great advance over the organization that had been in existence since June 1941. The Office of Chief of Air Corps and the Air Force Combat Command were dissolved, and all elements of the air arm were merged into the AAF under a single commanding general and a single air staff. Because it had been established by law, the Air Corps remained in existence as the chief component of the AAF, and officers continued to be commissioned in the Air Corps.

Secretary of War Henry L. Stimson looked on the March reorganization as a formal recognition of quasi-autonomy for the air arm. The official statement of the AAF's mission—"to procure and maintain equipment peculiar to the Army Air Forces, and to provide air force units" for assignment to combat—hardly suggested the full scope of the AAF's activities. During the course of the war, Arnold and his staff consciously worked to prepare the air arm for eventual independence by making it as self-contained as possible. To the already considerable logistical activities of the AAF, they added still others taken over from the Army Service Forces in the face of strong opposition from ASF's ambitious and energetic commander, Lt. Gen. Brehon B. Somervell.

One of the greatest steps up the ladder came with Arnold's inclusion as a member of the US Joint Chiefs of Staff and the Anglo-American Combined Chiefs of Staff. This was a tacit recognition that airpower had arrived as an equal of land and sea power. The existence of the Royal Air Force as an independent service contributed substantially to the decision to include the AAF in the top councils of the war. As a member of these bodies, General

Arnold did much to forward the interest of his command.

The AAF derived further influence from Arnold's position as Marshall's trusted adviser in all air matters. What the AAF commander recommended, Marshall usually ordered. Overseas, air commanders were made—and unmade—at Arnold's suggestion. Moreover, he exercised a strong personal influence on those commanders. Most of them had known him for years and regarded him as their boss, whatever the regulations might say. Although not

Lt. Gen. William S. Knudsen, head of ATSC, with J. E. Schaefer of Boeing and Brig. Gen. K. B. Wolfe, AAF.

fully authorized to do so, he exerted his influence through a flow of very personal letters filled with criticisms and suggestions. Spaatz, Kenney, Eaker, Stratemeyer, Harmon, and others heard from him often. In terms of prestige, Arnold towered over the commanders of the Army Ground Forces and the Army Service Forces and was almost a peer of the US Navy's Chief of Naval Operations.

Within the United States, the initial impulse was to create a new command every time a new problem arose. As this wore off, it was followed by a trend toward consolidation. The Flying Training Command and the Technical Training Command merged on July 7, 1943, to form the AAF Training Command under Maj. Gen. Barton K. Yount. The logistical function, splintered at the beginning of the war, was integrated again on August 31, 1944, when the Air Service Command and the Materiel Command were combined as the Air Technical Service Command (ATSC). Lt. Gen. William S. Knudsen, the production expert from General Motors Corporation who had directed the nation's industrial mobilization during 1940-41, headed ATSC until almost the end of the war. Organizations concerned with evaluation of tactics and equipment—including the AAF Tactical Center, the Proving Ground Command, and the AAF Board—were grouped under the AAF Center on June 1, 1945. And a new headquarters—Continental Air Forces—took control on May 8, 1945, of the First, Second, Third, and Fourth Air Forces and the I Troop Carrier Command in the United States. Still in operation at the end of the war was the Air Transport Command, headed from its beginning by Lt. Gen. Harold L. George.

Findings

The AAF made conscientious efforts to learn the lessons of the war even before it was over. In 1944, carefully chosen evaluation boards went to each of the major theaters of operations to study the air war and its meaning for the future. By far the most thorough analysis was made by the US Strategic Bombing Survey, which published hundreds of reports on almost every aspect of the strategic air war against Germany and Japan, after intense research and on-the-spot investigation in the theaters. From these and other sources the AAF derived strong confirmation of its belief in the dominion of the air in warfare of the future.

To Arnold it seemed that the most important lesson of the war for the AAF was that "the first essential of the airpower necessary for our national security is pre-eminence in research." As British radar had defeated the German bombers, as the P-38 had mastered the Zero, as the atomic bomb had broken the will of Japan, so victories in research and development would decide future conflicts.

For the nation, perhaps the greatest lesson of the war was that henceforth, as never before, the price of its liberty would be eternal vigilance. "Future attack on the United States," wrote Arnold, "may well be without warning." Besides vigilance the nation would need air superiority, both for offense and for defense. Surface forces would still play an important part, but the whole course of World War II had demonstrated that air superiority was a prerequisite to any successful ground or naval action.

Arnold Engineering Development Center, Tullahoma, Tenn., is today's testimonial to "Hap" Arnold's belief in research.

Chapter 8

THE ESTABLISHMENT

September 18, 1947

O N September 18, 1947, Chief Justice Fred M. Vinson administered the oath of office to the first Secretary of the Air Force, W. Stuart Symington. Gen. Carl Spaatz was sworn in as the first Chief of Staff, United States Air Force, on September 26.

Thus ended an association with the US Army that had endured for forty years. And thus began a new era in which airpower became firmly established as the nation's first line of defense and its chief hope for deterring war.

Progress Toward Autonomy

Almost from the beginning of military aviation in the United States, the idea of a separate air force caught the imagination of some members of the military, the Congress, and the public. Two ideas kept recurring in Congress and within the War Department. Should aeronautics be a separate department like War and Navy? Or should air be coordinate with ground and sea forces under a department of national defense?

As early as March 1916, Congressman Charles Lieb of Indiana introduced the first of a long series of bills for a separate department of aviation. Through the years that followed, other bills—well over fifty—were submitted, calling for autonomy for military aviation as a separate department or as a coequal under a national defense establishment. Congressional committees and presidential commissions made exhaustive studies to determine where the air arm should be on the military ladder. The recommendations of these groups, as the years passed, reflected the slow but certain recognition of the potentialities of airpower.

When the United States entered World War I in April 1917, its Army aviation was less than ten years old and insignificant in size. The problems that arose from the vast expansion of the tiny Aviation Section of the Signal Corps eventually persuaded President Wilson in May 1918 to raise aviation to the level of a branch of the Army, as the Air Service. American air units under Pershing in France had been organized into the Air Service, American Expeditionary Forces, since the summer of 1917. The Army

Reorganization Act of June 4, 1920, confirmed the legal status of the Air Service as a combatant arm of the Army and also gave to it the functions of a supply branch.

During the Mitchell era after the war, supporters of airpower clashed with opponents over the mission of the air arm and its proper place in the armed forces. The voices of Mitchell, Foulois, Patrick, and others were heard but not heeded. The Air Corps Act of July 1926 was little more than a token gesture toward greater responsibility. The new name—Air Corps—pointed up the potential striking power of the air arm rather than its auxiliary services to other branches of the Army, but there was little change in substance behind the name.

By the early 1930s, aeronautics was making remarkable progress. The Air Corps was poised on the brink of long-range flight, with all that this would mean for strategic air warfare. Greatly encouraged by this progress, airmen reconciled themselves to the proposition that autonomy could await the technological development. So they settled for the creation of the General Headquarters Air Force (GHQAF) on March 1, 1935. The GHQAF operated directly under the Chief of Staff as the air combat arm, while the Air Corps retained administrative and logistical responsibilities.

After the war began in Europe in 1939, General Marshall saw the need for a "simpler system" of organization for the divided air arm. In November 1940, he made General Arnold his Acting Deputy Chief of Staff (for Air). From this position, Arnold directed both the Air Corps and the GHQAF until a more satisfactory control was found. This came on June 20, 1941, less than six months before Pearl Harbor, when the War Department created the Army Air Forces to give a degree of autonomy to the air arm and to provide unity of command over the Air Corps and the Air Force Combat Command (the former GHQAF).

After Pearl Harbor, sentiment for an independent air force flared up strongly for a while, but Arnold and his advisers wisely settled for less. They knew that such a changeover in wartime could be extremely difficult and hazardous. Accordingly, the air leaders went along will-

Stuart Symington, left, takes oath of office as first Air Force Secretary, September 18, 1947. Others are Army Secretary Kenneth Royall, Defense Secretary James Forrestal, Chief Justice Fred Vinson, and Navy Secretary John Sullivan.

ingly with the March 1942 reorganization of the War Department, which gave the air arm a degree of autonomy short only of independence. The Army Air Forces was made coequal with the Army Ground Forces and the Army Service Forces, but it actually carried more weight than the other two from the beginning.

Further recognition of the status of the air arm came in July 1943 when the War Department stated its official position in Field Manual 100-20, *Command and Employment of Air Power:* "Land power and air power are co-equal and interdependent; neither is an auxiliary to the other."

To the end of the war the autonomous position of the Army Air Forces was not challenged. But it was not lasting, because the arrangement had been made by executive order of the President under the provisions of the First War Powers Act of 1941. The Army Air Forces would revert to its prewar position six months after the termination of hostilities unless legislation legalized its status.

The Question of Unity of Command

During the war, congressmen continued to introduce bills calling for an independent air force and a national military establishment, but these received little consideration while the war was in progress. The War Department reorganization of March 1942 was generally considered a satisfactory accommodation for the duration of the war. But the Army and Navy were alive to possibilities of a complete overhauling of the national defense structure after the war, and both services gave the subject most serious consideration.

The Special Planning Division of the War Department General Staff pointed out the need for a single department of national defense in a study prepared in October 1943. In March 1944 the War Department presented a plan in broad outline to the House of Representatives Select Committee on Post-War Military Policy (Woodrum Committee). Brig. Gen. Haywood S. Hansell, Jr., the key AAF witness before this committee, praised unity of command in the

theaters and recommended the establishment of a single, unified defense organization. Assistant Secretary of War for Air Robert A. Lovett also spoke for one over-all command, and Secretary of War Stimson and the other Army witnesses agreed.

But the Navy witnesses, in general, opposed unity of command. As Under Secretary of the Navy James V. Forrestal cautiously put it, he was "not prepared to say that the Navy believes that the consolidation into one department is desirable."

The Joint Chiefs of Staff appointed a committee of outstanding Army and Navy officers in May 1944 to examine thoroughly the practicability of three basic systems of defense organization: (1) two departments—War and Navy; (2) three departments—War, Navy, and Air; (3) one department—Defense.

After ten months of study and travel in every theater of war, interviews with fifty-six key military and naval leaders, and 100 separate meetings in Washington, D. C., the JCS Special Committee, in March 1945, recommended a plan for one Department of Armed Forces consisting of three coordinate branches. It advised prompt action to prevent reversion of the air arm to its prewar status and the loss of the gains in efficiency and cooperation made since 1942. The JCS plan included a military commander of the armed forces who would also be chief of staff to the President.

The Department of the Navy sponsored a study committee of its own in the summer of 1945 under the chairmanship of Ferdinand Eberstadt, a prominent New York investment banker with experience in government and military organizations. The Eberstadt Report, although it counseled against a single department of national defense, emphasized the cooperation between Army and Navy in World War II and recommended the organization of the nation's military forces into three coordinate departments: War, Navy, and Air. This would have transformed the Army Air Forces into the Military Department for Air, but the Navy would have retained its air fleet. The Joint Chiefs of Staff would be the major link between the three departments, and a National Security Council, immediately under the President, would coordinate the armed forces with the civilian agencies. The Navy adopted most of this report as its program for national security, except that Forrestal, who had succeeded Frank Knox as Secretary of the Navy in April 1944, did not accept the idea of a separate department of air.

In October 1945, Lt. Gen. J. Lawton Collins, representing the War Department, submitted to the Senate Committee on Military Affairs a plan for a single Department of Armed Forces including Army, Navy, and Air Force. Each would have considerable autonomy but all would be under a chief of staff of the armed forces. There would also be a chief of staff to the President.

Meanwhile, in January 1945, Senator Lister Hill introduced a bill providing for a single Department of Armed Forces. In October 1945, Senator Edwin C. Johnson offered a bill for a single Department of Military Security containing six divisions, each with its own Under Secretary: Scientific Research and Development, Army, Navy, Air, Procurement, and Military Intelligence. During 1945 there were two other bills for a single department and four bills for a separate department of air, but these did not obtain hearings.

Hearings on the Hill and Johnson unification bills brought endorsements for a single department not only from Arnold, Spaatz, and other air leaders but from Secretary of War Robert P. Patterson, General Marshall, Gen. Omar N. Bradley, and other representatives of the War Department. But Forrestal, Adm. William D. Leahy, personal chief of staff to the President, and Admirals King, Halsey, and Nimitz opposed a single department. The Senate Committee on Military Affairs failed to submit a report on the bills when it concluded hearings in December 1945.

At this point, President Truman stepped into the picture. On December 19 he asked Congress for legislation to combine the War and Navy Departments into "one single department of national defense" along the lines proposed by the JCS and General Collins. Truman wanted parity for airpower and, like Arnold, he called for prompt action to prevent a reversion to the prewar status of the air arm. The President told Congress:

"Air power has been developed to a point where its responsibilities are equal to those of land and sea power, and its contribution to our strategic planning is as great. Parity for air power can be achieved in one department or in three, but not in two. As between one department and three, the former is infinitely to be preferred."

In calling for quick action to place the air arm on an equal basis with land and sea forces, Truman took the War Department and JCS views and blended in some Navy recommendations from the Eberstadt Report. His plan would set up a Department of National Defense with War, Navy, and Air as the three coordinate branches. The Navy would retain its carrier and water-based aviation and its Marine Corps. Besides the civilian Secretary of National Defense there would be a military Chief of Staff of National Defense, an office of short tenure to rotate among the three branches. Truman advised that unification must be regarded as a long-term process for which legislation should provide only the objective and the initial means.

In response to the President's message, a subcommittee of the Senate Committee on Military Affairs, under Senator Elbert D. Thomas, began working on a unification bill with the representatives of the Army and Navy—Maj. Gen. Lauris Norstad and Vice Adm. Arthur W. Radford. Numerous conferences with top leaders of the services followed, and nine separate drafts were prepared. The last draft was introduced as a bill in April 1946 and accepted by the full committee in May.

This bill (S. 2044) became known as the proposed Common Defense Act of 1946, because it provided for a Department of Common Defense comprising three coordinate arms. There would be a civilian Secretary of Common Defense, a Secretary and a commander for each of the arms, a Chief of Staff of Common Defense to rank above all other officers of the armed forces, a Council of Common Defense, a National Security Resources Board, and a Central Intelligence Agency. This bill offered no assurance that the Army and Navy could retain their special air units.

The fate of S. 2044 was not long in doubt. Even before the Senate Committee on Military Affairs accepted the bill, the Senate Committee on Naval Affairs held hearings that revealed the Navy's strong opposition to it. Except for Senator Thomas and Senator Warren R. Austin, who explained its provisions, every witness called before the naval committee opposed this bill, described by Forrestal as "an administrative monstrosity." Aside from Eberstadt and Charles E. Wilson, President of General Electric Company, all of the opposing witnesses were administrative officials of the Department of the Navy or naval officers.

Basically, the Navy witnesses objected to giving to a single individual, the Secretary of Common Defense, the only full statutory access to the President. They also disliked the proposal for a single Chief of Staff of Common Defense. And finally, underlying their reluctance to accept a Department of Air Force was the fear of losing the Navy's land-based air strength.

One of the witnesses, Adm. Richmond K. Turner, gave the most candid explanation of the Navy's opposition to unification. Admiral Turner told the committee:

"Frankly, I believe that the Navy as a whole objects to so-called unification because under any system the Navy will be in a numerical minority and the Army and Air Force, a military majority and scattered throughout the country, will always be in a better political position than the Navy. In spite of any possible degree of good will on the part of the Army and Air Force, I think the superior political position of those services will be used to the disadvantage of the Navy unless the Navy has at all times free and direct access to the President and Congress.

"Because the Navy has had and should retain in the future its position as the first line of military security for the United States, I believe the Navy will never willingly agree to a consolidation of national military forces in any manner that will silence the Navy's voice in military affairs or materially restrict its present responsibilities."

The Army and the Navy Get Together

On May 13, 1946, at the White House, President Truman asked Secretaries Patterson and Forrestal to get together and identify their points of agreement and disagreement. The Secretaries submitted their report to the President at the end of May, listing eight points of general agreement, including the elimination of the proposed single chief of staff. But they disagreed on three major points: the creation of a single department of national defense, the over-all status of military aviation, and the position of the Marine Corps. The Navy still preferred three military departments to one, if it had to choose.

The President hoped that unification legislation would be enacted speedily. He called the Army and Navy leaders into conference again in early June, but when he saw that the differences were deep rooted, he presented his own program for unification. Though leaning toward the position of the War Department, Truman's decisions were in the nature of a compromise. He insisted upon a single Department of National Defense, but with each of the three coordinate branches retaining its integrity and autonomy. He eliminated the Chief of Staff of Common Defense. He stated that naval aviation should be given every "opportunity to develop its maximum usefulness," yet land-based planes for naval reconnaissance, antisubmarine warfare, and protection of shipping should be manned by Air Force personnel. The Navy should keep the Marine Corps.

The Senate Committee on Military Affairs revised the Senate bill in late June, but the Navy adherents still opposed the unification bill, which died by default. In particular, the Marines and the naval aviators disliked the bill. Again President Truman proved his belief in unification, proposing in September that a new bill be drawn up that could win the approval of the next Congress.

When the Eightieth Congress met in January 1947, Army and Navy leaders were ready with a new measure acceptable to both departments. In November 1946, Secretary Forrestal had taken a leading part in reexamining the problem of unification. The services agreed at that time to have General Norstad and Vice Adm. Forrest P. Sherman work out an agreement to be offered as a basis for the legislation.

The two officers soon decided that the question of unified commands in overseas theaters was the most urgent question. They recommended to the Joint Chiefs of Staff a comprehensive system of unified military commands overseas, each with a single commander responsible for the conduct of operations by the land, naval, and air forces in that area. The JCS endorsed the proposal to the President in December. He promptly ordered the establishment of five such commands: the Far East Command, the Pacific Command, the Alaskan Command, the Northeast Command, and the European Command. Plans were also made to set up the Caribbean and the Atlantic Commands.

Norstad and Sherman reached agreement on functions and general organization of the military departments in a draft bill that received the hearty approval of President Truman. Further concessions to the Navy were evident in the completed draft of the bill, entitled National Security Act of 1947, that went to Congress at the end of February 1947. The Senate bill (S. 758) provided for a Secretary of National Defense and stipulated that the Department of the Navy would continue to include aviation units and the Marine Corps.

The situation in the new Congress was more favorable for passage of the legislation than it had been in the previous one. An administrative reorganization of both houses had merged the committees on naval affairs and military affairs into single committees on armed services. This eliminated the special forums each of the services had enjoyed and helped the committee members to take a broader view of national defense problems.

From March 18 to May 9 the Senate Committee on Armed Services conducted extensive hearings on S. 758. The House Committee on Expenditures in the Executive Departments held hearings from April 2 to July 1. The majority of the many witnesses favored the bill and called for its adoption. But it was no secret that there still remained much opposition to unification among Navy and Marine officers, particularly in the lower echelons.

Criticism of the unification bill centered around the status and powers of the proposed Secretary of National Defense. Navy witnesses and some congressmen voiced fears of a "super-secretary" who might wield dictatorial powers over the departments of Army, Navy, and Air Force. Demands were made for adequate safeguards to guarantee that each individual service would remain autonomous in matters of internal administration. As finally passed by Congress, the act differed considerably from the original Senate and House bills, for a number of changes had been incorporated.

The National Security Act of 1947

The National Security Act of 1947 became law on July 26, 1947. The lawmakers stated their intentions at the begin-

James V. Forrestal became first Secretary of Defense.

ning of the act in a Declaration of Policy: to provide a comprehensive program for the future security of the United States; to provide three military departments—the Army, the Navy (including naval aviation and the Marine Corps), and the Air Force; to provide for their coordination and unified direction under civilian control but not to merge them; and to provide for the effective strategic direction and operation of the armed forces under unified control.

To coordinate national security matters, Title I of the act established the National Security Council (NSC), the Central Intelligence Agency under the NSC, and the National Security Resources Board.

Title II created the National Military Establishment as an executive department, headed by a civilian Secretary of Defense appointed by the President. Within the National Military Establishment, the three coordinate departments were then established: Department of the Army, Department of the Navy, and Department of the Air Force.

Congress helped to still Navy misgivings by restricting the power of the Secretary of Defense and by spelling out the functions and missions of the Navy, including naval aviation and the Marine Corps with its aviation units. The National Security Act also established within the Department of Defense the War Council, the Joint Chiefs of Staff and the Joint Staff, the Munitions Board, and the Research and Development Board.

The law created the civilian position of Secretary of the Air Force, to be filled by presidential appointment. The functions assigned to the Commanding General, Army Air Forces, were to be transferred to the Department of the Air Force. The act provided for an orderly transfer of these functions as well as property, personnel, and records over a two-year period.

The United States Air Force was established within the Department of the Air Force. The Army Air Forces (and the Army Air Corps and the Air Force Combat Command) would be transferred to the United States Air Force, and the agencies themselves would cease to exist. Under the

Meeting with Navy Secretary Forrestal and Secretary of War Patterson in 1946 to discuss unification, are, from left: Maj. Gen. Lauris Norstad, Adm. William Leahy, Gen. Dwight Eisenhower, Adm. Chester Nimitz, Vice Adm. Forrest Sherman.

Secretary of the Air Force, the Chief of Staff, USAF, was to exercise command over the United States Air Force.

The act stated the composition and mission of the Air Force in the broadest terms:

"In general the United States Air Force shall include aviation forces both combat and service not otherwise assigned. It shall be organized, trained, and equipped primarily for prompt and sustained offensive and defensive air operations. The Air Force shall be responsible for the preparation of the air forces necessary for the effective prosecution of war except as otherwise assigned and, in accordance with integrated joint mobilization plans, for the expansion of the peacetime components of the Air Force to meet the needs of war."

On July 26, immediately after formally approving the National Security Act, President Truman signed Executive Order 9877, which prescribed the functions and roles of the three services. The specific functions of the United States Air Force were listed as follows:

"1. To organize, train, and equip air forces for:
  a. Air operations including joint operations.
  b. Gaining and maintaining general air supremacy.
  c. Establishing local air superiority where and as required.
  d. The strategic air force of the United States and strategic air reconnaissance.
  e. Air lift and support for airborne operations.
  f. Air support to land forces and naval forces, including support of occupation forces.
  g. Air transport for the armed forces, except as provided by the Navy in accordance with paragraph 1*f* of Section III.

"2. To develop weapons, tactics, technique, organization and equipment of Air Force combat and service elements, coordinating with the Army and Navy on all aspects of joint concern, including those which pertain to amphibious and airborne operations.

"3. To provide, as directed by proper authority, such missions and detachments for service in foreign countries as may be required to support the national policies and interests of the United States.

"4. To provide the means for coordination of air defense among all services.

"5. To assist the Army and Navy in accomplishment of their missions, including the provision of common services and supplies as determined by proper authority."

The National Security Act and the President's order confirmed to the Air Force a status that it had almost attained in all but name. But the birth certificate was a legal necessity before the Air Force could become truly independent on September 18 and embark on a new career of military responsibility.

Close cooperation between Symington and General Spaatz, USAF Chief of Staff, enabled them to announce the new organizational setup of the Air Force by October 1, 1947.

Chapter 9

THE ESTABLISHMENT

The Worldwide Air Force

ETWEEN September 1945 and March 1947 the United States retreated headlong from its powerful positions of military responsibility around the world. From China and India, from the Middle East and North Africa, from Italy and France, American troops departed with a haste that reflected the traditional postwar temper of the American people. Only in Germany and Japan and at a few strategic outposts like Okinawa did we leave garrisons, and these were but tokens of military strength. This hasty exodus from the arenas of war left power vacuums in many areas of the world, and the Communists rushed in to fill the void. Our closest ally, Great Britain, had neither the military nor economic strength to play its historic role of maintaining the balance of power in Europe and Asia.

By 1947 the outlines of the Cold War had become discernible to American leaders, and they responded to the Communist challenge with a dynamic policy of economic and military aid to other nations. The Truman Doctrine of aid to countries threatened by aggression and the Marshall Plan for economic aid to the war-ravaged countries of Europe were translated into action during 1947 and helped greatly to turn back the tide of Communist expansion. But these measures could be applied successfully against the bitter opposition of the Communist bloc only because of the implicit warning that American military power stood behind them. And this military power rested squarely on the possession of the atomic bomb and the means to deliver it. After the end of World War II, therefore, the United States Air Force was the keystone of American military power, and its role in the national security structure grew steadily greater.

Demobilization

During the eighteen months immediately preceding enunciation of the Truman Doctrine on March 12, 1947,

the United States almost completely dismantled the mighty Army Air Forces that had ruled the skies over Europe and Asia in 1944-45. By the end of 1945, overseas commanders no longer had enough manpower to carry out effectively their assigned missions. From a strength of 2,253,000 men on V-J Day, the Army Air Forces declined to 485,000 at the end of April 1946 and to 303,000 at the end of May 1947. Aircrew personnel fell from 413,890 on V-J Day to 24,079 in June 1947.

This headlong dissipation of strength naturally resulted in a striking loss of operational efficiency. In January 1945, fifty-four percent of the Air Force's first-line combat aircraft were available for immediate use; by October 31, 1946, only eighteen percent of the combat aircraft were combat ready. This directly reflected a drop in the number of aircraft maintenance men from more than 350,000 to fewer than 30,000. Effective combat units—the most meaningful measure of combat strength—melted away from 218 groups on V-J Day to two groups in December 1946. At that time, to be sure, the Air Force had a total of fifty-two groups, but fully fifty of these were ineffective.

The wing of a giant USAF transport high over the top of the world symbolizes global activities of the new USAF.

Thousands of warplanes, like these up-ended P-40s, ended honorable careers under the wrecker's torch and hammer.

105

Separation from the Army

Separation from the Army moved along smoothly because the Air Force had already gone a long way toward autonomy prior to September 18, 1947. The Army and the Air Force had begun in July 1947 to put in final form a joint plan for the orderly transfer of functions to the Department of the Air Force and the United States Air Force. The new Secretary of Defense, James V. Forrestal, approved the plan, which consisted of some 200 Army-Air Force agreements, as the framework within which the formal transfer orders would gradually be issued. On September 26, Forrestal approved Order No. 1, which transferred the military and civilian personnel of the Army Air Forces to the Department of the Air Force and the United States Air Force.

By June 30, 1948, some sixty percent of the transfer projects had been completed, and the entire administrative changeover was concluded with the signing of the final transfer order on July 22, 1949. The transfer of responsibilities for functions included almost every area of staff and command activity: personnel, administration, intelligence, training, operations, research and development, procurement, supply, fiscal.

There were those within the Department of Defense as well as without who looked on these changes as being more in the nature of "triplication" than unification, and indeed much of the activity of this period was in the direction of separation. But there were also genuine elements of unification in the process. Unnecessary duplication was avoided by having the Army continue to perform for the Air Force certain services. For instance, the Army Chief of Engineers continued to be responsible for real estate and construction for both services. In turn, the Air Force served the Army in certain fields where it had specialized competence—chief among them the development, procurement, and maintenance of small aircraft. The trend toward a single service performing functions for all three accelerated with the passing years, as successive Secretaries of Defense applied pressure toward this end.

Reorganization

As relations between the Free and Communist worlds deteriorated steadily during 1946-47, it became vitally necessary to bring order out of the near-chaotic condition to which the US armed forces had been reduced by too rapid demobilization. Cold war on the political and economic fronts could be waged successfully only from a position of real military strength, for, as Winston Churchill put it, "no foreign policy can have any validity if there is no adequate force behind it." And for a period after World War II, US military power rested on a handful of atomic bombs and a few hundred near-obsolescent bombers.

Air leaders like Arnold and Spaatz suffered acutely during the dismantling of the mighty airpower machine they had done so much to build. They were especially disturbed because for two years after V-J Day there was not enough stability to create effective combat strength. Men who had learned the lesson of Pearl Harbor—that modern wars begin with air attacks—could not help but be dismayed that in June 1947 the AAF could muster only eleven combat groups ready for battle. They knew, furthermore, that the technological revolution in aeronautics and atomic energy would make future air attacks more deadly and decisive than before. Obviously, no longer would there be time to prepare for a war after it actually began. The only logical conclusion was that the United States must have in being a peacetime air force in a state of the highest readiness.

When Spaatz succeeded Arnold as commanding general of the Army Air Forces on February 15, 1946, he already had in hand from the Air Staff a program for rebuilding the AAF. The program called for the reorganization of AAF headquarters as well as the field commands and the creation of a combat force of seventy groups and twenty-two specialized squadrons together with adequate supporting units. Until the Korean War changed the whole perspective of requirements for national defense, seventy remained the magic number for the Air Force—the number of groups it needed to do its job.

Fortunately, the AAF could reorganize its field structure without encountering the roadblocks, chiefly lack of funds, that frustrated efforts to expand to seventy groups. The roots of the new organization were embedded in the experience of World War II, which had confirmed AAF leaders in their belief that airpower was global in nature and that long-range bombers must be the hard core of American airpower. Although the dust of demobilization had not yet settled, Spaatz decided to anticipate an independent air force by grouping the combat forces in the United States, including the numbered air forces, under three new functional commands. The creation of the Strategic Air, Tactical Air, and Air Defense Commands on March 21, 1946, provided the fundamental framework for a lasting organization of the Air Force.

The remainder of the framework consisted of five supporting commands in the United States and five overseas commands that followed the traditional pattern of theater air commands established in World War II. Foremost among the overseas commands were the United States Air Forces in Europe and the Far East Air Forces, which accounted for most of the combat strength outside of the United States.

This organizational framework of the Army Air Forces in 1946 carried over with no changes into the US Air Force in September 1947. Important new commands, added after 1947, were the Air Research and Development Command, Continental Air Command, and the joint Military Air Transport Service.

Unlike the Army and the Navy, the Air Force had no congressional charter for its composition and organization, for the National Security Act had spoken only in broad terms. This had its compensations because it permitted more flexibility in organizing both the headquarters and the field structure. The Air Force took full advantage of the opportunity to profit from the organizational experiences of the two older services. It created a streamlined, functional structure that operated smoothly enough to invite from the Army and Navy the sincerest form of flattery—a considerable degree of imitation.

But there were also advantages in having the sanction of law for its organization, so the Air Force worked for legislation that would confirm the framework it desired. The first step in this direction came with the passage of the Army and Air Force Authorization Act on July 10, 1950, which allowed a peacetime air force of 502,000 officers and men and 24,000 serviceable aircraft organized into a maximum of seventy combat groups plus separate squadrons. Ironically, this authorization came two weeks after the outbreak of the Korean War. Only three weeks later, on August 3, Congress suspended this limitation, which had really been a goal for the Air Force, and USAF strength thereafter was adjusted to needs far transcending those of peacetime.

The internal organization of the Air Force was established by law in the Air Force Organization Act of 1951, approved on September 19, 1951. The act made the Secretary of the Air Force responsible for all Air Force affairs and gave him the necessary authority and assistants to carry out his responsibilities. It provided for the Air

THE AIR STAFF, HEADQUARTERS UNITED STATES AIR FORCE
October 10, 1947

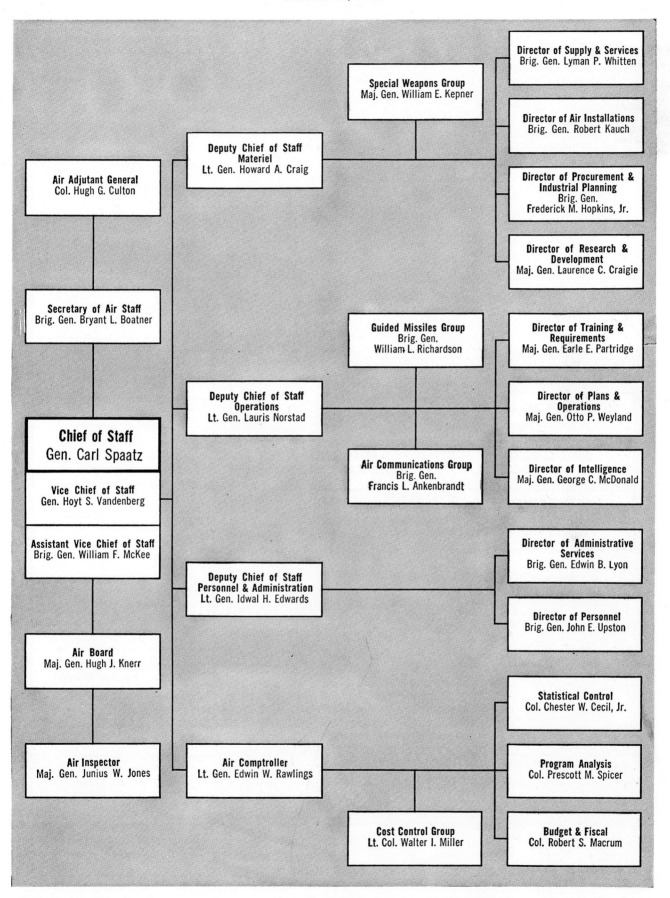

Director of Supply & Services
Brig. Gen. Lyman P. Whitten

Director of Air Installations
Brig. Gen. Robert Kauch

Special Weapons Group
Maj. Gen. William E. Kepner

Director of Procurement &
Industrial Planning
Brig. Gen.
Frederick M. Hopkins, Jr.

Deputy Chief of Staff
Materiel
Lt. Gen. Howard A. Craig

Director of Research &
Development
Maj. Gen. Laurence C. Craigie

Air Adjutant General
Col. Hugh G. Culton

Guided Missiles Group
Brig. Gen.
William L. Richardson

Director of Training &
Requirements
Maj. Gen. Earle E. Partridge

Secretary of Air Staff
Brig. Gen. Bryant L. Boatner

Deputy Chief of Staff
Operations
Lt. Gen. Lauris Norstad

Director of Plans &
Operations
Maj. Gen. Otto P. Weyland

Air Communications Group
Brig. Gen.
Francis L. Ankenbrandt

Director of Intelligence
Maj. Gen. George C. McDonald

Chief of Staff
Gen. Carl Spaatz

Vice Chief of Staff
Gen. Hoyt S. Vandenberg

Director of Administrative
Services
Brig. Gen. Edwin B. Lyon

Assistant Vice Chief of Staff
Brig. Gen. William F. McKee

Deputy Chief of Staff
Personnel & Administration
Lt. Gen. Idwal H. Edwards

Director of Personnel
Brig. Gen. John E. Upston

Air Board
Maj. Gen. Hugh J. Knerr

Statistical Control
Col. Chester W. Cecil, Jr.

Air Inspector
Maj. Gen. Junius W. Jones

Air Comptroller
Lt. Gen. Edwin W. Rawlings

Program Analysis
Col. Prescott M. Spicer

Cost Control Group
Lt. Col. Walter I. Miller

Budget & Fiscal
Col. Robert S. Macrum

DEPARTMENT OF THE AIR FORCE
October 10, 1947

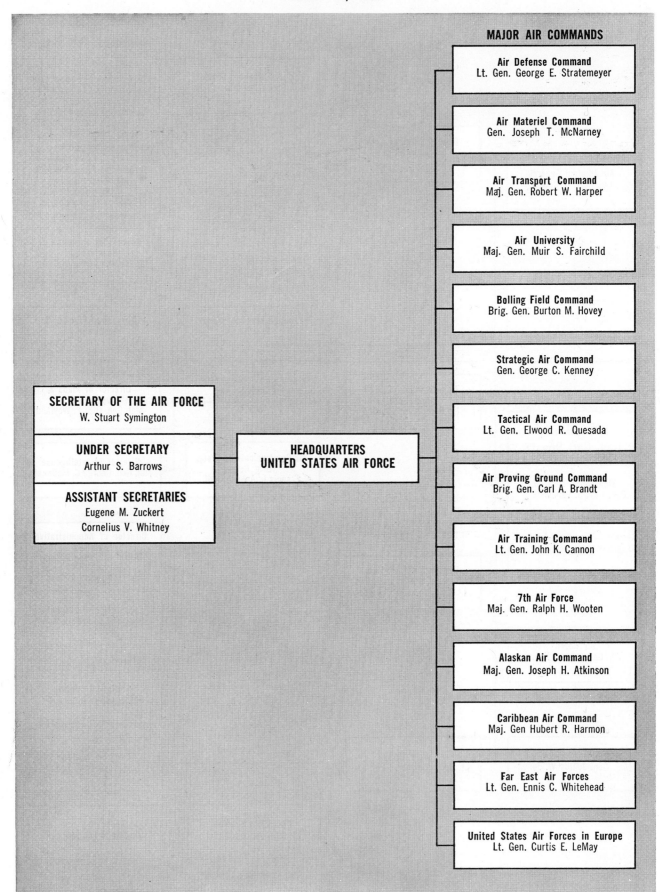

Air Force Organization Act of 1951 put internal AF organization on legal basis. President Truman signs, with Gen. Vandenberg, Rep. Overton Brooks, and Secretary Finletter.

war declared by the President or Congress. By granting broad discretionary powers to the Secretary, Congress guarded against the rigidity of structure that had sometimes handicapped the activities of the Army and Navy in the past. The Air Force retained a degree of flexibility that made it possible to change and strengthen its organization as circumstances might demand.

The Washington Headquarters

With sure hands that came from previous experience, Symington and Spaatz fashioned a sound and enduring organizational structure for the Air Force. Symington opened the Office of the Secretary of the Air Force in September 1947 with a nucleus of four officers and eleven civilians he brought with him from the Office of the Assistant Secretary of War for Air. Aided by an under secretary and two assistant secretaries, Symington made his office an effective agency for discharging his responsibilities and, in 1950, bequeathed to his successor, Thomas K. Finletter, a staff rich in knowledge and experience. The expansion of the Air Force after 1950 and its increasingly important role in the national security structure intensified the activities of the Secretariat and resulted in the addition of two more assistant secretaries and a number of special assistants. By 1957 more than 500 military and civilian personnel were employed in the Office of the Secretary.

Headquarters United States Air Force was new in name only, for there was no break in continuity from its previous existence as Headquarters Army Air Forces. Military and civilian personnel remained the same, and usually in the same jobs. In order to distribute the workload of the Chief of Staff more effectively, the staff structure was streamlined on October 10, 1947, to group most of the functions under a few key officers. This relieved the Chief of Staff of most of the administrative burden and permitted him to concentrate on the major problems of the Air Force, assisted by the Vice Chief and Assistant Vice Chief of Staff.

At top staff level, under the Chief of Staff, were four Deputy Chiefs of Staff—Personnel and Administration,

Staff organization, consisting of the Chief of Staff, Vice Chief of Staff, not more than five Deputy Chiefs of Staff, and such additional military and civilian members as the Secretary found necessary. The Chief of Staff was given command over the major commands and supervision over all other portions of the Air Force. Three major commands—Strategic Air, Tactical Air, and Air Defense—were established, and the Secretary was empowered to set up other commands and organizations when necessary. The Secretary could abolish or consolidate the three major commands or establish new ones in time of emergency or

At USAF commanders' meeting, 1949. Seated from left: Lt. Gen. George E. Stratemeyer, FEAF; Gen. George C. Kenney, Air University; Gen. Hoyt S. Vandenberg, Chief of Staff; Lt. Gen. Ennis C. Whitehead, CONAC; Lt. Gen. John K. Cannon, USAFE. Standing, from left: Gen. Muir S. Fairchild, Vice Chief of Staff; Brig. Gen. Frank A. Armstrong, Alaskan Air Command; Maj. Gen. William E. Kepner, Air Proving Ground; Lt. Gen. Benjamin W. Chidlaw, AMC; Brig. Gen. Robert F. Travis, Pacific Air Command; Maj. Gen. Gordon P. Saville, ADC; Maj. Gen. Robert M. Lee, TAC; Maj. Gen. Willis H. Hale, Caribbean Air Command; Maj. Gen. Laurence S. Kuter, MATS; Maj. Gen. Robert W. Harper, Air Training Command; Lt. Gen. Curtis E. LeMay, SAC; Maj. Gen. Leon W. Johnson, 3d Air Div.; Col. Sydney D. Grubbs, Hqs. Command.

Operations, Materiel, and Comptroller. Although the Comptroller did not officially become a deputy chief until 1949, from the beginning he was the equivalent of one. Within their areas of interest, the deputy chiefs were responsible for policies, plans, and programs, and they exercised broad supervision of USAF field commands engaged in activities related to their interests. The offices of the deputies remained quite small, for they discharged their functions through directorates under their control.

This structure was based largely on considerations other than the traditional military ones. Rapid technological advances, the greatly expanded role of logistics, and the increasing emphasis on fiscal management all combined to demand new and highly rationalized forms of organization. Changes in the headquarters organization after 1947 were simply elaborations of the original structure, giving recognition to new or enhanced functions. Among the most important of these were the establishment of the Office of the Inspector General, given a broad charter of activities in 1948, and the Deputy Chief of Staff, Development, in 1950. The special importance of guided missiles eventually led to the creation of an Assistant Chief of Staff for Guided Missiles in April 1954. Two other offices—Installations and Reserve Forces—had already been placed at the Assistant Chief of Staff level and made directly responsible to the Chief of Staff.

From the beginning, the chief architects of the new organization—Spaatz, Vandenberg, Norstad, and Maj. Gen. William F. McKee, the Assistant Vice Chief of Staff—had intended that Headquarters USAF be a small policy-making and supervisory body, leaving operations to the field commands. Although this proved to be impossible, important operating responsibilities were decentralized to the Air Materiel Command, Air Research and Development Command, and Air Training Command. Conscientious efforts were made to limit the size of the headquarters, even during the expansion caused by the Korean War. Thanks largely to the policy of decentralizing operations, in 1957 the Air Force headquarters in Washington was much smaller than that of either the Army or Navy.

Probably the most important development affecting policy-making in the headquarters was the establishment of the Air Force Council in 1951. Composed of the Vice Chief of Staff, the five deputy chiefs of staff, and the Inspector General, the council had responsibility for drawing up Air Force policies and objectives, reviewing and approving programs, and giving guidance to the Air Staff. The council relieved the Chief of Staff of much of the detailed work of policy-making, presenting to him for approval only formal recommendations. This permitted the Chief of Staff to devote more of his time to interservice and international problems.

Still another device—the Headquarters USAF Command Post—served the Chief of Staff as the focal point for the direction of USAF field operations after it was set up in 1950. Located underground, in the basement of the Pentagon, it was the chief communications center of the headquarters and a clearing house of the latest information for the Secretary of the Air Force and the Chief of Staff. The Air Staff also provided for an alternate headquarters in the field in the event the Pentagon was destroyed or made untenable in time of war.

From Washington, Headquarters USAF directed the commands, which handled all of the activities of the Air Force. This absorbed the greater part of the time and energies of the Air Staff. But the task of representing the Air Force at the seat of government became increasingly complex and required the services of an increasing number of people in the Office of the Secretary and in Headquarters USAF. Responsibility for the all-important budget and for relations with Congress, although centralized

under offices especially set up for the purpose, took much of the time of Headquarters and the Secretariat.

In one form or another, the Air Force was represented at all of the top levels of the national security organization: the National Security Council, Operations Coordinating Board, Office of Secretary of Defense, Joint Chiefs of Staff, Central Intelligence Agency. In all, the Air Force had to maintain a remarkable network of relationships involving some 200 agencies and offices, mostly in Washington. These relationships ran the gamut of administrative responsibilities, ranging from command through supervision and liaison to a purely informational relationship.

Overseas Deployment

The end of World War II did not terminate American political and military responsibilities in certain parts of the world. Occupation forces in Germany and Japan represented most of our overseas military strength for a period after the war, but there soon developed other reasons for deploying additional forces overseas.

The Truman Doctrine initiated a military foreign aid program which eventually included a large number of countries throughout the world and required a great deal of manpower and resources from the US military services. The continuing Russian threat to western Europe, driven home by the year-long blockade of Berlin, impelled the members of the Atlantic Community to form the North Atlantic Treaty Organization (NATO) in April 1949. As a leading member of NATO, the United States undertook to do its share—a large one—in defending western Europe. This required the dispatch of additional American forces, including strong USAF tactical air units, to Europe, where they were stationed in several of the NATO countries—principally Great Britain and France—in addition to Germany.

After the United States drew the line against Communist aggression in Korea in 1950, there was a great buildup of Air Force strength in the Pacific. And the uneasy armistice after July 1953 required the continued presence of strong USAF forces in Korea and Japan.

The air defense of North America assumed vital importance after the Russians demonstrated their ability to produce atomic and hydrogen bombs and long-range bombers. Because the arctic region appeared to offer the most likely routes for attack against the United States, the Air Force advanced its defense outposts as far to the north as possible. The Alaskan Air Command and the Northeast Air Command, in Canada and Greenland, became important links in the air defense chain stretching across the top of North America.

The Strategic Air Command also reached out to overseas areas for advanced airfields from which its bombers could strike more quickly against any aggressor. Huge new bases in the United Kingdom, North Africa, and Spain greatly added to SAC's bombardment capability, for even in 1957 most of its bombers did not have an intercontinental range.

USAF overseas commands were parts of larger theater organizations. In December 1946, on the recommendation of the Joint Chiefs of Staff, President Truman ordered the overseas military forces to be organized as unified, or interservice, commands, with responsibility for land, sea, and air operations in each area under a single commander. The overseas air commands remained under Headquarters USAF for administrative and technical matters, but they were under the operational control of the commander in chief of the unified command to which they were assigned. SAC units on duty outside of the United States were an exception; they remained under the command of SAC. And SAC itself was regarded as a JCS command from December 1946, although the Joint Chiefs of Staff did not issue a formal directive to SAC until April 1949.

The Air Force also participated in two international commands—the United Nations Command in Korea and the Supreme Headquarters Allied Powers Europe (SHAPE). As the Air Force grew in strength in Europe and NATO placed greater and greater reliance on airpower as the major deterrent to aggression, it was logical that an air officer should eventually succeed to the command of SHAPE, originally held by Gen. Dwight D. Eisenhower in 1951-52. In November 1956, Gen. Lauris Norstad of the US Air Force became Supreme Allied Commander, after almost six years of experience in Europe in high command positions, including that of Deputy Supreme Allied Commander.

In the years after 1945 the strength of the overseas air commands ebbed and flowed in accordance with changing conditions and strategic concepts. But regardless of their size, these commands were a pledge of American determination to resist aggression wherever it might occur throughout the world. They were the farthest-advanced line of American defense, and their evolution is worthy of examination.

United States Air Forces in Europe

Direct successor to the mightiest of the AAF's wartime combat commands, the United States Air Forces in Europe (USAFE) settled down in the early postwar years to the routine duties of an occupation air force in Germany and Austria. From its headquarters in the spa town of Wiesbaden, near Frankfort, USAFE carried out the demilitarization of the Luftwaffe, including destruction of its equipment. A decade later the wheel had made a full turn, and it became USAFE's mission to provide equipment and assistance for a new German Air Force.

The demobilization of US military forces after V-J Day reduced USAFE to a shadow; by mid-1948 it had dropped to fewer than 20,000 officers and men and a handful of combat units. The Russian blockade of Berlin helped to turn the tide in the opposite direction, and additional forces were dispatched to Europe. USAFE's strength grew steadily as it assumed responsibilities for providing tactical air forces for NATO and for a host of other duties stemming from American rearmament. These duties included direction of the Berlin Airlift in 1948-49; ferrying large numbers of aircraft to countries receiving mutual aid assistance; training pilots and maintenance men for these countries; and furnishing support to SAC units

COMBAT AND TROOP CARRIER WINGS IN THE AAF AND USAF—JUNE 1946 TO DECEMBER 1956

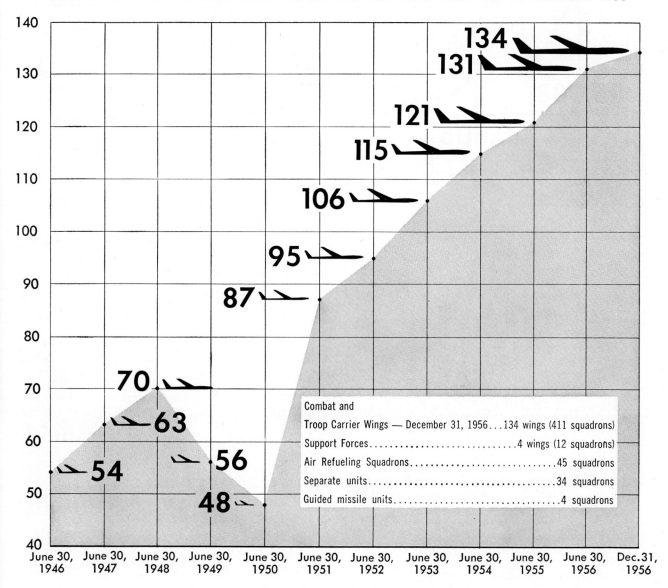

Combat and
Troop Carrier Wings — December 31, 1956...134 wings (411 squadrons)
Support Forces............................4 wings (12 squadrons)
Air Refueling Squadrons...........................45 squadrons
Separate units.................................34 squadrons
Guided missile units.............................4 squadrons

TOTAL AIRCRAFT INVENTORY IN THE AAF AND USAF—JUNE 1945 TO DECEMBER 1956

on training missions to Europe and North Africa. The command eventually stretched from the big depot at Burtonwood in the west of England to the air-conditioned base at Dhahran, in the Saudi Arabian desert.

The quickened pace of the NATO buildup after 1950 led to the reestablishment by USAFE of the Third and Twelfth Air Forces in January 1951 and the creation of the Seventeenth in April 1953. In 1957 these three air forces had control of all USAFE combat units—fighter, fighter-bomber, light bomber, and reconnaissance—while troop carrier units operated under the 322d Air Division (Combat Cargo). The combat units of the tactical air forces were allocated to one or another of the major international air commands established under SHAPE.

In the United Kingdom the Third Air Force, in addition to its tactical mission, also supported SAC's 7th Air Division, stationed in England. From its headquarters at Ramstein, Germany, the Twelfth Air Force directed the operation of all USAFE tactical air units on the European continent. The Seventeenth Air Force was responsible for the Mediterranean and North African areas, including support for SAC's 5th Air Division in Morocco.

Largest of the Air Force's overseas commands, USAFE had more than 79,000 officers and men at the beginning of 1957. Under a succession of able commanders, including Lt. Gens. John K. Cannon, Curtis E. LeMay, Lauris Norstad, and William H. Tunner, at one time or another

USAFE conducted US Air Force activities in most of the thirty-five countries included in its area of responsibility.

Far East Air Forces

The only USAF command to engage in combat after World War II, the Far East Air Forces (FEAF) had administrative and logistical responsibility for all Air Force activities westward from Hawaii to Japan, Korea, Formosa, the Philippines, and Indochina. It confined its sphere of operations, in the main, to Japan and Korea, and from 1945 to 1957 its headquarters was at Tokyo. For its operations in Japan and Korea it answered to the Far East Command, a unified command for which the Army acted as executive agent. To this major outpost of American airpower, the Air Force assigned some of its best commanders: Gen. George C. Kenney, World War II commander of FEAF, Lt. Gens. Ennis C. Whitehead and George E. Stratemeyer, and Gens. Otto P. Weyland, Earle E. Partridge, and Laurence S. Kuter.

FEAF's largest air force—the Fifth—acted as the occupation air force in Japan. In 1950 the Fifth moved forward to Korea, where it ruled the air over the battlefields and up to the Yalu River until the armistice was signed in 1953. Other FEAF subcommands included the 315th Air Division (Combat Cargo), which airlifted more than three million passengers and one billion pounds of high-priority cargo during the Korean War; the Japan Air Defense Force, which protected Japan while the Fifth fought in Korea; and FEAF Bomber Command, which controlled the B-29s that bombed North Korea during 1950-53. FEAF carried out its responsibilities in other areas of the Pacific through additional subcommands in the Philippines, the Marianas, the Ryukyus, and Hawaii. It also helped organize and train the air forces of Korea, Nationalist China, Japan, Thailand, and the Philippines.

After the end of the Korean War, the United States gradually reduced its forces in Japan and Korea, as national policy came to be based increasingly on the deterrent effect of strategic airpower. Also, the continued presence of American troops after the return of Japanese sovereignty created a sensitive situation in Japan that could best be minimized by reducing our forces. Accordingly, the Department of Defense dissolved the Far East Command on July 1, 1957, and placed all military forces in the Pacific under the Commander in Chief, Pacific Command (CINCPAC), a unified command for which the US Navy acted as executive agent. FEAF moved its headquarters to Hawaii in 1956-57, where CINCPAC had been ever since World War II, and exercised control of all US Air Force units in the Pacific from there.

On July 1, 1957, the historic name of Far East Air Forces was changed to Pacific Air Forces. The Fifth Air Force remained in Japan, from where it also directed units in Korea and Okinawa. The 315th Air Division (Combat Cargo) in Japan and the Thirteenth Air Force in the Philippines were other major subcommands. Throughout its farflung domain—the millions of square miles of the Pacific that stretched from Hawaii to the continent of Asia—FEAF had a strength of some 60,000 officers and men at the beginning of 1957.

Alaskan Air Command

In the 1920s, Billy Mitchell had singled out Alaska as an area of great strategic importance to the United States and urged that it be strongly fortified. Japanese assaults on the Aleutians in the early years of World War II confirmed Mitchell's theory that Alaska could serve as a springboard for attack on the United States. In the years after the war, Alaska took on still greater importance because its proximity to the Soviet Union made it a natural air route between Siberia and North America.

Since the possibility of large-scale ground operations in the Arctic was unlikely, Alaska became primarily an air theater, and the Air Force directed the unified Alaskan Command, set up in December 1946. The theater's air mission continued to be the responsibility of the Alaskan Air Command (AAC), which succeeded the wartime Eleventh Air Force in December 1945. Known in military vernacular as a "cold-weather" command, AAC covered an area stretching from the Yukon to the Bering Sea and from the Arctic Ocean to the end of the Aleutians, thousands of miles to the southwest.

AAC's mission was threefold: to furnish early warning of attack on the United States by means of an extensive radar and communications system; to defend Alaska from the air; and to provide bases for retaliatory SAC aircraft. Its varied functions included cold-weather experimentation and testing; air rescue in collaboration with the Navy; support of geological expeditions, polar research, map surveys, and other scientific work. The enormous difficulties of flying under arctic conditions required a continuing program to overcome such problems as high winds, drifting snow, permafrost, and tundra. Scientists at the Arctic Aeromedical Laboratory, at Ladd AFB, searched constantly for new equipment and procedures to withstand the rigors of ice and extreme cold.

The AAC headquarters at Elmendorf AFB, just outside Anchorage, operated through the 10th and 11th Air Divisions. The two air divisions divided their areas of defense by an arbitrary line roughly paralleling the Alaska Range. On September 1, 1956, AAC came under the operational control of the Commander in Chief, Continental Air Defense Command. This was one of the steps toward consolidating responsibility for continental air defense under a single authority.

Northeast Air Command

As the possibility of air attack on the United States via the polar regions became technically feasible, the northeast approaches to the American continent took on an importance comparable to the northwest approaches via Alaska. Just before World War II the United States began developing bases in Newfoundland, Labrador, and Greenland, which it used chiefly for ferrying and antisubmarine operations during the war. By January 1951 the importance of the region to the air defense of the United States had led to the establishment of the Northeast Air Command (NEAC) under the unified Northeast Command, for which the AF acted as the executive agent.

NEAC's mission was to defend the northeast approaches of the United States and Canada against air attack and to provide air-base and route support for SAC, MATS, and other friendly forces in the area. The command worked closely with the authorities of Canada and Denmark, within whose territory the radar network and all NEAC bases were located.

NEAC increased its strength and built new air bases and enlarged existing ones. The great air base at Thule, only 900 miles from the North Pole, had an important role in Air Force strategic plans. A cold-weather command, also, NEAC faced the same problems of operations in the Arctic that plagued the Alaskan Air Command. On April 1, 1957, the Northeast Air Command headquarters went out of existence, as the Continental Air Defense Command completely integrated under its control all elements in the area involved in the defense of North America. The 64th Air Defense Division took over the air defense mission for the area, and SAC took over the remaining missions and most of the bases.

Caribbean Air Command

The strategic significance of the Caribbean declined after World War II, as the fulcrum of potential world conflict moved far to the north. As a result, the Caribbean Air Command, set up in July 1946 as a successor to the wartime Sixth Air Force, remained the smallest of the Air Force's overseas commands during the decade that followed.

Although its prime mission was defense of the Panama Canal Zone and the approaches thereto, the Caribbean Air Command devoted much of its effort to helping the air forces of the nations of Latin America. The command furnished technical assistance to fourteen Central and South American countries, the eventual goal being to develop an inter-American defense system with standardized equipment, terminology, tactics, and techniques. In 1947 the Caribbean Air Command established a technical training school at Albrook AFB, Canal Zone, which graduated 2,500 officers and airmen from eighteen Latin American countries during the next nine years.

In addition to these activities, the command also gave considerable time to administration of mutual defense assistance, support of the Inter-American Geodetic Survey, disaster assistance, airlift operations, and mapping and charting surveys. To a greater extent than most US military commands overseas, it was able to engage in international activities that promoted good will and friendly relations with other nations.

Chapter 10

THE ESTABLISHMENT

Roles and Missions

AS Symington, Spaatz, and Vandenberg carried forward the separation from the Army in 1947-48, they found that the National Security Act did not furnish an adequate guide to action for the new Department of the Air Force. Unlike the Army and the Navy, which had permanent legislation fixing their powers and composition, the Air Force had only the President's Executive Order 9877 of July 26, 1947, specifying the functions of the three services in general terms. It became clear that the lack of a clear-cut definitive statement of the mission of the Air Force vitally affected the plans and programs of all three services. Forrestal put the problem simply: "What is to be the use, and who is to be the user of air power?"

The fundamental cause of disagreement among the services, and especially between the Navy and Air Force, could be found in the changing nature of warfare itself. The remarkable technological advances of the past and the enormous promise of the future pointed to a mode of warfare in which the air would be the dominant element. The Navy was acutely aware of the limitations on its air mission while mindful that the aircraft carrier was its prime weapon. The Army also saw a need to share in the airpower mission that promised to dominate the future.

The disagreements among the services over missions came into sharper focus after the creation of the Department of the Air Force and the Office of the Secretary of Defense because of competition for funds allocated to the Department of Defense. The military services were aware that their future would be influenced in large measure by the divi-

sion of funds among them—and these funds were severely limited prior to the Korean War. After 1947, therefore, the defense dollar was one of the major facts of military life in Washington.

At the heart of the differences between the Air Force and the Navy lay the role of strategic airpower. Navy strategists challenged the capabilities of the long-range bomber and, on occasion, the very concept of strategic bombing itself. Air Force leaders considered large carrier task forces incapable of accomplishing long-range strategic air operations. In the Navy's plans to build supercarriers, they foresaw the allocation of defense funds already too limited to permit the buildup of the Air Force to the minimum level for national defense recommended by the President's Air Policy Commission in 1947.

Concerned by the harmful implications of the contro-

Left: The traditional sharp delineation of roles and missions according to the medium in which a service operates —air, land, or sea—has tended to become blurred under the impact of rapid technological advances in modern weapons.

Right: B-36s over the Capitol. This big bomber was the object of a special congressional investigation in 1949.

versy, and aware that he would have to use his powers as Secretary of Defense to bring about agreement on the delineation of missions, Forrestal held conferences with the Joint Chiefs of Staff at Key West, Fla., from March 12 to 14, and at Newport, R. I., from August 20 to 22, 1948. Out of these meetings came clear-cut assignments of primary responsibility for strategic air warfare to the Air Force and for control of the seas to the Navy. All of the services were assigned collateral functions, which meant that in carrying out its missions each service would seek maximum assistance from the other services. Adm. Louis E. Denfeld's understanding was that the Air Force recognized that "the Navy will be able to make significant contributions to any Strategic Air Plan," and General Vandenberg pledged that he would "seek out aggressively" contributions of the other services to Air Force functions.

But the Key West and Newport agreements did not lay at rest the underlying causes of the controversy, although the statements of understanding by the participants were genuinely sincere and well intentioned. The competition for funds inevitably persisted and Forrestal's successor, Louis A. Johnson, acknowledged in 1949 that it is "primarily over the apportionment of funds that disagreements among the services arise."

By 1949 the Air Force was forced to abandon its program for a seventy-group force, although Congress had voted funds in 1948 to begin a five-year aircraft-purchase program to equip such a force. When President Truman requested fiscal year 1950 funds sufficient for only a forty-eight-group force, this meant a cutback rather than an expansion, because the Air Force had climbed to a total of fifty-nine groups in December 1948 from the low of fifty-two groups in 1946-47. And it appeared that further limitations on the defense budget would make it difficult to maintain even a forty-eight-group force.

The B-36 Controversy

Impressed with the importance of reducing the cost of national defense, Johnson ordered reviews of major programs, including that for the construction of supercarriers. After a majority (Admiral Denfeld dissented) of the Joint Chiefs of Staff recommended abandonment of the project, Johnson canceled plans on April 23, 1949, for building the $188 million supercarrier *United States*.

In April and May 1949 there circulated in press, congressional, and aircraft-industry circles an anonymous document charging that the new B-36 heavy bomber, in addition to being selected through corruption, did not have the performance characteristics claimed for it by the Air Force. Still another anonymous document in August charged that the Air Force had greatly exaggerated the effectiveness of strategic air warfare. The Committee on Armed Services of the House of Representatives investigated the B-36 charges and, after extensive hearings, concluded in August:

"There has not been . . . one iota, not one scintilla of evidence offered thus far in these hearings that would support charges that collusion, fraud, corruption, influence, or favoritism played any part whatsoever in the procurement of the B-36 bomber. There has been very substantial and compelling evidence that the Air Force procured this bomber solely on the ground that this is the best aircraft for its purpose available to the nation today."

This disposed of the corruption charges, and in October the committee resumed hearings on the other aspects of the "B-36 Case." Uniformed Navy leaders aired the frustrations and fears that had beset them under the Department of Defense during the past two years. Essentially, their testimony constituted an indictment of strategic bombing as serving no useful purpose and as being morally wrong. Furthermore, they believed that the Air Force had made a mistake in the B-36 and that it had neglected both air defense and tactical air in its obsession with long-range bombers. By contrast, the carrier, and especially the supercarrier, was a necessary and vital weapon for the future.

The Navy's real concern was a budgetary one. SAC was expensive to maintain, and as long as it enjoyed a high-priority mission it would take a large share of the defense budget. Admiral Denfeld stated the Navy's position: "Our concern is with arbitrary Navy reductions that impair or eliminate essential Navy functions." But as Gen. Omar N. Bradley, Chairman of the Joint Chiefs of Staff, testified "the Air Force and the Army can make the same complaint with equal or greater validity."

The Air Force answered the criticisms of the B-36 program to the satisfaction of most of the public and press. Under Symington's leadership it responded with restraint to the charges against it and relied on the House Committee on Armed Services to bring out the true facts. From the Air Force point of view, the entire episode served the useful purpose of directing the attention of Congress to the vital strategic issues involved and educating the public on the subject of airpower.

The B-36 investigation did not settle the problem of the division of airpower between the Air Force and Navy any more effectively than had the Key West and Newport agreements. In spite of its criticism of the effectiveness of both the atomic bomb and strategic airpower, the Navy, as General Bradley pointed out during the hearings, had been arguing right along that it "should be permitted to use the atomic bomb, both strategically and tactically." Limitation of the use of Navy air—the largest and most important combat element of the fleet—to antisubmarine, fleet defense, and amphibious operations would inevitably bring about a drastic reduction in size and operations of the Navy.

On the other hand there was a positive aspect to the Navy position, and this was a sincere belief in the ability of carrier aviation to continue the proud tradition established in World War II. With a zeal fully equal to that of the Air Force, the Navy pressed forward with technological developments and operational concepts which it hoped

Left: At congressional hearing in 1948. From left, Gen. Hoyt S. Vandenberg, USAF Chief of Staff; Adm. Louis E. Denfeld, Chief of Naval Operations; Gen. Omar N. Bradley, Army Chief of Staff.

Louis A. Johnson, Secretary of Defense, 1949-50.

would make its carriers capable of all types of air operations.

Dividing the Dollar

It was inevitable that there should continue to be disagreement between two services as strongly dedicated as were the Air Force and the Navy. From the Air Force point of view, continued adherence to the so-called "balance-of-forces" or "division-by-services" budget only compounded the difficulty. This was simply a three-way split of the money among the services so that each received roughly the same amount. Such a system of compromise, which could not make full allowance for rising costs of new weapons or for priorities among the missions of the services, might be damaging to the military posture of the United States. The Joint Chiefs could not always agree on mission priorities. It was often difficult, in view of new weapons and their capabilities, to define a truly balanced military force and set the priorities for achieving it. In terms of money, this meant that the Air Force mission was not regarded as of any greater importance than those of the Army and Navy.

But the Air Force felt that its mission was more imperative than that of the other services and that it required a larger share of defense funds to accomplish the missions for which it was responsible. The weapons of air warfare were changing more rapidly and radically than those of either land or sea warfare. Technological progress was revolutionary and the frontiers of aeronautical science almost limitless. Land aircraft, related weapons, and control systems—always expensive items—were becoming more so. In a single decade after 1944 the cost of a heavy bomber increased from $500,000 for a B-29 to $8 million for a B-52.

In the years following World War II the Air Force increasingly felt its responsibility for the military security of the United States. The rapid obsolescence of its equipment, to a greater extent than the other services, confronted it with the continuing dilemma of how to divide its limited funds between the needs of the present and the future. Because the threat of atomic aerial attack against the United States itself grew steadily from the time the Soviet Union exploded its first atomic bomb in August 1949, there was enormous pressure on the Air Force to maintain a force-in-being powerful enough to deter attack. At the same time, because of the technological progress of the Soviet Union, there was equally powerful pressure to make certain that the Air Force would continuously reequip its units with the most advanced weapons. And these weapons were still needed in quantity despite their great destructive power.

Under these circumstances, the Air Force remained in a state of almost constant alarm because of appropriation ceilings that it considered too low to permit it to carry out its mission. The civilian and military leaders made repeated and anxious appraisals of the needs of the present versus those of the future.

Korea helped resolve the dilemma of priorities, but only temporarily. Appropriations for the military services, which differ somewhat from new obligational authority, increased from $14.2 billion for fiscal year 1950, the year before Korea, to $47.3 billion for fiscal year 1951, and to $59.9 billion for 1952. These funds went far beyond the needs of the Korean War because they also took into account NATO requirements and the growing military threat from the Soviet Union. Defense officials planned to build to a high plateau of preparedness and maintain it.

On the eve of the Korean War the Air Force found itself in the difficult position of trying to maintain forty-eight wings with funds which it found sufficient for only forty-two combat-effective wings. During the Korean War, for the first time since World War II, it became possible to state military requirements and to have some assurance of getting the funds needed to meet the goals. As the threat to American security grew during 1950-51, the Joint Chiefs of Staff approved first a goal of ninety-five wings and eventually, in November 1951, 143 wings, to be reached by mid-1955.

The end of the Korean War in 1953 brought a gradual reduction in military appropriations, which totaled $48.4 billion and $33.7 billion for fiscal years 1953 and 1954, respectively. The military requirements stated in 1951 were subjected to a "new look" by the Joint Chiefs of Staff and the National Security Council in 1953. As a result, the Air Force goal of 143 wings was temporarily replaced by an "interim" goal of 120 wings to be attained by the end of June 1956. In December 1953, President Eisenhower approved a goal of 137 wings to be reached by the end of June 1957. Total defense appropriations of $29.1 billion for fiscal year 1955 and $31.4 billion for fiscal year 1956 made it quite clear that if the Air Force goals were to be met, there would have to be a statement of priorities of missions among the services.

That the chief threat to the security of the United States came from Russian atomic airpower and that the Strategic Air Command was our chief deterrent to attack were generally accepted by Congress and the public. And at the higher levels of government it also came to be realized that airpower would have to be given a priority over other military missions in the allocation of funds. The progression in this direction, in terms of billions of dollars of new obligational authority (a slightly different figure from appropriations), was as follows:

For Fiscal Year	Army	Navy	Air Force
1950	4.2	4.1	4.7
1951	19.4	12.5	15.9
1952	21.6	16.1	22.3
1953	13.6	12.5	20.3
1954	13.0	9.4	11.4
1955	7.1	9.7	11.6
1956	7.1	9.6	15.7
1957	7.8	10.4	17.7

The increasing emphasis on airpower (both Air Force and Navy) is also revealed in the percentage of total military expenditures used for aircraft. From 4 percent in fiscal year 1947 and 5.9 per cent in 1948, the percentage rose to 18.1 in 1953, 22.9 in 1954, and 24.7 in 1955. The large increase reflected not only the expansion of air strength but also the cost of more frequent reequipping of units and the generally high and ever rising cost of aircraft and related items.

An Air Force for the Army?

The priority given the Air Force after 1954 did not provide as positive an answer to the question of who should use airpower as the Air Force had hoped. All three services sought for an answer that would assure each a viable role in the military establishment of the future.

Because Korea was essentially a land war, the Army had expanded more than either the Navy or the Air Force and had exercised executive responsibility for fighting the war. Immediately after the war, the cutbacks in Army strength and functions seemed to presage a change in the Army's position within the military establishment. Alone among the three services, the Army did not have a single major air mission.

Army leaders adhered staunchly and with a great deal of logic to a strategic concept that envisioned airborne and land forces equipped with atomic weapons continuing to play a major part in future wars—especially those of the "brushfire" variety. To do this they would have to have adequate and effective tactical air support, including tactical airlift. Many Army leaders did not believe that the Air Force was providing such air support. Their thinking included the corollary that the Army should have, if not its own tactical air force, at least the control of tactical aviation allotted to it by the Air Force.

Before World War II the Army ground commanders had assigned to them their own air support units. But they had yielded this control to the Army Air Forces during the war, recognizing the desirability of concentrating forces instead of dispersing them. After September 1947, by agreement with the Air Force, the Army had continued to maintain a number of small specialized types of aircraft, some of which it had operated during the war as organic parts of ground combat units. At the Key West meeting in March 1948 the services had agreed that the Air Force should have the mission of furnishing close combat and logistical air support to the Army.

During the B-36 hearings in 1949, General Bradley and Gen. J. Lawton Collins supported the Air Force against Navy allegations that tactical air support had been neglected by the Air Force since the end of World War II. There was strong criticism of the handling of USAF tactical airpower in Korea all through the war, but Gen. James A. Van Fleet, commander of the Eighth Army, stated in 1953 that tactical air support in Korea had, on the whole, been satisfactory to the Army. Many ground commanders continued to feel that the Army should have exercised more control over the air units. They were supported in this belief by Marine and Navy critics, who argued that their own system of tactical air support was superior.

The prospect of a return to a tactical air support concept thoroughly disproved in World War II, not to mention the loss of part of its tactical air function, alarmed the Air Force. Even before Korea the Army had begun to add to its small air fleet, which was intended for use within the battle zone. During the Korean War, impressed by the contribution of its small aircraft to the mobility of its forces, the Army had greatly increased the number of its liaison aircraft and helicopters. These planes tended to grow larger in size as well as number. In order to avoid duplication of forces and to provide guidance for the future, the Secretaries of the two services concluded a series of agreements during 1951 and 1952. The last of these, a memorandum signed by Secretary of the Army Frank Pace and Secretary of the Air Force Thomas K. Finletter on November 4, 1952, placed a limit of 5,000 pounds on all Army aircraft except helicopters and more clearly defined the ground support functions of the aircraft of the two services. This agreement somewhat enlarged the Army's role, especially its transport and medical evacuation functions in the combat zone.

The Pace-Finletter agreement did not lessen the pressure within the Army for more and larger Army planes and for an extension of Army air responsibilities beyond the immediate liaison, observation, transport, and aeromedical evacuation duties. Army spokesmen, both officially and unofficially, held that the Air Force was not doing enough for tactical air support of the Army. They believed that their new mobile atomic forces would need more air transport than the Air Force could provide. The Army attitude was reinforced late in 1953 when the Air Force reduced its planned troop carrier wings from seventeen to eleven as part of its readjustment from the 143- to the 137-wing program.

The inability of the two services to see eye to eye on the Army's use of aircraft continued as the Army added to its air fleet, particularly helicopters. After long and careful study of the problem, Secretary of Defense Charles E. Wilson issued a memorandum on March 18, 1957, which superseded while reaffirming most of the provisions of the Pace-Finletter memorandum specifying the use of aircraft by the Army. Within the battle zone, normally extending about 100 miles each way from the front lines, the Army could operate aircraft for the following purposes: command, liaison, and communications; observation, reconnaissance, fire-adjustment, and topographical survey; airlift of Army personnel and materiel; aeromedical evacuation. Helicopters could have a maximum empty weight of 20,000 pounds; all other Army aircraft were not to exceed 5,000 pounds empty. Specific exceptions to the limitation might be granted by the Secretary of Defense. As a "basic objective," the Army should develop planes with the "capability of operations from unimproved fields." The memorandum confirmed the role of the Air Force in strategic and tactical airlift, tactical reconnaissance, interdiction of the battlefield, and close combat air support. In an earlier memorandum on November 26, 1956, Wilson had suggested that the development of guided missiles for close support of Army field operations would permit a reduction in the tactical air strength of the Air Force and asked the Joint Chiefs of Staff to study the subject and make recommendations.

The Guided Missile Era

Long before 1956, the services had begun to realize that the development of guided missiles would have a profound effect on their missions. Efforts to arrive at understandings on this point dated back to World War II. As progress accelerated after 1950 and the era of the guided missile appeared to be much closer than had been thought possible in the 1940s, competition among the services became keen. They appeared to be proceeding on the general principle that the developer of a weapon could use it, although there were agreements for mutual use of certain weapons. This could easily result in all three services performing the same functions. Secretary Forrestal's question of 1948 could be rephrased to ask, "Who is to develop and who is to be the user of guided missiles?"

Once again it became necessary to seek definitions of responsibilities in order to avoid duplication and make the most effective use of the limited funds and technical resources available. All of the services tended to push their developmental work to the logical extremes. The Air Force and the Navy, because of their broader air missions, had an advantage over the Army in the variety of missiles they required. But the Army, too, gradually broadened its missile development and, by 1955, announced progress on a so-called intermediate-range ballistic missile (IRBM) of 1,500 miles. At the opposite extremes from this missile were the short-range tactical and air defense missiles and the long-range intercontinental ballistic missile (ICBM).

The Air Force projects included ground-to-air, air-to-ground, air-to-air, and ground-to-ground guided missiles. In this last category fell the intermediate-range and long-range strategic missiles. Over long-range missiles the Air Force had exclusive jurisdiction, and its projects included air-breathing pilotless aircraft like the Snark, as well as the ballistic types—Atlas and Titan. The Navy developed missiles in all of the same fields except the intercontinental ballistic missile. The Army developed ground-to-air and ground-to-ground missiles. The duplications, therefore, were mainly in the ground-to-air and the intermediate-range missiles. The competition among the services was heightened by the greater emphasis on ballistic missiles in 1954-55 and the President's action in the fall of 1955 which gave the ballistic missile program the highest national priority.

The Joint Chiefs of Staff and the Secretaries of the services could not arrive at agreements that were satisfactory to all. For this reason, in his memorandum of November 26, 1956, Secretary of Defense Wilson clarified the responsibilities of the services for developing and using guided missiles. He distinguished between point air defense of specified geographical areas—cities and vital installations—and area defense—interception of enemy attacks far from and without reference to cities or installations. He assigned to the Army responsibility for point defense and, therefore, the development, procurement, and manning of land-based surface-to-air missiles with a horizontal range of 100 nautical miles. The Air Force would have similar responsibilities in providing and using land-based missiles for area defense. The Navy retained responsibility for ship-based air defense weapons.

Wilson directed the Army to limit development and use of surface-to-surface missiles for close support of ground operations to a range of about 200 miles. Beyond that limit, the Air Force would provide and employ tactical air support missiles. He further directed that the Army would not "plan at this time for the operational employment of the intermediate-range ballistic missile or for any other missiles with ranges beyond 200 miles." In addition to giving the Air Force sole responsibility for the operational use of the land-based IRBM, he confirmed its responsibility for use of the ICBM. The Navy continued its own approach to the development of a ship-based IRBM.

Toward Merger

In 1956-57 the three services were still seeking to maximize their existing missions. But forces at work in the opposite direction promised to bring about, at least in some measure, a greater unification of military effort— the underlying hope of the National Security Act. Chief among these forces was the tendency for the strategic concepts of all three services to converge on the same or similar weapon systems—most of them related to airpower, and primarily in the form of guided missiles. This made it difficult, if not impossible, to draw absolute lines between the missions of the services.

It appeared to some that the overlapping missions and the service rivalries pointed to a need for merging of the armed forces. In June 1956, General Spaatz (Ret.) proposed a single chief of staff and a general staff for the three armed forces. At the same time, Thomas K. Finletter, former Secretary of the Air Force, called for a single armed service in one uniform, with a single chief of staff and a general staff. This represented the ultimate in unification, and some senators regarded it as a wholly unacceptable approach to unification because, among other reasons, it might concentrate too much power in the hands of the military. But a ranking officer of the Air Force, Vice Chief of Staff Gen. Thomas D. White, saw merit in the idea of a single service and expressed his belief that the military services would "move toward more complete unification." Because most of the support for more unification came from people connected with the Air Force, opponents

looked on the idea with suspicion and tended to interpret it to mean that the Air Force expected to dominate the military establishment of the future. Certainly, at the end of the first decade of unification, it appeared that in the name of greater economy and efficiency, there would be further actions to merge duplicating functions of the services, if not the services themselves.

One of the major efforts toward unification of functions was in the field of transportation. MATS, which represented a merger of Navy and Air Force agencies, had been organized in 1948 as a unified command under the Secretary of Defense, with the Air Force as executive agent. But within a few short years the Navy and the Air Force were once more operating some transports under their own control. Although it, too, had a great need for airlift, the Army could not operate transports, except in the immediate battle area, and had to rely on MATS and the Tactical Air Command.

In a major step in December 1956, Secretary of Defense Wilson ordered the Navy and Air Force to transfer to MATS more of their large transports, including the equivalent of four groups of USAF heavy troop carriers. Transfers of additional transport planes from both services were planned, and it seemed that MATS would acquire the strength to carry out effectively its prime mission of supporting all three services in the event of war. The steps toward further integration of the air transport function during the closing days of the first decade of unification probably foreshadowed even more positive moves toward the same goal in the years ahead.

The pressure of events—specifically the growing long-range striking power of the Soviet Air Force—had resulted in the establishment on September 1, 1954, of a joint command with effective control over all available military forces for defense of the United States against air attack. The Continental Air Defense Command (CONAD), headed by a USAF general, included elements of the Army, Air Force, Navy, and Marine Corps, with the USAF Air Defense Command and the Army Antiaircraft Command as its chief components. The Department of the Air Force exercised executive control over CONAD.

At the end of its first decade of independent existence, the Air Force stood on the threshold of a new order of airpower. During the ten years, it had succeeded in keeping its mission substantially intact. It had maintained that land-based airpower, with certain exceptions (especially the Marines), was indivisible, and the executive and legislative branches of the government as well as the public had generally agreed. To some civilian and military leaders in 1957 it seemed logical that the new order of air warfare, based on guided missiles and atomic energy, might well transcend the missions of all three services and lead to their eventual merger. The Air Force felt confident that in any event airpower would continue to play its role as the main military instrument of national policy.

The composition of the Joint Chiefs of Staff after August 15, 1957. From left, Army Chief of Staff Gen. Maxwell D. Taylor; Marine Commandant Gen. Randolph McC. Pate; USAF Gen. Nathan F. Twining, Chairman; Chief of Naval Operations Adm. Arleigh A. Burke; USAF Chief of Staff Gen. Thomas D. White.

Chapter 11

THE MISSIONS

Strategic Air Command— The Deterrent Force

THE leaders of the Army Air Forces came out of World War II convinced that their long-cherished faith in strategic bombardment had been vindicated by the record. Their conviction was borne out by the final judgment of the United States Strategic Bombing Survey: "Allied airpower was decisive in the war in western Europe. . . . It brought the economy which sustained the enemy's armed forces to virtual collapse, although the full effects of this collapse had not reached the enemy's front lines when they were overrun by Allied forces." And enemy leaders like Albert Speer, the German production chief, and Premier Kantaro Suzuki of Japan testified feelingly to the decisive role that strategic bombardment had played in the defeat of their countries.

No accurate assessment of exactly how much strategic bombardment contributed to the defeat of Germany and Japan is possible. Not even the leaders of the AAF claimed that victory could have been won by strategic bombardment alone within the framework of the war as actually fought. But as a test of the theories of the major prophets of airpower—Mitchell, Andrews, Douhet, and Trenchard— World War II proved to be more than adequate. If it did not prove them right beyond question, it demonstrated that it was only a matter of time before they would be wholly correct.

Arnold and Spaatz, architects of the mighty bomber forces which wrecked Germany and Japan, insisted that American airpower of the future be built around the strategic air arm. It was fitting that Spaatz, the wartime commander of the AAF's strategic air forces in both Europe and the Pacific, should have the satisfaction of establishing the Strategic Air Command on March 21, 1946. That it came only five weeks after he succeeded Arnold as commanding general of the Army Air Forces betokened his determination to brook no delay.

The selection of Gen. George C. Kenney as the first commander of SAC was also a measure of the command's top priority. Second only to Spaatz among combat leaders of the AAF, Kenney reacted to his new job with characteristic vigor and competence and devoted the next two and a half years to building SAC into an effective fighting force.

When Kenney opened his headquarters at Bolling Field, Washington, D. C., early in the spring of 1946, his assets were not only meager but pitifully inadequate. It was appropriate that the first two air forces assigned to SAC should be the Fifteenth and the Eighth, but, aside from the names, they bore little resemblance to the great strategic air forces that had dealt Germany such terrible blows during World War II. Between them they could muster only nine bombardment groups and two fighter groups. The bombardment groups were equipped with B-29s and B-17s, and there were even two-engine B-25s in the command's inventory. The fighter groups had World War II P-47s and P-51s. Among the 600 aircraft assigned to the Strategic Air Command, there were only three jet planes— P-80 Shooting Stars.

The command's mission was to be prepared to conduct long-range operations in any part of the world at any time, but its ability to do this in 1946 fell so short as to be almost negligible. The B-29s could not attack intercontinental targets from the United States, and the B-17s were already obsolescent. Nor were there adequate bases overseas to be used in an emergency. Even in the United States there were not enough base facilities to accommodate the larger bombers. But this was still not the whole picture. Demobilization had ripped the organizational fabric of most of the units into shreds, and they could not muster enough combat and ground crews to be classed as effective combat groups.

In itself, SAC could hardly be regarded in 1946 as the deterrent to aggression that its creators had intended it should be. But the United States also possessed the atomic bomb, and even though the means of delivering the bomb on the target were limited at best, the lesson of Hiroshima

SAC's strength and its weakness. It has the best trained pilots and crews in the world, has trouble keeping them.

Top left, first of SAC's three commanders, Gen. George C. Kenney, took over in 1946.

Above, Gen. Curtis E. LeMay guided SAC destinies for almost nine years, until 1957.

Left, Gen. Thomas S. Power came from ARDC to succeed LeMay as SAC commander.

and Nagasaki remained fresh and unmistakable. The bomb was undeniably a strategic weapon, and it was logical that SAC should be the first command to be given the responsibility of using it in time of war. At the time it received the responsibility, on May 1, 1946, SAC had only one unit—the 509th Composite Group at Roswell Field, N. M.—capable of delivering atomic weapons. Fortunately, the 509th, which had dropped the atomic bombs on Japan, happened also to be capable of sustained combat operations—the only such group in SAC at the time. It would serve as the nucleus around which SAC would build an all-atomic striking force.

Although SAC consistently received top priority among the Air Force's combat commands from the beginning, this was not an overriding priority. Like the rest of the Air Force in the postwar years, SAC lacked planes, bases, equipment, and trained men. Like the others, it had to learn how to do its job in spite of inadequate resources.

When Lt. Gen. Curtis E. LeMay succeeded Kenney as commander of SAC in October 1948, the command stood on the threshold of a rejuvenation of strength and spirit to which LeMay himself would contribute a great deal. One of the most experienced and successful bomber commanders of World War II, LeMay had displayed unusual originality and daring as a strategist and tactician during the air assaults on Germany and Japan. In the longest tenure of major command in the history of the Air Force—1948 to 1957—LeMay became uniquely identified with SAC. Both a leader and a driver of men, he impressed on the command his own singlemindedness of purpose and iron resolution. His insistence on the highest standards of readiness and performance eventually gave the command the *élan* and the pride of service that have always distinguished the great military forces of history.

In November 1948, a month after taking over SAC, LeMay moved his headquarters from Andrews AFB, near Washington, D.C., to Offutt AFB, at Omaha, Neb. This was a more central location from which to control the command that grew into a global air force during the next half-dozen years.

Buildup of Strength

From the beginning, SAC urgently needed to be modernized and expanded, but the Air Force did not have the resources to do this until 1950. Few of the sixteen bombardment and five fighter groups on hand by the end of 1947 were fully manned or operational, even though the number of planes had almost doubled during the year and personnel strength had gone up to 50,000. The B-29s had become the backbone of bomber strength, and the command inventory included 120 F-80 jet fighters, but these were not really the stuff of which strategic airpower could be built. The F-80s could not qualify as escort fighters because they lacked range, and before the end of 1948 they were all transferred to the Continental Air Command. The first of the F-84 Thunderjets, a fighter with higher performance than the F-80, became available to SAC during 1948. At the end of the year, SAC had only two fighter wings, one equipped with F-51s and the other with F-84s. By this time the wing had replaced the group as the basic self-contained combat unit, and the Air Force measured its strength in wings rather than groups.

During 1948 the first improved postwar bombers—the B-50 and the B-36—arrived in the combat wings. The B-50 had greater speed and combat radius than the B-29 but was essentially an advanced model of the Superfortress. The B-36, on the other hand, was the largest bomber in the world with a range approaching that of the intercontinental bomber about which air leaders had been dreaming for a generation. Later versions were greatly improved by the addition of four jet engines to the six reciprocating engines that normally powered the B-36. The increased power gave the plane greater speed and altitude and unquestionably prolonged its effective life.

The addition of B-36s to its bomber fleet permitted SAC to form three heavy bombardment wings by the end of 1949. The B-29s, the very heavy bombers of World War II days, had been downgraded to medium bombers after the war, and the B-50s also fell in this category. The guides to classification included combat radius of action as well as size although, to be sure, the combat radius usually increased with the size of the plane. The eleven medium bombardment wings were all equipped with B-29s and B-50s. SAC also had two fighter wings and three strategic reconnaissance wings.

By 1950, SAC had grouped its strength under the Second, Eighth, and Fifteenth Air Forces. All had specialized missions: the Eighth operated medium and heavy bombers; the Fifteenth, medium bombers only; and the Second, reestablished in November 1949, reconnaissance planes only. Geographically, there were no clear lines between the air forces, so that the Fifteenth, from its headquarters in California, controlled MacDill AFB in Florida, while the Second, from its headquarters in Louisiana, controlled Travis AFB in California. A reorganization early in 1950 divided the country into geographical regions, with the Second responsible for the eastern United States, the Eighth for the central, and the Fifteenth for the western. In addition, all three air forces contained both bombardment and reconnaissance units, giving them a balance and flexibility they had not had before.

Rearmament after June 1950 permitted SAC to reequip its bombardment units with jet aircraft much more quickly than would otherwise have been possible. The first B-47 Stratojets arrived late in 1951 and were used to form new bombardment wings. The six-engine medium jet bomber had about the same radius as the B-29, but its performance in every other regard far exceeded that of SAC's other bombers. In 1953, B-29s and B-50s began going out of use as B-47s replaced them. By the end of 1954 all B-29s had gone, and by mid-1955 all B-50s were retired from bombardment units. In 1955 the huge B-52 Stratofortress all-jet heavy bomber arrived in SAC to begin replacing the B-36s, which had served their purpose well. Reconnaissance versions of the two all-jet bombers also gradually replaced the RB-50s and RB-36s, which had carried the burden of the reconnaissance mission.

The Korean War and related events sped up the acquisition of rights to overseas bases and the extension of direct SAC control to overseas areas vital to its operations. In the United Kingdom, where SAC bombardment units had been present most of the time since 1948, SAC was represented by the 7th Air Division from March 1951, in Morocco by the 5th Air Division from June 1951, and on Guam by the 3d Air Division from June 1954. The growing importance of the overseas bases led to the establishment in July 1956 of SAC's first overseas air force—the Sixteenth—in Spain. The 5th Air Division came under the control of the Sixteenth Air Force in 1957. Also in 1957, after the dissolution of the Northeast Air Command, SAC's Eighth Air Force took over direct control of a number of bases in Newfoundland, Labrador, and Greenland, including Thule. SAC's acquisition of direct control over its major overseas bases gave it a completely global character befitting its mission.

Fortunately, SAC's over-all growth between 1950 and 1957 was well balanced, including more modern aircraft and additional bases as well as more men and units. Personnel strength increased from about 70,000 to almost 200,000 (larger than the whole US Army in 1939) and aircraft from approximately 1,000 to more than 3,000. The number of combat wings grew from nineteen to fifty-

one, but the loss of all six fighter wings during 1957 reduced the total to forty-five wings. The growth in air refueling squadrons was correspondingly large. Men and units were not the full measure of the growth, for the aircraft strength of the heavy bombardment wings increased by fifty percent. Although the number of bases in the United States and overseas more than doubled, additional bases were still needed. The true combat effectiveness of SAC in 1957 in relation to 1950 was far greater than the inventory of aircraft and units would show.

At the beginning of 1955, SAC undertook a number of measures to increase this effectiveness and decrease vulnerability to attack. The strategic value of the northeastern United States as a base of operations against overseas targets was stressed increasingly in SAC's plans. Bombers taking off from New England instead of New Mexico, for instance, could reach their targets more quickly and with fewer refuelings or stops, since they would be closer to begin with. In June 1955, SAC moved the Eighth Air Force headquarters from Carswell AFB, Tex., to Westover AFB, Mass. The Eighth took over responsibility for bases, units, and personnel in the northeastern part of the United States and moved additional bombardment wings into that area.

In conjunction with this change, and for additional reasons, SAC planned to disperse its combat strength over a larger number of bases in the United States. There could be little doubt that SAC would be a priority target, probably even the No. 1 target, in the event of air attack on the United States. SAC's bases, a number of which housed two whole bombardment wings, would be especially tempting targets. At the minimum, SAC needed one base for each bombardment wing and additional bases to which it could disperse its aircraft. Keeping too many bombers on a few

Convair B-36, with 10,000-mile range, was long SAC's pride.

Boeing B-50 was refinement of World War II Superfortress.

Sleek Boeing B-47 Stratojet is SAC's medium jet bomber.

SAC's new heavy, Boeing B-52, can fly faster than 650 mph.

bases became too risky to be ignored, and in 1957 a start was made toward dispersal.

There was another important gain to be derived from more bases. A large base housing ninety bombers could not get its planes into the air as quickly as two bases housing forty-five planes each. And squadron airfields with only fifteen planes could cut the takeoff time to a bare minimum. In short, the speed with which SAC could get its bombers into the air might well mean the difference between success and failure. More bases would certainly improve the chances of success.

The Long Reach

The most important factor in strategic bombardment has always been combat radius—the maximum distance a plane can fly to the target with a bomb load. This is usually less than forty percent of combat range because provision must be made for time over the target and return to base. The chief problem of the "bomber boys" in the 1920s and 1930s had been to develop a plane with a long reach. Both the B-17 and B-24 of World War II had a practical combat radius of some 600 to 800 miles, while the B-29 eventually got up to 1,600 miles during the war. These planes could not have carried out sustained strategic bombardment campaigns without bases in England and the Marianas.

The need for an intercontinental bomber had been recognized even before World War II, and the development of the B-36 had begun in 1941. But until 1949 the Air Force had to rely almost entirely on the obsolescent B-29, which obviously could not reach targets in Europe or Asia from the United States. How would SAC carry out its mission if its planes could not fly to the targets and back? Even the B-36s, when they arrived, would not be able to reach all of the targets from bases in the United States. And since B-29s and B-50s would be in use for a number of years after 1948, something would have to be done to enable them to carry out their mission.

The obvious solution was to get overseas bases. But there were few or none available where SAC wanted them. Alaska and the Far East, to which SAC had sent bombardment squadrons for brief training periods even before 1948, were too far from the chief target areas. Germany and most of the European continent were too vulnerable. The increased sense of urgency imparted by the Berlin Airlift in 1948 helped bring about Anglo-American agreement for the construction of SAC bases in England. To provide for more flexible deployment of the bombers, the United States built additional bases in Morocco and Spain after 1950 by agreement with the governments concerned.

In the polar regions, the great base at Thule added another string to SAC's bow.

Bombardment units were not permanently stationed at the overseas bases. Housekeeping units maintained the bases, providing services to the bombers that came from time to time for training and orientation in the particular areas. These bases were the stepping stones between the home bases in the United States and the target areas.

But overseas bases were vulnerable to attack, and many of them might well be destroyed before they could be used. To provide an alternative the Air Force turned to a technique developed by the Air Service a quarter of a century before—aerial refueling. In 1948, as part of a program to make all its bombers capable of in-flight refueling, SAC organized the first two air refueling squadrons and began flying practice refueling missions. The *Lucky Lady II*, a B-50A, dramatized the possibilities of this method when it made the first nonstop round-the-world flight between February 26 and March 2, 1949. The flight covered 23,452 miles in ninety-four hours and one minute, and the plane was refueled in the air four times by B-29 tankers from the Azores, Saudi Arabia, the Philippines, and Hawaii. This flight helped greatly to develop advanced refueling procedures and to improve equipment.

Initially, SAC used the British trail-line or gravity-flow system. In 1950, Boeing developed the flying boom, a telescoping aluminum tube that could be used up, down, or to either side. The boom system sped up refueling and therefore provided a much greater degree of operational flexibility.

In the years after 1948, SAC greatly increased the number of its air refueling squadrons, first using modified B-29s as tankers and later adding KC-97s. Later models of the KC-97 were also used as personnel and cargo transports. The B-47 and the B-52 created a refueling problem because of the great difference in speed and altitude between the jet bombers and the tankers. SAC asked for jet tankers that could keep up with the latest bombers, and in 1957 began receiving KC-135s—tanker version of the Boeing Model 707 jet transport. The KC-135 refueled planes at speeds of 500 miles an hour and at altitudes above 35,000 feet.

In 1955, SAC had thirty-six air refueling squadrons assigned as integral parts of bombardment wings. In a departure from this practice, SAC organized two air refueling wings in 1955 and gave them geographical areas of responsibility, free of assignment to specific bombardment wings.

With aerial refueling, SAC's bomber fleet could reach targets anywhere in the world. The smaller B-47s, of course, needed more "drinks," as the bomber crews put it, than did the B-52. The F-84 jet fighters also greatly extended their combat radius by aerial refueling. In August

Boeing KC-97 tanker (above), still the backbone of SAC's refueling fleet, will eventually be replaced by jet KC-135s.

Right, *Lucky Lady II* refuels on training flight before round-the-world mission.

Left, KC-135 jet tanker refuels a B-52. Mid-air refueling is now routine in SAC.

1955, for instance, twelve F-84Fs flew nonstop from England to Texas in ten hours and forty-eight minutes. The leader of the flight breakfasted at Sturgate, near London, and lunched with his family in Austin, Tex., the same day.

Refueling attained precision status in the 1950s. Individual planes and mass formations alike were refueled on schedule, often in mid-ocean. The combat radius of the B-47 grew steadily, thanks to modifications, improved operating techniques, and air refueling. By 1956 the B-47 could fly three times its normal radius with two or more refuelings en route. Refueling became a normal part of almost every long-range flight. Early in 1956, SAC planes were averaging almost 3,000 aerial refuelings per week.

In 1957, SAC still depended on overseas bases and aerial refueling to give its bombers the long reach they needed to carry out their mission. And until the bomber with a combat radius of 6,000 or 7,000 miles or the intercontinental ballistic missile came along, SAC would remain dependent on these auxiliaries.

The Fighter Mission

World War II experience over Germany firmly implanted in the minds of Air Force tacticians the importance of fighter escort for strategic bombers faced with strong fighter opposition. For more than a decade after the war, SAC insisted on its own fighter units.

The classic concept of fighter escort called for relays of fighters to escort the bomber formations to and from the targets. But the development of air defense systems and the growing superiority of the jet interceptor over the bomber in combat made it clear after 1950 that the day of the bomber formation was drawing to a close. Furthermore, the jet fighter lacked the tactical combat radius to be a truly effective escort, given the conditions under which SAC bombers would have to operate. Finally, the number of fighters and advanced bases required for effective escort would be prohibitive.

SAC applied to the fighter the same principle of radius extension that it had applied to the bombers. The F-84 Thunderjet, its chief fighter of the 1950s, became adept at aerial refueling, and beginning in 1952, whole fighter wings moved overseas with the aid of two or three "drinks" over the Atlantic or the Pacific. Although this remarkable development helped to make the fighters almost as mobile as the bombers, it did not make fighter escort much more practicable.

In an effort to provide the bombers, especially the slower B-29s, B-50s, and B-36s, with some protection, the Air Force experimented with other possibilities. Wingtip coupling of bombers and fighters, which permitted the latter

to get a free ride part of the way, and the F-84 fighter riding into battle cradled in the bomb bay of the B-36 were promising developments that were eventually overtaken by events.

The major event was the replacement of the older bombers by the much swifter jets. The new planes changed SAC's tactics for penetrating enemy territory. In place of flying in large and vulnerable formations, the fast B-47s and B-52s would fly singly or in small formations under cover of darkness or bad weather, relying on speed, deception, and evasive tactics to get them to the target and back. This spelled the end of the escort fighters.

But SAC found other uses for them. In 1952 it directed that in the future the fighters would be equipped to use atomic weapons and employed as part of the strategic striking force. Their new mission included counterair operations against airfields and aircraft, attacks against strategic targets, diversionary strikes, and other operations supplementing the efforts of the big bombers. Like the bombers, fighter units rotated to England, Morocco, and other areas. For a while, the fighters had the task of helping defend SAC bases overseas, but they were looked on primarily as atomic fighter-bombers.

Even before 1957 it became apparent that the fighters had no truly legitimate mission in SAC. They were essentially fighter-bombers, and while they could use atomic weapons, so could the planes of the Tactical Air Command, where the Air Force's fighter-bombers were properly assigned. Furthermore, in the event of war, the fighter-bombers of TAC would supplement the strategic air offensive wherever possible. It was only logical, therefore, that most of SAC's fighter units should be transferred to TAC to strengthen the USAF fighter-bomber force. In 1957 the remaining SAC fighter wings were inactivated and their personnel used by SAC for other purposes.

SAC's Cold War

SAC's role as the deterrent force and, therefore, as the nation's first line of defense, imparted a sense of urgency throughout the command. As the ability of the Russians to launch a nuclear attack against the United States increased after 1949, SAC's importance as the shield of the Free World took on added meaning. Its ability to strike swift and overpowering blows against an aggressor became the paramount concern of its officers and men. They knew that there would be no time to get ready once the fighting had started.

SAC's mission required that in peacetime it behave as if it were at war. Obviously, there were limits to how far it could go in this direction, for it did not actually fly to wartime targets or drop real bombs. But SAC's training certainly became as demanding and realistic as was ever devised for a modern military force in peacetime, and its global scope was truly breathtaking.

SAC demanded a remarkable degree of mobility and flexibility from its bombardment and fighter units. Men and machines had to be prepared to take off at any time for flights to overseas bases or for simulated bombing missions. Whole bombardment squadrons and even wings had to be ready to pick up and move 5,000 or more miles away for a stay of days or months. And they had to take with them essential unit equipment and maintenance personnel. This meant a constant state of readiness throughout every unit of the command.

Such a state of readiness did not exist when SAC carried out its first temporary overseas deployment in November 1946. In order to get the necessary spares to support six B-29s in Germany for thirty days, the 43d Bombardment Group had to cannibalize other B-29s. Communication failures across the Atlantic and inadequate weather information further complicated the flight, but the B-29s finally arrived at Frankfort, Germany, on November 17, four days after leaving Davis-Monthan AFB, Ariz. After twelve days of training activities, the planes returned to the United States. This mission helped convince SAC that its units should be deployed periodically to overseas bases for intensified training under simulated wartime conditions.

Regular overseas rotations began in 1947. Between May and October, a number of SAC bombardment squadrons spent a month each at Yokota Air Base, Japan, practicing their reconnaissance and bombardment skills in the Far East. SAC placed heavy emphasis on the polar regions, and its units flew to Alaska from where they carried out important mapping and survey flights. Other units also flew training and good-will flights

to Great Britain, France, Holland, Belgium, Germany, and Italy, and a few individual planes reached Saudi Arabia.

Within the United States, SAC's units "attacked" such targets as New York, Chicago, and Kansas City. In the largest such mission during 1947, the command sent all of the B-29s it could put into the air—101—against New York City on May 16.

During 1948, as bases became available in England, the emphasis on overseas training shifted to Europe. Two B-29 groups each spent three months or more at bases in England, and one spent more than a month at Fürstenfeldbruck in Germany. After more bases were secured, SAC began a program for regular rotation of bombardment units to Europe. Three other B-29 groups rotated to the Far East during the year, and many individual flights were made to other parts of the world.

From 1948 on, the tempo of rotation and training flights increased steadily. Fifteen bombardment groups flew to European bases during 1949. The effectiveness of this intensive training was demonstrated in 1950 during the Korean War. Alerted on July 1, the B-29s of the 22d and 92d Bombardment Groups left the United States on July 5 and arrived two days later in Okinawa and Japan, respectively. They flew their first mission against the North Korean oil refinery at Wonsan on July 13. In all, SAC had four bombardment groups, a bombardment squadron, and a reconnaissance squadron operating over Korea in 1950.

In spite of the Korean War, SAC continued to rotate its bombardment and fighter units to other parts of the world. The first mass jet fighter flights were made to England and Germany before the end of 1950. As new bases were completed in England and Morocco, they became the chief overseas training areas for SAC's units. Units continued to fly to Alaska, Guam, Greenland, and other areas also, but usually in lesser strength than to Europe.

COMPOSITION OF A TYPICAL MEDIUM OR HEAVY JET BOMBARDMENT WING IN SAC

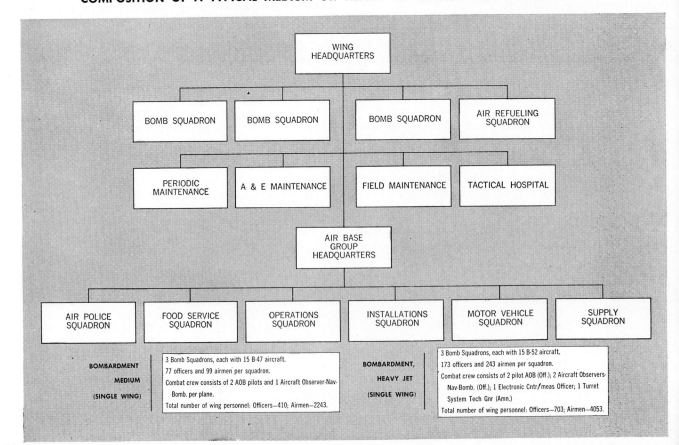

SAC planes made more than 3,400 overseas flights during the first six months of 1954. The 92d Bombardment Wing, first complete B-36 wing to be deployed overseas, flew 5,000 miles from Fairchild AFB, Spokane, Wash., to Andersen AFB, Guam, in October and spent ninety days on the island. By June 1955, SAC's jet bombers and fighters were flying approximately 50,000 hours per month, and the rate was rising steadily.

The deployments of 1955 were a far cry from the squadron and group deployments of 1948. In keeping with a commitment to NATO, SAC had to maintain bombardment wings at European bases at all times. As a result, whole wings, and sometimes two at a time, were deployed overseas for thirty- to ninety-day training periods after 1950. C-124 strategic support squadrons, assigned to SAC, airlifted the men and heavy equipment needed to maintain the units at the overseas bases.

As General LeMay put it, "Moving an entire combat wing is comparable to picking up one of our major domestic airlines, moving it across an ocean, and putting it back in operation all within a matter of hours. This is now accomplished as a routine training deployment." It was routine to the extent that each SAC unit normally moved to a base outside the United States for a three-month period of training and maneuvers annually. In addition, SAC planes flew to the far corners of the world on normal training missions. Obviously, such a scheme of deployment and training could operate only with a strong and mobile logistical system.

Planes flew test bombing missions constantly, regardless of weather and time of day or night. From altitudes of eight miles and higher, the bombers attacked American cities again and again under conditions as nearly approaching the real thing as could be managed. Their targets were specific buildings or corners of buildings, not whole cities, for even with the atomic and hydrogen bombs there was still a need for precision bombing. The bomb runs were carefully charted and scored by radar bomb-scoring detachments in order to determine the degree of accuracy.

SAC participated in most of the major atomic tests, beginning with Operation Crossroads in July 1946. During Crossroads, SAC provided bombers, photographic planes, and air logistic support for the task force off Bikini Atoll in the Pacific. This and subsequent tests permitted SAC to obtain accurate technical information that was vital to its effective use of atomic weapons. From time to time the command revised its plans, techniques, and operational procedures as a result of these tests.

SAC's potency as a deterrent force depended on its ability to deliver nuclear bombs on targets. From 1947 on, the command concentrated on adding as rapidly as possible to the number of planes and units that could drop the bombs. This involved aircraft modifications, provision of special equipment, and intensive training of combat crews and technicians. When the Korean War began, this program was still under way, and most of the earlier bombardment wings sent to the Far East had only a limited ability to drop atomic bombs. In the years that followed, almost all of the bombardment and fighter wings acquired the capacity to use atomic weapons. The development of the thermonuclear bomb in 1952 required further adjustments of aircraft and training programs. In 1957, SAC had the ability to use both atomic and thermonuclear weapons on a mass scale.

The importance of accurate navigation and bombing led SAC to start an annual bombing competition among its units in 1948. Picked crews had to make flights of thousands of miles and bomb visually and by radar from high altitudes. The success of the bombing competition resulted in the inauguration of the annual reconnaissance and navigation competition in 1952. According to LeMay, his crews could find their targets with certainty, coming within fifteen miles of any place on earth by celestial navigation alone. Radar navigation could take them precisely to their targets.

Still another competitive program yielded high dividends. This was the classification of bombardment crews into three categories of ability: "select," "lead," and "combat-ready." SAC based the ratings on a highly sophisticated system of records of achievement by all crews. Awarding "spot" promotions to select crews, begun in 1951, stimulated competition. If a select crew could not maintain the high standards of its rating, all members lost their promotions. Most of SAC's crews in 1957 were composed of mature professionals with an enormous amount of flying experience behind them. Under constant urging for higher performance, the crews worked harder and measured up increasingly well.

The Human Factor

Reaching and keeping the high standards of performance required by LeMay was not without its human cost. But an intensive flying safety program that emphasized accident prevention lessened the physical toll. The rate of accidents per 100,000 flying hours declined steadily from fifty-four in 1949 to forty-one in 1950 and to an all-time low of nine in 1956. SAC made this fine record in spite of the continual addition of new types of planes, for which the accident rate was normally higher. The increasing proficiency of the aircrews themselves contributed greatly to the achievement.

There was another human toll exacted by the mental and emotional stress of life in SAC. To the attitude of mixed exasperation and pride with which many officers and airmen viewed themselves, their activities, and their command, they gave the name "SAC-happy." The exasperation grew out of the tensions of living under a state of constant alert and flying frequent long-range flights. Flying at all hours of the day or night and frequent absences from home ranging up to three months further compounded this abnormal situation. Normal home life proved difficult to maintain, and both the flyers and their families suffered. Under these circumstances, the equivalent of combat fatigue in peacetime became a not uncommon phenomenon in SAC.

Other conditions, not confined to SAC alone, also affected the morale of the command. Poor housing was often the last straw that led officers to resign and airmen not to reenlist. Sometimes air and ground crews had to go as far as twenty miles from the base to find decent living quarters. Aside from the inconvenience, this created a serious operational problem, for it meant that SAC's planes might well be delayed in taking to the air in the event of an alert. Other conditions affecting morale included inadequate pay and allowances and inadequate medical care for dependents.

Part of SAC's hold on its men derived from the realization that the command was making a conscientious effort to remedy poor conditions. The men felt that LeMay and his staff cared about the well-being of all SAC people. And indeed SAC greatly improved living conditions on the bases, set up dependents' assistance programs, provided outlets for individual interests in the form of flying clubs and hobby shops, and worked faithfully to secure better housing and pay.

But over and above all material inducements there existed a sense of dedication and mission among many of SAC's people—ranging from the highest to the lowest—that kept them chained to their duties in spite of physical and mental hardships. Some cracked under the strain; some left before they cracked; others found the financial rewards of civilian life too tempting to resist. Those who stayed formed the hard core of professionals without which SAC could not endure. And for many of them the inspiration was that without SAC the nation might not endure.

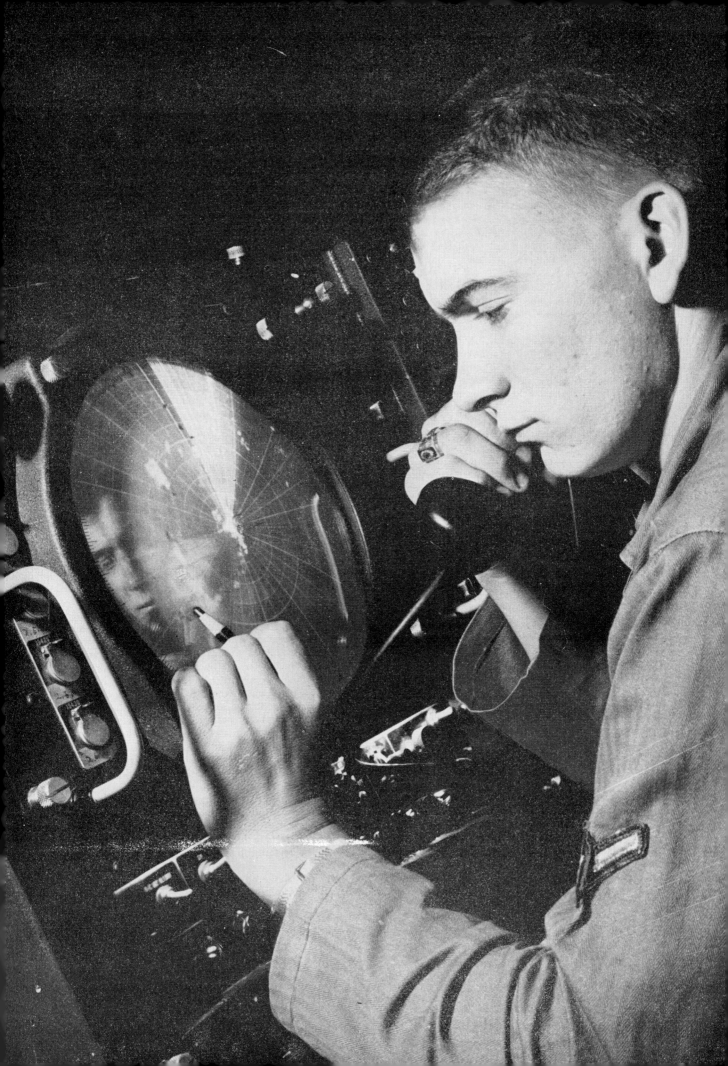

Chapter 12

THE MISSIONS

Air Defense of North America

ANY danger of an air attack on North America seemed remote at the end of World War II. Only the United States possessed the atomic bomb and the means to deliver it. But Army Air Forces leaders knew that this American monopoly was temporary. They reasoned that even though it might be years away, any future war would undoubtedly begin with an air attack. And since the United States was not an aggressor nation, they assumed that it would have to be prepared to defend itself against a surprise attack. Continental air defense, therefore, would be an important function of the peacetime military establishment, and it would be a job primarily for the AAF.

Discussion of defense during the first months of peace, however, was largely academic. Demobilization was the order of the day, and the AAF was quickly reduced to near-impotency. While its strength rapidly dwindled away, the AAF reorganized along functional lines in March 1946, establishing the Air Defense Command (ADC) as one of the three major combat commands. As the AAF's striking arm, SAC received first call on the AAF's limited manpower and materiel. The Air Defense Command, assigned a variety of missions, would have to get along with as little as possible.

ADC's first commander, Lt. Gen. George E. Stratemeyer, had as one of his missions the organization and administration of the integrated air defense of the continental United States. This meant an early-warning radar network and weapons to intercept and destroy attacking bombers. For the job, Stratemeyer had four understrength fighter squadrons and a single training unit equipped with a few World War II radar sets. In fact, the entire AAF did not have the means to fashion an effective air defense. And the relationship with the Army and Navy remained vague, awaiting the outcome of unification and the determination of roles and missions among the services. Stratemeyer's role as air defense commander would have to be one of training and planning.

Outside the AAF the absence of air defenses caused little concern. Most people believed that SAC and the atomic bomb, within limits imposed by the domestic economy, could be counted upon to deter potential aggressors. Other nations would obtain atomic bombs some day, but an air defense system could wait until then.

Air leaders knew better. British experience in World War II had shown that it took time to build an air defense system. And while the United States remained virtually defenseless, the Russians were building copies of the American B-29 good enough to make one-way attacks on the United States with high-explosive bombs. Even though the American atomic monopoly might last for years, the AAF believed that a temporary air defense system was necessary for training as well as defense.

The Temporary Expedients

After 1947 the newly independent US Air Force was in a stronger position to push its air defense views and to begin to set up at least a minimum system. Late in 1947 it approved a plan—known as Supremacy—for an aircraft control and warning (AC&W) network for the United States and Alaska. The proposed network would consist of 411 radar stations—374 of them in the United States—and would cost nearly $400 million. In December the Air Force gave General Stratemeyer formal responsibility for the air defense of the United States in an emergency. And, in the following March at the Key West Conference, the Joint Chiefs of Staff assigned to the Air Force primary responsibility for continental air defense.

Meanwhile, the need for an effective air defense was forcibly brought home by events in Europe. With Russian support, Communists seized power in Czechoslovakia in February 1948. By March 5 the situation looked serious enough to prompt Gen. Lucius D. Clay, the American military governor of Germany, to warn that World War III might break out with "dramatic suddenness" at any moment. With war seemingly so close, General Spaatz ordered ADC to establish air defenses in the northeast and northwest sections of the United States and in Alaska.

Radar acts as the electronic eyes of air defense, but human eyes are still needed to read and interpret the information.

Left, Lt. Gen. George E. Stratemeyer, first commander of Air Defense Command as part of CONAC.

Right, Maj. Gen. Gordon P. Saville who in 1948 decided the crying need was radar for early warning.

Far right, Lt. Gen. Ennis C. Whitehead, took over the reconstituted ADC in 1951.

The attempt to carry out this order underscored the precarious state of continental air defenses. Only one radar station was in operation in the United States. In Alaska, four radar sites operated for a few hours each day. The rest of the scanty equipment and the handful of men allocated to air defense were on a standby basis. To strengthen this feeble system, the Air Force sent one fighter group and additional radar sets to Alaska, while a second fighter group moved to McChord AFB, Wash.

By mid-April the immediate crisis was over. As a result of ADC's frantic efforts, a semblance of an air defense had been set up in the Northwest and in Alaska. In the Northeast, several World War II radar sites had been reoccupied. Although barely a beginning, Headquarters USAF directed ADC to retain the skeleton systems and to set up a similar one in the region of Albuquerque, N. M., an important atomic energy center.

While ADC tried to create an active air defense, Headquarters USAF sought funds to begin construction of the air defense system outlined in plan Supremacy. Despite Army and Navy concurrence, Congress adjourned in June 1948 without considering the plan.

This meant that Supremacy could not be considered until the next session of Congress, six months later. In fact, it seemed doubtful that Congress would approve in 1949, or even later, such an expensive program. In the summer of 1948, Headquarters USAF established an Air Defense Division, headed by Maj. Gen. Gordon P. Saville, a top air defense expert, to study the problem. Assuming that Congress would not approve any expenditure as large as that called for in Supremacy, the Air Force compromised. Saville's group decided that the most urgent need was radar for an early-warning network.

The division prepared the Modified program, which Saville presented to Secretary of Defense Forrestal late in 1948. It called for only $86 million to build a Permanent System of seventy-five early-warning radar stations and ten control centers in the United States and Alaska. These eighty-five installations, to be operational by 1952, would be equipped with obsolescent but usable radar sets already on hand and others of more advanced design that were on order. No new money, therefore, would be required for equipment.

Congress provided the funds for this compromise program in 1949. Although the radar coverage would still not give adequate protection against future threats, the Air Force could at least begin construction of air defenses for the important Northeast, Northwest, California, and New Mexico areas.

Since the completion date for the Permanent System lay several years in the future, the nation still remained virtually defenseless. To provide some protection in the meantime, the Air Force decided to expand the meager temporary network set up early in 1948. With no new funds available, the Air Force asked permission to divert money appropriated for other purposes to construct a temporary

network, known as Lashup, in California and in the vital northeastern and northwestern sections of the nation. For this purpose, the Air Force proposed to use government-owned lands as radar sites.

In August 1949, the Russians exploded an atomic device. The US monopoly was broken. The need for an effective round-the-clock system of air defense was becoming acute. Early in 1950 the Air Force gave priority to manning and equipping fighter and radar squadrons to extend the operating hours of the system. It also began to disperse its fighter-interceptor squadrons over more bases, and it started building the Permanent System toward an earlier completion date. The forty-four stations of the Lashup system were rushed to completion by mid-1950.

The Korean War dispelled any remaining doubts about the need for an effective air defense, but it did not bring about any overnight improvement. Further strengthening of continental air defenses began in the latter part of 1950. ADC used reservists recalled to active service to undertake full-time operation of the radar network. The number of fighter aircraft was greatly increased by calling Air National Guard units into active service. And, of great importance, the President authorized the air defense commander to begin actual interception of unknown aircraft.

It was clear that the air defense mission was too big and too important to be run as a vest-pocket operation, as was actually happening. This situation was the result of organizational changes dating back to December 1, 1948, when the Air Force had reduced both ADC and TAC to the level of "operational" commands under the new Continental Air Command (CONAC) headed by Stratemeyer. All units were assigned to CONAC, and the air defense mission also passed to the new headquarters. All ADC and TAC units were under one commander who could use them as the situation demanded for either air defense or tactical air missions. In the event of an air attack on the United States, there would be a more closely integrated fighter force on hand and under central direction.

ADC itself had been abolished on September 1, 1949, in favor of an Eastern Air Defense Force and a Western Air Defense Force. Both reported directly to CONAC's new commander, Lt. Gen. Ennis C. Whitehead, the World War II leader of the Fifth Air Force. Like his predecessor, Whitehead could not give full attention to air defense because he was also responsible for other important missions, including tactical air.

These conflicting pressures within CONAC were relieved in December 1950 when the Air Force separated the command into its major component parts. Tactical Air Command reemerged on December 1. Air Defense Command again became a major command on January 1, 1951, with headquarters at Colorado Springs, Colo. CONAC retained the mission of supervising the reserve components of the Air Force.

ADC took over the two air defense forces, the fighter

units, the AC&W groups and the radar squadrons, and all of the other USAF units with the primary duty of air defense. For the first time, a USAF command had the sole mission of air defense of the United States. Later in the year, Congress specified in the Air Force Organization Act of 1951 that an air defense command should be one of the permanent major commands of the Air Force.

Components of the Air Defense System

Construction of the Permanent System, begun in 1950, made slow progress. Following the outbreak of the Korean War, the Air Force attempted to speed up the construction program, but strikes and radar equipment shortages delayed completion of the network. Although construction work was finished in 1952, the seventy-five radar stations of the Permanent System were not fully operational until April 1953. The temporary Lashup system was gradually dismantled as the Permanent System came into operation.

The Air Force realized that a major weakness of the Permanent System would be its inability to warn of the approach of low-flying aircraft. Radar equipment to remedy this defect was under development, but in the meantime the Air Force would have to depend upon the eyesight of

Civilian volunteers of the Ground Observer Corps donate freely of their time to fill gaps in the radar network.

ground observers. In February 1950, Headquarters USAF authorized a Ground Observer Corps (GOC).

Composed of volunteers, the GOC depended for success largely upon public interest. From its inception, GOC recruiting lagged badly, and interest was difficult to sustain. By 1957 the corps consisted of more than 15,000 ground observer posts (about two-thirds the number required) manned by nearly 350,000 volunteers. The Canadian Ground Observer Corps, which worked closely with its American counterpart, had 80,000 volunteers. About seventy percent of the posts in the United States were considered active (operational at least two hours each day), while a few more than ten percent of the posts were on twenty-four-hour duty. Despite strenuous efforts, in 1957 the GOC remained an uncertain but necessary element in the air defense system.

Once detected by radar or ground observers, approaching aircraft had to be identified. Identification by electronic equipment would be the most effective means, but ADC had no reliable successor to the compromised World War II identification system (Mark III). Without electronic identification in its interim air defense system, the Air Force had to devise some other method of distinguishing between friend and foe.

As early as 1948, ADC began to use flight information furnished by the Civil Aeronautics Administration and the MATS Flight Service to keep track of aircraft flying over critical areas. From this meager beginning, a vast system for correlating the flight plans of all aircraft was set up and given legislative sanction. In general, the system depended on a number of air defense identification zones around the nation's borders. All pilots entering or leaving these zones had to file flight plans unless they were in very slow and low-flying aircraft. By this means, friendly aircraft were accounted for at all times; aircraft which were not accounted for were investigated at once. This procedure became the chief method of identification for air defense purposes.

For interception and destruction of hostile bombers, the fighter aircraft remained the best weapon. But in 1957 the Air Force still did not have the plane it wanted for air defense. While waiting for the "ultimate" aircraft, ADC used a number of "interim" interceptors.

World War II experience emphasized the importance of all-weather operations in air defense, and development of all-weather interceptors became a prime requirement of the postwar period. As a replacement for the World War II Northrop P-61 Black Widow night fighter, ADC investigated two jet models—the Curtiss-Wright XF-87 and the Northrop XF-89. Meanwhile the North American F-82 Twin Mustang was chosen to replace the obsolete P-61. Some 225 F-82s were in use by the end of 1948, but they were soon replaced, in turn, by the North American F-86 Sabrejet day fighter and the early models of the Lockheed F-94 Starfire. Although these aircraft strengthened the interceptor force, they did not meet the need for all-weather planes that could fly under any conditions, day or night.

The change-over to an all-weather fighter force began late in 1950, when ADC acquired improved versions of the F-94. In mid-1951 it began to receive early models of the

Above, Northrop F-89D all-weather interceptor carries 104 rockets in its wing pods.

Left, North American F-86D single-seat all-weather interceptor as it fires a rocket.

F-89 Scorpion, chosen over the XF-87. These aircraft were supplemented, beginning in 1953, by all-weather F-86Ds. By the end of 1954 the fifty-five squadrons of the interceptor force were equipped with all-weather F-94C, F-89D, and F-86D aircraft.

While these interceptors were coming into the fighter squadrons, the Air Force continued to develop aircraft it called "ultimate" because they were to be built around their own armament, intercept, and control equipment. In 1951 it settled on a Convair model designated the "1954 Interceptor." But it became quickly apparent that this plane would not be operational before 1955 or 1956. Since this delay meant that still another interim aircraft was needed, the Air Force decided to produce a version of the Convair 1954 Interceptor as the F-102A. But even the F-102A did not begin coming into ADC until 1956, and the ultimate fighter receded still further into the future. Although development of the ultimate fighters—the F-104 as well as the F-106 (redesignation of the 1954 Interceptor)—was progressing favorably in 1957, it appeared that they would not be ready for a few more years.

Along with improved performance, interceptors developed much greater destructive power. Most World War II fighters carried machine guns, as did most of the interceptors in use during the Korean War. Early models of the F-89 and F-94 carried cannon and some rocket projectiles. By the time the F-86D began joining the air defense system in 1953, air-to-air rockets had become the chief interceptor attack weapon. Soon, rockets had been added to most of the all-weather interceptors.

For the future, guided aircraft rockets and interceptor missiles appeared to have the most potential. In 1956, the F-89H and the F-102A appeared with the Falcon, a 100-pound air-to-air rocket with its own guidance system. These were to be followed by the more advanced interceptors

Lockheed F-94C all-weather interceptor is a direct descendant of the F-80, carries afterburner for added thrust.

with their special weapon systems and, finally, by the ground-to-air interceptor missiles such as Bomarc. In 1957, however, the air defense system still relied for the most part on manned interceptors armed with guided and unguided missiles.

Another major component of air defense, antiaircraft artillery, had remained with the Army when the Air Force became independent. On July 1, 1950, the Army Antiaircraft Command (ARAACOM) was established to control antiaircraft artillery as part of the continental air defense system. A month later the Army's Chief of Staff, Gen. J. Lawton Collins, and General Vandenberg reached an agreement that served as the basis for joint cooperation in air defense. All antiaircraft units remained under Army command, but they were placed under the operational control of the air defense commander. Such an arrangement, of course, required close cooperation at all levels of command.

At the beginning, the Army had little to add to the air

COMPOSITION OF A TYPICAL F-102A FIGHTER-INTERCEPTOR WING IN ADC

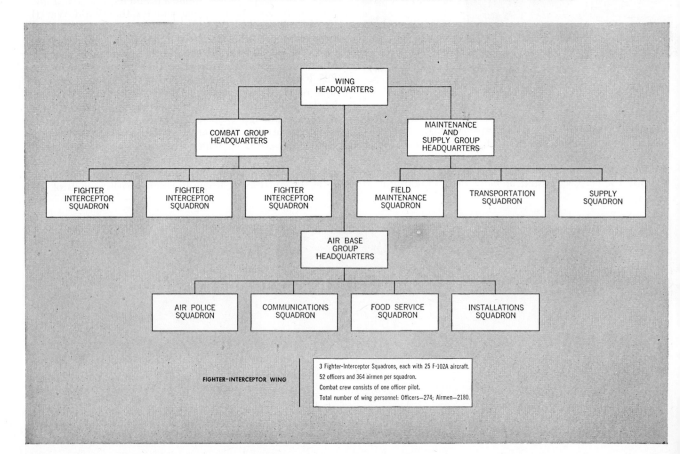

Convair F-102, supersonic all-weather interceptor, with delta-wing design and Hughes-built fire-control system.

Hughes GAR-1 Falcon guided air-to-air missiles, shown in launching position on the wing pod of an F-89H Scorpion.

defense system. But the new command expanded rapidly, and antiaircraft units were stationed around most of the nation's vital target areas. In 1957 the antiaircraft units in at least thirteen of these areas were equipped with the Nike, a radar-directed, short-range, ground-to-air guided missile. The other antiaircraft weapons on hand were 120-mm. and 90-mm. guns and the radar-controlled 75-mm. Skysweeper. In December 1956, Secretary of Defense Wilson decided to continue to vest in the Army development and control of short-range guided missiles. This meant that ARAACOM would continue to play an important role in the air defense of the United States.

By mid-1954, a nationwide integrated air defense system had become a reality. The Permanent System of early-warning radars was in operation, and a large interceptor force patrolled the skies. The Ground Observer Corps and antiaircraft units under ARAACOM had taken their places in the system. And furthermore, the Army and Navy had agreed to place at the disposal of the air defense commander in an emergency all forces of both services that could contribute to air defense.

Extending the Radar Screen

In spite of advances, the air defense system in 1954 still had a number of defects. Radar coverage was shallow and virtually nonexistent at low altitudes. Nor was there any early-warning coverage of the routes that an attacking force would most likely follow: over the seaward flanks and the polar regions. And on top of this, the entire system required too much time to transmit and display the information gathered from the early-warning radar sites.

Obviously, the nation could not afford to cover the whole country with radar. As ADC's commander, Gen. Benjamin W. Chidlaw, stated, complete coverage would require construction of an "impenetrable fence 10,500 miles long and eight to ten miles high around 3,000,000 miles of country." The Air Force decided instead to expand the existing radar

Gen. Benjamin W. Chidlaw, commander of ADC from 1951 to 1955, was also first CONAD commander.

system into a "double perimeter" arrangement. Two lines of radars would be set up to protect the nation's three most vital areas: the Northwest, California, and the Northeast (including much of the Middle West). This network would alert the air defenses so that enemy aircraft could be identified, intercepted, and attacked before they reached their targets. Smaller areas of importance, such as Albuquerque-Los Alamos in New Mexico, would be given island-type defenses. Other early-warning sites would be placed along the northern border of the United States. Interceptors and antiaircraft artillery would be based where they could take utmost advantage of the radar information.

Completion of this double perimeter system entailed a large expansion of the Permanent System network on land. To expand the network as rapidly and economically as possible, the Air Force decided to use mobile ground radar sets as a substitute for costly permanent facilities. This Mobile program, which provided for about 100 radar stations to be installed in three phases, was nearing completion in 1957.

Mobile radars could increase radar coverage but they could not fill the gaps in the system or materially improve low-altitude surveillance. To correct these shortcomings, the Air Force approved the Gap-Filler program in January 1954. As originally planned, this called for more than 300 small automatic radar sets to be placed between the larger radar stations. Further modifications delayed the program, but in 1957 it was partially completed.

The Air Force made greater progress in covering the most important approaches to the North American continent. The USAF commands guarding the northwestern and northeastern approach routes—the Alaskan Air Command and the Northeast Air Command—were integrated into the continental air defense system in 1956-57. Earlier, American negotiations with Canada led to an agreement in 1951 for the construction of a chain of radar stations, known as the Pinetree Line, across southern Canada. Completed by the end of 1955, the Pinetree system consisted of about thirty radar stations, two-thirds of which were built by the United States.

North of the Pinetree chain lay the vast expanse of Canada, reaching far up into the frozen Arctic. On the flanks of this immense area, the Alaskan Air Command and the Northeast Air Command stood guard against air attacks. But in between, the millions of square miles of unguarded air space over Canada offered likely avenues of approach to North America via the polar regions—the shortest air route between the Old and New Worlds. To maintain the first line of warning on the northern border of the United States was manifestly absurd when precious hours could be gained by having a warning line far to the north.

After long consideration, the United States and Canada finally agreed in 1953-54 to build two lines of radars across Canada. One, the Mid-Canada Line, would be built along the fifty-fifth parallel by the Canadian government. The

CONTINENTAL AIR DEFENSE RADAR LINES, AIR DEFENSE AREAS, AND ADIZ AREAS

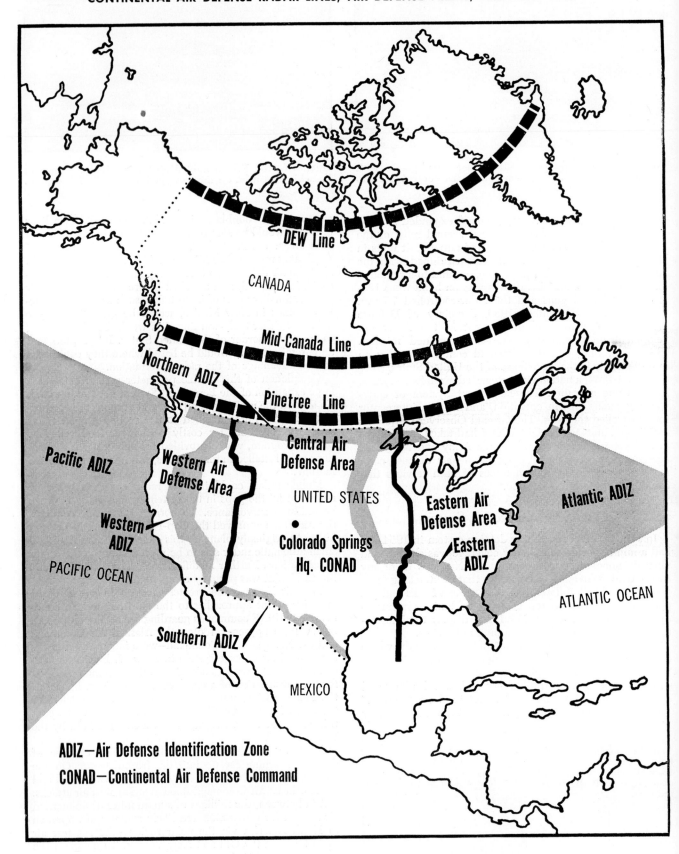

DEW Line

CANADA

Mid-Canada Line

Northern ADIZ

Pinetree Line

Central Air
Defense Area

Pacific ADIZ

Western Air
Defense Area

UNITED STATES

Eastern Air
Defense Area

Atlantic ADIZ

Western
ADIZ

Colorado Springs
Hq. CONAD

Eastern
ADIZ

PACIFIC OCEAN

ATLANTIC OCEAN

Southern ADIZ

MEXICO

ADIZ—Air Defense Identification Zone
CONAD—Continental Air Defense Command

other, the distant early-warning line, known as the DEW Line, would be built by the United States within the Arctic Circle.

Behind the decision to build the DEW Line lay a period of intensive study and analysis of air defense by the Air Force and the other services. As early as 1948, air defense planners had drawn a detailed plan for an early-warning line across Canada. Another study in 1949–50 concluded that continental air defense was inadequate and would not be substantially improved by the Permanent System then being installed. At this point, the Air Force called on the Massachusetts Institute of Technology (MIT) to conduct a broad study of air defense.

MIT formed Project Charles to make the study and later set up the Lincoln Laboratory to carry out the Charles recommendations and to work on improvements to existing radar equipment. The Charles report in 1951 confirmed the vulnerability of the nation to air attack.

Spurred on by the Charles findings, the Lincoln Laboratory organized the Summer Study Group in 1952. This special committee of prominent scientists, including Isidor I. Rabi, Jerrold R. Zacharias, Charles C. Lauritsen, Lloyd V. Berkner, and J. Robert Oppenheimer, reviewed the evolution and future development of continental air defense. The Summer Study Group's report to the Department of Defense at the end of August immediately attracted a great deal of interest.

Specifically, the Summer Study Group emphasized the inability of the nation to repel a surprise air attack. At the same time, the scientists believed that with three to six hours of early warning a strong air defense could be attained. This amount of early warning could be gotten by building a defense in depth northward, backed up by the double perimeter system then being installed.

The most important element of the defense recommended by the Summer Study Group was the DEW Line, running along the sixty-ninth parallel and connecting with the Alaskan Air Command and Northeast Air Command radar networks at either end. Building and equipping the DEW Line would cost an estimated $370 million, and maintenance an additional $100 million per year. The group believed that the DEW Line could be installed and placed in operation by the end of 1954.

Although neither the Air Force nor the Department of Defense had officially approved it, the Summer Study Group report was presented to the National Security Resources Board (NSRB) in September 1952. Because of the dangerous situation indicated by the report, NSRB referred it to the National Security Council and recommended immediate construction of the DEW Line. The board believed that construction would require an initial appropriation of $1 billion to cover the next three or four years.

The report of the Summer Study Group called for a crash program for construction of the DEW Line. Air Force leaders did not oppose the DEW Line as an element of the continental air defense system, but they agreed with the Department of Defense that the time was not right for its construction on a crash basis. The Air Force felt that development of the radar equipment needed for the DEW Line was not far enough advanced. Also, it believed that any available funds could be used more effectively to improve the air defense system then in existence.

But the NSRB and other governmental agencies continued to push the proposal. On December 31, 1952, President Truman approved a National Security Council policy statement calling for construction of the DEW Line as part of a strengthened continental air defense system. Following President Truman's action, Secretary of Defense Robert A. Lovett directed that the DEW Line be made ready by December 31, 1955. As a first step, the Air Force began testing equipment for the DEW Line in Canada during the arctic summer of 1953.

While preparations were being made, the entire concept of the DEW Line became the subject of a lengthy public discussion. Conflicting reports of the cost were made public in 1953, with estimates running as high as $150 billion for installation and maintenance. The reasons for Air Force reluctance to approve the crash DEW Line program were sometimes distorted. As often happens in a public debate on an important issue, sinister or selfish motives were attributed to those who strongly advocated or opposed con-

struction of the line. Some military leaders genuinely feared that the existence of the DEW Line would give the American people a Maginot Line psychology. The total effect of the public airing of the DEW Line issue may well have been harmful to national security. On the other hand, the increased public awareness of the danger of air attack on the United States was all to the good. The nation had become more air-defense-minded.

Early in 1954 the government made the final decision to build the DEW Line. Construction began early in 1955 on a chain of early-warning radar stations sited along a 3,000-mile semicircle near the sixty-ninth parallel. The line included a few main stations to serve as operations centers and a number of smaller stations to fill the gaps. Except for a nucleus of military personnel at the main stations, the line was to be manned by civilian technicians. The Air Force worked toward a completion date of July 1, 1957, and a month after that date—on August 1—announced that the DEW Line had become operational.

The DEW Line, of course, could furnish only early warning of the approach of an attacking force. Such a force would still have at least up to 1,000 miles in which to maneuver before coming within range of the Pinetree radars in southern Canada. This gap will be filled by the Mid-Canada Line along the fifty-fifth parallel, expected to be completed by the Canadians before the end of 1957.

In addition to the northward extensions of the Permanent System radar network, a seaward extension was needed to complete the double perimeter and to supplement the land-based network. Radar coverage could be extended seaward by three means: airborne early-warning and control (AEW&C) aircraft, picket ships, and "Texas Towers." The Air Force decided to use a combination of the three.

In 1951 the Air Force decided to organize AEW&C units. The Navy had developed the Lockheed Super Constellation as an AEW&C aircraft, and this aircraft—called RC-121 by the Air Force—seemed to meet the need.

Bulges atop and below fuselage of this Lockheed RC-121 early-warning aircraft contain some six tons of radar gear.

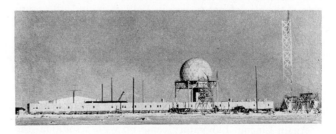

DEW (Distant Early Warning) Line station, part of a 3,000-mile chain of early-warning radar in the Arctic.

Above, Texas Tower off shore early-warning radar station, named for resemblance to oil-drilling platforms.

These radarscopes are connected to an electronic computer which is part of the SAGE air defense system.

Progress in filling Air Force requirements was slow—the first AEW&C squadron was not organized until October 1953. In 1957 the Air Force had several squadrons in operation off each coast as an integral part of the early-warning system. The Navy also operated three squadrons of AEW&C aircraft in the North Atlantic to extend radar coverage. For the future, the Air Force wanted planes superior in performance and equipment to the RC-121.

Possible use of AEW&C aircraft by the Air Force had given rise to some difference of opinion with the Navy as to which service would furnish the aircraft. On the other hand, there had never been any doubt about who would provide picket ships for sea-based radar extension. The Navy obviously was best equipped to do so. In 1950 the Air Force asked for ten picket-ship stations, six for the east coast. But the Navy could not spare the ships at that time, and it was only in late 1952 that it placed the first picket ship on twenty-four-hour duty. The number of picket ships—mainly destroyer escorts—in operation increased rapidly thereafter. In 1957 the Navy had a number of picket-ship stations off each coast. All were scheduled to be equipped with Liberty-type transports.

The third device for extending coverage seaward was the man-built radar island. In the summer of 1952 the Lincoln Laboratory proposed the construction of radar-equipped platforms 100 miles or so from the Atlantic Coast on a number of shoals between Nova Scotia and New Jersey. Since these platforms resembled oil-drilling platforms used in the Gulf of Mexico, they were named Texas Towers. A more stable radar platform than the picket ship, the tower was also cheaper to operate. The first Texas Tower became operational in December 1955, and two others were scheduled for completion in 1957.

Despite all these improvements, the interim air defense system was handicapped by the slow handling of data furnished by the radar sets. As one USAF committee said of the air defense system in 1949, it made "little sense for us to strengthen the muscles if there is no brain; and given a brain, it needs good eyesight." In an era of speeds measured in Mach numbers, this brain would have to perform almost instantaneous operations and be as nearly automatic as possible. The human mind could go only so far in controlling the vast complex of detailed information, and an automatic brain became a necessity for an age of supersonic bombers and missiles.

Again Lincoln Laboratory came up with a solution—the Lincoln Transition system—intended to strike "a balance between men and machines." Men would continue to make

basic decisions while machines would perform the intricate functions. The Air Force accepted the system early in 1953 and renamed it the Semi-Automatic Ground Environment (SAGE) system.

At the heart of the SAGE system, a high-speed, electronic digital computer received, processed, stored, and displayed air surveillance information. It sent the information or instructions to air defense units as directed. By means of the SAGE system, the entire air battle (or air traffic in peacetime) could be controlled. Technical facilities for the first SAGE installations had been built by 1957.

Testing the Air Defenses

From time to time the Air Defense Command tested the defenses it was building to protect the country against air attack. These exercises were also useful in training the various elements of the air defense system.

In an early maneuver in the spring of 1948, SAC bombers "attacked" the Seattle, Wash., area, probing the defense of the fighter wings and aircraft control and warning squadrons. In Operation Blackjack, a preliminary test of the Lashup system in the northeastern part of the United States in June 1949, ADC found the system to be uneven. Some radars performed excellently while others did not. The northwestern net was tested in November 1949 in Operation Drummerboy, with results similar to those of Blackjack.

Two months earlier, in September, ADC had tested the northeastern air defenses in Operation Lookout to determine whether a civilian ground observer organization would be useful. Aircraft made simulated attacks during daylight and darkness and at both high and low altitudes. The maneuver demonstrated that a ground observer system was indispensable. Lookout showed that there had been progress, but it underscored the need for replacing obsolescent and inadequate equipment. The exercise also revealed serious training deficiencies. Another test of the aircraft control and warning system in the Northwest in June 1950 showed that operating personnel were gaining experience.

In February 1951, and again in April, ADC's Eastern and Western Air Defense Forces, together with the other services and the Royal Canadian Air Force, tested their defenses. Day and night fighters, including some Navy units, trained in the techniques and tactics of air defense. SAC bomber units gained additional experience in penetrating a protected area. Royal Canadian Air Force units learned USAF methods. All the elements of the warning system received valuable training.

Between 1952 and 1955, ADC held four annual nation-wide air defense exercises. Each was held in July except for the one in December 1955. Fighters from TAC, SAC, Air Proving Ground Command, and Air Training Command also took part in these tests to show how they might augment air defenses in an emergency. Navy and Marine fighters joined with those of the Air National Guard and Air Force Reserve in these maneuvers. The fighters flew from their home bases and got into action quickly. ADC learned that an appreciable number of them could be ready in about the same time as its own combat force.

These exercises, especially the last, in December 1955, furnished important tests of the speed with which ADC interceptors could scramble once the initial alert sounded. Ideally, it would have been best to keep all fighters ready to take off at all times. But this was obviously impossible, if only because planes had to be serviced and pilots had to train and rest. Five states of preparedness were established to be used as the situation dictated: immediate takeoff, airborne within two, five, fifteen, or thirty minutes.

As tests of the permanent radar system, the exercises revealed defects. Some radars should have been better located. The data needed to be transmitted and used more efficiently. There were still personnel and training problems in operating the radar systems. These annual tests also revealed the degree of vulnerability of the system to electronic countermeasures.

The Continental Air Defense Command

The command structure for air defense expanded quickly after 1950. In 1951, the Central Air Defense Force joined the Eastern and Western Air Defense Forces as the third ADC force in the United States. Sectors within the air defense forces were assigned to air defense divisions, the first two of which had been formed in 1949. By 1957 there were sixteen air defense divisions operating throughout the United States. These had direct control of the fighter squadrons, which operated separately from small individual bases rather than from wing bases. This dispersal was needed for swift reaction and for maximum coverage. The number of divisions will be greatly reduced when SAGE comes into operation, because the new system will permit a greater decentralization of air defense functions below the division level.

The Air Force, to be sure, was the key element in the air defense of the United States, but the Army and Navy also had important roles to play. Since air defense involved all three services, after 1947 the Joint Chiefs of Staff periodically considered plans for a joint continental air defense command that would include forces of all three services. Each successive plan was shelved, usually because the three services could not agree on a command organization. Meanwhile, they agreed that the Air Force should command the air defense forces of all the services in an emergency until the JCS issued further orders. The Army Antiaircraft Command coordinated its activities closely with Air Defense Command beginning in 1950, and the Navy took some steps in the same direction.

In mid-1953, the Joint Chiefs of Staff agreed to form a joint command for continental air defense, but they took a long time to agree on the details. On September 1, 1954, the new Continental Air Defense Command (CONAD) was established directly under the JCS, with the Air Force as executive agent. The JCS charged the command with the air defense of the United States. The new headquarters was set up at Colorado Springs, Colo., under the command of General Chidlaw, head of ADC.

Chidlaw and his successor in 1955, Gen. Earle E. Partridge, exercised operational control over ADC, ARAACOM, and such naval forces as were allocated. In time of emergency CONAD would also control certain additional forces from all three services. These included fighter forces from the Air Force, Navy, and Marine Corps, and Army National Guard antiaircraft units. Senior representatives of the Army and Navy served as advisers directly under the commander of CONAD. The principle of joint command extended downward, and the headquarters of the air defense forces and air divisions became joint agencies, with Army and Navy representatives on hand.

In 1957 the outlook for air defense was promising. More and more the air defense of the North American continent was being treated for what it actually was—a single problem. Canada had begun building its national air defenses early in 1951. At about the same time, the United States and Canada began to integrate their defenses. On August 1, 1957, a new joint command was formed: North American Air Defense Command (NORAD). As commander, and with a Canadian deputy, General Partridge will control all American and Canadian air defense forces.

Lt. Gen. Joseph H. Atkinson, now the commander of ADC.

In CONAD command post, from left, Navy Capt. Dennis J. Sullivan; Maj. Gen. Frederic H. Smith, Jr., ADC vice commander; Gen. Earle E. Partridge, commander in chief.

Chapter 13

THE MISSIONS

The Tactical Air Arm

THE air battles of World War II demonstrated the amazing versatility of American tactical airpower. By controlling the skies over the battlefield, fighters protected the movement of Allied ground troops. Fighters and bombers isolated the combat zone and cut off enemy supplies and reinforcements by attacking railroads, bridges, and other lines of communications. They were also partners in common air-ground assaults against hostile troop columns and gun emplacements. As the eyes of both ground and air forces, reconnaissance planes brought back the photographic and visual information so vital to modern warfare. And troop carrier planes airlifted entire divisions behind the enemy's lines.

At first, each ground force commander wished to control the tactical aircraft within his zone. But World War II furnished abundant evidence that an air commander could use air forces more effectively. Remembering this, Gen. Dwight D. Eisenhower declared in November 1947 that "tactical air units belong under the Air Force rather than under the Army."

The Lean Years, 1946-50

The War Department recognized tactical air as one of the three pillars of modern airpower when it established the Tactical Air Command (TAC) on March 21, 1946, along with the Strategic Air Command and the Air Defense Command. Because it needed to work closely with the Army and Navy, TAC moved its headquarters from Tampa, Fla., to Langley Air Force Base, Va., in May. This site, near the headquarters of the Army Ground Forces at Fort Monroe and the Navy's Atlantic Fleet headquarters at Norfolk, remained its permanent location.

Although TAC was a new command, it inherited a great tradition from two combat air forces of World War II—the Ninth and Twelfth. And its first chief, Maj. Gen. Elwood R. Quesada, had been an outstanding fighter commander with the Ninth Air Force in North Africa and Europe. With the assignment of troop carrier units, TAC also controlled combat airlift in the United States.

In December 1948, the Air Force stripped TAC of its units and reduced it to an operational and planning headquarters under the newly created Continental Air Command (CONAC). The Ninth and Twelfth Air Forces, plus the separate units formerly assigned to TAC, became subordinate units of CONAC. TAC had neither administrative nor logistical control over tactical units, CONAC allocating them for specific missions or during special training maneuvers.

The size and strength of the tactical air arm fluctuated to meet changes in the unsettled international situation. Men and money had to be parceled out according to the importance of the mission. Since most of the money went

Maj. Gen. Elwood R. Quesada, the first chief of TAC.

Left, combat-ready TAC pilot stands by his F-86H, a supersonic plane that can deliver nuclear weapons, representing the fantastic destructive power one man controls in modern AF.

to SAC, the other commands had to bear the brunt of reduced budgets. At the close of 1946, TAC had six combat groups and 26,810 officers, airmen, and civilians. Even after an intensive effort to concentrate all tactical air units under it, TAC had only eleven groups and 31,731 men at the end of 1948. During the two years under CONAC, when it had neither units nor aircraft, TAC headquarters was manned by a staff of approximately 150.

The tactical aircraft that had served with distinction in World War II soon became obsolescent. In 1946, TAC had Republic P-47 and North American P-51 fighters, Douglas A-26 and North American B-25 bombers, and Curtiss C-46, Douglas C-47, and Douglas C-54 cargo and troop carrier aircraft. All but the A-26 were out of date. But also in 1946, TAC received its first jet plane, the Lockheed P-80 Shooting Star, as well as the Fairchild C-82 twin-boom cargo transport. One year later, two new jets, the four-engine North American B-45 bomber and the Republic

head within "enemy territory" and held its position until reinforcements could be flown in. At a large airborne-amphibious maneuver of the three services in the Caribbean early in 1950—Exercise Portrex—Air Force units furnished air defense and helped load and transport the airborne troops.

The most important of these maneuvers, from the Air Force viewpoint, was Exercise Swarmer. In the spring of 1950, 42,000 members of the three services, including 15,000 from the Air Force, joined forces in the destruction of an airhead established by the "enemy" in North Carolina. The Air Force maintained an aerial supply line for an airhead large enough to sustain a military offensive, tested technical developments in cargo-carrying aircraft and equipment, and gained valuable experience in joint tactical operations. During Swarmer, jet aircraft proved that they could provide close support for ground troops and destroy enemy targets.

Lockheed F-80, then known as the P-80, was the first jet aircraft received by Tactical Air Command back in 1946.

F-84 Thunderjet, began to replace the older aircraft. In June 1947 the Air Force changed the prefix for fighters from P to F and settled on B for all bombers. Thus the A-26 became the B-26.

The triumphs of World War II did not mean that all the problems of tactical air warfare had been solved. American fighter pilots had been able to stop the Germans by day but not by night. To attack around the clock, pilots had to learn how to navigate at low altitudes, identify pinpoint targets, and bomb them with precision. And the likelihood that the polar regions would become a center of air warfare created still more problems. Tactical units could operate in the Far North from prepared installations, but they needed to know how extreme cold affected men and machines, how to provide aerial transport for a field army, and how to rescue downed airmen in a land of ice and snow.

During the winter of 1947-48, TAC airlifted infantry companies from the United States to Alaska and back. It also took part in battalion-scale airborne maneuvers in severe cold and deep snow in upper New York state. Exercises with Army ski troops in 1948 proved that jet fighters could operate successfully in mountainous terrain. And in February 1950, Americans joined Canadians in an exercise in Canada and Alaska, the Air Force carrying troops and supplies and providing tactical support and reconnaissance.

The large joint training exercises proved of greatest value in gaining information and experience. In May 1948 the Ninth Air Force airlifted an Army regimental combat team about 500 miles. While tactical aircraft furnished both air cover and close support, an air-ground team set up an air-

But Swarmer also revealed that the Air Force was not getting the full benefit of these maneuvers, chiefly because there was no continuity from one exercise to the next. The practice was to gather from many different sources a temporary headquarters to control units attached for the duration of the exercise. At the end of a maneuver, this structure was dissolved, and the experience gained, even if put on paper, was lost for practical purposes. For the next maneuver a new headquarters would be organized and different units attached. The Air Force recognized the defects of this system and was seeking to overcome them when the Korean War broke out.

Expansion, 1950-53

In August 1950, shortly after the Korean War started, the Air Force began to rebuild TAC, returning to it the administrative and logistical control of its own units. The Ninth Air Force, although still assigned to CONAC, became TAC's field command. It moved from Langley to Pope AFB, N. C., in order to train units more effectively by working closely with the nearby Army airborne center at Fort Bragg. At the same time, TAC took over additional units and stations from other commands.

On December 1, 1950, the Air Force separated TAC from CONAC and restored it to the level of a major command. From Europe to take command in January 1951 came Lt. Gen. John K. Cannon, one of the great tactical air commanders of World War II. In reestablishing TAC, General Vandenberg noted that the Air Force would be able to put more emphasis on ground support now that it had money for an over-all expansion. The large buildup of Army ground forces, moreover, justified greater tactical air strength.

In one of his earliest moves, in March 1951, Cannon established a troop carrier air force—the Eighteenth—to handle TAC's troop carrier units and to train all the Air Force Reserve wings of this type that were called to active duty during the Korean War.

TAC's new position was reflected in its strength. At its peak in 1951, the command had twenty-five tactical wings and more than 60,000 men. Reserve units called up in 1950-51 began to leave the command toward the end of 1952, but most of them were replaced by Regular Air Force units and the number of wings declined only slightly. Because of transfers to FEAF and USAFE, TAC strength at the close of 1953 had fallen to twenty-one combat wings and 52,000 men.

When TAC regained control of tactical units from CONAC

the Far East. By the close of the Korean War, TAC had further shipped two fighter-bomber wings, a troop carrier wing, two troop carrier groups, and six specialized units, including a tactical reconnaissance squadron, to help repel the North Korean and Chinese Communist invaders.

The Tactical Air Command not only helped FEAF to hold the line in Korea but it played an important role in the defense of Europe. For the United States as well as for its more vulnerable allies, the defense of the nations belonging to the North Atlantic Treaty Organization was a matter of vital concern. Despite the revolution in techniques of warfare, the NATO powers still had to be prepared to resist aggression by enemy ground forces. Even if invading armies were crippled by air blows against their sources of supply, they might still be able to carry the war deep into western Europe. Tactical airpower could help repel such an attack and drive off enemy aircraft. But to counter an attack, the NATO forces needed enough strength on hand

The late Lt. Gen. John K. Cannon took over TAC in 1951.

One of TAC's overriding requirements was the ability to land and take off in short distances. Here a Republic F-84 is zero-launched experimentally from a truck-borne platform.

in August 1950, it took over 520 airplanes, some of recent, others of World War II vintage. They included B-26 and B-45 light bombers, F-51 and F-84 fighters, and C-46, C-47, C-82, and Fairchild C-119 transports. In 1951, TAC added reconnaissance aircraft and Douglas C-124 Globemasters as well as administrative, glider, and liaison planes and helicopters. By October 1952 the total number of aircraft had risen to about 1,400, with transport planes accounting for sixty percent of the total. During 1953 the veteran Curtiss C-46 left the inventory, and the North American F-86 Sabre replaced the F-51. By the end of the year, aircraft strength had dropped to less than 1,100.

Contribution to Overseas Commands

The Korean War provided the only combat test of American tactical airpower in the decade after World War II. When the United States rushed to the aid of South Korea in June 1950, FEAF fighter, fighter-bomber, light bomber, and troop carrier wings were the first American units to enter the battle. Since the air war on the peninsula was almost wholly tactical in nature, TAC made the most substantial air contribution from the United States to the fighting forces in the Far East.

Almost immediately after the North Koreans struck, TAC supplied FEAF with men and planes. During three years of war, it trained units of the Regular Air Force, Air National Guard, and Air Force Reserve, as well as replacement crews, and sent them to the Far East. In September 1950 the first crews trained at Langley AFB went overseas, and by the end of the year a troop carrier wing, a light bombardment wing, and a tactical control group had left for

to gain an advantage in the first round of any war. If they could not protect themselves against an atomic onslaught and deal the enemy heavier blows in return, General Vandenberg predicted that there would be no second round.

Even before NATO came into existence in April 1949, the Berlin Airlift had required deployment of the 313th Troop Carrier Wing to Germany in October 1948. TAC began its contribution to the NATO forces in August 1951, when it sent the 433d Troop Carrier Wing to Germany— the first Air Force combat unit permanently assigned to Europe since World War II. In December 1951 the 126th Bombardment Wing became the first US combat unit based in France since World War II. The largest unit sent to Europe, the 49th Air Division, went to England. Its two wings had the primary mission of conducting atomic operations in support of NATO against an aggressor. By June 1953, USAFE had received from TAC an air division, three fighter-bomber wings, two light bombardment wings, two troop carrier wings, one tactical reconnaissance wing, and some fifteen specialized units—including communications squadrons, reconnaissance technical squadrons, and aircraft control and warning squadrons.

Speedup in Training

TAC training went into high gear to meet the urgent demands for tactical air units in both Korea and Europe. In September 1950, TAC set up the School of Air-Ground Operations at Fort Bragg to familiarize Army officers with USAF tactical doctrines. The Air Force changed the name to USAF Air-Ground Operations School in February 1951 and moved it to Southern Pines, N. C.

Korean combat experience indicated where emphasis should be placed. When American control of the air over Korea in daytime forced the enemy to move his supplies almost exclusively at night, the Fifth Air Force used B-26s to harass the enemy supply lines. To meet the increased demand for B-26 pilots, TAC set up a specialized training unit. It also started a training program to overcome a shortage of tactical reconnaissance pilots for RF-80 units. The Eighteenth Air Force trained entire units as well as individual crews to serve with the Korean airlift and in other combat units. The war in Korea provided the Eighteenth with a good testing ground for the development of combat airlift techniques and doctrines.

In special programs, TAC trained forward air controllers and tactical air coordinators to direct aircraft to targets from their respective ground and air posts. For many of the pilots recalled to active duty it was necessary to offer refresher courses. TAC also had to place greater emphasis on general military training so that airmen could fight on the ground in Korea if it became necessary.

TAC applied the lessons of the Korean War in training units and testing weapons and techniques in extremely cold climates. In a winter test at Camp Drum, N. Y., early in 1952, forty-eight cargo planes resupplied a "threatened" area and dropped airborne troops behind "enemy" lines. A year later, new C-119s and C-124s airlifted an Army regimental combat team from the United States to Alaska and back. During the early months of 1953, TAC took part in training troop carrier and fighter-bomber units under severe weather conditions in New York and Vermont. In these and other exercises, TAC used new transports to test troop carrier procedures and techniques.

TAC drew upon wartime experience in two major joint maneuvers, Exercises Southern Pine and Longhorn. The first, held during the summer of 1951 at Fort Bragg, featured an airborne assault with ninety-six troop transports. In Exercise Longhorn, the largest maneuver since World War II, eight wings of the Eighteenth Air Force flew almost an entire infantry division from South Carolina to Texas in the spring of 1952, airlifting nearly 9,000 men and more than 500 tons of equipment.

Debate Over Doctrine

Throughout its early years, TAC needed to persuade the Army that jets were superior to conventional aircraft for the tactical air mission. During the Korean War, the press and public argued the relative merits of jet versus conventional aircraft in the close support role. Critics claimed that F-80 jets flew too fast to strafe ground troops or fight slow conventional planes and that they had too limited a range. In support of their contention, they noted that F-51s instead of F-80s had been sent to Korea early in the war.

But the Air Force had not sent the Mustang because it was superior to the Shooting Star. It was simply that the F-80 was vital to the training program in the United States and could not be spared at that time without seriously interfering with the output of jet pilots. When the AAF had faced similar dilemmas in World War II, it had often favored training over combat demands, sometimes even with the concurrence of the combat commander. As a temporary measure, therefore, the Air Force withdrew F-51s from the Air National Guard and from storage and sent them to Korea. Combat experience quickly proved that the F-80 was less vulnerable to ground fire than the F-51, and criticism tended to die down as jets began to dominate the air war.

The hot debate over the proper use and control of tactical airpower did not subside when the Korean War ended. Army critics and others charged that the Air Force devoted too much of its money and effort to strategic airpower and too little to the tactical air arm. They maintained that the Air Force did not pay enough attention

COMPOSITION OF A TYPICAL F-100D FIGHTER-BOMBER WING IN TAC

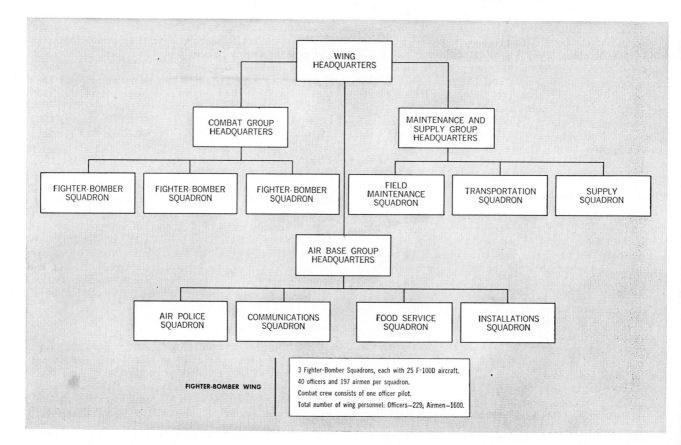

Gen. O. P. Weyland, veteran of tactical air war in ETO and Korea, has been TAC commander since 1954.

Right: this view of the F-84F gives an idea of the heavy armament it can carry for TAC close-support missions.

to close support of ground troops. And they concluded that the ground commander should control the air units supporting his troops.

To the Air Force, this adverse criticism showed a lack of understanding of tactical air doctrine. In explaining the relationship between strategic and tactical airpower, Gen. Otto P. Weyland, who succeeded General Cannon as TAC commander in April 1954, saw no clear line of demarcation between strategic and tactical airpower. They were simply opposite ends of the same spectrum.

Air leaders pointed to the fact that tactical aircraft could shift from one place to another or from one job to another. The tactical air units in the United States and overseas were ready to move quickly and in strength against a threatened attack at any time or place. In Korea, air commanders had been able to switch rapidly from interdiction of communications to close support. Transports were also versatile, for troop carriers took part in airborne operations, supply drops, and evacuation of wounded.

Because of these factors, the Air Force contended that any parceling out of tactical air strength among ground commanders would fritter it away. A single air commander in control of a theater air force could shift his full strength from one type of mission to another to meet threats or exploit successes. If each ground commander had his own little tactical air force to support local actions, the theater commander could not have a powerful air arm available when he needed it.

Critics also alleged that the Air Force did not devote sufficient attention to combat airlift. In November 1956, Secretary of Defense Wilson decided that this airlift was adequate. A month later, Wilson clarified the airlift roles of TAC and the Military Air Transport Service by directing the transfer from TAC to MATS of the equivalent of four heavy troop carrier groups.

In the face of dynamic technological developments and changing concepts of aerial warfare, the tactical air arm adjusted its doctrines and precepts. The Air Force recognized that tactical air could join strategic air in the first blows against the sources of enemy military strength. Modern tactical aircraft must move, regardless of distance, against their historic targets: communications centers, men, and equipment. But the Korean struggle and subsequent events indicated that the Soviet Union had an alternative to global war—the "brushfire" or peripheral war—which would require greater flexibility from American airpower. The ability of the United States to counter this type of "little" war depended in large measure on how successfully the Tactical Air Command could carry out its mission.

In 1957, TAC could adjust the size, composition, and firepower of its highly mobile strike forces to meet any given war situation. A typical strike force might contain fighter-bombers and tactical bombers—both carrying atomic weapons—reconnaissance aircraft, tankers for in-flight re-

fueling, and transports to airlift men and equipment. Aerial tankers were used to refuel TAC's fighters, fighter-bombers, and light bombers so that they could fly from the United States to any of the overseas bases. In September 1956 a mobile air strike force of North American F-100Cs, RF-84Fs, and Douglas B-66s flew nonstop from the United States to Europe—a distance of more than 4,000 miles. This new long reach promised still further changes in the future employment of tactical air.

Toward a Global Tactical Strike Force

In 1957, TAC consisted of three numbered air forces—the Ninth, Eighteenth, and Nineteenth—plus numerous specialized units. It had twenty-one combat wings and almost 58,000 officers and men. The Ninth Air Force, which moved to Shaw AFB, S.C., in September 1954, trained all of TAC's units except the troop carriers. This job was especially hard because units were reequipped so frequently with new aircraft and weapons that it was necessary to retrain them almost continually. The Eighteenth Air Force at Donaldson AFB, S.C., provided troop carrier airlift for the Air Force, the Army, and the Defense Department.

The newest air force, the Nineteenth, located at Foster AFB, Tex., was formed in July 1955 to direct USAF field training with Army forces in the United States and to act as a mobile task force headquarters. The Nineteenth was the answer to the problem of continuity in training, for it was a small permanent operational headquarters under which units trained or engaged in maneuvers. In an emergency, the Nineteenth would be the headquarters component of the Composite Air Strike Force and would be prepared to move overseas immediately. Fighter, fighter-bomber, light bomber, tanker, and other TAC units previously earmarked would join the Nineteenth when the time came to move out. These were fully trained units, prepared to carry out their missions under the control of the Nineteenth.

Overseas deployment of tactical units continued after the Korean War ended. Three fighter-bomber wings, one tactical reconnaissance wing, one troop carrier wing, and one troop carrier group went to USAFE, while a troop carrier wing and a troop carrier group left for FEAF. Fourteen specialized units also moved to Europe.

In the fall of 1954, TAC's fighter-bomber and troop carrier units earmarked for NATO began rotation flights to Europe. This rotation strengthened the air defenses of western Europe. Between 1954 and the beginning of 1957, eleven squadrons—seven fighter-bomber and four troop carrier—spent six-month training periods with USAFE.

TAC trained units for overseas commands, supported these units by sending abroad trained men and crews as replacements, and at the same time kept the units at home ready for combat. Because of overseas deployment and

Latest version of the Martin Matador tactical missile, known as the TM-61B.

Supersonic North American F-100C, both day fighter and fighter-bomber.

Martin B-57 tactical bomber replaced the B-26 in TAC inventory in 1956.

Douglas RB-66 (refueling below) is reconnaissance version of tactical bomber.

Fairchild C-123 assault transport is used by TAC troop carrier squadrons.

Lockheed C-130, turboprop-powered, shown with huge rear cargo door open.

rotation, the Air Force had more tactical air units stationed overseas than in the United States. This dispersal of strength made it difficult for TAC to meet its responsibilities for training and for rapid deployment to threatened areas. Since mobile tactical striking forces could be deployed anywhere in the world with great speed after 1954, TAC believed that it could meet local as well as global dangers more effectively if most of the USAF tactical air strength remained in the United States.

In the spring of 1956, Headquarters USAF began to consider such a concentration. TAC proposed that each combat wing in the United States maintain one of its squadrons overseas at all times, rotating squadrons at six-month intervals. These squadrons would go abroad without the men's families, whose presence normally detracted from the alertness and efficiency of a unit overseas. Under these circumstances, TAC believed, a single squadron would give a better account of itself in combat than would an entire wing under existing conditions. This proposal resembled SAC's rotation practice.

Increase in Firepower

In November 1950, Headquarters USAF directed TAC to develop tactics and techniques for the use of atomic weapons in tactical operations. At the time, only SAC's bombers could carry atomic weapons. Bombs designed for delivery by other types of aircraft were still in the development stage. In March 1951, Headquarters USAF further directed TAC to prepare to use guided missiles with atomic warheads. Although both tactical atomic bombs and the Martin Matador missile were still being developed, TAC planned to have an atomic bombardment wing ready by January 1952.

In a major effort that proved highly successful, TAC selected men for specialized training, created ground and aircraft equipment, and introduced new flying tactics and delivery techniques. Many unique training and guidance problems had to be solved, especially in the case of the Matador. Looking into the future, TAC decided that units scheduled to receive the F-84 would ultimately carry nuclear weapons, so it gave special schooling to these units.

By May 1952, the 49th Air Division, composed of a

B-45 wing and an F-84 wing, not only had the ability to use atomic weapons but had already been deployed to England for use with the NATO forces. Later, another fighter-bomber wing joined this atomic force. Since most of its atomic capability had gone with the 49th Air Division, TAC had to build anew. The Ninth Air Force began to train, organize, and equip several more fighter-bomber wings for atomic warfare.

The Air Force developed by 1953 a low-altitude bombing system that enabled fighter-bombers to deliver atomic weapons accurately and at the same time permitted the pilot and his craft to escape the ensuing blast. TAC modified F-84s during 1953 to use this new system. By 1954, TAC had available a variety of atomic bombs that could be used selectively against different kinds of targets.

In 1957, TAC was approaching the point where every one of its aircraft would be able to carry nuclear weapons, as well as rockets and high-explosive bombs. The only TAC missile, the TM-61 Matador, also could carry either high-explosive or atomic warheads.

This ability to deliver nuclear bombs made TAC second only to SAC as a deterrent force. One TAC fighter-bomber could strike with the force of 100,000 B-17s. General Weyland stated in 1956 that "with them [tactical nuclear weapons] we can be selective, limiting our air attacks to primary military targets with much greater effectiveness. This is especially true when you consider that our nation's stockpile of nuclear weapons now includes a range of yields which permit accurate and optimum attacks on the entire spectrum of targets."

Shift to New Weapons

Rapid obsolescence of aircraft gave TAC a never-ending problem. While its strength varied little after 1953—remaining at about 1,400 planes—the composition of the inventory underwent substantial changes.

The major changes took place among fighter-bombers and day fighters. During the first half of 1954, TAC shifted from the F-84G to the F-84F, a new airplane rather than a new model, and later in the year, from the F-86 Sabre to the supersonic F-100A. During 1955, TAC received the F-100C, both a day fighter and a fighter-bomber, and in 1956, the more advanced F-100D fighter-bomber. By February 1956, four wings were flying F-100s rather than F-86s—a jump in speed from the subsonic to the supersonic in level flight. On their way in 1957 were the Lockheed F-104 day fighter, fastest US aircraft to go into production, and the Republic F-105, to be used for both close support and interdiction. The RF-84F remained the standard fighter reconnaissance plane.

Among tactical bombers, the highly maneuverable and versatile jet Martin B-57—an American adaptation of the British Canberra—superseded the last of the World War II tactical bombers, the B-26, in the spring of 1956. A reconnaissance version, the RB-57B, had entered the inventory at the close of 1954. The new, speedy B-66, another jet, joined the small tactical bomber fleet early in 1956. The RB-66, an all-weather plane, also entered the reconnaissance wing at Shaw AFB during this period. To refuel both fighters and bombers, TAC received the Boeing KB-29 aerial tanker in 1954, and by the close of that year, two air refueling squadrons were equipped with this airplane. In 1956, the Boeing KB-50, using an improved probe and drogue refueling system, joined the tanker fleet. But like SAC, TAC badly needed a jet tanker like the Boeing KC-135 to refuel its supersonic jet aircraft on their nonstop flights overseas.

To reinforce fighter-bomber and light bomber units, the Air Force began organizing TM-61 Matador tactical missile units in 1951. The Matador was the first guided missile sent overseas by the Air Force and the first built in sections so that it could be shipped by air to any part of the world. The first Matador squadron went to Germany in March 1954, and by September 1955, three of the four squadrons in existence were stationed in Europe.

Army and Air Force plans for airborne operations called for troop carrier aircraft to load and unload troops and equipment rapidly, to operate from small unprepared fields, and to have greater speed and load capacity. The aircraft on hand in 1954—the C-119 and the huge C-124—did not have all of these qualities. To help meet the Army's needs, TAC began feeding the Fairchild C-123 Avitruc into the Eighteenth Air Force in July 1955. This two-engine assault transport, with a cargo capacity of 16,000 pounds or sixty troops, could get in and out of small unprepared fields. The large and versatile Lockheed C-130 Hercules entered the TAC inventory in December 1956. This turboprop, four-engine combat transport, even with a cargo capacity of 40,000 pounds, could land and take off in short distances. It proved useful for assault transport as well as for logistic support and air evacuation.

Maneuvers After 1953

Training exercises continued to bolster the effectiveness of the tactical air arm. In March 1954, US armed forces held the northernmost maneuver in their history at Thule AFB, Greenland, only 900 miles from the North Pole. During a mock airborne invasion, soldiers and airmen tested the ground defenses of air installations guarding

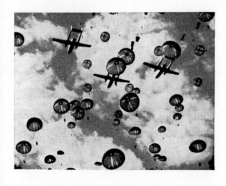

Paratroopers of 82d Airborne Division hit the silk from Fairchild C-119 Packets in training exercise.

the polar air routes. Air units at Thule participated, and C-124s of the 62d Troop Carrier Wing provided the airlift. One month later, TAC provided air elements for the Army's first simulated atomic field exercise in the Fort Bragg-Camp Mackall area of North Carolina. Ninth Air Force fighters and reconnaissance planes flew an average of 125 sorties daily for ten days, while Eighteenth Air Force troop carriers flew almost 1,500 troop carrier and aerial resupply sorties during the period.

Overseas, the Allied Air Forces, Central Europe, held a large air exercise in June 1955. More than 3,000 aircraft from eleven NATO nations, including planes from the Twelfth Air Force, took part in a simulated combat exercise called Carte Blanche.

All Eighteenth Air Force wings and many other TAC units joined in a large-scale Army-Air Force maneuver, Sagebrush, in the vicinity of Camp Polk, La., in November-December 1955. This marked the first appearance of the C-123 in tactical operations. The maneuver showed that the dispersal of highly mobile, self-sustaining Army units in strategic locations near the combat zone was preferable to the concentration of large masses of troops. This dispersal concept was further tested in November 1956 when the Eighteenth airlifted 14,000 Army troops from Fort Riley, Kan., to six bases from which C-119s and C-123s carried them to "forward areas."

In 1955 and 1956, TAC also tested its mobile strike forces to ensure that they could be deployed anywhere at any time. Within three weeks in September-October 1956, a token Composite Air Strike Force flew nonstop from the United States to Europe, participated in NATO exercises, and returned.

Assisting the Global Airlift

Aside from its training activities, TAC's Eighteenth Air Force contributed greatly to airlift operations, serving the United States and its allies in all parts of the world. When these flights followed established international transport routes, they were under the operational control of the Military Air Transport Service. In the spring of 1954, TAC airlifted 1,300 French paratroops halfway around the globe to Indochina to reinforce the doomed fort at Dien Bien Phu. Two of the Eighteenth's troop carrier wings, operating under MATS control, carried out the longest large-scale airlift in the history of the Air Force in July 1955. Forty C-124s lifted a US Army regimental combat team from Fort Campbell, Ky., to Japan and brought back another regimental combat team from Japan to Fort Bragg, N.C. In all, the troop carriers airlifted more than 7,000 troops in this rotation of units. When MATS diverted its scheduled flights to Europe to bring Hungarian refugees from Austria to the United States in December 1956, Eighteenth Air Force C-124s took over the MATS runs.

The Eighteenth also carried out special airlifts in support of continuing operations. Its big transports brought in equipment and supplies for the construction of the great air base at Thule, Greenland, the distant early-warning line in northern Canada, and the scientific research stations of Operation Deep Freeze in Antarctica. They carried missiles to their launching sites in this country and overseas. The Eighteenth's mobile disaster team, consisting of a thirty-six-bed hospital fully staffed and equipped, was ready to move to any spot where emergency or disaster might occur.

By its fifth anniversary in March 1956, the Eighteenth Air Force had made an impressive record. Its aircraft had flown more than 83,000,000 plane miles, 391,000,000 passenger miles, and 241,000,000 ton miles. And it had airlifted 407,000 tons of high-priority cargo for the Army and the Air Force.

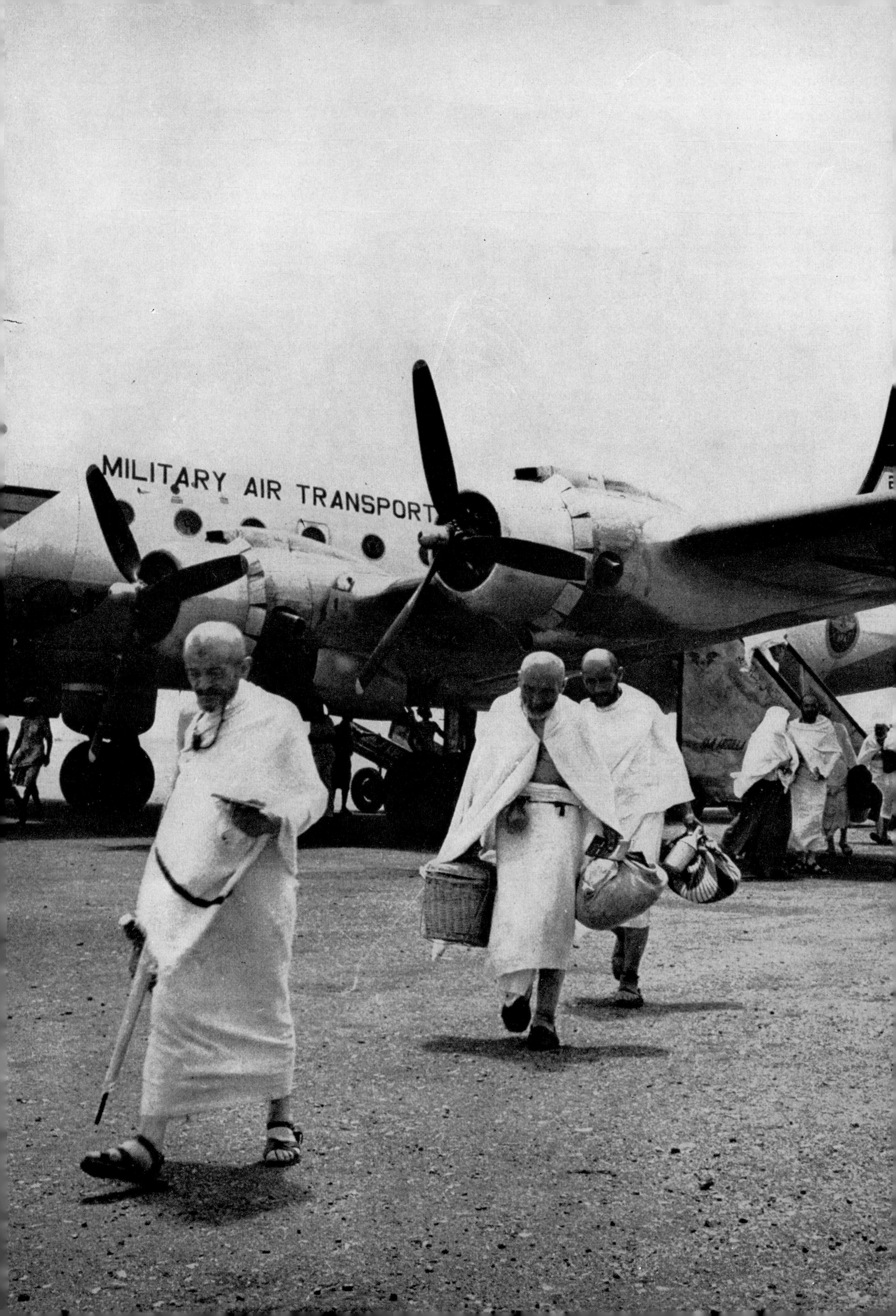
MILITARY AIR TRANSPORT

Chapter 14

THE MISSIONS

Global Airlift

THE strategic importance of airlift was amply demonstrated during World War II. Both the Army Air Forces and the Navy operated worldwide air transport systems that contributed greatly to the final triumph. But they duplicated each other's efforts in many areas, and the experience showed the desirability of a single military air transport system for the armed services. When this system came into being in 1948, it had as a firm foundation the existing Air Force and Navy air transport agencies.

The Forerunners

At the height of wartime transport operations in August 1945 the Air Transport Command (ATC) had 3,705 aircraft, 209,201 officers and enlisted men, and 104,667 civilians. At the same time, the smaller Naval Air Transport Service (NATS) had 431 aircraft and 26,134 officers and enlisted men. ATC's nine divisions—eight foreign and one domestic—operated on every continent.

Within a year of V-J Day, consolidations and inactivations had cut the number of transport divisions to three—the Pacific, Atlantic, and European. By December 1946, strength had dropped to 42,000 military and 17,000 civilian personnel. Demobilization at this rate threatened complete disruption of the ATC organization and involved a sharp, downward revision of its transport capacity. To bolster sagging operations and services, the command contracted with civil air carriers to supply airlift as well as civilian technicians for maintenance, communications, and weather services.

For greater efficiency and economy, a number of allied services were integrated with the Air Transport Command in March 1946. The Army Airways Communications System, AAF Weather Service, AAF Flight Service, AAF Rescue Service, AAF Aeronautical Chart Service, and the Office of Flying Safety were assigned to ATC and placed

An offbeat MATS mission. Four thousand Moslem pilgrims, stranded on way to Mecca, are rescued by American airlift.

at the same command level as the transport divisions.

General Arnold, meanwhile, had given serious thought to the peacetime role of the Air Transport Command. He believed that in peacetime ATC should provide routine flying services between the United States and overseas bases to ensure that in wartime AAF personnel could fly over any part of the earth's surface, regardless of weather, climate, or geography. In November 1945, Arnold envisioned an organization which, when combined with the reserve fleet of the civil airlines, would be large enough to airlift one Army corps to either Alaska or Iceland.

Arnold's thinking set the pattern for the future development of ATC, but lack of funds did not permit fulfillment of his program. No significant change in the command was to come until passage of the National Security Act of 1947 increased the pressure for unifying like functions of the military services. Both the President's Air Policy Commission and the Congressional Aviation Policy Board recommended that the Air Force and Navy air transport services be merged.

The Command Structure

The consolidation on June 1, 1948, of the Air Transport Command and the Naval Air Transport Service brought into being the Military Air Transport Service, known as MATS. A major USAF command, as well as a Department of Defense agency, MATS operated a global air transport system for the Department of Defense and other authorized government agencies. From its inception MATS also provided supporting air communications, weather, rescue, and flight services.

Established at the direction of Secretary of Defense Forrestal, the Military Air Transport Service set a pattern for unification. Early experience with MATS demonstrated beyond doubt that personnel and equipment from different services could function successfully within one command. Navy as well as Air Force officers and men manned the new organization.

The first commander was Maj. Gen. Laurence S. Kuter,

At 1951 MATS change of command. From left: General Twining; outgoing commander Kuter; his successor, Maj. Gen. Joseph Smith; his deputy, Maj. Gen. William Tunner.

from mid-November 1951 his successor, Lt. Gen. Joseph Smith. The basic mission remained the same until the late spring of 1950, when the emphasis shifted from providing peacetime airlift to meeting the D-day and, ultimately, the wartime airlift requirements of the Department of Defense. The organizational pattern of three air transport divisions—Continental, Atlantic, and Pacific—and four subordinate services—Airways and Air Communications, Air Weather, Air Rescue, and Flight—continued until April 1952, when the Air Photographic and Charting Service entered the MATS fold. The Airways and Air Communications Service absorbed the Flight Service in October 1956.

MATS felt the effect of world-shaking events before it was a month old. The Berlin Airlift began in late June 1948 and lasted until September 1949. By July 1950 the command had begun another great overseas operation—the Pacific Airlift. These operations were superb examples of strategic airlift: the mass movement by air of men and materiel to meet urgent military requirements in far corners of the world.

a topflight air strategist who had previous experience with ATC. The vice commander, Rear Adm. John P. Whitney, had been a director of the Naval Air Transport Service and a naval aviator since 1925. Subordinate to Kuter and Whitney were two deputy commanders—one for air transport and the other for the supporting services. Headquarters MATS, originally at Gravelly Point, Va., moved to Andrews AFB, Md., in November 1948.

The prime function of MATS was air transport of people, materiel, mail, strategic materials, and other cargo. Specifically excluded from its mission was responsibility for tactical air transport of airborne troops and their equipment and for the initial supply and resupply of units in forward combat areas. The supporting services were exclusively USAF organizations, the Navy participating only in the air transport operations.

Time brought little change in the top command, basic mission, and organizational pattern of MATS. By mid-1957 there had been only two commanders: General Kuter and

The MATS Global Circuit

General Kuter developed the concept of MATS as a new worldwide air-route command. In his words, such a command would be "capable of airlifting any required amount of personnel or cargo wherever needed in the national military interest in the shortest possible time, during peace or in war."

Fortunately, MATS had a strong foundation on which to build. A good nucleus of ATC routes and bases had survived the demobilization, and these were consolidated with NATS routes. Specifically, the Navy turned over to MATS its transcontinental, Caribbean, transatlantic, and transpacific routes—except for seaplane operations from the west coast to Hawaii. With the transfer went the four Navy R5D (C-54) squadrons, which had formerly operated these routes.

From the beginning, MATS routes circled the earth. The Atlantic Division operated across the Atlantic through

INTERNATIONAL ROUTES OF THE MILITARY AIR TRANSPORT SERVICE, DECEMBER 31, 1956

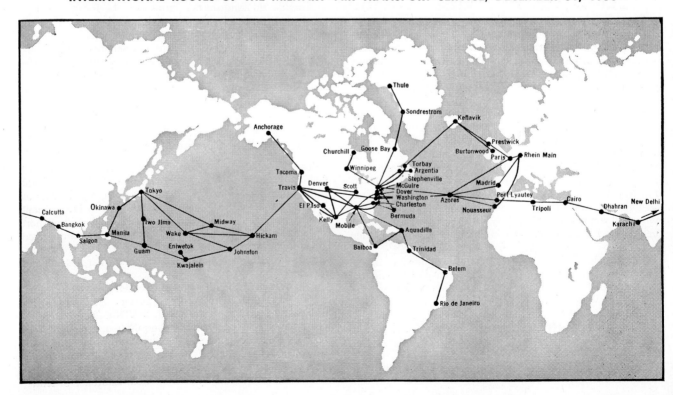

Europe and the Mediterranean as far east as Dhahran in Saudi Arabia. The Pacific Division served the island bases in the Pacific from Hawaii to Japan, Okinawa, and the Philippines, as well as the outposts on the Embassy run to Saigon, Bangkok, New Delhi, and Karachi. Its planes completed the MATS global circuit by connecting with the Atlantic Division transports at Dhahran. The Continental Division augmented the transocean operations of the other two divisions with flights in both the Atlantic and the Pacific. Its planes flew into the Caribbean, Panama, and South America, and its routes spanned the continental United States. By 1957, MATS had 115,000 miles of routes extending all over the world.

The MATS aerial ports of embarkation received, processed, and cleared aircraft, passengers, patients, cargo, and mail for movement by air between the continental United States and overseas areas. On the eastern seaboard, Westover AFB, Mass., was the first aerial port for the North Atlantic, European, Mediterranean, and Near East areas. In the spring of 1955 its air transport activities passed to two newly established MATS bases, McGuire in New Jersey and Dover in Delaware.

Headquarters for the Atlantic Division of MATS, McGuire AFB became one of the busiest military air terminals in the United States, handling passenger traffic across the Atlantic to the United Kingdom, Europe, North Africa, and the Middle East. The fast-growing Dover AFB specialized in air cargo shipments within the Atlantic area.

Washington National Airport, Washington, D. C., remained the aerial port for special-mission flights between the United States and overseas points. Here a crack outfit of veteran pilots and crewmen—the 1254th Air Transport Group—flew the VIPs, from the President on down.

In April 1954 a new aerial port at Charleston AFB, S. C., took over the Caribbean and South American passenger and cargo runs previously assigned to Brookley AFB at Mobile, Ala. Charleston also provided service to Bermuda, North Africa, and Saudi Arabia.

On the west coast, Travis AFB, Calif., remained the main gateway to the Pacific islands and the Far East. Home for some and departure point for others, it was the stateside terminal for the Pacific Airlift during the Korean War. MATS planes also flew into the USAF bases at Anchorage and Fairbanks, Alaska, from Great Falls AFB, Mont., until June 1953, when McChord AFB, Wash., became the aerial port for Alaska.

Overseas, MATS generally used bases under the control of other commands. Some, notably Dhahran Air Base in Saudi Arabia, operated primarily in the US national interest and only secondarily as MATS stations. Others, particularly in Bermuda, Libya, the Azores, and Hawaii, were predominantly route bases or major stops on the MATS global circuit. In some places MATS was in direct control, in others it shared control with a foreign government, and in still others it depended upon a private contractor.

Along the North Atlantic route to Europe the bases in Newfoundland and Labrador provided convenient stops and vital weather and communications facilities. Ernest Harmon AFB at Stephenville, Newfoundland, was a frequent stopover point, but landings could also be made at Argentia and St. John's in Newfoundland or at Goose Bay in Labrador.

A US air and naval base during World War II, Iceland remained an important way station on the long hop from North America to the British Isles. At Keflavik, an international airport, MATS and the Icelandic government used facilities jointly under an agreement signed in May 1951. Through Iceland, MATS moved a steady stream of passengers and cargo as well as jet planes on their way to the NATO countries.

Kindley AFB, in Bermuda, remained a main stop on the mid-Atlantic air route to Europe, Africa, and the Middle East. A refueling point for MATS aircraft, this base was also useful for weather reconnaissance and air search and rescue operations. USAFE's Wheelus Air Base in Libya served as a terminus and intransit base on the North African segment of the MATS route to the Middle East.

Busier than either Keflavik or Kindley, Lajes Field on the small island of Terceira in the Azores linked the Old World and the New. From this Portuguese island MATS routes reached out to France, Spain, and French Morocco.

About midway on the long stretch between Cairo and Karachi, the well-equipped airfield at Dhahran—in the Saudi Arabian desert only four miles from the Persian Gulf —linked the Atlantic and Pacific Divisions of MATS. The only American air base in the explosive Middle East, Dhahran served also as a training center for Saudi Arabians.

The first stop on the transpacific flight from Travis, Hickam AFB at Honolulu was the focal point for MATS operations in the vast Pacific Ocean area. From its runways, MATS aircraft flew to the Far East over three different island-hopping routes, via Midway, Wake, or Johnston Islands. In late November 1956 the MATS Pacific Division transferred its headquarters from Hickam to Parks AFB, Calif. Victim of the Pearl Harbor attack, Hickam AFB continued to play a key role in MATS operations.

At the Japanese end of the long Pacific flight was the Tokyo International Airport, the former Haneda Air Base. Under MATS command jurisdiction until October 1955, the Tokyo International Airport played an important part

A Navy contribution to global airlift. Navy designation, R6D; in the Air Force, C-118; commercially, the Douglas DC-6.

All C-124 Globemasters, like this one, previously assigned as TAC troop carriers, were transferred to MATS in 1957.

Air Rescue Service, part of MATS, made good use of the Sikorsky H-19 helicopter in rescue missions in Korea.

Boeing C-97 Stratofreighter, designed to carry heavy freight at high speeds, was a mainstay on Pacific hops.

in the evacuation of military patients by air from Korea to the United States.

The MATS Fleet

The Military Air Transport Service began operations with a miscellaneous assortment of airplanes, which by August 1, 1948, totaled 824. Of that number, the Air Force contributed 766, as against the fifty-eight aircraft received from the Navy. Mainly transports, the initial inventory included 234 Douglas C-54s and 239 Douglas C-47s. Products of World War II, these planes were largely outdated.

In recognition of the inadequacy of its aircraft, MATS immediately set up a replacement and modernization program, the results of which were reflected in the command's inventory by the end of 1956, when the MATS fleet numbered 1,435 aircraft. Of these, 610 were four-engine transports—C-54s, C-97s, C-118s (Navy R6D), C-121s (Navy R7V), and C-124s. All but the C-54s had rearward-facing seats, a safety innovation in air transport which MATS assisted in developing. But still most widely used in 1957 was the C-54 (Navy R5D) Skymaster, veteran work horse of the "Hump" operation of World War II, the Berlin Airlift, and the MATS trunk lines.

Among the nontransport aircraft in use in 1957 were the Grumman SA-16 amphibian aircraft and Sikorsky H-19 and Piasecki H-21 helicopters of the Air Rescue Service and the modified Boeing WB-50 of the Air Weather Service. All the MATS supporting services were in need of newer aircraft equipped to meet their special requirements.

Designed primarily for long-range air transport of bulky cargo at high speeds, the Boeing C-97A Stratofreighter was a mainstay in Pacific operations. Its built-in loading ramp facilitated the handling of howitzers, trucks, ambulances, and other mobile equipment. A troop carrier version, the C-97C, carried 130 troops or seventy-nine litter patients and four attendants.

The Douglas C-118, a passenger plane, operated in both the Atlantic and Pacific. A long-range, high-speed transport, the Lockheed C-121 Constellation lifted 40,000 pounds of cargo or forty-four passengers. The huge Douglas C-124 Globemaster II could carry as much as 74,000 pounds. Equipped with clamshell doors and its own roll-on, roll-off loading ramp, the C-124 easily accommodated a truck, a light tank, a disassembled H-19 helicopter, or a Matador missile.

Since its aircraft at best could furnish only the nucleus for an expanded wartime operation, MATS planned to call on the Civil Reserve Air Fleet (CRAF) as needed. The CRAF program involved the modification of designated aircraft from the civil airlines to enable a quick change-over to war service. In 1957 the Civil Reserve Air Fleet consisted of more than 300 four-engine transports belonging to twenty-three airlines. Most of these already had the standby wiring and brackets to accommodate the communications and navigation equipment required for long-range transocean operation.

The MATS Supporting Services

Aircraft alone do not make a global airlift system. Without a host of supporting services, any such system would soon fall apart and disappear. Accordingly, MATS paid special attention to the operation of its supporting services.

Airways and Air Communications Service

The Airways and Air Communications Service (AACS) provided airway communications facilities, navigational aids, and flight services for the Air Force. AACS utilized highly technical facilities and equipment, such as direction finders, radio ranges, ground-controlled-approach and in-

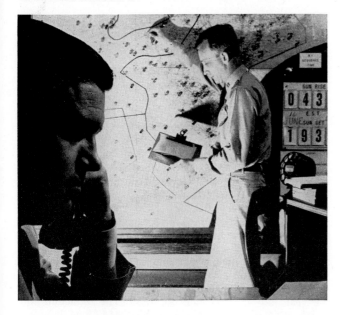

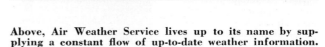

Above, Air Weather Service lives up to its name by supplying a constant flow of up-to-date weather information.

Officers of the Airways and Air Communications Service select alternate landing fields for use in foul weather.

strument-landing systems, radio and radar beacons, air-to-ground and point-to-point radio, message centers, and cryptocenters.

Global in concept and operations, AACS had stations at over 300 points throughout the world, ranging from Greenland to the Caribbean and from Germany to Japan. At the close of 1956, more than fifty percent of its 28,000 officers and men were serving outside the continental limits of the United States.

AACS had responsibility for the installation, operation, and maintenance of the USAF Strategic Communications System (STRATCOM), a worldwide, long-range, point-to-point, and ground-to-air communications system for the control of air operations. By furnishing round-the-clock support along its global communications chain, AACS assisted the Air Force in flying under all weather conditions anywhere in the world.

The work of the Flight Service remained unchanged when it came under AACS in October 1956. The only MATS activity confined to the continental United States, the Flight Service, through its seven centers, cleared all military flights from airfields where no other clearing authority was available. It also assisted aircraft lost or in distress, and it notified the Air Defense Command coordination centers of the movements of military aircraft. As General Arnold once put it: "AACS has taken the aloneness out of flying and with it whatever dread there might otherwise be of air routes over lonely and dangerous areas . . ."

Air Weather Service

The Air Weather Service (AWS) furnished vital weather information for the US Air Force and US Army. In 1957 it operated approximately 300 weather stations, twenty-four mobile weather teams, and seven aerial reconnaissance squadrons throughout the world. After May 1952, AWS furnished each major USAF command a specialized weather service to meet individual needs.

AWS gathered weather data from the North Pole to the tropics. Scheduled weather reconnaissance flights brought reports from the Arctic and from the North Atlantic and Pacific oceans, covering thousands of miles of remote ocean and land areas beyond the range of ground stations. AWS provided both operational and planning forecasts for any air route terminal or geographic location.

AWS planes regularly tracked hurricanes and typhoons in the Atlantic and Pacific areas. In August 1955, a WB-29 flying out of Bermuda made the first recorded night pene-

tration of Hurricane Connie. At Kansas City, Mo., the AWS Severe Weather Warning Center, working side by side with the US Weather Bureau, issued advisory forecasts for areas of the United States that could expect tornadoes, severe thunderstorms, or winds above fifty knots.

Air Rescue Service

The Air Rescue Service (ARS), with headquarters at Orlando AFB, Fla., carried out worldwide search and rescue operations over both land and water. Wherever MATS and other military or civil aircraft flew and whenever air disaster occurred, ARS was on the alert to save lives and to aid the injured.

Easily the most spectacular member of the MATS family, ARS had trained personnel and specialized equipment for immediate action in any climate or terrain. It rushed men to crash sites and assisted the survivors by the fastest possible means—by parachute drop of rescue teams, supply, and equipment from SC-47 and SC-54 aircraft; by helicopter and triphibian planes; or by jeeps, caterpillar-tread weasels, and trucks. Able to give emergency medical aid and skilled in the techniques of survival in arctic, jungle, mountain, or desert areas, the ARS personnel took over until the rescue operations were completed.

The record of ARS is replete with heroic deeds. One example will suffice. In July 1952, a British transport plane ditched in the Mediterranean and sent out distress calls. From Wheelus Field, in Libya, Capt. Kendrick U. Reeves took off in an SA-16 in search of the plane, sighted it, and reported to his base. Two British planes already overhead were not equipped for rescue operations. With the approval of his entire crew, Reeves decided to land, even though the sea was too choppy for a takeoff. The landing was made and the thirty-two survivors were brought aboard, wrapped in blankets, and given hot food and drink. A British destroyer soon picked up the rescued, but the rescuers stayed with their aircraft. Three days later the battered SA-16 was taxied and towed into port.

Despite its many mercy missions, ARS remained primarily a military force with a wartime mission of retrieving downed combat aircrews. But its humanitarian aspect was a satisfying byproduct of its peacetime activities.

Air Photographic and Charting Service

The newest of the MATS services, the Air Photographic and Charting Service (APCS) was responsible for the research, production, reproduction, worldwide distribution, and storage of aeronautical charts. It also handled air target

Above, Convair C-131A Samaritan aeromedical transport assigned to MATS. Inset shows how interior can be arranged to handle litter or ambulatory patients, or any combination.

materials and provided related cartographic services. One of its most important jobs was to perform aerial mapping photography and aerial electronic geodetic surveys for the Department of Defense. Under APCS the Air Force concentrated all of its still and motion picture production.

APCS maintained a large Aeronautical Chart and Information Center at St. Louis, Mo., staffed mostly by skilled civilians. During the year ending June 30, 1956, APCS distributed 100,000,000 copies of charts and publications.

MATS Operations

In practice, MATS operated as a transocean, intertheater carrier. The Joint Military Transportation Committee, an agency of the Joint Chiefs of Staff, determined over-all airlift requirements and allocated available airlift. Within his allocation, each user of MATS facilities decided what he wanted to move and determined the priority of shipment for each passenger and each item. MATS processed all passengers and cargo and obtained all the necessary air transportation from its own resources or by purchase from commercial operators.

In addition to furnishing technical support services for the Air Force, MATS had to be ready to airlift men and materiel for the SAC striking force should war come. The day-to-day flights of the transports were regarded as training for this all-important D-day mission—the real reason for the existence of MATS. General Smith believed that MATS had to "handle real passengers and real cargoes, in order to develop the techniques and procedures that will be effective in emergencies."

In a typical peacetime deployment of a SAC wing to the United Kingdom, for instance, MATS planes first flew a MATS control team into a SAC home base. After loading, the transports proceeded through an aerial port and on over the North Atlantic. In the United Kingdom, the same aircraft might pick up a SAC wing for rotation to the United States. Conducted under simulated wartime conditions, these movements gave valuable experience to both SAC and MATS. Of course, they required that MATS maintain considerable airlift above that needed for normal transport operations.

Throughout 1956, during every hour of the day, MATS airlifted about 100 passengers and patients and nearly twenty tons of cargo. In that banner year its planes moved approximately 850,000 patients and passengers and about 170,000 tons of cargo and mail. In 1956, MATS set the unprecedented record of one transocean flight every twenty-three minutes.

The regular transports brought back military patients

from overseas, usually to Travis AFB, Calif., or McGuire AFB, N.J. Within the United States, aeromedical evacuation squadrons picked up patients for delivery to military hospitals. Under this system, any patient wherever stationed could be certain of getting the best possible treatment and hospital care within a matter of hours. Specially equipped aircraft and trained medical attendants contributed to patient comfort and safety.

Because aircraft could do the job more quickly and effectively than any other type of transport, air evacuation became the accepted practice for all military patients. Through December 1953, 66,536 Korean War patients returned by air to the United States. To handle this traffic, the Air Force converted C-54, C-74, and C-97 aircraft into litter-carrying planes. On April 1, 1954, MATS took over its first Convair C-131A Samaritan, specially designed for domestic aeromedical evacuation.

Following the Korean War years, medical air evacuation assumed a more normal pattern. At the peak, during the year July 1, 1950-June 30, 1951, the patient movements worldwide totaled 131,639, as compared with 53,739 for the year July 1, 1955-June 30, 1956. The reduction and stabilization of the workload enabled MATS to improve its handling of medical evacuees.

MATS met airlift emergencies as they arose, whether in the United States, Germany, or Korea. During the twenty-four-day Operation Haylift ending in February 1949, MATS C-47 and C-82 aircraft dropped almost 1,900 tons of feed, rations, medical supplies, heaters, coal, and oil to isolated ranches in Nevada and Utah. With all surface transportation snowbound, the sky afforded the only access to this area, and MATS was ready with planes and crews.

In late August 1952, more than 3,700 Moslems, eager to make the religious pilgrimage to the holy city of Mecca, in Saudi Arabia, were stranded in Beirut, Lebanon, because of insufficient commercial transport. MATS rolled out a modern Magic Carpet—as the operation was naturally called—and provided immediate airlift to Mecca. And in the following February, when floods brought disaster to Holland, MATS aircraft took part in Operation Humanity, dropping food and other supplies for the stricken people and sandbags to reinforce the sagging dikes.

In November 1956, MATS airlifted 1,306 troops and 110 tons of equipment from Colombia and India to the United Nations staging area at Naples, Italy, for occupation duty in the Suez Canal area. On December 11, MATS began Operation Safe Haven—the movement of Hungarian refugees from Munich, Germany, to McGuire AFB, N. J. By April 27, 1957, MATS and its civil contract carriers had brought more than 13,000 Hungarians to the United States.

The original mission called for MATS to ferry aircraft both within the United States and outside. Less than sixty days after its creation, the command began ferrying transports used in the Berlin Airlift to and from reconditioning plants in the United States.

Completion of this emergency assignment brought only a temporary respite in overseas ferry operations. When the cold war intensified after Korea, it became necessary to deliver many more aircraft to USAF bases overseas and to the air forces of allied and friendly nations. Via the familiar North Atlantic ferry route of World War II, where ice, wind, and weather were frequent foes, MATS crews delivered T-33, F-84F, F-86, and F-100 jet aircraft to Europe. At the same time, domestic ferrying continued. Consisting mostly of Air National Guard and Air Force Reserve aircraft, the deliveries within the United States always outnumbered those to foreign destinations.

MATS achieved an outstanding safety record. Although

In Operation Haylift in 1949, MATS aircraft dropped tons of feed to starving cattle stranded in snow.

In 1956 Hungarian refugee children in GI chow line had good reason to be grateful to MATS.

its planes flew in all sorts of weather, the accident rate continued to decline, reaching an all-time low of 5.12 per 100,000 flying hours in 1956. This record prompted a leading underwriter to offer worldwide accident insurance protection to MATS crew members on scheduled passenger or cargo flights, at the same rates available to commercial airline pilots. Military and civilian passengers could also obtain air travel insurance at regular commercial airline rates on MATS scheduled flights.

MATS and the Korean War

Out of the gray morning mists on June 25, 1950, four North Korean fighter planes swooped down on Kimpo Airfield near Seoul, strafing a MATS C-54 transport about to take off on a scheduled flight to Tokyo. The attackers disappeared within minutes, leaving behind the smoldering wreckage of the first American plane lost in the Korean conflict.

MATS and its supporting services reacted quickly to the emergency. The Atlantic and Continental Divisions immediately diverted forty four-engine aircraft—all they could spare—to the Pacific Division for the support of the Korean operation. Thus began the Pacific Airlift, the longest aerial supply line in history. Meanwhile, the Air Force called upon the commercial airlines for assistance. The first contract carrier, a DC-4 already equipped for the long Pacific haul, left for Tokyo on July 3. By late August 1950, MATS had sixty-six four-engine transports under charter from seventeen airlines. In addition, Canada and Belgium contributed aircraft. Headquarters USAF also assigned TAC's 61st and 62d Troop Carrier Groups with approximately seventy-five C-54s to the airlift. Until mid-November 1950, when its job was completed, the provisional airlift task force at Travis AFB expedited the MATS airlift to Japan.

During the first three months of the conflict the number of four-engine transports operating in the Pacific Airlift increased from about sixty to 250, and aircraft utilization climbed from 2.5 hours to almost six hours per aircraft per day. Cargo delivered to Japan rose from approximately 2½ tons daily before the airlift to an average of 106 tons daily.

Fortunately, MATS could use the already established transpacific routes fanning out from Hawaii to Japan as well as the shorter but more hazardous great-circle route via Alaska and the Aleutians. The same aircraft that flew critical cargo to Japan brought back the sick and wounded from Korea to the United States.

Beginning in 1951 the Korean airlift requirements eased to the extent that both MATS and commercial aircraft could resume their regular runs. In March 1952, approximately sixty MATS, sixty commercial, and fifteen United Nations transports were participating in the Pacific Airlift. Despite diminished demands, during the year July 1, 1951-June 30, 1952, the Pacific Division of MATS transported 16,766 tons of cargo and mail and 53,904 passengers to Japan, and returned 17,968 medical evacuees to the United States. When the war ended, MATS was still using civil contract carriers to meet its commitments in Korea and elsewhere.

In addition to air transport, MATS furnished vital air communications, weather, and rescue services in Korea. Following the outbreak of hostilities, the Airways and Air Communications Service rushed highly skilled personnel and specialized communications equipment to the theater. AACS got its first Korean combat experience in August 1950, during the evacuation of the airfield at Pohang. One unit had to be moved over twelve miles of sniper-infested highway to the seaport where it was loaded onto a waiting ship. The forty-five men in the detachment escaped without injury, although they spent the last two nights in foxholes helping to defend the perimeter of the doomed airfield.

The Air Weather Service moved quickly into war-torn Korea, establishing its first weather station at Taegu on June 27, 1950. Small detachments stationed at the principal Korean airfields and two-man weather-observation teams attached to US Eighth Army units supplied direct, on-the-spot weather data for all United Nations forces. Portable weather stations proved more adaptable in Korea than mobile ones, since the former could be airlifted while the latter were difficult to move over the poor roads. Regularly scheduled, daily reconnaissance flights furnished additional weather coverage, as did also the aerial weather observers placed aboard bombers and reconnaissance aircraft operating over North Korea.

The 3d Air Rescue Squadron became one of the most honored and decorated units of the Korean War. Its Sikorsky H-5 helicopters proved invaluable in rescuing airmen and wounded ground troops. In mid-February 1951, H-5 pilots braved a forty-knot wind and a blinding snowstorm to evacuate fifty-two wounded men, after delivering blankets, blood plasma, and medical supplies to elements of the US 2d Division surrounded at Chinyong. During March 1951, helicopters saved six out of seven pilots forced down behind enemy lines, one pickup taking place twenty minutes after the pilot was shot down and another involving hazardous night flying. Many pilots, including jet ace Capt. Joseph McConnell, lived to fly and fight again because of the Air Rescue Service.

Although the helicopters stole the show, the Grumman SA-16 amphibians performed equally dramatic and hazardous rescues of UN personnel from the coastal waters and rivers of Korea. On the night of June 11, 1951, an SA-16 pilot landed in the shallow, debris-filled Taedong River to rescue an F-51 pilot, while the downed pilot's squadron mates beat off heavy enemy fire and provided some illumination with their landing lights. On September 13, 1951, a jet pilot whose engine failed at 27,000 feet notified a patroling SA-16 and indicated where he would bail out. When he landed, the rescue plane was already there, and in three minutes he was safe on board.

At the end of hostilities on July 27, 1953, the 3d Air Rescue Squadron was credited with a total of 9,680 rescues within the combat area. Of this number, 996 were UN personnel saved from behind enemy lines.

Chapter 15

THE   MEN

The Leaders

DURING its first ten years the Air Force was fortunate in the quality of its top leadership. The men who held the posts of civilian Secretary and military Chief of Staff generally worked together closely and effectively. Mutual respect and understanding resulted in a mature and constructive approach to problems. Air Force leadership inspired trust and confidence, not only in the Air Force but in the nation as a whole.

Stuart Symington

When Stuart Symington took the oath of office as the first Secretary of the Air Force on September 18, 1947, it marked the official beginning of the Department of the Air Force. President Truman chose for this important position a fellow-Missourian who had been Assistant Secretary of War for Air since January 1946. Symington had headed a company that built thousands of power-driven turrets for American bombers during World War II.

Symington's greatest contribution to the Air Force was his single-minded—some said fanatical—devotion to the concept of the seventy-group Air Force, which he deemed "the irreducible minimum" needed to maintain national safety. In 1947 and 1948 he was one of the first public figures to call attention to the necessity of confronting the Communist nations with the threat of overwhelming retaliation against aggression.

The Secretary's insistence upon seventy groups found increasing favor in Congress but sometimes left him in disagreement with his superiors, President Truman and Secretary of Defense Forrestal. This was the era of the "balanced-forces" concept and rigid budgetary ceilings. Symington insisted that "balance" did not mean that the Army, Navy,

and Air Force should be maintained at the same size, man for man, or dollar for dollar.

During the B-36 controversy with the Navy in 1949, Symington used the opportunity to give wider dissemination to Air Force ideas and doctrines. He completely vindicated USAF procurement of the B-36 and, in the process, convinced both the public and Congress that the Air Force position on major issues of national security was a valid one.

Another of Symington's valuable contributions was the promotion of management and cost-control concepts within the Air Force. He established the comptroller organization and fostered its growth. Faced with the task of rebuilding the Air Force with limited funds after its frenzied demobilization, he insisted on the creation and use of management tools that would bring about more effective and economical Air Force operations. He called his plan "Management Control Through Cost Control."

Symington resigned as Secretary of the Air Force on April 24, 1950, to become chairman of the National Security Resources Board. Subsequently, he served as head of the Reconstruction Finance Corporation. In 1952 he was elected US Senator from Missouri. In the Senate, he devoted much of his time and attention to the problems and needs of the Air Force.

General Carl Spaatz

Carl Spaatz became the first Chief of Staff of the United States Air Force on September 26, 1947—thirty-three years after his graduation from West Point and almost thirty-two years after he learned to fly at the Signal Corps Aviation School at San Diego, Calif. The new honor followed nineteen months as commanding general of the Army Air Forces.

The foremost American combat air commander of World War II, Spaatz had had the unique experience of commanding the American strategic air assaults on both Germany and Japan. After the victory in Europe, Spaatz moved

Three great air leaders in order of command succession: Gen. Arnold, the AAF's World War II chief; Gen. Spaatz, first Chief of Staff, USAF; Gen. Vandenberg, his successor.

First Chief of Staff with the first Secretary of the Air Force: Gen. Carl Spaatz, left, and Stuart Symington.

to the Pacific in time to guide the final B-29 campaign against Japan, including the atomic bomb-drops on Hiroshima and Nagasaki. He was also present at all three signings of unconditional surrender by the enemy—at Reims, Berlin, and Tokyo.

His combat experiences convinced Spaatz that the Air Force could accomplish its mission only if it maintained a force in being of adequate size and proper composition, strategically deployed and in a high and constant state of readiness. He believed that the first priority should be given to a strong strategic air force, but he also spoke out for adequate tactical cooperation among air, ground, and sea forces. To keep a powerful Air Force in being, Spaatz wanted a strong Air National Guard and Air Force Reserve to provide trained replacements and units in time of emergency or war. To support this Air Force in being, Spaatz urged a well-balanced, forward-looking program of research and technical development, an alert, readily expandable aeronautical industry, and an informed and enlightened public opinion.

The years immediately following World War II proved frustrating for Spaatz because he found it so difficult to put his ideas into practice. Beset by the problems growing out of rapid demobilization, the Air Force could not maintain an effective striking force. The United States relied on the atomic bomb for its military security, but the effectiveness of the bomb was severely limited by the lack of combat-ready units in the Air Force.

To meet the growing threat of aggression, Spaatz worked hard to secure approval for the seventy-group Air Force. He contended that this was the minimum for warding off any attack and at the same time striking a decisive retaliatory blow. By the spring of 1948 the Air Force reached the fifty-five-group phase of the projected seventy-group program. But the postwar era of fiscal retrenchment had not yet ended, and the Air Force reduced its program to fifty-five groups.

The administrative duties of Chief of Staff weighed heavily on Spaatz. They proved especially irksome after

his satisfying experience as a wartime combat commander. In April 1948, he retired. In retirement, he continued to impress on the American public the need for keeping the Air Force strong at all times, because in a future war there would no longer be an extended period of mobilization.

General Hoyt S. Vandenberg

Hoyt S. Vandenberg succeeded Spaatz as Chief of Staff on April 30, 1948, and held that position for more than five years—until his retirement on June 30, 1953. His death on April 2, 1954, at the age of fifty-five, ended a long and brilliant military career.

After graduating from West Point in 1923, Vandenberg spent his entire military life in the Army air arm that grew into the US Air Force. During World War II his most important assignment was as commander of the Ninth Air Force in Europe in 1944-45. After the war he served successively as Director of Central Intelligence and Vice Chief of Staff of the Air Force, until he became Chief of Staff.

Vandenberg undertook to clarify in the minds of the public and of Congress the position of the Air Force in the defense of the United States, as outlined by the Joint Chiefs of Staff at the Key West and Newport conferences in 1948. The Air Force would meet aggression against the United States by launching immediately a powerful, strategic air offensive against the basic sources of an enemy's warmaking capacity. At the same time, it would defend the United States and our essential bases against attack by air. It would also provide tactical support of the Army and Navy in exploitation of the opportunity presented through successful prosecution of the first two tasks.

Vandenberg's greatest problem, perhaps, was to reconcile the Air Force needs of the present and future with each other as well as with the over-all needs of the nation as determined by Congress. This was further complicated when the President refused in 1949 to release funds voted by Congress to expand the Air Force. Vandenberg hoped desperately for a degree of permanency in Air Force goals that would make it possible to reduce to a minimum the uncertainty and costly changes. But international events, technological progress, and economic and political considerations combined to produce frequent changes.

Vandenberg felt strongly that limiting Air Force funds for research and development, procurement, and manpower had resulted in a "shoestring" air force with which to fight the Korean War. For that reason, he advised against bombing across the Yalu River in 1951. He argued that the Air Force in being at the time could "peck at the periphery" of the Communist world by wiping out the sources of Communist power in China or it could destroy the industrial centers of the Soviet Union. But it could not do both. If the peripheral concept were followed, the losses by attrition would be so great that the Air Force would not be able to defend other areas of the world. Accordingly, in 1951, Vandenberg asked for an air force that would be large enough to handle most contingencies. He sought and obtained official adoption of a 143-wing program for the Air Force. In the spring of 1953, shortly before he retired, he made a valiant but unsuccessful effort to convince Congress that the 143-wing program should not be cut back.

Thomas K. Finletter

Thomas K. Finletter became the second Secretary of the Air Force on April 24, 1950. After service in the Army Field Artillery during World War I, he had practiced law until 1941. From 1941 until 1944 he was a special assistant to the Secretary of State, and in 1945 he was a consultant to the American delegation to the United Nations Conference on International Organization at San Francisco.

Gen. Hoyt S. Vandenberg succeeded Spaatz in 1948, served as Chief of Staff for more than five years, died in 1954.

Thomas K. Finletter, second AF Secretary, guided the Department of the Air Force through most of the Korean War.

As chairman of the President's Air Policy Commission in 1947, he had a major part in preparing its report—*Survival in the Air Age*—which recommended a seventy-group Air Force.

An outspoken advocate of airpower, Finletter saw "air-atomic power" (his favorite phrase) in the mid-twentieth century as playing the role of world policeman similar to that played by the British Navy in the nineteenth century. Because of his interest in warfare and its larger implications, Finletter reviewed and discussed strategic planning with Air Force generals, especially General LeMay, SAC's commander. He wanted to know and understand the fundamental reasons for the operational concepts on which requirements were based. His penetrating analysis of strategic thinking led him to place major emphasis on the Strategic Air Command and its mission.

From the beginning Finletter recognized that to be effective, SAC needed overseas bases. He devoted a great deal of his energies to securing agreements with NATO countries for construction of bases for SAC and other USAF commands. Finletter also helped pave the way for the Spanish base negotiations.

When the Department of Defense decided on the 143-wing program in October 1951, it forced a change in the traditional practice of distributing military funds equally among the three services. The change was based on the principle of allocating money in accordance with the priorities assigned to the missions of the services. Finletter had labored hard for this principle. He called the change "a milestone in the history of the Air Force, . . . a recognition of the key position in military operations today of land-based airpower."

When the Air Force was accused of having neglected its tactical air arm during the Korean War, Finletter pointed out that FEAF was handicapped by two major restrictions: first, it could not use atomic weapons; and second, it could not bomb beyond the Yalu River boundary between North Korea and China, nor could it pursue enemy planes beyond that river line. And Finletter did not let others forget the

crucial fact that the Korean "police action" did not explode into World War III principally because of SAC, the deterrent ace-in-the-hole.

When Finletter left office with the change of administration in January 1953, it was with the knowledge that he had been one of the principal architects of the Air Force of the future.

Harold E. Talbott

Harold E. Talbott took office as Secretary of the Air Force on February 4, 1953. After duty as a major in the Air Service during World War I, Talbott had extensive experience in the aircraft and automobile industries in the years between wars. For a period during World War II he directed aircraft production under the War Production Board.

During Talbott's two and a half years in office the major concern of the Air Force shifted from problems of materiel, installations, and research and development to problems of money and personnel. It fell to Talbott and Twining to defend and carry forward the large Air Force expansion for which Finletter and Vandenberg had obtained agreement.

With the end of the Korean War, the bottom began to drop out of the skilled manpower pool of the Air Force. Reenlistment rates dropped from fifty-five percent to twenty-four percent by 1954. For certain critical Air Force skills the first-term reenlistment rate dropped to as low as ten percent. Talbott appreciated the full significance of the problem. He pointed out that it cost $14,000 to train an airman in a basic job and $75,000 to train an electronic expert who, at the earliest opportunity, would leave to take a higher-paid job in private industry.

Talbott traveled widely to get the story from the airmen and to tell the public—and Congress—what should be done about the situation. He listened to Air Force personnel of all ranks and grades, and to their wives and families. With a vast acquaintance in the business and pro-

Harold E. Talbott was the airman's friend. Here he swears in M/Sgt. Horst Tittel as the latter begins his 47th year.

Donald A. Quarles as Secretary and Gen. Nathan F. Twining as Chief of Staff were a close and effective team.

fessional worlds, he could persuade many people and organizations to help the Air Force improve conditions. He repeatedly called attention to the decline in the so-called "fringe benefits"—medical care, dependent housing, and recreational facilities—which service personnel had traditionally received. Talbott worked hard for passage of the Career Incentive Act in 1955.

Talbott personally supervised planning for the establishment of the Air Force Academy. He worked to get from Congress the necessary legislation as well as the money to build it. As one of his last major acts of public office, and one that gave him the greatest satisfaction, Talbott dedicated the Air Force Academy on July 11, 1955. It was the culmination of a generation-old Air Force dream.

Talbott resigned on August 1, 1955. He died on March 2, 1957, at the age of sixty-eight.

General Nathan F. Twining

Nathan Farragut Twining, as his middle name indicates, was probably intended for a naval career, in keeping with family tradition. But the future Air Force Chief of Staff started out in the Oregon National Guard, was graduated from the US Military Academy as an infantry officer in 1918, and got into flying nearly five years later.

During World War II, he had the distinction of commanding three combat air forces—the Thirteenth, Fifteenth, and Twentieth. His more than three years of wartime experience in both tactical and strategic air operations in Europe and the Pacific were probably more extensive than that of any other air commander. After the war he successively commanded the Air Materiel Command and the Alaskan Command. He became Vice Chief of Staff on October 10, 1950, and succeeded General Vandenberg as Chief of Staff on June 30, 1953.

Twining took office at a critical moment in the history of the Air Force. At the direction of the President, the Joint Chiefs of Staff were engaged in a "new look" at the military services in order to reassess expansion programs. Twining was credited with playing a delicate but important part in the adoption of the 137-wing program by the JCS in the fall of 1953. This replaced a 120-wing program, successor for a brief time during 1953 to the 143-wing program.

Twining insisted that war machines were only an extension of man's powers. "Readiness" could be reached only when the men who manned the aircraft and other Air Force weapons were adequately trained. Twining said,

"We speak continually of the importance of scientific and technological breakthroughs. I know of no single breakthrough that I would trade for the assurance that the USAF would get—and be able to keep—the skilled men it needs in the years ahead."

Twining believed that the Soviet Union, long ahead of the United States in quantity production of aircraft, had also gone ahead in the speed with which it developed new types. One reason was that Russian schools graduated more than 50,000 engineers in 1954 while American universities graduated only 20,000, fewer than half the number needed by the nation's industrial establishment and the government. Twining warned: "Years ago it was said that the battle of Waterloo was won on the playing fields of Eton. Let us hope it can never be said that the battle for the Free World was lost in the classrooms of American high schools and colleges."

At the invitation of the Russian government and the direction of the President, Twining visited the Soviet Union in June 1956. The visit convinced him that Russian aeronautical progress not only justified American emphasis on research and development but warranted a still greater effort.

Months before Twining completed his tour of office on June 30, 1957, President Eisenhower announced his appointment as Chairman of the Joint Chiefs of Staff, effective August 15, 1957. It was a fitting climax to a long and successful career.

Donald A. Quarles

Donald A. Quarles was the first Secretary of the Air Force with a background in engineering and science. He came to the position on August 15, 1955, after almost two years as Assistant Secretary of Defense for Research and Development.

After serving as a captain in the Army Field Artillery during World War I, Quarles spent a long and fruitful career with Bell Telephone Laboratories and the Western Electric Company. Later, he was president of the Sandia Corporation, a main laboratory operating under contract with the Atomic Energy Commission. As Assistant Secretary of Defense, Quarles served on the National Advisory Committee for Aeronautics and headed a group that made a detailed study of the guided missile program for the three services.

Quarles brought to his job in the Air Force both a theoretical and a practical knowledge of nuclear power and missiles. In November 1955 the President directed that the ballistic missile programs receive the highest national priority. Quarles' knowledge proved of particular value a year later when the Secretary of Defense delegated to the Air Force operational control of all land-based missiles with a range of more than 200 miles.

Quarles followed closely the construction of the important DEW Line above the Arctic Circle. He gave encouragement and technical advice in the construction of the vast Semi-Automatic Ground Environment (SAGE) facilities being built under Air Force auspices, a role for which he was eminently qualified.

By the end of 1956 the Air Force counted its assets at $70 billion. In supervising the biggest business in the United States, Quarles demonstrated superior managerial ability. His interests were broad, he kept informed on all aspects of Air Force problems, and he had the happy faculty of putting his fingers on the key problems.

Hopefully, Quarles suggested that we might have already arrived at a point in international arms competition where atomic weapons themselves would impose a peace upon mankind. He said:

"As long as both sides have these terrible weapons and the means of delivering them, there is no way for one side to initiate total war without disaster to itself. No matter which side decided to start total war, destruction would be so tremendous and so general that no one could dream of victory."

On May 1, 1957, Quarles left the Air Force to become Deputy Secretary of Defense.

James H. Douglas, Jr.

James H. Douglas, Jr., became Secretary of the Air Force on May 1, 1957, after more than four years as Under Secretary. He was an Army lieutenant in World War I while still in his teens. Following his graduation from Harvard Law School in 1924, Douglas practiced law and engaged in investment banking. In 1932–33 he served as Assistant Secretary of the Treasury. On duty with the Army Air Forces as a colonel in World War II, he held the posts of deputy chief of staff and chief of staff of the Air Transport Command. After World War II he returned to the practice of law until his appointment in 1953 as Under Secretary.

His extensive knowledge and experience made Douglas the logical man to ride close herd on the Military Air Transport Service. This was an important task, for the Air Force was responsible for the operation of MATS—a vital link in the nation's military system. In addition to super-

vising MATS affairs, Douglas was responsible for another major Air Force activity—installations. He also served as chairman of the Requirements Review Board, an informal but influential agency at the Secretariat level that reviewed all USAF requirements. As Under Secretary, he also dealt with USAF intelligence activities.

Past experience enabled Douglas to establish a close personal relationship between the military and civilian leaders of the Air Force. As Under Secretary, he was kept informed of the work of the Joint Chiefs of Staff so that he understood both the military and civilian approaches to problems. Because of this broad knowledge and a faculty for reconciling different points of view, Douglas was well qualified for the Secretary's job.

Douglas became Secretary at a time when the Air Force stood on the threshold of a major transition from piloted aircraft to guided missiles. Shortly after he took office, General White became Chief of Staff, ensuring continuation of a strong working relationship that had lasted for four years.

General Thomas D. White

Thomas D. White completed thirty-seven years of military service on July 1, 1957, the day he became the fourth Chief of Staff of the US Air Force. After graduation from West Point in 1920, before his nineteenth birthday, he served in the infantry until he entered the primary flying school at Brooks Field, Tex., in 1924.

From 1927 to 1942, White spent much of his time as a military attaché—in China, the Soviet Union, Italy, Greece, and Brazil. He learned to speak Chinese, Italian, Portuguese, Russian, and Spanish fluently.

During World War II, White was Assistant Chief of Air Staff, Intelligence, at Headquarters AAF and later commanding general of the Seventh Air Force on Okinawa. After further duty in the Pacific following the war, he served in responsible staff positions in Washington until July 1951, when he became the Deputy Chief of Staff, Operations. From this key office in the Air Staff, White moved up to become Vice Chief of Staff on June 30, 1953.

As Vice Chief, White became an outspoken advocate of strategic airpower. He insisted that airpower could bring greater force to bear on an enemy with less danger to fewer men than could any other military force available to the United States. Yet he did not lose sight of the importance of teamwork among the three services. White declared that airpower was not *the* answer to our security problem, but rather "one of many vital components which must be employed in a coordinated fashion to bring us closer to our goal of national security and in the process protect our basic freedoms."

He disclaimed for the Air Force any desire for bureaucratic expansion. "The day of the empire builder is long past," he said. "We are looking for men who can do more with less." But to do a bigger job with fewer people, the Air Force needed topnotch men. "Our number one problem in the Air Force," he maintained, "is holding on to our good people." But aware that national survival might well depend on having an adequate air force, White insisted that combat effectiveness come before economies within the Air Force. "Every saving, every management method must be measured against its effect on our fighting ability," he said.

White stated clearly and tersely the basic American approach to national security in the postwar era:

"There is a far better way to protect our homes and our people than to fight and win a great war. The better way . . . is to be so obviously superior in our ability to carry the war to an enemy that he will not take the risk of starting one."

Latest to take over the two top US Air Force posts: Secretary James H. Douglas and Gen. Thomas D. White.

Chapter 16

THE MEN

Manpower

"TODAY the greatest weakness of America is lack of manpower. Of resources and technology and arms we have much; of men we have few." To the Air Force, this statement by the Senate Committee on Armed Services in 1951 epitomized its own experience, particularly after 1949.

The essence of the manpower problem was not simply numbers. It was the quality of the people—their professional and technical knowledge. As the world's foremost industrial power, the United States naturally had a great many skilled people in its population. But the Air Force had to compete with the civilian economy for trained manpower, and it had great difficulty recruiting the people it needed.

The Air Force problem was further complicated by the need to increase its striking power markedly while severely limiting its manpower. Between July 1, 1952, and June 30, 1956, it increased its combat strength from ninety-five to 131 wings while reducing its military manpower by nearly 64,000 people. How far this practice could be carried remained one of the major questions facing the Air Force at the end of its first decade.

Demobilization and Reorganization

Many of the Air Force's later manpower difficulties had their roots in the chaotic demobilization after World War II. The Japanese surrender in August 1945 came suddenly. The United States had anticipated that it would take twelve to eighteen months after the end of the war in Europe to defeat the Japanese, during which few men could be released from the Army Air Forces. When the Germans gave up in May, most AAF men were overseas, and transportation to the United States had been reserved for forces on their way to the Pacific. The continuing demand for technicians prevented the discharge of more than a

token number of officers and enlisted men, even in the United States. As a result, when the Japanese quit, the AAF was nearly as large as it had been when the war ended in Europe.

After V-J Day—September 2, 1945—military authorities could not resist the public demand for swift demobilization. On V-J Day the AAF had 2,253,000 military personnel. By the end of December 1945 only 888,769 remained, and by May 31, 1947, AAF military strength reached its low point of about 303,600. The number of civilians employed by the Army Air Forces dropped from 318,154 in September 1945 to a few more than 110,000 at the end of June 1947.

By the end of 1945, troop strength had been cut so drastically that overseas commanders did not have enough people to carry out their responsibilities. At unmanned or undermanned installations all over the world great quantities of materials, from trucks and aircraft engines to pipes and copper wire, rapidly deteriorated into useless junk. Rapid, uncontrolled demobilization left combat units ineffective and disrupted both maintenance and training. Airplanes were stranded in all parts of the world for lack of trained mechanics. Thousands of engines, bombsights, guns, and instruments never got through the repair shops. Even new aircraft rapidly deteriorated because there was nobody to prepare them for storage.

To man the seventy groups adopted as its goal in 1946, the AAF believed it would need 502,000 officers and airmen. And this was arrived at only by cutting ground-crew strength per group to eighty percent of wartime strength and reducing the number of aircrews to one per plane. The number of civilians required to serve the Air Force in the United States was set at 129,187. This did not take into account all of the functions likely to be transferred from the Army to the Air Force under terms of the National Security Act of 1947 or the number of civilians needed overseas.

Within a few months after the end of the war, the AAF decided to man its units with volunteers to the greatest extent possible. Shortly thereafter, it launched a vigorous recruiting campaign for three-year volunteers, and in May

Disintegration of an air force. These overseas veterans are on way out during post-World War II demobilization.

1946 it prohibited twelve- and eighteen-month enlistments. By 1948 only three-, four-, five-, and six-year enlistments were accepted, since experience had demonstrated the unsoundness of trying to man the Air Force with people who stayed less than three years. The Air Force also raised the educational requirement for enlisted men to a higher level than that of the Army or Navy.

Years of Uncertainty

In March 1947, when the AAF learned that there would not be enough money to start on the seventy-group program, it decided on fifty-five groups as a first step. In July it directed that the fifty-five groups be organized, manned, and placed in some degree of operational efficiency by January 1, 1948. Men were available to fill the positions, but the lack of trained and experienced people to handle the increasingly complex tools of war caused difficulty. The Air Force succeeded in manning the fifty-five groups by January, and inspections revealed that the units were reasonably efficient. But the mobility of some combat units was reduced because civilians had to be hired to fill military vacancies.

In the meantime, Secretary Symington had adopted a "four-year program" designed to create by 1952 an Air Force capable of meeting any international crisis that might be forced upon the United States. There would be seventy groups by late 1949 and the qualified personnel to man them soon afterward. The military manpower goal was set at 444,500 officers and airmen for the end of June 1949.

By July 1949 total military personnel strength reached 419,347, but a year later it had dropped to 411,277. Failure to reach the planned goal was the result of a decision by President Truman in December 1948 that the country could afford no more than a forty-eight-group Air Force. By this time the Air Force had activated fifty-nine groups and was busily planning for the increase to seventy. With the new announcement, it had to shift quickly from expansion to contraction.

During 1948-49, the Berlin Airlift further complicated the task of organizing and manning an effective Air Force. Nearly all of the major commands, both in the United States and overseas, had to furnish men and planes for this huge operation. Many of the best-qualified flying, maintenance, and service people had to be withdrawn from active combat units. The Air Force recalled some reserve officers to active duty and diverted to the airlift men previously scheduled for other assignments. Not until the spring of

1949 could emphasis be shifted back to improving the combat readiness of the tactical commands.

As it slowly trained and organized its manpower during the two years before the outbreak of war in Korea, the Air Force faced a manpower problem of growing intensity. Enlisting men presented no particular problem, but getting qualified men and keeping those that had been trained proved difficult. Partly because of the opportunities for good jobs in industry, there was always a large turnover of high-grade technicians, and the training of replacements imposed an expensive burden. Inadequate housing, too frequent moves as a result of changes in programs and such operations as the Berlin Airlift, a relatively low pay scale—all these aggravated the situation.

As early as 1948, military and civilian leaders expressed concern because the Air Force had no adequate source of professionally trained officers. Moreover, the percentage of college-trained officers in the Air Force was considerably below that in the Army or Navy. Most of the new officers came from four sources—aviation cadet schools, officer candidate schools (OCS), Air Force Reserve Officer Training Corps (AFROTC), and West Point or Annapolis. In 1949 the Army and Navy agreed to allow twenty-five percent of the graduating classes at West Point and Annapolis to accept commissions in the Regular Air Force. This provided no permanent solution, however, since the other two services were also short of well-trained junior officers.

In November 1949, Secretary Symington appointed a board, headed by General Spaatz, to find a suitable location for an Air Force academy. The following month, President Truman and Secretary of Defense Johnson endorsed the idea of an Air Force academy, and Lt. Gen. Hubert R. Harmon was appointed to manage planning for the academy.

The shortage of housing for military people and their families plagued the Air Force continuously from the end of World War II. In a 1948 report, Symington stated that family quarters on Air Force bases in the United States were available for only one-fourth of the officers and enlisted men legally entitled to them. About half of these were makeshift conversions of barracks and other buildings unfit for families to live in. Bachelor troops were only a little better off. Accommodations off the bases cost far more than the government allowed men for rent and were often

ROTC is prime source of AF officers. These cadets will accompany active-duty bomber crews on training mission.

These WAFs have interesting duty as stewardesses on transatlantic flights for the Military Air Transport Service.

grossly inadequate—in some cases shocking. In August 1949, Congress authorized a $500 million fund with which the Federal Housing Administration could insure mortgages for rental housing built by private industry on military posts. Although it by no means solved the problem, this Wherry-Spence act did eventually bring some relief.

On June 12, 1948, Congress passed the Women's Armed Service Integration Act, establishing Women in the Air Force (WAF) as a permanent part of the Air Force. The office of the director, first occupied by Col. Geraldine F. May, was set up on June 16. Since the law limited the number in the WAF to 300 officers and 4,000 enlisted women for the first two years, the Air Force could be highly selective in enlisting women. The number in the WAF did not rise above this figure until after the outbreak of the Korean War. During the first three years of its existence, the WAF encountered numerous difficulties arising from a lack of clarity on enlistment standards and a failure at top levels of the Air Staff to decide on the proper function of the WAF.

Because of the 1948 cutback and the prospect that the Air Force would shrink rather than expand, the reserve forces took on added significance during the two years preceding the Korean War. In June 1948, Symington noted that the air reserve program had not succeeded in its two main objectives: (1) to create a pool of qualified and quickly available officers and airmen to augment the Regular establishment in time of war, and (2) to develop proficiency in the individual participants. During 1948-50, the Air Force worked to raise the Organized Air Reserve to the same level of effectiveness that the Air National Guard had attained. By the middle of 1949, the ANG had 406 of its 514 units in full training, and the Air Force had come to place great reliance on the Guard.

A new program, pushed in 1949 and 1950, stressed the establishment of twenty-three Air Force Reserve training centers, 300 training units attached to Regular Air Force units at about fifty bases, and a mobilization assignment program for 12,523 reserve officers. To attract volunteers, Congress provided incentives in the form of liberal retire-

ment benefits, inactive-duty training pay, and greater protection in the event of death or disability. The twenty-five Air Force Reserve wings organized at the twenty-three centers included twenty troop carrier and five light bombardment wings. These types were selected because the Air National Guard was composed mainly of fighter units and because resources were not available for the operation of medium and heavy bombers by reserve units.

Among civilian employees, the reduction in manpower after V-J Day created a serious morale problem. Although the reduction took place within the framework of Civil Service regulations, it created a widespread feeling of insecurity, for the great majority of civilians did not have permanent Civil Service status. The Air Force found it difficult during 1947 and 1948 to stabilize its civilian work force. Turnover was excessive, totaling eighty-nine percent during the period from July 1, 1947, to June 30, 1948.

As the Air Force rebuilt its manpower strength, the steady gain in the number of civilians cut down the rate of turnover and largely solved the morale problem. From the low point of 110,070 in June 1947, the number of civilian workers climbed to nearly 169,000 by June 30, 1949. Another cutback brought the total down to 153,000 by the end of 1950, just at the start of the Korean War. About 24,000 of these employees were overseas.

In spite of the general reduction in the number of civilians, the growing complexity of weapons and operational techniques made it necessary to recruit technical specialists and scientists. The Civil Service Commission permitted the Air Force to employ certain categories of scientists and highly specialized people without regard to normal hiring procedures. The Air Force also made a particular effort to train and develop men of outstanding ability into key executives.

On the eve of the Korean War, Department of Defense officials seemed unable to agree upon the size of the force needed to ensure the country's security. Only three years earlier, a seventy-group Air Force, with more than 500,000 military personnel supported by a strong reserve, had been regarded as a bare minimum. Then, changes in programs had led to reductions in strength that were still under way when the North Koreans moved across the thirty-eighth

Civilian technicians play an important role in the Air Force. These are checking telemetering research equipment.

SAC crews leave little to chance. This is parachute inspection of a tanker crew prior to refueling mission.

parallel in June 1950. Comparatively heavy cuts in officer strength, especially in pilots, occurred during the year before Korea, and in 1950 the Department of Defense proposed further reductions for the next year.

Korea and the Great Expansion

The Korean War revealed our weakness in human resources. The problem was not so much one of enough manpower as it was one of trained manpower. During the year following the North Korean attack, the Air Force grappled with the task of creating as rapidly as possible a trained and balanced fighting machine and sustaining it indefinitely. To bring units in the Far East up to combat strength, train replacements, and develop additional forces required a great effort. Only by drawing on the reserves and Selective Service could the most urgent needs be met during 1950.

The Buildup

Starting with forty-eight wings and a military strength of 411,277, the Air Force increased its military manpower to 788,381 officers and airmen within a year of the outbreak of war. To achieve this increase the Air Force had to resort to involuntary recall of reservists. By October 1951, however, it became possible to end the forced recall except for officers possessing special qualifications.

On January 12, 1951, the President authorized the Air Force to build to ninety-five wings and 1,061,000 troops by the end of June 1952. Heavy enlistments permitted the Air Force to limit involuntary recalls primarily to officers.

During the first year of the Korean War, the Air Force called into active service twenty-two of the twenty-seven Air National Guard wings and all of the twenty-five wings and eighty-two percent of the men of the Organized Air Reserve. These provided the only readily available trained

combat and service units. To obtain a balanced expansion, however, it became necessary to call up only certain kinds of units and to dissolve others in order to use their personnel effectively. Many individual specialists were also called. The fact that the Korean War required a partial rather than a full mobilization left the Air Force reserve program thoroughly disrupted.

Because the many involuntary recalls created hardships for reservists and could have had unfortunate effects on essential civilian and government activities, the Air Force tried to give careful consideration to such cases and permitted delays whenever possible. With rapid expansion came greater demands for all kinds of people to fill important positions. WAFs replaced many men in staff positions in the United States, Europe, and Asia.

To permit the most effective support of the fighting forces in Korea and reduce transport, the Air Force suspended normal rotation of men from overseas from July 1950 to January 1951. For FEAF the suspension lasted until June 1951, except for combat crews, whose rotation began in December 1950. Many returning veterans were assigned to training units where they taught the reservists valuable lessons learned in Korea.

The shortage of enlisted men was eased when Congress extended for one year all enlistments expiring between July 27, 1950, and July 8, 1951. To meet the expanding needs for enlisted technicians, the Air Force allowed civilians with previous military service, Air Force Reservists, and National Guard airmen to enlist in the grades they had held when they were discharged.

Civilian strength increased to 260,000 by the end of June 1951. Skilled people were scarce and hard to hold, especially since wages in industry were rising and civilian jobs were plentiful. As international tension mounted, the recruiting and retention of people for overseas jobs became especially difficult.

Before the end of 1951 the Air Force adopted a new program of expansion. In November 1951 the President approved a 143-wing program, to be completed by the middle of 1955. Budget restrictions and the magnitude of the proposed expansion called for stringent manpower economies. The fifty percent increase in combat strength—from ninety-five to 143 wings—was to be attained with an increase of only fourteen percent in military personnel. The Air Force treated military and civilian manpower as an entity and tried to determine more accurately the number of men needed by each command to carry out its mission.

Teamwork is necessary even in single-seat fighters. This new wingman is checked out by instructor before takeoff.

High-speed aircraft have placed a heavier burden on the navigator, who also serves as radar man and bombardier.

Cutting out some group headquarters in SAC and ADC saved the spaces of about 6,600 officers and airmen. By eliminating duplication, abolishing some functions, and delegating more responsibilities to noncommissioned officers, the Air Force did away with more than 38,300 authorized positions between July 1952 and June 1953.

The ninety-five-wing program called for 1,061,000 military personnel, but by retrenching in administration and certain support functions, the Air Force manned ninety-five wings with 973,500 as of June 30, 1952. For the 143-wing establishment, 1,210,000 officers and airmen would be required. The Air Staff hoped to have 106 wings and 1,061,000 officers and airmen by June 30, 1953. The desired wing strength was attained by that date, but military strength increased only 4,000 to 977,500.

Meanwhile, certain members of the Air Staff had been doing some hard thinking on manpower problems. In the fall of 1952, Lt. Gen. Laurence S. Kuter, DCS/Personnel, expressed the opinion that within a year or two manpower would become the limiting factor in Air Force expansion. Although he believed that the estimate of 1,210,000 officers and airmen for the 143-wing Air Force was low, Kuter became convinced by November 1952 that the Department of Defense would never approve even this figure because of the great cost. For the Air Staff to base its plans on this program too long, he believed, could be dangerous.

The general shortage of manpower, the increased destructive power of modern weapons, and the great financial burden of the military establishment prompted the new administration to take a "new look" at the nation's military requirements in 1953. Before a full study could be completed, Secretary Wilson announced in May a new budget and manpower program that temporarily reduced the Air Force goal to 120 wings. Military personnel would be cut back to about 960,000 by the end of June 1954, although wing strength would be increased to not less than 110. The civilian work force would be reduced from 302,300 to 298,500 during the same period.

Special Flying Problems

A serious shortage of volunteers for flying developed in the fall of 1951 and continued for the next two years. It was especially difficult to find enough applicants to fill the training quotas for pilots, navigators, bombardiers, and

other flyers. In order to obtain men to replace experienced combat crews, educational requirements for flying training had to be lowered. The gap was temporarily filled by allowing high school graduates to apply and permitting men with two years of college to sign up for only two-year terms. In 1952-53 an especially critical shortage developed in applicants for nonpilot flying positions: navigators, bombardiers, and radar men. To get more volunteers for navigator training, the Air Force tried to persuade pilot applicants to switch to navigator training and stepped up the recruiting of aviation cadets at colleges and universities.

Between January and April 1952 an abnormally large number of reservists on active duty asked to be released from flying duties. These "fear of flying" cases received nationwide publicity and created concern throughout the Air Force. Maj. Gen. Kenneth P. McNaughton, vice commander of the Air Training Command, declared that they posed a serious threat to the Air Force's ability to fill crew positions and maintain high morale. On April 16, with Secretary Finletter's approval, General Vandenberg ruled that qualified officers who refused to fly would be separated from the service. Flying duty had always been and would remain voluntary, but a qualified pilot or observer would be expected to fly after completing his training. Any man found suffering from psychoneurosis would be grounded and given proper medical treatment.

Although fear of flying was not widespread enough after June 1952 to cause undue alarm, this episode did emphasize the urgency of obtaining newly trained young flyers to replace reserve pilots and navigators, most of whom were veterans of World War II. General Kuter started an educational campaign to ensure that the Air Force's flying training program instilled in its graduates a willingness to perform any duty, no matter how difficult or dangerous.

Manpower Problems of Peacetime Preparedness

The 120-wing program set by the Department of Defense in May 1953 remained the target only until the JCS could complete a full study and arrive at a new assessment. After the Korean War, the JCS developed a new Air Force program of 137 wings and 975,000 officers and men, to be reached by the end of June 1957. President Eisenhower gave his approval in December 1953.

It became increasingly clear before the end of 1953 that holding the manpower to operate a 137-wing Air Force would be a most critical problem. And this problem might grow worse, since the end of the Korean War brought little reduction in Air Force responsibilities while creating a semblance of peace and lessening public interest in military service.

The program adopted in December 1953 involved a decision to maintain a strong force with far less manpower than previously had been considered possible. This meant the utmost economy in the use of men, the substitution of machines for men wherever possible, and a higher degree of skill on the part of Air Force personnel. As equipment grew steadily more complicated and the techniques of operating and maintaining it more difficult to master, a greater proportion of an airman's time had to be devoted to training. This situation presented the Air Force with its greatest manpower problem, for highly skilled men showed the least inclination to remain in the military service.

Economizing on Manpower

After the fall of 1953 the Air Force added combat wings while its military manpower strength gradually declined. By July 1954, wing strength reached 115, but military personnel fell to about 948,000. At the end of 1956 the Air Force was manning 131 wings with only 914,000 officers and men. This decline resulted from the release of airmen

USAF MANPOWER—AS OF DECEMBER 31, 1956		
USAF Military Personnel		914,073
Officers—141,296	Airmen—772,777	
Rated Officers		76,516
Pilots—56,847	Others—19,669	
AF Military Personnel Overseas		264,490
Officers—33,118	Airmen—231,372	
Civilian Personnel		429,737
Air Force Reserve		389,817
Officers—146,211	Airmen—243,606	
Air National Guard		64,880
Officers—7,777	Airmen—57,103	

who had enlisted during the Korean War and the transfer of about 28,000 engineer troops back to the Army. The number of civilians employed by the Air Force also declined slightly during the first year after the Korean War, falling to 298,600 on June 30, 1954. During the next two years, however, civilian employment rose as the Air Force found it economical to fill many semiskilled and technical military positions with civilian workers. By the end of 1956, Air Force civilian employees numbered a few more than 350,000.

The determination of the administration and Congress to keep both military and civilian manpower at minimum levels prompted the Air Force to exercise stringent manpower controls. One project, known as Native Son, substituted natives of foreign countries for Air Force personnel in overseas commands. By July 1954, 34,000 officers and airmen had been released for other military duties under this program. Between July 1953 and June 1954, about 14,000 civilian positions were eliminated at air materiel depots. The great shortage of airmen was relieved somewhat the following year by filling about 9,200 positions with civilians. The Air Force also decided to man the land-based portion of the DEW Line with civilians under contract.

Changes in methods of operation and far-reaching technological developments compelled the Air Force to add new activities and expand existing ones. By early 1956, SAC needed more men to disperse its forces over a larger number of bases and expand its B-52 units. Additional manpower would also be needed to handle new and more complex aircraft coming into use, to build up aircraft control and warning squadrons for air defense, and to speed up research and development.

But the people for these vital activities were not available under the manpower ceiling imposed by the Department of Defense in December 1953. At the end of 1956 it appeared that the Air Force faced growing deficits in manpower for some years to come. Held under a rigid ceiling, it had no choice but to try to reduce requirements and use manpower more efficiently. The constant effort to economize helped relieve the manpower deficits but did not overcome them.

The Crisis in Reenlistments

A certain amount of turnover in personnel is normal in a large military organization, but the Air Force's loss of trained people after 1953 was so large and constant that it seriously threatened to impair operations. In March 1956 the Air Force revealed that the situation had reached the point where it was not buying all the equipment it needed because there were not enough qualified technicians to operate or maintain it.

Talbott, Quarles, and Twining all believed that the ability of the Air Force to perform its mission depended greatly on whether it could keep experienced technicians. The trend of airmen reenlistments showed that this was a

serious problem. Between 1949 and 1955 the reenlistment rate fell from sixty percent to twenty-three percent. Although the rate rose after July 1955, it was not enough. Most serious were the facts that highly skilled men were harder to hold than the unskilled and that about eighty percent of both groups failed to reenlist after serving only four years. Aside from the threat to combat effectiveness, this rapid turnover cost extra billions for the training of replacements.

Much study was devoted to the problem of high turnover without producing an agreement on its cause. Perhaps the natural reluctance of young Americans to pursue a military career in peacetime was fundamental. M/Sgt. Frank Clifford, writing under the nom de plume of Norman Winfield in AIR FORCE Magazine of January 1954, maintained that even the three top grades—staff, technical, and master sergeants—had come to the conclusion that a career in the Air Force afforded little satisfaction. Housing was substandard, both for bachelors and men with families, transfers came too often and sometimes for no apparent reason, and frequent and prolonged temporary duty raised living costs and deprived men of deserved promotions.

When Congress cut down on base exchanges and refused to appropriate money to furnish comfortable housing, many men felt that the government had failed them and that the advertised security in the military service was a mirage. The married noncom could depend on medical care for his family only if he was lucky enough to be stationed near a large military installation, and even then, there were often too many troops for the medical facilities to handle. Last but not least, advancement usually stopped for an enlisted man before he reached thirty years of age.

A related picture emerged from the letter of resignation submitted by a Regular lieutenant colonel in 1954. He, too, resented the government's failure to live up to its promises, but in addition his sole remaining incentive—professional pride—had been destroyed. He felt that public scorn had become the chief reward for achieving high military rank. The press, many congressmen, and even high civilian officials in the Department of Defense constantly criticized the "wasteful brass" who lived in unearned luxury and "squandered the taxpayers' money to build mysterious

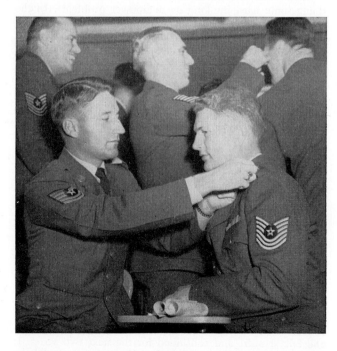

Students at a noncommissioned officers school switch shoulder loops from left to right to signify "graduation."

Highly trained technicians, like S/Sgt. Harold E. Aycock, are hard to come by, even harder to keep in the service.

and unnecessary empires." As a result, the lieutenant colonel complained, ". . . the uniform I once wore with pride is now regarded by most civilians as a badge of mediocrity, of a parasite unable to earn an honest living outside."

The Air Force could do little about this sort of complaint, but many of its own personnel policies appeared irrational and haphazard to its officers and men. Promotion policy did not seem to be uniform, malassignment was frequent, and men were rotated from station to station with bewildering frequency. They placed much of the blame for this situation on professional personnel officers. But certainly many of these defects must have arisen from the impersonality characteristic of all large organizations.

In August 1954, Secretary Talbott declared that his biggest worry since taking office had been the rising turnover of skilled men. He estimated that the Air Force was losing more than $2 billion a year in trained manpower. Talbott's investigations had convinced him that the men's complaints were justified, and that they would stay in the service if their living standards could be raised. He attributed the exodus of skilled people to low pay, inadequate housing, insufficient medical facilities, frequent and sudden changes of station, and the reduction of commissary and base exchange privileges. For each one percent rise in the over-all reenlistment rate, he estimated that the Air Force would save about $100 million in training costs during each four-year enlistment period.

Talbott and other officials who grappled with the turnover problem probably had no means of coming to grips with its fundamental cause. Some doubted whether making service life more attractive would really keep the men in. By mid-1954, opinion surveys showed that a large segment of the American people had never favored intervention in Korea and that an even larger proportion opposed any further involvement in the Far East. Now that we were not in a war, most people weighed the advantages and disadvantages of military service in terms of personal gain and comfort. It was extremely difficult to persuade the American public that if war came it would probably come suddenly and that the decisive air engagements would be fought within a few days or hours by men already in uniform.

Americans, moreover, appeared to be weary after years of war and crisis, and many were disillusioned because the sacrifices of men and resources seemed to have brought us no closer to a peaceful world than before. In a period during which the civilian economy offered unprecedented job opportunities, many intelligent and enterprising young men considered military service a waste of time. They preferred to sell real estate, manufacture household appliances, or build roads rather than prepare for a crisis which might never come.

Renewed Efforts to Hold the Men

With the help of constructive legislation and administrative actions, the Air Force made intensive efforts to hold men in service. At the end of March 1955, Congress passed the Career Incentive Act, which raised military pay an average of about twelve percent. This act departed from the traditional practice of giving the same percentage increase to all personnel. Instead, it provided higher raises for selected people, establishing special incentives to keep them in the service. The largest raises went to the younger commissioned officers and men in the middle enlisted grades who were at an age to assume family responsibilities and make decisions about their future careers.

Included in this act were increases in pay for hazardous duty, per diem allowances for official travel, and moving expenses for family men changing their permanent duty stations. Cadets and midshipmen of the service academies received half the pay of a second lieutenant, and aviation cadets for the first time were given hazardous-duty pay. Congress also increased retirement benefits and reenlistment bonuses and provided mortgage insurance for homes purchased by servicemen.

Legislation between the fall of 1954 and the summer of 1956 attacked the continuing shortage of family housing. Thousands of new units were authorized for construction on permanent installations, largely as a result of the Capehart amendment to the National Housing Act. Money from the sale of surplus agricultural products became available to build troop housing overseas, and some foreign countries agreed to build family quarters when the United States guaranteed rents. These measures helped to reduce the critical housing shortage, but they fell far short of meeting even minimum needs.

The Dependents' Medical Care Act, effective in December 1956, improved a serviceman's chances of obtaining medical care for his family by giving the Secretary of Defense power to contract for civilian medical service. An act passed in July 1956 permitted the Air Force to more than double the number of its Regular officers. This was expected to benefit lower-ranking officers holding reserve commissions who had become discouraged about their chances for advancement.

Within the Air Force there developed a growing awareness of the importance of good human relations and the need for commanders to make special efforts to hold airmen in the service. Commanding officers and supervisors personally interviewed men whose enlistments were about to expire. In addition, the Air Force expanded the concurrent travel privilege permitting a man's family to accompany him overseas, provided more information about living conditions overseas, built up social and recreational programs, and expanded overseas schools.

With the help of these measures, the Air Force succeeded, during the year ending June 30, 1956, in raising the over-all reenlistment rate from the previous year's twenty-three percent to forty-four percent. During the following six months it rose to forty-seven, but the true

A quick engine change by a SAC crew at annual bombing and navigation competition typifies AF technical needs.

rate was substantially lower, since about thirty percent of these men took a "short discharge" and reenlisted after serving only half of their four-year tours.

In September 1956, General Twining revealed that lack of qualified personnel was the chief reason why many wings were not yet at peak combat readiness. He declared that the 137-wing force could not possibly be effective if manned by technicians of doubtful skill and limited experience. Twining emphasized that during the past five years the requirement for trained technicians had increased twice as fast as the need for other types of people.

By late 1956, most defense leaders recognized that this problem was broader than the mere retention of technically and scientifically trained persons in the Air Force. The shortage of technological skills was nationwide, and the solution would have to be a national one.

New Emphasis on the Reserve Forces

In setting tight ceilings on the size of the military forces, the President and Congress assumed that the active establishment would be supplemented by large, well-trained reserve components. But ever since World War II all three military services had found it difficult to develop and maintain stable reserve programs. And since the next war might be fought entirely by forces already on hand, the reserve programs appeared less meaningful to many leaders. Nevertheless, other kinds of war were also possible, and the nation continued to require a large military reserve program, even though it did not always provide the means to carry it out.

Before the Korean War was over, the Air Force set about rebuilding its badly depleted reserve forces. By mid-1952, four reserve districts under the Continental Air Com-

mand had assumed control of the administration, training, and supply of the Air Force Reserve, Air National Guard, Civil Air Patrol, and the Air Explorer programs. In addition, five specialist training centers had been set up to supplement the twenty-five Air Force Reserve training centers already operating, and arrangements had been made for reservists to receive training at civilian colleges and universities near their homes.

To comply with the Armed Forces Reserve Act of 1952, the Air Force divided its reserves into Ready, Standby, and Retired, placing all members in one of these three categories. All units of the Air National Guard became members of the Ready Reserve. Without a steady influx of trained young men released from active service, the Ready Reserve, aside from the ANG units, tended to become a pool of trained manpower rather than a well-organized, well-trained reserve. This was partly the result of the government's failure to enforce the reserve obligations imposed on young men by the Universal Military Training and Service Act of 1950.

After November 1951 few reservists were ordered to active duty involuntarily, and after April 1952 the Air Force authorized the major commands to release large numbers of men. This enabled the reserve units to gradually build up their manpower. The twenty-three flying training stations opened in July 1952 grew slowly but steadily, and new nonflying training centers were opened later. To ensure greater participation in training, the Air Force stipulated that individuals in paid reserve positions would have to take part in active-duty training or lose their assignments. Reserve wings had to participate in active-duty unit training each year.

By the end of June 1955, the Air Force's reserve establishment was large, but not enough of the men were maintaining their military proficiency. Of the more than 166,000 members of the Ready Reserve, for example, only about 52,000 were receiving instruction. In 1956, about 60,000 out of nearly 288,000 trained actively. On the other hand, practically all of the 63,500 Air National Guardsmen trained actively during 1956.

By October 1954, seventeen ANG units were furnishing jet aircraft and combat-ready crews to ADC every day for active participation in air defense. These units reached a high state of readiness, unequaled by any other reserve components. By the end of June 1955, twenty-three of the twenty-seven ANG wings had been converted from fighter-bomber to interceptor units and given mobilization assignments with ADC. A big step toward an effective reserve was the establishment in January 1955 of a firm requirement for fifty-one combat wings in the Air Force Reserve and the Air National Guard. At the same time, the Air Force Reserve began converting pilot training wings to combat wings.

In November 1955 the Air Force declared all AFR combat wings, support units, and individual mobilization positions "Ready," in keeping with current war plans. All men assigned to these units and positions were required to have a Ready status for at least two years and to be immediately available for active military duty in case of an emergency. In August 1956, however, Maj. Gen. William E. Hall, Assistant Chief of Staff for Reserve Forces, reported that serious difficulties had arisen in selecting men for the Ready category. Airline pilots, for example, belonged to some of the reserve flying units and could be used effectively by reserve troop carrier wings. Unfortunately, they would not be available on D-day because they would have to man the Civil Reserve Air Fleet, augmenting the stupendous airlift the country would require in a wartime emergency.

The Ready requirement affected many people in the ANG and the Reserve, such as airway-operation specialists of the CAA and other technical experts working for the government and defense industries. Any officer or airman whose civil occupation would keep him from being available at once, in an emergency, could not serve in a Ready unit, but would have to be transferred to some other status. Finding replacements for these people constituted a big job during 1956.

The reserve forces made steady progress in equipping their flying units with modern aircraft. By August 1956 all of the AFR's fighters and most of the ANG's were jets. During 1956, jet aircraft were transferred to the reserve units as rapidly as the newer models for USAF units came from the factories. By December the ANG could have equipped all of its fighter units with jets if it had possessed fields large enough to accommodate them.

The thirteen AFR troop carrier wings and six ANG air resupply and transport squadrons had not reached full combat readiness by 1957. Most of their aircraft were obsolescent C-46s. Some C-119s were coming into the units, but they were too few and too badly worn to meet the need.

In August 1956, General Hall pointed out that the most serious difficulty facing the reserve forces was the shortage of facilities, especially for flying training. This problem plagued the whole Air Force, but the reserves had the especially complicated problem of finding bases near the larger cities where most of the men lived. Getting funds was hard enough since active units received priority, but this was only part of the problem. Public resistance to placing reserve units at municipal airports had been growing stronger because jet aircraft were noisy and could be dangerous. Special Air Force projects to minimize the noise and danger promised help in overcoming these objections.

Air National Guard pilots check hits on an aerial sleeve target during the annual two-week summer training period.

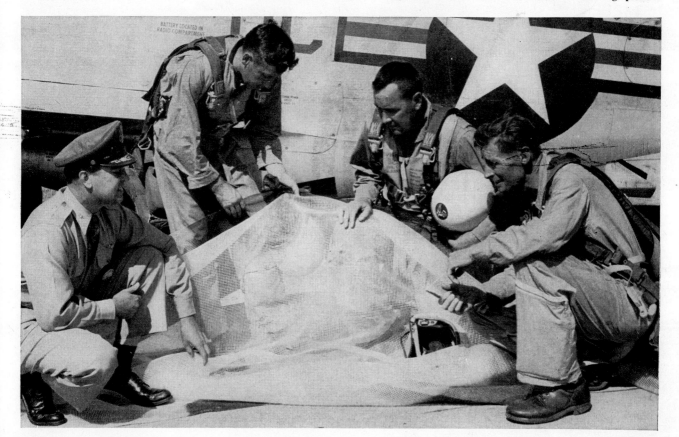

Chapter 17

THE MEN

Military Training

DEMOBILIZATION after World War II seriously disrupted the Air Force's training establishment. So many instructors were lost that effective training had become extremely difficult by the end of 1946. Students and recent graduates of the AAF Training Command had to keep the training program going. As a result, few of the training stations and schools could be adequately manned. Basic training was reduced to speed up the flow of students into technical schools.

The need for advanced training in the hundred or more military specialties became acute during the first year following the war. The large backlog of students, accumulated before V-J Day, kept the number of graduates high until the end of October 1945. After V-J Day, however, the Training Command could obtain few students, and by February 1946 the number of graduates from all courses had dropped sharply. Because the need for even partially trained technicians was so great, the command relaxed entrance requirements for some of the technical courses.

During the first eight months of 1945, the Air Force graduated each month an average of more than 20,000 flyers—pilots, navigators, bombardiers, radar observers, and gunners—but this figure fell to 322 in December 1945. Because of the surplus of well-trained flyers on hand, pilot and navigator-bombardier training almost stopped in 1946, and gunnery training ceased entirely. By 1948 the Air Force's training courses were gradually increasing their output, but the shortage still remained critical.

The postwar training establishment was built around the Air Training Command (ATC) and the Air University. The Air Training Command sent a steady flow of skilled men into every USAF unit. After 1945, new and highly advanced equipment demanded newer and more exacting courses of instruction. The transition to jet aircraft, for example, required not only new training for the men who flew them but special courses for mechanics and other maintenance men. Instrument specialists had to be brought up to date on jets, and an expanded field of electronics had to be mastered.

After World War II, ATC reorganized its program to make the best use of its facilities. At Lackland AFB, Tex., all enlistees received basic military training before going on to technical schools to learn their future specialties. The Officer Candidate School for nonflying officers was also at Lackland.

The Technical Training Division schooled all ground crews, technical specialists, and administrative personnel in more than a hundred separate courses. The Flying Training Division managed all USAF flying training. The headquarters of Air Training Command moved from Barksdale AFB, La., to Scott AFB, Ill., in October 1949, from where it supervised the over-all training program.

The Air University, established in September 1946 at Maxwell AFB, Ala., directed the professional education of Air Force officers. Many of the features of Air University that made it a rather unique military organization originated with Maj. Gen. Muir S. Fairchild, the first commander. He set up the Board of Visitors, which provided a link with the best civilian colleges and universities, and employed civilian educational experts. He also originated the idea of an Air University Library as a research institution modeled after the leading civilian university libraries.

At its schools—Air War College, Air Command and Staff School, Institute of Technology, and School of Aviation Medicine—Air University trained leaders and planners. Here, current technological developments were related to strategy, tactics, and techniques, and their effect on future operations was analyzed. The Air Force sent selected officers through the different schools according to age, experience, and length of service.

Air University also administered the educational program of Air Force officers attending civilian colleges and universities. After April 1950, Air University managed this program through the Air Force Institute of Technology (AFIT), which also conducted a resident college at Wright-Patterson AFB, Ohio. In addition, the Extension Course Institute, established in 1948, offered many courses which airmen and officers could pursue when off duty.

Lockheed's T-33 was USAF's first jet trainer. Transition from piston engines to jets posed a big training problem.

Maj. Gen. Muir S. Fairchild, who served as the Air University's first chief.

Lt. Gen. Dean C. Strother, who became commander of the Air University in 1955.

Air view of the new plant of the Air Command and Staff College at Maxwell Air Force Base, near Montgomery, Ala.

All armed services are represented in the classes of the Air War College, part of the Air University complex.

Rebuilding the Training Program, 1948-50

By 1948 the Air Force could see its surplus of pilots, trained before the end of the war, gradually dwindling away. To prevent future shortages, it had revived pilot training in 1946, but not on a large enough scale to man the Air Force being planned. In 1948, Headquarters USAF set the pilot training goal at 3,000 for the next year, but by the end of June 1950 this goal still had not been reached. To supply the projected seventy-group force and provide pilots for a reserve required the graduation of 6,000 students a year. Even though the seventy-group goal was soon cut to forty-eight, too few pilots were trained between 1948 and 1950, partly because of the lack of enough volunteers with the proper qualifications. Many students were eliminated before completing their courses, and in April 1950, after the Air Force raised entrance requirements, the number accepted for instruction fell off appreciably.

After 1948, newly graduated pilots had to fly types of planes which a few years earlier would have been reserved for men with years of experience. The new crews mastered aircraft far advanced beyond those of World War II—

planes that flew much faster and higher and were more complicated. To prepare for this change the training schools consolidated the early phases of instruction, developed a new basic trainer, and put the student in tactical aircraft more quickly.

The functions of navigator, bombardier, and radar observer were consolidated in one crewman. Since this man might become even more important than the pilot, ATC gave special attention to his educational background and training. Up through 1948, only experienced navigators or bombardiers were instructed in this specialty, but the Air Force soon had to start putting untrained men in the program.

To develop pilot ability to operate in all kinds of weather, the Air Force maintained an instrument school. Although it would have been desirable to allow every flying officer to attend this school, it was possible to train only instrument instructors, who could pass on the skill to their respective units. ATC also maintained a school to train fighter gunnery instructors and another to train liaison and helicopter pilots for the Army.

A drastic cut in civilian personnel in May and June 1947 forced ATC to dismiss many of its experienced instructors. This severely affected the quality of technical training as well as the number who could be trained. Not until after the outbreak of the Korean War could the Air Force devote enough manpower and capital to technical training to produce the skilled specialists it needed.

To compensate for the deficiency in numbers, the Air Force adopted a system of broader and less specialized technical training. Many of the specialized wartime courses were grouped into single courses. The Air Force expected a graduate of one of these courses, with a minimum of on-the-job training, to handle any one of a number of technical specialties.

In the spring of 1948, a survey of the combat commands revealed that ATC graduates of aircraft maintenance, administrative, radar, and communications courses lacked certain skills and knowledge which the commands believed essential. Many of the deficiencies were the result of poor school facilities and obsolescent equipment, difficulty of night study in barracks, and the fact that many of the students were young and immature.

Despite these handicaps, ATC managed to expand and improve the program. The demand for technicians exceeded the capacity of the five schools operating in 1949, and a new school had to be established at Sheppard AFB,

Student navigator takes reading. Air Training Command emphasized job of welding individuals into combat crews.

Tex. In 1949, also, ATC launched a recruiting campaign to find technicians with teaching ability. In addition, it doubled the number of civilian instructors between July 1948 and June 1949.

The Years of Expansion, 1950-53

The Korean War and related events expanded the training establishment and created new and more serious shortages in facilities and trained manpower. One shortage aggravated another, as the great demand for skilled technicians and flying personnel increased the need for training facilities.

Between May and August 1951, Air Training Command set up two new agencies, Flying Training Air Force (Fly TAF) and Technical Training Air Force (Tech TAF). This move, designed to decentralize training supervision, placed responsibility for graduating pilots, navigators, and radar observers on Fly TAF, with headquarters at James Connally AFB, Tex.

Flying Training

The undergraduate pilot training program in effect in July 1950 had been designed to produce 3,000 pilots a year, but even this modest program had been reduced temporarily to 2,200 because of a lack of applicants with two years of college education. When the ninety-five-wing goal was approved in January 1951, the Air Force thought it would require a pilot graduation rate of 7,200 per year by January 1952. For the 143-wing program, the Air Force made plans in the fall of 1951 to expand pilot training to a rate of 12,000 a year by 1956, but it did not quite achieve even the 7,200-per-year program.

As a first step, ATC contracted with civilian training schools for the early phases of instruction at eleven private flying stations. In addition, ATC operated eight advanced fighter schools and two advanced bomber schools. Most of the new fighter pilots learned to fly jets, but early in the Korean War a shortage of jet trainers made it impossible to instruct the numbers needed.

After the war began in Korea, ATC took over most combat crew training, thereby relieving combat commands of much of their burden. During the first year of the war, the Air Force recalled to active duty a large number of reserve navigators, bombardiers, radar observers, and other non-pilot flyers and gave them refresher training. In June 1952 aircrew training in the B-47 jet bomber began at Wichita AFB (later renamed McConnell AFB), Kan., close by the Boeing plant that produced the planes.

By the spring of 1952 it became evident that the Flying Training Air Force would be unable to do more than train basic flyers. Involved in the instruction of thousands of cadet pilots and navigators, Fly TAF could not give the close supervision needed to turn out finished crews. Nor could the combat commands take the time to prepare newly graduated flyers to work effectively as combat teams. Getting the men ready for combat became the task of Crew Training Air Force (Crew TAF), established at Randolph AFB, Tex., in April 1952. By September 1952, Crew TAF was operating six bases and supervising the "postgraduate" courses in medium bomber, fighter, and interceptor operation, plus instrument training and gunnery.

By mid-1953 the Air Force had settled on a program designed to graduate about 7,200 new pilots a year through fiscal year 1956. To do this job, ATC operated ten primary training stations, eight basic and nine advanced schools, and one pilot instructor school. Pilots received three months of preflight instruction, six months of primary, five months of basic, and about three months of combat training. The first phase of primary training— flying in light planes—eliminated most of the deficient students before they reached the more difficult and expensive stages. Advanced or combat training, in which the young pilots made their transition to first-line jet aircraft, expanded greatly by 1953.

Aircraft observers—navigators, bombardiers, and radar specialists—offered the most problems. Largely because they had less opportunity to advance into command positions, observers left the Air Force faster than replacements could be trained. At the end of 1953, no improvement was in sight.

Basic and Technical Training

A great technical training establishment transformed raw recruits into aircraft mechanics, weather observers,

Airmen learning stacking procedure in air traffic control course at Keesler Air Force Base, Miss., technical school.

electronics repairmen, and other specialists. Every new air-man received basic military training from the Technical Training Air Force. From basic training, most went to technical schools. The remainder received on-the-job training in their first assignments.

During the fall and winter of 1950-51 enlistments increased so rapidly that the Air Force had temporary difficulty in accommodating the recruits. Lackland and a part of Sheppard AFB were the only basic training centers at the time. By January 1951, after the number of men in basic training had increased to 67,800 from the 13,600 of the previous July, Lackland became seriously overcrowded. More than 19,000 men were sleeping in tents, and the "Lackland story" received nationwide publicity. Senator Lyndon Johnson's investigating subcommittee severely criticized the Air Force for accepting more men than it could house, but the stories of a pneumonia epidemic, high incidence of AWOL, and suicides proved to be unfounded.

The Air Force maintained that it needed large numbers of men and was justified in taking them when they were available. Secretary Finletter admitted, however, that the Air Force had made a mistake in not coordinating enlistments more closely with base facilities. Overcrowding was remedied by reducing basic training from thirteen to eight weeks, by using Lackland only as a processing center during January 1951, and by suspending enlistments entirely between January 16 and February 1. On the latter date Sampson AFB, N. Y., opened as a basic training center, and in March 1952 another opened at Parks AFB, Calif.

By January 1951, ATC had begun expanding its facilities to meet the increased need for technicians. Within six months the number of airmen graduating from technical schools had nearly doubled. The six schools already operating went on multiple shifts, and a new one was established at Amarillo AFB, Tex. In addition, the Air Force contracted with civilian schools to instruct airmen in aircraft maintenance and related technical subjects. Factory schools taught key people to operate and maintain new equipment. By mid-1951, twenty-one percent of the USAF technical students were being taught in civilian schools.

In 1951, ATC started instructing technical students in the characteristics and maintenance of guided missiles. At first this training consisted chiefly of acquainting certain instructors and supervisors with Air Force plans in the guided missile field, but by mid-1952 Tech TAF had set up five courses in this specialty.

As a part of its policy to emphasize the military applications of atomic energy, the Air Force stepped up training in the use of atomic energy weapons. Beginning in 1952, officers and airmen received orientation courses at Air University, aircrews were instructed in the delivery of weapons, and technicians received training in the assembly of arms. ATC also established courses in radiological defense and in the maintenance of instruments for detecting radiation.

In February 1952, ATC undertook another great expansion of technical training in response to the 143-wing program. More use had to be made of the civilian contract and factory schools. Between July 1951 and June 1952, about 5,000 Air Force technicians went to factories for instruction on new equipment. The Air Force spent more money for factory training during these twelve months than during any year since World War II.

By spring of 1953 the Air Force could foresee that the technical training establishment would not long be able to do its job. Already, despite the relatively high graduation rate and additional on-the-job training, the Air Force faced a critical worldwide shortage of technical supervisors and highly skilled workers. The big problem, however, lay just ahead. The large number of men who enlisted after the outbreak of war in Korea would become eligible for

release in 1954 and 1955. Not only would they have to be replaced, but many more would have to be trained to take care of the Air Force's planned expansion.

Most of the technical training was handled by schools at Sheppard AFB, Tex., Keesler AFB, Miss., Scott AFB, Ill., Lowry AFB, Colo., and Chanute AFB, Ill. Training displays of aircraft engines were shown to prospective engine mechanics, and as they progressed in their courses, the displays grew in size and detail until the students became thoroughly familiar with every part of the engine and its functions. Instructors used the same methods in courses on radio, radar, and other machinery.

Rapid changes in operational equipment complicated the training task. Before new aircraft could be assigned to a combat unit, trained men had to be on hand to maintain and operate them. Technical schools were among the first units to receive new models of planes and equipment so that men could learn to maintain them before they appeared in quantity. Whenever the Air Force changed the types or numbers of aircraft in production, Tech TAF made corresponding changes in its courses.

From its headquarters at Chanute, the 3499th Mobile Training Group sent mobile training detachments all over the world to instruct men at their home bases. Skilled instructors went to the combat commands to familiarize technicians with new aircraft, engines, and equipment. These traveling instructors were usually recent graduates of factory courses.

Tech TAF also managed an important on-the-job training advisory service. Since formal schooling could not supply all of the required instruction, the combat commands had to provide on-the-job training. The commands also used this method to broaden and extend the knowledge and skill of their technicians. Specialists from Tech TAF furnished teaching materials, established courses, and evaluated the results of training conducted in other commands.

Professional Education

Professional education in the Air Force suffered a temporary setback during the first year of the Korean War. The war and the expansion required the services of most of the senior and flying officers who would ordinarily have made up the student body of the professional courses. Headquarters USAF decided, however, that the professional schools should not be closed entirely.

Air University consolidated and shortened most of its courses and intensified instruction during 1950-51. During 1952 and 1953 the schools of Air University gradually built back to their pre-Korean War status. The Air Command and Staff School added several courses, especially in the types and uses of air weapons, and expanded its student body as much as housing facilities permitted. By 1953, the school was graduating about 1,950 students a year from eleven courses. The Air War College, which had suspended for a while during 1950-51, had about 160 students enrolled by the end of 1952 but did not expand beyond that figure.

The Air Force Institute of Technology was transferred from Air Materiel Command to Air University in April 1950. It took on new importance even though it had to restrict its program to essential courses in scientific and technical fields during the first year of the Korean War. In January 1951 it began a resident graduate program with the enrollment of eight officers in an advanced engineering management class.

Through its Resident College, Civilian Institutions Program, and Installations Engineering School, AFIT offered graduate programs in engineering and industrial administration and senior-level undergraduate programs in the engineering sciences. Located at Wright-Patterson AFB, the institute was in an excellent position to prepare student officers to cope with the growing technological problems of the future.

AFIT did not expand its Resident College program above 300 students a year, partly for lack of facilities, but the number of students sent to civilian colleges and universities increased from about 600 in 1951 to about 900 in 1953. Air University continued to give considerable training in foreign languages, sending people to civilian colleges and to the Army's language school at Monterey, Calif. In June 1953 the Foreign Service Institute of the Department of State established a language course for Air Force personnel serving with Latin American missions. Altogether, the Air Force furnished instruction in about thirty-eight different languages and dialects.

Two educational programs supervised from Headquarters USAF gained added importance in 1952 and 1953. The first, called Operation Bootstrap, was intended to raise the general educational level of Air Force officers and airmen by enabling them to attend college in off-duty hours. By 1953 more than 200 colleges and universities were participating in the program and about 100,000 students had enrolled in courses. Operation Midnight Oil assisted troops to become more proficient in their specialties by taking correspondence and extension courses in their spare time.

Air Force ROTC

The major source of junior officers after World War II was the Air Force Reserve Officers Training Corps (AF-ROTC). This expanded rapidly after 1950, the number of colleges and universities with AFROTC units growing to 187 in 1953. In August 1952, Air University took over administrative responsibility for ROTC from the Continental Air Command.

The Air Force ROTC program began to run into difficulty in late 1952 and early 1953. Men qualified for and willing to undergo flying training were needed most, but only a small percentage of ROTC students volunteered for flying. In March 1953 the Air Force had to restrict the number who could enroll in the nonflying specialties and considerably reduce the whole AFROTC program. Although this action caused a good deal of concern in the educational institutions, the Air Force could afford to train only men needed in the active establishment. To encourage volunteers for flight training, the Air Force cut their active tours of duty to three years. Since the proportion desiring flight training still remained too low, enrollment was reduced again in July 1953. To satisfy the Air Force requirement for junior officers, about eighty percent of the graduates had to be prospective flyers, with the other twenty percent mainly engineers and scientists.

On August 1, 1956, President Eisenhower signed a bill which permitted the armed services to include flight instruction as a part of the ROTC program. The Air Force hoped that this would stimulate interest in flying among college students. In addition, it could serve to eliminate students naturally unsuited for flying.

Training the Modern Air Force

After the Korean War the Air Force had to make an orderly transition from expansion to sustained readiness. The buildup to 137 wings continued, but personnel strength declined. When men who signed up early in the Korean War reached the end of their enlistments, there was a heavy loss of trained specialists that made the training job particularly difficult. To the harassed commanders and instructors, it seemed that they were schooling a whole new Air Force every few years. Limited in both instructors and facilities, ATC could not handle the training job by itself, and the combat commands were forced to assume an ever growing burden of on-the-job training.

Lt. Gen. Charles T. Myers, who became commander of Air Training Command in 1954.

North American T-6 trainer has been work horse of AF.

The T-28 primary trainer has two seats in tandem style.

Convair T-29 "Flying Classroom" for navigator-bombardiers.

Cessna T-37 primary jet trainer has side-by-side seats.

Flying Training

During 1954-56 the Air Force graduated between 6,200 and 6,800 new pilots a year, including Air National Guard and foreign students. This fell short of the plan to train approximately 7,000 a year, a slight reduction from the previous training program for 7,200. A number of factors intervened: the over-all reduction in military manpower, the fall-off in volunteers for flying training, and the limited capacity of ATC. Until December 1956, when the job was transferred to the Army, the Air Force also trained liaison and helicopter pilots at Edward Gary AFB, Tex.

The Air Force found that it was giving advanced (or combat) training to many graduates of the basic flying schools who did not stay in service long enough to justify the time and effort. After August 1954, only those students who signed four-year contracts received combat training and assignment to crew positions in tactical units.

Assignment of first-line fighters simultaneously to ATC and tactical units began in 1956. North American F-100s and F-86Hs began replacing Republic F-84Fs in the flying schools. Although fighter-pilot graduations declined at first because the new planes presented difficult teaching and maintenance problems, the Air Force decided to go ahead. Headquarters USAF directed ATC to prepare a course of training for interceptor crews culminating in Convair F-102 instruction, which would probably begin in the summer of 1958.

In 1954 and again in 1955 the Air Force revised the training for aircraft observers—navigators, bombardiers, and radar men—because of the new standards for operating highly technical and rapidly changing electronic equipment. Observers especially needed more intensive schooling in aerial navigation. Veterans, skilled only in narrow specialized fields, were given the broad training required to operate modern aircraft.

In 1955 the Air Force began qualifying all new aircraft observers as navigators before assigning them to combat units. Only experienced navigators were taught the more specialized subjects, such as radar bombardment, electronic countermeasures, and radar interception. To encourage the recruitment of observer cadets and retain experienced men, the Air Force improved command opportunities and created a new rating of Senior Aircraft Observers.

Modern Aircrew Training

Crew TAF had the job of preparing the young officer to use his plane in combat. It conducted approximately thirty-five major courses of combat instruction at nine bases. With a nearly constant enrollment of about 2,000 students, the courses graduated approximately 18,000 a year. These included pilots and observers, instructors, instrument specialists, aircraft controllers, special-weapon students, and experts in survival techniques. Aircrew courses lasted from six weeks to four and one-half months.

The crew-training bases covered nearly 9,000,000 acres, 6,000,000 of which lay in open country—desert and mountain regions—used for gunnery and bombing ranges and maneuvers. Another 1,500,000 acres served to train men in advanced survival methods. Of the approximately 1,600 planes assigned to crew training in late 1955, ninety percent were jets. More than 500 were first-line fighters. The crew-training planes flew about 700,000 hours a year.

Aircrew training was divided into three types or "complexes"—fighter, interceptor, and bomber and transport. For special reasons, SAC continued to direct advanced training in the heavy bombers, where it used only men with long experience.

Each category of fighter training included five phases. First came transition to first-line aircraft, including acrobatics. Second was tactical formation flying, followed by air-to-ground gunnery instruction, including practice with machine guns, rockets, bombs, and special weapons. The fourth phase taught air-to-air gunnery. In the last phase—tactics—students had to search out and attack typical enemy targets such as airfields, railroads, gun emplacements, and convoys. Tactics also included fighter-vs.-fighter action, in which the gun camera showed the accuracy of the gunners.

Interceptor training with the Lockheed F-94C, Northrop F-89D, and North American F-86D concentrated on teaching radar interception techniques. In the two-place planes—the F-94C and F-89D—an observer operated the radar, but in the F-86D the pilot flew the plane and also operated the radar. Since interceptors flew in any kind of weather and at night, the pilots had to be well qualified in instrument flying. Steering information furnished by the radar and a computer were shown to the pilot on a radarscope. He had to act on it immediately and accurately in order to center the aircraft's fire on the target. The first phase of interceptor training stressed instrument techniques and the fundamentals of weather flying. Next, the men learned to operate first-line aircraft and practice simple interceptions of Lockheed T-33s. The final phase consisted of making radar contacts with tow targets and firing rockets at them.

In the training of interceptor pilots and radar operators, difficult compromises had to be made between quantity and quality. During late 1955 and 1956, ADC's need for interceptor pilots was so great that the courses were shortened. Although the graduates were well schooled in their planes and the basic techniques of interception, their proficiency against fast, high-flying, multiple targets fell below the desired standard. They had to learn on the job in their combat units.

In the bomber and transport schools, Crew TAF gave three courses in bomber aircraft and one in transports. At McConnell AFB, Kan., pilots and navigators learned to operate the Boeing B-47 under all kinds of flight conditions. They soon achieved combat readiness after joining their bombardment units. In a course at Randolph, former Douglas B-26 crews learned to operate Martin B-57 jet bombers. Transport crews received instruction in the Fairchild C-119 and the Douglas C-54. The Boeing B-29 courses trained crews for four-engine aircraft and for later instruction in the Boeing KC-97 tanker.

Introduction of more advanced jets—North American F-100, McDonnell F-101, and Convair F-102—into schools

---

NUMBER OF GRADUATES—PILOT TRAINING AND TECHNICAL SCHOOLS—BY FISCAL YEARS

FISCAL YEAR	PILOTS	TECHNICAL TRAINING	
		OFFICERS	AIRMEN
1951	2,345	4,424	129,798
1952	2,702	6,475	171,007
1953	4,595	6,087	158,912
1954	5,315	6,261	128,158
1955	2,633	8,507	124,061
1956	5,701	8,616	130,778
1957*	2,865	2,880	64,731

*Until December 31, 1956.

Technical training schools must work at peak capacity to fill the gaps created by AF's too-low reenlistment rate.

was expected to create new problems. Crew TAF did not believe that basic flying school graduates were experienced enough to fly these faster planes safely. A transition trainer with higher performance than the T-33 was badly needed. Since the new supersonic Northrop T-38 was not expected to be available before 1960, Crew TAF intended to use existing first-line fighters and interceptors to bridge the gap.

Another problem concerned the new planes themselves. In the light of past experience, Crew TAF anticipated spare engine and parts shortages, a high rate of failure of aircraft parts, and frequent failure of weapon systems and equipment. For these reasons, plus the high cost of operation of the new aircraft, Crew TAF believed it would be more practical to teach fundamental fighter gunnery and tactics in older first-line models before shifting to the advanced planes.

On July 1, 1957, the Air Force disbanded Crew TAF and transferred its functions back to Fly TAF. This consolidation became possible because fewer flyers were being trained at fewer bases than at any time since the beginning of the Korean War.

Technical Training

As equipment became more intricate and expensive after 1953, training became complicated, expensive, and prolonged. At the same time, the great turnover of skilled men continued, making it necessary to train an excessive number of replacements. During fiscal year 1956, for example, nearly 126,000 airmen failed to reenlist after serving one four-year term. Many of these men had spent up to two years in training costing over $20,000 per man. In fiscal year 1954, USAF technical schools graduated 98,500 students; in fiscal year 1955, 124,061; and during fiscal year 1956, 111,877.

The Air Force's technical training system, developed in 1947-48, was intended to produce technicians with broad backgrounds. After short periods of on-the-job instruction, the men who had graduated from technical schools could work at any one of a number of related jobs. Under such a system, based on the assumption that a specialist would serve about twenty years, the school courses were fairly comprehensive and lengthy. By 1955, however, it appeared that this program would have to be modified. Since a majority of the technicians were serving only four years,

Above: The late Lt. Gen. Hubert R. Harmon, who was the first superintendent of the new Air Force Academy.

Left: Air Force instructional aid to NATO forces began in 1949. American sergeant with students at Turkish AF Communications School at Izmir.

the Air Force could not afford to spend so much time schooling them.

In January 1955, Gen. Thomas D. White, the Vice Chief of Staff, directed that some way be found to get more value from the time and money spent on technical training. The Air Force needed, particularly, to get the most it could from the four-year men. As a first step, ATC shortened many courses as much as seventeen days by omitting information not essential to the airman's job. Three of the schools began to experiment with narrow instruction for specific jobs in place of the broader schooling employed previously.

Under this approach, ATC shortened the early training and got the men ready for jobs sooner. After they left school, the students received instruction in their assigned units from mobile training detachments and through on-the-job training. If a man decided to make a career of the Air Force, he could go back to school for more general training, which would prepare him to become a master technician and supervisor. The Air Staff expected that, within a year or two, all new airmen could receive some technical schooling before going to operational units. In 1956 only about sixty-five percent went to technical schools, chiefly because of the lack of facilities.

Although experiments with the new plan during late 1955 and 1956 indicated that it was working satisfactorily, certain serious risks were involved. The narrow specialized training would require closer control of assignments. In addition, mobile training detachments would have to be expanded and field units would assume a heavier training burden. This might cost as much as the shortening of formal instruction would save.

During 1956 the Air Force began integrating basic military and technical training. ATC first shortened basic military training to six weeks for airmen going on to technical schools, and in July reduced it to four weeks. The airmen received their remaining five weeks of basic instruction as extra duty at the technical schools. This permitted the concentration at Lackland of all military basic training except that done at the technical schools.

Training of Foreigners

After the formation of NATO in 1949 and the inauguration of the Mutual Defense Assistance Program, the Air Force provided training for military personnel of allied and friendly countries to make sure that they could operate and maintain the US equipment furnished them. The United States not only trained foreign students in its schools and combat units but helped other countries set up their own training programs.

Foreign personnel received instruction in flying, aircraft and aeronautical equipment maintenance, armament, electronics, communications, supply, and administration. The language barrier posed the greatest difficulty. Although foreign students were supposed to know English before entering an American school, their knowledge of the language was often inadequate to learn new techniques rapidly.

Between 1949 and 1956, this training furnished approximately 37,000 spaces for foreigners in Air Force schools in the United States and overseas. The program trained more than 3,200 pilots, in addition to thousands who received specialized flying training, formal technical instruction, and on-the-job training.

The Problem of Officer Education

During 1954–56, Air University reestablished its officer education program on a long-term basis and largely overcame the disrupting effects of the Korean War. In September 1954 the Air Command and Staff School set up a nine-month course, attended by about 900 majors and lieutenant colonels annually. It also operated a Squadron Officers School for lieutenants and captains, an academic instructors course, and four air-weapon courses. The Air Command and Staff School was redesignated Air Command and Staff College in November 1954.

AFIT was accredited by the Engineers' Council for Professional Development in time for the March 1956 class of the Resident College to be awarded academic degrees. The college was authorized to give both undergraduate and graduate degrees in engineering.

The Air Force's educational program had to take into account the growing shortage of scientists and engineers. Estimates indicated that by 1960 the Soviet Union would have about 300,000 more scientists and engineers than the United States. A small proportion of the Air Force's scientists, engineers, and technicians remained in the service beyond their first tour of duty, and an even smaller number made the service a career. In competing with industry for college graduates, the Air Force was at a distinct disadvantage.

This situation made it imperative that the Air Force train more of its own specialists, but AFIT had difficulty finding qualified applicants. In 1956 the institute could fill only seventy percent of its quota of students in the engineering and scientific courses, indicating that the shortage would continue to be acute.

After many years of planning, the Air Force finally obtained legislation for a service academy in March 1954. Lt. Gen. Hubert R. Harmon, who had supervised planning for the academy since 1949, became the first superintendent.

In June 1954 a commission selected a site near Colorado Springs, Colo., as the permanent location of the academy, but until facilities could be built at the new site, the school would operate at Lowry AFB, at Denver. The Air Force Academy admitted its first class of about 300 cadets in July 1955.

Academy cadets were required to meet physical qualifications for pilot training. Because of the increasing demand for scientists and engineers and the growing importance of guided missiles, some doubts arose over this prerequisite. A board of Air Force generals, which met at Air University in October 1956 to evaluate the professional education program, recommended that academy students be trained as pilots and four or five years later be given advanced instruction in engineering and science by Air University. Those who for any reason did not become pilots ought to receive postgraduate scientific training immediately after graduation from the academy.

At the end of 1956 the USAF professional education program faced serious difficulties. Air University and its branches did not have the money to educate enough officers to meet the future needs of the Air Force, particularly in the scientific and technological fields. In addition, the operating commands often felt that they could not spare qualified officers from their regular assignments to attend school. Many officers were not qualified to attend AFIT or lacked interest in becoming proficient in specialized fields.

Another side of the problem was revealed by Col. Oliver G. Haywood, former chief of the Office of Scientific Research, Air Research and Development Command, who resigned from the Air Force in 1953. In an article in the *Air University Quarterly Review* in the summer of 1955, Haywood, who had an A.B. and M.A. from Harvard and a Sc.D. from MIT, declared that technical competence sometimes handicapped a man who wanted to get ahead. A considerable number of officers were convinced that qualifications in a technical field impaired their chances of getting good assignments and advancement. They were apt to be retained as staff consultants in their technical specialties, while promotions went to men in operational and management jobs.

The crucial need for professionally trained people seemed likely to put an end to this kind of mismanagement. A board headed by Gen. Edwin W. Rawlings, commander of AMC, reviewed the Air Force's educational program in October 1956. It recommended to the Chief of Staff that additional incentives be given officers attending scientific courses, including preference in promotion. The board also proposed that Air University be allowed more funds to expand its educational program and to construct new facilities for the AFIT Resident College as soon as possible.

In 1949-50 there had been recommendations that the Resident College be gradually converted into a graduate school, leaving undergraduate study to civilian institutions. The Rawlings Board, however, found that the need for undergraduate courses in science and engineering remained as great in 1956 as it had been in 1950. Since a large proportion of the officer corps still lacked bachelor's degrees and sufficient background to do graduate work, the board recommended that both undergraduate and graduate studies be continued by the Air Force.

Finally, the Rawlings Board noted that only fifty-six percent of Regular officers and forty-six percent of reserve officers on active duty possessed bachelor's degrees. Since it believed that all officers should have bachelor's degrees and many needed graduate study, the board recommended that the Air Force place greater emphasis on the value of education for an officer or airman. Effectiveness reports should indicate what officers were doing to remedy their educational deficiencies.

Air Force Academy cadet puzzles over a bit of research. Academy opened its doors in July 1955 at Lowry AFB, Denver, is scheduled to move eventually to Colorado Springs.

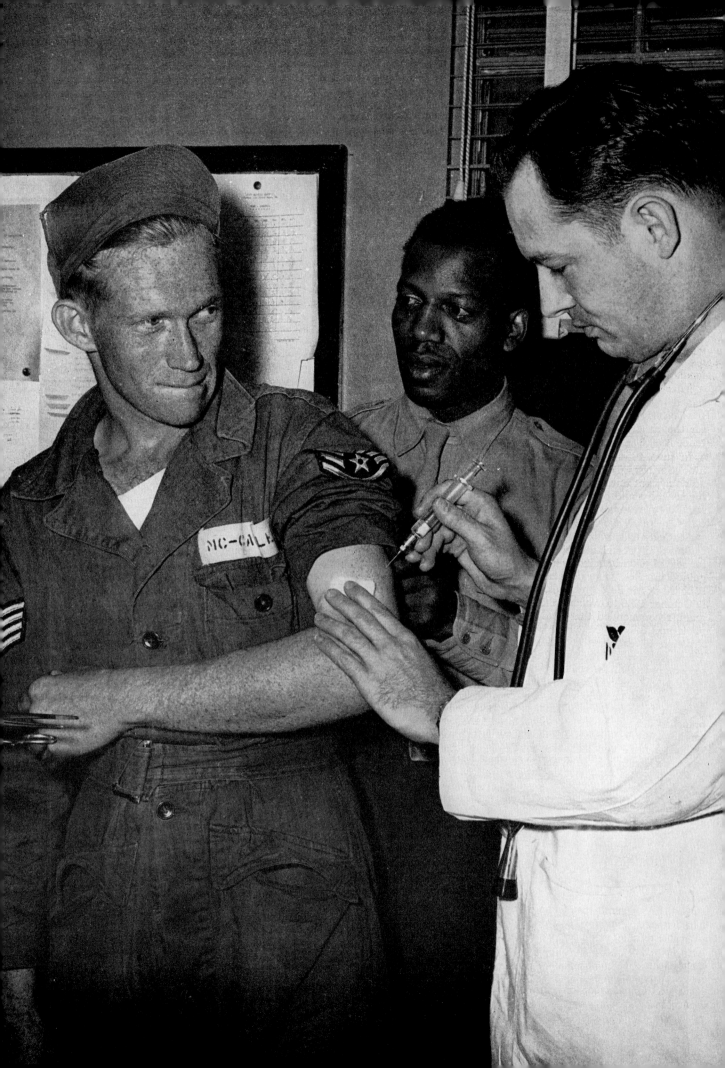

Chapter 18

THE MEN

Health, Welfare, and Safety

INCREASINGLY, the Air Force came to realize that its manpower and training problems were closely related to a host of morale factors. Among the foremost of these were the health, welfare, and safety of its men and their families. The Air Force made a determined effort to meet the needs of its people and provide them with the incentives to good work that most men need.

Medical Care of the Air Force

Because human beings will always be the decisive element no matter how mechanized war may become, the health of a military force is a major factor. For the Air Force, the problem of maintaining a physically sound force was complicated by the growing hazards of new high speeds and altitudes. The American Medical Association recognized the uniqueness of the problem in February 1953 when it declared aviation medicine a distinct specialty.

Aviation medicine in the United States can trace its origins to the efforts in 1917 of Col. Theodore C. Lyster, the first surgeon of the Aviation Section of the Signal Corps. During World War II the Air Surgeon, Maj. Gen. David N. W. Grant, aggressively worked to improve the stature of aviation medicine and the quality of the care given to AAF units. This work was continued after the war by Maj. Gen. Malcolm C. Grow, who led the fight for a separate USAF medical service.

The National Security Act of 1947 did not provide for a separate medical service for the Air Force, and debate arose over the merits of a single medical department for all the armed services as opposed to three medical services. Secretary Symington and General Vandenberg supported General Grow in his contention that the new US Air Force should have its own medical service—that command responsibility for health could not be assigned to another

department. Finally, Secretary of Defense Johnson ordered the transfer of certain medical functions and the people performing them from the Army to the Air Force by July 1, 1949. An Army-Air Force agreement called for the Air Force to perform its own basic medical services and the Army to continue providing general hospital service, with the Air Force sharing proportionate responsibility for staffing the hospitals and buying materials.

The USAF Medical Service, headed by General Grow as the first Surgeon General, was established on July 1, 1949. It provided services in preventive medicine, general medicine, aviation medicine, dentistry, nursing, occupational and physical therapy, public health, food hygiene and sanitation, and nutrition. It also performed research in all these fields.

Two main principles guided the USAF Medical Service. First, it engaged in coordinated action with the Army and the Navy under the policy control of the Secretary of Defense. Second, it became an integral part of the Air Force. According to Maj. Gen. Harry G. Armstrong, Surgeon General from 1949 to 1954, this meant a medical service "which is planned by air-minded doctors . . . geared to aeronautical operations, and . . . can be fitted into airplanes."

The safety of the individual in flight and the health of the military family on the base were the central concerns of the Medical Service. Since most Air Force people lived on or near air bases, each base constituted an individual community. In isolated areas, especially, Air Force families needed local medical facilities. To meet these needs, the Air Force developed a community-type medical service at its air bases. This kind of service received encouragement from the Dependents' Medical Care Act of 1956, which broadened the responsibilities of the military services for dependent medical care.

The Medical Service tried to give the largest amount of care at the place of duty. Using the concept of group practice, it staffed the smaller facilities with general practitioners and with the broader medical specialties. When the size of a base warranted, the more limited specialties

The familiar inoculations make up but a small part of the extensive medical program the Air Force provides its people.

Maj. Gen. David N. W. Grant, Air Surgeon, AAF, WW II.

Maj. Gen. Malcolm C. Grow, first Surgeon General, USAF.

Maj. Gen. Harry G. Armstrong, Surgeon General, 1949-54.

Maj. Gen. Dan C. Ogle, General Armstrong's successor.

were furnished; only at the largest bases were all the medical specialties represented, supported by specialized nursing, technical help, and the latest equipment. The largest hospitals became medical centers for consultation and acceptance of problem cases transferred from smaller facilities.

Doctors, Dentists, and Nurses

The first major problem for the Air Force Medical Service was to get enough qualified professional personnel. The number of officers selected for transfer from the Army in July 1949 was 3,706.

Expansion to meet the Korean crisis intensified the need for doctors, dentists, nurses, and other medical personnel. The armed services used various methods to attract them, but it soon became clear that further legislation would be necessary to obtain enough doctors. Special-inducement pay had already been in use since October 1949. Congress responded by passing the so-called doctor draft act in September 1950.

To encourage medical careers, the Air Force introduced postgraduate training courses in hospitals and universities, offered opportunities for research and specialty practice, and adopted other inducements. In 1956, additional bonus pay was made available to doctors and dentists. The number of physicians and dentists entering the Air Force became encouraging enough in 1957 to permit ending the doctor draft. Nevertheless, the paramount problem facing the Medical Service was its difficulty in persuading its professional men to make a career of the Air Force.

The shortage of nurses and medical specialists—dietitians, occupational therapists, and physical therapists—remained serious. Because of the shortage of qualified women to fill the officer vacancies, both the Nurse Corps and the Medical Specialist Corps were opened to men in August 1955.

The Medical Service Corps also suffered shortages. This corps performed technical and administrative specialties, and its officers were used to save the time of physicians for care of the sick and injured. The many specialties included pharmacy, sanitary and industrial-hygiene engineering, physiology, and psychology.

Civilian consultants stimulated professional interest and trained junior medical officers. They advised the Surgeon General at Headquarters USAF on over-all policy, while at base hospitals they advised medical officers on special clinical matters.

At the end of 1956, the Medical Service had 35,714 military personnel on duty, representing almost four percent of the entire Air Force strength. The 10,623 commissioned officers included 3,266 physicians, 2,184 dentists, and 2,793 nurses.

Medical airmen received basic, advanced, and special technical training courses in sixty-four specialties. A special assistant to the Surgeon General devoted full attention to airman careers.

Hospitals

The Medical Service early adopted a policy of treating the patient at his place of duty. And since the Air Force had bases all over the world, doctors and medical facilities were needed in many faraway places.

In December 1949 the Air Force was operating seventy-five World War II hospitals of temporary construction with a capacity of 6,850 beds. When the Korean War began, hospital construction became the major problem, with first priority going to facilities for evacuated patients. Within two years, by July 1952, the Air Force had 164 medical facilities providing 18,730 beds.

After 1953, there was less demand for hospital beds

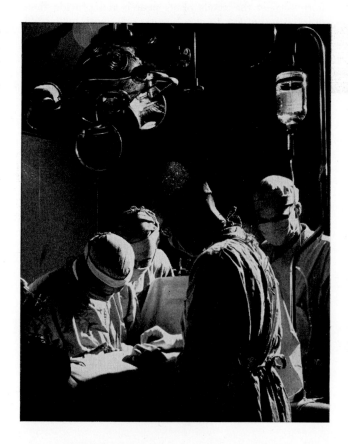

The Medical Service prefers to treat a patient at his place of duty. An appendectomy at Bolling AFB, Washington, D. C.

because manpower in the Air Force declined slightly and health consistently improved. But to give adequate care to its widely dispersed units, the Air Force had to increase the number of hospitals and dispensaries. At the end of December 1956, new construction had brought the total number of Air Force hospitals and Class A dispensaries (up to twenty-five beds) to 204, but the number of hospital beds dropped to 14,000. At this time, Air Force facilities were caring for 79.8 percent of all Air Force patients requiring hospitalization.

Of the 204 total, there were ninety-one hospitals and thirty-five Class A dispensaries in the United States and forty-two hospitals and thirty-six Class A dispensaries in overseas areas. The two largest hospitals were the 400-bed, seven-story hospital at Elmendorf AFB, Alaska, completed in 1955, and the 300-bed hospital capable of expansion to 500, at Wright-Patterson AFB, Ohio, completed in 1956. Because of the emphasis on definitive diagnosis and outpatient treatment, these modern hospitals gave more space for services such as X-ray, laboratory, and pharmacy.

Health in the Air Force

In 1952, General Armstrong announced: "The level of health is higher in the Air Force than it has ever been in any large military force in history and each year the Air Force has successively exceeded its previous record." And the record continued to improve in each succeeding year. In 1957, Maj. Gen. Dan C. Ogle, USAF Surgeon General after July 1954, reported that health and physical efficiency in the Air Force were "at an all-time high."

The Air Force used several measurements of health. The noneffective ratio told the number of persons out of every 100 in the Air Force excused from duty on an average day because of noncombat medical reasons. This ratio reached an all-time low of 1.02 for 1956, compared with 1.64 for 1950. The admission rate told the number per thousand admitted for treatment during one year. This rate fell to 265 for 1956 compared to 343 for the year July 1, 1949–June 30, 1950. A third index was the daily proportion of personnel occupying hospital beds, and this hospitalization ratio reached another low in 1956 of 0.80 per 100.

Dental health was also good. The high rate of turnover made it difficult to improve dental health, but the Dental Service estimated a ten percent improvement between 1950 and 1953. Since about ninety-five percent of recruits required dental treatment, the Dental Service intensified its preventive dentistry program. It also conducted a busy research program, studying the effects on teeth and dental appliances of high altitude, high speed, explosive decompression, prolonged exposure to oxygen, horizontal-position flying, and excessive fatigue.

The Korean War brought new health problems. The rapid influx of unseasoned troops caused a higher illness rate in the winter months of 1951, and the movement of units brought new demands on the Medical Service. It responded with intensified preventive medicine, more rigid maintenance of health standards, more careful selection of Air Force personnel, and wider immunization.

The Air Force mortality rate for 1956 of 2.15 per 1,000, a decrease of twenty-one percent from the 1951 noncombat rate, was largely the result of a lower death rate from aircraft accidents. The death rate from disease was only 0.36 per 1,000, about the same as in previous years.

A number of special factors affected the disease and mortality rates in the Air Force. During 1951-56, when the strength of the Air Force averaged more than 900,000, at least seventy-five percent of USAF personnel were under thirty years of age. These younger people were more susceptible to infectious and contagious diseases and more prone to accidents. Also affecting the general

"Tilting chair" device built by aeromedical researchers delving into visual problems encountered in night flight.

level of health unfavorably were the considerable turnover of personnel, particularly among young airmen, and the worldwide deployment which exposed unseasoned troops to uncommon diseases. Immunization against all diseases was not possible.

Aviation Medicine

The new problems that medical science faced when men began to fly multiplied with the capabilities of flight. How much faster and how much higher men will be able to fly may depend upon how well medical scientists do their work. "Space medicine" came into the language as research moved on to interstellar travel and man's chances of survival in airless regions.

Advances in aircraft design taxed the minds and physiques of the men who flew the new air weapons. To safeguard the flyers, the Air Force carried on extensive research programs. The Medical Service advised and cooperated with ARDC, Air University, and other USAF agencies dealing with flight and ground safety. It trained flight surgeons; planned and supervised programs to improve the health, safety, and effectiveness of aircrews; and evaluated personal, protective, and survival equipment.

High speed and high altitude caused most of the aeromedical problems. Associated with these problems was the one of selecting men who could best adjust to the environment and the equipment. Among the factors studied were the pathological and psychological aspects of flight and aerial combat. Problems included oxygen supply, decompression phenomena, fatigue, noise of jet engines, vision difficulties, in-flight food kits, bail-out and survival equipment, restraining harnesses, safety clothing, and effects of cosmic-ray nuclei and high temperatures.

The Air Force centered its major research at the USAF School of Aviation Medicine (SAM) at Randolph AFB, Tex., and at the Aero Medical Laboratory at Wright-Patterson AFB, Ohio. Additional research activities were conducted at the Air Force Flight Test Center at Edwards AFB, Calif., and at the Holloman Air Development Center, N. M. Also, the Environmental Health Laboratory at Wright-Patterson and various hospitals did research in aviation medicine. The Arctic Aeromedical Laboratory, at Ladd AFB, Alaska, investigated health and safety problems that have proved peculiar to cold-weather operations.

At Randolph the laboratories worked on all aspects of aeromedical research except aeronautical engineering. The Aero Medical Laboratory at Wright-Patterson collaborated closely with the Engineering Division at Air Materiel Command in the design of aircraft and equipment to best satisfy the human factors of flying.

The School of Aviation Medicine had trained more than 8,000 flight surgeons by 1957. Air Force nurses, medical technicians, physiological training officers, and equipment specialists attended a branch school at Gunter AFB, Ala. Young physicians, fresh from internships, took an intensive nine-week course at Randolph and graduated as aviation medical examiners. Then they completed a year of supervised field practice before becoming flight surgeons. The school also offered refresher and graduate courses for senior flight surgeons.

Aeromedical Evacuation

Perhaps the earliest aeromedical evacuation occurred during the siege of Paris by the Prussians in 1870, when 160 wounded were successfully removed by balloon. During World War I, there was some air evacuation, but the small planes did not allow adequate space for patients. Although the AAF made extensive use of air evacuation during World War II, its full potentialities were not realized until the Korean test.

Air evacuation of patients during the Korean War succeeded famously. Helicopters lifted the wounded from near the front lines to airstrips where troop carrier planes airlifted them to hospitals in Japan, and MATS transports hurried them home across the Pacific. Doctors, nurses, and medical technicians waited for the wounded at the airstrips in Korea and cared for the patients aboard the

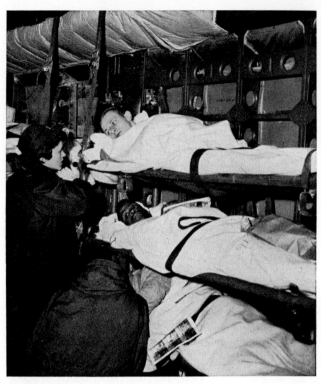

Air evacuation of sick and wounded saved thousands of lives in Korea. A flight nurse checks comfort of patient.

transports. These teams, assigned to FEAF aeromedical evacuation squadrons, attended 296,328 patients within Korea and Japan and more than 63,000 patients on transpacific flights. During the Korean conflict, ninety-five percent of all medical evacuations were by air.

The largest and most notable evacuation occurred in December 1950 when American Marines, fighting in bitter, below-zero weather in North Korea, were surrounded by Communist Chinese. In a hazardous five-day airlift, C-47s evacuated 4,689 casualties over enemy lines to medical care and safety.

The Surgeon General credited air evacuation with being a major cause of the low death rate among American soldiers during the Korean War. Deaths fell from 4.5 per 100 injured men who reached aid stations in World War II to two per 100 in Korea. General Armstrong specified increased use of blood and its derivatives and new drug therapy as the other chief causes for this improvement.

In carrying out its responsibility for evacuating patients of all the armed forces, the Air Force operated a worldwide system. The USAF aeromedical units worked in coordination with troop carrier units within a theater, and USAF medical personnel operated the terminal hospitals and holdover stations. Transport planes, fitted out as "flying hospitals" with up to fifty beds, could be flown into combat areas for on-the-spot emergency treatment.

To further develop these techniques, Headquarters USAF set up a Tactical Medical Center under the Eighteenth Air Force at Donaldson AFB, S. C. Aeromedical units participated in many joint exercises in a quest for speed, mobility, and flexibility. In August 1953, they airlifted a fifty-bed hospital, consisting of 36,740 pounds of equipment and fifty-four persons, a distance of 1,000 miles to Altus AFB, Okla., in twelve hours.

Air Force Chaplains

A small building topped by a steeple graced every Air Force base. Military chaplains, representing the Catholic

Lt. Col. John P. Stapp, Air Force flight surgeon, acts as his own guinea pig in deceleration tests on high-speed sled.

and Jewish faiths and sixty-nine Protestant denominations, held religious services in these chapels and in many ways gave meaning and guidance to the lives of Air Force men and women and their families.

The Senate Committee on Armed Services stated in 1955 its firm conviction that "the American way of life is in no small way predicated on the spiritual welfare of the individual." It desired "that facilities for worship be ready and available wherever possible prior to stationing of large bodies of troops at these installations." In April 1957 there were 466 chapels in use at air bases throughout the world.

The Chief of Air Force Chaplains, (Maj. Gen.) Charles I. Carpenter, advised the Chief of Staff on religious and related matters affecting Air Force personnel and their families. Each command had a chaplain on its staff, and chaplains were further assigned down through wings, and in some cases groups. All chaplains were advisers to their commanders, and they were free to develop and participate in all types of activities that improved recreational and social outlets for the men and relieved personal and family hardships. Although their primary interest was in the religious life of Air Force people, the chaplains had a deep concern for maintaining morale and encouraging cultural activities. The Chief of Air Force Chaplains and his staff at Headquarters USAF kept close personal contact with USAF chaplains, frequently visiting air bases to learn of problems firsthand.

At the peak of World War II there were 2,200 chaplains in the Army Air Forces. But when chaplain officers were transferred from the Army on July 1, 1949, the Air Force received only 141 Regular officer authorizations for chaplains. These and the reserve chaplains on active duty totaled 458, including 302 Protestant, 149 Catholic, and seven Jewish chaplains. The Air Force received only 573 chaplains from the Army's inactive reserve list. This number proved far too small when the Korean War expansion occurred.

The Air Force followed a policy of involuntary recall to active military duty in 1951, to protect the best interests of the chaplain reserves on return to their parishes after the emergency. But in 1952 the basis was changed to voluntary indefinite to bring the chaplain procedure in

**Maj. Gen. Charles I. Carpenter,
Chief of Air Force Chaplains.**

line with over-all Air Force policy. By June 1952 there were 995 chaplains on active duty in the Air Force, and by the end of March 1957, 1,202.

Beginning in 1952, ROTC graduates could receive commissions as second lieutenants with designation of "chaplain trainee," which they carried through their religious training at a seminary before entering the Air Force. After becoming chaplains, officers attended the specialized chaplain training course at Fort Slocum, N. Y. In July 1953 the Air Force integrated this training with the basic military course for officers at Lackland AFB, Tex. Many airmen also found career opportunities as chaplain helpers.

The chaplaincy developed a Six-Point Program in 1950-51. The first and most important point (1) concerned religious worship and pastoral functions, including rites, visits, and ministrations. The other points were (2) moral and religious education, including the character-guidance program; (3) personal counseling on problems of religion, welfare, marital relationships, rehabilitation of prisoners, and wholesome adjustments; (4) humanitarian services to victims of underprivilege or disaster; (5) development of public understanding and good will in community relationships; (6) cultural leadership.

The chaplains helped the individual commander, and through him the entire Air Force, by the information they gathered for the Chaplain's Monthly Report. Since this report listed the numbers and types of consultations held, without divulging confidences, the nature of the problems revealed provided a key to Air Force morale.

Judge Advocate General

Military justice was always of utmost importance in the Air Force. But, as with the Medical Service and the Chaplains, the Air Force did not have its own Judge Ad-

Air Force chaplains employ modern communications techniques to reach their charges. A TV show at Loring AFB, Me.

**Maj. Gen. Reginald C. Harmon,
Judge Advocate General, USAF.**

vocate General's Department independent of the Army until 1949. In January it came into existence as the legal agency of the Air Force, with the prime function of administering military justice. From February 1950 on, the Judge Advocate General (JAG), Maj. Gen. Reginald C. Harmon, had direct access to the Chief of Staff. General Harmon was the first and still the only USAF Judge Advocate General in 1957.

Officers, designated as judge advocates, were assigned to duty for the administration of military justice and other legal matters at USAF installations all over the world. In July 1949 there were only 339 officer-lawyers in the JAG Department, but by July 1951 the number had grown to 929. In March 1957 there were 1,262 on duty.

By 1956 enough AFROTC graduates were entering the JAG Department as second lieutenants to eliminate the need for direct appointments. Two new problems then arose—how to retain young lawyers in the service and how to give them more military and legal experience. Air University had conducted an orientation course for new judge advocates for several years, but this was discontinued in 1955 in favor of allowing the new officers to train in their first duty positions.

The administration of military justice was based on the Uniform Code of Military Justice, which became effective May 1, 1951, as a result of legislation passed in 1950. Representatives of the Army, Navy, and Air Force joined in the preparation of a single manual of interpretation of the new law, called *Manual for Courts-Martial, United States, 1951.* Briefly, the code redefined the punitive articles, changed the requirements for qualified personnel administering the code, and provided for a revised system of appellate review.

Court-martial cases fell into the categories of summary, special, and general, the last two involving the more serious cases. Only the special with bad-conduct discharge and the general were reviewed by the Office of the Judge Advocate General. The JAG Department administered its general court-martial responsibilities through jurisdictions, of which there were ninety-two in June 1957.

Although the Office of the Judge Advocate General reviewed all records of general court-martial trials, the law required that certain ones be reviewed by special boards of review within the office. There were six such boards in 1957. The cases included those involving imprisonment for one or more years. The office provided both defense counsel and government counsel in all appeal cases.

The Air Force also concerned itself with aspects of civil law. The JAG gave opinions on international law and laws that governed USAF organization, administration, and personnel. It supervised a legal assistance program and advised the Air Force on laws relating to claims, patents, taxes, and litigation. It told the Air Staff when legislation was necessary to accomplish its aims.

Flight Safety

From its earliest days, flying took a toll of dead and injured in peacetime as well as wartime. The Air Force and its predecessors had always sought safety precautions to reduce the hazards of flight. To give the proper emphasis to flight safety the Air Force established a directorate under the Inspector General in December 1949.

A new concept in accident prevention, adopted in 1950, demanded constant stress on safety factors in the design, production, and maintenance of aircraft. Since pilot error caused most aircraft accidents and since maintenance error was also an important cause, the Air Force conducted an aggressive educational campaign among flying and maintenance personnel in the fundamental principles of safe flying. It prepared and circulated special studies of such

problems as the human and weather factors in aircraft accidents, jet fighter forced landings, and air and ground aircraft collisions. It issued informative accident summaries for specific types of aircraft and sponsored safety conferences and symposiums. In addition, it published two magazines, the *Aircraft Accident and Maintenance Review* and *Flying Safety,* the latter carrying the well-known cartoon depicting the mishaps of that fictitious bungler "Mal Function."

Day or night, information on each aircraft accident was immediately flashed to the Directorate of Flight Safety Research, which decided whether its personnel or those of a local base would conduct the investigation. Directorate personnel actually investigated only a small percentage of the USAF major accidents, selected because they involved new aircraft, indicated new accident trends, or presented unusual technical difficulties. In particularly important or complicated accidents, the directorate drew upon the technical knowledge of ARDC and AMC and the aircraft industry to assist in on-the-spot investigations. Once the

MAJOR AIRCRAFT ACCIDENT RATE WORLDWIDE
(Rates per 100,000 flying hours)

For Calendar Year

YEAR	RATE
1946	61
1947[a]	44
1948	40
1949	37
1950[b]	36
1951	33
1952	29
1953	24
1954	20
1955	17

a. Accident data for ANG are included only since 1947.
b. Accidents and flying hours of Navy units flying for MATS included since 1950.

SOURCE: USAF STATISTICAL DIGEST

AIRCRAFT FATALITIES WORLDWIDE
(Rates per 100,000 flying hours)

For Calendar Year

YEAR	RATE
1946	24
1947	17
1948	14
1949	12
1950	16
1951	15
1952	15
1953	11
1954	9
1955	9

SOURCE: USAF STATISTICAL DIGEST

Aeromedical research has had much to do with the evolution of flying garb from boots and breeches to the G-suit.

cause was known, experts directed every effort toward corrective action.

Flight safety was of vital concern to the Air Force, not only because of the tremendous cost of aircraft accidents in life and property but also for the very practical necessity of conserving combat capability for wartime. The crash of a B-52 meant a loss of about $8 million; of a C-124, about $1.7 million. Thanks in large part to the accident-prevention campaign, the major aircraft accident rate declined steadily from forty-four per 100,000 flying hours for 1947 to an all-time low of fifteen for 1956. The Air Force classified accidents as major when they re-

**Maj. Gen. Joseph D. Caldara
Director, Flight Safety Research.**

quired more than a certain number of man-hours to repair the aircraft. The number varied with the type of plane.

The fatality rate also declined but not as precipitately as the major accident rate. As aircraft increased their performance and speed, any single accident was likely to be more serious than ever before. For example, during the 1930s, an average of one out of every thirteen major accidents was a fatal one. In 1956, one out of every five major accidents resulted in one or more fatalities. Because of the greater operating hazards, in 1956 jet fighters and jet trainers had a higher accident rate than any other type of USAF airplane. The annual fatality rate per 100,000 flying hours dropped from seventeen in 1947 to eight in 1956. One-third of all fatalities in the Air Force during 1956 resulted from aircraft accidents, with an average of three men each day suffering fatal or major injuries.

Ground Safety

The Air Force was vitally concerned with the safety of its men on the ground as well as in flight. Its commands carried on programs to promote safety in ground activities at air bases, on the flight line and in the shops, on and off the job.

The USAF ground safety record was particularly impressive after 1950. In April 1957 the Air Force received for the seventh consecutive year the Award of Honor for outstanding achievement in safety from the National Safety Council. The 1957 award was based on a reduction of 5.8 percent in ground accident rates and costs during 1956 as compared with the average experience for 1954 and 1955. Over the seven-year period 1949-56, the Air Force reduced its accident rates and costs as much as twenty-five percent.

The specific improvements in the 1956 record included reductions in the military injury rate, civilian injury rate, the USAF (government-owned) vehicle accident rate, and ground accident costs per capita strength. These rates were determined through accident indexes used in a system of ground accident investigation, reporting, and analysis.

As in civilian life the motor car caused the highest proportion of injuries. And by far the greater number occurred in privately owned vehicles. Although injuries and fatalities declined in 1956, 612 Air Force personnel were killed in private motor cars and twenty-three in government-owned cars. This almost equaled the number of fatalities from aircraft accidents. The second largest number of injuries and deaths on the ground came from participation in sports, especially water sports. Accidental deaths from sources other than the operation of motor vehicles were reduced by four percent in 1956.

Engineering and research studies uncovered the causes of ground accidents, both human and material, and indicated corrective measures. Research projects included studies on motor-car crashes, jet aircraft air-intake hazards, noise problems in aviation, use of reflectorized material, refueling of aircraft by trailers, vapor-control systems, liquid-petroleum exhaust purifiers, and methods of handling dangerous materials.

A training program offered graduate courses in safety engineering to officers. Airmen also could make a career field out of ground safety. Inspectors checked the progress of safety education in the commands. And safety engineering standards were included in all ground operations and planning.

The Air Force cooperated with private, industrial, and governmental organizations in the development of safety programs. It was particularly interested in cooperating with local communities for safety measures of benefit to airmen and civilians alike.

Chapter 19

THE TOOLS

Bases

ADEQUATE bases and facilities are perhaps the first requisite for the operation and maintenance of a modern air force. A modern air base—with its runways, taxiways, warmup and parking aprons, hangars, and shops—is a complicated and costly establishment. It must have control towers and navigational aids, storage tanks for great amounts of fuel, warehouses, and housing for its personnel. Air bases have grown steadily larger and their facilities more numerous and complex. The construction of a worldwide system of modern air bases was one of the Air Force's most important tasks in the period after World War II.

Period of Transition, 1945-50

During World War II the AAF built a vast array of bases throughout the world. At the end of September 1945, the AAF had 1,895 air installations, including 1,333 within the United States. Peace brought a rapid reduction in the number of these stations, and by the end of June 1948 the Air Force had only 290 major installations. Of the 112 in the United States, only ninety were active, while overseas 133 out of 178 were active.

The closing down of many air installations after the war naturally led the public to believe that no new bases and facilities would be needed for many years. But almost all of the bases built during World War II were temporary, and they soon deteriorated to the point where it became uneconomical to use them. Most of those in the United States had been used as training bases and did not suit the changed strategic situation after 1945. It had not been necessary to build many combat bases in the United States, and as a result, the Air Force did not have enough

Air Force bases span the world. This is the first sunrise of the season at Thule Air Base, in Greenland.

to meet its requirements in the years following World War II. Bases were not in the right places, nor could they accommodate the faster and heavier aircraft coming into use.

SAC and ADC were the commands most concerned about bases after 1945. From its beginning in 1946, SAC needed strategically located bases. This often meant new ones with more extensive facilities. The increased emphasis on air defense after August 1949 forced ADC to seek more bases at strategic locations. Overseas, SAC bases posed much the same problems. The Air Force made more progress overseas, especially in the Pacific and North Atlantic areas where the most pressing requirements existed. By 1950, work was moving ahead on Okinawa, at Elmendorf, Ladd, and Eielson AF bases in Alaska, at Ernest Harmon AFB in Newfoundland, and at Keflavik Airport in Iceland.

The decision at the end of 1948 to cut the Air Force back from fifty-five to forty-eight groups instead of expanding it to seventy changed the whole base construction picture for 1949-50. The Air Force consolidated activities on fewer bases, reducing its major installations to 180. The fact that this smaller group structure still required $2.2 billion in new construction indicated the extent to which existing facilities would have failed to meet the needs of a seventy-group Air Force. Aside from housing, then, the Air Force placed its main effort before 1950 on modernizing and maintaining existing installations. Even this task could not be done properly because of lack of funds. As a result, the outbreak of war in Korea found the Air Force woefully short of bases and facilities.

Housing for men and their families posed one of the Air Force's most critical problems after 1945. The normal postwar housing shortages were complicated by the location of certain bases far from urban centers. Although the Air Force did what it could with the funds available, the situation continued to grow worse. By mid-1950, about 55,000 officers and enlisted men legally entitled to government-furnished family quarters did not have them. About 63,000 more men urgently needed family housing. Such a situation inevitably lowered morale, and many men left the Air Force because they could not obtain decent housing for their families.

Government construction failed to alleviate the situation. The 1,300 houses authorized by the Eightieth Congress were almost completed by June 1950, but they satisfied only about 1½ percent of the need. Within the United States the Air Force relied chiefly on family housing constructed under the Wherry-Spence Act of August 1949. This law permitted the Federal Housing Administration to insure privately financed housing on or near military installations to the extent of $500 million, or up to $1 billion with the consent of the President.

The Air Force planned to construct 26,595 units at forty-nine bases in the United States, but by mid-June 1950, work had begun on only 4,292 of these. Even if the complete program could have been finished, it would have provided less than half of the required houses. Because of the high cost of utilities and construction, private builders did not display much interest in the 3,000 to 4,000 units planned for Alaska. The need for cold-weather housing in Alaska and typhoon-proof housing on Okinawa made both these areas difficult problems. Firms in Japan and the Philippines handled most of the construction projects on Okinawa.

At the beginning of 1950 more than half of the 207,000 bachelor airmen still lived in temporary wartime barracks, and the remainder lived in obsolete permanent-type barracks. The old Army squad room, uncomfortable and unhealthy, was home for tens of thousands of airmen. The Air Force drew up new dormitory designs calling for two to four men in a room and costing from $2,000 to $2,300 per man to build. In 1950 the Eighty-first Congress authorized the Air Force to build enough of these to house only 5,250 airmen in the United States and 700 overseas.

More than half of the USAF bases in 1950 were temporaries and had been deteriorating for five years. This created a big recurrent maintenance job, further complicated by the chronic shortage of money. In 1950 the Air Force estimated that a five-year program of major repairs would cost $90 million.

Emergency repairs and base modifications used up most of the funds appropriated for repair and maintenance during 1945-50. Money often had to be diverted from one base to pay for badly needed repairs at another. Typhoons did $6.5 million worth of damage on Okinawa and Guam in 1949. Tornadoes and fires during the first six months of 1950 cost $800,000 in repairs to base facilities in the United States. The Air Force installed fire-prevention devices and sprinkler systems and bought new fire-fighting equipment for many bases. Air Force fire losses were serious, running to about $150,000 a month in the United States and even more overseas. They were particularly heavy in arctic regions like Alaska.

After September 1947 the Air Force became fully responsible for the management, expansion, and repair of its own base facilities. This included determination of requirements and, beginning with fiscal year 1950, the preparation and defense of budgets. In most cases, the Army Corps of Engineers continued to handle real estate purchases and to contract for the actual construction. At times, particularly overseas, field commanders used aviation engineers for construction work. These were Army engineer troops serving with and under control of the Air Force.

Planning and managing construction activities was a complicated business, since all projects had to be approved by the Air Force, the Department of Defense, the Bureau of the Budget, and Congress. In August 1950, Brig. Gen. Colby M. Myers, USAF Director of Installations, stated that "the cycle of construction programming and execution is constantly passing through so many echelons of control and review that the Air Force must foresee and plan its construction requirements at least three years in advance."

Rebuilding the Bases, 1950-53

During its rapid expansion after June 1950 the Air Force found that lack of adequate base facilities was as serious a handicap as the shortage of men and weapons. Since the base structure in the summer of 1950 was insufficient even for the existing forty-eight wings, it was hopelessly inadequate to support the ninety-five wings planned during the fall and winter of 1950-51. Then, in the fall of 1951, came the decision to expand to 143 wings. The long time-lapse between the adoption of programs and completion of usable facilities meant that the Air Force faced a long and difficult struggle to house its units. It also meant that the first year or two following the outbreak of the Korean War would witness a frantic, worldwide emergency construction program.

The selection and construction of new bases and the repair and modernization of old ones became a major task during 1950-53. In June 1950, nearly all of the training bases needed more and better facilities. All-weather flying required newer and better types of navigational aids. Adequate troop housing and suitable operations, administration, depot, fuel storage, and medical facilities had to be provided.

After June 1950 the Air Force began an emergency base construction program in the Far East and other overseas areas. At the same time, it laid plans for a long-range construction program that included bases overseas. Congress appropriated $1.4 billion for Air Force military construction in fiscal year 1951 and $2.1 billion in fiscal year 1952.

One of the largest amounts was earmarked to modernize permanent installations and to finance major repairs and necessary facilities at reopened World War II bases. Millions of dollars went for aircraft control and warning stations, the Long Range Proving Ground, and construction in Okinawa and Alaska and elsewhere overseas. FEAF

MAJOR INSTALLATIONS, USAF	
AS OF END OF FY	NUMBER
1950	278
1951	355
1952	426
1953*	262
1954	285
1955	278
1956	279
As of DECEMBER 31, 1956	276

*As a result of the classification of installations in accordance with AFR 87-5, installations were broken down into various categories. The totals, starting with FY 1953, represent the totals of the first four (Operational, Training, Research and Test, and Logistical) categories of installations.

Night view of a scramble hangar housing all-weather F-86D interceptors on alert at Itazuke Air Base, in Japan.

built six advanced airfields in Korea and improved thirteen in Japan. On Okinawa, the Air Force constructed airfields at Kadena and Naha, storage tanks for aviation gasoline, utilities, and living quarters for officers, airmen, and civilian workers.

The rise in construction costs during the first year of the Korean War led President Truman to direct the Air Force to build new bases only if no suitable existing base could be modernized or no surplus base belonging to one of the other armed services could be transferred. This was only a partial solution, because the older installations were not always strategically located and it was sometimes cheaper to build a new base than modernize an old one. Nevertheless, as Secretary Finletter observed in July 1951, few of the installations within the continental United States were really new since they had been used during World War II. But most of the foreign bases were new.

The construction program suffered a temporary setback in 1953 after the change in administration. In an effort to cut government expenses, President Eisenhower directed that all expenditures be reviewed and pared as much as possible. The Director of the Bureau of the Budget and the Secretary of Defense announced in early February 1953 that work should continue only on those projects which were clearly essential and "consistent with the objectives of the Eisenhower Administration." On the essential projects the "strictest standards of economy" would be employed. No construction contracts would be awarded after February 7, 1953, until each project had been reviewed and specifically cleared by the Secretary of the Air Force, the Secretary of Defense, and the Bureau of the Budget. Secretary of Defense Wilson also directed that advertisements for bids should cease on March 1, except on those construction contracts reapproved by the Secretaries of the Air Force and Defense.

The review of projects placed an enormous administrative burden on Air Force agencies and delayed about $700 million of new construction work for a minimum of two months. About 180 items considered no longer essential were reduced or eliminated from programs. Action on more than $1.9 billion of Air Force construction was suspended for varying periods of time. In May 1953, when the Department of Defense temporarily cut the USAF goal from 143 wings to 120, another readjustment became necessary. This changed plans for the use of seventeen bases in the continental United States and seventeen overseas. Construction was deferred on fourteen bases in

the United States and six overseas. The Air Force canceled projects already under contract and, in some cases, where construction had begun.

Foreign Bases

In 1950 the United States already possessed bases— mostly developed during World War II—in the Far East, Alaska, Newfoundland, Germany, and Great Britain. Other bases, such as Kindley AFB in Bermuda, Lajes Field in the Azores, Wheelus Field in Libya, and Dhahran Airfield in Saudi Arabia, also dated from the war but in 1950 were being used mainly for air transport operations. But existing airfields did not meet the need for alternate strategic bases which the Air Force had come to consider vital for its operations.

As early as 1948 the Air Force had considered setting up a depot in French Morocco to support strategic operations. Planning in early 1950 contemplated an air-base complex in the neighborhood of Casablanca, and in October the Joint Chiefs of Staff approved a USAF proposal to build a system of SAC bases in French Morocco. Because of the great urgency, General Vandenberg had already directed the Air Staff to make preparations in anticipation of approval. Begun in great haste, the French Moroccan project experienced difficulties for nearly three years and probably aroused more controversy than any construction job the Air Force attempted.

On December 22, 1950, the French government agreed to permit the Air Force to build five air bases in Morocco. The Americans were to pay all costs and turn the installations over to the French when the emergency ended. Negotiations early in 1951 for a technical agreement covering use and occupancy of the bases ran up against a major obstacle. When the French realized the magnitude of the project and the number of Americans who would be coming to Morocco, they were disturbed by the possible effect on the local economy and on the rising tide of Moroccan nationalism. As a result, the Air Force agreed to limit severely the number of units and people it would assign to Morocco at any one time.

Meanwhile, the Air Force had issued construction directives to the Corps of Engineers, and Congress had provided money to get the airfields started. The Engineers, in turn, engaged the Atlas Constructors—a joint syndicate of five American contractors—to build the bases. Atlas employed a large force and amassed considerable equipment, which

lay idle in Casablanca while negotiations continued between the Air Force and the French. This delay not only
postponed the completion of badly needed bases but added
greatly to the expense.

To minimize the possibility of political and economic
disturbances, Gen. Alphonse Juin, the Resident General in
Morocco, suggested that the new bases be located in
isolated areas. The Americans agreed, chiefly because of
the urgent need to get on with the job, but the isolated
locations meant that the bases would have to be built
from scratch. Instead of enlarging four French installations
and building one new one, the Air Force would have to
build five new ones far out in the desert where transportation was difficult.

In May 1951 the French signed the technical agreement
and allowed construction to begin at Nouasseur and Sidi
Slimane. Usable runways had been laid down at these
two bases by July 15, 1951. By June 1952, additional sites
had been chosen at Benguérir, El Djema Sahim, and
Boulhaut, but construction was slow. Building of pipelines,
pumping stations, and fuel storage tanks moved slowly,
too, partly because the French insisted on building and
controlling facilities not located on air bases. Despite many
difficulties, four great bases, with runways up to 14,000
feet long, were completed by June 1955—El Djema Sahim
having been eliminated during the economy drive in 1953.

There was controversy within the Department of Defense and, especially, in Congress over the high cost of the
bases—about $390 million. Critics alleged that the Air
Force failed to supervise the construction closely, that
the Army Engineers bungled, that Atlas Constructors kept
faulty accounts and did sloppy work on some of the
pavements, and that too much efficiency was sacrificed for
speed. All of these charges probably contained some
truth, but the job was extremely difficult, and the Air
Force and the Corps of Engineers had many other large
construction projects under way at the same time. The
Air Force, particularly, did not have a professional staff
large enough to handle its vast construction program. The
"extremely urgent" label, which the Air Force kept on the
project until January of 1952, probably contributed to
inefficiency in the rush to get some usable runways as
quickly as possible. However, many defense officials, including the President, considered war perilously near in
the winter and spring of 1951. If the bases at Nouasseur
and Sidi Slimane, which became operational in July,
helped to prevent war, the French Moroccan project was
cheap at almost any price.

Requirements for bases in Newfoundland, Labrador,
and Greenland took on added importance after the middle
of 1950. The Air Force had retained operational rights
since World War II at such bases as Ernest Harmon and
Pepperrell in Newfoundland, Goose Bay in Labrador, and
Sondrestrom and Narsarssuak in southwestern Greenland,
but these no longer satisfied strategic needs. Representatives of interested combat commands—especially SAC—
called for another base in this area. A board of USAF officers decided in November that Thule, in northwestern
Greenland, about 900 miles from the North Pole, offered
the most suitable site. The JCS approved the project
before the end of 1950.

Thule, which had early been recommended as an air
base site by the Danish explorer Knud Rasmussen and
later by Col. Bernt Balchen, lay within striking distance
of much of the Soviet Union. B-47s could reach targets
with only one aerial refueling: Moscow, 2,700 miles away;
the Ural industrial area, about 3,000. Thule could also
serve as a base for intercepting bomber attacks along the
northeasterly approaches to Canada and the United States.

Like the French Moroccan venture, construction of the
Thule base was a rush job, and the arctic conditions made

In 1950 the Joint Chiefs approved plans for system of SAC
bases in French Morocco. This is construction at Boulhaut.

it costly. Original estimates called for spending about $168
million, but unforeseen difficulties ran it to about $220 mil-
lion. When the survey party landed on the small Danish
strip at Thule in February 1951, it encountered temperatures of −30° to −40° and winds up to 100 knots. Preliminary work got under way in March when MATS delivered
the early construction force and such essentials as bulldozers, power shovels, road graders, trucks, gasoline, and
oil. Transports flew in supplies from Westover AFB, Mass.
North of Goose Bay these planes had to depend on the
dilapidated bases at Frobisher Bay and Sondrestrom, and
they faced uncertain courses, radio blackouts, and lack of
navigational aids and rescue stations.

The Navy carried the bulk of the men, supplies, and
equipment by water. This operation had to be carefully
timed, for sea lanes to Thule were open to shipping only
six or seven weeks during midsummer. Major construction,
again supervised by the Corps of Engineers, got under way
in the summer of 1951.

During the first season, construction workers lived on
the ships and in winterized huts until permanent barracks
could be built. Gradually, a small city emerged, with barracks, warehouses, heating and power plants, hangars, and
fuel storage facilities. Prefabricated sections made of aluminum, plywood, and insulation materials were used for
most of the buildings. By November 1952, when the Air
Force took control of the base from the Engineers, Thule
was considered operational—its runways capable of handling any type of plane that might operate in the Arctic.
By the fall of 1953 the bulk of construction had been completed, and Thule took its place as a major USAF base.

Elsewhere overseas, the Air Force expanded and improved its bases. Expansion of Wheelus Field, Libya,
began in the spring of 1951 and continued until it became
one of the largest and busiest of American overseas bases.
Most of the actual building in France and Germany, where
the Air Force had more than twenty bases, was done by
French and German contractors and workers. American
firms often received the architectural-engineering contracts
for these projects. In the United Kingdom, the British
handled construction. FEAF supervised construction in the
Far East, and in Korea it used aviation engineer troops to
build the bases.

Spain seemed to offer an especially favorable location
for air and naval bases to strengthen NATO defenses.
Shielded by the Pyrenees from swift overland attack, aircraft based in Spain could exert a powerful influence on
military operations anywhere in western Europe and the
Mediterranean area and could reinforce strategic operations from Great Britain and French Morocco. After more
than two years of negotiations, the United States and Spain
signed an agreement in late September 1953. Spain author-

ized the United States to build four air bases and one naval base and a 485-mile petroleum pipeline connecting them with the port facilities at Rota, five miles from Cadiz.

The Navy Bureau of Yards and Docks directed the over-all construction program. Beginning in October 1954, it let contracts for air bases at Terrejon de Ardoz, fifteen miles northeast of Madrid, Zaragoza, in northeast Spain, Morón de la Frontera, twenty-five miles south of Seville, and an Air Force supply depot at San Pablo, five miles northeast of Seville. The Navy built an air station and port facilities at Rota. A syndicate of American firms did the architectural and engineering work. A large part of the construction was carried out by Spanish firms under sub-contracts, using local labor and materials. Much of the construction equipment was brought from French Morocco and overhauled.

By the fall of 1955 work had gotten under way on the giant air bases at Terrejon, Zaragoza, and Morón, where runways up to 13,400 feet were to accommodate both fighters and bombers. Right-of-way for the pipeline had been obtained and pipe laid out for about thirty miles along the right-of-way north from Rota. The system included ten- and twelve-inch pipe, pumping stations, and underground tank ranches, with storage tanks up to 80,000-barrel capacity. The Spanish base project was not rushed, and the Air Force estimated in January 1957 that the job, for which about $187 million had been authorized, was only half finished.

Air Defense Facilities

Construction of the DEW Line was a major USAF project after 1953. The Air Force contracted with the Western Electric Company, a subsidiary of the Bell System, to manage the DEW line project. Western Electric, in turn, sub-contracted the actual construction work.

Before definite agreements had been reached on the DEW Line stations, preliminary tests were made in the vicinity of Point Barrow, Alaska, to determine if a major project of this type so far north were feasible. During early 1953, airfields were scraped out in the ice and snow, and cargo planes delivered tractors, machinery, building materials, and other supplies. When the ice broke in summer, the Navy sent in the bulk of the necessary materials through the Bering Strait. Work began on six preliminary radar stations in August 1953, and by the end of 1954 these had been completed and tested. In February 1955 the job of selecting sites and constructing the main stations of the DEW Line got under way.

Selecting sites for radar stations had to be carried on in cold and darkness without exact information about the terrain. The engineers used aerial photographs and all available maps, many of which were inaccurate or incomplete. They depended on the bush pilots, flying skiplanes, to find suitable sites. Each area had to be surveyed for landing strips, building locations, and gravel, or rock that could be crushed into gravel.

With the help of seven-ton tractors dropped by parachute, the first airstrips were usually scraped out on lakes frozen to depths of five or six feet. C-119s and C-124s, weighing up to 168,000 pounds, touched down on these strips and unloaded twenty-ton tractors and other heavy equipment with which work could be started in earnest.

The frozen, isolated lands beyond the Arctic Circle posed tremendous construction problems. Aside from the cold, lack of transportation facilities, and remoteness from sources of supply, the job of building on permafrost was formidable. To prevent buildings, roads, and airstrips from sinking underground, the engineers placed them on thick pads of gravel or other insulation material. To set piling in the ground, they used jets of steam to melt the permafrost. Despite these obstacles, the project moved ahead with

Right: DEW Line sites above Arctic Circle posed tough building problems.

Below, right: F-84s over operations building at Furstenfeldbruck, Germany.

Below: Spaniards help build air bases under the supervision of Americans.

commendable speed. In February 1957, Headquarters USAF estimated that the job was approximately eighty-five percent completed. Total cost of the DEW Line was expected to be almost $400 million.

The construction of Texas Towers in shoal waters off the Atlantic Coast was handled for the Air Force by the Navy's Bureau of Yards and Docks. Placed on pilings driven into the ocean floor, the platforms were built high enough above water to escape flooding during stormy weather. They had a helicopter landing space and docking facilities. The first tower went into operation on Georges Shoal off Cape Cod in December 1955. A second tower was towed into place early in 1957, and by June a third was ready to be towed to its site.

The Air Force decision in mid-1953 to adopt the SAGE system to augment air defense communication facilities also required extensive construction. By mid-1957, four facilities had been completed and ten others were being built. Completed facilities were still being tested during 1957.

The Air Force gave the over-all contract for SAGE to the Western Electric Company as a package deal. Headquarters USAF believed that the design and construction of SAGE direction centers and similar facilities were so closely related to the installation of complex equipment that all should be under single management.

The Eternal Housing Problem

Obtaining family housing for its officers and airmen at rentals they could afford continued to present difficulties that the Air Force could not overcome. In 1954, for example, the Air Force needed at its semipermanent installations 185,000 housing units—160,000 in the United States, its territories, and possessions. It had only 64,000 units of all kinds available, including trailers and temporary housing. In the United States the Air Force depended on Title VIII of the National Housing Act (Wherry housing). Although never enough, Wherry housing helped relieve the shortage. But overseas and at isolated locations such as aircraft control and warning stations, building was difficult and shortages remained acute.

In August 1955, Roger Lewis, Assistant Secretary of the Air Force, reported that lack of adequate housing was still a severe handicap to combat effectiveness. Some pilots and other aircrew members had to live an hour and a half away from their bases in order to have suitable housing. Some officers and airmen continued to live in areas no better than slums. Lewis insisted that adequate housing on the bases was a *must* to keep men in service.

Except for appropriated funds, which were always short, Public Law 534 (1952), Eighty-second Congress, provided the only authority to build family housing overseas. Until 1954, Department of Defense regulations permitted the Air Force to guarantee a private builder ninety-five percent occupancy of housing units for five years at a rental not to exceed $125 per month. But the Air Force could not interest enough qualified builders or money lenders to ease the critical housing shortages at overseas bases. This particularly held true in places like North Africa and Newfoundland, where housing in isolated areas would be virtually worthless if American forces should be withdrawn. To overcome the reluctance of builders, Congress approved, in 1954, guaranty of up to ten years' occupancy.

This rental-guaranty arrangement relieved to a considerable degree the critical housing shortage in foreign countries, especially France and Morocco. By June 1957 almost all of the 2,686 units contracted for in France and all of the 700 in Morocco were completed. Most of the latter were at Nouasseur, Sidi Slimane, and Benguérir. In Spain, 1,518 rental-guaranty units were under construction in 1957. As an emergency measure, in the fall of 1955

the Air Force bought 2,689 trailers to house troops in Europe and North Africa—897 of these being for North Africa.

Rental guarantees did not work well in the United Kingdom because of high taxes. The Air Force secured new financing, however, under an arrangement whereby surplus agricultural products held by the US Commodity Credit Corporation were sold for British money which was used to pay for construction of family housing. In 1955 the Air Force raised $15 million in this way—enough to finance 1,800 to 1,900 units. The British Air Ministry managed the program, and by June 1957, 927 out of 1,481 units under construction were completed. A new surplus-commodity agreement totaling $12 million was signed with the British in 1956. At the end of May 1957 the Air Force arranged for the construction of 16,700 housing units in France under surplus-commodity financing.

In August 1955, Congress passed the Capehart Amendment to Title VIII of the National Housing Act. This amendment permitted expansion of Wherry housing by authorizing the use of quarters allowances of occupants to pay off the mortgages. The Air Force contracted for housing to be built on government land in the United States or its territories. The average cost of quarters was not to exceed $13,500 per unit. By June 1956, the Air Force had drawn up plans to build more than 46,500 of these units at eighty-eight bases. In July, construction began on large developments at Dyess AFB, Tex., and Eglin AFB, Fla. Between July 1956 and May 1957 work started on 9,367 additional units on thirteen bases in the United States.

Air-Base Problems

By 1955 the Air Force system of bases extended three-quarters of the way around the world. It might have seemed that the USAF base structure was about complete and that the necessity of pouring additional millions into runways, fuel storage tanks, pipelines, and other such facilities had ended. But this was not so. General Twining put the Air Force case in March 1956:

"If war should ever strike this nation again, our airfields . . . could very well be one of our most priceless assets. In an atomic war, the more airfields we have the better our chances of successful retaliation against an aggressor. More airfields mean more dispersal. More dispersal means more of our retaliatory force could survive an atomic onslaught. More airfields mean more division of an enemy's effort. More airfields would make his job tougher and our job easier."

During 1955-56 the Air Force opened five new SAC bases within the United States—at Abilene, Tex.; Homestead, Fla.; Portsmouth, N. H.; Plattsburg, N. Y.; and Little Rock, Ark. Another bomber base—Clinton Sherman at Burns Flat, Okla.—was under construction in 1957. Even with these additions, SAC did not have enough bases over which to disperse its units.

The growing danger of a devastating air attack on the United States brought a realization of the need for more strategically located air defense bases. In 1955, Congress approved construction of six ADC interceptor bases just below the Canadian border. By June 1957, five of these—located at Klamath Falls, Ore.; Glasgow, Mont.; Minot and Grand Forks, N. D.; and Marquette, Mich.—were in operation. The sixth, originally planned for Kalkaska, Mich., was delayed by the failure of Congress to agree on its location. The bases at Minot and Grand Forks were also to support a squadron of heavy bombers in addition to the interceptors. Construction began on two new Tactical Air Command bases in April 1955—at Goldsboro, N. C., and Myrtle Beach, S. C., the latter becoming operational in 1957.

Base Exchange at Dyess Air Force Base, Abilene, Tex., one of the newest, most modern bases in the Air Force.

As the tempo of flying operations increased—accompanied by mass parking, servicing, and refueling of aircraft—the problems of maintenance, fire-fighting, and rescue operations grew more complex. Hazards associated with the new and more powerful weapons further complicated these problems. The Air Force improved the fire-protective quality of new construction and eliminated many of the hazards in existing structures. It made particular use of safer construction materials and automatic sprinkler and fire-detection systems and removed highly combustible interior-surfacing materials from most buildings.

Pavement failures were a constant maintenance problem. During the period of feverish expansion after 1950, most runways and taxiways, particularly on bases not considered permanent, were built of flexible or asphalt pavement. Asphalt did not stand up as well as concrete built of portland cement, but even with the additional maintenance costs, asphalt was less expensive. On the refueling aprons and warmup pads, however, asphalt always presented difficulties because spilled jet fuel caused it to disintegrate. As planes became heavier and the number of takeoffs and landings increased, asphalt pavement failures became more frequent. Finally, in early 1956, Headquarters USAF decided that all primary airfield pavement for combat or combat support aircraft would thereafter be constructed of concrete made with portland cement. It also changed the design of heavy-load pavements to make them support greater weight, shock, and strain.

The advent of new aircraft and new weapons greatly aggravated certain construction problems. New types of jet aircraft required much more space than earlier models. Fighters needed a 10,000-foot runway, 200 feet wide; bombers, an 11,000-foot runway, 300 feet wide. Because runways on most of its fighter bases were less than 9,000 feet long, ADC paid a high price in smashed planes and crippled men. High landing speeds required longer overruns—clear zones—at the ends of the runways in order to give the pilot who made a slight error a chance to save his life. The Air Force tried to provide its bases with approach and takeoff corridors seven miles long and four miles wide. About sixty percent of all takeoff and landing accidents occurred within these corridors. For this, as well as other reasons, the Air Force sought to locate its new bases at least fifteen miles from the nearest major community.

Major aircraft accident rates fell from 467 per 100,000 hours flown in 1921 to forty-four in 1947 and fifteen in 1956. But as the frequency of accidents came down, noise, unfortunately, went up and up. The noise from the F-86D was just under the decibel point that causes pain in the ears; from the F-102 it was just over that point. The F-102 had to get up two miles before its noise no longer interfered with conversation on the ground. Fortunately, it got there quickly.

Not all air base hazards were connected with the flight of aircraft. ADC interceptors were loaded with weapons when on alert. The F-89D, for example, carried 100 2.75-inch rockets, each with the blast power of a three-inch artillery shell. And in 1957 it seemed likely that atomic weapons would soon be stored on many bases and carried by planes in flight. Even with all possible safety precautions, the potential hazard to inhabitants of surrounding communities and civilian aircraft could not help but grow. The Air Force was determined to remove military flying from civilian airports as soon as possible, but the tremendous cost of relocation was a major obstacle.

The final problem was air traffic control. Once the jets got off the ground, they became projectiles themselves, streaking along at least as fast as a bullet fired from a pistol. The new fighters were expected to climb at 40,000 to 50,000 feet per minute and cruise at terrific speeds. Without a traffic system to control them continuously from takeoff to landing, the mingling of these lightning-like objects with slower aircraft around airports would create ever growing hazards.

The increasing awareness by communities near the air bases of the noise and potential hazards from jet aircraft and weapons created a serious problem for the Air Force. Some communities demanded that the Air Force move its jet units elsewhere. It seemed likely that the demands would increase and become more insistent as both civil and military air traffic over urban areas grew heavier.

In February 1956, General Partridge, Commander in Chief of CONAD, described this development as a national problem requiring a national solution. Community growth, the change in an air base's mission, the introduction of more powerful weapons, and faster aircraft would inevitably magnify the problem. But noise and danger were part of the price the nation would have to pay for security and the advancement of technology. The Air Force could follow three broad courses of action to lessen the difficulties: (1) try to obtain public understanding of the necessity for inconvenience, (2) decrease noise and hazard by scientific research, and (3) move flying units farther away from urban communities.

The last possibility, usually proposed by the communities themselves, would be the most costly of all. In 1957 the Air Force had about $7 billion invested in air bases. It would have to spend $3 billion more for new bases in order to accommodate the units whose removal had been requested by adjacent communities. And such removals might be only temporary because new urban areas would spring up adjacent to the new bases. Over a long period of time, the process could be an endless one.

Chapter 20

THE TOOLS

Weapons

FROM the bow and arrow to the thermonuclear bomb, weapons have shaped the ways of war, and superior weapons have often meant the difference between victory and defeat. As warfare became increasingly mechanized, the military man came to rely more and more upon the scientists for newer and better tools of war. In the mid-twentieth century this quest for new weapons produced a revolution in the art of war, and particularly in the art of air war, that had fateful implications for all mankind.

Research and Development in the Air Force

In World War II the American scientist played a far more influential role than in any previous conflict. Nevertheless, the United States often took calculated risks during the war by subordinating research and development to mass production. Looking ahead, the Army Air Forces hoped to strike a better balance between quantity and quality in the postwar period. During the closing months of the war, Dr. Theodore von Karman, world-renowned aerodynamicist, headed a committee of scientists who analyzed the achievements of the warring powers and concluded that science had become the key to aerial supremacy. But it took time to give research and development the high priority that the scientists wanted.

In the debate over organization, supporters of the *status quo* argued that Air Materiel Command should retain responsibility for research and development as well as for procurement and production. They believed that these activities were so intertwined that separation would be ruinous. Proponents of change replied that AMC could not concentrate on the weapons of tomorrow because it was absorbed in current production.

In 1949 a group of scientists, headed by Dr. Louis N. Ridenour, and a group of military experts at Air University both recommended that USAF research and development activities be concentrated under a separate command. The Air Force then decided to disentangle the scientific from the logistical and set up a direct line of

Dr. Theodore von Karman set the Research and Development pattern.

Dr. Louis N. Ridenour recommended an R&D command.

authority for scientific matters. In January 1950 it created the office of the Deputy Chief of Staff, Development, in Headquarters USAF to provide top-level staff supervision of all research and development. At the same time it established a single agency, the Air Research and Development Command (ARDC), to carry out the research and development programs. But ARDC did not actually take over control of the function until April 1951. In the summer of 1951 it moved from Wright-Patterson AFB to Baltimore, Md.

Research and development also received recognition at the Secretarial level. On March 1, 1955, Trevor Gardner, an experienced engineer and administrator, became the first Assistant Secretary of the Air Force for Research and Development. Gardner, who had served as a special assistant to the Secretary for research and development matters from 1953 to 1955, resigned in February 1956 because of a disagreement with the Secretary of Defense over the priorities given the Air Force guided missile program. Richard E. Horner was appointed to fill the vacancy in June 1957.

The success or failure of the new organization rested upon the quality of the new weapons and the speed of their development. Planning in terms of weapon systems,

Boeing Bomarc IM-99 interceptor missile roars straight up in test at AF Missile Test Center, Patrick AFB, Fla.

first considered in 1949, became an important method for attaining these goals. To the Air Force, a weapon system included not only the airframe but all the component parts and supporting equipment that enabled it to carry out its mission. Thus, a typical weapon system would include such items as the propulsion unit, navigation, fire-control, bombing, communications, and armament systems and related ground equipment.

Because of the ever increasing technical complexity of its weapons and equipment, the Air Force adopted this approach to ensure that the various parts of a weapon system would be compatible. The design of an airplane had always been shaped in large part by the design of its propulsion system. As aircraft and missiles moved into the supersonic realm, a component could no longer be judged on its own merits alone but only as part of the whole. When the people responsible for the design, production, and eventual use and maintenance of a weapon system worked together during its earliest stages, the transition of the new weapon from development to production was not as difficult, and both the time and the cost of introducing it into the USAF inventory were reduced.

A typical weapon system originated in the minds of the development planners. The Air Staff then told ARDC why a weapon system was necessary and how it should perform. ARDC drew up specifications, evaluated the contractors' proposals, and prepared a development plan. After Air Staff approval, ARDC let a development contract. The contractor converted ideas into actualities and built an experimental model. The weapon then ran the gantlet of exhaustive tests to see whether it met specifications and worked satisfactorily under simulated combat conditions. The development of a new weapon system usually took from four to eight years, depending upon its complexity.

Men, Money, and Facilities

In managing the research and development program, the Air Force was fortunate to have such experienced technical leaders as Lt. Gen. Donald L. Putt, Lt. Gen. Laurence C. Craigie, Maj. Gen. Donald N. Yates, Maj. Gen. Albert Boyd, Maj. Gen. Ralph R. Swofford, Jr., Maj. Gen. James McCormack, Jr., and Brig. Gen. Benjamin S. Kelsey. These men had the counsel of a group of civilian consultants, known as the Scientific Advisory Board, who kept the Air Force informed of latest developments and evaluated long-range plans. The chairmen of the board were, in turn, Dr. von Karman; Dr. Mervin J. Kelly, a prominent director of industrial scientific work; and Lt. Gen. James H. Doolittle (Ret.), distinguished both as combat commander and engineer.

The Air Force also set up the Rand Corporation, a nonprofit organization, to do specific research jobs and to help the Air Force select the most promising development programs. This organization, located at Santa Monica, Calif., worked closely with the Air Staff. Universities under contract carried out major research projects to determine requirements for accomplishing a basic air mission. MIT's Lincoln Laboratory, for example, provided the basic data which enabled the Air Force to develop the latest weapons for air defense.

At the end of the war the Air Force recruited German scientists and engineers, particularly in the field of missiles. The Air Force also stimulated aeronautical research in western Europe. At the suggestion of the Scientific Advisory Board, the directors of aeronautical science in seven NATO nations met in February 1951 and decided to set up an advisory group for aeronautical research and development within the NATO framework. The group was established in May 1952, with Dr. von Karman as its first chairman.

First meeting of USAF Scientific Advisory Board, June 17, 1946, in the Pentagon. Seated, from left: Dr. George E. Valley, Jr., Dr. Frank L. Wattendorf, Dr. George A. Morton, Dr. Nathan M. Newmark, Dr. Walter S. Hunter, Dr. Lee A. DuBridge, Dr. Detlev Bronk, Dr. Theodore von Karman, Dr. Charles W. Bray, Dr. C. Richard Soderberg, Dr. Courtland D. Perkins, Dr. Charles S. Draper, Dr. Harold T. Friis, Dr. William R. Sears. Standing, from left: Dr. Pol E. Duwez, Dr. Hsue-shen Tsien, Dr. William H. Pickering, Dr. Ivan A. Getting, Dr. W. J. Sweeney, Dr. W. Randolph Lovelace, II, Dr. Julius A. Stratton, Dr. Duncan P. MacDougall, Dr. Edward M. Purcell, Dr. Vladimir K. Zworykin, Dr. Fritz Zwicky, Dr. Robert H. Kent, Col. William S. Stone, and Col. Roscoe C. Wilson. The SAB members not present at this meeting were Prof. Enrico Fermi, Dr. George Gamow, Dr. Hugh L. Dryden, Dr. Walter A. MacNair, and Col. Benjamin C. Holzman.

Lt. Gen. Donald L. Putt, Deputy Chief of Staff, Development, guided the program from Hq. USAF after April 1954.

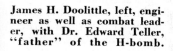

James H. Doolittle, left, engineer as well as combat leader, with Dr. Edward Teller, "father" of the H-bomb.

Like a surrealist cyclops, this specially instrumented F-86 stands poised on a desert runway at Edwards AFB, Calif., as pilot climbs aboard for a research flight.

During fiscal years 1946 through 1948, the Air Force received an annual average of about $155 million for research and development, not enough to start new prototypes and barely enough to keep alive those started with wartime funds. During the two years before the Korean War, there was some increase, but only after war began did money become plentiful. During the three years of war, the amount rose to an annual high of $533 million, and many old projects of merit were revived and new projects started. When the Eisenhower Administration reexamined the program, it reduced the funds for fiscal year 1955 to $420.4 million. But funds had to be increased during the next two years because of inflation, the urgent need for new weapons, and the inclusion under research and development of items such as operation of facilities that had previously come under different appropriations. The appropriation reached a new high of $720.5 million for fiscal year 1957.

An important share of this money went for building new facilities or improving existing ones. Under ARDC, ten research and development centers checked the scientific work of industry and universities, determined weapon specifications and standards, and evaluated the final products. They also did research work in highly specialized military areas. The equipment at the centers varied in size from tiny transistor crystals, smaller than the head of a pin, to gigantic wind tunnels.

The largest of these centers, the Wright Air Development Center at Dayton, Ohio, supervised the development of most weapon systems, airborne components, ground equipment, and materials. The Special Weapons Center, Kirtland AFB, N. M., helped in the development of nuclear weapons and related equipment. At the Flight Test Center, Edwards AFB, Calif., the aircraft of the future were put through their earliest tests. Short-range missiles were tested at the Holloman Air Development Center, Alamogordo, N. M., and long-range missiles at the Missile Test Center, Patrick AFB, Fla. The Armament Center at Eglin AFB, Fla., worked with the Army Ordnance and Chemical Corps in testing aircraft guns, rockets, and other weapons. Problems in aerodynamics and propulsion were studied at the Arnold Engineering Development Center, Tullahoma, Tenn. The Cambridge Research Center, Cambridge, Mass., worked in the fields of geophysics, nuclear physics, and electronics, while the Rome Air Development Center, Rome, N. Y., concentrated on both ground and airborne equipment. And the Personnel and Training Research Center, Lackland AFB, Tex., built equipment and prepared procedures for selecting, assigning, and training officers and airmen.

Three other USAF organizations engaged in research, development, and testing. The Air Proving Ground Command at Eglin AFB, Fla., a major command, had the important job of conducting operational tests of weapon systems and other equipment. Under simulated combat conditions, USAF pilots flew the planes and airmen maintained them. This type of testing revealed deficiencies and helped eliminate costly future modifications. These tests also helped the Air Force to devise new concepts of tactical employment. Air University's School for Aviation Medicine, at Randolph AFB, performed medical and aero-medical research. Problems of a similar nature relating to cold-weather operations were investigated at the Arctic Aeromedical Laboratory, Fairbanks, Alaska, a part of the Alaskan Air Command.

The need for larger test facilities became obvious late in World War II, and the AAF's scientific advisers proposed that the Air Force build a large development testing center. In October 1949, Congress authorized the construction of a center, which the Air Force named the Arnold Engineering Development Center in 1951, in honor of the late Gen. Henry H. Arnold. It included facilities

for testing engines, including an addition for testing ramjets, a gas dynamics facility permitting simulation of the flight of a missile, and a huge propulsion wind tunnel. Operations began on a small scale in 1952, but in 1957 the Air Force did not expect the entire structure to be completed as planned until 1959.

The Air Force Missile Test Center, at Cape Canaveral on the Florida coast, and its down-range stations covered more area than any other USAF installation. The three services had chosen this site in 1946 for launching their guided missiles. Two years later, the Navy transferred the Banana River Naval Air Station to the Air Force, and work began on the Cape site and the island stations. Originally known as the Joint Long Range Proving Ground, it was operated jointly by the three services and administered by the Air Force until June 1951, when the range was placed under the Air Force alone and its name changed to Air Force Missile Test Center.

Concrete pads, set in the sand at Cape Canaveral served as launching platforms for the missiles. The missiles could fly southeast over water past the Bahamas, the Dominican Republic, and Puerto Rico as far as Ascension Island in the South Atlantic. On the islands, stations equipped with electronic and optical equipment recorded the performance of the missiles. In February 1957, Brazil agreed to construction of a station on the island of Fernando de Noronha, off the bulge of Brazil. In February 1954 the Air Force completed its negotiations with Pan American Airways Corporation to operate the down-range stations, with the Radio Corporation of America acting as major subcontractor.

Nuclear Weapons

The most far-reaching of all the scientific achievements of World War II was the military application of atomic energy. The awesome mushroom cloud became a symbol of the hopes and fears of the modern age. So that this new force might be used in the best interests of the entire nation, its control was placed in the hands of the Atomic Energy Commission (AEC). The armed service maintained a close association with the AEC through the Military Liaison Committee. The Armed Forces Special Weapons Project served the military departments jointly in atomic energy matters.

During World War II the AAF had little to do with the development of the atomic bomb. But it participated in other phases of the program, and in August 1945 it dropped atomic bombs on Hiroshima and Nagasaki. Air Staff officers saw the importance of this new weapon for the air arm and the need for special organizations to handle atomic matters and deal with AEC. Much had to be done before the Air Force could use atomic weapons on a large scale. In December 1949 the Air Force set up the Special Weapons Command for the development testing of atomic weapons. This command worked closely with AEC's prime contractors—the Sandia Corporation and the Los Alamos Scientific Laboratory. In April 1952 the Command became the Special Weapons Center under ARDC. Within the Air Staff, the Assistant for Atomic Energy, Deputy Chief of Staff, Operations, coordinated atomic energy matters.

The first step toward a nuclear Air Force was to strengthen the ability of SAC to deliver atomic weapons, and in 1946 the Air Staff directed that all new bombers be able to carry atomic as well as high-explosive bombs. The second step, decided upon in 1949, was to integrate atomic weapons wherever possible in its activities. In 1951 the Air Staff decided that TAC's fighter-bombers should have the same dual capability as the strategic bombers. There were two major problems in using nuclear weapons: adapting various types of weapon carriers and atomic

Telemetry antenna at Air Force Missile Test Center, Patrick AFB, Fla., receives such data as speed, altitude, and temperature of a test missile in flight, relays it to tape recorders.

DEPARTMENT OF THE AIR FORCE
RESEARCH AND DEVELOPMENT NET EXPENDITURE DATA BY FISCAL YEARS

FY 1950	$62,304,923	FY 1954	$439,228,279
FY 1951	177,164,348	FY 1955	445,746,520
FY 1952	346,556,491	FY 1956	622,546,652
FY 1953	460,445,070	FY 1957 (through December 31, 1956)	351,305,276

SOURCE: Monthly Report on Status of Appropriations

---

bombs to each other and developing bombing systems that would be effective and yet permit the airplane to escape safely. The first problem was primarily aerodynamic, arising as the aircraft reached supersonic speeds. Working with AEC, the Air Force overcame the difficulties of making weapons compatible with delivery systems. The Air Force also perfected techniques for delivering weapons at high and low altitudes and at the same time protecting airplane crews.

In January 1950, President Truman directed AEC to emphasize its thermonuclear research. The Air Force immediately began to make preparations for delivering thermonuclear weapons, and early in 1954 it was ready. By 1957 it could deliver nuclear weapons ranging from a few kilotons (thousands of tons) to several megatons (millions of tons) in explosive power.

Guided Missiles

The first true guided ballistic missile—the German V-2 rocket of 1944-45—carried less than a ton of high explosive in its warhead. This was a most expensive way to deliver a small bomb on a target, and for all the brilliance of the technical achievement the V-2 did not promise to replace the manned aircraft. But with the appearance of the atomic bomb, it became clear that if the guided missile could be married with a nuclear warhead it would probably become the dominant weapon of the future. And, with the availability of thermonuclear warheads after 1953, there could be little question about the future role of the guided missile.

The great value of the guided missile lay in the fact that potentially it could fly faster, farther, and higher than manned airplanes and was less vulnerable. But because the missile had to be fully automatic, it required a higher degree of reliability than any previous weapon, and this was its great weakness.

Even before World War II ended, the AAF began to work on guided missiles. Expenditures increased steadily after 1950 until, by fiscal year 1956, spending for research and development of guided missiles virtually equaled that for aircraft. Four percent of the money for aircraft and related procurement went for guided missiles in fiscal year 1952 and twelve percent four years later. It was anticipated that the percentage would be twenty-five in fiscal year 1959.

As a result of preliminary studies, the Air Force began to develop four types of missiles: air-to-air, surface-to-air, air-to-surface, and surface-to-surface. Through changes in nomenclature, the air-to-air missiles became guided aircraft rockets launched from interceptors against enemy aircraft or from our bombers against enemy interceptors. Surface-to-air missiles became long-range interceptor missiles for defending an area against hostile bombers. Air-to-surface missiles, eventually redesignated guided aircraft missiles, would be directed at highly defended enemy targets by bombers attacking from a distance. Surface-to-surface missiles were either tactical weapons for supporting ground forces or long-range strategic weapons.

The unique feature of a missile was its guidance system—its brain and nerves. There were a number of different guidance systems under development by 1957, but they fell into two general categories: those to be used against aerial targets and those directed against fixed surface targets. Whether launched from the ground or the air against air targets, the missile faced the major problem of detecting the oncoming air vehicle. Several approaches warranted investigation. A missile equipped with radar could send out electronic pulses to sweep the sky until they struck the target and determined its range and direction. The missile could then be directed to the target on the basis of this information. Since aircraft and missiles gave out a great deal of heat as they flew through a cold sky, a seeker in the interceptor missile sensitive to heat or infrared radiation could detect and track the invader. Other approaches involved an acoustic system to detect sounds made by air vehicles and an air-wake detector to pick up disturbances in the air created by these vehicles.

Against fixed-surface targets, the inertial guidance system was of great importance. Using an intricate arrangement of gyroscopes, built-in computers, and other complex equipment, the guidance system could calcuate the position of the missile and signal its control system to place it on course to its target. Enemy electronic devices could not jam this type of system, since it did not depend on radar to determine its path. Another type of system, which could be used in combination with the inertial system, was the automatic star tracker. This used the stars to figure the position of the missile over the earth in the manner of a seagoing captain using celestial navigation.

The most powerful potential weapon in the USAF arsenal of the future promised to be the ballistic missile. Guided during the upward part of its trajectory, this weapon became a free-falling body during the latter stages of its flight through the atmosphere. It had four basic parts —the warhead, the guidance system, the airframe, and the propulsion system. The Air Force began work on ballistic missiles after the war, but had to cancel the program in 1947 for lack of funds. Four years later, it gave a contract to Convair Division of General Dynamics Corporation that led to work on the intercontinental Atlas missile, with a range to exceed 5,500 miles.

Trevor Gardner (left) was Assistant Secretary for Research and Development when Maj. Gen. Bernard A. Schriever, head of ARDC's Ballistic Missile Division, got second star in 1955.

In 1952-53, a most significant event in the development of ballistic missiles took place—the so-called thermonuclear breakthrough, which made it possible to build smaller thermonuclear warheads. After a group of eminent scientists recommended in February 1954 the development of an intercontinental ballistic missile as quickly as possible, the Air Force assigned highest priority to this program. The Western Development Division of ARDC, under Brig. Gen. Bernard A. Schriever, was placed in control of development and production.

The Air Force also awarded a contract to Glenn L. Martin to develop a second ICBM—the Titan—which was to use many of the components being developed for the

Atlas. In December 1955 the Air Force contracted with Douglas to develop its first intermediate-range missile—the Thor. Some components of the intercontinental ballistic missiles were to be used for this shorter-range missile.

Basic Research

Underlying all major technological advances have been the basic facts and principles upon which science rests. The atomic bomb may be traced to Albert Einstein's conclusion that $E=MC^2$ (energy equals mass times the square of the speed of light) and the guided missile to Isaac Newton's third law of motion: "For every action there is an equal and opposite reaction." In our time, theoretical knowledge has become a prerequisite to national security. The basic research that advances scientific frontiers is a responsibility of the entire nation, since all applications, military or otherwise, flow from this common reservoir of knowledge.

In World War II, American scientists left the seclusion of the campus to improve and perfect existing weapons. Aside from the atomic bomb, they introduced no revolutionary weapons of aeronautical warfare. At the same time, the war almost ruined European science, from which the United States had always gotten good ideas. These factors, plus the shortage of trained men and the advent of controlled atomic energy, left a void in the field of pure research. The Air Force tried to fill this gap by stimulating interest in the fundamentals of the sciences.

The Air Force cooperated closely with scientific organizations to make the best use of their discoveries. It also sponsored basic research that others could not do either because of the expense or the purely military nature of the work. Even most of this work was carried out on a contract basis with industry, universities, scientific organizations, and other government agencies. Since funds for this purpose were limited, the Air Force selected the most promising areas for research and concentrated on those most likely to succeed.

In aeronautics the Air Force could make a distinctive contribution itself through its special series of X-planes, which were actually flying laboratories. These research planes added to an ever growing storehouse of aerodynamic knowledge.

For years the speed of sound appeared to be an invisible barrier that fixed a limit to the speed of flight. Then, on October 14, 1947, Capt. Charles E. Yeager flew the experi-

Left: As Capt. Charles E. Yeager was awarded the Mackay Trophy, Gen. Vandenberg (right) called his faster-than-sound flight in the X-1 the "greatest achievement since Kitty Hawk."

Right: Bell X-1, which Yeager piloted through so-called sonic barrier, was first manned aircraft to fly supersonically.

Nearly all the operational aircraft—for combat and support—in the US Air Force are shown in this "family portrait" made at the Air Proving Ground Command, Eglin AFB, Fla. In the center of the two concentric circles is the Sikorsky H-19 helicopter. Toward the front of the picture from it is the Cessna T-37 jet trainer. To the viewer's left of the T-37 is the North American F-86D Sabre interceptor. Continuing clockwise around the inner circle are the Lockheed F-94C Starfire jet interceptor; the Lockheed RC-121 Super Constellation reconnaissance plane; the Boeing KC-97 tanker; the Republic F-84F Thunderstreak jet fighter; and the North American F-86 Sabre jet fighter. Reading clockwise along the outer circle, starting from the lower center of the picture, are the Convair F-102 delta-wing, supersonic interceptor; the North American F-100 Super Sabre supersonic fighter; the Martin B-57 Canberra jet bomber; the Douglas B-66 Destroyer jet bomber; the Boeing B-47 Stratojet jet bomber; the Boeing KC-135 Stratotanker jet tanker; the Boeing B-52 Stratofortress heavy jet bomber; the Convair B-36 bomber; the Douglas C-124 transport; the Boeing KB-50 tanker; the Lockheed C-130 Hercules turboprop transport; the Grumman SA-16 Albatross rescue amphibian; the Northrop F-89D Scorpion jet interceptor; and theMcDonnell RF-101 Voodoo, supersonic reconnaissance aircraft.

mental X-1 faster than the speed of sound over the sprawling desert acres of the Air Force Flight Test Center in California. General Vandenberg called it the greatest aeronautical achievement since the flight of the Wright brothers at Kitty Hawk.

To determine the most efficient shapes for aircraft and missiles, USAF engineers studied the forces acting on bodies moving through the air. Among the early aircraft

with new and previously untested designs were the tailless X-4 and the adjustable-wing X-5. In November 1953 the Air Force unveiled a huge Flying Stiletto, the X-3, which it used to determine the aircraft features suitable for sustained flights at extremely high speed.

For the future, the Air Force planned air vehicles capable of fantastic speeds. It appeared likely, for example, that the intercontinental ballistic missile would have a

Maj. Arthur Murray flew the X-1A to an altitude of 94,000 feet in 1954; at that time no US plane had ever flown higher.

velocity of more than 10,000 miles per hour as it reentered the earth's atmosphere. Long before air weapons reach such speeds, air friction generates such intense heat that parts begin to disintegrate. When an aircraft or missile made of aluminum goes beyond a speed of Mach 1.5 (Mach 1 equals the speed of sound, about 740 miles per hour at sea level), it nears this "thermal barrier." Titanium, lighter than steel and its superior in many ways, can be used as a substitute for aluminum for speeds of up to Mach 3. For still higher speeds, scientists must either discover new materials or make existing materials more heat resistant.

In 1955 the AF's rocket-powered Bell X-2 began to

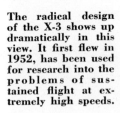

The radical design of the X-3 shows up dramatically in this view. It first flew in 1952, has been used for research into the problems of sustained flight at extremely high speeds.

probe the thermal barrier. Like the X-1 and its sister ship, the X-1A which exceeded 1,650 miles an hour in December 1953, the X-2 rode in a mother plane to the altitude from which it began its flight. Before Capt. Milburn G. Apt crashed to his death in the X-2 in September 1956, he had flown at a reported 2,178 miles an hour—the fastest speed to that date.

The achievement of supersonic and, potentially, of ultrasonic speeds was made possible by extraordinary developments in propulsion. At the end of World War II, the turbojet, ramjet, and aircraft rocket engines were in the early stages. The turbojet used a gas turbine to drive an air compressor and engine accessories. The early British turbojet, the Whittle engine of 1941, had a thrust of 850 pounds. In February 1953 the Air Force put into production the J-57 with a thrust of around 10,000 pounds.

The ramjet type of engine, sometimes called the "flying stovepipe," was planned for speeds above Mach 2. Without compressor or turbine, it is essentially a tube open at both ends in which fuel is burned continuously to create the jet thrust. The X-7 experimental vehicle is driven by a rocket up to the speed where the ramjet power system can take over. Rockets are promising propulsion systems for future space flight beyond the earth's atmosphere. They move forward by ejecting a stream of hot gases to the rear. Carrying their own oxidizers, such as liquid oxygen, they are independent of the atmosphere.

Much remains to be discovered about the vast atmospheric envelope in which these aircraft and missiles soar. The Air Force must understand the nature of the stratosphere that begins seven miles above the earth's surface, for this is the environment of high-speed aircraft and missiles. Above this stratum, at heights beyond twenty-five miles, is the ionosphere, where layers of ionized air particles influence the transmission and reception of radio communications. To probe the heights, the Air Force fired V-2s and other rockets carrying highly specialized instruments in the warheads. In 1951 a number of fully equipped rockets rose higher than fifty miles. To study the weather, the Air Force floated large plastic balloons carrying instruments for recording atmospheric information. By 1953, balloons in the United States and selected overseas areas had obtained data on winds, temperatures, turbulence, and cloud formations above 50,000 feet. Three years later, this meteorological survey, known as Moby Dick, was expanded to include other areas of the world.

The Air Force studied the earth as well as the sky. In 1947, reconnaissance pilots of the Alaskan Air Command called attention to huge floating masses of glacial ice in the Arctic Ocean. In March 1952 the Air Force set up a weather station on one of these masses, Fletcher's Ice Island (T-3). The island was abandoned in May 1954 after it had served as a base for providing weather data and as a source of valuable information on the physiological and

Right: Rocket-powered X-2 is carried aloft beneath a B-50, released at the desired altitude, then rockets are cut in.

Lt. Col. Frank Everest in cockpit of X-2 in which he set speed record in 1956 during tests probing the thermal barrier. Capt. Milburn G. Apt was killed in the same plane after flying more than 2,100 mph—fastest man had flown.

psychological effects of severe arctic environment on man.

The Air Force knew that the never ending pursuit of greater speed, height, and range might reach a point where the human being could not tolerate the stresses and strains. Aeromedical research attempted to learn how much man could endure without risk to health, safety, or efficiency. In July 1952 a rocket carried monkeys and mice up to 200,000 feet, indicating the possibility that humans might survive where gravity did not exist.

To safeguard its men, the Air Force needed an effective means of escape from high-speed aircraft. In August 1954, two USAF officers, using a new type of ejection seat, parachuted safely from a B-47 moving at a speed of 570 miles an hour at an altitude of 45,200 feet. Then, in December 1954, Lt. Col. John P. Stapp rode a rocket-propelled sled at a record speed of 632 miles per hour on a high-speed track at the Holloman Air Development Center, N.M. He demonstrated that a pilot's body could withstand a wind blast equivalent to that received if ejected from an airplane flying at 35,000 feet and at twice the speed of sound. These experiments in acceleration and deceleration justified the continued use of the ejection seat.

The Weapons of Air War

The revolution in aeronautics after 1945 sent the aircraft of World War II the way of the Spad and the Fokker of World War I. To keep the lead in the race for supremacy, new weapons superseded old at a bewildering speed. But certain basic trends were visible despite the continuing change and the ever mounting list of types and models. The Air Force became increasingly an atomic air force as nuclear weapons began to enter into every phase of USAF activity. Aircraft also moved out into higher and higher speeds, from the supersonic to the ultrasonic, and they were always reaching upward. And finally, the weapons of war became more and more auto-

matic, for only electronic devices could react with the lightning-like speed so vital to modern war.

Many weapons that reached various stages of development and even production did not meet USAF needs and had to be abandoned. There was no way to be sure that the plane on the drawing board would be effective except by building it and flying it. To ensure against failure, several paths usually had to be explored. And those planes that did not pass the tests usually added to the fund of aeronautical knowledge and paved the way for more successful weapons.

The Air Force continually altered its successful aircraft to meet the demands of modern warfare. All types of planes became heavier, if not larger. Airframes had to be heavier and stronger in order to carry the increasing weight of complex equipment. And as the planes became heavier, they required still more powerful engines and more fuel to attain the necessary higher performance.

The following table shows the increase in gross weight between 1945 and 1957:

Bombers	Pounds
B-17H	55,000
B-29B	133,500
B-36D	358,000
B-52D	400,000

Fighters	Pounds
F-51H	12,000
F-80C	16,000
F-84F	25,000
F-89H	45,000

The constant changes in aircraft were reflected in an increasing number of types and models. The type, representing class and tactical employment, was indicated by a letter—B, F, C, for bomber, fighter, cargo; the model, a general design within a type, by a number; and the

Flight-test research deals with conventional aircraft as well as radical experimental models. Here a B-47 roars from the runway at Edwards AFB in a cloud of smoke. As part of maximum loading tests, the plane uses special JATO units.

model series that showed each major change in the model, by a final letter. A prefixed letter showed special use of the plane as, for instance, R for reconnaissance and K for tanker. Thus, the RB-47E was the E series of the 47th bomber design since the system was inaugurated in the 1920s, and the plane was modified for reconnaissance purposes.

The model series letters traced the evolution of a plane throughout its production life. It did not necessarily follow that the series letter indicated either the order of production or the degree of improvement of the weapon. Sometimes an F version of a plane actually went into production and service before a D version. And an E version might be more powerful and have a higher performance than a G version.

Strategic Air Weapons

The mainstay of SAC during much of the decade after World War II was the B-36. Begun in 1941, it flew for the first time on August 8, 1946, and entered tactical units in 1948. It was greatly improved in the D version of 1949. The addition of four jet engines to the six piston engines of the earlier models almost doubled its power. The last B-36 to roll off production lines in August 1954 was the sixth production version, the B-36J.

In mid-1945, a year before the B-36 flew for the first time, the AAF asked industry for a faster, more powerful heavy bomber. The Boeing design that won the competition in 1946 proved unsatisfactory because a new turboprop engine did not live up to expectations. Boeing's development difficulties continued until the Air Force decided in October 1948 to use the sweptback wing and the still-experimental J-57 turbojet engine for the B-52 Stratofortress. In 1951 the cockpit of the eight-engine Stratofortress was altered to permit side-by-side seating, and the gross weight was increased to gain more range and take advantage of engine improvements. The six-man B-52 first flew in April 1952, and the first production model was ready in August 1954. The B-52D of 1957 was faster and heavier than the A version.

The B-29 and the B-50 were the backbone of SAC's medium bomber fleet until they were replaced in 1953-54 by the six-engine B-47 Stratojet, the first large jet-propelled aircraft fitted with sweptback wings and tail surfaces. The B-47 had originally been planned as a conventional straight-wing bomber. Before the end of World War II, the Air Force had held a competition for a jet-propelled medium bomber that was won by Boeing. In designing the B-47, Boeing demonstrated experimentally that a plane with the conventional wing could not take full advantage of the turbojet engine because it would encounter a rapid rise in the resistance and turbulence of the air as it approached the speed of sound. When Americans discovered that German successes with the sweptback wing corroborated their theories, the Stratojet was born.

The original prototype first flew in December 1947 and the B-47A two and a half years later. SAC received its first plane in October 1951, but it was not until the B-47 successfully passed service tests in January 1953 that it became SAC's work horse. Although somewhat similar in appearance to the B-52, the B-47 had a tandem seating arrangement and the more familiar bicycle landing gear. Later versions of the B-47 had newer and more powerful engines, increasing the thrust from 4,000 to 6,000 pounds per engine. Boeing produced almost 1,400 B-47s at its Wichita, Kan., plant before production ceased in October 1956.

In 1957 the Air Force was approaching the day when it would begin using the supersonic bomber. The first of these, Convair's four-engine medium bomber, the B-58 Hustler, took to the air in November 1956. The Hustler embodied an aerodynamic principle discovered by the National Advisory Committee for Aeronautics (NACA). The NACA found that air resistance to the motion of an airplane traveling at supersonic speeds could be decreased by extending the nose, indenting the fuselage,

The nation's first supersonic bomber, the Convair B-58 Hustler. Instead of the bomb bay being an integral part of the airplane, the weapons are carried in a pod slung beneath the belly. Pods may be interchanged for varied tasks.

Northrop SM-62 Snark, intercontinental, air-breathing subsonic missile, being launched during tests at AF Missile Test Center, Patrick AFB, Fla.

Lockheed X-17 test vehicle, used in ballistic missile nose-cone research.

or otherwise reworking its shape to reduce resistance. The B-58 was the first bomber given a long fuselage with a "coke-bottle" or "wasp-waist" shape. Research scientists also revealed that when certain metals were sandwiched, their union was stronger and more heat-resistant than any one metal alone. This discovery was used to create an airframe skin for the B-58.

After 1946, the Air Force, together with industry and other government agencies, sponsored an extensive research program in an effort to apply nuclear energy to the propulsion of aircraft. A nuclear-powered plane would have virtually unlimited range, enabling it to bomb any target in the world from the United States without having to rely on foreign bases or inflight refueling. Before this goal could be attained, there were problems in materials, reactors, shielding, and airframe design that had to be solved. In January 1956 the Air Force announced airborne experiments in a B-36 which had been modified to carry an atomic reactor.

Looking into the future, the Air Force saw a strategic air arm composed of both manned aircraft and missiles. Aside from the ballistic missiles, the Air Force worked on two long-range pilotless bombers officially known as air-breathing missiles—Northrop's SM-62 Snark and North American's SM-64 Navaho. The Snark, launched from a platform, needed two booster rockets to take off because of its size and weight. A number of successful launchings of the Snark were made at Patrick AFB in 1956-57. Powered by the J-57 turbojet engine, the Snark had a long, slender fuselage, a sharply pointed nose, swept wings, and a tail consisting only of a vertical stabilizer.

After extensive tests at Edwards AFB, the Navaho began its flight tests at Patrick AFB. Designed to fly faster than the Snark, the Navaho was not as far along in development. To check on advanced aeronautical designs as well as the Navaho's electronic system and general flight characteristics, the Air Force flew a test vehicle, the X-10. But development of the Navaho came to an end

in July 1957 when the Air Force canceled the project for financial and other reasons.

Also under development was Bell's GAM-63 Rascal, a rocket-powered missile fired from piloted bombers at very high speeds to knock out vital targets far from the bomber. Like other strategic missiles, the Rascal was to be capable of carrying a nuclear warhead. The Air Force looked on the Rascal as a means of improving the bomber's chances of survival, because it would not have to fly into the heart of heavily defended targets.

Air Defense Weapons

In defending their homeland in World War II, the British proved that German night attacks could be countered by radar-equipped interceptors directed to their targets from a radar station on the ground. The first American plane designed specifically for fighting at night was the P-61 Black Widow.

The prime requirement after the war was for an all-weather fighter that could fly at any time of day or night, and in any kind of weather. In 1946, Northrop began to manufacture for the Air Force the F-89 Scorpion, a two-place jet fighter whose electronic devices enabled it to intercept aircraft at night and in inclement weather and to sight and fire automatically. The Scorpion first flew in August 1948, but the Air Force, impatient to get an all-weather plane into its combat units quickly, converted the T-33 jet trainer into the two-place F-94 Starfire in 1949. An advanced model, the Lockheed F-94C, was heavier and more powerful than the earlier models.

By 1952 the F-86D interceptor version of the Sabre, the F-89, and the F-94 joined the air defense fleet and within two years had replaced earlier planes. The F-86D, a single-seater, had a powerful engine and an afterburner. Later F-89 series, sent to Alaska and Thule, contained an advanced fire-control system, Mighty Mouse 2.75-inch aerial rockets, and the Falcon missile.

The weapon system idea was first applied to interceptors. In May 1949 the Air Force and industry agreed that they should decide upon the fire-control system first and then build the plane around it. This weapon system would be for use during 1954-60. One year later, the Air Force chose Hughes Aircraft Company to build the integrated electronic control system, known as the MA-1, and in September 1951 it selected Convair to manufacture the new interceptor. An interim version of this plane, the wasp-waisted F-102A, whose prototype flew in October 1953, began to enter air defense units in 1956. It could fly at supersonic speeds and at altitudes above 50,000 feet. The F-106A, known as the ultimate interceptor, was being tested in 1957.

A distinctive feature of the F-102A was its delta wings, an aerodynamic innovation that had originated in the wind tunnels of wartime Germany, although the NACA had also studied its possibilities. After exhaustive tests, Convair had built an experimental delta-wing XF-92, which first flew in September 1948. The triangular shape, adopted for the advanced interceptors, gave them a relative freedom from drag when they neared the speed of sound, while its sweepback and its thinness avoided buffeting at high speeds.

In 1956 the F-89H and the F-102A were armed with the deadly GAR-1 Falcon guided aircraft rocket, developed by Hughes Aircraft. The Falcon weighed a little more than 100 pounds, was about six feet long, and was powered by solid-rocket propellants. With previous guns and rockets, the pilot had to get into a firing position near the target while flying at high speed. The Falcon flew a true collision course to its target despite any error in launching or enemy maneuvering, since an electronic guidance system made all the necessary corrections. This air-to-air missile could also be launched from a distance to streak upward toward the target, giving the interceptor crew a greater margin of safety and saving precious time.

The Air Force also had under development a surface-to-air interceptor missile—Boeing's IM-99 Bomarc. This long-range pilotless aircraft, launched from the ground, could seek out and destroy enemy aircraft at great distances from the area to be defended. Powered by two ramjet engines, it could be launched quickly by rocket and ascend vertically at supersonic speed to high altitudes. There were successful experimental launchings of the Bomarc at Patrick AFB. The Air Force was also interested in the Navy-developed Talos, but Secretary of Defense Wilson decided in November 1956 that the Talos was a weapon for local rather than area defense and placed it under the control of the Army.

In air defense, the performance of the airplane, and especially its fire-control system, depended on the way electronic equipment on the ground guided the plane to the vicinity of the target. The British first used ground radar early in World War II to warn of the Luftwaffe's approach, and by the end of the war it was possible to distinguish friendly from hostile aircraft when they were a mile apart. But in a future war, it might be necessary to control large numbers of high-speed interceptors flying to meet an armada of enemy bombers or missiles. Such a degree of precise control could be exercised only by a system of precise instruments. Accordingly, the Air Force turned to the SAGE system developed by the Lincoln Laboratory.

The brain of the SAGE is a giant computer that accepts information, "memorizes" it, and finally presents on a

Bell GAM-63 Rascal air-to-ground guided missile is designed to be launched from bomber at a safe distance from enemy defense. The rocket-powered missile then goes on to target while the bomber turns back to its home base.

radarscope the location, speed, and direction of all planes within a given area. The computer automatically calculates the best way to use interceptors, missiles, and antiaircraft guns against the enemy. It transmits this data to computers near the scene of action and, through radio-data links, guides interceptors and missiles automatically toward their target. Although the complete SAGE system was still in the future in 1957, the interceptor was reaching a point where its entire flight, except for takeoff and landing, would be performed automatically.

Tactical Air Weapons

For its first few years, TAC relied on piston-engine World War II aircraft except for the Lockheed jet F-80. This plane had flown in January 1944 but did not engage in combat until it fought the first jet air battle in history in Korea on November 8, 1950. A versatile plane that went through three models, it was modified into the T-33 trainer and then the F-94 interceptor.

The F-86 Sabre, the only American plane to counter the Russian MIGs successfully in Korea, was also the first USAF operational fighter with swept wings. In 1944 the Air Force needed a medium-range day fighter that could double as escort fighter and dive bomber. A plane with straight wings could not reach the desired speed of 600 miles per hour. In the spring of 1945, technical representatives of American aircraft companies visited Europe and brought back data on the swept wing. North American proposed that the XF-86 adopt this design, and General Craigie, then engineering chief at Wright Field, approved. A captured sweptwing Messerschmitt provided a pattern for the XF-86 design. The design proved highly satisfac-

tory and six versions of the Sabre were manufactured by 1957.

The F-100 Super Sabre, successor of the F-86, was originally called the Sabre 45 because of its forty-five-degree sweepback as compared with the thirty-five degrees of the other models. For a while, the F-100C held the world's speed record of 822 miles per hour, set over the California desert in August 1955.

When the Air Force adopted the sweptwing F-86 in 1945, it decided to develop the straight-wing F-84 Thunderjet as insurance against possible failure of a sweptback plane. Republic's F-84 first flew in 1946, and each later version had more powerful engines, inflight refueling equipment, or other improvements. The F-84F Thunderstreak, although in the same series, was a more advanced plane with sweptback wings and a far more powerful engine, a modified British Sapphire redesignated the J-65. Although these alterations in design and engine proved difficult, the F flew in February 1951, and in 1954 it replaced the G in TAC units.

The replacement for the F-84F was McDonnell's sweptwing, twin-jet F-101 Voodoo, originally intended as a long-range strategic fighter for SAC. An early design of this plane was evaluated in 1949 and 1950, but the Air Force had to terminate an experimental contract because of a cutback in defense funds and a change in tactical requirements. In 1951, however, interest revived and an advanced version was ordered into production as the F-101. On its first flight in September 1954, the F-101 exceeded the speed of sound.

On the way were two other aircraft in the "Century" series—the F-104 and the F-105. Lockheed's F-104, a

National Advisory Committee for Aeronautics plays major role in AF flight research. Here is an F-84 mounted in the forty-by-eighty-foot wind tunnel at NACA's Ames Aeronautical Laboratory, Moffett Field, Calif., near San Francisco.

Dramatic view of ground test of Lockheed F-104 Starfighter at Edwards AFB. The F-104 is a supersonic interceptor, which Gen. Twining called "the fastest, highest flying fighter in the air." It can go supersonic straight up.

lightweight air superiority fighter, first flew in February 1954, and a new model scheduled for TAC was in accelerated production in 1957. General Twining called the F-104A Starfighter the "fastest, highest flying fighter in the air." This plane could reach ultrasonic speeds and climb as fast as it could fly horizontally.

Republic developed the F-105 to meet the need for a supersonic fighter-bomber that could deliver nuclear weapons as well as heavy loads of high-explosive bombs and rockets at extremely high speeds and at great distances. The F-105, which first flew in October 1955, had short, very thin sweptback wings, a long cylindrical fuselage, and radar equipment in its needle nose.

The tactical bomber also came a long way after World War II. The B-26 Invader was the last propeller-driven light bomber to remain in USAF units. In 1947, TAC received its first jet bomber, the four-engine B-45 Tornado, and the reconnaissance version of this plane fought in Korea.

In 1951 the Air Force decided to manufacture the British Canberra, first jet to cross the Atlantic without refueling, under the designation of B-57. Before this plane could serve USAF purposes, Glenn L. Martin had to make substantial changes, including the addition of a rotary bomb door to make bombing at high speeds more accurate. In speed and altitude, the two-engine B-57 light bomber compared favorably with a jet fighter. TAC received its first B-57s in June 1954. Douglas' high-speed two-engine B-66 Destroyer, the USAF version of the Navy's A3D, first entered USAF combat units in March 1956.

The only tactical missile actually deployed overseas was Martin's TM-61 Matador. This missile, which first flew in

January 1949, had a range of several hundred miles. Powered by a jet engine, it was launched from the ground by a booster rocket and controlled electronically in its flight by men on the ground. The TM-61B, longer and faster with greater range, had a better guidance system. The C model was expected to be still more accurate and less vulnerable to electronic countermeasures.

Reconnaissance Aircraft

At first the Air Force modified B-29s to perform long-range strategic reconnaissance, but the first suitable plane for such missions was the RB-50. This plane, approved for production in 1950, was soon supplemented by the RB-45, the first multijet reconnaissance plane. For truly long-range reconnaissance, the RB-36, also approved in 1950, carried fourteen different cameras in the forward bomb bay as well as other special equipment, probably the largest photographic setup devised for any plane. The long-nosed RB-47E, with seven cameras, became a medium-range reconnaissance aircraft, although inflight refueling permitted this plane to make long flights.

Standard aircraft were also adapted for reconnaissance purposes. The bomb bays of the B-52B and C were fitted with a capsule containing photographic and electronic equipment, enabling them to shift quickly from a bombing to a reconnaissance mission. Strategic fighters, too, were modified for photographic purposes. The RF-84F Thunderflash, slightly longer than the F-84F, carried camera equipment in its nose. The Air Force ingeniously extended its range by converting a number of RB-36s into carriers for the RF-84F so that the two could be capable of combined flight. Under this project, formerly known as FICON

(Fighter Conveyor), the RB-36s used special gear to launch and retrieve the fighter in flight.

For future long-range strategic reconnaissance, the Air Force considered using surface-to-surface missiles. They would be equipped with the proper gear, launched on their mission, and then recovered. The Air Force was also interested in the future possibilities of the small space satellite being developed by the Navy. If a large unmanned space satellite were developed, it could provide invaluable electronic, photographic, and weather information.

Tactical reconnaissance, the first mission assigned to the earliest military planes, remained a prime USAF function. During the Korean War, a photographic version of the jet F-80 as well as the veteran propeller-driven RF-51 carried out this mission. The successor to the RF-80, the more advanced RF-84F Thunderflash, first flew in September 1953. The heavier, elongated Thunderflash carried special cameras for taking pictures by night as well as by day and a trimetrogon camera for mapping purposes. In May 1957, TAC units started to receive the RF-101, the first truly supersonic reconnaissance aircraft.

Two tactical reconnaissance versions of bombers—the four-engine jet RB-45 and the propeller-driven RB-26—saw service in the Korean War. The Air Force used the RB-45C for high-altitude photo reconnaissance by day or night. In 1957, TAC had available the reconnaissance versions of the B-57 and the B-66. The RB-57A could reach speeds of over 550 miles per hour, and the RB-66B could do 600 to 700 miles per hour. General Weyland hailed the RB-66B, which entered tactical units in January 1956, as a fast reconnaissance bomber capable of carrying out its mission at night and in all kinds of weather.

Supporting Aircraft

SAC needed a jet tanker because its bombers were jets, and the standard tanker in use—the KC-97G—did not have the speed and altitude to refuel jets efficiently. The refueling of one B-47 by another proved the feasibility of a jet tanker. In September 1954, the Air Force ordered into production an advanced jet tanker, the Boeing KC-135 Stratotanker. This plane had a speed of 550 miles per hour at heights above 42,000 feet.

Inflight refueling also multiplied the range of TAC's fighters and bombers. In 1954, TAC began to use the KB-29 aerial tanker with flying boom to refuel its combat aircraft, and in 1956 it added the KB-50. TAC also desired a jet tanker like the KC-135 to refuel aircraft making nonstop flights overseas.

At the end of World War II, the Air Force had on hand such veteran cargo and troop carrier planes as the C-46 and C-47 as well as two that had appeared late in the war, the C-74 Globemaster I and the C-82 Packet. To obtain a better carrier with longer range for large, heavy Army items, the Air Force modified the C-74 into the C-124, which first flew in November 1949.

Fairchild modified the medium transport C-82 Packet to improve its performance and enable it to carry larger cargoes. Redesignated the C-119, it made its first flight late in 1947 and was subsequently further improved. Used primarily by troop carrier wings, the C-119G carried sixty-two troops, or twenty more than the C-82.

The turboprop engine that harnessed jet power to conventional propellers offered great promise for future transports. In 1951 the Air Force began to develop a new turboprop plane, the C-130 Hercules, to succeed the C-119. This assault transport, which first flew in April 1955, received the tasks of carrying troops and supplies to the front and returning casualties to the rear. It could carry ninety troops with full equipment or seventy litters with six attendants, and it could drop a ten-ton cargo in seconds.

Further test flights in 1955-56 of three transports fitted with turboprop engines—the YC-131C, YC-97J, and YC-121F—provided data for improvements in the engines. The first plane specifically designed for the air logistic mission was the Douglas C-133A, which made its first flight in April 1956. This long-range heavy transport could carry a cargo weighing over 50,000 pounds.

Both the Air Force and the Army needed an aircraft to operate from rough, unprepared fields. The Chase C-122, a powered version of the G-20 glider, did well under adverse conditions, and the Air Force decided that an airplane could perform this mission better than a glider. The C-123, manufactured by Fairchild, first entered TAC units in the summer of 1955.

The Air Force used Boeing's versatile C-97 not only as a tanker but as a carrier of cargo, passengers, troops, and sick and wounded. It also adapted commercial aircraft that required but few changes to make them acceptable for military use. The C-118 Liftmaster, a civilian airliner converted for MATS, served as a litter carrier and cargo and troop transport. The two-engine C-131 had the primary mission of transporting disabled or convalescent men. The YC-121F version of the Super Constellation, fastest propeller-driven transport, carried 106 passengers or fifty-three to seventy-three litters.

By the end of World War II, the Air Force knew that the helicopter, although its range and payload were limited, could be useful for rescue work or for carrying bulky items into hard-to-reach areas. Its success in Korea stimulated further interest in its development. The largest rotary-wing plane built, Vertol's YH-16A, carried forty passengers or thirty-two litters, but it was not put into production. Among the other helicopters of importance were Sikorsky's H-19, which first flew in 1942, and the H-21C, designed for arctic missions. The Air Force also developed for the Army the one-man XH-26, which was collapsible and could travel in a jeep trailer.

If aircraft could take off and land vertically or from very short runways, large and vulnerable air bases would no longer be necessary and aircraft could be dispersed more easily. Boundary layer control and aerodynamic devices enabled aircraft to rise quickly at a slow speed. One way to eliminate runways was to shoot piloted aircraft from a launching platform mounted on a truck. In January 1955 the Air Force awarded a contract for a jet, vertical takeoff airplane. Ryan developed the X-13 Vertijet for the purpose of investigating problems relating to this type of flight.

The Air Force also developed convertiplanes that took off vertically like a helicopter and flew at high speeds like a conventional airplane. The McDonnell XV-1, a two-place liaison vehicle carrying either three passengers or two stretcher patients and an attendant, first flew in April 1955. The Air Force hoped that this plane would lead to the development of larger assault and transport craft. Bell also developed the XV-3 convertiplane to explore a tilting-rotor design. This plane flew in August 1955.

The standard elementary training plane in the Air Force, familiar to all pilot trainees during World War II and after, was the T-6 Texan. This plane, which first flew in October 1939, did not go out of service until July 1956. After the war, North American received a contract to develop a plane to be used in all training up to the advanced stage. This plane, the T-28A, was faster than the T-6, and its tricycle landing gear resembled that of the tactical aircraft the student would later fly. The student continued his training in the F-80 jet modified into a two-place trainer and designated the T-33.

In the summer of 1954, Beech's T-34A came into training units to replace the T-6. This plane was faster than the T-6, easier to handle, and also had the tricycle landing gear. Cessna's jet T-37A, in production in 1957, was scheduled to replace the T-28 as an intermediate two-place trainer. The experimental version of this plane made its first test flight in October 1954. This lightweight twin-jet trainer, first USAF jet plane specifically designed as a trainer, would acquaint prospective pilots with the complexities of high-speed jet aircraft at an early stage of their training. A low-wing monoplane, it had the advantages of high speed in flight, low landing speed, and side-by-side seating, a good feature for instruction purposes. To meet the need for a supersonic trainer to replace the T-33, the Air Force selected Northrop's two-engine jet T-38. This airplane, still under development in 1957, had many of the flight characteristics of advanced fighters.

Ryan X-13 Vertijet, jet-powered vertical takeoff and landing research airplane. Rising and descending on a column of exhaust gases, the X-13 went through its first complete flight sequence at Edwards AFB, Calif., on April 11, 1957.

Chapter 21

THE TOOLS

Logistics

IT SEEMS appropriate that Dayton, Ohio, the home of the Wright brothers, should have become the center of the Air Force logistical system. In 1957 the Air Force could look back on forty years of continuous tenure in Dayton, thirty of them at Wright-Patterson AFB, still popularly referred to by its earlier name—Wright Field. From Dayton, the Air Technical Service Command and its predecessors made a great contribution to the triumph of American arms in World War II. Redesignated Air Materiel Command in March 1946, this huge field command remained the operating arm of the USAF logistical structure after September 1947. At Headquarters USAF, the Deputy Chief of Staff, Materiel, exercised staff supervision over logistics after this date.

By 1952, AMC had become so large and complex that the Dayton area was overcrowded. Additional facilities would have cost too much, and the desirability of further centralization was dubious. So AMC decentralized many of its activities by delegating responsibilities to subordinate commands. In January 1956, AMC became a worldwide command when it took over Air Materiel Force, European Area, including North Africa. Three months earlier, it had placed depots in the Far East under its Air Materiel Force, Pacific Area. By 1957, AMC controlled eight air materiel areas in the United States as well as seven specialized depots. Five air materiel areas operated under the two intermediate headquarters overseas.

Industrial Mobilization

The United States won the air battles of World War II because it had time to build the production lines that turned out the hundreds of thousands of planes and other weapons for the fighting forces. And these production lines worked unmolested behind the vast ocean barriers on which the country had come to rely for protection. But

after the war, swift technological advances made it evident that distance would no longer buy the time to rearm after the fighting began.

Industrial Planning

Basing industrial planning upon these new realities, the Air Force contracted with its manufacturers late in 1945 for studies of the best ways to cut the time between the beginning of a future mobilization and peak production. The manufacturers indicated the space, tools, raw materials, men, and subcontractors that they would need to meet a specific mobilization schedule, and they prepared for mass production by redesigning products, changing methods, and obtaining new tools. The Air Force analyzed these preparedness measures and incorporated them into mobilization plans.

These plans were based on maintenance of a stable aircraft industry. But the sharp cutback in military orders after World War II threatened to put many companies out of business and narrow the whole mobilization base. On the other hand, some manufacturers of components had shifted to consumer goods and showed little interest in returning to military production. During 1947 and 1948 the Air Force tried to keep the aircraft industry running efficiently and profitably by distributing its business among producers considered most reliable. Since components, not airframes, were the limiting factor in production, AMC examined each type of aircraft scheduled for mobilization to prevent any component from becoming a bottleneck.

The basis of USAF industrial planning was the mobilization production schedule—a detailed estimate of the maximum rate of aircraft production expected in an all-out effort. But the schedule would be of little value unless manufacturers could meet it in an emergency. Since competitive purchasing by the armed forces had impaired the mobilization effort in previous wars, key industrial plants were allocated among the three services, beginning in 1947. Using the mobilization schedule as a guide, the Air Force then drew up tentative production schedules with the managers of plants assigned to it. It wanted to discover

Part of Wright-Patterson Air Force Base, Dayton, Ohio, home of Air Materiel Command and hub of USAF logistics.

in peacetime what manufacturers needed, how their sub-contracting systems worked, and where bottlenecks might develop. The manufacturer learned what he was to produce, for whom, and how much.

In planning with contractors, the Air Force also took into account subcontractors and certain manufacturers, known as licensees, who produced aircraft or other major items under license from the prime contractors. Licensees exchanged production data and engineering drawings with prime contractors, and each became familiar with the manufacturing methods of the other. Prime contractors also kept track of the capabilities of their major subcontractors. Since one contractor bought more than 15,000 different parts for a heavy bomber from 1,578 firms, the Air Force had to be sure that subcontractors could easily convert to war production.

In 1950, American industry once again became an "arsenal of democracy," although, to be sure, on a smaller scale than in World War II. American manufacturers produced weapons and equipment for a rapidly rearming United States, the fighting forces in Korea, and our allies overseas. But unlike World War II, the Korean War was a limited war and required only a partial mobilization of industry. Since planning prior to 1950 had been for a full mobilization, the partial mobilization had to be improvised. Fortunately, many measures and procedures of the prewar period proved of great assistance. To prevent shortages of civilian goods, the government superimposed a limited wartime economy upon the existing peacetime structure. This policy prevented a serious economic dislocation, but it gave rise to many mobilization problems during the first year of war.

During the second half of 1950 the Air Force began to create a larger and stronger industrial base, equipping plants and assembly lines beyond those needed to fill current orders for equipment and weapons. The Air Force used these extra facilities and a larger number of subcontractors in January 1951 to speed up production for the ninety-five-wing program. By the close of 1952 the number of operating airframe factories had doubled, and the

Air Force had more than a thousand additional producers of airframe parts and equipment.

In allocating production the Air Force succeeded far better in 1950-51 than a decade earlier. In 1940, permission to negotiate contracts came only after rearmament had begun, by which time the allocation plans had already been scrambled. By contrast, when the Korean mobilization got into high gear in December 1950, the Secretary of Defense permitted procurement through negotiation, while foreign aid under the Mutual Defense Assistance Program was closely coordinated with USAF rearmament. During the Korean War, AMC placed orders with firms under USAF jurisdiction according to plan. With mobilization actually taking place, the Air Force no longer needed to spend as much money on industrial preparedness. It reassigned funds to buy tools and industrial equipment for current use.

The United States emerged from the Korean War with a vast potential for industrial mobilization. The Air Force no longer needed to expand its industrial base except to develop new types of weapons and equipment. Under these circumstances, it permitted plants no longer required for military production to shift to the manufacture of civilian goods or it placed them on a standby basis. Plants owned by the government and not needed for mobilization were sold outright. In retaining plants as a production reserve, the Air Force gave priority to those especially adapted for development work and those capable of rapid expansion of production.

In January 1954 the Defense Department made a major revision in the production allocation program for the first time since 1947. The services concentrated on allocating the production of especially critical items or components that might become bottlenecks, eliminating items that could be purchased on the open market or put into production without any difficulty. The Air Force also began to integrate procurement more closely with mobilization plans in December 1954. It tried to arrange for more than one source of supply for items and to spread its orders throughout the country as a precaution against air attack.

In November 1955 the Air Force based industrial planning on an industrial structure that had to be ready at all times to support the forces in being. The production base would have to be adjustable to USAF missions, equipment, and available resources. In the event of a general war, American industry would try to deliver every possible piece of critical equipment during the first sixty to ninety days.

Industrial Facilities

In the industrial demobilization after World War II, the Air Force retained some plants and released others to private enterprise. The National Reserve Act of 1948 set up a military reserve of important government-owned plants that could not easily manufacture civilian goods. The act also set up a national reserve of facilities built at government expense that were sold or leased but could be recaptured by the government in the event of war. Under a national security clause, the current owners had to keep these plants ready for reconversion to wartime production on 120 days' notice.

The Korean emergency demonstrated the wisdom of keeping standby facilities. By July 1951, thirty-three of the thirty-six plants in the USAF portion of the military reserve were in operation. While standby plants provided a base for expansion, the Air Force also had to build new facilities or enlarge existing ones. Congress appropriated $2.2 billion for the purchase of land, buildings, and machine tools to help manufacturers who could not enlarge their own facilities. The Air Force contracted for about $2 billion of this amount and kept the rest for additional expansion. The government also tried to induce manufacturers to use their own capital.

Following a World War II precedent, in September 1950, Congress permitted manufacturers to write off the cost of new plants and additions over a five-year period rather than over the normal twenty-year span. The Air Force endorsed approximately 1,200 tax amortizations totaling about $1.3 billion during the Korean War. The government also made direct loans to private enterprise. By the end of June 1953 the Air Force had sponsored seventy-eight of these loans, amounting to about $26.5 million.

By the close of 1953, most major expansion projects were well on their way to completion, and the number of new projects was falling steadily. The Air Force did not need to ask for new money during the immediate postwar period because it had leftover sums from the war years to finance new projects or supplement old ones. Accelerated tax amortizations remained popular, but the number of applications and the dollar amount of contracts dropped substantially. In reviewing requests for industrial expansion, AMC tried to maintain normal industrial competition. If a contractor used government-owned machine tools or facilities without charge, he paid the government in the form of a reduced cost of the product or contractor's service.

During 1955-56 the Air Force spent far more to expand industrial plants than it had originally intended, primarily because of the accelerated development of ballistic missiles. The speedup in B-52 production also demanded additional facilities for the manufacture of the J-57 engine, the airframe, and component parts.

Industrial Equipment

The sale of large quantities of government-owned tools after World War II caused the civilian market to shrink and the manufacturers of machine tools to reduce their output and capacity. Emergency supplies of machine tools and production equipment were set up in military and national reserves in 1948. The Air Force portion of the military reserve contained 36,967 machine tools in June 1950.

At the start of the Korean War, the machine-tool indus-

This Convair production line at its San Diego, Calif., plant is representative of modern aircraft production.

try was operating at less than ten percent of its World War II peak rate. The resulting shortage of machine tools, a repetition of the events of a decade before, was the biggest single bottleneck to production. The Air Force helped meet the shortage by withdrawing about half of the items in its portion of the military reserve and by getting additional tools from the national reserve. By July 1953, contractors serving the Air Force had received more than 30,000 items from government reserves. But many of the reserve tools could not be used to produce the newer types of weapons. Tools designed to build radial engines, for example, could not build jet engines. There was a need to keep the machine-tool reserve in step with technological changes.

In supplying critical new tools to contractors, the government adopted the pool-order plan used successfully in World War II. Beginning in February 1951, it placed large orders with tool builders, based on the needs of manufacturers, and then sold the tools to individual contractors. This was an efficient approach to the problems of scheduling and allocating machine-tool production. As production increased, the urgency of the machine-tool problem decreased. Although a considerable backlog of orders remained, especially for more complicated tools, shipments finally exceeded orders by April 1952. Three months later, the government relaxed its controls over the distribution of machine tools.

The new policy of production readiness, adopted in November 1955, called for a maximum number of machine tools in use and a minimum number in the inactive reserve. The Air Force ordered new items worth $69 million to be used as delivered instead of stockpiling them. It also reconditioned idle tools, whenever possible, instead of buying new ones. By July 1956, there were 147,420 items valued at $1.3 billion in the AMC inventory of machine tools owned by the Air Force. Of this number, 104,892 were in use.

The heavy press was of great interest to the Air Force because it could fabricate large structures in one piece. In aircraft design, a structure made of one piece was preferable to one fashioned from several smaller pieces, for

Lt. Gen. K. B. Wolfe saw the advantages of heavy presses.

it enabled aircraft to better withstand the severe aerodynamic stresses of high-speed flight. In 1945, Maj. Gen. Kenneth B. Wolfe sent a technical mission from the Air Technical Service Command to Germany to acquire heavy forging and extrusion presses developed by the Germans. The Russians, also recognizing their value, seized the largest item, a 33,000-ton forging press. The Air Force obtained several smaller ones as reparations and installed them in various plants in the United States. In 1948, General Wolfe proposed that the Air Force build heavy presses, if the aircraft industry would redesign parts so that they could be forged. This idea slowly gained favor, and in the summer of 1950 the Air Force got $210 million to buy twenty heavy presses. A year later, six firms received contracts to build eight forging and nine extrusion presses.

The forging and extruding of heavy structural members was a relatively new technique and involved numerous engineering problems in both aircraft design and metallurgy. In 1953 the Defense Department cut the number of machines to four forging and six extrusion presses. By April 1957, nine heavy presses were in operation, including two 50,000-ton forging presses and a 12,000-ton extrusion press.

Procurement Policies

Air Force procurement was quite different from that of private industry. In purchasing goods it had to avoid competing unnecessarily with the Army and the Navy. In selecting firms to manufacture weapons and equipment, it had to allocate an adequate share to small business and promote subcontracting. Nor did usual pricing procedures apply on exclusively military goods.

AMC bought airframes, engines, and other major USAF items, while the air materiel areas and depots contracted for aircraft accessories and supporting equipment. Air procurement districts or USAF plant representatives administered these contracts, checking on production, helping

Fruit of the Air Force heavy press program. In foreground, a hydraulic forging press of 50,000-ton capacity.

to eliminate work stoppages, analyzing contractors' costs, and controlling the quality of the product.

One of the first tasks in the postwar period was to settle the thousands of contracts let during World War II. Between the defeat of Germany and the end of 1947, the Air Force terminated more than 18,000 contracts totaling over $22 billion and recovered $2.5 billion through renegotiation.

The Armed Services Procurement Act of 1947, which went into effect in May 1948, reaffirmed the traditional method of formal advertising and competitive bidding on government contracts. Under one of the seventeen exceptions to this general rule, the government could buy goods by negotiation when the President or Congress declared a national emergency.

In December 1950 the President declared a state of national emergency, and Secretary of Defense Marshall called for a speedup in purchasing and broadening the industrial base. Invoking the emergency clause of the 1947 act, the Air Force sped up purchasing by negotiating contracts, although it encouraged competition and formal advertising whenever possible. During the buildup period the Air Force used the incentive type of contract extensively, increasing profits when costs decreased. The commanding general of AMC became "the sole head of the procurement activity" in February 1951, supervising purchasing overseas as well as in the United States.

Until January 1956 the Air Force negotiated virtually all contracts under the national emergency clause of the 1947 act. After this date, it used this exception only in special cases and made most of its determinations under the other exceptions to the act. Contracting became more complex, since the Office of the Secretary of the Air Force had to approve a large number of decisions that field agencies formerly would have handled.

Following government policy, the Air Force placed as many contracts as possible with small business concerns —those employing fewer than 500 people, independently owned, and not dominant in their respective fields. AMC helped small businessmen secure contracts, subcontracts, and adequate financing. When the Air Force let contracts amounting to more than $14.2 billion during the last year of the Korean War, it placed orders for $609 million of this amount with small businesses. This was 72.8 percent of the value of items and services considered within small-business capabilities. With Air Force encouragement, a considerable portion of the total amount found its way into small business through subcontracting. In 1953, more than 100 USAF prime contractors reported that they had placed with small business subcontractors $3.3 billion worth of business, or twenty-one percent of the $15.56 billion in contracts they themselves held.

The Air Force wanted prices that were fair and reasonable and at the same time encouraged efficiency and economy in production. It emphasized prompt and satisfactory performance and took into account the risk of the individual contractor. After studying profits in the aircraft industry, both in the aggregate and for individual companies for the period January 1942-December 1955, the Air Force related these profits to those of comparable industrial groups and concluded that they were fair and reasonable. Subsequently, a House of Representatives subcommittee agreed that the government was receiving "substantial value" for its money.

Production Programs and Problems

One of the most important factors affecting aircraft production after World War II was the fluctuation in Air Force programs. Between July 1, 1946, and June 30, 1947, the 604 aircraft accepted by the AAF were not enough to replace the aircraft that had become obsolete. In its support of the seventy-group program, the congressional Aviation Policy Board held in 1948 that the Air Force should buy 86,000,000 pounds of airframe weight annually by 1953. In May 1948, Congress granted almost $2 billion to the Air Force to meet the needs of the first year of a five-year buying program. But this buying spurt ended in December when the prospect of reduced funds in future years compelled the Air Force to cut back to forty-eight groups. Even a force of this small size required an annual production of 31,000,000 pounds of airframe weight, but the Air Force got only 20,154,000 and 26,315,000 pounds in fiscal years 1949 and 1950, respectively.

After the Korean War began, USAF goals shot upward. For the ninety-five-wing force, the Air Force planned in July 1951 to spend about $6.86 billion of its fiscal year 1952 funds to buy 5,604 planes. Then, in late 1951, the goal became 143 wings to be reached by 1955. During the latter half of 1952, the Air Force directed AMC to buy 6,032 planes with fiscal year 1953 funds of about $7.4 billion.

Despite shifting programs and production problems, the American aircraft industry increased production fivefold. In December 1952, Under Secretary Roswell L. Gilpatric noted that manufacturers were building about 650 planes per month as compared with 130 per month two years earlier. During the first six months of 1953 aircraft deliveries totaled more than 4,000.

The end of the Korean War, new production goals, and the decision to arm for the "long pull" rather than for an imminent date of maximum danger all profoundly affected aircraft procurement. During 1953 the fluctuation in the wing programs from 143 to 120 and then back

---

NUMBER OF AIRCRAFT ACCEPTED FOR THE USAF 1948 TO DECEMBER 31, 1956		
	UNITS	WEIGHT (Thousands of Pounds)
FY 1948	876	8,358.2
1949	1,278	20,154.0
1950	1,652	26,315.0
1951	1,756	27,800.7
1952	2,814	54,239.5
1953	4,723	83,243.3
1954	5,662	101,810.4
1955	4,830	94,585.4
1956	3,086	65,141.0
1957*	1,228	30,739.0
(*As of December 31, 1956)		

NUMBER OF LINE ITEMS AND ESTIMATED QUANTITY OF ALL ITEMS IN USAF SUPPLY SYSTEM		
	TOTAL INVENTORY OF LINE ITEMS	ESTIMATED TOTAL QUANTITY OF ALL ITEMS
As of June 30, 1947	310,808	360,848,088
As of June 30, 1956	1,087,634	957,117,920
As of December 31, 1956	1,147,145	999,163,295

to 137 wings resulted in cutting the numbers of trainers, transports, and supporting aircraft to be purchased. Because of the continued stretchout of aircraft schedules, aircraft production remained at a more even keel during the latter half of 1954, declined in 1955, and leveled off in 1956.

Even with more stable production programs, important changes in procurement and production continued. As more money went for guided missiles, less went for airframes. Individual companies felt the effects of this decline in aircraft deliveries. The Air Force expected money for engines and armaments to remain fairly constant, but there would be a substantial increase in funds for electronic equipment. During fiscal year 1956 the Air Force released more than $8 billion for procurement, about half going for the purchase of new aircraft and spares, one-fifth for missiles, and the balance for modifications, facilities, and supporting activities. Original plans called for the purchase of 2,375 planes, but program changes enabled the Air Force to add another 402 without new appropriations. By price redeterminations, changes in requirements for spares, and other adjustments, the Air Force recouped about $1 billion during fiscal year 1956, enough to buy 100 B-52s or 1,000 fighters. The money actually went for a variety of weapons.

Immediately after World War II, the Air Force could do little to assist the aircraft industry, which had been hard hit by a decline in production from a wartime high of nearly 100,000 planes a year to less than 1,000 in 1947. When the Air Force scheduled more planes to be built in 1948, the industry was ill prepared to cope with even a moderate expansion. Aircraft had become more difficult to build, for reciprocating engines and airframes of light sheet metal had given way to jet engines and airframes of heavy sheet metal. During World War II the Air Force bought standardized weapons in enormous quantities, permitting full play to the American flair for mass production. But quality was more important in the age of atomic power and jet propulsion, and mass production was more difficult to come by.

Major strides in technology gave the Air Force planes with far better performance, but their complexity often ruled out the fullest application of mass production techniques that would have saved both time and money. Aircraft contained extremely complex superjet engines and highly intricate electronic systems. Each of the 6,000 bolt-holes in the wing of a B-47 had to be accurate within one- to two-thousandths of an inch—less than the thickness of a human hair. To make the thin wings of the latest fighters strong enough to withstand the stresses of supersonic flight, they were almost hand-carved from solid metal. Giant forging and extrusion presses that shaped whole plane sections promised to solve this problem.

The production difficulties of aircraft manufacturers were multiplied during the early years of the Korean War. Slippage, the amount that deliveries fall behind schedule, became a familiar term. In May 1952, General Rawlings, AMC commander, pointed out that there had been substantial slippages in the effort to meet the ninety-five-wing program and that even schedules that had been stretched out had not been met.

Many production problems were inescapable during a limited mobilization when industry continued to produce civilian goods and when military requirements were superimposed upon an existing industrial base. Machine tools, components, and parts became bottlenecks, and strikes affected industry. Modifications on the production line, although essential if planes were to become reliable and superior combat weapons, affected schedules also. To balance demands for new and better planes against the criticism that too frequent changes on the production line

Gen. Edwin W. Rawlings, who has been commander of the Air Materiel Command from July 1951 to the present.

inhibited mass production, the DCS/Materiel decided when to freeze designs or permit deviations.

Lead time, the period between the placement of an order and the delivery of a finished product, remained a controlling factor in military production. The events that took place during this period were time-consuming, but they normally had to occur in sequence. Because of lead time, the great production effort of the Korean War did not bear fruit until the summer of 1952 when the first aircraft ordered after June 1950 rolled off the production lines. In 1952 a modern fighter required an average of twenty-one to twenty-four months in lead time, while big bombers took thirty to thirty-six months.

To reduce time and costs, in 1953 the Air Force applied the weapon system approach to procurement and permitted the manufacturer to subcontract for many items of equipment. Previously, it had bought most components and supplied them to the airframe manufacturer, but this grew increasingly awkward as airframe and components became more interdependent. This new method utilized the engineering and managerial skills of the aircraft industry to a far greater extent. The Air Force still bought separately certain major components such as engines.

Supply

Modern air warfare demanded military equipment on a scale that was truly bewildering. By 1957 there were about 1,150,000 separate items in the Air Force inventory. During 1955 alone, AMC handled more than 41,600,000 items weighing about 4,500,000 tons. Keeping track of this vast quantity and variety of goods was a fantastic problem in supply management.

The Supply System

The Air Force bought most of its supplies direct from the manufacturer. Whenever practicable, it coordinated purchases with the other services. A single military depart-

The airlift of high-priority cargo like jet engines proved itself in the Korean War as saving both time and money.

ment bought for all three certain items in common use. The Air Force, for example, bought photographic equipment for all the services, while the Army bought food for all three. Joint agencies under the Secretary of Defense bought such items as petroleum products and medical supplies. In December 1955 the three services decided to exchange information on inventories and, if possible, transfer materiel instead of buying new goods. Of the eight groups set up for this purpose, the Air Force headed those handling vehicles and chemical products.

While AMC did most of the purchasing, an Air Force installation could also buy certain inexpensive goods directly from a local civilian merchant or manufacturer. This local purchasing helped the Air Force keep down the number of items in its supply system, reduced the cost of record-keeping, and eased the problem of storage space. Beginning in 1952, USAF bases bought from General Services Administration depots when their prices and services compared favorably with those of commercial stores. Of 145,000 items authorized for local purchase in 1956, GSA supplied 2.8 percent.

The Air Force distribution system was built around the air materiel area depots and the specialized depots. In January 1949 the Air Force divided the United States, and in a sense the world, into eastern and western supply zones. Each area depot supplied units in its locale with items in common use. Specialized depots carried particular items of supply, and generally only one in each zone carried these items. Thus, only two depots in the United States would stock F-84 parts, one in the east and the other in the west.

For shipments overseas, certain depots in the United States acted as control points, checking requisitions from

abroad and ensuring that they would be filled. In January 1950 the Army and the Air Force agreed that the predominant service in an overseas area would have responsibility for supply of items in common use in that area. Among the areas for which the Air Force assumed supply responsibility were the United Kingdom and the Philippines.

As atomic weapons began to enter into all USAF activities, they had to be integrated into the supply system. The process began early in 1950 with the establishment of a separate class of atomic energy property. In 1951, by agreement with the Department of Defense and the Atomic Energy Commission, the Air Force began to operate atomic storage sites. AMC assumed responsibility for storing and maintaining weapons. Except for the bombs themselves and certain specialized items, most atomic materials came within the USAF logistical and budgetary system.

Supporting the Combat Forces

The striking power of the Air Force hinged upon the preparedness of the USAF supply system. Early in 1949 the Air Force began to prestock supplies at selected overseas bases to sustain SAC forces in combat for ninety days. Combat units liable to deployment on short notice also had flyaway kits, packages of spare parts and supplies that could keep a plane flying for thirty days.

During the Korean War the Air Force concentrated on equipping combat wings and limited the size of the materiel reserve to be kept for all-out mobilization. In 1954, however, it began to accumulate stocks for its mobilization reserve. In building up this materiel reserve, the Air Force took into account the fact that certain

Antiquated logistic methods of World War II forced stockpiling on global basis, piled up large surpluses like this.

items might soon become obsolete and that it would have to replace them from time to time. It began to emphasize those items required during the critical initial period of a full-scale war.

Considering the tempo of modern warfare, it was apparent that the supply system did not give sufficient support to aircraft included in war plans. In February 1955 the Air Force began to give preferential treatment to these planes in time of peace to ensure that as many of them as possible would be ready at all times. It based priorities on the importance of the mission for which the items were needed and the period within which the request had to be met. When the first B-52 wing encountered shortages of supporting equipment, AMC depots worked hard and fast to overcome the deficiencies.

Since the Air Force stocked more than a half-million items for spare parts and engines, it was extremely difficult to order the right part in the right amount and be sure that it went to the right place at the right time. A year's supply of spare parts was delivered along with new aircraft. Aside from these initial spares, additional parts went to factories when there were major modifications on the production line and to units when worn-out items needed replacing. In June 1955 the value of spare engines and parts exceeded $8.6 billion.

In 1948 the Air Force began to study ways to reduce the cost of spares. The sum requested for initial spares in fiscal year 1951 amounted to 44.2 percent of the total cost of the aircraft program. But by fiscal year 1956 the Air Force brought this staggering percentage down to 28.1. The cost of spare engines was a major factor. By making minor repairs at air bases, maintenance men lengthened the useful life of a jet engine and reduced these costs substantially. Using the modern actuarial methods of the life insurance business, the Air Force made more accurate forecasts of the life expectancy of engines, saving millions of dollars.

Strict control over the delivery, stockage, issuance, and repair of the few most expensive items also cut the cost of spares. Seventy-six percent of the dollars spent

for airborne electronic equipment went for twenty-nine items, less than one percent of the total number of items in this category. The Air Force saved large sums by cutting down the time spent to repair these high-value items and the time that they were kept in stock.

Oil was the blood stream of the air arm. When an oil workers' strike in 1952 cut deliveries of aviation gasoline and jet fuel by almost thirty-five percent, the Air Force could maintain an adequate reserve of fuel only by restricting flying in all commands except FEAF. The Air Force decided that pipelines delivered gasoline and oil with less danger of fire than railroad cars or tank trucks and at less cost in time and manpower. By 1956, commercial pipelines were supplying ten USAF installations with vital petroleum products. The Air Force also tested the possibility of storing jet fuel in underground salt caverns in Kansas.

Airlift and Automation

In World War II, supplies moved to troops at a speed of only three and one half miles per hour, no great improvement over the one and one-third miles per hour of the American Revolution. Critical and expensive items were transported by ship and rail and stockpiled at forward depots. The need for swifter supply for a global air force was self-evident, and the Air Force looked to airlift and automation to do the job.

While the airlift of materiel was difficult, it was the only way that goods could be delivered to overseas bases in time to support the combat forces in the initial and crucial stage of a war. For this purpose, frequency of aerial delivery was a much better measure of effectiveness than total tonnage delivered or tons per mile. Airlift also eliminated the need for large stockpiles of expensive items in forward depots, cut down the time between procurement and use, and permitted the purchase of fewer critical items, such as engines. Early in 1955, the Air Force began the routine airlift of certain types of aircraft engines and other valuable and critical items to overseas areas directly from depots in the United States. AMC determined

A part of the logistic function is the maintenance of materiel. This machine shop is at Albrook AFB, Canal Zone.

engine requirements and tonnage and pickup and delivery points, while MATS operated the airlift, deciding routes, schedules, and standards of service.

Automatic machines could also help solve the problem of rapid delivery. It was not unusual for the Air Force to spend about eighty percent of the time between the requisition of supplies and their receipt in processing the data and handling materials. An electronic communications system cut about ten days off the requisitioning time. The heart of this system was the transceiver, an electronic device that transmitted information by wire or radio at tremendous speeds and without error. By January 1957 this equipment had been installed at all depots throughout the world and at overseas bases.

Supply Management

Fortunately, measures which contributed to speed and flexibility also offered substantial savings. And proper supply management, such as disposal of surpluses, inventory control, and standardized procedures, contributed to the efficiency of USAF operations.

The disposal of billions of dollars of surplus items after World War II helped ease the problem of storage space until the Korean War, when it became acute again. The Air Force built warehouses, leased commercial space, and recaptured facilities formerly operated by the government. In December 1954, AMC opened one of the largest and most modern warehouses in the world at Wilkins Air Force Station, Ohio. During 1955 the Air Force took over from the Army seven depots, with about 10,000,-000 square feet of storage space.

The Air Force had to know the cost as well as the number of each item it used. By 1955, it had applied mone-

tary values to inventories and supply transactions at bases and depots both at home and abroad. Since items costing less than $10 made up 75.5 percent of the total number but only eighteen percent in terms of dollars, the Air Force decided in 1953 to concentrate on controlling the more expensive items.

Considering the staggering number of items in USAF inventories and their constant modification or replacement, the paper work involved in processing data and controlling inventories would be virtually impossible to handle manually. After 1947 the Air Force experimented with electronic computers as a solution. UNIVAC proved its worth in computing requirements for fiscal year 1957. Another computer handled the paper work involved in filling a requisition from depot stocks in about one second.

Conveyors and other mechanical devices saved time, men, and money in the handling of materials. Packaging alone cost the Air Force about $1 billion each year. The three military departments tried to use uniform methods parallel to those of private industry. In January 1954, transportation experts took over this important activity.

The Air Force joined the other services in standardizing procedures to eliminate duplication. A major step in this direction was the preparation of a single catalog for all items used by the military. The slow and arduous task of identifying, describing, and numbering millions of articles began in 1947, and by 1957, more than 360,000 USAF items, about one-third of the total, had been catalogued.

Maintenance

Maintenance at three levels kept USAF weapons and equipment ready for combat: organizational, field, and

Mothballed B-29s, later broken out and used in Korea. Technical progress has virtually outdated such methods.

depot. Squadrons serviced their own aircraft and equipment on the flight line, inspected them before and after flight, and replaced parts. Field maintenance, performed in hangars and shops at USAF bases, involved the minor repair and modification of equipment. And air materiel area depots and private plants completely overhauled aircraft and components and made major modifications. In July 1951 the Air Force set up the first of its specialized maintenance depots at Kirtland AFB, N. M., to keep test equipment for atomic weapons ready for use.

Maintenance made heavy demands on USAF resources. In 1957, one-third of the military and civilian members of the Air Force were maintenance men. Their tasks ranged from installing electronic countermeasure equipment in B-52s to painting radomes on DEW Line stations in the Arctic. The cost of maintenance grew as the cost and number of aircraft increased. Frequent modifications of weapons

and their increasing complexity also raised maintenance costs. In fiscal year 1956, the Air Force spent $1.4 billion for maintenance and modification.

The rapid demobilization after World War II almost ended all USAF maintenance work. By November 1946, when the number of maintenance men had dropped to eight percent of the total on hand in January 1945, only eighteen percent of first-line aircraft were ready for combat. The situation eased somewhat by 1948, when AMC was able to help overseas commands clear up their backlogs of items needing repair. During the pre-Korean years, the Air Force also modernized World War II planes. It equipped most of its B-29s with new engines and electric propellers so that they could reach higher altitudes.

The Berlin Airlift created a major maintenance problem in 1948-49. C-54s underwent extensive 200-hour inspections amounting to minor overhauls at the Burtonwood de-

Lt. Gen. Clarence S. Irvine, Deputy Chief of Staff, Materiel.

between overhauls and kept jet fighter units in a higher state of operational readiness. The average span between major overhauls of the J-33 engine was extended from ninety-six to 237 hours.

Minor overhaul plus better maintenance saved men and money as well as decreasing the need for new engines. Since litter on runways and taxiways damaged jet engines, the Air Force improved the surface conditions of the runways and impressed maintenance men with the importance of keeping them clear of debris.

After 1950 the most important stress was placed on staying ready for action. AMC organized about 4,000 highly skilled civilians into sixty mobile maintenance teams ready to move at any hour to repair battle damage or help SAC bases get aircraft into action. During SAC exercises, some of these teams moved to SAC bases; others repaired aircraft landing at depots without advance notice.

The shortage of experienced technicians caused the Air Force to resort to contract maintenance. By 1949, private enterprise handled a considerable portion of the work of repairing USAF transports. This not only relieved USAF depots of some of their workload but helped support the aircraft industry. After the Korean War, there was a steady increase in the amount of contract work. Aside from maintaining jet engines, civilian contractors repaired certain complex armament and radar equipment because there were too few airmen able to work on these items. During 1956 the Air Force spent $75 million to hire civilian technicians and expected this cost to continue to rise. But skilled airmen were also necessary because there were many places where only military people could be used. Furthermore, in time of war, industry would have to shift from repairing aircraft to producing them.

One of the most important contract jobs was that of keeping the giant B-36 ready to fly. Beginning in 1952, the manufacturer of the plane, Convair, spent many thousands of man-hours modernizing and reconditioning each plane every two years. The craft was reconditioned and improved but not made like new, thus saving money and reducing the time the plane was out of commission. Convair also performed necessary field maintenance on the B-36 from 1952 on.

The reconditioning program followed the procedure known as "inspect and repair as necessary" (IRAN), under which the Air Force began to work in August 1952. Previously, in overhauling a plane, mechanics disassembled it and replaced many parts that could have continued to function. Under the new system, the maintenance records of the plane and its components, plus flight tests and equipment tests, determined the extent to which the plane would be taken apart and repaired. This procedure reduced the costs of overhaul sharply, enabling the Air Force to repair three aircraft of the same type for the previous price of two. In the case of the C-47, IRAN cut the cost of repairs on each plane from $60,000 to $13,000.

Until the Korean War created emergencies, the Air Force had made progress in repairing damaged or worn-out equipment. After the war ended, USAF depots inspected and classified each item worth repairing to see how much maintenance was needed. Repairmen at air bases also screened items to decide whether they could be fixed. From October 1952 to July 1954, USAF depots checked about 12,500,000 items and found that ten percent were serviceable, ten percent required minor repairs, sixty-seven percent needed overhaul, and thirteen percent could be reclaimed or condemned. During this period, major commands also inspected more than 1,350,000 items and reported that twenty-five percent were serviceable, thirty-five percent could be repaired at bases, thirty-four percent would have to go to USAF depots, and six percent could be reclaimed or condemned.

pot in England. AMC depots also overhauled engines, while civilian contractors in the United States under AMC technical supervision carried out "cycled reconditioning" of aircraft after every thousand hours of flight. When Operation Vittles ended in September 1949, the Air Force returned virtually all the planes in the airlift to the United States and reconditioned them.

In 1950 there was an immediate demand for aircraft for the Korean War, for additional wings, and for foreign aid. The Air Force withdrew B-29s, F-51s, and other World War II planes from storage and reconditioned them for combat. USAF depots and civilian contractors fitted these planes with improved engines, armament, and equipment. New aircraft coming into use developed unsatisfactory mechanical conditions and needed repairs. Maintenance men installed and maintained radar and communications equipment at aircraft control and warning sites and converted communications equipment in aircraft and ground facilities to ultrahigh frequency.

During the Korean War, the Air Force did not have enough aircraft on hand to follow the World War II practice of declaring aircraft "war weary" when they needed extensive repairs. The modern airplane was also six to seven times as expensive as its predecessor of a decade before. During the early stages of the war, certain maintenance units dragged heavy equipment into forward areas and built small maintenance shops. This practice proved unsatisfactory, and after a year of war, FEAF units set up relatively complete facilities in rear areas. These shops relieved two or more combat groups of their normal responsibilities for field maintenance, major inspections, and minor repair of engines.

The Air Force greatly improved jet engine maintenance after 1946. In 1947-48 the number of jet engines in USAF depots tripled. Engineers developed techniques for making these new engines more reliable and durable. Beginning in 1949 the Air Force authorized minor repairs of jet engines at air bases. This step increased the average length of time

Chapter 22

THE TOOLS

Management

WITH assets of more than $70 billion and a budget of almost $18 billion for fiscal year 1957, the Air Force might well be described as the biggest business in the United States. Effective management of an enterprise of such magnitude called for the utmost efficiency and economy of operation.

Secretary Symington early recognized the importance of management in the new Air Force and appointed his former special assistant, Eugene M. Zuckert, as Assistant Secretary (Management) on September 26, 1947. During a tenure of more than four years of responsibility for budgetary policy and control, Zuckert laid the groundwork for an effective system of management control throughout the Air Force. He was instrumental in developing a cost-control system that enabled the Air Force to account more clearly for its use of public funds and to present its budget in the terms appropriate for a large enterprise.

Within the Air Force, two major staff officers, the Comptroller and the Inspector General, exercised the principal management controls. In a small way, the Air Adjutant General also assisted in the managerial process through his records management program. The Comptroller idea was a comparatively recent development taken over from private enterprise, while the Inspector General basically continued a traditional inspection system but with additional police and security functions.

Comptroller Management

The Air Force pioneered among the military services in adopting the modern business concept of comptrollership to help solve its management problems. Confronted with limitations on personnel and funds and increased operating and procurement costs at the end of World War II, the Assistant Secretary of War for Air, Robert A. Lovett, saw the need of a comptroller organization to ensure the maximum return on every dollar spent. This approach culmi-

The air policeman represents the field arm of the Provost Marshal, part of the Air Force management organization.

As Assistant Secretary, Eugene Zuckert laid foundation for management control.

nated in the establishment in the AAF of the Office of the Air Comptroller on June 7, 1946, headed by Brig. Gen. Grandison Gardner. Gardner's deputy, Brig. Gen. Edwin W. Rawlings, took over in mid-November 1946. Able and energetic, Rawlings guided the new office through its formative years—1946-51. His initial efforts went into bringing budgetary, fiscal, and statistical functions together into a smooth-working organization.

Establishment of the Department of the Air Force brought new responsibilities to Rawlings, whose office was redesignated Comptroller, USAF, in December 1947. These functions included preparation and support of its own budget, operation of its own accounting and disbursing network, assumption of its own auditing functions, and enlargement of the statistical reporting system to include personnel strength accounting, casualty reporting, and the collection and compilation of medical statistics.

In 1949, Congress recognized the worth of the comptroller concept by the passage of Public Law 216. It required the appointment of a comptroller for each of the military departments, with responsibility for all budgeting, accounting, progress and statistical reporting, and internal auditing. Since the Air Force had already anticipated this action, the

Lt. Gen. Charles B. Stone, Deputy Chief of Staff, Comptroller, 1951-55.

Lt. Gen. Manuel J. Asensio, who succeeded Gen. Stone in mid-December 1955.

essential effect of the law was to make the Comptroller responsible to the Secretary of the Air Force as well as to the Chief of Staff. The act stipulated that the Comptroller might be either military—the rule in the Air Force—or civilian, but that if military he must have a civilian deputy.

The comptroller organization continued to expand and, by 1948, had begun to operate on a worldwide basis. A special recruitment and training program was set up to obtain properly qualified personnel. The Comptroller kept a close check on the entire system by means of a program of recurring visits begun in November 1949.

By the close of July 1951, when Lt. Gen. Charles B. Stone, III, succeeded General Rawlings as Deputy Chief of Staff, Comptroller, the comptroller organization throughout the Air Force totaled approximately 22,375, almost equally divided between military and civilian personnel. Lt. Gen. Manuel J. Asensio, who had previously served as the USAF Director of Budget, replaced General Stone in mid-December 1955. At the close of 1956, Asensio supervised 43,177 persons, of whom 25,925 were civilians.

Budgeting

Every year the Air Force prepared its budget for the next year—an estimate of the amount of money it needed to carry out its program for the fiscal year. The amount of money appropriated by Congress determined the size and composition of the Air Force. Despite the recurrent stress on economy, the mounting cost of modern air weapons precluded any real or lasting reduction in USAF budget requirements. After the Korean War, the Air Force got the biggest slice of the defense dollar.

The military budget for fiscal year 1950 presented for the first time in one estimate and one series of appropriations all the direct requirements of the Air Force. A new creation arising from the separation of Air Force and Army budgeting, the main budget structure consisted of twelve appropriations corresponding to the major elements in the USAF program. Primarily functional, it grouped homogeneous and related programs within a single appropriation. This change resulted in the so-called performance type of budget, and its adoption promised more effective management of appropriated funds.

Subsequently, the Air Force reduced the number of appropriation categories to eight: aircraft and related procurement, other procurement, military construction, research and development, operation and maintenance, military personnel, reserve personnel, and Air National Guard. Under the first four appropriations, called no-year appropriations, the funds authorized remained available for obligation and expenditure for an indefinite period. This continuing availability of money, authorized by Congress in 1950, was of great importance to the Air Force because of its costly, long-range programs for base construction, weapon research and development, and aircraft procure-

ment. The last four categories were annual appropriations available for obligation for one fiscal year and for expenditure for two additional fiscal years. In the 1950s, the two procurement appropriations accounted for about forty percent of the USAF budget request, while day-to-day operating costs—operation and maintenance and military personnel—required about fifty percent.

The USAF budget process began with the compilation of program data, based on fundamental assumptions provided by the Office of the Secretary of Defense. The next step, issuance by the USAF Director of Budget of the Call for Estimates, provided program guidance and budgeting instructions to all the major commands and estimating agencies of the Air Force. Normally, this document was released in mid-January of each calendar year and applied to the budget estimate for the second succeeding fiscal year. The fiscal year 1955 call, for example, went out on January 15, 1953.

Upon receipt at Headquarters USAF, the completed estimates underwent an intensive review by the Air Staff. From

---

DEPARTMENT OF THE AIR FORCE AIRCRAFT AND RELATED PROCUREMENT EXPENDITURES BY FISCAL YEAR

FY 1950	
Net Expenditures:	$1,198,750,160
FY 1951	
Net Expenditures:	1,931,394,935
FY 1952	
Net Expenditures:	4,340,909,236
FY 1953	
Net Expenditures:	6,472,188,217
FY 1954	
Net Expenditures:	6,909,219,635
FY 1955	
Net Expenditures:	6,959,282,055
FY 1956	
Net Expenditures:	6,073,788,654
FY 1957 (Through December 31, 1956)	
Net Expenditures:	3,402,533,647

---

the reviewing process, which ultimately involved the USAF Budget Advisory Committee, the Office of the Secretary of Defense, and the Bureau of the Budget, emerged the USAF fund requests forwarded by the President to the Congress in his annual budget message. As a rule, the Office of the Secretary of Defense and the Bureau of the Budget, insisted on reductions. The USAF Director of Budget, however, could protest such cuts either informally or by a formal reclama—from the Spanish word for complaint. In the final analysis, Congress, of course, decided how much money the Air Force would get.

Congressional action began in the House of Representatives with the drafting of an appropriation bill, followed by extensive hearings before a subcommittee of the House Committee on Appropriations. The House hearings usually opened with general statements by the Secretary of the Air Force and the Chief of Staff outlining in broad terms the requirements, objectives, and problems of the Air Force. Thereafter, the USAF witnesses presented the detailed justifications for the various programs and projects. The

Director of Budget organized and supervised all USAF budget presentations before Congress.

Congressmen asked all sorts of questions during the hearings and USAF witnesses had to provide the answers, whether the subject was the wearing of suspenders by military personnel, the number of gadgets on aircraft, the construction of bakeries and laundries, or the procurement of heavy presses. At times also the going was rough, as when USAF witnesses had to refute the perennial charges of waste and extravagance or demonstrate that the Air Force needed more rather than less manpower.

Once the appropriation measure passed the House and Senate hurdles and received the approval of the President, the USAF Director of Budget took over the task of administering the funds made available to the Air Force. This was the final step in the budgeting process, which by general agreement never allowed enough time for computation, required too much detail, and was always subject to change.

The Air Force achieved autonomy during a period when economy was the watchword in Washington. In general, defense budgets prior to the Korean War were kept under tight dollar ceilings. In fiscal year 1950, Congress appropriated $4.7 billion for the Air Force.

The Korean War brought a sharp increase to $15.9 billion in new USAF money appropriated for fiscal year 1951. The wartime peak of $22.3 billion came in the following fiscal year. The "new look" resulted in low figures of $11.4 billion for fiscal year 1954 and $11.6 billion the following year. In fiscal year 1956 the Air Force received $15.7 billion, and in 1957, $17.7 billion.

Most of the rise in the total new money for 1956 came in the appropriation for aircraft and related procurement. This resulted from two factors: an increase in the number and cost of aircraft to be procured and the lack of any carry-over funds from prior years that could be applied for that purpose. The major portion of the additional $2 billion for 1957 came in the appropriations for procurement and military construction and resulted principally from the acceleration of the B-52 and KC-135 production programs.

In each of fiscal years 1950 through 1957 the Air Force got more money than the Navy, and in only two years—1951 and 1954—did it get less than the Army.

Finance

With autonomy achieved, the Air Force gradually took over its own finance activities from the Army. The establishment of a USAF finance center was the final major step in the separation of Army and Air Force finance activities. After the Air Force Finance Center, located at Denver, Colo., began operating in July 1951, the Comptroller had responsibility for the entire USAF disbursing network. Because of its size and location, the center functioned under the Air Force Finance Division, a separate operating agency with the responsibilities of a command.

The Korean War greatly increased the workload of the center, but by the spring of 1952 effective management permitted a sizable cutback in civilian personnel as well as other economies. Significant savings also resulted from the substitution of punch-card checks for conventional paper checks, a change later extended to other USAF installations. Punch-card checks cost less and their use made possible an additional economy through mechanized operations.

A beehive of activity, the Air Force Finance Center handled personnel finance matters that required centralized control. It processed and issued allotments; paid allotments, retired pay, and administrative expense accounts; processed accounting documents; accounted for, audited, and kept military pay records; and made collections and adjustments. A tremendous enterprise, this operation directly or indirectly touched the lives—and pocketbooks—of most USAF personnel throughout the world.

Allotment activities overshadowed all others, whether measured by volume or by importance. If the allotment check failed to arrive promptly, an airman's dependents might suffer or an officer's life insurance policy might lapse. The processing included three types of action—authorizations, discontinuances, and changes. Processing actions in 1957 averaged approximately 150,000 per month. Allotment checks, which made up about ninety-five percent of the entire number issued by the center, exceeded 640,000 and totaled $70 million per month.

The center made every effort to lighten the workload and reduce the cost of its extensive allotment activity. In July 1952, it began a recurring annual review to determine whether the parents of airmen were actually dependents as claimed. The initial result was the discontinuance of 2,686 allotments at a saving of $148,027 per month. In the same year, additional economies came from the consolidation in one check of the premium payments due each large commercial insurance company from individual allot-

Finance Center, Denver, Colo., keeps records of total expenditures of the Air Force, about $17.8 billion in 1957.

The Finance Center's Allotment Division sets up, services, and maintains more than 640,000 allotments for USAF people.

Modern electronic business machines enable the center's Accounting Division to process 400,000 vouchers a month.

ments. Under this arrangement, the center issued a single check to each of sixty-nine insurance companies, in place of the 144,554 individual checks previously required.

During the Korean emergency, as in World War II, civilian contractors received financial assistance from the government to expedite defense production. Beginning in late 1950 the Directorate of Finance began to process applications from USAF contractors for the guaranteed loans provided by the Defense Production Act of 1950. During the period from July 1, 1950, through May 31, 1953, the Air Force received 365 applications for guaranteed loans and authorized 326 of them. The total value of these loans was $886.2 million, of which the Air Force guaranteed the repayment of $702.8 million. The principle of revolving credits was applied to defense contract financing, and the same contractor might use the money again and again.

Accounting, Auditing, Capital Funds

In 1951 the Air Force began to develop an integrated accounting system. The approach adopted was, first, to improve and interrelate all existing systems into a single accounting system for the entire Air Force, and, second, to devise procedures that would place USAF assets under accounting control, using the available stock, industrial, and management funds whenever appropriate. Harvard University and several nationally known commercial ac-

counting firms gave advice and assistance in setting up the new system. On July 1, 1954, the AF installed an integrated commercial-type accounting system at all air bases.

After tests in February 1953, monetary inventory accounting was extended to stocks at all USAF depots and bases. This system made possible a USAF inventory expressed in terms of dollars as well as units. Using the dollar as the common denominator, the supply manager could determine where stocks were heavy and had to be reduced in order to lessen handling costs and warehouse requirements.

The USAF auditing system operated on four continents and in nineteen countries with an organization of approximately 2,500 persons. It had the large task of auditing internal USAF financial activities and all procurement contracts. Its importance as the "Watchdog of the Air Force Dollar" grew with the expansion of the Air Force.

The Korean War brought a substantial increase in contract auditing. About ninety percent of the dollar value of procurement contracts required auditing because they were either of the cost-reimbursement type or were fixed-price contracts containing price-redetermination clauses. The contract auditors—mostly civilians—audited the accounts and cost records of the contractors and surveyed their accounting methods and internal controls for accuracy and reliability. By agreement, the military service having the predominant procurement interest at one industrial location took responsibility for the related audits of the other services.

Contract auditing paid for itself many times over by uncovering excessive or improper charges for labor, materials, or administrative expenses. During fiscal year 1956 the auditing of approximately $9 billion in procurement contracts resulted in cost reductions totaling an estimated $325 million. Based on an expenditure of $7 million for contract-audit salaries, each $1,000 spent for audit resulted in a cost reduction of $46,000.

The Air Force benefited materially from two types of working capital funds. In use from 1950, the stock fund financed inventories of stores, supplies, materials, and equipment, while the industrial fund furnished working capital for industrial and commercial-type activities. These were revolving funds, which meant that the selling or producing enterprise got the money derived from the sale of goods or services and used it to finance continued operation.

The Air Force Stock Fund in 1957 consisted of six divisions: Aviation Fuels, Clothing, Medical-Dental, Commissary, Air Force Academy, and General Supplies. These buying and selling organizations operated in areas where studies indicated that the stock fund could bring about more efficient management of USAF resources.

Clothing is handled through a revolving fund whereby the seller uses money from sales to finance the operation.

The Air Force pioneered among the military services in developing and using high-speed electronic computers to help solve its planning, programming, and operating problems. USAF funds were used to develop the Standards Eastern Automatic Computer (SEAC), an experimental model placed in operation in 1950. In June 1952, Headquarters USAF received its first high-speed, digital computer, the Eckert-Mauchly UNIVAC. Another UNIVAC, installed in July 1954 at Headquarters AMC, lightened the huge burden of materiel computation. Well suited to processing huge masses of data, the UNIVAC saved a lot of time.

The Comptroller furnished accurate, timely, integrated statistical data on all USAF activities. A worldwide reporting system highlighted accomplishments and signaled potential trouble spots. In 1957, the Comptroller issued 729 recurring reports, of which almost fifty percent originated from requests by agencies outside the Air Force.

The Air Force used modern mechanized techniques to

Air Materiel Command uses UNIVAC high-speed digital computer to process huge masses of data, saves precious time.

In 1957 there were eight printing plants under the Air Force Industrial Fund. Except for the absence of the profit motive, each operated like any other commercial printing plant, buying its own materials and supplies, paying for its own labor, and selling its finished product to defense activities in the neighboring area.

USAF laundry and dry-cleaning plants at fifty installations began operating under the industrial fund on July 1, 1955. The Secretary of Defense, in December 1955, directed the Air Force to apply this principle to the air transport operations of MATS at the earliest practicable time. Because of organizational difficulties, this change had not yet been completed in mid-1957.

Analysis and Reporting

The Air Force carefully analyzed its missions, programs, and operations, measuring effectiveness against objectives in terms of quality, quantity, and cost. Management analysis, established as a staff function under the Comptroller, sought to provide reliable data as a basis for making sound command and staff decisions.

Progress analyses pointed up the major factors affecting USAF operations, and cost analyses made possible evaluation and comparison on a dollar basis. Where alternate courses of action could be undertaken, knowledge of costs helped in making a final decision.

transmit and process the massive data needed for its operations. It used electrical accounting equipment and the much faster electronic data-processing machines known as digital computers. The newly developed transceivers made possible the instantaneous transmission and verification of punch-card data via radio, telegraph, and telephone. Continued mechanization of operations at the base level promised more timely, accurate, and useful data while, at the same time, freeing much-needed manpower for reassignment in other areas.

The Inspection Function

The Office of the Inspector General determined and reported upon the combat readiness, efficiency, and economy of the Air Force, investigated aircraft accidents, promoted flight safety, and ensured the maintenance of discipline and security. It also provided a centrally directed criminal, counterintelligence, and special investigative service to all USAF commands in the zone of interior, Puerto Rico, Bermuda, and Iceland.

The Office of the Inspector General was established in January 1948, under Maj. Gen. Hugh J. Knerr. By 1951 all inspection activities had been decentralized to the field, and eventually they were all concentrated at Norton AFB, Calif. In 1957, the Inspector General, Lt. Gen. Elmer J.

Rogers, Jr., carried out his duties through two deputies—one for inspection and the other for security.

Lt. Gen. Howard A. Craig, who succeeded General Knerr as the Inspector General in September 1949, insisted that inspection should not be a career field for officers. In his opinion, officers tended to lose contact with the field and its problems after prolonged inspection duty. Furthermore, in order to function effectively, the inspection system required a steady influx of new men with a fresh approach and a firsthand knowledge of current problems. Craig therefore established a rotation policy whereby officers would normally serve a maximum of three years on inspection duty.

Both General Craig and his successor, Lt. Gen. Bryant L. Boatner, who became Inspector General in late July 1952, held that inspection reports were confidential and privileged documents intended for use only within the Air Force. Secretaries Finletter and Talbott supported this stand. In the same vein, the reports of investigations of aircraft accidents were considered privileged documents not to be released to outside agencies, since such action would be prejudicial to the efficient operation of the Air Force and not in the public interest. A court decision in March 1953 upheld this contention.

Inspection

Perhaps the most important function in the inspection system was to ascertain the operational readiness of the Air Force. Operational readiness inspections brought out the factors, such as shortages of equipment and personnel turnover, which limited the effectiveness of combat and support units. Aircraft accident investigation was part of the flight safety activity.

Readiness and materiel inspections and surveys covered all USAF activities except procurement. This broad approach was typified by the survey of USAF capability to support the war plans of the Strategic Air Command.

Inspection teams examined weapon systems and paid particular attention to the B-52 aircraft program and special weapon activities. They analyzed and evaluated USAF administrative, supply, health, and morale programs and looked into the effectiveness of the command and inspection system. Sizable savings resulted from elimination of planned construction that did not meet immediate or projected requirements. In addition to pointing out faulty maintenance, the inspectors suggested improvements in aircraft design, specifications, and production standards.

Expansion of the Air Force after June 1950 naturally increased the importance of procurement inspection. Here the objective was to ensure the maximum return from each dollar spent. Procurement inspectors kept a continuing close watch on USAF contractor facilities and performance and on all USAF procurement activity. Because AMC was the largest single buyer for the Air Force, inspectors paid it special attention and made many recommendations to improve its procurement program.

During 1953 the emphasis shifted from inspection of the individual facilities of a contractor to the survey of an entire procurement program. To make certain that the Air Force received items of high quality, inspectors made searching inquiries into all phases of the procurement cycle—from planning and design to final purchase. They conducted these inspections as early as possible in the production stage, so that corrective action could be taken with the least expense and delay.

Police and Security

The Provost Marshal and the Director of Special Investigations shared the responsibility for police and security functions in the Air Force. After September 1950, these agencies were under the Deputy Inspector General for

Keeping track of literally millions of individual items, large and small, presents a formidable inventory problem.

USAF air police have found trained sentry dogs a valuable asset in their mission of safeguarding government property.

Security, a position still occupied in 1957 by Maj. Gen. Joseph F. Carroll, a former FBI official.

The Directorate of Special Investigations (OSI), set up in August 1948, combined three previously separate investigative units into one centrally directed agency, which served the entire Air Force. From its inception, the Directorate of Special Investigations carried an increasingly heavy load of personnel security investigations. The high rate of turnover of personnel, the steady growth of classified equipment and materiel, and ever increasing security consciousness combined to magnify the USAF security problem. As a result, between July 1, 1955, and June 30, 1956, the total number of personnel security investigations soared to approximately 360,000, an increase of about 80,000 over the previous year.

The directorate also investigated all cases involving suspicion of bribery or fraud in the procurement or disposition of USAF property. OSI personnel, like FBI agents, gathered evidence but did not draw conclusions, leaving appropriate action to the particular commands.

The Air Force forbade its personnel to accept gifts, no matter how small, from any person or firm doing or planning to do business with it. But occasionally there were transgressions of this rule. One such case involved a junior officer who reportedly had two new cars, a $30,000 home, and plenty of spending money. Subsequent investigation by the OSI and FBI disclosed that the officer had been selling surplus property and had received "gratuities" totaling $24,700 for favors shown to one of the bidders. All of the guilty parties—military and civilian—were tried and given sentences ranging from five to eight years.

The Provost Marshal supervised the internal security program at all USAF installations and industrial establishments. A well trained and well equipped air police force maintained discipline and enforced law and order. The Provost Marshal was responsible for the confinement and rehabilitation of USAF prisoners. In time of war his office also dealt with censorship, travel control, and enemy prisoners of war within the jurisdiction of the Air Force.

Because of increased security consciousness, the Provost Marshal put greater emphasis on protecting USAF installations and equipment against sabotage. This concern led to the setting up of many additional physical safeguards, such as chain-link fences, guard towers, floodlights, and warning systems. Considerable progress was also made in developing local ground defenses for all air bases.

Records Management

The rapid wartime growth of its files led the AAF to set up a records management program in 1944. At that time it had more than 2,000,000 cubic feet of records in the zone of interior alone, and the end of the war was not yet in sight. The first task naturally was to reduce the great bulk of this material and to retire to records centers the relatively small number of documents still needed. As the result of continuing effort, by June 30, 1956, approximately 4,200,000 cubic feet of records had been disposed of.

Even after 1947, the Air Force leaned heavily on Army practices and facilities in its records management. The Air Adjutant General, who directed this activity for the Air Force, worked steadily toward the creation of a USAF records system. In September 1953 he prescribed in detail the proper procedure for the maintenance of current USAF records and replaced the obsolete Army filing system with an entirely new system.

To reduce its reliance upon the Army, the Air Force opened a large records center at St. Louis, Mo., on July 1, 1956. The center took over the noncurrent organizational records of the Air Force, previously held by the Army in Kansas City, Mo. These records, originally totaling 150,000 cubic feet, had been reduced to about 45,000 cubic feet when the transfer occurred.

Meanwhile, beginning in June 1952, the Air Force set up low-cost records staging areas, which provided for noncurrent records until they were retired to a records center or became eligible for destruction. This avoided the expense of transfer to a records center of much material that eventually would have to be destroyed. The records at staging areas remained available for temporary local use.

Although USAF expansion meant many more records, the Air Force kept the rate of increase within manageable bounds. Systematic disposition of records and extensive use of records staging areas saved valuable office space and filing equipment. The total Air Force records holdings on June 30, 1956, amounted to 1,933,683 cubic feet, of which 1,377,038 were in current files, 261,145 in records staging areas, and 295,500 in records centers.

Chapter 23

THE DEEDS

The Berlin Airlift

AT THE close of World War II, Berlin became an island entirely surrounded by the Russian Zone of occupied Germany. By agreement, the United States, Great Britain, and France took over West Berlin, leaving East Berlin to the Russians. Even though access by land could be blocked, the Western Powers fortunately had been guaranteed the free use of three twenty-mile-wide air corridors leading directly into the city from the British and US zones.

By early 1948 the Russians were fast becoming difficult, if not downright unfriendly, neighbors within Berlin. In March they proposed to curtail the air rights of the Western Powers but were rebuffed. During the following month the Americans, British, and French refused to permit inspection of their Berlin-bound trains by Soviet guards. As a result, for eleven days the United States resorted to airlifting Allied passengers and supplies into the city, a temporary measure that provided valuable experience for the future. Beginning early in June 1948, progressive Russian restrictions on all travel by rail and road through their zone foreshadowed the ultimate stopping of all surface traffic into Berlin.

Buildup of the Airlift

By June 22, 1948, the Russians had cut off all rail, barge, and highway traffic into that part of Berlin occupied by the Americans, British, and French, leaving it isolated. The Western Powers then had the choice either of withdrawing their forces and abandoning West Berlin to the Russians or of supplying the necessities of life to the military community and to more than 2,000,000 Germans by the only remaining means of transportation—air.

Gen. Lucius D. Clay, the United States military governor, and his British and French associates, refused to give

Berliners gathered by the hundred around Tempelhof Air Base to cheer the planes bringing precious food and fuel.

up and ordered the beginning of what came to be known as the Berlin Airlift. A joint enterprise, it was Operation Vittles to the Americans and Operation Plainfare to the British. Luckily there was a small reserve on hand in West Berlin, since the last food train got through on June 21, but an assured source of supply was needed quickly.

The task of organizing and operating the initial airlift fell to General LeMay's US Air Forces in Europe (USAFE). On Sunday, June 26, by plucking "chairborne" flyers from their desks and utilizing the only available transports—C-47s —USAFE flew eighty tons of milk, flour, and medicine into Berlin's Tempelhof Air Base from Wiesbaden Air Base near Frankfort. On the same day LeMay requested additional transports and crews from Headquarters USAF, and soon hundreds of pilots and airmen were winging their way into West Germany from such widely separated areas as Alaska, Hawaii, and Texas. On June 29, Brig. Gen. Joseph Smith took command of the short-lived Berlin Airlift Task Force, which during the next four weeks laid the groundwork for the operation. By July 20 he had fifty-four C-54s and 105 C-47s with a maximum daily lift of 1,500 tons. Despite the assistance of the British Yorks and Dakotas that could carry a maximum of 750 tons, the combined airlift remained insufficient for the job to be done.

As the Russian blockade persisted, it became increasingly evident that the daily airlift requirement—roughly 3,000 tons for the American and French sectors and 1,500 tons for the British sector—could be met only by a full-scale operation. Accordingly, on July 23, General Vandenberg directed MATS to send to Germany seventy-two C-54s (eight squadrons) and enough men to form a task force headquarters to direct the Berlin Airlift under the operational control of USAFE. This required more than 2,500 men—three crews per aircraft, a headquarters staff, traffic supervisors, and maintenance men. Sent across the Atlantic at the rate of two per week, the MATS squadrons began operating at once. By July 31, for the first time, the US airlift to Berlin topped the 2,000-ton mark.

On July 29 a new Airlift Task Force (Provisional) came into being with headquarters at Wiesbaden. On the following day Maj. Gen. William H. Tunner took command of this unit, which three months later was redesignated the 1st Airlift Task Force. A veteran of the Hump airlift to China, Tunner was then Deputy Commander for Air Transport, MATS. He also headed the Combined Airlift Task Force, set up in mid-October to merge the previously co-ordinated but independent American and British efforts.

The Berlin Airlift was not only a combined operation but also—on the American side—a joint enterprise involving the US Army, Navy, and Air Force. The Army's Transportation Corps trucked cargo to and from the planes, and its Engineer Corps troops built additional runways as well as an entirely new airfield. From the beginning, Navy tankers delivered huge quantities of aviation gas to Bremerhaven to provide fuel for the airlift. Later, Navy planes and crews assisted the Air Force in furnishing round-the-clock delivery service. The arrival in November 1948 of the twenty-four Navy R5Ds (C-54s) of Squadrons VR-6 and VR-8 brought into the operation two highly efficient units, well supplied and fully manned with skilled maintenance personnel.

The C-47s could carry only three and a half tons, but by the end of September they were replaced by C-54s, which lifted about three times that much. Dependable and rugged, the C-54s had been designed for passenger and not cargo transport. Nevertheless, through ingenuity and improvisation, they performed splendidly on the coal and food run. In mid-August a C-74 Globemaster arrived in Germany with eighteen C-54 engines. Before returning to the United States, the C-74 delivered almost thirty tons of heavy engineering equipment to Berlin for the construction of new runways. In September, five C-82s joined the lift, primarily to carry vehicles.

The C-54s remained the backbone of the fleet, and ultimately as many as 319 of about 400 in active service joined the airlift. Of these 319 C-54s, nineteen were used for the pilot and aircrew replacement training program set up at Great Falls AFB, Mont., in October 1948. The maintenance pipeline usually absorbed seventy-five C-54s at any one time, and the remaining 225 C-54s had to be on hand in Europe to keep the airlift going. The British used an average of about 140 military and civil aircraft, many of them smaller than the C-54.

Maj. Gen. William H. Tunner, who ran the airlift.

C-47s, in line at Tempelhof, discharged cargoes ranging from engine crates to milk bottles. They bore the brunt of early airlift, were later replaced by bigger C-54s.

Coal-hauling C-54s based at Fassberg in the British Zone being unloaded at beleagured Berlin's Gatow airport. Even the residue from unloading operations was not wasted. Swept into neat piles, it was rebagged and distributed.

Operation of C-54 aircraft created a tremendous maintenance problem because of the abnormal wear and strain of the maximum-load takeoffs and landings and the almost continuous use. Only basic maintenance could be performed in Berlin, but intermediate inspections for every fifty hours of flying time were made at air bases within the US Zone of West Germany. Beginning in August 1948, 200-hour inspections took place at the air depot in Bavaria called Oberpfaffenhofen, a jawbreaker soon shortened to Obie. In November, USAFE transferred this activity to Burtonwood Air Base, in England, but the Erding depot in Germany continued to provide supply and maintenance services for the airlift. After 1,000 hours of flying, C-54s returned to the United States for cycled reconditioning (progressive overhaul) by civilian contractors. This program proved successful beyond expectation. Reconditioned C-54s returned to the airlift in like-new condition.

At the outset, maintenance suffered from a critical shortage of trained personnel, later relieved by the employment of German nationals. Following the arrival of additional supplies and replacement parts, transported mainly by air from the United States, few aircraft had to be grounded for lack of parts. Engines for C-54s, however, were in short supply. The need for washing and cleaning facilities was serious because the planes soon became filthy from coal dust and flour. House brooms and isopropyl alcohol were the main weapons against the cold-weather nuisances—ice, frost, and snow.

The Operational Pattern

All flights had to keep within the three twenty-mile-wide corridors that offered the Allies their only access to Berlin. Fanning out from Berlin like spokes in a wheel, the shorter northern and central corridors terminated in the British Zone while the longer southern corridor ended in the US Zone. Initially, the Air Force flew into Berlin from its two big bases in the Frankfort area—Rhein-Main and Wiesbaden. As ground and air traffic increased at these points, USAF transports began operating over much shorter routes from the British Zone, first from Fassberg in August and next from Celle in December 1948. Operationally, all these bases had the advantage of being near the entrances to the corridors and near the supply points for the commodities hauled—principally coal and food.

Within their respective sectors in Berlin, the Americans originally utilized Tempelhof while the British used Gatow airfield. Despite the addition of more runways, Tempelhof soon became congested, and another field for USAF planes had to be constructed. Located at Tegel in the French

sector and built from the rubble of Berlin by German men and women toiling day and night, the new airfield opened officially on December 7, 1948. All told, US aircraft used seven fields. The four loading fields were at Rhein-Main, Wiesbaden, Fassberg, and Celle. The three turn-around (unloading) fields—all in Berlin—were Tempelhof, Gatow, and Tegel. Because of the continuous pounding from heavily loaded aircraft, maintenance of these fields was a major problem.

Letting down into Tempelhof, over a cemetery. The towers are part of the high-intensity approach light system.

Long hours, little sleep, and foul weather told heavily upon air and ground crews. The arrival in July of additional personnel brought much-needed relief. During August and September unexpected rain and fog often blanketed Germany. Said one former B-29 pilot, "Everything was soup from Rhein-Main and Wiesbaden, all the way down the corridor to Tempelhof." Fortunately, the adverse conditions were largely overcome by weather, communications, and traffic-control experts from the MATS technical services and the Civil Aeronautics Administration.

Air traffic control was a *must* from the start because of the limited air space and terminal airfields, as well as the large number of aircraft involved. All flying in the corridors and into Berlin was under strict control, and the pilots were carefully briefed. Check pilots made sure that all aircrews complied with required flight procedures. Airway traffic control was handled by the centers at Frankfort in the US Zone and Bad Eilsen in the British Zone and by the Berlin Air Safety Center in which the Russians also were represented. In addition, at the insistence of the British, a new Joint Traffic Control Center was established at Tempelhof in December 1948.

THE APPROACHES TO BERLIN DURING THE BERLIN AIRLIFT—JUNE 26, 1948—SEPTEMBER 30, 1949

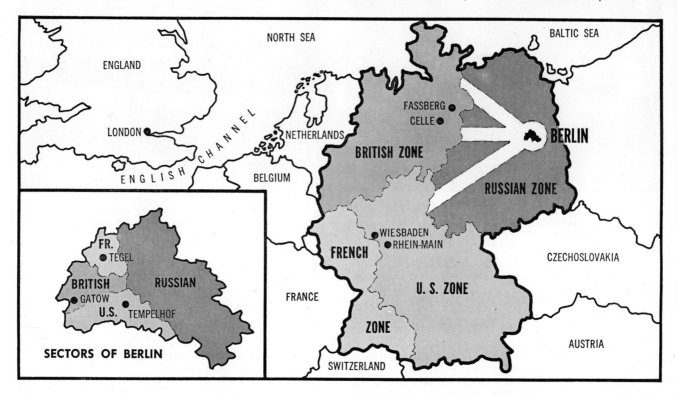

All pilots had to fly at a specified altitude and airspeed. Initially, six separate altitudes were tried, with the first level at 5,000 feet, the second at 6,000 feet, and so on to 10,000 feet. Intervals between aircraft were determined by the capabilities of the terminal airfields to accept incoming planes.

In effect, this system resulted in a series of ladders of aircraft proceeding to Berlin. Later, the number of altitudes was reduced as experience showed that two were adequate for safety. Frequent checks of spacing over designated fixes (known locations) by each pilot showed that a six-minute separation between aircraft at the same altitude was sufficient, which meant three-minute intervals at takeoff.

Because the aircraft from Rhein-Main and Wiesbaden operated in the same corridor into Tempelhof, it was necessary to coordinate the traffic from these bases. This was done initially by a "block system," whereby each base was allotted alternate four-hour periods in which to dispatch its aircraft. In order to fill the block, as many as twenty to thirty aircraft lined up near the takeoff position with their engines idling. The subsequent adoption of an hourly block system materially reduced idling time and greatly increased aircraft utilization.

Pilots had to follow the prescribed routes religiously and regardless of weather, since even the slightest variation could lead to disaster. These routes were designed to eliminate interference with traffic from other bases and to provide a six-mile final leg into Berlin. Radio and radar beacons, radio ranges, visual-aural ranges, and radar surveillance were all part of the predetermined pattern governing the pilot's flight.

To illustrate, the pilot taking off in a C-54 from Rhein-Main to Berlin first gained an altitude of 900 feet and then in succession passed over the Darmstadt beacon and the Aschaffenburg beacon, continuing to climb until he reached his assigned altitude. Next, he headed for Fulda range station on the border of the US Zone, his last directional guide before Berlin. Approaching Fulda, he listened carefully for the required time and position report from the aircraft just ahead, which told him whether

he was on schedule and properly spaced. After reaching Fulda and reporting his time and position for the aircraft behind him, the pilot started on the last 211-mile lap to Tempelhof. With Russians on both sides of the narrow corridor and with no beacons for guidance, he had to steer by dead reckoning while maintaining his assigned altitude and an exact air speed of 170 mph.

Precisely forty minutes after leaving the Fulda range station, the pilot tuned in his radio to Tempelhof and received an altimeter setting and a time check. He was next directed to the Wedding beacon inside Berlin, and, reducing his speed gradually to 140 mph, he descended and turned for the final approach. If the weather was clear, the control tower brought him into Tempelhof. But in foggy weather, GCA took over, guiding the transport by radar and radio to a safe landing. After time out for unloading and for a short stop at a mobile snack bar, plane and crew headed out through the central corridor to the home base in the US Zone.

Weather constituted the greatest single threat to the success of the airlift, especially during the winter. Although bad weather seldom closed a field, it did necessitate instrument flying, which meant fewer completed flights. Fog was the major hazard in November 1948 and again in February 1949. Turbulent weather and icing proved much less serious than anticipated.

With the approach of winter, the Air Weather Service (AWS) increased its efforts on behalf of the airlift. AWS furnished both long- and short-range forecasts for planning and logistical purposes. By daily telephone conferences among all stations on the routes, it produced a composite weather forecast available to all pilots at all bases.

When visibility fell below a mile, a weather observer was stationed on the landing end of each runway. In this position, he observed actual runway visibility by counting the visible runway lights and reported by field telephone to the weather office. In late November 1948 a weather reconnaissance squadron of B-29s, based in England, began making regular flights over the North Sea and reporting on the weather that would be over the corridors in twenty-four to forty-eight hours. Airlift pilots also reported regularly on weather conditions encountered in flight. All weather information was passed along as rapidly as possible.

The airlift highlighted the limitations of weather forecasting. During marginal weather, when the ceiling ranged from 200 to 400 feet and visibility from one-half to one mile, it was not possible to forecast accurately the changes over a period longer than thirty minutes. This was a distinct drawback, since it was important to know exactly when a field would have to be closed and the incoming aircraft diverted. Experience also demonstrated that observation and measurement by the human eye to determine ceiling and visibility were not accurate enough, and that electronic equipment was the only solution.

Perhaps the factor contributing most to the success of the Berlin Airlift was the installation and efficient operation of GCA (ground-controlled approach) equipment. With proper training, GCA controllers could bring the aircraft in at three-minute intervals. GCA was the primary aid used in all landings in Berlin during marginal and instrument conditions. Each incoming plane got one try at the approach. If it missed, the pilot returned to his home base. In this way, airlift traffic was kept moving and stacking of planes in the air over Berlin was eliminated.

Other electronic and visual landing aids contributed appreciably to the success and safety of the operation. These included mobile radio and radar equipment, as well as additional communications facilities and lighting systems for all key airfields. Tempelhof, in particular, was most troublesome during thick weather. Despite its great size, the field was almost completely encircled by high apartment buildings, a serious menace to incoming aircraft. To help solve this problem, high-intensity approach lights were installed in late 1948 in the best available area, which happened to be in a narrow cemetery adjacent to one of the main runways. The Germans cooperated fully, even to the extent of moving several graves, thereby giving Russian propagandists a chance to charge the Americans with desecrating the dead.

By 1949 the airlift had become a highly effective and almost routine operation, which winter weather hampered but never halted completely. At the close of February each USAF airlift base had two GCA sets ready for operation at all times. At Tempelhof, a new CPS-5 (traffic-control search radar), contributed substantially to the safety of air traffic. By giving the accurate position of each aircraft in the Berlin area, it made possible a minimum spacing interval during marginal and instrument conditions.

A C-54 roars past a ground-controlled approach unit on takeoff from Rhein-Main Air Base at Frankfort, Germany.

Handling the Cargo

During the summer and fall of 1948 the US Air Force and the US Army, in conjunction with the Royal Air Force, developed an effective ground support system for the airlift. The objective was to load and unload the airlift planes as swiftly as possible. On the US side, this was the task of the Army Transportation Corps, and it was made no easier by having to contend with the ever present German pedestrians, bicyclists, and automobile drivers on the roads to and from the airlift bases. As a sympathetic USAF observer remarked, a single German on foot sometimes seemed a greater traffic hazard than a half-million New Yorkers in Times Square.

After the shakedown period of the airlift in July, the Transportation Corps was loading a block of seventy C-54s every six hours, day and night. Six truck-tractors assigned to each of the two railheads at Rhein-Main brought a steady stream of loaded ten-ton trailers into the airfield. In an endless and automatic routine, the drivers then returned the empties to the freight cars and switched to full loads. DPs (displaced persons) and, later, German laborers actually loaded the cargo aboard the planes, supervised by an Air Force technician. Since idle aircraft were nonproductive, every effort was made to reduce the time spent in loading and unloading. The average turnaround time at the loading base was one hour and twenty-five minutes and at the unloading base forty-nine minutes.

Proper payload had to be maintained in keeping with

Night at Tempelhof was a pattern of lights. Only forty-nine minutes after a plane landed it was unloaded and airborne.

the dictates of safety as to weight and balance. Floor stresses, load distribution by compartment, and proper tie-down of cargo were the primary factors that determined whether or not the aircraft was safely balanced for take-off and landing. Overloading could be tragic, while under-loading led to an expensive and irretrievable loss of tonnage.

In order to attain the best use of load capacity, it was necessary to "marry" commodities of high density with those of low density. A load of macaroni, for example, would fill all available cargo space in a C-54 but weighed only about 6,000 pounds. Therefore, loads containing macaroni were "married" with sacks of sugar to get the desired weight and bulk. This mixing process took place when the trailers were being loaded, so that there would be no delay in placing cargo aboard the airplane.

Weights were carefully checked, and savings made wherever feasible. Dehydration reduced the daily require-ments for potatoes from 900 to 180 tons. Sacking cereals for air shipment proved more economical than packaging. Even that sturdy work horse, the C-54, could be reduced in weight. By removing the equipment not essential to operation, its over-all payload was increased by about 2,500 pounds.

The tempo of the airlift demanded a safe and efficient system for assuring weight and balance control. To this end, a single loading diagram, specifying the total allow-able loads for the available spaces, was prepared and posted inside each plane. Loading crews found this very helpful.

The Payoff

From the first, airlift tonnage into Berlin climbed stead-ily until September 18, 1948, when US planes delivered 5,583 tons of coal to the beleaguered city. The daily minimum airlift requirement for West Berlin, initially estimated at 4,500 tons, was increased on October 20, 1948, to 5,620 tons. The change permitted an improved daily ration. The new figure was broken down as follows:

	Tons
Food	1,435
Coal	3,084
Commercial and industrial items	255
Newsprint	35
Liquid fuel	16
Medical supplies	2
Total for the German populace	4,827
For US, British, and French military	763
For three C-54 passenger flights daily	30
TOTAL	5,620

Coal constituted approximately two-thirds of all ton-nage airlifted, and without it Berlin could not have sur-vived. At first, coal appeared relatively easy to handle as it was compactly sacked. But the sharp and abrasive dust seeped into the inner fuselage, wings, and engines, creating a serious maintenance problem. Dampening the 110-pound cloth sacks, laying tarpaulins on the floor, and thorough sweeping helped, but not enough. Better results in dust control came through the use in February 1949 of smaller —fifty-five pound—multiwall paper sacks, which lasted for three to five trips, and by sealing the floors with a special compound.

Second on the tonnage list was food, including flour, potatoes, frozen meats, fish, vegetables, cereals, sugar, fats, milk, salt, coffee, cheese, and yeast. Frozen foods and meats moved so rapidly that no appreciable loss occurred.

USAF Lt. Gail S. Halvorsen (above, with admirers) started Operation Little Vittles by dropping candy in tiny chutes.

Left, below: Small recipient of Little Vittles candy packages wastes no time in opening her welcome prize.

Right, below: Meanwhile the big version of Operation Vittles goes on, as German workers unload sacks of flour.

Pilferage was a major problem, since food at this time was more valuable than money to the Germans.

Initially, petroleum, oil, and lubricants moved in the familiar fifty-five gallon metal drums. When this method proved uneconomical, a British fleet of chartered tankers took over the airlift of all liquid fuels. Fast and efficient, these tankers operated between British bases and the Berlin airfields of Gatow and Tegel, where underground pipes and storage tanks permitted unloading by gravity flow. The average daily capacity was 550 tons of liquid lift.

Also airlifted into Berlin were raw materials to keep the city's industry alive, heavy equipment for new air-field construction, urgently needed medical supplies, huge rolls of newsprint, clothing, mail, and parcel post. Out-bound cargo included manufactured items such as machine tools. In addition, there was considerable passenger traffic to and from Berlin, mostly via British aircraft.

The most publicized of the miscellaneous items flown was the candy dropped to the German children in the vicinity of Tempelhof. This was "Little Vittles," an un-official operation started in July 1948 by Lt. Gail S. Halvorsen and continued by others. Halvorsen, a MATS pilot, knew from past experience overseas that children everywhere liked candy and chewing gum. So he told the Berlin small fry to gather at the end of the runway on the next day and wait there for the first airdrop of the candy lift. From the start the operation drew bigger and bigger crowds of children. The only problem was to find enough handkerchiefs and other pieces of clothing to parachute gum and candy to the ground.

By January 1949 the combined USAF and RAF efforts had accomplished the chief goal of the airlift, that of pro-viding sufficient food for the people of West Berlin. During that month the food ration was raised from 1,600 to

1,880 calories a day. The coal requirements of the city proved harder to fill. Except in September, when the airlift concentrated on coal shipments, the deliveries in 1948 lagged. However, enough coal was lifted to provide the most essential services, although the rations of electric power and gas to the Germans had to be cut. Monthly deliveries of coal climbed steadily during 1949, reaching a cumulative total of 1,586,029 tons on September 30. During the same period, food shipments also increased but not as sharply as coal, attaining a cumulative total of 536,705 tons at the close of September 1949.

Operational efficiency improved steadily, culminating in the spectacular performance of mid-April 1949 known as the Easter Parade. On that day 1,398 aircraft reached Berlin with an all-time record tonnage of 12,940.9. The Russians no doubt were impressed, and the rumor spread that they might become reasonable. In any event, less than a month later, the Soviet authorities announced the end of the blockade of Berlin, effective May 12, 1949.

Mission Accomplished

The airlift continued until the reserve stocks in Berlin reached a satisfactory level and the international situation became clarified. On July 30, the date for the termination of the airlift was announced officially as October 31, 1949. Early in August the first C-54 aircraft left Rhein-Main for the United States. Later in the same month the two US Navy transport squadrons were withdrawn. And on September 1, General Tunner's Combined Airlift Task Force went out of business. On September 30, at 1845 hours, the last C-54 left Rhein-Main for Berlin, ending Operation Vittles one month ahead of schedule.

The Anglo-American airlift delivered a total of 2.325 million tons of food, fuel, and supplies to Berlin. The Americans delivered 1.783 million tons and the British, 0.542 million tons. The airlift demonstrated to the satisfaction of the leaders and flyers that, given the proper support, anything within reason could be moved by air anywhere in the world with minimum concern for geography or weather.

Despite fears for the worst, the operation proved surprisingly safe. The average monthly accident rate for USAF personnel in the airlift was less than fifty percent of that for the entire Air Force. Although traffic was heavy, only one mid-air collision took place between aircraft. Pilot error was a prominent factor in the great majority of aircraft accidents. The most usual type of mishap was the taxiing accident. Altogether, thirty-one Americans lost their lives in twelve crashes. Astonishingly low, these figures reflect the constant and uncompromising efforts made to keep the airlift as safe as humanly possible.

Operation Vittles achieved its purpose but at a huge cost. US Air Force and Navy participation in the project from June 26, 1948, to May 12, 1949, cost an estimated $181.3 million. That total included $57.5 million for operating costs and $64.7 million for support costs. Wrecked aircraft accounted for $7.5 million, and depreciation of aircraft for $11 million. In addition, the Army estimated that from July 1, 1948, through June 30, 1949, its direct costs in support of the airlift totaled $8.8 million.

The airlift furnished an excellent example of the three US armed services effectively working together for a common goal. It also provided a striking demonstration of international teamwork by British and American forces. American planes carried most of the tonnage in their C-54s. The British used several different types of planes and, in 1949, lifted all the petroleum products needed in West Berlin.

As a proving ground for air transport, Operation Vittles could not have been excelled. It underlined both the importance and the feasibility of sustained, round-the-clock mass movement of cargo by air. It showed that with GCA and other aids, an airlift could function satisfactorily almost without regard for the weather. It brought valuable experience in operational techniques, in air traffic control, and in the maintenance and reconditioning of aircraft.

According to General Tunner, experience in the airlift proved that the future of military air transport lay in big aircraft. Had they been available in the summer of 1948, sixty-eight C-74s could have done the work of the 178 C-54s required to lift the 4,500 tons needed each day in Berlin. Use of C-74s would have meant fewer flights, fewer men, less fuel, and less maintenance. The C-54s turned in a magnificent performance, but bigger planes could have done even better.

The allied airlift flew its 100,000th plane into blockaded Berlin on New Year's Eve, 1949, 189th day of lift.

A Navy crew of the joint airlift force celebrates the ending of the blockade by the Russians on May 12, 1949.

"MIG ALLEY" 200 MILES

Chapter 24

THE DEEDS

The Korean War

THE division of Korea after the Japanese surrender in 1945 caused continuing friction between the northern and southern parts of the country. The Soviet Union, by agreement with the Allies, occupied northern Korea down to the thirty-eighth parallel in order to accept the surrender of Japanese forces in the area. Even though they had agreed at Potsdam in July 1945 that Korea should become a free and independent nation, the Russians organized in the north a "People's Democratic Republic of Korea" under the control of Red China and the Soviet Union. The new regime refused to permit the United Nations to hold free elections there.

South Korea, occupied by American forces in 1945, held free elections in 1948 that resulted in the establishment of the Republic of Korea (ROK). The United States helped the new republic to build internal security forces and, by July 1949, had withdrawn all of its own forces except a small military advisory group. At the time, it informed the South Koreans that they must be prepared to defend themselves against attack but that, if aggression proved too great, they could look to the United Nations and the United States for help.

North of the thirty-eighth parallel, the Communists prepared to conquer South Korea. Communist China transferred battle-seasoned cadres and entire military units to the North Koreans, and the Soviet Union "sold" them offensive weapons. Soviet airmen trained and equipped a small but eager North Korean air force. Before dawn on the morning of June 25, 1950 (June 24 in the United States), the North Koreans attacked the Republic of Korea —an act of naked aggression in the tradition of Hitler and Stalin.

For months before June 25, Lt. Gen. George E. Stratemeyer, commander of the Far East Air Forces, and his staff had been anxiously watching the worsening situation in the peninsula. As part of the Far East Command (FEC)

under General MacArthur, FEAF was charged with defense of American bases in Japan, Okinawa, the Philippines, and the Marianas. In case of war in Korea, FEC had the mission of evacuating American nationals from the battle zone.

FEAF learned of the North Korean attack at 0945 on June 25, but it could do nothing until US Ambassador John J. Muccio in Seoul asked, at a few minutes before midnight on June 25, that American dependents be evacuated by surface vessel from the port of Inchon and that FEAF's Fifth Air Force provide fighter cover. Flights of F-82 all-weather fighters from the 8th Fighter-Bomber Wing's base at Itazuke, in southern Japan, stood guard in relays throughout June 26 while the evacuation vessel loaded and got under way.

On the night of June 26, with the North Koreans storming at the gates of Seoul, Muccio asked for emergency aerial evacuation of the remaining dependents. Maj. Gen. Earle E. Partridge, commander of the Fifth Air Force, directed his 374th Troop Carrier Wing to do the job. Since the North Korean air force had been active, General Partridge told the 8th Wing commander to permit no interference with the air evacuation mission. These precautions were wise, for shortly before noon on June 27, a flight of F-82s spotted five YAK fighters headed for Kimpo Airfield, where the transports were loading passengers. Within a few minutes, the F-82 pilots shot down three of the enemy fighters, with the first victory of the war going to Lt. William G. Hudson of the 68th Fighter Squadron (All-Weather). The unarmed transports completed their task without hindrance, carrying a total of 851 refugees to safety in Japan on June 27 and 28.

Back in America, US and UN officials watched the Korean situation with growing alarm. On the afternoon of June 25 (June 26 in the Far East), the United Nations Security Council adopted a resolution calling on the North Koreans to cease their aggression and withdraw to the thirty-eighth parallel. The North Koreans intensified their attack.

On the evening of June 26, President Truman sent new

Two F-86 pilots of the 4th Fighter-Interceptor Wing on first leg of a journey to meet Red MIGs up near the Yalu.

An American casualty early in the Korean War. A C-54 transport burns on a South Korean landing strip after being strafed by Communist fighters.

Gen. Vandenberg (right) hears report of Maj. Gen. Earle Partridge, 5th AF.

instructions to Tokyo. He directed MacArthur to employ American air and naval forces to support the ROK army. Except under emergency conditions, however, no air or naval attacks would be made north of the thirty-eighth parallel. On June 27, the UN Security Council approved a second resolution recommending that the "Members of the United Nations furnish such assistance to the Republic of Korea as may be necessary to repel armed attack and restore international peace and security in the area."

Late on the afternoon of June 27, General MacArthur ordered FEAF to strike the North Korean ground forces with everything it had. From their bases on Honshu, the 35th Fighter-Interceptor and 49th Fighter-Bomber Groups began to move, each with two squadrons of F-80s, down to Itazuke and Ashiya, on Kyushu, the southernmost of the Japanese islands. That night, a few B-26s of the 3d Bombardment Group went to Korea, but the weather was so bad that they accomplished little. On the next day—June 28—the weather was still bad at Itazuke and Ashiya, but F-80 jet fighters and B-26s attacked hostile targets along the roads north of the Han River. Late that afternoon, four 19th Bombardment Group B-29s, which had just moved from Guam to Okinawa, bombed targets on the two main roads leading into Seoul. On June 29 a larger formation of B-29s bombed Kimpo Airfield, which had fallen into enemy hands.

The order from Washington to stay below the thirty-eighth parallel hindered FEAF's air operations. Although Fifth Air Force fighter patrols destroyed some Communist aircraft, others got through to attack USAF transports unloading ammunition at Suwon Airfield. On the afternoon of June 29, General Stratemeyer explained the problem to General MacArthur, who verbally authorized air attacks against enemy airfields north of the thirty-eighth parallel. At dusk, the 3d Bombardment Group sent its two squadrons of B-26s against the enemy's main airfield at Pyongyang. This raid—the first against a target in North Korea—marked the beginning of a rapid demise of the North Korean air force.

On June 30 the President authorized air attacks against military targets in North Korea and the dispatch from Japan of combat and service troops to safeguard the South Korean ports of Pusan and Chinhae. But MacArthur notified Washington on the same day that ROK troops could not stop the attack and that American ground forces were needed in Korea. Within a few hours, President Truman gave MacArthur permission to use Army forces in Korea,

subject only to requirements for the safety of Japan. To wage the war, the United Nations set up a United Nations Command under General MacArthur, and British, Australian, Turkish, and other forces joined the Americans and the South Koreans in the fight against the aggressors. Air units from other UN countries served under FEAF.

Tactical Air Warfare and the Pusan Perimeter

FEAF was primarily a defensive force, and a thousand things had to be done to prepare it for the tactical air war in Korea. Yet, without a day of respite for any cause, FEAF planes carried the war to the enemy, night and day, in all kinds of weather.

The first objective was to secure air superiority. Small to begin with, North Korean air strength dwindled rapidly. By August 10, UN pilots estimated that they had destroyed 110 enemy planes, leaving the North Koreans with perhaps twenty-two aircraft.

Air superiority was gained without great difficulty. Stratemeyer believed that the lack of determined enemy air opposition in the initial stage of the Korean operations was the "paramount feature" of the war. Because of this, UN naval forces could operate close inshore, Air Force planes remained virtually unchallenged in the air, and UN ground troops under the US Eighth Army had nothing to fear from enemy air assault.

FEAF's second major task was to prevent the movement of enemy troops and supplies to the South Korean battleground, where the North Koreans already outnumbered the UN forces. World War II had shown that the best way to stop an enemy's attack was to destroy his supplies at their source. The next most efficient way was to knock out or interdict enemy manpower and supplies before they scattered out along the front lines.

General Vandenberg, the USAF Chief of Staff, knew the wisdom of these lessons. Early in July he sent two of SAC's B-29 groups—the 22d and 92d—to the Far East. On July 8, General Stratemeyer organized the FEAF Bomber Command (Provisional), under the command of Maj. Gen. Emmett O'Donnell, Jr., to control the medium bombers. Stratemeyer directed O'Donnell to use the B-29s against deep interdiction targets and war-production industries within North Korea. But, at the time, MacArthur did not like this mission because of the perilous situation of the ground forces. He directed Stratemeyer to use the B-29s in the immediate vicinity of the battlefield, either

KOREA, SHOWING THE PRINCIPAL CITIES, MAIN ROADS, RAILROADS, AND RIVERS

AND INDICATING THE MAXIMUM ADVANCE OF THE COMMUNIST FORCES

AND THE MAXIMUM ADVANCE OF THE UNITED NATIONS FORCES DURING THE KOREAN WAR

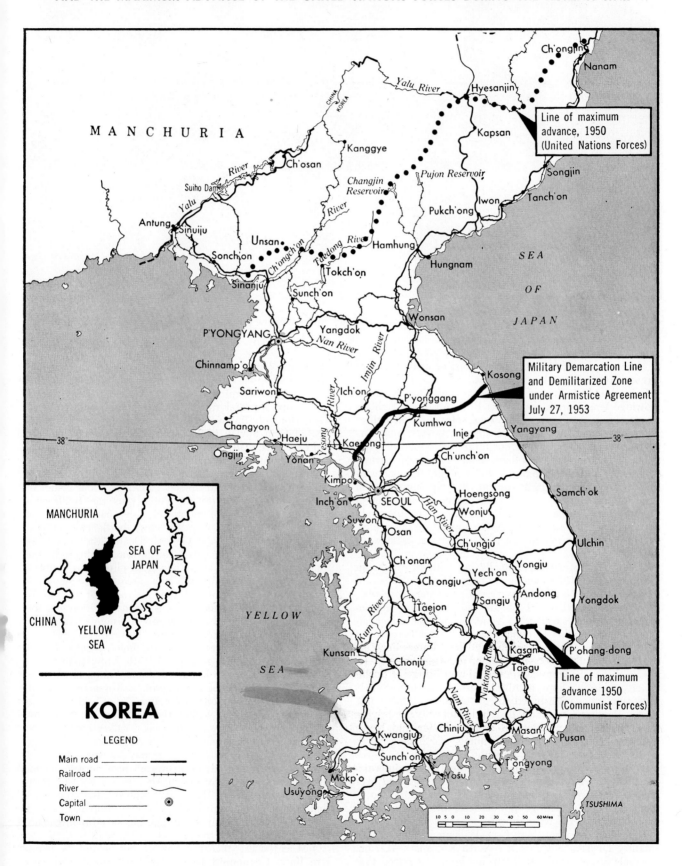

A B-26 crew is briefed before night mission takeoff. The medium bombers did valiant work in interdiction campaign.

in close support of Eighth Army troops or against bridge targets a few miles behind the front.

From the first days of the Korean hostilities, General Partridge employed a few of his Fifth Air Force fighters on armed reconnaissance missions. He ordered fighter pilots who could not get close support targets from forward air controllers to seek out targets of opportunity on the roads. During the early days, before the enemy learned to disperse and to move and fight at night, armed reconnaissance was particularly fruitful. But the emphasis on close support and the lack of a comprehensive interdiction program handicapped the effort. Fighter pilots commonly devoted their attention to the main communications routes, permitting the enemy to use back roads and trails with little interruption.

On July 26, Stratemeyer finally got authority to begin a comprehensive interdiction campaign based on a careful selection of railway and highway bridges. Once these were rendered impassable, all of the enemy's transportation routes would be severed. In general, the Han River divided FEAF Bomber Command and Fifth Air Force areas of interdiction. The carrier planes of Naval Forces Far East could attack all targets in both areas.

Except for the steel cantilever railway bridge at Seoul, which required a large number of attacks by both Superfortresses and carrier-based aircraft before it finally fell, FEAF Bomber Command had little difficulty destroying its assigned bridge targets. B-29s ranged far into North Korea, cutting bridges and bombing marshalling yards on the enemy's main railway routes. The Fifth Air Force used approximately one-third of its fighters for interdiction, and it sent its pilots on armed reconnaissance over secondary as well as primary roads. To stop hostile movements at night, Partridge put most of the 3d Bombardment Group's B-26s on night intruder work.

Early in July, when Maj. Gen. William F. Dean's 24th Infantry Division engaged the North Koreans at Taejon, Generals Stratemeyer and Partridge both recognized that

the lightly armed American divisions sent to Korea would need effective close support to make up for their lack of artillery. To control this support, Partridge sent a team to help set up and run the Joint Operations Center at Taejon on July 5. Two tactical air control parties had retreated from Suwon to Taejon on the night of June 30, and they were ready for action when General Dean's troops arrived in that city several days later.

During the critical days after July 12, when the 24th Division battled to hold the key communications center of Taejon, the entire Fifth Air Force plus the B-29s supported it. During the month of July, 61.5 percent of FEAF's total sorties were for close battlefield support. "Without question," said General Dean, "the Air Force definitely blunted the initial North Korean thrust to the southward. Without this continuing air effort, it is doubtful if the courageous combat soldiers, spread thinly along the line, could have withstood the onslaught of the vastly numerically superior enemy." But Dean's division was too far outnumbered by the five enemy divisions attacking it, and on July 20 the Red Koreans captured Taejon.

Three weeks of air action and the holding battle fought by the 24th Division gave the Eighth Army time to get other ground troops to Korea. Lt. Gen. Walton H. Walker, who took command of the Eighth in Korea on July 13, retreated to the Naktong River and Taegu and formed a perimeter defense to shelter the key port of Pusan. As he built up his defensive positions, Walker continued to get strong support from the Fifth Air Force, an average of 340 fighter-bomber sorties per day between August 1 and 10. On August 11, he expressed his appreciation for the "all-out" support that Fifth Air Force pilots had given to the Eighth Army: "They have destroyed enemy tanks that had penetrated our lines. . . . Their effort has been of tremendous value to our forces and has saved many, many lives of our infantry troops."

Just as the Eighth Army was settling behind its defensive lines, Communist troops appeared to be gathering across the Naktong for a thrust at Taegu. To relieve this threat, on August 16, General O'Donnell led ninety-eight B-29s on a carpet-bombing mission against a strip of terrain near Waegwan. The attack apparently had more psychological than direct military effect.

Although Walker received reinforcements, the length of his defensive line around Pusan during August compelled him to deploy practically all of his forces. "Sometimes," he said, "I had only a company in reserve." The Fifth Air Force flew an average of 239 close-support sorties each day during August. This period furnished a brilliant example of air and ground cooperation at its best. Generals Walker and Partridge had adjacent headquarters in Taegu, and at evening or early morning conferences they carefully coordinated their operations for each day. If the tide of battle changed, airpower moved immediately to fill a breach. When the enemy achieved penetrations that could not be stopped immediately, Walker called on Partridge to blunt the enemy thrust until ground reserves could be concentrated against it.

By the end of August the UN aerial interdiction campaign had reduced the North Korean army to desperate straits. The North Korean generals evidently decided they had to win quickly or lose everything. Shortly before midnight on August 31, the North Koreans began to cross the Naktong River. In the next few days the Communists threw elements of six divisions against the US 2d and 25th Infantry Divisions at the southwestern end of the perimeter. In this emergency, the Fifth Air Force went all out.

On September 3, Maj. Gen. William B. Kean, commanding the 25th Division, reported that "the close air support strikes rendered by the Fifth Air Force again saved this Division, as they have many times before." Maj. Gen. Laurence B. Keiser, commander of the 2d Infantry Division, stated that one day's combined air-ground action resulted in a confirmed destruction of approximately 1,500 enemy troops and their equipment. During the course of this battle, B-29s and Navy carrier planes switched their efforts to the battle area.

The battles of early September 1950 marked the end of the North Korean People's Army as a fighting force. Cut off from his source of supplies by air attacks, the enemy had sustained these last offensives only by sheer desperation. Attacks against the 2d Division in the Yongsan area on September 9, for example, came in five waves: the first three waves were armed, and the last two were sent onto the battlefield unarmed, with instructions to secure their weapons from the dead and dying. After the first week of September 1950, the North Koreans had few combat troops left in the rearward areas.

Strategic Bombing of North Korea

Throughout the war, Communist forces in Korea drew most of their support from sources in China and Russia, which were off limits to UN air attack. In the early months of the war, however, the North Korean army drew substantial support from industries within North Korea. On July 29, the Joint Chiefs of Staff offered to send two additional B-29 groups to the Far East, provided they were used to destroy industrial targets in North Korea. General MacArthur accepted the proposal, and SAC dispatched the 98th and 307th Bombardment Groups in August.

Nearly all the strategic targets marked for destruction lay within Pyongyang, Chongjin, Wonsan, Hungnam, and Rashin. To simplify the bombing problem and to achieve psychological gains, FEAF recommended using area bombing tactics and incendiary munitions. Washington, anxious to avoid civilian casualties, hesitated to authorize any air attacks that Communist propaganda might exploit. The indiscriminate use of incendiaries was not sanctioned. Other aspects of the plan were approved.

On August 8, Stratemeyer ordered O'Donnell to make the attacks with a maximum effort of two groups every third day. Use of high-explosive bombs instead of incendiaries meant additional sorties, but the B-29s bettered the peak records of World War II for both sorties flown and tons of bombs per plane delivered on targets. The SAC groups, moreover, proved so adept at radar bombing that weather did not hinder them as much as FEAF planners had expected.

Once strategic bombardment began in earnest, it moved rapidly. Everywhere except at Rashin—deleted from the target list because it was so near the Siberian border—the B-29s destroyed their assigned targets. By September 15, 1950, Stratemeyer could state that "practically all of the major military industrial targets strategically important to the enemy forces and to their war potential have now been neutralized." On September 26 the JCS informed MacArthur that further attacks against targets of relatively long-term military significance should be suspended. The strategic bomber offensive over North Korea had been completed in less than two months.

Invasion at Inchon

While UN ground forces were retreating southward in the summer of 1950, MacArthur had been planning an amphibious encirclement of the North Korean army. On August 30, he issued his operations order. The US X Corps, commanded by Maj. Gen. Edward M. Almond, would land at Inchon on the west coast on September 15 and, in conjunction with a D-plus-one attack by the Eighth Army, would destroy the North Korean army. Navy Task Force 77 was to gain air superiority and furnish deep support and interdiction strikes for the landing. Once ashore, 1st Marine Aircraft Wing would provide air support for X Corps. FEAF would support the Eighth Army, carry out an airborne operation with the 187th Airborne Regimental Combat Team (RCT), and provide cargo airlift.

Mindful of the air transport commitments, General Stratemeyer had secured additional units and set up the FEAF Combat Cargo Command (Provisional) on August 26, under Maj. Gen. William H. Tunner. Late in August, the 314th Troop Carrier Group brought its C-119s to Japan from the United States.

During the week of September 10-16 a typhoon called "Kezia" centered over southern Japan. Alerted in time, the 8th and 18th Fighter-Bomber Groups moved their F-51 Mustang fighters to barely serviceable airstrips in Korea. This arrangement permitted an increase in the sortie rate, and aircraft under FEAF control flew 3,257 sorties of all types during the week. Seeking to cut off possible enemy reinforcements, B-29s struck rail lines and marshalling yards from Seoul to Wonsan to Pyongyang. Reconnaissance planes plotted enemy movements, and when FEC discovered a few days before the landing that no one knew the height of a seawall that would have to be scaled at Inchon, two RF-80s of the 8th Tactical Reconnaissance Squadron went in at low level to photograph the invasion area.

At Inchon, X Corps went ashore at dawn on September 15. FEAF Combat Cargo Command provided important airlift for the corps, sending the first C-54 into Kimpo at 1426 hours on September 19. Full-scale airlift operations began on the next day. Late in September, when the need for an airborne operation had not developed, transports airlifted the 187th Airborne RCT to Kimpo.

With strong Fifth Air Force support, the Eighth Army broke out of the Pusan perimeter without difficulty and attacked northward. On September 17, fighters set on fire the "walled city" of Yongchon, a strong fortification in the

Return to Seoul. View taken from inside ruined operations building at Kimpo Airfield after Pusan breakout.

path of the ground advance. The next day, forty-two B-29s blanketed two areas west and northwest of Waegwan with bombs, achieving excellent results. By September 22, Eighth Army regiments were attacking in column, a tactic possible only because the Fifth Air Force spearheaded the advance and cleared the regimental flanks. Other Fifth Air Force fighters supported ROK troops as they moved up the east coast of Korea.

At this nadir of their hopes, many North Korean soldiers surrendered. Others sought safety in flight, and as they headed northward, Fifth Air Force fighter pilots slaughtered them. Pilots returned from missions with tales of North Korean soldiers dragging field pieces northward and refusing to disperse even when they were strafed. But by September 28, fighters were returning to their bases with bombs still in their shackles. Most enemy ground units had been badly broken, and sizable troop concentrations were fast disappearing.

Victory in South Korea came quickly, once the Red Korean army was dislodged from its positions around the Pusan perimeter. A few minutes before midnight on September 26, Eighth Army troops made contact with elements of X Corps near Osan. At the same time, on the east coast of Korea, ROK troops were approaching the thirty-eighth parallel. The government of the Republic of Korea returned to Seoul on September 29. The United Nations had achieved its stated objective of clearing the aggressors from South Korea.

Advance to the Yalu

In the early autumn of 1950, the United Nations cause in Korea appeared completely victorious. Flushed with military success, on October 7, 1950, the General Assembly of the United Nations approved a resolution that "all necessary steps be taken to ensure conditions of peace throughout the whole of Korea." MacArthur did not believe that the mopping-up task would be difficult and quickly launched an offensive into North Korea. His strategy required the Eighth Army to attack northward along the Kaesong-Sariwon-Pyongyang axis, while X Corps made another amphibious landing at the east-coast port city of

Wonsan. Navy Task Force 77 and the 1st Marine Aircraft Wing would support the X Corps operation. FEAF would support the advance of the Eighth Army.

In preparation for the campaign in North Korea, Partridge bent every effort to get the Fifth Air Force established at airfields in southern Korea. Headquarters Fifth Air Force in Korea, accompanied by the Joint Operations Center, opened in Seoul on October 15. At this time the 502d Tactical Control Group arrived from the United States, replacing the improvised tactical control system. Three F-51 fighter groups—the 8th, 18th, and 35th—moved from Japan to fields at Kimpo, Pusan, and Pohang. Two F-80 jet fighter groups—the 49th and 51st—settled at Taegu and Kimpo. These movements were made with difficulty, for the Eighth Army and X Corps enjoyed overriding claims on all available land and sea transportation. General Walker, moreover, frankly admitted that he wanted air transportation much more than he wanted air support.

Displaying scant regard for enemy opposition, the Eighth Army used only two American divisions and four ROK divisions in its initial thrust toward Pyongyang. Covered by Fifth Air Force fighters, which scouted ahead and guarded the flanks, this mobile force entered the city on October 19.

Capture of Pyongyang, seat of the North Korean government, was a significant victory, but MacArthur wanted to snare as many of the enemy as possible. On October 20, Combat Cargo Command dropped the 187th Airborne RCT astride the main transportation routes about thirty miles north of Pyongyang, near the villages of Sukchon and Sunchon. By 1500 hours seventy-one C-119s and forty C-47s had delivered 2,860 paratroopers and 301.2 tons of supply and equipment. The success of the jump was matched by the air attacks. Prior to the drop, 137 fighters and five light bombers had worked over the drop zones. This "softening-up" attack, together with the sudden airdrop, so startled North Korean troops that they abandoned strong defensive positions, leaving loaded guns with ammunition alongside.

Over on the east coast of Korea, the ROK I Corps, supported by Fifth Air Force and Marine fighters, captured Wonsan on October 10, ten days before the American X Corps was scheduled to land there. Because the Reds had mined the waters of the harbor, X Corps did not get ashore until October 26. Supported by the 1st Marine Aircraft Wing, it quickly fanned out along the coastal routes of eastern Korea against light resistance.

The rapidity of the United Nations advance into North Korea made necessary a new interdiction plan, issued on

Russian-built MIG, its landing gear damaged by US pilot's fire, burst into flames seconds after picture was taken.

October 6. This emphasized destruction of thirty-two key highway and rail bridges, most of them on the three routes northward from Sinanju. Eight days later, all except six had been destroyed. On October 25, because of the scarcity of medium bomber targets, MacArthur authorized the return of the 22d and 92d Bombardment Groups to the United States.

During the last week of October, the ground-oriented strategy of the United Nations Command seemed everywhere successful, but as November progressed a series of actions indicated the possible full intervention of the Chinese Communists in the war. On November 1, six hostile jet fighters, at once identified as MIG-15s, unsuccessfully jumped a flight of Mustangs just south of the Yalu. On November 8, the first all-jet air battle in history occurred at the Yalu when 51st Fighter-Interceptor Wing F-80s met MIG-15s. The old F-80Cs were no match for the swept-wing MIGs, but Lt. Russell J. Brown managed to shoot down a MIG-15, the first enemy jet aircraft destroyed in the Korean War. On the ground, a Communist force penetrated and encircled elements of the US 8th Cavalry Regiment near Unsan on November 2.

To meet the new threat, Partridge opened an aircraft warning radar closer to the front lines, instituted air patrols over Sinuiju, and moved the three Mustang groups up into North Korea. Since crossing the thirty-eighth parallel, General Walker had been supplied chiefly by air. Now he had to pause, regroup his forces, and build up his supplies. On November 3, he ordered the bulk of the Eighth Army to withdraw to the south bank of the Chongchon River. For the moment, at least, the United Nations campaign had stalled.

In hopes of discouraging Chinese intervention, MacArthur directed Stratemeyer on November 5 to make a maximum air effort for two weeks. From the Yalu southward to the battle line, FEAF was "to destroy every means of communication and every installation, factory, city and village." FEAF was also directed to destroy the first over-water span of the international bridges across the Yalu between North Korea and Red China.

On November 8, a massive B-29 incendiary attack against Sinuiju virtually eliminated the first of ten communications and supply centers designated for attack. As of November 28, photo reconnaissance showed that the other cities on the list were also substantially destroyed. Other B-29 crews directed their efforts against the international bridges. Enemy flak forced the bombers up to 20,000 feet where MIGs threatened them. Orders forbidding violations of Manchurian territory limited the axes of attack, crosswinds complicated precision bombing, and all of the bridges were major steel structures. On November 12 carrier-based crews joined the fray, only to find the bridges to be every bit as tough as the medium bomber crews had reported. By the end of November, the combined effort had cut at least four of the international bridges and had damaged most of the others. Early in December the Yalu froze over, and the bridge attacks were suspended.

MacArthur believed on November 18 that the ten days of all-out air effort had largely isolated the battle area from added enemy reinforcements. Both Walker and Partridge were completing preparations for the renewed offensive in northwestern Korea. All seemed to be nearing readiness, and MacArthur fixed November 24 as the day for the main Eighth Army attack.

Retreat from North Korea

The Eighth Army attacked northward as scheduled, and for two days it advanced toward the Manchurian border. But on November 26, a Chinese counterattack halted the advance. On the X Corps front, an enemy force cut the supply routes behind two regiments of Marines northwest of the Changjin Reservoir. Confronted with an entirely new war, all United Nations ground troops sought safety in retreat.

During bleak December, UN airpower once again had to save the ground troops from destruction. FEAF had three functions: to protect UN forces from hostile air attacks, to destroy the Chinese on the ground and so permit Walker and Almond to disengage their forces and rally them to the southward, and to assist the withdrawals with air transportation. In no phase of the Korean fighting would airpower be of greater assistance to the ground forces. Yet it would be incorrect to regard all air activities against the enemy ground forces merely as support operations. Actually, with the Eighth Army and X Corps in full retreat and generally out of contact with the enemy, only UN air forces were carrying the fight to the advancing Communists.

From the moment that the Chinese unveiled their MIG-15 fighters, the success of UN ground and air operations depended on the maintenance of air superiority. Fortunately, the enemy pilots were not aggressive during the weeks in which the Fifth Air Force possessed no aircraft that could battle on equal terms with the MIG-15. By the middle of December the 4th Fighter-Interceptor Wing (F-86 Sabres) and the 27th Fighter-Escort Wing (F-84 Thunderjets) had arrived in Korea from the United States. The F-86A Sabres of the 4th Wing drew the task of opposing the MIGs over northwestern Korea, getting their first kills on December 17, when they shot down four MIGs. Under the conditions of combat in northwestern Korea, the MIG-15 was superior in performance to the F-86; but the Sabre pilots were more skilled, and during December they destroyed eight MIG-15s. For the moment, at least, the appearance of USAF Sabres had abated the threat of the Chinese Communist air force.

As Eighth Army units broke away from the initial Red assaults, air support often made the difference between escape and destruction. Fifth Air Force fighter-bombers gave especially valiant close support to the US 2d Infantry Division on December 2, as it retreated from Kunu-ri toward Sunchon. Unknown to the American troops, the Chinese had emplaced machine guns along a five-mile stretch of the escape route. Once the 2d Division's motor columns encountered this ambuscade, they had no choice but to try to run the gantlet of fire. The division's only salvation was close air support, and throughout the day Fifth Air Force fighter-bombers bored into the hostile gun emplacements with rockets, napalm, and bullets. The commander of the 2d Division later tendered high praise for the effective air support, without which, he said, the division might never have weathered the Chinese fire.

After the first week of December the Eighth Army was generally out of contact with the enemy, and it began to mass in defensive positions north of Seoul, along the Imjin River. Now the air task was to delay and destroy the advancing Chinese armies. FEAF Bomber Command began a planned interdiction program designed to limit troop movements and resupply by railroad. Fifth Air Force fighter-bombers reaped heavy casualties among the masses of Chinese jamming the roads in bold daylight movements. When the enemy crossed the Chongchon River, 49th Group F-80 pilots made the water run red with enemy blood. By mid-December, Stratemeyer estimated that 33,000 enemy troops, the equivalent of four full-strength Chinese divisions, had been killed or wounded in UN air attacks.

After two weeks of punishing air action, the Chinese grew more cautious. They practiced camouflage and marched their troops at night. Although FEAF pilots got poorer results, they estimated that they had killed another 6,700 Communist soldiers during the second half of December.

Meanwhile, at the end of November, the US X Corps had received orders to evacuate northeast Korea. It found itself in a serious plight. The embattled Marines, fighting both frigid weather and the Chinese at the Changjin Reservoir, needed air supply as much as they needed aerial firepower. General Tunner moved promptly. In the thirteen days that the Marines were cut off, Combat Cargo Command dropped 1,580 tons of supplies and equipment, including an eight-span treadway bridge, each span of which weighed an even two tons when packaged. While they were besieged, the Marines scratched out rocky airstrips at Hagaru-ri and Koto-ri, where transports landed replacements and supplies and brought out 4,689 casualties on return flights.

When the Marines were back within the Hamhung-Hungnam defense perimeter on December 11, X Corps began wholesale evacuation. General Almond asked for a maximum air evacuation from Yonpo Airfield. Fortunately, Combat Cargo Command had been recently reinforced by two troop carrier groups. With all transport groups working, the air evacuation from Yonpo got under way on December 14. Before infiltrating Chinese ended it at nightfall on December 17, this maximum effort lifted 228 patients, 3,891 passengers, and 20,088 tons of cargo from Yonpo. Naval transports took off the bulk of X Corps, completing the evacuation on the afternoon of December 24.

The Fifth Air Force also retreated southward during December 1950. The Mustang groups went to airfields in southern Korea. The units at Kimpo remained there as long as possible and then evacuated to southern Japan. Fifth Air Force headquarters at Seoul moved back to Taegu on December 20. Meanwhile, FEAF underwent a general reorganization—effective December 1, 1950—which recognized that the war was going to continue indefinitely. The Fifth transferred its responsibilities for the air defense of Japan to the new 314th Air Division and concentrated its attention on Korea. On January 25, 1951, the FEAF Combat Cargo Command (Provisional) was replaced by the 315th Air Division (Combat Cargo).

Defeat of the Chinese Communists

During December 1950 the US government recognized that any further attempt to bring about Korean unification by military force would incur the grave risk of a world war. To avoid this catastrophe, the United States sponsored and the UN General Assembly adopted on December 15 a resolution that immediate steps be taken to end the fighting in Korea and settle the existing issues by peaceful means.

The strategy of the United Nations Command was now to inflict the maximum damage on the enemy in order to compel Communist China and North Korea to seek a military armistice. The UN air commanders understood their duties under the new strategy. They had to maintain air superiority. They had to deprive the enemy of logistical support, mobility, and combat effectiveness by relentless attacks behind his lines. They had to provide the UN ground forces with strong air support, especially against Chinese ground attacks. Lt. Gen. Matthew B. Ridgway, who took command of the Eighth Army on December 26 following General Walker's accidental death, had a firm grasp of the ground actions required by the new strategy. UN ground forces would maneuver before Chinese ground offensives, trading space as necessary for enemy casualties. When a Red offensive waned, UN ground forces would counterattack and inflict more casualties.

Having lost the advanced airfields at Kimpo and Suwon, FEAF had trouble maintaining air superiority over northwestern Korea during January and February 1951. Since the Sabres had withdrawn to Japan, the MIG-15s enjoyed a wider freedom of action in the area between the Yalu and

FEAF Bomber Command airmen work in a bitter, snow-laden wind at the delicate task of arming bombs for mission.

Chongchon rivers, called "MIG Alley." Long-range F-84E aircraft of the 27th Fighter-Escort Wing escorted B-29 missions into this zone. On January 23, in the largest all-jet battle to date, thirty-three F-84s engaged about twenty-five MIGs near the Yalu and destroyed at least three of the hostile planes without loss. Rather than divert fighters to escort duties, however, FEAF generally kept the B-29s out of MIG Alley during February. Late that month, the Fifth Air Force returned two urgently needed squadrons of Sabres to Korea.

The Fifth did not get the F-86s back into action any too soon, for in March the Chinese Communist air force launched its first serious offensive effort. A captured report of a Red air staff group described the enemy plans in some detail. The Chinese clearly recognized that their ground campaigns could not succeed without air support. At bases in Manchuria they had enough aircraft to wage offensive attacks, but like the UN air commanders the Red airmen operated under political restrictions. Because of a fear of reprisals, the Red airmen were not permitted to attack UN positions from air bases above the Yalu. They were permitted, however, to stage offensive strikes from airfields in North Korea. But FEAF Bomber Command had already neutralized all of the airfields in North Korea. The Chinese air staff group went into North Korea early in 1951 to supervise airfield repair, and in March, Fifth Air Force reconnaissance pilots reported that the enemy was rehabilitating airfields all over North Korea.

According to standing policy, Brig. Gen. James E. Briggs, O'Donnell's successor as commander of FEAF Bomber Command, took no action until the Communist airfields neared serviceability. On April 13 the B-29s swung into action. Scheduling an average of twelve planes daily, Bomber Command cratered the runways at nine airfields. Larger bomber forces hit Pyongyang's two airfields hard on April 16 and 19. And on May 9, Partridge sent 312 Fifth Air Force, Marine, and Navy planes against Sinuiju Airfield to knock out some forty planes there. As a result, the enemy could make only a few night heckling attacks with small biplanes against the United Nations forces during the spring of 1951. In a bitter report, the Red air staff group concluded, "If we had had a strong

Fifth Air Force F-84 Thunderjets gave close air support to UN ground troops, pounded interdiction targets too.

air support, we could have driven the enemy into the sea."

Behind the enemy battle lines in Korea, the UN air forces waged a continual war of interdiction and destruction. The B-29s attacked railway bridges, marshalling yards, and supply centers, while fighter-bombers and night intruders turned in a mounting total of destruction. Fifth Air Force pilots claimed destruction of 599 enemy vehicles in January, 1,366 in February, and 2,261 in March. According to air intelligence estimates, the damage inflicted upon Communist supply lines by airpower was preventing as much as eighty percent of the enemy's supplies from reaching his front-line troops.

Far away to the north, the ice-covered Yalu River began to thaw late in March. In spite of bad weather, the B-29s made three highly effective attacks against the international bridges on March 30, April 7, and April 12. These attacks severed all of the bridges in northwestern Korea, except for the much-damaged steel railway bridge at Sinuiju. But the raids were costly, for MIG fighters intercepted each mission and destroyed four of the bombers. In the furious action on April 12, Superfortress gunners were credited with the destruction of several MIGs. But for the Sabre and Thunderjet escort, B-29 losses would have been much heavier. Two facts became obvious: the old Superfortresses were extremely vulnerable to jet interceptors, and the Thunderjets were badly outclassed by the superior speed of the MIG-15s.

Although the air attacks in the rear of the Chinese armies proved highly effective, the enemy front-line forces were able to accumulate enough supplies to undertake four ground offensives during the first half of 1951. In deference to United Nations airpower they timed each offensive to concide with periods of bad weather. The long-awaited enemy attack against the Imjin River line came on the last night of 1950. Eighth Army troops fell back by January 6, 1951, to prearranged defensive positions on a line running across the peninsula between Pyongtaek and Samchok. Although fighting continued for some days about the key junction of Wonju, the weaker-

F-86 Sabrejets, off on one more sweep over MIG Alley.

American fighter-bombers wreaked havoc on Communist rail lines and rolling stock with rockets and napalm fire bombs.

than-anticipated Red offensive ran out of steam after five days.

UN pilots defied terrible flying weather to exact a heavy toll from the Red "human wave" assaults. Chinese prisoners confirmed that UN airpower had not only cut off their supplies but had inflicted fully fifty percent of their casualties. Aerial resupply and air evacuation of casualties increased the mobility of Eighth Army units. With its experience in North Korea in mind, X Corps scraped out strips at Wonju, Chungju, and Andong, and Combat Cargo Command C-46s and C-47s landed supplies there.

Recognizing that the Chinese hordes could be defeated, General Ridgway announced on January 20, 1951, a series of limited offensives. Behind air strikes, the Eighth Army forged northward to the Han River, recaptured Suwon Airfield on January 25, and Kimpo Airfield and the port of Inchon on February 10.

Although obviously suffering from shortages of supplies, the Communists unleashed a violent attack against X Corps on the night of February 11. Elements of the US 2d Division, surrounded for three days in the middle of February, were supplied by air. With strong support from the Fifth Air Force, they held their position. Maj. Gen. Clark L. Ruffner, commander of the 2d Division, wrote that, after one napalm attack around the Chipyong perimeter, he had observed more enemy dead than he had ever seen before. By February 24, X Corps was driving the enemy northward.

Eighth Army troops captured the central-front communications center of Hongchon on March 12, and the Communists, fearing a flanking attack against Seoul, hurriedly evacuated the South Korean capital. Hoping to exploit the enemy retreat, Generals Partridge and Ridgway arranged to drop the 187th RCT on the village of Munsan-ni, lying athwart the Seoul-Kaesong road. The airborne operation on March 23 was a technical success, but few enemy troops were captured or killed. The Reds were retreating faster than had been anticipated.

Early in April, UN ground forces continued to advance toward the thirty-eighth parallel, but they were expecting the Communists to launch a spring offensive. The Red offensive struck the US I and IX Corps on the night of April 22. The ROK 6th Division broke south of Kumhwa, leaving a gapping hole in the IX Corps line. Partridge threw fighter-bombers by day and radar-directed bombers by night into the breach, enabling IX Corps to close the gap and to counterattack by April 26. On the western front, I Corps was forced back to a line about three miles north of Seoul, where it held.

Assisted by a blanket of fog and rain, the Reds launched the "second impulse" of their spring offensive against X Corps in the center of the Korean peninsula on the night of May 15. Between May 10 and June 5, the Fifth Air Force flew 2,380 fighter sorties in close support of X Corps. The initial enemy thrust drove to within twenty miles of the key communications hub of Wonju, but the toll taken by artillery fire and airpower was too much. During the offensive, X Corps estimated that air attacks killed 16,700 of the enemy on its front.

During the Communist spring offensives, B-29s and B-26s using night radar made highly destructive bombing attacks. The US IX corps reported that a radar-directed strike against a large troop concentration in front of its lines "completely stopped preparation for attack and friendly units received no further attack that night at all." On the nights of May 20 and 21, in the X Corps area, B-29s under ground radar guidance destroyed an enemy regiment, 4,000 dead being verified by actual count. General Almond called radar-directed bombing "an epic in our warfare."

The spring campaign brought demands for increased air transportation. Lt. Gen. James A. Van Fleet, who took command of Eighth Army on April 11, 1951, later explained that the army's ammunition supply, never large enough, fell below the danger point and had to be fed by an airlift from Japan. During several days of furious fighting, trucks stacked up fifty to 100 at a time at a small airfield only six miles behind the X Corps command post, waiting to take ammunition from the transports to the batteries at the front. By airlift and airdrop, the 315th Air Division delivered to Korea 15,900 tons of cargo in April, 21,300 tons in May, and 22,472 tons in June.

On May 19 the Eighth Army attacked on all fronts. As the Chinese fled, Fifth Air Force pilots redoubled their efforts and harried the enemy unmercifully. On June 10, Eighth Army troops drove into the base of the enemy's "Iron Triangle," a bastion area just north of the thirty-eighth parallel. The Reds stood on the brink of a major military disaster. They had had enough of the war. On June 23, 1951, Jacob A. Malik, the Soviet delegate to the United Nations Security Council, proposed immediate cease-fire discussions. The offer was accepted.

What had gone wrong with the Chinese plan to drive the UN troops into the sea? In the truce discussions later, Lt. Gen. Nam Il, the chief North Korean delegate, supplied the answer: "Without the support of the indiscriminate bombing and bombardment of your air and naval forces, your ground forces would have long ago been driven out of the Korean peninsula by our powerful and battle skilled ground forces."

Railway Interdiction

As delegates of the United Nations Command, the North Korean People's Army, and the Chinese Communist Forces sat down to negotiate armistice terms at Kaesong on July 10, 1951, the course of Korean hostilities began to change. Shortly after he became Commander in Chief of the United Nations Command on April 10, 1951, General Ridgway had announced: "Our principal objective is to keep the United States out of war and in Korea to restore international peace and security and to repel aggressions. The job of unifying all Korea, while desirable, is not an element of this principal mission."

A C-119 of the 314th Troop Carrier Group, loaded with supplies for isolated unit on ground, circles prior to drop.

What would be the UN air mission during the truce talks? On June 10, 1951, the same day that he became commander of FEAF, Lt. Gen. Otto P. Weyland had stated that FEAF now had "its first real opportunity to prove the efficacy of airpower in more than a supporting role." Airpower could range far and wide over hostile Korea and, by selective attack, motivate the enemy to accept the United Nations terms. But, for more than a year, FEAF would not be allowed to do this. Taking into consideration the climate of world opinion, the JCS stated the rule: "If armistice discussions fail, it is of the greatest importance that clear responsibility for failure rest upon the Communists."

During the first two weeks of July the Eighth Army carefully watched the enemy. What it saw was alarming. The Chinese, no longer expending supplies in active combat, were stockpiling materiel at an estimated 800 tons per day. If such activity went unchecked, the Eighth Army feared that the enemy would "reach a degree of preparedness previously unparalleled in the Korean War." On July 6, Ridgway informed the Joint Chiefs that numerous sources "indicate a planned large-scale offensive effort to be launched in the event . . . peace overtures fail."

At Seoul, Army and USAF intelligence officers concluded that the North Korean railways were the enemy's best means of transportation. The Fifth Air Force decided that the North Korean rail lines could best be interdicted by a heavy effort against railway tracks and enough effort against key railway bridges to immobilize the enemy's heavy rail repair equipment. Since the eight USAF wings in Korea did not have enough strength to do the job alone, Lt. Gen. Frank F. Everest, who had assumed command of the Fifth on June 1, 1951, asked for the help of the Naval Forces Far East and FEAF Bomber Command. The Navy was asked to interdict rail tracks in east central Korea; Bomber Command was requested to keep the railway bridges at Pyongyang, Sonchon, Sunchon, and Sinanju out of operation.

The Fifth Air Force realized that this interdiction could not be 100 percent successful. The enemy could reduce his effort along the battle line and thus conserve his supplies. He could also keep enough trucks in operation to meet his minimum needs. The stated objective of the railway interdiction campaign was thus a limited one: "To interfere with and disrupt the enemy's line of communication to such an extent that he will be unable to contain a determined offensive by friendly forces or be unable to mount a sustained offensive himself."

Formally initiated on August 18, 1951, the comprehensive railway interdiction campaign had good results for nearly three months. Floods washed out temporary bridges at Sinanju and Anju, and the B-29s kept the other assigned bridges out of operation for much of the time. Twice daily, fighter-bombers attacked selected stretches of railway track. In September and October, they destroyed track faster than the enemy could rebuild and repair. By the middle of November it looked as though the campaign could be completed by destroying one short key length of railway connecting the towns of Kunu-ri and Sunchon.

Caught by surprise, the Communists were compelled to jam the roads at night with truck convoys. In August an observer in a C-47 flare plane counted 150 lighted vehicles in a fifteen-minute period. Both the 3d and 452d Bombardment Wings were flying night intruder missions at this time, and their soaring claims of vehicles destroyed later proved to be somewhat exaggerated.

Provoked to action by the success of the railway bombing, the enemy made a determined bid to establish air superiority over northwestern Korea. On September 1, FEAF estimated that the Chinese had 1,255 aircraft. This figure included 525 MIG-15 fighters, compared with 105

US F-86 Sabres. Beginning in September, the Reds attempted to overwhelm UN air forces. Using superior numbers of jet fighters, the enemy tried "pincers and envelopment" tactics. "Trains" of MIGs evaded or broke through the Sabre screens and converged over Pyongyang, where they dropped down to 15,000 feet and then swept back northward looking for fighter-bombers. MIG attacks destroyed twelve UN fighter-bombers in the last four months of 1951 and forced other fighter-bomber pilots to jettison their bombs and seek safety in flight. To meet the threat, the Fifth equipped a second wing—the 51st Fighter-Interceptor—with F-86s. The enlarged Sabre force destroyed thirty-one MIGs during January 1952, and in the latter part of the month the Reds broke up their "trains" into smaller formations, which usually remained north of the Chongchon River.

In October, Fifth Air Force reconnaissance crews discovered that the Reds were building three new jet airfields just north of the Chongchon River and within a twenty-mile radius of each other. If the Reds could establish these bases at the southern end of MIG Alley, they could effectively challenge UN fighter-bombers in the area where railway interdiction attacks were centered. On October 18, 22, and 23, Superforts attacked the new airfields and drew the full force of MIG interception. On these three days, the MIG-15s overwhelmed escorting F-84s and destroyed four Superforts.

Rumors that the B-29s were finished did not reckon with the versatility of the SAC crews who flew them. Using Shoran bombing techniques, the medium bombers began to operate entirely at night, and in November they blasted the three airfields without loss. The Chinese abandoned sustained efforts to build or rehabilitate airfields in North Korea.

The Chinese failed in their bid for air superiority, but their less spectacular measures against the railway interdiction campaign proved effective. Along the railway lines they concentrated automatic weapons that not only took a toll of fighter-bombers but markedly reduced the bombing accuracy. The Reds also mobilized a labor force of half a million civilians that repaired rail cuts quickly and built temporary bypass bridges at the key river crossings. By December 23 the Fifth Air Force recognized that the enemy had "broken our railroad blockade of Pyongyang and . . . won . . . the use of all key rail arteries."

In January 1952, Weyland and Everest requested permission to attack more decisive targets in Korea, but Ridgway held the UN forces to the job of railway interdiction. The interdiction operations, he said, were slowing and seriously affecting the enemy's supply operations.

During early 1952, the railway interdiction attacks proved even less effective because the enemy could repair rail cuts almost as fast as the fighter-bombers could make them. This brought a change in Fifth Air Force tactics. The fighter-bomber wings would concentrate against short sections of rail track and completely devastate them. Since the Reds made their rail repairs at night, the B-26s would harass such efforts with periodic attacks during the hours of darkness. The B-29s would concentrate their strikes against the multiple rail bridges at Sinanju and Sunchon.

Early in March, bad weather hampered attacks on the rail lines. Finally, on March 25 and 26, fighter-bombers made 468 sorties against a stretch of track between Chongju and Sinanju, and at night eight B-26s attacked. But by March 30, only five days after the initial attack, the Reds had almost completely rebuilt the roadbed, and they replaced the tracks on the following day. Similar attacks during April showed that the new tactics required too much fighter-bomber effort. The entire UN air strength could possibly have maintained six major cuts on the enemy's rail lines, but several times six cuts would have been required for proper railway interdiction. By the end of April, morever, Fifth Air Force planners could no longer outguess the enemy and select undefended sections of railway for attack. The key rail lines were so well defended that there were no flak-free targets.

In May 1952 the ten months of comprehensive railway interdiction were drawing to a close. What had been accomplished? From the beginning, both Generals Vandenberg and Weyland had regarded the railway attacks as a unique form of limited interdiction—limited because of the short distance to the Manchurian sanctuary and the fact that the enemy did not have to use his supplies in active ground combat. Unfortunately, however, someone at Fifth Air Force headquarters (even General Weyland was never sure who did it) had tagged the railway interdiction operations with the name "Strangle." This misnomer gave those who did not understand the real objective of the railway interdiction campaign a vehicle for proclaiming its failure.

Viewed in terms of its stated purpose, the rail interdiction campaign had not failed. The operations had delayed the enemy's efforts to stockpile supplies, they had destroyed some Communist materiel, and in the course of ten months the UN air forces had retained a whip hand over North Korea. The battered rail system could never again provide the sustained logistical support for a major ground campaign. But the campaign did not hurt the Communists badly enough to make them agree to end hostilities.

The Air Pressure Campaign

First at Kaesong and then at Panmunjom, UN truce negotiators sought patiently but firmly to come to armistice agreements with the Communists. But in April 1952 the truce negotiations were headed for a stalemate. There was only one outstanding problem—the disposition of prisoners of war. The United Nations insisted that all prisoners be permitted to accept or reject repatriation. The Communists demanded that all prisoners be repatriated, and insisted that it made no difference whether or not they desired to return home.

General Weyland had long argued that United Nations airpower, through cumulative destruction of appropriate targets in North Korea, could force the Communists to accept UN truce terms. Weyland could not test his concepts before May 1952, when the Communists rebuffed final compromise offers. Gen. Mark W. Clark, who took over the United Nations Command on May 12, firmly believed that "only through forceful action could the Communists be made to agree to an armistice the United States considered honorable."

Early in June, Weyland explained to Clark the significance of North Korea's hydroelectric power-generating complex. Suiho, on the Yalu River about thirty miles northeast of Antung, was one of the world's largest power-generating plants when it was built. All the North Korean power plants produced electricity for military purposes, and Suiho was transmitting much of its production into Manchuria. Higher levels of command had ruled earlier that the military importance of these facilities was outweighed by their political significance. The "choicest plum" —Suiho—lay on the Yalu and could not be attacked without approval of the Joint Chiefs. After studying FEAF's plans, Clark directed on June 17 that FEAF and the Naval Forces Far East attack all the generating plants except Suiho. Shortly after, the Joint Chiefs informed Clark that the President had approved attacks on Suiho.

Late on the afternoon of June 23, UN aircraft struck Suiho. Strangely enough, there was no enemy air opposi-

T-6 trainers were put to work as "mosquito" spotter planes to find targets and direct fire for jet fighter-bombers.

tion; most of the 250 MIGs that had been counted on the airfields at Antung just before the strike fled into Manchuria. On that day and the two following days, UN aircraft put out of operation more than ninety percent of North Korea's electric power potential.

Beyond doubt the enemy was hurt. Intelligence reports confirmed FEAF predictions that the loss of electric power would curtail military production in many small North Korean factories, themselves so dispersed as to be impracticable air targets. Information from Manchuria indicated that the neutralization of Suiho meant the loss of twenty-three percent of northeast China's power requirements for 1952. As a result of power shortages, thirty out of fifty-one key industries in Port Arthur, Dairen, and other cities failed to meet their annual production quotas.

On July 10, FEAF issued a directive outlining the goals of the new air strategy of continuous pressure through selective destruction. First priority was to control the air. Second priority was to do the maximum damage to selected targets, making the Korean conflict as costly as possible for the enemy. Third was to reduce the immediate threat by the Chinese ground armies. The small size of FEAF's striking force demanded great care in the choice of targets. There appeared to be few lucrative targets left in North Korea, but careful analysis turned up a good many.

The air pressure strategy eventually had two major facets. FEAF made sustained air attacks against targets whose destruction would make the war as costly as possible to the enemy in terms of equipment, supplies, facilities, and personnel. In addition, psychological pressure was brought to bear by concentrations of force at decisive times and places. The air pressure operations, however, were seriously limited by General Clark's ruling that every effort would be made "to attack military targets only, and to avoid needless civilian casualties."

The F-86 pilots continued to hold the enemy air force at bay. This was a grave responsibility, for by June 1952, China's twenty-two air divisions had an estimated strength of 1,830 aircraft, including 1,000 jet fighters. Destroying Communist aircraft also had a high priority, because the loss of modern combat aircraft would hurt the Chinese.

Continuous pressure through selective destruction was FEAF's strategy. Rail bridges and tunnels were favorite targets.

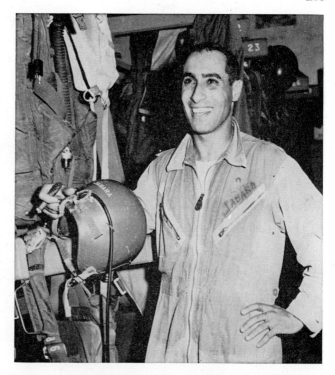

Maj. James Jabara became the Air Force's first jet ace on May 20, 1951. His final score over MIG Alley—15 planes.

Lt. Gen. Glenn O. Barcus, who took command of the Fifth Air Force on May 30, 1952, accordingly sought to increase the effectiveness of his interceptor force and to give his Sabre pilots a maximum of combat action.

During the autumn of 1952 the Fifth did not need to think up strategems to make the Red pilots fight. Galled by UN air attacks near the Yalu, the Red airmen surged into action in August and fought like angry hornets during September. The Sabre interceptor pilots got a chance to fight, and some of them now possessed improved F-86Fs which met the MIGs on more even terms. At a cost of six planes, the Sabres destroyed sixty-three MIGs in September. The Reds paused to lick their wounds. During the winter of 1952-53, most Red pilots did not seem eager to fight, and so long as they stayed up at high altitudes the Sabre pilots could do little.

After January 1953, when the 8th and 18th Fighter-Bomber Wings began to get F-86F fighter-bombers, the Fifth could look forward to using the Sabre fighter-bombers as interceptors if necessary. To force the Reds to fight, psychological warfare officers commenced an intensified campaign on a single theme: "Where is the Communist Air Force?" Whether because of this taunt or some other unknown reason, the MIG pilots suddenly became more aggressive in mid-May 1953. Numerous aircraft with Red Chinese insignia appeared, and the enemy pilots, some of whom may have been other than Chinese, displayed "more enthusiasm than know-how." In May 1953 the Sabres destroyed fifty-six MIGs; their only loss was one F-86, and the pilot was rescued.

In June the Sabre pilots reached their peak in victories —seventy-five MIGs destroyed, and no Sabres lost. The new F-86Fs could operate at higher altitudes, and the MIGs, seeking to dodge under low-flying clouds and engage the fighter-bombers, came down MIG Alley at lower heights than before. For the first time, Sabre pilots initiated most of the engagements, and the MIGs suffered accordingly. Smarting from this major defeat, the enemy risked few planes in July 1953, the last month of the war, and the Sabres got only thirty-two kills.

Covered by the F-86s, other UN pilots attacked targets in North Korea during 1952-53. Weyland obtained per-

Capt. Joseph McConnell, Jr., topped the jet aces with 16 victories, was later killed in crash of test plane in US.

mission to launch massive fighter-bomber attacks against military targets in Pyongyang. On July 11, 1952, the Fifth Air Force and the Navy carriers sent 822 sorties against Pyongyang. They sent 1,080 sorties to attack other military targets in the city on August 29. Before each of these massive attacks, the Fifth dropped leaflets urging civilians to stay away from military installations of any kind.

Japan-based B-29s of the 98th Bomb Wing line up on the runway for another shot at Communist targets in North Korea.

FEAF target planners discovered that North Korean industries were still producing some war materiel. Some plants had been overlooked; others had recuperated from earlier air attacks. Shoran-bombing B-29s went to the banks of the Yalu to bomb such targets as the Oriental Light Metals Company, the Nakwon Munitions Plant, and the Namsan-ni Chemical Plant. Other UN aircraft attacked North Korean mines, smelters, and ore-concentrating facilities.

The Chinese armies in North Korea, together with their supplies and equipment, also represented a huge outlay of capital. At the front lines, enemy troops and supplies were so dug-in and dispersed that they made poor air targets. Because of the impact of the railway interdiction campaigns, however, the Chinese had moved many of their combat troops to billets in the rear, closer to Manchuria and easier to supply. The Reds had also established supply storage areas in road-junction cities and at many villages along their main communications routes.

These concentrations of men and supplies were worthwhile air objectives. Fifth Air Force intelligence officers drew up a list of seventy-eight towns known to serve as vehicular repair stations, supply centers, or troop billets. On July 20, 1952, streams of 3d and 17th (formerly 452d) Wing B-26 light bombers, flying at night against targets marked by skilled pathfinder crews, began to destroy these centers with incendiary bombs. To reduce civilian casualties, the Fifth Air Force dropped warning leaflets, and on August 5, General Barcus publicly announced the names of the seventy-eight towns to be bombed.

Other supply targets unsuited for visual bombing were allotted to the Shoran-bombing B-29s. In November 1952 the B-29s methodically began to eliminate each month forty to fifty of the 200 targets assigned to them. Although many of these targets appeared to be civilian communities, the attacks set off so many secondary explosions that it

was apparent the villages were being used as storage areas.

To keep the interdiction campaign going meanwhile, Barcus concentrated the most experienced light bombardment crews in two night intruder squadrons. Recognizing that a lone wolf light bomber had small chance of destroying scattered, moving vehicles, the new night intruder specialists used tactics for concentrating enemy vehicles. While some aircraft made roadblocks on well-traveled roads, others followed and attacked stalled vehicles. These tactics paid good dividends.

On three occasions in January, March, and April 1953, the Fifth Air Force and FEAF Bomber Command cooperated in interdiction attacks to sever rail bridges across the Chongchon estuary north of Sinanju. Then they destroyed the rolling stock accumulated in marshalling yards up and down the main west coast rail line. Late in March and early in April, Fifth Air Force fighter-bombers and light bombers joined in cutting road bridges at first and last light of day. The light bombers attacked the vehicles stalled after dusk, while the fighter-bombers got those that could not secure shelter after dawn. The Fifth claimed destruction of 2,005 enemy vehicles in March and 2,732 in April.

As early as December 1952, discussions in the United Nations indicated that Communist China was much more eager to end the fighting in Korea than was Soviet Russia. After the death of Joseph Stalin on March 5, 1953, Chinese Premier Chou En-lai made it quite apparent that the Chinese were anxious to terminate their costly venture in Korea. When the truce negotiations began again on April 26, 1953, however, the Communists seemed as intractable as ever. With General Clark's full support, General Weyland continued to hammer at targets calculated to compel the Communists to accept suitable armistice terms.

In the last months of the war, UN aircraft pounded

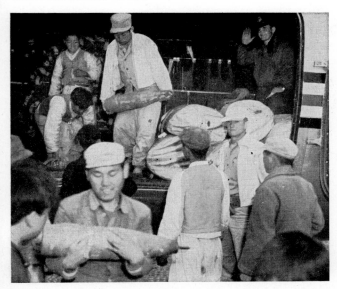

Artillery shells for the UN ground forces are unloaded by South Koreans from a cargo aircraft at a forward strip.

targets along the Yalu River, but it is likely that no single air operation so gravely concerned the Communists as the destruction of two agricultural irrigation dams in northwestern Korea. These strikes demonstrated that FEAF could devastate the most important segment of North Korea's agricultural economy. After three years of war, agriculture remained the only part of the enemy's economy that had escaped air attack. Under rigid police controls, North Korea's rice and grain production fed Communist soldiers. Nearly all of North Korea's rice lands required some form of controlled irrigation from impounded waters, and the Koreans customarily stored water in reservoirs for use in the rice-growing season.

These irrigation dams were excellent targets whose destruction would have a powerful effect on the enemy. Analysis showed that loss of all of the dams would greatly diminish the amount of arable land in North Korea and that the yield from much of the remaining acreage would fall far below normal. Weyland was not yet ready to approve the devastation of the enemy's agriculture. But he did not hesitate to authorize irrigation dam attacks where the resultant flash floods would accomplish military objectives, as was true of most of the dams. About twenty miles north of Pyongyang, the Toksan irrigation dam loomed over the main Pyongyang-to-Sinanju rail line and dominated a principal highway. On May 13, fifty-nine F-84s attacked the dam and, by dusk, water was seeping down its face from bomb craters. Sometime that night the impounded water broke through. The results of the raging flood exceeded all expectation. "The breaching of the Toksan Dam," General Clark jubilantly informed the JCS, "has been as effective as weeks of rail interdiction."

Weyland immediately ordered the Fifth to destroy the Chasan irrigation dam, whose impounded waters would wash out the railway line connecting Pyongyang with Sunchon. On May 16, ninety Thunderjets attacked in three waves to open a break in the dam which was pounded out by the hydraulic pressure of bomb explosions in the water of the reservoir. Here, again, the flood damage was terrible to behold. At the end of the Korean fighting Weyland remarked that two particular fighter-bomber strikes stood out in his mind as "spectacular on their own merit." One was the hydroelectric attack of June 1952, and the other—"perhaps the most spectacular of the war"— was the breaching of the Toksan and Chasan dams in May 1953.

The Communists had had a touch of total war, and they did not like it. Vitriolic propaganda indictments showed that the Communists were deeply impressed. How much the bombing of the dams influenced their decision to agree to armistice terms in conjectural, but Weyland believed that it was a major factor. On May 27, General Clark let the enemy know that the United Nations had made its final offer. After a short adjournment, the enemy speedily came to agreement, and on June 8, 1953, the Reds signed the terms of reference for a neutral nation repatriation commission. These terms marked a complete Communist capitulation on the prisoner of war issue: after 120 days, the prisoners who did not wish to go back to Communist rule could be freed as civilians.

The fighting in Korea should have ended in mid-June, but the Communists, with their usual callous disregard for human life, seemed determined to end the fighting on some note of victory. As early as May 27, FEAF aerial reconnaissance indicated that the enemy was preparing for a major ground offensive. On the night of June 10, the Reds attacked the ROK II Corps near Kumhwa. Recognizing that the UN ground situation was perilous, Lt. Gen. Samuel E. Anderson, who had taken command of the Fifth Air Force on May 31, 1953, called for an all-out air effort against the enemy's ground attack. On June 15, both the Fifth Air Force and Navy Task Force 77 mounted a maximum effort in support of the Eighth Army. The Reds had not yet had enough, and on the night of July 13 they threw three divisions against the right flank of the US IX Corps near Kumsong. The curtain of fire laid down by UN aircraft permitted the Eighth Army to establish a new main line of resistance along the Kumsong River.

UN ground forces were out of danger by July 20. At Panmunjom the truce negotiators were rapidly approaching agreement on all outstanding points of difference. Under the terms of the armistice agreement, the Chinese could not bring aircraft into North Korea after the cease-fire went into effect. To ensure that the enemy would have no airfields in North Korea capable of receiving aircraft during the closing hours of hostilities, General Weyland called on all air commands on July 20 to attack the fields. Except at Uiju, where reconnaissance revealed a number of MIGs in revetments, there were no Communist aircraft at any of the airfields in North Korea. The work was therefore mainly one of precautionary bombing. On the night of July 21, B-29s strewed fragmentation bombs on the MIGs at Uiju, knocking out thirty-six. Just before dusk on July 27, photographic reconnaissance showed that all North Korean airfields had been rendered unserviceable.

Elsewhere in the air over Korea on July 27, the UN air forces fought until the last moments of the war. During the day, Sabre interceptors saw only twelve MIGs in the air, all headed for home in Manchuria. At twilight, however, up on the Yalu near Manpojin, Capt. Ralph S. Parr of the 4th Fighter-Interceptor Wing met and shot down an IL-12 transport apparently far off course. This was the last enemy aircraft destroyed during the hostilities. Exactly twenty-four minutes before the cease-fire went into effect, a 3d Bombardment Wing B-26 crew dropped the last bombs of the Korean hostilities. Thus the Korean War ended at 2200 hours, July 27, 1953, exactly three years, one month, and two days after its beginning.

These years of war brought no final solution to the Korean problem, but the United Nations' effort was not in vain. The Republic of Korea was spared the Communist yoke, and the United Nations' courage in opposing naked aggression gave heart to the free countries of the world. To Americans the Korean War emphasized an old lesson: the price of peace is eternal vigilance—vigilance to detect and halt aggression wherever it appears.

Select Bibliography

BOOKS

Arnold, Henry H. *Global Mission*. New York, 1949.

Arnold, Henry H., and Eaker, Ira C. *Winged Warfare*. New York, 1941.

Baxter, James P., 3d. *Scientists Against Time*. Boston, 1946.

Brereton, Lewis H. *The Brereton Diaries*. New York, 1946.

Bridgman, Leonard. *Jane's All The World's Aircraft* (Series) 1947-1956. New York.

Cannon, M. Hamlin. *Leyte: The Return to the Philippines*. (*United States Army in World War II: The War in the Pacific*.) Washington, 1953.

Chandler, Charles DeF., and Lahm, Frank P. *How Our Army Grew Wings*. New York, 1943.

Chennault, Claire L. *Way of a Fighter: The Memoirs of Claire Lee Chennault*. New York, 1949.

Cline, Ray S. *Washington Command Post: The Operations Division*. (*United States Army in World War II: The War Department*.) Washington, 1951.

Collier, Basil. *The Defence of the United Kingdom*. London, 1957.

Compton, Arthur H. *Atomic Quest*. New York, 1956.

Craven, Wesley F., and Cate, James L., eds. *The Army Air Forces in World War II*. Vol. I, *Plans and Early Operations, January 1939 to August 1942*. Vol. II, *Europe: Torch to Point Blank, August 1942 to December 1943*. Vol. III, *Europe: Argument to V-E Day, January 1944 to May 1945*. Vol. IV, *The Pacific: Guadalcanal to Saipan, August 1942 to July 1944*. Vol. V, *The Pacific: Matterhorn to Nagasaki, June 1944 to August 1945*. Vol. VI, *Men and Planes*. Chicago, 1948-1955.

Davy, M. J. B. *Interpretive History of Flight*. London, 1948.

De Fonville, Wilfred (tr. by John S. Keltie). *Adventures in the Air*. London, 1877.

Dornberger, Walter. *V-2*. New York, 1954.

Edmonds, Walter D. *They Fought with What They Had*. Boston, 1951.

Eisenhower, Dwight D. *Crusade in Europe*. Garden City, N. Y., 1948.

Fahey, James C., ed. *United States Air Force and United States Army Aircraft, 1947-1956*. Falls Church, Va., 1956.

Fahey, James C., ed. *U.S. Army Aircraft, 1908-1946*. New York, 1946.

Fechet, James E., *et al. Parachutes*. New York, 1942.

Finletter, Thomas K. *Power and Policy*. New York, 1954.

Galland, Adolf. *The First and the Last*. New York, 1954.

Gavin, James M. *Airborne Warfare*. Washington, 1947.

Gorrell, Edgar S. *The Measure of America's World War Aeronautical Effort*. Northfield, Vt., 1940.

Harris, Arthur T. *Bomber Offensive*. New York, 1947.

Haugland, Vern. *The AAF Against Japan*. New York, 1948.

Holley, Irving B., Jr. *Ideas and Weapons*. New Haven, 1953.

Howard, Clive, and Whitley, Joe. *One Damned Island After Another*. Chapel Hill, N. C., 1947.

Ismay, Lord. *NATO, The First Five Years, 1949-1954*. Utrecht, Netherlands, 1955.

Kelly, Fred C. *The Wright Brothers*. New York, 1943.

Kenney, George C. *General Kenney Reports*. New York, 1949.

La Farge, Oliver. *The Eagle in the Egg*. Boston, 1949.

Lilley, Tom, *et al. Problems of accelerating Aircraft Production During World War II*. Boston, 1947.

Lord, Walter. *Day of Infamy*. New York, 1957.

McClendon, R. Earl. *Army Aviation, 1947-1953*. Documentary Research Division, Air University, 1954.

McClendon, R. Earl. *The Question of Autonomy for the United States Air Arm, 1907-1945*. 2 vols. Documentary Research Division, Air University, 1950.

McClendon, R. Earl. *Unification of the Armed Forces: Administrative and Legislative Developments, 1945-1949*. Documentary Research Division, Air University, 1952.

Mansfield, Harold. *Vision: A Saga of the Sky*. New York, 1957.

Marshall, George C., Arnold, H. H., and King, E. J. *The War Reports of General of the Army George C. Marshall, General of the Army H. H. Arnold and Fleet Admiral Ernest J. King*. Philadelphia, 1947.

Milner, Samuel L. *Victory in Papua*. (*United States Army in World War II: The War in the Pacific*.) Washington, 1957.

Mixter, G. W., and Emmons, H. H. *U.S. Army Aircraft Production Facts*. Washington, 1919.

Morison, Samuel E. *History of United States Naval Operations in World War II*, Vols. I-IX. Boston, 1947-54.

Morton, Louis. *The Fall of the Philippines*. (*United States Army in World War II: The War in the Pacific*.) Washington, 1953.

Okumiya, Masatake; Horikoshi, J.; and Caidin, Martin. *Zero*. New York, 1956.

Patrick, Mason M. *The United States in the Air*. New York, 1928.

Reynolds, Quentin. *The Amazing Mr. Doolittle*. New York, 1953.

Richards, Denis, and Saunders, H. St. G. *Royal Air Force, 1939-1945*. 3 vols. London, 1953-54.

Saunders, Hilary St. G. *Per Ardua: The Rise of British Air Power, 1911-1939*. London, 1945.

Sherrod, Robert. *History of Marine Corps Aviation in World War II*. Washington, 1952.

Smith, Robert R. *The Approach to the Philippines*. (*United States Army in World War II: The War in the Pacific*.) Washington, 1953.

Straubel, James H., ed. *Air Force Diary.* New York, 1947.

Strausz-Hupé, Robert, and Possony, Stefan T., eds. *Air Power and National Security.* Philadelphia, 1955.

Sweetser, A. W. *The American Air Service.* New York, 1919.

Taylor, Frank J., and Wright, Lawton. *Democracy's Air Arsenal.* New York, 1947.

Toulmin, H. A., Jr. *Air Service, A.E.F., 1918.* New York, 1927.

Watson, Mark S. *Chief of Staff: Prewar Plans and Preparations. (United States Army in World War II: The War Department.)* Washington, 1950.

•   •   •

The Aircraft Year Book (Series), 1949-1955. Aircraft Industries Assn., Inc. Washington.

A Brief History of the Air Corps and its Late Development. Air Corps Tactical School [Clayton L. Bissell]. Langley Field, Va., 1927.

Civil Defense in the United States: Federal, State and Local. Public Affairs Bulletin No. 92. Washington, 1951.

Korea—1950. Office, Chief of Military History, Department of the Army. Washington, 1952.

Korea—1951-53. Office, Chief of Military History, Department of the Army. Washington, 1956.

Official Munitions Production of the United States, 1 July 1940-31 August 1945. Civilian Production Administration. Washington, 1947.

The Official Pictorial History of the AAF. AAF Historical Office. New York, 1947.

Survival in the Air Age. A Report by the President's Air Policy Commission. Washington, 1948.

U.S. Strategic Bombing Survey: Over-all Report, European War. U.S. Strategic Bombing Survey. Washington, 1945.

MAGAZINE ARTICLES

Berkner, Lloyd B. "Continental Defense," *Current History,* May 1954, pp. 257-62.

Berry, Maj. Margaret V. "Unification—The Next Step," *Air Force,* October 1956, pp. 43-48.

Brinkley, Bill. "Birth of a Base," *Life,* September 22, 1952, pp. 130-51.

Butcher, Lt. Col. Chester J., and Koelle, Capt. J. B. "The Growth of ADC's Counter-Weapon Arsenal," *Air Force,* June 1956, pp. 56-68.

Carter, Maj. Gen. Warren R. "USAF Pilot Training," *Air University Quarterly Review,* Winter 1952-53, pp. 3-21.

Combs, Brig. Gen. Cecil E. "Air Crew Training in the Atomic Age," *Air University Quarterly Review,* Summer 1955, pp. 3-9.

Davis, Louis W. "How the Program Looks to a Reserve Wing," *Pegasus,* January 1955, pp. 1-6.

Demler, Brig. Gen. Marvin C. "Problems and Pitfalls in Guided Missile Research," *Air Force,* September 1956, pp. 114-16.

Dodd, Everett E. "Here's Why They Leave the Air Force," *Air Force,* March 1954, pp. 32-36.

Fisher, Paul. "The Berlin Airlift," *The Bee-Hive,* Fall 1948, pp. 3-31.

Greene, Jerry. "A New Deal for the Air Reserve," *Pegasus,* January 1955, pp. 1-6.

Hall, Maj. Gen. William E. "Facilities and Equipment; Biggest Reserve Headache," *Air Force,* September 1956, pp. 150-52.

Harper, Lt. Gen. Robert W. "Air Force Training," *Army Information Digest,* October 1952, pp. 47-54.

Harper, Maj. Gen. Robert W. "The Air Transport Command, USAF," *Armed Force,* November 1, 1947, pp. 3, 8.

Haywood, Col. Oliver G. "Technology and Military Men," *Air University Quarterly Review,* Summer 1955, pp. 83-87.

Key, William G. "Route Command for Air Power," *Pegasus,* December 1951, pp. 1-15.

Killian, James H., Jr., and Hill, A. G. "For a Continental Defense," *The Atlantic Monthly,* November 1953, pp. 37-41.

Lee, June. "Women's Work is Never Done," *Pegasus,* May 1951, pp. 9-12.

Lee, Maj. Gen. Robert M. "Troop Carrier—Its Tactical Role," *Pegasus,* November 1949, pp. 1-5.

Lindsay, Maj. Gen. Richard C. "How the Air Force Will Use Its Missiles," *Air Force,* September 1956, pp. 98-103.

Loesch, Col. L. F., and Low, Col. C. R. "Air Force Headquarters: Its Mission and Organization," *Air University Quarterly Review,* Summer 1956, pp. 102-8.

McClendon, R. Earl. "The Rise of Air Power," *Current History,* May 1954, pp. 276-83.

Miller, Ed Mack. "How ADC Builds a Wall Twelve Miles High," *Air Force,* June 1956, pp. 46-54.

Mosley, Col. Lawson S., Jr. "Aircrew Training—Whose Responsibility," *Air University Quarterly Review,* Summer 1950, pp. 43-52.

Murphy, Charles J. V. "The United States as a Bombing Target," *Fortune,* November 1953, pp. 118-21, 219-28.

Nelson, Maj. Carl G. "REMCO, A Korean War Development," *Air University Quarterly Review,* Summer 1953, pp. 78-85.

Newlon, Lt. Col. F. Clarke. "Billions for Equipment and Peanuts for Men," *Pegasus,* December 1956, pp. 1-6.

Newlon, Lt. Col. F. Clarke. "Report on Spain," *Pegasus,* November 1955, pp. 11-13.

O'Donnell, James P. "What's Behind the Air-Base Scandals?" *Saturday Evening Post,* June 28, 1952, pp. 17-19, 90-92, 97.

Ostrander, Brig. Gen. Donald R. "Who is Doing What in Ballistic Missile Research?" *Air Force,* September 1956, pp. 119-24.

Palmer, C. B. "Our Great Base on Top of the World," *New York Times Magazine,* December 13, 1953, pp. 10, 53-57.

Putt, Lt. Gen. Donald L. "All-Weather Weapon Systems," *Air Force,* September 1956, pp. 94-95.

Quesada, Maj. Gen. Elwood R. "The TAC Today," *Military Review,* September 1947, pp. 3-8.

Ransom, Harry H. "Lord Trenchard, Architect of Air Power," *Air University Quarterly Review,* Summer 1956, pp. 59-67.

Rawlings, Gen. Edwin W. "A New Equation for Jet Age Logistics," *Air University Quarterly Review,* Spring 1955, pp. 8-29.

Rawlings, Gen. Edwin W. "What's Ahead in Logistics," *Air Force,* October 1955, p. 84.

Rentz, Col. William E. "Technical Training Air Force," *Pegasus,* August 1952, pp. 11-15.

Rogers, Brig. Gen. Turner C. "Crew TAF," *Pegasus,* October 1952, pp. 11-13.

Scharlemann, Chaplain (Lt. Col.) Martin H. "The Chaplain at Work," *Army Information Digest,* September 1952.

Scholin, Maj. Allan R. "The Air Training Command," *Pegasus,* July 1952, pp. 7-11.

Smith, Brig. Gen. Dale O. "For a Revised Profession of Arms," *Pegasus,* December 1956, pp. 7-9.

Smith, Maj. Gen. Frederic H., Jr. "How Air Defense is Part of the Great Deterrent," *Air Force,* June 1956, pp. 90-93.

Smith, Lt. Col. Gerald T. "Too Much Detail or Too Little Management?" *Air University Quarterly Review,* Fall 1953, pp. 79-90.

Spaatz, Gen. Carl (Rtd.). "If We Should Have to Fight Again," *Life,* July 5, 1948.

Spaatz, Gen. Carl (Rtd.). "Phase II, Air War," *Life,* Aug. 16, 1948.

Stapleton, Bill. "What are We Doing in Spain?" *Colliers,* January 11, 1954, pp. 84-89.

Talbott, Harold E. "Millions for Equipment, Nickels for Men," *Air Force*, October 1954, pp. 29-30, 60-63.

Teller, Dr. Edward. "Science in the United States," *Air Force*, April 1957, pp. 102-7.

Thompson, Maj. A. G. "TAC's Global Combat Airlift Air Force," *Pegasus*, April 1956, pp. 1-6.

Timberlake, Maj. Gen. Edward J. "Tactical Air Doctrine," *Air Force*, July 1955, pp. 44-46.

Twining, Gen. Nathan F. "Behind the Manpower Eight Ball," *Air Force*, September 1956, pp. 55-59.

Vicellio, Brig. Gen. Henry P. "Composite Air Strike Force," *Air University Quarterly Review*, Winter 1956-57, pp. 127-38.

Walkowicz, Lt. Col. T. F. "Birth of Sweepback," *Air Force*, April 1952, pp. 30-32, 72.

Weyland, Gen. Otto P. "The Air Campaign in Korea," *Air University Quarterly Review*, Fall 1953, pp. 3-28.

Weyland, Gen. Otto P. "The Role of TAC in the 'Long Pull,'" *Air Force*, May 1956, pp. 52, 55.

Weyland, Gen. Otto P. "Tactical Airpower—Worldwide," *Air Force*, July 1955, pp. 39-44.

White, Gen. Thomas D. "Community Relations—Military Aviation," *Air Force*, April 1957, pp. 57-60.

White, Gen. Thomas D. "We Cannot Have Complete Protection Here at Home," *U.S. Air Services*, December 1953, pp. 9-11.

Wilber, Maj. Allen W. "The Pattern of Air Defense," *Army Information Digest*, February 1952, pp. 53-60.

Winchester, James. "The DEW Line Story," *Flying*, February 1957, pp. 27-31, 76.

Winfield, M/Sgt. Norman. "Cause of the Pause," *Air Force*, January 1954, pp. 28, 30-31.

Yates, Maj. Gen. Donald N. "Test Programs—Path to Missile Pay-Off," *Air Force*, September 1956, pp. 116-19.

• • •

"Air Materiel Command, USAF," *Aviation Week*, August 16, 1954.

"Air Research and Development Command," *Aviation Week*, August 17, 1953.

"The Builders of Bases" (Editorial), *Fortune*, December 1951, pp. 93-97.

"Canada's Air Defenses," *Aircraft* (Canada), October 1954.

"CONAD: An Inter-Service Team Geared for Continental Defense," *All Hands*, September 1956, pp. 16-19.

"The Greenland Ice Plateau" (Editorial), *Air University Quarterly Review*, Spring 1955, pp. 78-90.

"The Hungarian Airlift," *The Bee-Hive*, January 1957, pp. 2-16.

"Lessons of the Airlift," *Pegasus*, June 1949, pp. 1-5.

"Million Alumni" (Editorial), *Pegasus*, December 1954, pp. 7-10.

"Project East River—The Strategy of Civil Defense," *Bulletin of the Atomic Scientists*, September 1953, pp. 247-52, 288.

"Project Mint Julep" (Editorial), *Air University Quarterly Review*, Winter 1954-55, pp. 96-105.

"A Special Study of Operation Vittles," *Aviation Operations Magazine*, April 1949, pp. 1-120.

"The Strategic Air Command—A Special Report," *Air Force*, April 1956, pp. 39-128.

HISTORICAL STUDIES

USAF Historical Studies

USAF Historical Study No. 6, The Development of the Heavy Bomber, 1918-1944. 1951.

USAF Historical Study No. 10, *Organization of the Army Air Arm, 1935-1945* (Rev.). 1956.

USAF Historical Study No. 25, Organization of Military Aeronautics, 1907-1935 (Congressional and War Department Action). 1944.

USAF Historical Study No. 39, Legislation Relating to the Air Corps Personnel and Training Programs, 1907-1939. 1945.

USAF Historical Study No. 46, Organization of Military Aeronautics, 1935-1945 (Executive, Congressional, and War Department Action). 1946.

USAF Historical Study No. 50, Materiel Research and Development in the Army Air Arm, 1914-1945. 1946.

USAF Historical Study No. 71, *United States Air Force Operations in the Korean Conflict, 25 June-1 November 1950*. 1952.

USAF Historical Study No. 72, *United States Air Force Operations in the Korean Conflict, 1 November 1950-30 June 1952*. 1955.

USAF Historical Study No. 81 (draft), The Air Service in World War I.

USAF Historical Study No. 84, *Legislative History of the AAF and USAF, 1941-1951*. 1953.

USAF Historical Study No. 89, Development of Air Doctrine in the Army Air Arm, 1917-1941. 1953.

USAF Historical Study No. 98 (draft), The Army Air Arm, 1861-1917.

USAF Historical Study No. 100, *History of the Air Corps Tactical School*. 1955.

USAF Historical Study No. 126, The Development of Continental Air Defense to 1 September 1954. 1956.

USAF Historical Study No. 127 (draft), United States Air Force Operations in the Korean Conflict, 1 July 1952-27 July 1953.

Other Studies

Air University Since its Founding. Air University. 1957.

The Air Weather Service Reorganization, Fiscal Year 1952. Air Weather Service Historical Study No. 1. November 1952.

The Berlin Air Lift. Part I: 21 June-31 December 1948; Part II: 1 January-30 September 1949. European Command. 1952.

Berlin Airlift, a USAFE Summary . . ., 26 June 1948-30 September 1949. United States Air Forces in Europe.

A Chronological History of the Eighteenth Air Force, 1951-1956. Eighteenth Air Force. December 1956.

A Decade of Continental Air Defense, 1946-1956. Continental Air Defense Command.

Early History of the Air Research and Development Command. Air Research and Development Command. May 1953.

History of the United States Air Force Medical Service, 1947-1957. Office of the Surgeon General, USAF. 1957.

History of U.S. Air Service, 1862-1920. Office, Chief of Air Service. Washington, 1920.

MATS Participation in the Korean Crisis (Pacific Airlift), June-December 1950. 2 vols. Military Air Transport Service. December 1950.

Organization and Responsibility for Air Defense, March 1946-September 1956. Continental Air Defense Command Historical Study No. 9.

The Progressive Development of Strategic Air Command, 1946-1956. Strategic Air Command. 1957.

Report on the Korean War. 2 vols. Far East Air Forces. March 1954.

TAC Highlights, 1946-1956. Tactical Air Command. December 1956.

Tactical Air Command Historical Chronology. Tactical Air Command. December 1956.

USAFE and the Berlin Airlift 1948: Supply and Operational Aspects. United States Air Forces in Europe. April 1949.

USAFE and the Berlin Airlift: Supply and Operational Aspects. United States Air Forces in Europe. February 1950.

COMMAND AND STAFF HISTORIES

Headquarters USAF Histories

History of Headquarters USAF, 1 July 1949 to 30 June 1950. Washington, 1954.

History of Headquarters USAF, 1 July 1950 to 30 June 1951. Washington, 1955.

History of Headquarters USAF (draft), 1 July 1951 to 30 June 1953.

Semiannual Headquarters USAF Staff Histories, 1949-56.

Air Adjutant General, USAF

Assistant for Ground Safety, Deputy Chief of Staff, Personnel

Chief of Air Force Chaplains, USAF

Deputy Chief of Staff, Comptroller, directorates and offices

Inspector General

Judge Advocate General, USAF

Surgeon General, USAF

Command Histories

Air Materiel Command. 1 July 1954-30 June 1955.

Air Transport Command. 1 October 1945-31 December 1946.

Military Air Transport Service. 1948, 1949, January-June 1950.

Strategic Air Command. 1 July 1950-30 June 1953.

Tactical Air Command. 1 January-30 November 1948, 1 January-31 December 1949, 1 July-30 November 1950, 1 January-30 June 1955.

OFFICIAL PUBLICATIONS

Recurring Reports

Annual Reports, Air Material Command. 1948 through 1955.

Annual Reports, Chief of Air Corps, U.S. Army. 1927-39.

Annual Reports, Chief of Air Service, U.S. Army. 1918-26.

Annual Reports, USAF Medical Service. 1 July 1949-30 June 1952, 1 July 1952-30 June 1954, 1 July 1954-30 June 1955, 1 July 1955-30 June 1956. Office of the Surgeon General, USAF.

Final Report of Chief of Air Service, A.E.F. Washington, 1921.

Final Report of the Chief of Staff of the United States Army to the Secretary of the Army, 7 February 1948. Washington, 1948.

First Report of the Secretary of Defense, 1948. Washington, 1948.

Report of the Chief of Staff, United States Air Force, to the Secretary of the Air Force, 30 June 1948. Washington, 1948.

Report of Director of Military Aeronautics, U.S. Army, 1918. Washington, 1918.

Report of the Secretary of the Air Force to the Secretary of Defense for Fiscal Year 1948. Washington, 1949.

Reports of the Military Air Transport Service to the Secretary of Defense. First Quarterly, 30 September 1948; 1 October-31 December 1948; Fiscal year 1949 with Statistical Summary; Semiannual, January 1952-December 1954; Annual, July 1955-June 1956.

Second Report of the Secretary of Defense and the Annual Reports of the Secretary of the Army, Secretary of the Navy, and Secretary of the Air Force for Fiscal Year 1949. Washington, 1950.

Semiannual Report of the Secretary of the Air Force, July 1-December 31, 1949. Washington, 1950.

Semiannual Report of the Secretary of Defense and the Semiannual Reports of the Secretary of the Army,

Secretary of the Navy, and Secretary of the Air Force, 1950 through 1956. Washington, 1950-1957.

USAF Publications

AAF Statistical Digest. *Aircraft Accident and Maintenance Review.* Air Force Bulletins, Information Services Letter, Manuals, Pamphlets, Personnel Newsletter, Public Information Letter, Public Relations Letter, Regulations. Comptroller News. Directory of United States Air Force Organizations. *Flying Safety.* Hq. USAF Daily Staff Digest. Hq. USAF Information Bulletin. Hq. USAF Organization and Functions Chartbook. Supply and Services Newsletter. USAF Command Organization and Functions. USAF Medical Service Digest. *USAF Research and Development Quarterly Review.* USAF Roster of Key Personnel. USAF Statistical Digest.

Air Force Bulletin No. 1, Functions of the Armed Forces and the Joint Chiefs of Staff, 21 May 1948.

Air Force Bulletin No. 4, Functions of the Armed Forces and the Joint Chiefs of Staff, 9 September 1948.

Air Force Bulletin No. 9, Functions of the Armed Forces and the Joint Chiefs of Staff, 9 July 1954.

Air Force Manual 1-2, United States Air Force Basic Doctrine. 1955.

Air Force Manual 1-4, Air Defense Operations. 1954.

Air Force Manual 1-7, Theater Air Forces in Counter Air, Interdiction and Close Air Support Operations. 1954.

Air Force Manual 1-8, Strategic Air Operations. 1954.

Air Force Manual 1-9, Theater Airlift Operations.

Air Force Pamphlet 210-1-1, Historical Data. A Chronology of American Aviation Events. 1955.

DOCUMENTS

Congressional

Air Force Organization Act of 1951. Public Law 150, 82d Congress, September 19, 1951. 65 *Stat.* 326.

National Security Act of 1947. Public Law 253, 80th Congress, July 26, 1947. 61 *Stat.* 495.

5th Report of Senate Preparedness Investigating Subcommittee, Committee on Armed Services, 82d Congress, 1st Session, *Investigation of the Preparedness Program: Interim Report on Lackland AFB.* Washington, 1951.

42d Report of the Senate Preparedness Investigating Subcommittee, Committee on Armed Services, 82d Congress, 2d Session, *Interim Report on Moroccan Air Base Construction.* Washington, 1952.

44th Report of Senate Preparedness Investigating Subcommittee, Committee on Armed Services, 83d Congress, 1st Session, *Second Report on Moroccan Air Base Construction.* Washington, 1953.

Hearings before a Subcommittee of the Committee on Appropriations, House of Representatives, 82d Congress, 1st Session, *Military Public Works Appropriations for 1952.* Washington, 1951.

Hearings before a Subcommittee of the Committee on Appropriations, House of Representatives, 82d Congress, 2d Session, *Investigation of Military Public Works, Part 2, Department of the Air Force; Part 4, Moroccan Air Base Construction; Part 4 (Continued).* Washington, 1952.

Hearings before the Subcommittee of the Committee on Appropriations, House of Representatives, 84th Congress, 2d Session, *Department of the Air Force Appropriations for 1957.* Washington, 1956.

Other Documents

The Air Force Budget, Fiscal Year 1956. Department of the Air Force. March 1955.

The Air Force Budget, Fiscal Year 1957 (Rev). Department of the Air Force. August 1956.

Air Force Industrial Production Readiness Policy. Office of the Secretary of the Air Force. November 23, 1955.

Air Force Institute of Technology, Air University, Catalogue, 1956-1957. Wright-Patterson Air Force Base, Ohio, 1957.

The Air Photographic and Charting Service of MATS. Air Photographic and Charting Service. February 1956.

Clarification of Roles and Missions of the Army and the Air Force Regarding Use of Aircraft. Office of the Secretary of Defense. March 18, 1957.

Clarification of Roles and Missions to Improve the Effectiveness of Operations of the Department of Defense. Office of the Secretary of Defense. November 26, 1956.

Command and Employment of Air Power. War Department Field Manual 100-20. July 21, 1943.

Conditions at Lackland AFB. Analysis Division, Directorate of Legislation and Liaison, Office of Secretary of the Air Force. 1951.

Deputy Chief of Staff, Comptroller, USAF (Handbook). September 1956.

An Educational System for Officers of the Army Air Forces: A Summary of the Gerow Board Report, 1946. Air University. July 1956.

Fact Sheet. Tactical Air Command. August 1956.

Guide to Air University, 1956-1957. Air University, 1957.

High Point in Operation Safe Haven. Military Air Transport Service. 26 December 1956.

Mecca Airlift. Military Air Transport Service. 1952.

Mercy Ship. Military Air Transport Service. March 19, 1954.

The Military Air Transport Service in 1952. MATS in 1953. The Military Air Transport Service in 1954. 1955 MATS Yearly Round-Up. MATS Round-Up of 1956. MATS Facts, Military Air Transport Service, November 1956. MATS Ninth Anniversary, Hq. Military Air Transport Service, 1 June 1957. Chronology of the Military Air Transport Service, June 1, 1948-May 31, 1949. First Anniversary, 1 June 1949, Military Air Transport Service, USAF. The Story of MATS, U.S. Air Force, 1951.

The Mission, Functions, Organization and Accomplishments of the Office of Special Investigations, The Inspector General, USAF, July 1948 to July 1952.

Outline of Organization and Mission of Air University. Air University, 1956.

Past Educational Conferences. Air University. 1956.

Personnel. Air Command and Staff College, Air University. 1956.

Releasable Information on U.S. Air Force Aircraft. Security Review Branch, Office of Secretary of Defense. December 1, 1956.

A Report on the Airlift Berlin Mission, the Operational and Internal Aspects of the Advance Element. Combined Airlift Task Force, n.d.

Report on Comptrollership Within the Air Force, 1946-1951, by Lt. Gen. E. W. Rawlings.

Report of the USAF Educational Conference of 18-19 October 1956. Air University, 1956.

Report of the USAF Military Educational Board on the Professional Education System for USAF Officers. Air University, 1950.

Summary of the Berlin Airlift. Office of Public Information, National Military Establishment, May 13, 1949.

USAF Air Weather Service. Air Weather Service. February 29, 1956.

The U.S. Air Force Chaplain Program. Office, Chief of Air Force Chaplains. 1953.

United States Air Force Institute of Technology, Air University, Resident College Catalogue, 1954-1955. Wright-Patterson Air Force Base, Ohio, 1954.

SPEECHES AND PRESS RELEASES

Speeches

Gardner, Trevor. Address on guided missiles. September 20, 1955.

Kuter, Maj. Gen. Laurence S. Before the Aviation Writers Association, Washington Chapter. November 16, 1950.

Lewis, Honorable Roger. Before the Ninth Annual Convention of the Air Force Association, San Francisco, Calif. August 13, 1955.

McCormack, Maj. Gen. James, Jr. Trends in Weapon Systems Development. August 21, 1953.

Partridge, Gen. Earle E. Before the Jet Age Conference of the Air Force Association, Washington. February 3, 1956.

Rawlings, Gen. Edwin W. Air Logistics in Total War. August 1, 1956.

Smith, Honorable David S. Before the Annual Convention of the National Guard Association of the United States, New Orleans, La. October 19, 1955.

Smith, Maj. Gen. Phillips W. Air Force Procurement in World War II and Today. February 3, 1955.

Smith, Maj. Gen. Phillips W. Is Production Engineering our Dangerous Blind Spot? October 22, 1954.

Stever, Dr. H. Guyford. Technical Commitments of the Aeronautical Engineering Community. March 17, 1956.

Talbott, Harold E. Before Convention of the Air Force Association, Washington. August 22, 1953.

Talbott, Harold E. Before University Club, New York City. October 14, 1954.

Twining, Gen. Nathan F. Air Force Academy Dedication, Denver, Colo. July 11, 1955.

Twining, Gen. Nathan F. Dedication of Military Air Transport Service Terminal, Charleston Air Force Base. March 16, 1956.

Twining, Gen. Nathan F. At National Aircraft Show, Philadelphia, Pa. September 3, 1955.

Twining, Gen. Nathan F. At Scott Air Force Base, Belleville, Ill. December 3, 1953.

White, Gen. Thos. D. Before the Management Course, George Washington University. September 21, 1954.

White, Gen. Thos. D. Before National Security Industrial Association, Washington. October 15, 1953.

Vandenberg, Gen. Hoyt S. At Air University, Montgomery, Ala. April 6, 1948.

Press Releases, Department of Defense

Air Force Designated Agent for Spanish Base Program. October 9, 1953.

Air Force Meteorological Survey Expanded in Northern Hemisphere. January 8, 1956.

Air Force Reveals Radical Design of Douglas X-3 Research Plane. November 16, 1953.

Convertiplane Being Developed for Army Flown for First Time in Texas. August 24, 1955.

Fact Sheet on Guided Missiles. May 25, 1956.

Newport Conference Discussed before Senior Military Officers. August 24, 1948.

Releasable List of Overseas Air Bases Used by the USAF. December 7, 1955.

Rocket Powered Bell X-2 to Probe Thermal Barrier. August 11, 1955.

USAF Installations in the Continental United States. December 7, 1955, and June 1, 1956.

Yeager Flight in X-1A. December 16, 1953.

Index

F

Lend-Lease Act, 48
Lepere aircraft (French), 16
Le Rhone engine, 16-18
Leuna, 72
Lewis, Col. Isaac N., 7
Lewis, Assistant Secretary Roger, 194
Lewis gun, 7
Leyte, 81
Liberator. *See* B-24.
Liberty engine, 16, 18, 33, 37
Libya, 57-58, 60, 64, 149, 151, 191-92
Lieb, Congressman Charles, 99
Liége, 71, 73
Liftmaster. *See* C-118.
Lightning. *See* P-38.
Lilienthal, Otto, 2
Lille, 58
Lincoln Laboratory, 135-36, 198, 209
Lingayen Gulf, 75-76, 81
"Little Vittles," 240
Lockheed Aircraft Corporation, 91, 93, 131, 135, 140, 145,
    150, 208, 210
Lodge, Senator Henry Cabot, Jr., 48
Logistics: before WW II, 4-6, 10-11, 13-18, 29, 33, 37, 43-44;
    during WW II, 84, 91-93, 97; since WW II, 215-24
Loire River, 68, 70
London, 1, 30, 54, 57-58, 71, 125
Longhorn, Exercise, 142
Long Range Proving Ground, 190
Lookout, Operation, 136
Los Alamos, 133; Scientific Laboratory, 200
Los Angeles, "Battle of," 89
Losey Field, Puerto Rico, 52
Lovett, Secretary Robert A., 51, 100, 135, 227
Lowe, Thaddeus S. C., 1
Lowry Air Force Base, Colo., 50, 174, 179
Lucky Lady II, 124
Lufbery, Maj. Raoul, 27
Luftwaffe, 43-45, 47, 66-69, 71, 73, 111, 209
Luke, Lt. Frank, 27
Luke Field, Ariz., 50
Luzon, 75-77, 81
Lyon, Alfred J., 37
Lyster, Col. Theodore C., 181

Mc

MacArthur, Gen. Douglas, 38, 52-53, 75-77, 80-81, 87, 243-44,
    246-49
McChord, Col. William C., 35-36
McChord Air Force Base, Wash., 130, 149
McConnell, Capt. Joe, 153
McConnell Air Force Base, Kan., 173, 176
McCook Field, Ohio, 33-34, 37
McCormack, Maj. Gen. James, Jr., 198
MacDill, Col. Leslie, 35-37
MacDill Air Force Base, Fla., 122
McDonnell Aircraft Corporation, 210, 212
McGuire Air Force Base, N. J., 149, 152
McKee, Maj. Gen. William F., 110
McNaughton, Maj. Gen. Kenneth P., 165

M

Mach number, 204
Macready, Lt. John A., 34
Madrid, 193
Magic Carpet, Operation, 152
Maintenance, aircraft and equipment: Berlin Airlift, 224-25,
    236-37, 241; IRAN, 225; jet engine, 225; Korean War,
    225; pers & tng, 95, 105; types, 223-25; WW II, 93
Maintenance, base, 189-90, 195
Maitland, Lt. Lester J., 37
Malaya, 55, 77
Malik, Jacob A., 252
Malta, 60-61
Management, 227-33; analysis, 231; control, 155, 227
Manchuria, 47, 87, 249-50, 254, 256-57
Mandalay, 83
Manila, 7, 53, 75-77, 81; Bay, 76-77
Mannock, Edward, 18
Manpojin, 257
Manpower: buildup, 164; demob, 161, 171; leg, 167; limita-
    tions, 163, 165-67, 176-77; recruiting, 161, 164; reserve,
    168-69; shortage, 157-59, 161-67, 232-33
Marauder. *See* B-26.
March Field, Calif., 40
Mareth Line, 58, 60
Marianas, 84-87, 93, 113, 124, 243
Marine Corps: Korean War, 184, 248-50; mission, 101-2, 118-
    19, 137; WW II, 55, 78, 80, 82, 84-85

Markham Valley, 80
Marne River, 25
Marrett, Lt. Samuel H., 76
Marseille, 71
Marshall, Gen. George C., 43-44, 48, 51-52, 95-96, 99, 101, 219
Marshall Islands, 53, 84-85
Marshall Plan, 105
Martin, Maj. Gen. Frederick L., 52, 54
Martin, Glenn L., 9
Martin Company, Glenn L., 16, 30, 34, 38, 91, 144-45, 202,
    211
Massachusetts Institute of Technology, 19, 135, 179, 198
Matador missile, 144-45, 150, 211
Materiel, Deputy Chief of Staff, 109-10, 215, 220
Materiel Command, 97
Materiel Division, 37, 41, 51
Mather Field, Calif., 50
Matterhorn, Operation, 84
Maughan, Lt. Russell L., 34
Maxim, Sir Hiram, 2
Maxwell Air Force Base, Ala., 34, 171
May, Col. Geraldine F., 163
MB-2, 16, 30, 32, 34
ME-109 (German), 45
ME-262 (German), 71
Mecca, 152
Mechanics. *See* Technicians.
Medical Service, USAF, 181-84; specialized corps, 182
Mediterranean Air Command, 60, 62
Mediterranean Allied Air Forces, 62-63; Strategic and Tactical
    Air Forces, 62
Mediterranean area, 58-63, 67, 71, 90, 112, 148-49, 151, 192;
    AAF/MTO, 62
Menoher, Maj. Gen. Charles T., 30
Mercy missions, 37, 145, 151-52
"Merrill's Marauders," 83
Merseburg, 72
Messerschmitt aircraft (German), 45, 65, 71, 210
Messina, Strait of, 61
Meuse River, 26, 71
Mexico: Border incidents, 7, 9-10, 34, 37; Gulf, 90, 136
Mid-Canada Line, 133, 135
Middle East, 53, 57-58, 60, 82, 105, 149
Midnight Oil, Operation, 175
Midway, 53, 77, 90, 149; Battle of, 77, 89
MIG-15 (Russian), 210, 249-51, 235-55, 257
"MIG Alley," 250, 253, 255
Mighty Mouse rocket, 208
Military Aeronautics, Division of, 15
Military Air Transport Service: aerial POEs, 149; Berlin Airlift,
    235, 237; divs, 148-49, 153; Korean War, 148-49, 153;
    Navy role, 147-48; opns, 152-53, 184, 192; orgn, 106, 119,
    147-48; safety record, 152-53; supporting svs, 148, 150-53;
    trans fleet, 143, 145, 150
Military justice, 185-86
Military Liaison Committee, 200
Military Security, Department of, proposed, 101
Militia Bureau, 6
Milling, Brig. Gen. Thomas DeWitt, 6-7, 10, 23
Mindanao, 53, 75-76, 81
Mindoro, 81
Missile Test Center, Air Force, 199-200. *See also* Long Range
    Proving Ground.
Missouri, 87
Mitchell, Brig. Gen. William, 8, 11, 34, 43; air doctrine, 29-33,
    99, 113, 121; WW I, 21-23, 25-27
Mitchell bomber. *See* B-25.
Mobilization, industrial, 91, 215-18
Moby Dick survey, 205
Modification, aircraft, 91-92, 220, 224. *See also* Maintenance.
Montebourg, 68
Montgolfier brothers, 1
Montgomery, Gen. Bernard L., 58, 60
Montgomery, John, 2
Montreal, 53
Moore, Lt. Joseph H., 76
Morale, 7, 23, 162, 166, 185, 190. *See also* Welfare.
Morocco: Spanish, 58. *See also* French Morocco.
Morón de la Frontera, 193
Morotai, 81
Morrow, Dwight W., 36; Board, 36
Mortain, 69
Moscow, 192
Moselle River, 70
Moslems, 152
Mount Etna, 61
Muccio, U. S. Ambassador John J., 243
Munich, 42-43, 152
Munitions Board, 102